This is Spain

RICHARD F. PATTEE

THE BRUCE PUBLISHING COMPANY
1951 MILWAUKEE

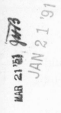

PREFACE BY THE GENERAL EDITOR

WE ARE presenting herewith a book of unique interest for our times. It is an accurate and most readable account of Spain, from its earliest beginnings to the final great event of the Spanish Civil War within our own recent memory. The outcome of this broke the strength of red radicalism and saved a Christian nation from ruin.

The writer himself, through long familiarity with Spain, its people, and with every section of the land, is perhaps the one man best fitted for this task. Consultant on International Affairs of the N.C.W.C. of the United States of America, he is equally prominent in Spain itself and in Spanish countries throughout the world.

Perfect in the use of the Spanish tongue, he is no less thoroughly familiar with the purely subversive literature spawned by the radicals in Spain — socialists, communists, and anarchists — than with the Christian contributions issued in defense of a peace-loving people, desirous to be left unmolested, and yet not unwilling to protect their churches and their firesides against the aggressive promoters of a universal godlessness.

A writer in Spanish no less than in the English language, Richard Pattee has spent extensive periods not only in Spain, where he is familiar with every inch of ground, we might say, but in the Spanish American countries as well. His intimate acquaintance with South America dates back to 1929 and 1930, when he was still in his twenties; with Central America and the West Indies, to 1938. In 1944 he held the rank of visiting professor at the University of Mexico.

In more recent times no fewer than fifty lectures were delivered by him throughout Spain itself during the year 1947, while in the following two years we find him lecturing at the Santander International Summer School in Spain, and later appearing as delegate to the Apologetics Congress at Vich in 1949. Surely no man could be more intimately acquainted with Spain and with Spanish-speaking countries.

In his literary capacity Pattee has been regular contributor to a full half-dozen Spanish periodicals, including at least two dailies: *El Grafico* in Venezuela and *El Pueblo* in Buenos Aires, the remaining papers appearing in Madrid. In addition he has provided regular articles to the Spanish news agency, "Logos." Evidently no one can fail to perceive his intimate connection with Spanish events and the Spanish people!

Particularly worthy of note, however, is the fact that among the books written by him no fewer than five are in the Spanish language, the first of these appearing in 1939 and the most recent in 1949. Significantly the title of this latter book is *Informe sobre España,* or as you might render it into English: "What You Should Know About Spain."

Obviously, then, if there is one person qualified reliably to inform the world about Spain today, it is this scrupulously exact and careful author, who in the writing of his present work has spared no pains and labor to give us an authentic and at the same time most interesting account for which the entire English-speaking world, still so badly misinformed upon this question, can never be too grateful.

As manifesting in a specific way the author's long-continued and universal interest in the History of Spain, to which this book is dedicated as a most significant contribution, we need but further mention his present membership in the Academies of History established respectively in Ecuador, Panama, Colombia, Nicaragua, and Venezuela, while he also holds today affiliation with the Geographical Society of Lisbon.

All this external evidence is backed by the absolute reliability of this book and the ease with which the author uncovers the factual errors and often, no doubt, the positive falsehoods that abound in the present-day literature in Spain. As for the thoroughly paganized products of the extreme socialist, communist, and anarchist combination that has striven to submerge Spain under their own godless and destructive rule, there can be nothing but utter contempt. They are not writing history but are merely laboring to promote their own red dogmatism. Yet Spain has been cluttered with such abominations, too often taken seriously by the world at large.

Every letter in the work issued by the present writer is backed by facts and evidence to the ultimate degree. But what still further characterizes this book is the author's conscientious accuracy, giving to all men and to every group of men, independently of their religious or social affiliations, the perfect measure of justice, whether there be question of praise or blame. There is nothing iconoclastic in these pages. On the other hand, the reading done by the author is amazing, and the judgment passed by him on the innumerable citations given is always to the point, if a judgment is at all called for.

Now indeed, if ever, Spain needs the fellowship and confidence of the anticommunist world, while this, in turn, badly needs Spain. Let us be helpful one to the other, or else perhaps in these tremendous times we might willfully expose ourselves to go down to ruin together. Spain, it is true, may still be far from ultimate perfection, but so too are we!

JOSEPH HUSSLEIN, S.J., PH.D.
General Editor, Science and Culture Series

St. Louis University
February 14, 1950

ACKNOWLEDGMENTS

I HAVE to acknowledge indebtedness to the editor of *Columbia,* organ of the Knights of Columbus, for permission to use certain material that first appeared in the pages of that publication. The list of persons in Spain to whom I am deeply indebted would fill many pages. I am particularly grateful to Manuel Jiménez Quílez, Manuel Berlanga Borba, Manuel Martínez Pereiro, Fernando Martín Sánchez Juliá, Father Ramón Puig Cunill of Barcelona, Alfredo Sánchez Bella, Director of the *Instituto de Cultura Hispánica,* Santiago Magariños, His Excellency Joaquín Ruíz Jiménez, Spanish ambassador to the Holy See, and a host of other friends whose ideas and opinions have aided me considerably in arriving at conclusions regarding contemporary Spain. I cannot fail to mention the endless courtesies and materials made available by the *Oficina de Información Diplomática,* under the able direction of Luis María Lojendío, and the Hemeroteca of Madrid with its splendid newspaper and pamphlet collections.

None of these friends is responsible, of course, for opinions or conclusions at which the author arrives.

CONTENTS

This Is SPAIN

Chapter 1. THE HISPANIC TEMPERAMENT

"We have invented nothing, but we have had faith and courage. We have discovered and conquered lands; we have fought everywhere in the world. For spiritual satisfaction during peace, we have achieved mysticism. To occupy our leisure we have conceived a magnificent art and to arouse our emotions we have developed bull fighting" (Angel Ganivet).

IN THESE words the Spanish mind is summarized by one of the most penetrating observers of the past century. It stresses the three elements that constitute the synthesis of the Spanish people: the resolute refusal to succumb to the modern mania for gadgets and the mechanized society; a profound sentiment of religion; and a very high degree of emotional capacity. It is a simple statement of the fact that Spain has been out of step with the rest of the world, a discrepancy which springs from clinging to values which the rest of the world — and I refer naturally to the western European and American — has too often discarded as painfully outmoded.

After all, what is Spain? Some writers have preferred the term "The Spains" as a more accurate description of the diversity within unity that is a basic feature of the peninsula.[1] Physically, Spain is a microscopic world in itself. Diversity is so startling as to disturb the casual traveler who finds himself in a maze of transformation and contradictions as he moves from province to province.

There is the undefinable majesty of the *Basque provinces.* No city in Spain conjures up quite the same sentiments as Pamplona. It is, in many ways, a very ordinary town. But there hangs over it an aura of militancy and intransigent adherence to conviction that is unequaled in the peninsula. The Navarrese belong to a sturdy branch of humanity, tough, resilient, and profoundly attached to their soil. The contem-

[1] Carles Cardo, *Histoire spirituelle des Espagnes,* Paris, 1946.

porary visitor to Spain is all too often provoked by what he calls, for the sake of a better name, the "reaction" of Navarre. It is infallibly annoying to the modern mind to discover that there are people in this world who are not eager for "progress" and who are quite ready to resist the inroads of modernism. Navarre fought for decades the losing battle for the Carlist successor. The patriarchal family farm system produced an almost unanimous adherence to the crusade against the Republic when it broke in 1936. The bright red berets of the Traditionalists, their simple political and social creed, their unswerving loyalty made them one of the unconquerable ramparts of Hispanism.

There are other Basque provinces too, from *Guipúzcoa* with the effete San Sebastián, to the rugged mountain country behind Bilbao. The Basques have long constituted a nucleus of unexplained origin in the main body of Spanish territory. Their industriousness is proverbial; their family organization splendid; their fierce local loyalty a source of strength. Basque nationalism is a factor of no small importance in the history of contemporary Spain.

To the west lies *Asturias*, a kindly region, endowed by nature with resources and a diligent people. It was here that the tiny nuclei of Christian resistance formed to thrust back the Moslem after the first great wave of Islamic conquest swept over the land. Vast numbers of Asturians have migrated to settle the western hemisphere and bring riches back to their province.

Beyond Asturias is *Galicia,* as different from harsh, dry Castile as though it belonged to another world. Its lush climate, exuberant vegetation, heavy rainfall, and soft landscape, have made the Galician akin to the Portuguese in temperament. His language is very nearly that of neighboring Portugal. The melancholy and sweet sadness that makes Portugal so different from Spain forms a part of the spiritual heritage of Galicia. The *rías* of Galicia are minor fiords along the Atlantic seaboard. This and the Cantabrian coast have long been Spain's window out on the world, and especially on America. Its fisherfolk supply a large part of the seafood that constitutes so vital a part of the Iberian diet. It looks out across the ocean in a way contrasting with the deep introspection of Castile.

Catalonia conjures up Barcelona and the magnificent Mediterranean coast. It is a compact area with a language and a culture of its own, the Mediterranean being its outlet. Contact with France has influenced its culture. Its people have long enjoyed fame for their extraordinary industriousness and capacity for competition in the modern world of business and trade. They are, perhaps, the one Spanish element which has achieved real incorporation with the economic trends of the times. Catalonia means a great deal to Spain, for much of its industry is concentrated here. Its spiritual inheritance is no less significant, for it is the link between the predominant Castilian form of expression and the French and Italian.

Running parallel to Portugal is *Extremadura,* which merges with León in the north. The brown dryness of Extremadura has long been the synonym of poverty, and grinding, heartless landlessness. Its peasantry has struggled for centuries in this inhospitable land to eke out a bare living from its barren soil. Its population is sparse, its territory reeking with history. It is not by mere chance that so many of the conquerors of America came from Extremadura, with Pizarro and Cortes typical products of its soil. Rough and unlettered, these Extremaduran peasants performed miracles of intrepidity and gave Spain a large segment of its empire.

To the south lies *Andalucía.* Here every major city is colorful and meaningful. The traces of the Moslem occupation are visible in the architecture, the customs, and the people. Seville is not merely a city concerning which the tourist agencies conjure up alluring adjectives, but a synthesis of Spanish history in the imperial period. Along the Andalucian coast — Málaga, Almería, Algeciras, Cádiz — there is poverty, for meager resources have made it one of the socially most depressed areas of the entire peninsula. The contrast is overwhelming between the solid prosperity of Barcelona and the Catalan hinterland, or between the frugal well-being of the north and this sunny, underprivileged Mediterranean coast. There is an Andalucian temperament, terribly overromanticized by foreign visitors; visions of guitars, tight trousers, haunting music, and moonlight that befog its harsh realities. Strong in its vitality — for no people of Spain have more sheer animal spirits — it has never pulled its weight in the struggle for social and economic betterment. There are whole regions of indescribable depression, despite the natural charm of the people and scenery. Lesser areas should not be forgotten. There is the Mancha, of Don Quixote fame, some of its windmills still whirling in the breeze and dust, its villages reminiscent of the scenes of the dreams and heroism of the cavalier of the Mancha and his sturdy attendant, Sancho.

Castile is the hard core of things Spanish, culturally and historically. It has been described a thousand times in the prose of a dozen languages with its bleak tablelands, broken here and there by chains of mountains, and the austere vastness of its plains. Miguel de Unamuno in his exquisite *En torno al casticismo* depicts it as a "petrified sea full of sky." The Castilian landscape does not provoke sentiments of softness or of voluptuosity. It is hard, real, earthy, and filled with the spirit of constant struggle against the adverse elements of nature. A poor soil, a magnificent, endless sky, rugged bare mountains; this is the physical backdrop of Castile. Life in Castile is not easy. Nature provides a hard and exhausting living for the tenacious Castilians who till its barrenness generation after generation. This is no land of light-hearted, flighty folk, devoted to the good things of life. It is the land of a meditative, introspective, transcendental people, whose awareness of God is accentuated by the sobering influence of a harsh milieu. Cold in winter, blazing hot in summer, Castile squeezes its inhabitants. Its peasantry has acquired the complexion of the land it works. Heroes and saints are more likely to come from this unpromising atmosphere than men of indifference or the easy life. Castile has given the tone to all Spain. It is the everlasting miracle of a land that has nothing in its favor except the will of its people, but which has given form and spirit to the entire peninsula. Expanded beyond the seas, it has created a unique and steadfast culture. Castile is tradition and introspection at the same time. Let one but visit Salamanca, whose whiteness stands out against the uniform gray as one approaches from the other side of the Tormes. Let him visit austere Valladolid which gives the impression of the quintessence of the Castilian. Let him stop midway between Madrid and Valladolid, in the empty waste of the plain, and feel the silence and the restraint that have molded the Castilian character. It is the heart and soul of Spain and is the reason for its greatness and its weakness. There is toughness, hardihood, obstinate refusal to succumb, and ability to bear adversity in the fiber of the Castilian people. Let anyone who thinks of the Spanish as soft Mediterraneans, engrossed in the business of pleasure and self-indulgence, visit Castile. Its peasants and its merchants, its townsmen and its shepherds have produced almost every element of greatness the nation has ever known.

There is a striking similarity between Spain and Palestine; not merely in the external aspects of aridity, vegetation, and often physical appearance, but in the more profound spiritual characteristics. In Palestine and Spain there is continuity of tradition — not traditionalism as a political idea, but the fundamentally uninterrupted way of life and sense of values that partake of the whole of man's presence in a particular territory. Spain, says Maurice Legendre, "is a Biblical land."[2] It is a land of prophets and of saints. It is a land of fervor and repentance. Spain, like Palestine, is a singular anachronism in the twentieth century, not because it is queer or obtuse, but because it has retained perhaps more than any other European people a standard of values which are no longer those of the so-called "advanced nations." There are, to be sure, innumerable Spaniards who belong to the cosmopolitan world about them. There is a legion of intellectuals during the past and present centuries who are Spanish only in the language they employ for expression and who have broken with the tradition that still prevails for the immense majority of their fellow countrymen.

Spain has always been a land of peasants. The inroads of industrialism have changed the face of some of its large cities and a bit of its countryside, but it still remains what it has been from the dawn of history: a nation of humble folk, tucked away in their villages and farms, rooted solidly to the ground, unafraid of the challenge of the times, and not particularly moved by the proposal that they adapt themselves to the modern way of life. Even the proletariat in the large cities, in direct contact with the new economic order, has looked at it and found it wanting. One of the secrets of the Spanish labor movement, and especially of its extreme expression, anarchism, was precisely that the anarchist reacted not against capitalism itself, but against the introduction of capitalism. This is perhaps the basic reason why the Spanish, when they threw off traditionalism in the spiritual sense, swung over to the opposite extreme, and embraced the most devastating doctrine of all — anarchism.

If there is a single reason for prefacing this story of modern Spain with this little disquisition on the Hispanic temperament, it is to establish one important premise, without which the understanding of the Spanish experience is out of focus, and that is the need for comprehending the scale of values to which the Spanish adhere. It is not a question whether these values are good or bad; whether we like them or not; whether they ought to be changed or not.

One of the platitudes about Spain is the intense individualism of its people. The Spaniard has been judged more than once to be ungovernable because of his refusal to sacrifice any part of his own individuality to the common good. Miguel de Unamuno has established

[2] Maurice Legendre, *Semblanza de España,* Madrid, 1944, p. 41.

a subtle distinction between what he calls the "individualism" and the "personalism" of the Spaniard. Martin Hume, the historian, speaks of the "introspective individuality of the Spaniards." At another point he uses the expression "overwhelming individuality."[3]

This individuality proceeds from a number of sources. In the first place, it is a reflection of the Christian conception of the value of the individual with the conviction that the business of saving one's soul is personal and not collective. Secondly, it reflects the Spanish insistence on making things concrete. The Spaniard is no friend of vague abstractions. It is for this reason that principles have often been sacrificed in Spain to flesh-and-blood human beings. Humanity means nothing; the individual human being who makes up that humanity means a very great deal indeed. It would be inconceivable, for instance, that Auguste Comte should ever exert the slightest influence on the Spanish mind. The cult of humanity, which is often what our so-called humanism today becomes, has never penetrated Spain to any appreciable degree. This insistence on personalizing reality reveals itself in the precise and direct form with which God, the Blessed Virgin, and the saints are depicted. God could never be designated merely as "The Supreme Being," or even simply as the "Deity." Our Lady is presented in innumerable invocations in terms that satisfy the Spanish yearning for the concrete.

Charity evidences itself in the same way. The Spaniard conceives of charity in the abstract with great difficulty. Whereas in America or in Britain, organized charities function normally and people can be moved to give money for the relief of Tibetan victims of a disaster, even though they may never have laid eyes on a Tibetan in their lives, the Spaniard tends to make his charity a direct personal relation. The beggar on the street or in the square, who is a flesh-and-blood human being, in need of the charity of his fellow men, arouses the charitable instincts of the passer-by. This impulse toward charity is construed in terms of a visible, known, and tangible object.

Much of the attitude and spirit of the Spanish is related directly to the problem of religion. No proper understanding of the history or institutions of Spain is possible without an appraisal of the precise place of religion in the life of both the individuals and the community. This is unquestionably the major hurdle for the modern student of

[3] Martin Hume, *The Spanish People, Their Origin, Growth and Influence,* London, 1901, pp. 375 and 12. A most stimulating essay on the "problem of Spain" is that of Pedro Laín Entralgo, *España como problema,* Madrid, 1948.

things Spanish. The idea that religion really forms a fundamental part of life and that people take it seriously has gone out of our existence in all too many cases. The result is that modern-minded observers search frantically for any explanation except the obvious one. To the modern mind, human beings can be explained on almost any ground except their concern about God and their anxiety about the hereafter. Yet Spanish history and conduct is meaningless if God is removed from the equation.

"The moment Christianity was introduced into Spain it rooted itself so firmly there that it was soon the essential element of the national character."[4] The celebrated American Hispanist, Ticknor, has said that "No sooner did Spain become Christian than it became mystic." The flowering of mysticism has been a significant phase of the whole spiritual odyssey of the Spanish nation. Much has been written on the subject, but this is obviously not the place to do more than call attention to the fact that mysticism plays an exceedingly important role in the story of the spiritual development of the country. Spanish mysticism must be fitted into that equally complex picture of the peculiar Hispanic insistence on a combination of the divine and the human. "Nowhere is the divine and the human so intimately linked as in the Hispanic world."[5]

This happy blending of the world and the other world, the flesh and the spirit, the body and the soul, permeates every aspect of Spanish life and is particularly evident in literature. A large body of the early Hispanic literary tradition is popular in nature; it springs from the wit and wisdom of the ordinary people: peasants, tradesmen, and petty bourgeoisie. The *Romancero* is an endless mine of this popular tradition. The Quixote, itself a compendium of the Hispanic mind, reveals not a cavalier detached from the realities of his *milieu,* but a very human and often pathetic man, beset by difficulties and disturbed by obstacles. Don Quixote has sometimes been looked upon as the most unreal creature ever to parade through the pages of literature. On the contrary, he is one of the most earthy of our literary heroes. His eye is constantly on the goal he has set for himself, which is sublime. His feet are invariably placed very squarely on the solid earth from which he sprang. It is a supreme achievement that he manages to rise above the ordinary shackles that bind him to a mundane and prosaic existence

4 David Rubio, O.S.A., *The Mystic Soul of Spain,* New York, 1946, p. 27.

5 Pfandl, *Historia de la literatura nacional española en la edad de oro,* Barcelona, 1933, p. 5.

to strive for that which is sometimes elusive and intangible. Honor, gallantry, courage, and an unflinching devotion to what he conceives to be his duty is a reflection of the thirst of the Spanish race for transcendent values; for a touch of the divine. Sancho Panza, who follows him in triumph and adversity, has been depicted as the vulgar, gross attendant, concerned more with filling his belly than with the ideals of his master. But the devotion and endurance of a Sancho and his willingness to be convinced even if his eyes do not see, is again a part of the collective portrait of the Spanish people. Sancho is an everlasting testimony to the ability of coarse matter to catch a glimpse at least of the eternal.

It would take pages to describe how this conception prevails throughout Hispanic culture. Take, as an example, the magnificent picture, the *Death of the Conde de Orgaz* of El Greco. Here we have the death of a nobleman depicted with no softening, no lessening of the sharp reality, and no glossing over of the harsh fact of death. Above and beyond the scene of death is the vision of eternity, an image that is a sort of preview of the destiny of all men. It is earth and heaven; man and God; the transient character of this life and the glory of the next. No single example more eloquently illustrates the double nature of the Spanish mind in all of its activities and anxieties.

The reader need not think of the Spanish mysticism to which I have referred as a cold, emaciated thing. It was no perpetual state of ecstasy of bloodless men and women who languished in monastic cells out of contact with the world. Mysticism was, to be sure, more than mere piety and even more than saintliness. It was a communication with God; a prevision, so to speak, of beatitude. It has been given to few men to achieve this intimate communion with God. But the Spaniards who achieved it were often men and women who also attained a most competent communion with the society of their time.

St. Teresa was by all odds one of the most remarkable of this army of mystics. Read her own writings, written at the command of her superiors and despite her own protestations of literary inability. Her language is frequently incorrect, but her thought is of pristine clarity, going straight to the heart of both the mystical visions with which she was rewarded and the affairs of the world in which she was engaged as one of the most remarkable administrators of her time. St. John of the Cross devoted his early days to care of the sick. St. Thomas of Villanova, Archbishop of Valencia, was literally a wholesaler in almsgiving and the succor of the poor and afflicted. St. John of God founded an order. Luis of Granada recommends with insistence the visit to the sick, aid to the needy, and constant care of those in misery. Ticknor has spoken of this band of mystics as having in superlative quantities one of the great virtues which so many lacked in a harsh age: compassion and mercy.

The Spanish mystics emphasized introspection, attaining a delicacy and profundity of psychoanalysis rarely equaled and perhaps never surpassed in the annals of human experience. These strong men and women, so devoted to the works of God and to communion with Him, were superb defenders of the Faith, and with it of the integrity of Europe and the Church. The mystics made Spain's Christianity a living, real thing. Hence the special character of the Hispanic Renaissance, so profoundly different from that of the rest of the Continent. In the chapter on the history of Spain we shall have occasion to refer to certain of the major features of this enlightenment and the way in which Spain wedded orthodoxy to survival.

The Spanish preoccupation with death, combined with the absolute naturalness with which he accepts its reality, is another characteristic that puzzles and sometimes shocks the foreign observer, and very particularly the Anglo-American mind. To an age in which the fact of death must be covered up with endless euphemisms, it is not surprising that the Spanish forthrightness in face of it should prove profoundly disconcerting. Death is ever present in the Spanish mind. It is the supreme fact of life; the normal dividing line and the threshold beyond which lies the realization of the boundless promises of Christ. Death is ever present and its presence is taken with that remarkable matter-of-factness that astonishes the foreign observer. We all remember perhaps the story of an officer in the late civil war who, driving with a foreign correspondent over a road close to the firing line, stopped the car for the purpose of examining some imperfection. Bullets were whizzing all over the place and the foreigner suggested, with some trepidation, that perhaps it might be well to seek shelter before they became a target for the shooting. The Spanish officer was startled. "But you are in a state of grace, are you not? If you are, what difference does it make whether a bullet hits us or not?"

The disdain for death accompanied by a yearning for immortality, that is, the projection of life beyond death itself, is not the consequence of cynicism, brutishness, or fatalism. It is the product of faith, of unbreakable, unbounded, limitless faith that is called by those to whom faith is a strange and archaic thing, fanaticism. The Spaniard is naturally a believer, and if his faith in revealed religion is destroyed he is likely to become an equally ardent atheist, or a violent partisan of some form of extremism. Let it be mentioned in passing that with the enthusiasm and ardor that the Spanish put into everything, the individual who loses his Catholic faith is almost certain to become strongly anticlerical, vigorously hostile to the Church, and quite possibly its persecutor. Unamuno has called attention to the fact that the fallen-away Catholic is not likely to continue as a passive, indifferent human being. He will put his faith in something. He may be a great saint or a very great burner of convents or flayer of the clergy, but he is not going to do either job half-heartedly. The idea of compromise and the happy medium is something quite out of keeping with the Spanish temperament.

The major difficulty in the way of parliamentary government springs from this incapacity to compromise. The Spanish character tends to draw the ultimate consequences from any principle that it embraces. If a republic is established, it must be absolutely republican and all traces of monarchism must be effaced. If anarchism becomes the principle for which the Spaniard is ready to live and die, it must be absolute. There is no room for sharing and mutual concession. Spanish Catholicism partakes of this quality and for this reason is so sadly misunderstood abroad. One of the most discouraging things is the hostility, veiled or open, that so many non-Spanish Catholics have shown regarding Spain and its Church. In later chapters I shall have occasion to call attention to some of these criticisms. Many of them are caustic, not a few of them are bitingly ironical, and almost none of them reveals the slightest conception of the Spanish background, the tribulations and trials of its Spanish peoples, or the inherent character of their race. There is altogether too much of a tendency to conceive of Catholicism in Spain as bad and ineffective because it does not operate precisely as it does in Chicago or Philadelphia. The Spanish Catholic does not cease to be a Spaniard simply because he is a Catholic. He brings to bear on his religious conduct long centuries of experience, outlook, and conditioning. The least the foreigner can do is to appraise this background as the indispensable prelude to the present scene. This understanding will help us to grasp, for example, the Spanish insistence on religious unity, the reluctance to make concessions to heretical religious groups, the so-called intolerance of Spain, and the particular thesis of the Spanish on the relations of Church and State. Several of the recent *Conversaciones*

Católicas, held annually at San Sebastián, have treated of this problem, where the discrepancy between the Spanish on one side, and, let us say, the Belgians and French on the other, is noteworthy. It is the product of those who have lived under religious unity, who prize it above everything else, and who believe the defense of orthodoxy a primary need of our time against those who live in mixed communities or who are more concerned with meeting the challenge of an age that seems to demand flexibility.

Again and again in these pages it will be emphasized that religion is the main link in the unity of Spain. That this unity is basic, real, and enduring admits of no doubt. Havelock Ellis has called attention to the general unity despite the innumerable elements of disunity. Religion, and specifically the Roman Catholic and Apostolic religion, serves the purpose of providing an *external* force above and beyond the myriad of disrupting elements in Spanish society. Precisely because Spaniards are divided in politics, social conceptions, and a hundred other things, combined with the hardy, obdurate individuality that makes of each Spaniard a little island fortress of its own, religion provides the basis of union outside of these preoccupations. It is superior to the ordinary loyalties precisely because it is revealed by God and not concocted by man. Even the monarchy, despite its tremendous prestige and antiquity, could never provide quite the same buttress for Spanish society as does revealed religion. It has held Spanish society in place, while within the social order the countless elements of discord and anarchy held sway.

The predominance of the Catholic faith and monarchical institutions have never made the Spaniard anything but a democrat at heart. Hispanic democracy is basically aristocratic for the simple reason that the individual Spaniard's sense of his own intrinsic value is very high. In a society where every man is conscious of his worth and sometimes capable of overvaluating it, there is no place for an undemocratic order. Even at historical moments, when the royal power was at its height, the attitude of the ordinary Spaniard was that of rigid distinction between those things that belonged to Caesar and those things that belonged to God. Even before the King, no Spaniard quaked in helpless fear. Personal dignity and the sense of individual worth made it impossible. The King was never confused with the State. His function was always carefully delimited. His authority was never to be taken as that of the institutions themselves over which he presided.

Al Rey la hacienda y la vida se ha de dar; pero el honor es patrimonio del alma y solo se debe a Dios.[6]

A strong sense of equality pervades all Spanish society. The dignity of the peasant has become proverbial. There is a famous anecdote of how a humble peasant spoke his mind to Charles V, unhesitatingly and without recourse to the slightest subtlety. This passion for equality, combined with a love of a hierarchized society — and the ideas are not contradictory — is revealed in a hundred ways. Ramiro de Maeztu tells of the case of the distinguished Spanish medical man, Ramón y Cajal, who, as a medical student, was annoyed that no Spanish names figured among the authorities cited in his textbooks. So indignant was he that he set out to prove that what British, French, Germans, and Americans could do, Spaniards also were capable of achieving. He did not abandon his microscope until his name became one of the greatest in the history of contemporary medicine.[7] This personal dignity and the strong traditionalism that has endured in Spain so unbrokenly has produced a remarkably high level of general culture.

Indeed, this last phrase requires a word of explanation. Someone is bound to rise up and announce that statistically it can be demonstrated that there has always been a high degree of illiteracy in Spain; that compared to other European countries, Spain can hardly be considered as advanced. This is quite true for the person who still thinks that literacy and culture are the same thing, or that the number of schoolhouses necessarily produces a society of cultivated folk. It takes no account of the brutal fact of our own age in which the number of illiterates who know how to read and write is inordinately large. G. K. Chesterton once remarked that he was touched and moved on a visit to Spain by the deep culture of many of its unlettered peasantry. The explanation is that these peasants retain a very rich heritage of tradition and oral culture, all so often forgotten in our mania to believe that culture can only be contained in a printed page. Spanish culture itself has always been extremely close to the mass of its people, and its literature is full of evidence of how the more refined forms of expressions have found their source in the immense quarry of popular tradition, folkways, and the wisdom of the anonymous

---

[6] "To the King must be given goods and life, but honor is the patrimony of the soul and belongs only to God," Calderón, *Alcalde de Zalamea.*

[7] Maeztu, *Defensa de la Hispanidad,* Madrid, 1946, 5 ed., p. 65.

masses of the peoples. Let it be remarked, too, that if we should avoid the confusion of culture with either literacy or education, we must not presume either that it is the equivalent of civilization.[8]

It is true that in the strictly material order Spain is woefully out of step with the world. Comfort as such has never been a matter of primary concern to the Spanish mind. There is a current throughout its history of positive disdain for the material and in every expression of the Hispanic ideal there is attached a singularly small value to possessions as such. Leadership, eminence, and authority have never had anything to do with what a man was, but what he believes. Nothing is more revelatory of this state of mind than the fact that even at the height of its power in the world, Spain was consistently in financial straits. Don Quixote has perhaps expressed it most succinctly: "Where-ever I am, that is the head." It is the individual and his worth that represent the supreme determinant of the place he holds in the social order.

There is unquestionably something that for the sake of a better term we may call the "Spanish way of Life." Manuel García Morente has devoted numerous pages to the subject and has concluded that "neither race, blood, territory, or language really suffice to explain the essence of a nationality." There is something more fundamental than any of these accidents to explain that subtle and elusive thing called a "style," a "way of life," a "temperament." "Spain displays a unity of style. There is a Spanish way of life. It cannot be violated and the nation cannot be called upon to engage in an enterprise that runs counter to that style or way."[9] García Morente has undertaken to discover what the Spanish ideal really is and how it can be examined in the concrete. He finds that the Christian knight — using the term in a very broad sense — represents the synthesis of this Hispanic ideal. This knight is distinguished by a lively and realistic faith, for the Spaniard is normally incapable of vague sentimentality or pure rationalism. He sees in both tendencies a perversion of real faith. And he is entirely disposed to follow his faith to the ultimate conclusion regardless of circumstances and without reference to any of the ordinary contingencies that curb and modify most human conduct. He is, to use the brilliant expression of this same writer, a man of *"más pálpito que*

---

[8] A remarkably illuminating little essay on the Spanish character is that of E. D. Gannon, "Portrait of a Spaniard," published as No. 21, Vol. VIII (London, December, 1947) of *The British Survey* series.

[9] García Morente, *Idea de la Hispanidad,* Madrid, 1947, 3 ed., p. 27.

cálculo," that is to say, he depends for the source of his action far more on the ideal than on the practical; he rejects studied calculation of advantage and benefit as undignified and unbefitting a gentleman and a Christian. This willingness to sacrifice for the ideal without reference to material advantages might be meditated by unthinking statesmen who believe that Spain can be made to change her government or institutions simply because some international group does not like them. The most superficial acquaintance with the character and past of the Spanish race would teach them that coercion of this sort or the threat of economic sanctions would produce the opposite effect. The Spaniard probably feels a certain exhilaration and zest in finding himself alone against the world. This has been, incidentally, his normal position down through the ages, and he is not disconcerted to discover himself in mortal combat with the world once more. Aside from political considerations, pressure of this kind is a psychological blunder of the first order.

The Spaniard displays at the same time a joyous disrespect for established authority in the form of administration, bureaucracy, and the like. Spanish letters are full of rogues who have devised clever ways for outwitting officialdom. No literature contains more vigorous satire against the authorities or the administrators of the laws. Don Quixote, releasing the prisoners on their way to the galleys, performs a typically Spanish action. Sancho Panza's eternal fear of the *Santa Hermandad* is an equally characteristic reaction. Reverence for authority and a willingness to defy it in numerous petty ways go hand in hand. It is the same as the devout respect with which the Spanish treat religion and, simultaneously, the familiar manner they have with so many religious things and institutions. In language and conduct, in proper names and devotions, a sense of personal *rapport* with religion is constantly evident.

Much of this attitude derives from the highly developed Spanish sense of the absurd. Administrators, and especially people connected with tax collecting, are likely to be extremely tiresome. Their profession lends itself to endless fun, while solemnity either in high or low classes of society is mercilessly satirized. This overwhelming sense of the ridiculous is one of the major saving graces of Spain. Without it, hopelessness might very well have overtaken the nation long ago. Certainly by the standards of objective history and human criteria Spain has not been a particularly fortunate country, but the redeeming grace of humor and an appreciation of the comic have saved it from that enormous self-pity that becomes so often an obsession of the Germanic mind.

This self-criticism often reaches extreme heights and becomes biting aspersion on everything national. Joaquin María Bartrina has expressed it in one of his epigrams:

> Listening to a person makes it easy
> To learn from where he comes,
> If he praises England he is English,
> If he speaks ill of Prussia, he is French
> If he speaks ill of Spain, he is Spanish.

Against this Spanish background everything must be measured in a different way than in other countries. Some writers are prone to apply the same terminology to Spanish affairs as elsewhere in Europe, thus leading to complete confusion. Liberalism, totalitarianism, republicanism — all are terms that in their universal application fail to fit the special circumstances of Spain. "Spanish liberalism has little in common with those convictions which are labelled with the name in Europe. In Spain it is simply synonymous with anticlericalism."[10] This is one of the numerous terms that must be defined with careful precision when Spain is concerned.

This brief survey of some of the salient characteristics of the Spanish spirit has of necessity left a great many things unsaid. It would have been wise, perhaps, to apply the general principles laid down in these opening pages to some of the problems of our day. The reader, however, will quickly grasp the relation between this analysis of temperament and some of the problems that face contemporary Spain. He should see among other things that the individuality, balance, deep spiritual force, and equanimity of the Spanish makes anything like real totalitarianism an impossibility in the Iberian peninsula.[11]

---

[10] Franz Borkenau, *The Spanish Cockpit* (London: Faber and Faber, Ltd., 1937), pp. 7–8.

[11] A few judicious selections may be made from voluminous literature on the Spanish mind and temperament. One of the most admirable is the long introduction from the pen of Ramón Menéndez Pidal in his *Historia de España. España prehistórica,* Vol. I, Madrid, 1947. The English translation of these observations is to be found in *The Spaniards in Their History* of Walter Starkie, London, 1950. An excellent short analysis is "Spain: the Country, Its Peoples and Languages," by William C. Atkinson: *Spain, a Companion to Spanish Studies,* ed. by E. Allison Peers, 4th ed., London, 1948. A suggestive essay is Rafael Calvo Serer, *España, sin problema,* Madrid, 1949.

Chapter 2. A SYNTHESIS OF SPANISH HISTORY: MAIN TRENDS TO THE FORMATION OF THE FIRST REPUBLIC

MIGUEL DE UNAMUNO raises the question: "Are we Spaniards fundamentally incapable of Europeanization and modernization? Is there no other life than the European and modern? Is there no other form of culture whatever it may be called?"[1] The essential character of Spain has been one of the constants in the preoccupation of Hispanic thinkers. Time and again, sometimes with anguish, sometimes with fierce pride, the peculiar historical personality of Spain has been emphasized by its own intellectuals as impossible of classification among the normal current of European development. Spain is something apart, set aside as a vast promontory reaching out toward Africa to the south and toward the western hemisphere across the ocean.

Of all the modern nations of Europe, Spain reveals perhaps the highest degree of historical continuity. Tradition became in the peninsula a deep-rooted and enduring thing. Factors of geography, ethnic fusion, and early political unity, gave Spain "a sometimes subtle, often striking originality."[2] The result was an undefinable combination of qualities and virtues which resists facile generalization. "Spain, the world's great aristocracy," was the expression used by Barrès to describe what is at the same time certainly one of the most democratic peoples on earth.

The main currents of Spanish history may be suggested as follows: (1) The long process of assimilation of numerous racial and cultural streams, giving Spain as rich a variety of elements as any modern European nation. (2) The Christianization of Spain brought with it an attachment to Catholicism which has been one of the most intense of all Spanish loyalties and allowed the nation to play an exceptionally

[1] *Sobre la europeización, Ensayos,* Vol. I, Madrid, 1945, p. 890.
[2] Pierre Vilar, *Histoire de l'Espagne,* Paris, 1947, p. 5.

important role in the evolution of Christian belief and life in the world. (3) Spain is the one European nation that received and assimilated to a very high degree the cultural heritage of the Arab world. (4) The expansion of Spain beyond the seas in the era of discovery and exploration made possible a new type of empire and a veritable society of nations under the aegis of the Spanish crown. (5) Spain was among the first of the European states to become a modern nation in the contemporary sense of the word, with the creation of a modern army and administrative structure. (6) The Spanish Golden Age represented a period of unparalleled brilliance not only for Spanish culture but for Europe at large. (7) The so-called decadence of Spain, reaching from the eighteenth through the nineteenth centuries is due to causes and factors alien to the Spanish genius itself, and largely the result of external influences.

These central ideas in Spanish history have been phrased in another way by an exceptionally qualified historian of things Hispanic:

> The Iberian tradition, emerging strong from pre-history and capable of enrichment through the Roman conquest and the evangelization of the peninsula, became national as a consequence of the numerous invasions from north and south. In the Golden Age this tradition achieved an imperial and universal value which protected it against the inroads of Revolution and gave it the strength to react to Revolution. This reaction was demonstrated first in a religious way in the sixteenth century; in a political in the nineteenth and in a social in the present century.[3]

A more recent historian of Spain, Albert Mousset, has expressed his astonishment that even with the improved means of communication and subsequent opportunity for a knowledge of Spain and its characteristics, there is no indication that this has come about. The same thick curtain of misunderstanding and *parti pris* prevails today as in the past. The present-day adverse opinion regarding the regime of General Francisco Franco is no different in essence than the views held contemporaneously regarding Philip II, Charles V, or other Spanish rulers. The same persistent refusal to understand Spain by Spanish standards; to penetrate beneath the superficialities to the basic elements that explain the course of events — this continues today in as virulent a form as in past centuries.

"The truth is that the history of Spain, like that of Russia, develops with a rhythm quite different from that of the other western peoples. But to consider it because of this difference as fundamentally

---

[3] Maurice Legendre, *Nouvelle histoire d'Espagne,* Paris, 1938, p. 7.

incoherent, is simply intellectual blindness."[4] The difficulty is that the Spanish tradition as revealed in its history retains certain values which the modern world rejects as outmoded and archaic. These values form an integral part of the backbone of the Hispanic way of life and are particularly in evidence in the history of Spain during periods of great strain and stress. No European nation was ever so profoundly impregnated with religion as Spain, nor is there a country in which nationality and religion are so intimately bound together. Few great literatures contain so many illustrious names of clerics who have gone down in history as creators of imperishable literary works.[5] Almost every characteristic of Spain in the modern age is to be found in the remote past, and particularly in the combination of religious conviction, missionary zeal, and unyielding devotion to independence.

Spain contrasts powerfully with neighboring France. In the latter country, the river systems form the unifying element of the people. There is no natural center in Spain, as Paris and London are the nuclei of French and British life. Spain's isolation springs in part from the Pyrenean barrier and the abundance of climatic and natural zones within the peninsula.

This is not an attempt to reduce to a few pages a systematic history of the Spanish people. This cursory survey of the main elements that go to make up the historical background may be suggested under three main heads:

1. The formation of the Spanish tradition;
2. The propagation of this tradition in the world influenced by Spain;
3. The defense of this tradition.

Around these three basic points the whole history of the country may be conceived to revolve. The formation of the Spanish tradition is the story of the elements that have gone into the making of the spiritual and social structure that we call the Spanish people. The expansion of that tradition is the story of Spain's influence in the world, both European and American, and the role she achieved at various moments in history elevating her to the plane of a universal

---

[4] Mousset, *Histoire d'Espagne,* Paris, 1947, p. 10. The so-called Black Legend, *Leyenda negra,* concerns not only the work of Spain in America, but the history and institutions of Spain itself. See Julián Juderías, *La leyenda negra. Estudios acerca del concepto de España en el extranjero,* Madrid, 1914 and 1917; Rómulo Carbia, *Historia de la leyenda negra hispanoamericana,* Madrid, 1944.

[5] The list of names in Spanish letters who were priests or religious would be interminable. Lope de Vega was a priest and member of the Inquisition. Tirso de Molina, Góngora, the historian Mariana, Gracián, and Calderón were all priests.

force. The defense of the tradition is simply the refusal to capitulate to the forces that make for revolution and transformation. Spain has been throughout history fundamentally antirevolutionary. The reaction against revolution, be it religious, political, or social, has been consistent and vigorous. The total hostility to heresy in the sixteenth century constituted a chapter in the process of rejection of liberalism and later of socialism in the nineteenth and twentieth centuries. Spain is one of the most perfect cases of a people that would not consent to transformation by external agencies.

From the earliest period until well into the eighth century of the present era Spain was the crossroads of conquest and migration. It has been spoken of as the *El Dorado;* the "Far West" of primitive Europe, to which the most heterogeneous peoples and cultures flocked in search of wealth or an abode. Celts and Iberians mingled in the far-off twilight of Spain's prehistory. A millennium before the birth of our Lord, the Phoenicians founded Cádiz and for five centuries they reigned supreme until the arrival of the first Greeks. The older Spanish historians, with an almost Hebraic fervor, describe the ancient origins of their people, pushing the beginning back to Tubal, son of Japhet, and connecting the evolution of the peninsula with Egypt. With the foundation of Marseilles the Greek navigators and merchants penetrated the West, and Spain was not exempt from their influence. Titus Livius tells us that "The Spanish, ignorant of the sea, were fond of trading with the Greeks." The primitive Iberians received the impact of the Near East to their advantage. The discovery in 1897 of the famous sculptured head called the Lady of Elche, demonstrated the close relations between the two extremes of the Mediterranean. Carthage contributed its share to the formation of the Spanish people, although even the more significant Carthaginian settlements, such as Cartagena and Cádiz, were never heavily populated.

Gaul required seven years for its conquest by the Romans. The subjugation of Spain began with the Second Punic War, in 218 B.C., and was terminated under Augustus almost at the beginning of the Christian era. The conquest was slow and erratic. Long before the final incorporation of the Iberian peninsula as a Roman province, the domination was virtually complete. The final pacification came in the closing years before the Christian period. The name of Augustus has been retained in numerous Spanish cities: Emérita Augusta (Mérida), Caesaraugusta (Zaragoza), and others. Roman rule proved to be a golden period during which great material changes were instituted.

Pax Augusta (Badajoz)

Spain contributed a brilliant company to the splendor of Rome: Martial, Quintillian, Séneca, Trajan, Hadrian, and Lucan. Roman rule declined after the third century, and by the fifth the Barbarian infiltrations brought in that steady stream of Gothic and Germanic influence that was to add one more ingredient to the already complex racial strain of the emerging Spanish people. The structure of Roman society was so strong that even the impact of the semi-Romanized Arian Christians who came under the name of Barbarians did not produce its collapse. The Visigothic center at Toledo became the focal point for an Iberian unity which was both administratively real and spiritually significant. The grandeur of this obscure period during which figures of the dimensions of Isadore of Seville flourished was rapidly transformed as Spanish society became decadent and the victim of innumerable internal conflicts.

The foundations of Christian Spain were laid firmly from the very beginning of the Evangelization. If the visit of St. James is shrouded in legend and supposition, we have the words of St. Paul regarding his voyage to Spain.[6] The powerful influence of the Latinized milieu made the spread of Christianity relatively rapid. By the third century Spanish soil was watered with the blood of martyrs at Huesca and Tarragona. The veneration of St. Eulalia still holds a very high place at Mérida and the memory of St. Engracia and the other martyrs is revered in Zaragoza.

Spain passed very rapidly from a mission country to a missionary one. Scarcely had Christianity shot its roots down deep into Iberian soil than Spain became one of the major forces in the Church militant. In the days of Arianism it was Osius of Córdoba who combated the heresy at the Council of Nicaea and was in large part responsible for the definitive statement of the creed that concluded the deliberations. Spain appeared even in that remote day in the form of champion of orthodoxy. This role is the central thread in the spiritual history of the nation. From Osius to Ignatius; from the martyrs of Tarragona to the Council of Trent; and down to our own time, the Spanish have demonstrated a rare discernment for the basic issues. Cutting through the rhetoric and verbiage within which so many questions are enveloped, an almost instinctive perception of the essential elements in controversy emerges. St. Damasus I, Pope, and Theodosius, Emperor of the West, were Spaniards. During the Visigothic period the bare out-

[6] Rom. 15:23, 28.

lines of the institutional life of the nation began to emerge. The development of Spanish legal principles from this primitive period is of supreme importance in understanding the Spain of today.[7]

Lord Acton has called the Councils of Toledo one of the most democratic of institutions and a sort of forerunner of modern parliamentary practice. This period gave the world the *Lex Visigothorum* and other legal codifications which were to constitute an important contribution to the juridical thought of Europe and the decided penchant of Spain for the moral and juridical sciences was clear from the earliest period.

The Spanish peninsula was overrun by the Arabs in the seven years from 711 to 718. The story of the Islamic occupation must be told very briefly although its influence on the Spanish mentality and customs was unquestionably considerable. The so-called Moslem "empire" was a short-lived affair, centering at Córdoba, but very soon broken up into innumerable minor kingdoms and *taifas* which in turn succumbed to the Christian Reconquest. Soon after the year 1000 this fragmentation of Arab Spain was almost complete, while after 1212 the Reconquest made great strides until the final expulsion of the Arabs from Granada. The influence of Islam lasted from three to eight centuries, varying in profundity in different areas.

The study of Islamic influence on Spain has experienced considerable modifications in recent years. The serious approach to the problem has done away with the facile generalizations about the Barbarians of the north against the refined and cultivated Arabs in the south. If Islamic culture attained a high level and exerted an undoubted influence on the rest of Spain and Europe itself, it was equally true that there were destructive elements in the presence of the Moslems in the peninsula. The term *Arab* is in many ways a misnomer. The actual Moslem population consisted largely of Berber from North Africa, more akin to the inhabitants of the peninsula than the Moslem conquerors out of the Middle East.

It is equally absurd to suppose that for seven long centuries Christian and Moslem fought an unending battle for supremacy. In fact

[7] "In Spanish political thought from the earliest times, justice was not only the end of human society, it was the norm and method of regulating civil society, and in fact the civil state has no other justification save that through it justice was secured. The state as an entity, either abstract or concrete, to which people owed allegiance and which had rights over the people composing it, never entered into the concept of Spanish legal thinking." Marie R. Madden, *Political Theory and Law in Medieval Spain* (New York: Fordham University Press, 1930), p. 33.

the Reconquest, although extending over many centuries, was characterized by spurts and stops. In some areas the conflict raged more persistently than in others, while elsewhere Moslem and Christian lived side by side in relative peace. There were Christians who turned Moslem; there were others who acquired the Arabic tongue, but retained their Christian faith, for every combination was possible during these long centuries of common occupation of the peninsula. The Moslems themselves were profoundly influenced by the contact with Christianity. Much of the splendid architecture and painting in the Spain of the Mussulman was the work of Spaniards. Despite the prohibition in the Koran to the depicting of human figures in religious art, Islamic artistic expression in Spain was distinguished by a strong Christian influence in this direction. The emergence of a form of ascetic life, even monastic, among the Moslems may be traced to contact with Christianity. This interplay of influences formed the basis of the complex and fascinating culture that grew up in the Spain divided between Moslems and Christians with a very strong Judaic influence added.[8] These mutual influences manifested themselves in language, in customs, and in thought, and Father Asín Palacios has shown in his *La Escatología musulmana en la Divina Comedia* (Madrid, 1919) how Dante borrowed heavily from Islam for certain of his descriptions of Paradise.

The Christian Reconquest had its beginnings in the tiny mountain kingdoms of the north. In the shadow of the Pyrenees, the minute Christian reducts became the nuclei of the forward movement that was to regain control of the peninsula and this ebb and flow of influences and conquest is another of the constants in Spanish history. The Moslems never established themselves properly beyond a line which crossed the peninsula from Coimbra in Portugal to Toledo, Guadalajara, and the Mediterranean coast. In Asturias, Galicia, and the Basque country, Christian resistance never wavered, although at times it was pushed very close to extinction, while the area of Burgos and León, although unincorporated in the Moslem realms, was a kind of no man's land, subject to razzias and largely depopulated.

[8] See Louis Bertrand, *Histoire d'Espagne*, Paris, 1932. The bibliography in Spanish on the Moslem period is extremely rich. The works of Asín Palacios are particularly significant. There is at Granada a center of Arab studies which is one of the most important sources for the interpretation of the cultural and historical places of the Moslems in Spain. Particularly interesting also is his *Huellas del Islam*, Madrid, 1941.

From 785 to 811 the Christians were on the defensive. This period of waiting was not unproductive, for it allowed the Franks to penetrate the east and convert the area of Barcelona into a Frankish march. After 840 the kingdom of Asturias expanded, fixing its capital at León. Toward the year 932 Burgos became the nucleus of a little kingdom which was to develop in time into Castile. Navarre also came into being and northern Spain was dotted with little kingdoms. In 1080 the Christians crossed the mountains and took Toledo and toward the end of that century the Cid Campeador carved out a little domain in the region of Valencia. The twelfth century belonged to Aragón. This kingdom was centered at Zaragoza, and with the marriage union with Barcelona began the new jurisdiction that was to become the Aragonese-Catalan kingdom. The thirteenth century was that of the great drive toward the south. The Battle of Navas de Tolosa in 1212 assured the Christians of sufficient unity to make the advance effective; James of Aragón took the Balearic Islands and Córdoba and Seville fell. By 1270 the Moslems retained scarcely more than Granada and an area about Huelva and the Reconquest appeared to have been stopped short. Portugal turned its eyes toward the ocean and toward Africa. Aragón became involved in Mediterranean projects and Castile was torn from time to time by dynastic strife.

Legislation flourished in Castile as in the days of the Visigothic monarchs. Ferdinand III codified the laws of the realm; his son Alfonso X, surnamed the "Wise," continued the work under the title of the *Siete Partidas*. Alfonso XI in the middle of the fourteenth century concluded this vast labor, a tribute to the scholarship and juridical spirit of medieval Castile.

The long duration of the Reconquest contributed certain traits to the Spanish character. For one thing it made warfare, and especially internal warfare, a more or less natural thing. In the second place it imposed an austerity which became a common feature of Spanish life. The spirit of medieval Spain was founded on the double conviction of a religious mission and the need for expansion. The Reconquest represented a permanent policy of colonization, since the areas taken over by the Christians were frequently depopulated and was, in a sense, a minor rehearsal of the great performance of the conquest of America. It produced a breed of men engaged in war and the expulsion of the enemy as their business. There was in this long period of struggle a very strong element of religion and the belief that the Christian enterprise was that of a holy war.[9]

The Reconquest saw the emergence of the social pattern that was to prevail in Spain for centuries and the salient features of the Spanish social order have their origin in this period. The role, for example, of the lesser nobility, the landowning class with a minimum of resources, was most important in the fighting forces that reconquered Spain. These were the *hidalgos,* the *Hijos de algo* — that is, the sons of something — who in a later period served in the armies of Flanders and Italy, went overseas and engaged in what was called the "professions of arms." They were to be found in the person of Don Quixote and in many of the picaresque tales. In our time the small landowner and the small-town lawyer reflect the sentiments and heritage of this class. The clergy too was molded by the influence of the Reconquest. Its militancy was the natural product of the mood and demands of the time; its authority and influence were enhanced by the nature of the struggle in which as a class it was of necessity in the vanguard.

But if the nobility and clergy enjoyed a special position in this social order, it must not be overlooked that the Reconquest was also a movement that contributed very powerfully to the maintenance of a profoundly democratic tradition. Nothing is more inaccurate than the notion that Spain was a land of retrograde absolutism where the "masses" possessed neither rights nor a voice. Few societies have combined more extraordinarily egalitarian and class distinctions at the same time. The Reconquest increased the royal authority and retarded feudalism while the peasant and urban communities were rapidly developing as strong and semi-autonomous groups. The resettlement of the lands taken from the Moslems made it necessary to create new communities, and these communities were granted privileges and the *fueros* extended to them formed the basis of a high degree of self-government. In fact the medieval tradition became so profound a part of the Spanish way of life that a sort of agrarian collectivism arose that has endured down to the present century. The existence of the Cortes in medieval Spanish practice provided a very early example of parliamentary institutions. It probably originated in León, and during the Middle Ages it flourished in all the Hispanic kingdoms: Castile, Valencia, Aragón,

[9] Joseph Calmette remarks: "The reconquest became for generation after generation the unfailing program of Spanish Christianity," *La formation de l'unité espagnole,* Paris, 1946, p. 7.

Catalonia, and Navarre. It received the king's oath to support the *fueros,* provided subsidies out of taxation, and presented the complaints of the citizenry to the monarch. "It is true that few peoples have participated more directly in their government in the course of their history than did the Spanish people in the Middle Ages."[10]

The twelfth century was a brilliant one for Christian Spain. St. Ferdinand ruled in Castile. A crusader for the expansion of the Faith, he was nevertheless a man of wide tolerance and spoke of himself as "king over the three religions" (Christian, Judaic, and Moslem). In Aragón James the Conqueror, poet and warrior, ruled, surrounded by men of great stature: Ramón de Peñafort, Ramón Llull, and others. Cathedrals were rising and Islam was pushed back into the recesses of Andalucía. Spain was not a united whole by any means, for each monarch of the separate Christian kingdoms tended to claim for himself the legitimate Visigothic heritage.

Leaving aside smaller divisions, the broad outline of the peninsula in the late Middle Ages was Portugal on the west, Castile in the center, and the combined Aragón-Catalonia-Valencia on the east. Around these three nuclei the history of Spain henceforth was to revolve. The force of attraction tended to pull each of the three kingdoms in a different direction. Portugal, under the Aviz dynasty and after the defeat of the Castilians at Aljubarrota, turned its eyes toward the ocean and along the coast of Africa. Portugal's frontier was fixed, and it remains so to our day as the most permanent unchanging international line of demarcation in Europe. Aragón and Catalonia became a Mediterranean power and, with the strength of the kingdom concentrated on the coast, it was in this direction that Aragonese-Catalan expansion veered. Its monarchs occupied Tunis in 1280, intervened in Sicily, obtained privileges in Sardinia and Corsica, fought with Venice against Pisa and Genoa, and secured a commercial foothold in the Near East and Greece. Spanish interests in Italy date

---

[10] Pierre Vilar, *Histoire de l'Espagne,* Paris, 1947, pp. 21–22.

"The government of these kingdoms, up to that time aristocratic and theocratic . . . was modified and developed a democratic tendency through general participation of the mass of people, represented by the delegates of towns, cities, and villages. . . . Popular liberties and the royal power were to be the two great political forces which opposed the feudal nobility and served as a solid foundation to our representative institutions." Manuel de Bofarull y Romaná, *Las antiguas Cortes, et moderno parlamento, el régimen representativo orgánico,* Alcalá de Henares, 1945, p. 35.

from the first intervention of the Aragonese kings in Italian affairs.

Castile, as a largely inland kingdom, was the only Hispanic state to pursue the war against Islam. The consolidation of its internal position became the primary preoccupation. The story of the fourteenth century holds the explanation of the rivalries of Portugal and Spain — the conflict of Catalan and Castilian and the reasons that led the Aragón-Catalan combination to resist the primacy of Castile. In 1410 the crisis came. The Catalan dynasty was extinguished and the Aragonese crown fell to a prince of Castilian origin. After ten years of confusion in Catalonia, James II came to the throne (1472). One of the major elements in his policy was the Castilian marriage of his son Ferdinand. By this process, Catalonia was inevitably doomed to the position of a province, a role to which the energetic and ambitious Catalans adapted themselves with the greatest reluctance.

Castile, on the other hand, was forging the instruments of power during the course of the fifteenth century. John II and Henry IV were not strong monarchs, but the natural consequences of Castilian expansions was beginning to bear fruit. The outlets to the sea through Andalucía and the Cantabric coast produced an economic upsurge, and wool production, the great industry of the Castilian highlands, brought wealth to Burgos and Bilbao. The middle class became increasingly important while the clergy and lesser nobility reacted against the turbulent condition of the higher nobility and the laxity of the court. There was a strong religious undercurrent favorable to unity. The influence of Jews and Moors in the Castilian court produced a reaction in favor of the older Christian tradition. Much of the conflict that distinguished the fourteenth and fifteenth centuries derived precisely from the fact that Spain was not a docile, easily managed nation, in which the will of a strong monarch was sufficient to produce order and stability. Contrary to the usual interpretation, the Spain of the late Middle Ages possessed a strong middle class, a firm mercantile foundation of its economy, and a very keen and highly developed political sense at the municipal level. The popular will was so strong that it insisted on the right to pass judgment on the monarch himself. "The nobles, and even the cities and clergy, proclaimed the right to depose the monarch."[11] In the midst of what appeared to be travail of the severest kind, the Spain of the late Middle Ages was dominated by the ideal of chivalry, of sanctity, and of crusade. It was the era

---

[11] Legendre, *op. cit.*, p. 148.

of Ramón Llull, of whom mention has been made, St. Vincent Ferrer, and a host of others who are the glory of medieval thought and spirituality.

Isabel, sister of Henry IV, was destined to carry on the tradition of the great monarchs and realize the miracle of peninsular unity. She had been married to the heir of the Aragonese throne for five years when Henry IV died in 1474. It was a decisive moment for the history of the Iberian peninsula — and for the world. Juana, the daughter of Henry IV and possible successor, was asked in marriage by the King of Portugal. The succession and marriage settlements could determine whether Castile was to ally itself with Aragón and achieve its own destiny, or with Portugal. The decision in favor of Aragón meant that henceforth Spain and Portugal would go their separate ways, each carving out its own place in the sun. The genius of Isabel meant quite simply that Spain was to be placed henceforth under the guidance of pastoral and warrior Castile, in the spirit that had animated the Reconquest. The mercantile *motif* of the Mediterranean ports was subordinated; the economic motivation of expansion was secondary. A territorial and religious sentiment dominated the work of their Catholic Majesties. Isabel found Spain a moral ruin at the time of her accession, for the court of Henry IV was anything but edifying and the degree of desolation throughout the land was incredible. Her reign literally transformed Spain within a few years:

> It is a transformation such as is rarely registered in history. It is unnecessary to go into details regarding the moral and political misery that prevailed in Castile under Henry. . . . Isabel, who knew better than anyone the state of affairs . . . turned her attention to the remedy, applying the most rigid and inflexible standards of justice.[12]

Spain was on the threshold of the greatest period in her history. The magnificent vitality that was latent in the Spanish people; the extraordinary historical juncture that led to triumph at home and conquest abroad, all converged to make the great and glorious Golden Age. Spain was dedicated not merely to the problem of construction in politics; she was embarked on the greatest enterprise to which human hand had up to that time been turned, the conquest of a new world. And in the peninsula there flourished the splendid fruits of erudition, intellect, the spirit, and the arts.

No single act of their Catholic Majesties has aroused the same

[12] Feliciano Cereceda, S.J., *Semblanza espiritual de Isabel la Catolica,* Madrid, 1946, p. 114.

passionate criticism as the decree expelling the Jews from Spain, signed March 31, 1492. The modern mind has chosen to see in this a kind of remote forerunner of the Nürnberg legislation. Nothing is further from the truth. Spain was not then and has never been in the slightest degree the promotor of racism. Certainly no European nation has been more free from this stigma than Spain, unless it be Portugal. The reasons for the expulsions were deep rooted and formed part of the outburst of religious and national fervor that came with the conquest of Granada. There was friction and misunderstanding between the Christians and Jews, for religion, let it be repeated once more, was taken as an essential element of nationality — one would almost say nationalism. This point is fundamental to the proper understanding of the Spanish mind and its history. The expulsion of the Jews and even the forced conversions, although the Jews were given the choice between conversion or exile, forms a part, too, of the spirit of the epoch. There is no more reason for indicting Ferdinand and Isabel for heartless cruelty than it is to pass over in silence similar actions in England, Germany, Switzerland, and every other country of Europe. Ludwig Pfandl, the eminent German Hispanist, has written: "Those who wax indignant regarding the ethics of the expulsion in Spain are recommended to study carefully the Reformation in England and Switzerland. There they will find forced conversions, by the side of which the solution of Ferdinand and Isabel is child's play."[13] The much maligned Inquisition was in large part an instrument of national policy and a guarantee that national unity should be maintained. This is not the place, obviously, to enter upon a detailed discussion of the Inquisition. If Spain became great and retained the bases of its unity for a hundred spectacular years it was due in no small part to the inflexible will of the Catholic kings and their immediate successors to maintain the religious unity of the nation without which Spain would have been incapable of her achievements.

The bridge between the Middle Ages and the modern period is the century and a quarter from 1479 to 1598. Three reigns take up this epoch and the Spanish people reached the pinnacle of their greatness before the seventeenth century sapped the foundations of this glory. The union of Castile and Aragón was followed by the conquest of Granada, the discovery of the New World, the incorporation of Navarre, and the new conception of empire. If Charles V fell just

---

[13] *Juana la Loca, su vida, su tiempo su culpa,* Madrid, 1938, 2 ed., p. 44.

short of the union of the entire peninsula, Philip II achieved this end with the fusion of the Portuguese and Spanish empires during his reign.

It must not be supposed that peninsular unity effaced all traces of the traditional local autonomy that had grown up in Spain ever since the formation of the primitive Christian states. The strong regional sentiment, which was destined to play so large a part in modern Spanish history, was not stiffled, but simply subordinated. Aragón had retained its administrative machinery even after the union, for it was really a confederation together with the Balearic Islands, Catalonia, and Valencia. This area retained its own coinage, its customs service, and chiefly the local Cortes. Even under Charles V, as a single sovereign, viceroys were maintained in the regional capitals, as the former kingdoms were never completely won over to the idea of officials and other functionaries from Castile, which was still regarded an alien land. The only possibility of unity in this case was a flexible administration on the part of the central government and a very high degree of prestige on the part of the monarch. This was amply achieved under Charles and Philip. Soon after the accession to the throne of Spain of Philip II, one of his first acts was a curtailment of the rights of Aragón, whereupon the local Aragonese authority called him to order without hesitation, insisting that its *fueros* be rigidly respected. Even in the seventeenth century when the first flush of enthusiasm and fervor had passed, the attempts of Count Olivares to promote centralization met with the flat refusal of Catalonia, which threatened to secede and join France.

The major work of the Catholic kings was to produce unity on the only basis on which it could possibly be achieved in Spain, the maintenance of religious orthodoxy. At the same time a sweeping religious reform was introduced to oblige the clergy to refrain from nonecclesiastical activities. The military orders ceased to be semi-autonomous states, the royal power was respected and obeyed and the mission of Spain is defined for the first time with precision and foresight. Spain was destined henceforth to play its role in the world either as the bulwark of traditional Christianity or not at all. The uncompromising Spanish mind, peculiarly unadapted to half measures, saw survival and security in unity around orthodoxy, and it was this principle which guided Spain at each moment of her greatness.[14]

[14] The interpretation is developed in detail in Julián M. Rubio, *Los ideales y los hombres en la España imperial,* Madrid, 1942, p. 34 sq.

There were very definite signs that religious heterodoxy was capable of finding its way through chinks in the solid armor of Hispanic orthodoxy. Illuminism, Erasmism, and the extremism of certain Spanish reformers such as Valdés and Serveto showed that Spain was not immune to such penetration. The growth of Erasmism was stopped by 1535, and under Philip II steps were taken against incipient Protestantism. Religious plurality as an idea gained no foothold and by the end of the sixteenth century was totally alien to the Spanish mind.

Historically the fact remains that Spain found greatness in religious uniformity. Two schools of thought have developed around this problem. There are many, and their number is legion today in Spain, who see in this unity the source of Spain's strength and the violation of this conception as the cause of the ills and infirmities that have beset the nation. The second school believed firmly that Spain was religiously isolated and narrowly sectarian, that this rigidity bred obscurantism and, what the extreme Left called, "fanaticism." This was the view that dominated much of the thinking in the nineteenth century, that presided over the republic's birth, and that led to the introduction of new philosophical and cultural currents into Spain.

The error in the second judgment rests on the confusion of time and conditions. In the late fifteenth and sixteenth centuries there was a rare convergence of popular sentiment, the will of the State, and the wish of the Church in favor of a policy of religious unity. The work of the Catholic kings translated that almost unanimous will into action. There was no violation of either opinion or sentiment by the State. Fanaticism was not the dominating characteristic of either Isabel or that remarkable man, Cardinal Cisneros, in so many ways the architect of the Spain of their Catholic Majesties. Cisneros was tireless in his efforts to root out heresy, but he was at the same time one of the precursors of the Catholic reform itself; a reformer of the monastic orders, founder of the University of Alcalá, and the patron of the Polyglot Bible. Spain had reached a remarkable point of strength and power when she was able to assimilate Charles V, the Fleming, and make of him a champion of things Hispanic. The ability of Spain to conquer half the world, evangelize it, and take the lead in the Counter Reformation, speaks eloquently of the internal vitality of the people, and no little credit for these achievements is due to the unification in mind and in spirit that preceded them.

The period of Charles V and Philip II is rich in material and spiritual conquests. Charles arrived in Spain in 1517. The guiding principle of his reign was the increase of his wealth and power. Philip II, on the contrary, was devoted to the conservation of what had already been gained. Both rulers were consecrated to tasks which we may call, for the sake of a better word, "extra-Spanish," that is the expansion of the faith beyond the seas and the defense of that Faith in the Europe torn asunder by the religious strife of the sixteenth century. Charles, in a sense, belonged to Europe rather than to Spain alone. It is extraordinary how completely he became Hispanized and how zealous he became even in the defense of the Spanish, or Castilian language as the preferable instrument for diplomatic intercourse. But his concerns were Germany, Italy, and the Low Countries at the same time. Philip II was intensely and introspectively peninsular, whose reign began in 1556. In September, 1559, he landed in Spain from abroad and was never again to abandon its territory. Charles was a perpetual imperial wanderer; Philip was in the environment that best suited him in the austere and massive Escorial.

Charles maintained the classic spirit of combat for the faith that had animated and exhilarated the Spanish for so long against Islam. The challenge in Europe, evidenced in the wars of religion, was an extraordinary opportunity for the exercise of this conviction. The conquest of America with its hazards and its promise was equally an outlet for the abundant energies of which the Hispanic race has always given ample evidence.

Charles V dreamed of that elusive unity to which Europeans have given thought from time immemorial. The vast stretches of his empire, the unity of its institutions and religion were factors that led to the hope that as the Holy Roman Empire and Spain had come under a single crown, so too could the western world be united. The illusion that perhaps universal empire might be achieved was awakened at this crucial point in the ascending destiny of Spain.[15]

Charles fell exhausted in the face of the multiplicity of enterprises to which he devoted himself. The young and vigorous victor at Pavia was a far different man from the weary recluse at Yuste toward the end of his life. The grandiose idea of empire contrasted with the

---

[15] Regarding the idea of empire and the Hispanic conception, see Eleuterio Elorduy, S.J., *La idea del imperio en el pensamiento espanol y de otros pueblos,* Madrid, 1944. An excellent brief account is that of the distinguished Spanish philologist, Ramón Menéndez Pidal, *El ideal imperial de Carlos V,* Madrid, 1940.

penury of resources, for Spain never ceased to be a poor country and even the wealth of the Indies was insufficient to modify this normal condition. The Castilian Cortes never ceased to call the attention of the monarch to the gigantic expenses that expansion and imperial conquest represented; none of this was in conformity with the modest budget and expenditures which represented the *modo de Castilla* (the Castilian Way).

Charles borrowed money from the great bankers of his day; the Fuggers and the Welsers granting him funds on the guarantee of the wealth of the American continent. Philip II opened his reign by complaining bitterly that he was quite unable to pay the wages of the soldiery. His primary task was to preserve what had been won and beat back the incursions of heresy and foreign rivalry wherever they might manifest themselves. Lepanto was won against the Turks and Europe saved from their scourge; the Low Countries were in rebellion and must be pacified; British ambitions were crystallizing and must be curbed. There was danger that the Flanders-Castile combination, so essential to the material welfare of the empire, would be ruined. The Armada sought to destroy the English menace and, with its failure, Spain was definitely faced with the rising prestige of northern Europe.

Within Spain, everything contrasted with the outside world of doubt and clash. It was the Golden Age and one of the culminating points in the whole history of the human mind and the scene was dominated by the towering personality of Philip II. It was he who was responsible above all else for the restoration of the prestige of the monarchical idea which had been seriously threatened under Charles at the time of the *Comunero* revolt. The revival of the prestige of the kingship was carried out with vigor. During the formative centuries, the Hispanic monarchy had been little more than a tumultuous republic under the leadership of a king. The Cid Campeador had obliged Alfonso VI to swear three times on holy scripture that he had not been implicated in the murder of his brother; Alfonso X had been summarily deposed and Henry IV humiliated at Ávila. Even under Charles V the monarchy was still reminiscent of the turbulence and rebellious nature of the primitive Christian kingdoms. Philip was responsible for a new conception in which the monarchy became the central institution, intimately connected with the defense of the national interests, the protection of religion, and the stability of institutions.

The largest achievement of this brilliant period — brilliant in successes as well as in magnificent failures — was the maintenance of the intimate link between the institution of the monarchy and the mass of the people. Probably at no time in the history of Spain was the monarch so completely attuned to the feelings, sentiments, and hopes of the Spanish people. It was no tyranny. When a chaplain ventured to preach in Philip's presence that the King in his will could do as he pleased with his subjects and their property, the Inquisition intervened at once and Philip demanded that the friar retract from the same pulpit this absolutist thesis. There was very real democracy both in the service of the State and Church. The aged Duke of Alba was imprisoned for failing to keep a promise; the humblest peasant, if talented, could aspire to the highest posts in the administration. Philip encouraged the spirit of social equality, inherited from the Reconquest, making of the Philippine monarchy a rare union of the supremacy of God in heaven and the King on earth.

Philip more than anyone else was the leader of the Counter Reformation. Under his impulse the Spanish threw themselves joyously into the crusade against error.[16] The work of Philip in the Council of Trent and the contribution of the Spanish theologians in general can hardly be underestimated. Within Spain, Philip had in St. Teresa of Ávila a formidable and devoted collaborator, whose work may be compared in many ways to that of St. Ignatius in the broader arena of struggle with heresy.

The Spanish renaissance flowered with particular brilliance in the peninsular universities. The country was dotted with university centers that had had their beginning in Palencia, Valladolid, and Salamanca. At Valencia, Barcelona, and Zaragoza universities were erected with papal approval and at the end of the period the university college of Sacro Monte was established at Granada, in 1605. This latter period witnessed the founding of the institution of the Escuelas Pías by St. José de Calasanz. The Jesuits played a very large role in the work of education and particularly in the development of a system of secondary schools. Spanish humanism was enriched by the contributions of a galaxy of outstanding figures: Luis Vives, Luis de León, and Arias Montano, among others. Luis de Granada represented among other things one of the most significant moralists in the Spain of his time. No more important contribution was made to human progress than that of the Spanish jurists and theologians of this epoch. The

---

[16] Lope de Vega, a volunteer in the Armada, wrote: *Para la católica jornada, no se excusaba generoso mozo*—"From this Catholic undertaking, no generous youth could be excused." (or "would excuse himself")

great Jesuit, Father Suárez, was called the *doctor eximius et pius*. Bossuet was prone to say that he who knew Suárez knew the entire Church, so great was the sweep of his mind and the multiplicity of the fields in which he wrote. His *De legibus ac Deo Legislatore* exerted a very great influence on the political thought of his day. Francisco de Vitoria has been hailed as the founder of international law and no serious student today disputes his primacy in developing a conception of the international community.[17] At the side of Suárez, although perhaps less influential than he, was the extraordinary Melchior Cano. Philosophy and theology were represented by others of the first order: Bartolomé de Medina, Juan de Santo Tomás, and Domingo Báñez.[18]

Biblical exegesis was inseparable in this period from the development of scholasticism and the Counter Reformation. Although the Bible in the vernacular was prohibited by the Index Valdés in 1559 in view of the multiplicity of versions and editions, some of which were far from accurate, the Vulgate was always available and it would be improper to assume that Spain was deprived of the Bible as some writers have undertaken to prove. The field of mysticism and asceticism was highly developed and Spanish literature was rich in writing, reflecting the urge of man to establish contact with God.

Spanish literature was the handmaiden of this remarkable renaissance of culture. The end of the fifteenth century saw the publication of *La Celestina,* and before the end of the following century Cervantes had published his *Galatea*. Juan de Ortega and Pedro Juan Núñez gave luster to the mathematical sciences. Magellan and Elcano contributed to the state of knowledge of navigation. Linguistics, and especially the Spanish language, were fixed with grammar and rules by the great philologist Antonio de Nebrija. Biology received a great impulse under Miguel Servet, and medicine under Daza de Valdés.

Spanish culture was not limited to the peninsula. Its influence spread to all Europe. Ernest Renan has declared that Vitoria, Soto, Báñez, and Juan de Santo Tomás were as influential and as revolutionary in their time as Descartes and Diderot in a later day. The thesis can no longer be held that the Spanish men of letters and

---

[17] *Fray Francisco de Vitoria, Fundador del Derecho Internacional Moderno,* collection of lectures, Madrid, 1946.

[18] Ludwig Pfandl, *Historia de la literatura nacional española en la edad de oro,* Barcelona, 1933, p. 22 sq.

science were routine repeaters of the scholastic tradition with no element of novelty or originality.

Spain was literally the determinant of all current European history. Its far-flung empire, far-reaching intervention, and the aid given the crown by the Society of Jesus and the theologians, made of Spain a bulwark and an important factor in the destinies of western Europe.

Art and architecture was by no means forgotten in this resplendent bursting of culture. The Escorial itself is the supreme monument to the sentiment and the culture of the Spain of the sixteenth century. El Greco in art represented that magnificent blending of the other-worldly and the mundane which is so significant a trait of the Hispanic character. Outstanding were Ribera with his paintings of the Immaculate Conception, Murillo at the end of the sixteenth century, Zurbarán who was born almost at the moment of the death of Philip II, Valdez Leal, Veláquez, and others.

The Golden Age of greatness led straight into what has been called the Spanish decadence. "The gold of this Golden Age . . . is of imperishable purity in the work of the great Catholics of letters and arts, and in the institutional work of Loyola, Francis Xavier, Francis Borgia, Teresa de Ávila, St. John of the Cross and the host of others who contributed to the enrichment of the world."[19] The decline set in after Philip II although some Spaniards have denied the existence of any such decay. Asorín asserted: *"No hay tal decadencia"* (There was no such decadence).

If the period of Charles and Philip was distinguished by the triumph of Spain over the religious revolution, the country was next faced by a political revolution of an entirely different character. The same inflexible genius and the same resolute will that had opposed a literal dike to the penetration of heresy was not there to combat the rising political currents which were to invade the Iberian peninsula and produce the same confusion that beset the rest of western Europe. The religious breakdown had led to anarchy and to dictatorship. England had known the iron rule of Cromwell; the Netherlands, the severe rule of William of Orange. The political revolution that succeeded the religious was in many ways an intellectualist undertaking, promoted by men of letters, writers, and lawyers. Spain, as has been pointed out,

[19] Maurice Legendre, *op. cit.*, p. 192.

weathered the storm of religious anarchy, although weakened and impoverished. The political revolution, stemming from Great Britain and France, was far more subtle and penetrating. It found a Spain with its guard down, whose rulers were far less astute in their perceptions than Charles and Philip.[20]

The Spain that existed between the death of Philip to the extinction of the Habsburgs in 1700 was a declining influence, piloted by mediocre and inept monarchs. Under Philip III, Philip IV, and Charles II, Spain was as opaque and colorless on the stage of world affairs as France was brilliant under Louis XIII, Richelieu, and Louis XIV. The Spanish royal advisers, with the possible exception of Olivares, were mediocre intriguers. Portugal broke away and became independent once more in 1640. Catalonia rebelled and, despite temporary failure, attained autonomy between 1700 and 1714. The treaties of 1648 confirmed the independence of the Low Countries and Sardinia and Roussillon were lost while parts of Flanders were ceded to Louis XIV. By 1713 the descending index of Spain had reached its lowest point with Gibraltar and Minorca gone to a rising England. There was the usual complex combination of causes contributing to this; the idea of monarchy was weakened by the ineptitude of the crown and economic factors played a large role with the loss of maritime supremacy and foreign markets. The decrease of population in Castile played its role, and the exhausting experience of the conquest of the New World and part of the Far East was another element in the general breakdown of Spanish hegemony and grandeur. The existence of inflation and disorder in the economic and monetary life of the country was also part of the explanation although certainly not all of it.

Another interpretation is that western Europe was gradually developing the primitive elements of modern capitalism. Castile was by all odds the least mercantile-minded area of Spain. The Catalans, Jews, Flemings, and Genoese had traditionally played the largest role economically in Spanish affairs while the Castilians showed a singular inadaptation to the demands of a commercial society, and, in fact, the failure of Spain to respond to the exigencies of capitalism may indeed have their beginnings in this period of the eighteenth century. The decadence may be explained further in terms of the shift in equilibrium between the provinces. The central provinces had played the dominant

---

20 See Appendix 1, "Chronology of Spanish History at Its Zenith."

role in the fifteenth and sixteenth centuries, in part because they possessed a larger population and a sounder economy in terms of the needs of the times. It was an unusual coincidence of economic power, population, and political impulse. For two centuries the maritime provinces of the east suffered a decline. Once they had lost the position of economic solvency which had been theirs for so long, combined with the unfavorable factors already described in the case of Castile, a reversal of the roles became inevitable.

There were signs in the eighteenth century of a reaction against the apathy and passivity of Spanish life. Commercially there was a period of considerable promise. The great mercantile companies were formed such as the *Real Compañía Guipuzcoana de Caracas,* the Philippine company, and others, and Cádiz, Barcelona, and other parts knew a prosperity long denied them. A great minister, Count Aranda, envisaged a form of commercial policy that would increase trade and remove restrictions and perhaps, if it had been put into effect, forestall the later secession of the American colonies. The idea of a purely political empire was giving way even in Spain to that of an economic one. The eighteenth century was, despite the appearance of absolute decline, a great colonial period for Spain. Capital was organized, raw materials flowed in, and population again began to grow. In Catalonia cotton began to replace wool and industrial techniques were introduced very soon after they were set up in England.

No more pathetic a political failure could be imagined than the weak Charles II who, in his agony, was forced to admit the succession of the very house which had been the most consistent enemy of Spain, the Bourbons. The end of the Habsburgs and the beginning of Bourbon rule meant more than a mere change of dynasty, for it was the end of an era and the commencement of another. The new dynasty was alien to Spain, far less integrated with its traditions and customs than the Habsburgs had been. It was to take generations before the new dynasty could sink its roots into Spanish soil in the profound way that had characterized the House of Austria.

During the eighteenth century the winds of political revolt were blowing across Europe. The expulsion of the Jesuits, in Spain and Portugal, is perhaps the best reminder of the sectarian and secularist trend already violently manifest. The Spanish people have a remarkable power of resistance to influences from abroad as they demonstrated in rejecting outright everything savoring of religious reform in the heretical sense and they revealed the same instinct regarding politics. If the eighteenth century was a period of infiltration, the early nineteenth gave the masses the opportunity to overcome the very influences which their rulers had allowed to penetrate. Spain is a land where foreign influence has a very slight chance of success and where alien ideas and formulas, systems, and ideas contrary to the nature of the Hispanic spirit, have repeatedly been stopped at the frontier or expelled. It happened to the Lutherans and, in a different way, it was the remote cause for the rejection of liberalism and, above all, socialism in the twentieth century. History has revealed that Spain cannot be made to the image and likeness of anyone or of any external system that does not coincide with its own genius.

Spain was fundamentally impervious to the influences of French encyclopedism. The *Esprit des Lois* of Montesquieu was not known in Spanish translation until five years after the Bourbon restoration in France (1820). The resistance to politically revolutionary ideas was not merely negative; it was also positive. There were writers and thinkers who carried on the great Spanish tradition of the Golden Age. Father Jerónimo Feijoo, who died in 1764, while not one of the great Spanish writers, was nevertheless a very considerable influence in the Spain of his day. Gregorio Marañón has called him the "creator of the Spanish scientific language." Gaspar Melchor de Jovellanos, who lived until 1811, was another encyclopedic mind of comparable proportions to Father Feijoo, and his major interest in the moral and economic sciences coupled with his vast erudition made him one of the most enlightened intellects of his century.

There was a host of popular writers and preachers who represented the traditionalist idea in Spain. The country was open to many French influences, although it cannot be assumed that French thought marched in unobstructed to take over what had been heretofore the invincible product of a national culture, fiercely proud of its integrity and autonomy. The endurance of traditionalism and popular influences, even in the highest spheres, is no better depicted than in the paintings of Goya, who has left for us an unforgettable visual image of the turbulent and at the same time placid Spanish life of the eighteenth and early nineteenth centuries.

Charles IV has often been looked upon as a weak, vacillating monarch without character and will although he showed a remarkable shrewdness in his appraisal of the events in France during the Revolution. He was of the opinion that Louis XVI had been forced to accept the constitution, and that this acceptance was scarcely valid in the light of the constraints placed on the French monarch. Spain was still strong in its popular will to resist whatever might come from across the Pyrenees, but its weakness derived from the turpitude of the dynasty, the intrigues of the court, the character of the Queen, and the anticlerical sentiments of Floridablanca Aranda; all tending to weaken resistance against the threatened encroachments of the French. It was Godoy, later to be known as the Prince of Peace, who succeeded finally and guided Spain through the tumultuous years that were to follow. On March 7, 1793, after the execution of Louis XVI, the French Convention declared war on Spain, pushing the latter into an alliance with Great Britain. The Spanish people responded with alacrity to the call to arms against the revolution. From 1793 to 1815 Spain was involved in conflict with France; a conflict of such serious repercussions that the whole nineteenth century was to feel the result. The instability of the British alliance threw Spain into the arms of France itself, at the time of the Directory, and produced the alliance that was to play such a role at the naval disaster of Trafalgar. The relations with France were costly, for Spain lost Santo Domingo, Louisiana, and Trinidad among other possessions. Trafalgar was the decisive moment, for the victory of British sea power determined the fate of the Spanish overseas empire. Henceforth the colonies, left to themselves, evolved straight toward separatism. The British naval victory had done the trick and produced the situation in which the reality of empire could no longer conform to its theory, leading Godoy to obtain benefits from Napoleon and create for himself a brilliant position. The continental blockade so hampered Spain that the tension grew until the inevitable invasion by the French forces became necessary to maintain Spain within the continental bloc formed to bring England to her knees.

The war of independence in 1808 was a spontaneous, popular, unanimous uprising of an indignant and outraged people to defend their homes and their land. The movement was a literal storm of passion let loose. During May, 1808, Galicia, Asturias, and Aragón refused obedience to the French authorities, while the news of the designation of Joseph Bonaparte as king produced an outburst of hostility from the masses. The exiled Ferdinand became a legend and around his name gathered the forces of opposition, with motives, as usual, hopelessly mixed. In 1808 as in 1936 there was evident a wide variety of hopes and convictions. Some of the opposition to the French in 1808 was simply antiforeign; another sector believed that Spain might well imitate France in its institutions and thought, the better to combat it, while others were in favor of a patriarchal absolutism, inclined toward the maintenance of the ancient *fueros* and the close coordination of the religious and the political. In a word, in the early years of the nineteenth century, what was later to become "liberal Spain," "Carlist Spain," and anticlerical, leftist Spain was taking shape. The dim outline was clearly visible, and the tendencies that found it possible to merge temporarily against the common French foe were to develop along lines that would shake the structure of Spanish society for the ensuing hundred years.

The war against the French usurper was conducted very largely on a religious basis and once again the strength and force of Spain sprang directly from the fusion of the religious motive with the political. The French were denounced "atheists"; the guerrilla fighters in the mountains and towns wore scapulars and carried holy pictures and the celebrated Virgin of the Pillar in her shrine in Zaragoza was invoked against the invader, since she "did not want to become French." The war for independence brought to the surface such bizarre and heterogeneous elements that Joseph Bonaparte compared the Spanish militia fighting against him with the Parisians who achieved control in the second year of the Revolution. The outburst of popular sentiment in the name of religion and tradition was sometimes so fragile that perspicacious observers foresaw that this aggressive action of the masses might in time be turned against the very religion they so zealously defended.

The leadership of these masses was limited, for Spain did not possess a contingent of statesmen and leaders capable of channeling this upsurge of emotion and patriotism. The aged Floridablanca and Jovellanos were members of the central committee for the Resistance. The Cortes that met at Cádiz, as the authentic expression of the Spanish will, reflected the most diverse tendencies, although there were no elections and no consultation of public opinion. Intellectuals, lawyers, merchants, and many Spanish from the overseas possessions sat in this essentially "liberal" parliament in such a motley array that Karl Marx remarked, and in this he was singularly correct, that the guerrilla fighters were men of action without ideas; the Cortes was filled to overflowing with ideas but with no evidence of action. There was a complete and radical divorce between the popular resistance and the political leadership and this characteristic was to dominate the rest of the nineteenth century.

The past century gives the peculiar impression of two levels of activity within the same framework, each quite independent of the other; the political and administrative life of Spain functioning more or less separately from the more sluggish movement of the mass of the people. Ideas were launched in the name of the Spanish people that in reality were the ideas of a very small and often unrepresentative minority in power. Spain returned in the days of the war against France to extreme localism with mayors here and there declaring war against Napoleon with no regard whatever for the action of the central *juntas,* while in one case the Asturian junta actually undertook direct negotiations with Great Britain.

The chaotic and insensate fury with which the war was conducted astonished the French. Napoleon himself in his conversations at St. Helena recalled the blind alley that Spain had represented for his hopes, and confessed that the combination of popular resistance and awakened nationalism had been the cause of his defeat.[21] A modern historian describes the situation in these terms:

> Their cavalier, desperate, and unyielding reaction, the first the Emperor had encountered, was not that of a modern people but of a medieval society, ready to perish all together in defense of their faith. It was in vain that Napoleon sought effective collaborators. The most that he could obtain from the functionaries who remained in office was a reticent passiveness.[22]

The Spanish liberalism in evidence at Cádiz did not pretend to run counter to the religious tradition of the nation. It did, however, in the constitution adopted by the Cortes for the future Spain, include provision for restrictions in what were called at the time the material wealth of the Church and suppressed the Inquisition. The return of Ferdinand in 1813 was followed by the repudiation of the work of the Cádiz Cortes, for the restoration simply lumped liberals and collaborators with the French in the same category and swept them off the scene. The failure to achieve a balance in the years following the withdrawal of the French was one of the primordial causes of the crises of the nineteenth century.

The history of Spain from 1813 to the end of the century is a consistent story of intrigue, improvisation, and experimentation. The American provinces separated from the mother country to go their independent way. In 1820 an army officer, Riego, whose name remains in history largely because the hymn of the second Spanish republic was the "Himno de Riego," undertook a "liberal" rebellion. French

[21] Las Cases, *Le Mémorial de Sainte-Helène.*

[22] Alberic Varenne, *Quand la France occupait l'Europe,* Paris, 1948, p. 269.

intervention in 1823 restored the balance but without affording a permanent solution to the alternative of the weak, capricious Ferdinand and the liberalistic pulsations that were stirring within the country. Ferdinand was politically handicapped by the absence of an heir, for in his four marriages he had managed to obtain only a daughter. The logical heir in this event would have been Don Carlos, his brother, and the latter refused point-blank to entertain the notion of a woman in the succession. This in a few words was the immediate backdrop of the dynastic struggle on which Spain was about to embark and which was to form so conspicuous a part of her nineteenth-century history. María Cristina, in 1833, sought to rally the liberal forces both at home and abroad, while Don Carlos was supported by the stanch traditionalists of the Basque provinces. His claim was not a purely "reactionary" one but was rooted in a program of local autonomy, the legitimacy of the succession and hostility to the centralizing tendencies of the Bourbons.

María Cristina was regent in the name of her daughter Isabel II. The partisans of Don Carlos proclaimed him king, and for seven years the first Carlist war shook Spain. The pretender Don Carlos was not endowed with great perspicacity or audacity and his conduct nullified the military achievements of his commander, Zumalacáregui, one of the most extraordinary and colorful personalities Spain has produced. The period became one of *pronunciamientos,* and uninterrupted ministerial crises. In 1836 the Regent was forced to accept the constitution of Cádiz and a year later she substituted for it a more moderate document. The fact that the Regent had been forced to call on the army generals for support against the Carlists led to the direct intervention of the generals in political life. General Espartero had forced the Carlists to lift the siege of Bilbao and the Regent authorized him to sign the peace terms at Vergara in 1839 so that in a sense the regency was now subject to the will of the victorious military. Espartero became dictator of Spain for a short period which terminated with the retirement of the Queen Mother into exile and he was designated regent in 1841 until such a time as Isabel II became of age. Riots and rebellion characterized this period; in Barcelona a republic was proclaimed and the city was bombarded for its pains; in Pamplona the more moderate generals raised the standard of rebellion and were quickly put down. The Cortes was dissolved five times in five months until finally Espartero, in the face of almost universal hostility, was forced into exile.

In 1843 Isabel was declared of age. The "moderates," as they were called, imposed their will on Isabel, and General Narvaez was named to head the ministry. Under him the constitution of 1845 was proclaimed, strengthening the royal authority and the Council of State. The severe policy of Narvaez prevented any considerable reaction in Spain to the Revolution of 1848 in France with no subsequent wave of insurrection that washed across Europe. In 1854 a *coup d'état* took place under the leadership of General Leopoldo O'Donnell and Espartero, who had returned from exile. These so-called "progressives," as they were known, held power for two years. O'Donnell formed a political group known as the "Unión Nacional" of liberal tendency. There was a generous rash of new political parties during this period. The Republicans appeared under Castelar and Salmerón; and federalism under the Catalan leader, Pi y Margall.

The various foreign interventions of Spain: Morocco, Mexico, and Chile brought to the forefront new generals ready and willing to venture into politics: Prim and Serrano. General Prim rose in rebellion seven times in four years and promoted seven *pronunciamientos* in the classical tradition. Narvaez and O'Donnell died in 1868. When the Queen left for the French frontier to treat with Napoleon III, two generals, Prim and Serrano, with Admiral Topete formed a triumvirate. The fleet mutinied at Cádiz to cries of "Down with the Bourbons" and a full-dress rebellion followed. The troops of Isabel were defeated at Alcolea, and after the Queen had crossed into France a provisional government was set up. This was the country's first experience with a revolution, modern style. Prim was extremely popular and took over the war ministry in the new government. One of the members of this provisional arrangement was a political leader who was to play a large role in the future, Sagasta. A Cortes elected on the basis of universal suffrage met and drafted a liberal constitution, although retaining the monarchy. The difficulty was to find a king. On December 30, 1870, when Amadeo, son of the Italian king, arrived to take the throne, Prim was assassinated. The new King, a stranger in the atmosphere of Spanish politics, was soon weary of his functions and the constant intrigue in which he was called upon to live. There were rivalries between politicians and a renewal of the Carlist wars. The political scene was a confusion of Carlists, republicans, unionists, progressives, radicals, and liberals; there were Alfonists who favored the return of the traditional Bourbons, under Alfonso XII and Carlists devoted to the pretentions of Charles VII. On February 11, 1873, Amadeo abdicated and stated it as his studied opinion that Spain was ungovernable. There was a strong undercurrent of extremism in the Spain of that day, and an anarchist sentiment was one of the forces that made the republic unworkable. On the night of February 11, 1873, the Republic was proclaimed. It was conceived as the reply to the confused situation of personal rivalries and irreconcilable feuding between the pretenders, but the Republic, the first in Spanish history, was destined to endure less than a year.

Chapter 3. FROM REPUBLIC TO REPUBLIC

THE panorama of nineteenth-century Spain was that of a nation in constant flux and reflux; in an expenditure of its own energies and resources to no other end than its own destruction. The idea that Spain in the past century was exhausted spiritually and materially does not stand up under close examination. There was no exhaustion; on the contrary, there was a reservoir of energy and vitality, but it was directed to sterile ends. If that same energy had gone into constructive activity, Spain might well have regained its prominent place on the European stage. There was an abundance of first-rate personalities and men of action: leaders of talent, whose efforts ended invariably in frustration and failure. In some ways Spain was endowed during the past century with as many outstanding figures as in the sixteenth century; the difference lay in the way their abilities were harnessed. In the sixteenth century Spain poured forth her energies in productive achievements both abroad and at home, while in the past century these same efforts were wasted in hopeless strife within the peninsula. One Spanish historian has called the nineteenth century that of "fratricidal introspection."[1]

The last years of the monarchy were distinguished by the increase of party strife and a widening gap between class and mass. The Cortes of the years 1868 to 1873 were distinguished by the presence of a legion of outstanding theorists of politics, brilliant orators, competent constitutionalists and clever parliamentarians, with Emilio Castelar the *vedette* of these performances. His oratory, very much in the mid-century style, charmed and captivated in its eloquence. But the tragedy was that it was poured into a vacuum. The country was in a state of uproar with the republicans becoming more and more active, while the Carlists were on the point of another civil war. The formal abdication of Isabel

---

[1] Eduardo Aunós Pérez, *Itinerario histórico de la España contemporánea 1808–1936*, Barcelona, 1940, p. 160.

in 1870, leaving the throne to her son, Don Alfonso, only added fuel to the flames. The meteoric reign of King Amadeo had contributed nothing to the stabilization of Spain. The King himself, on his return to Italy, was still under the impression of the stupor that his adventure in Spain had produced. "I feel as if I had made a trip to the moon," was his pithy comment. By 258 votes against 32 the Republic was proclaimed. This Republic came in somewhat surreptitiously and lasted precisely ten months and twenty days. Few regimes in history have ever had so painful and inert an existence. Every branch of Spanish republicanism joined in an initial burst of good will in forming the government. Pi y Margall was there. So were the Salmerón brothers, and also Echegaray, the dramatist, who was to attain fame under the Restoration, and Castelar. The Republican government was one of academicians and has been called rightly a government of professors. In this sense there is a close analogy with the Second Republic, in which the intellectuals also played a very large part. Few cases in modern European history illustrate more effectively the truth that between political theory and the facts of political life there is often an abysmal gap.

One of the first causes of strife was the decision as to how this freshly created Republic was to be managed. The republicans in high position felt that the Republic ought to be for them, as its architects. Another large sector of opinion, made up of persons who had voted for the Republic but were not active in support of the idea, claimed, with perhaps some justice, that the Republic belonged to all Spaniards. It was a monarchical parliament that had voted the Republic in and it was this same Republic that expelled countless monarchists from administrative posts because they belonged to that familiar class called collaborationists with the old regime. The republicans themselves were soon divided between unitarians and federalists, the latter advocating a high degree of local autonomy and recognition of the regional differences of Spain while the former were in favor of the continuation of the centralistic tradition under republican auspices. This conflict, incidentally, is reflected perfectly in the Second Republic and remains as one of the thorniest of Spanish problems, for the nation has never been able to find the solution of centralism versus regionalism. The tendency has been to oscillate back and forth between one and the other, according to the mood and demands of the times. Pi y Margall advocated a complex arrangement whereby there was to be a national structure based on federalism and at the same time an internal or domestic federalism based on regionalism.[2] The close alliance of regionalism in the constitutional sense and republicanism is clear in the fact that much of the republican sentiment in 1873 sprang from Catalonia.[3]

When Pi y Margall entered upon his duties as president, it was the signal for the almost total submersion of Spain in hopeless anarchy. The fact that an advocate of federalism occupied the executive position persuaded a great many regionalists that immediate action was imperative, leading to the establishment of a kind of independent canton in Málaga, Cádiz, Granada, Seville, Valencia, and Cartagena. Each of these areas considered itself completely independent of the central authority, established its own finance machinery, and proceeded to act as though the national government no longer existed. Since the major part of the Spanish navy was in Cartagena harbor, the local government simply ordered the vessels to place themselves in its service and cruise up and down the coast pillaging and looting. It was not long before there were diplomatic repercussions and the action of the local Cartagena regime came close to provoking an international incident. Pi y Margall was reluctant to take drastic action, but the parliament, faced by the creeping anarchy, deposed him and placed Salmerón in the executive chair. The new president set about putting down the centers of insurrection and holding the line at least with the Carlists. His extreme scruples, especially regarding capital punishment for the insurrectionists, led to his resignation. Three chief executives had already preceded him when Emilio Castelar became the fourth president of the Republic.

Castelar admittedly did a better job than his predecessors, for he put down the Cartagena uprising, fought the Carlists effectively, and even went so far, despite an absence of devotion to its authority, as to negotiate with the Holy See for the filling of several vacant bishoprics. The president found it necessary to govern with the Cortes in recess, for the turbulent, intractable nature of the legislative body made the work of government almost impossible. At a given moment, General Pavia, the military governor of Madrid, offered to place the armed forces at the disposal of the president to make possible his action if the Cortes proved too rebellious. The meeting of the Cortes on January 3, 1874, represented, as anticipated, the defeat of Castelar.

[2] A. Rovira i Virgili, *Catalunya i la república,* Barcelona, 1931, p. 14.

[3] *Idem, Resum d'Historia del catalanisme,* Barcelona, 1936, p. 41: "Catalonia was the cradle of the Republican movement in the last century."

General Pavia, who had nothing of the political theorist in his make-up, proceeded to clear the parliament by the simple expedient of a fusillade at the ceiling. Pavia was a very different type from the military who had been responsible during much of the century for the eternal *pronunciamientos*. He was not conspiring with one group to oust another, nor was he particularly interested in any regime as such. His intention, as near as one can judge, was to put a stop to the frightful anarchy that was sapping the vitality of Spain and rendering the nation incapable of an orderly evolution. General Pavia proceeded at once to convoke the members of the parliament and proposed that they do something about setting up a new government. The one member who was willing to take a clear-cut position, in accord with the demands of the times, was Cánovas de Castillo, who suggested that the only solution was the restoration of the monarchy under Don Alfonso. A provisional government was in fact set up presided over by Serrano, the Cortes dissolved, and the constitutional guarantees suspended. The result was a hybrid sort of regime, half republic and half dictatorship, which lasted for some months.

The monarchists, needless to say, were extremely active. Isabel II was launching projects from her exile, and among them was a regency under the aged Espartero for her son Alfonso. No more absurd solution could be found, for it was the substitution of one shadowy, lifeless form of government for another. Isabel was done for and Cánovas de Castillo with rare perception realized that a restoration did not mean going back to what had existed before the advent of the Republic. The former Queen abdicated formally on June 25, 1870, and Cánovas became the director and strategist of the Restoration, and for over fifteen years he was to be the dominant figure in Spain.

Cánovas recognized perfectly the liberal trend of his times. He was aware that Spain could not resist the impact of the ideas that were becoming dominant everywhere at the end of the century. Nor was he so inflexible as to pretend that the Pyrenees could become a permanent barrier permitting Spain to work out a regime completely peninsular and isolated in character. Instead of employing the time-honored method of the military coup, Cánovas used a different procedure. Prince Alfonso issued a manifesto in December, 1874, addressed to those in Spain who had wished him well on his birthday, the document being drafted by Cánovas himself. It was a sober, realistic, and singularly felicitous pronouncement, and in emphasizing the necessity for the restoration of harmony and good will, it insisted that the monarchy when restored must be constitutional in character. The restoration itself came about through General Martínez Campos in Sagunto, who called for the return of Don Alfonso.

The Restoration occupies the period that extends from 1875 to 1917 when World War I produced a crisis of a different kind, and is the opening of the strictly contemporary period. The constitution of 1876 was a clever document, with the prestige of the monarch assured by the fact that he convoked the elections for the constituent Cortes that was to prepare the new charter. The King was proclaimed inviolable and his authority confirmed by the "Grace of God," a return to the classical formula of the Spanish monarchy. There was wide latitude in the constitution and a considerable recognition of regional and local rights while Cánovas laid the foundation for a more orderly interplay of political and party forces. The new era found Spain with a parliamentary regime and a liberal-conservative counterbalance. Outside the two major tendencies, the Carlists and the republicans represented a mere theoretical opposition. Cánovas had attained, if nothing else, a restoration of the national equilibrium which in itself was no small achievement after the chaos with which he had been faced. There was, to be sure, a certain artificiality about this whole parliamentary structure. Cánovas recognized as did most of his contemporaries, that the Spanish climate was not particularly propitious for the instant fruition of a full-blown, effective parliamentary system, modeled on that of Great Britain. He managed, however, to provide a strong authority through the externals of parliamentarianism with its play of party interests, while retaining for himself the indispensable power to assure order and tranquillity. Spain was mortally tired at this moment in its history of the confusion and internecine warfare that had plagued it. The soft hand of Cánovas and the firm direction he gave public affairs were a welcome respite.

The major defect was that the system was not a product of the Spanish tradition and experience, nor did it reflect the mature judgment of the people for whom it was intended. Hence, the premature death of Alfonso XII at the age of twenty-eight plunged Spain into the deepest crisis. The young King had been highly esteemed and remarkably prudent. Spain was once again at a critical crossroads in her history. Cánovas and Sagasta, the liberal leader, immediately met to issue a statement which for all practical purposes established an exclusive two-party system with the guarantee that each of the parties would have access to power. Cánovas gave way at once to Sagasta, and the new leader proposed a series of "advanced" measures aimed largely at disarming the Left and very particularly the republicans. María Cristina became Regent of Spain. The birth of Don Alfonso in 1886, six months after the death of his father, assured the succession and gave considerable relief to those who feared that an indefinite regency might endanger the bases of the monarchy.

The last part of the century was characterized by the increasing demand of the liberals for reforms and measures distinguished by their audacity. They were accused of betraying the pact of 1885 and sought the alliance of groups and parties outside the government. The *Memorias* of that remarkable political figure, Count Romanones, show clearly how this tendency became more and more evident as the years passed. The monarchy increasingly became the institution of the conservatives, while the liberals did not hesitate to seek the support of socialists and republicans. The result was a growing chasm between the parties, not on the temporary issues of everyday political conflict, but with reference to the fundamental institutions of Spain itself. Cánovas began to suffer the first consequences of unpopularity.

New political trends now began to manifest themselves. In 1892 a new group of Catalan politicians appeared under the name of *Unió Catalanista* and with a program called the Manresa principles. In 1893 the Spanish forces in Melilla in Morocco suffered a defeat that showed the whole country the tragic situation of Spanish authority in North Africa. The situation in Cuba was an open sore which no government had been able to heal. The overseas' difficulties dated from the days of Prim. Under the liberal regime in 1893 the young Minister of Overseas Affairs, Antonio Maura, proposed a series of reforms to satisfy the demands of the Cuban insurgents. They were not accepted and the last chance was lost to maintain Spanish sovereignty in the West Indies. Anarchy was again raising its head in Spain. Between 1893 and 1896, three terrorist attempts had been made in Barcelona. The bomb that exploded in 1896 during the Corpus Christi procession revealed perhaps more eloquently than anything else the state of affairs within Spain. The regime had become too rigid and too formalistic. There were strange and new undercurrents, the effects of which burst through to the surface now and again, as a warning of the fundamentally unstable position of the political regime. In 1897 Cánovas was assassinated and Spain once more was faced by the perplexity of a way out.

The work of Cánovas de Castillo was unquestionably fundamental for the salvation of Spain. Whereas other statesmen had proceeded with recklessness in the attempt to "modernize" Spain, Cánovas was more sensitive to the peculiarly unmodern mentality of his people. He draped the external garments of parliamentarianism on the figure of Spain without seeking to transform the body itself. The disappearance of Cánovas from the scene and the establishment of the Sagasta cabinet was followed by a worsening of the situation in Cuba. The insurrection in the West Indies was complicated by the equally insoluble rebellion in the Philippines where José Rizal had been shot and catapulted promptly into martyrdom. And now, too, the *Maine* incident, that touched off the Spanish-American War, came as an added shock to Spanish public opinion, for it was like a thunderclap in the sky, since the people had been uninformed of the course of events in America.

The war found Spain ill equipped and without friends abroad. The complete concern with domestic affairs and the absence of a sense of international politics was not the fault of Cánovas alone, but the characteristic failure of many Spanish regimes. The tendency to think in terms of the peninsula exclusively; the inability to grasp the combinations and alignments of the major powers have often left Spain in an insecure and isolated position precisely when she was most in need of support. An incredible aspect of this tragedy was the utter ignorance of the Spanish people of what was really happening to them. So ill informed were they that scarcely anyone perceived the inevitable outcome of the struggle nor appraised with a sense of reality the strength of the United States. The defeat at Cavite disconcerted opinion and the sense of national honor demanded action with the result that Sagasta ordered Admiral Cervera to put to sea from his refuge in Santiago de Cuba, an order that doomed him to certain defeat.

The naval and military calamities of the war led straight to the Treaty of Paris, to the loss of the last colonial possessions in America and the Far East, and to the whole spiritual crisis that goes by the name of the "Generation of '98." The Spanish people themselves reacted with remarkable indifference to the disaster. The Sunday when the news of the destruction of the fleet reached Madrid was characterized by the customary bullfight, with crowds of people in the streets. It was not indifference to the results of a tragic war; it was rather the utter weariness of the Spanish with the colonial problem which had faced them for an entire century. No matter what was done, the colonies seemed to fall away from the national sovereignty and the conviction became overwhelming that there was in fact nothing to do about it and that the sooner the colonies vanished the better.

The real problem is to be found in the deeper spiritual crisis that these events provoked. Or, perhaps, the gigantic failures in politics and war were rather the consequence of the spiritual state in which Spain found itself. The Spanish intellectual leadership, however, was plunged into pessimism and brooding melancholy. "The Spaniard once more displayed his misery with a fierce pride. His criticism of the national values was negative and painful. The pessimistic character in literature was reflected in the painting of Zuloaga; somber hues, melancholy little villages without life, tired and parchment-like faces — this was the plastic setting for the literature of '98."[4]

In 1896 Angel Ganivet wrote his *Idearium Español.* This profound and penetrating analysis of the essence of things Hispanic was no superficial eulogy of the past and of the virtues of the Iberian race. It was a critical, cold dissection of Hispanism, a work distinguished by an objectivity and honesty rarely found in nations that seek to disentangle the intricacies of their own collective past. "The undisciplined individualism," he explained, "that weakens us today and makes it impossible for us to raise our heads, may one day become an interior, creative individualism leading us to the accomplishment of our ideal."

So, too, no foreigner could have seized on the weaknesses of Spain with more telling directness than Miguel de Unamuno in his essays. Thus in his short *"Sobre el marasmo actual de España,"* the epigrammatic rector of Salamanca analyzed the defects of the Spain of his day. There is no youth and no youthful enthusiasm, he claims. "We live in a poor country and our economic poverty explains our mental anemia."[5]

The problem of 1898 concerned the future of Spain. Was the nation to decline into the morass of sterility, conscientious self-pity, or was it to make a superhuman effort to adapt itself to the demands of

---

[4] Angel Valbuena Prat, *Historia de la Literatura Española,* Barcelona, 1937, Vol. II, p. 836.

[5] In "En torno ad casticismo," *Ensayos,* Madrid, 1945, Vol. I, p. 132.

Salvador de Madariaga has remarked that the four dominant figures of the "Generation of '98" were Joaquín Costa, Angel Ganivet, Miguel de Unamuno, and José Ortega y Gasset. Costa was a remarkable figure about whom one is tempted to devote many pages, "one of those many-sided minds which are typical of a country so rebellious to specialization as Spain" (*Spain* [London: Jonathan Cape, 1943; New York: Creative Age Press, Inc., 1943], second impression, p. 81).

modern industrial society and compete with more powerful rivals on their own terms? The question is at the basis of the whole evolution of Spain and Miguel de Unamuno is the synthesis of this contradiction. His active intellectual life runs from the disaster of 1898 to the civil war in 1936. He lived through the very years in which Spain wrestled with its own soul and sought with agonizing perplexity a solution to the ills to which it had fallen heir. Unamuno was tormented and torn with doubt. His magnificent paradoxes and sometimes cruel thrusts reveal a spirit that cannot find certainty; that is lost in savage criticism of the existing order with all its defects and the inability to point the way to a more balanced society. His *El Sentimiento trágico de la vida* is the eloquent and moving confession of this impotency.

Spain was ripe for novelty and ready for almost any innovation. Krausism came in from Germany and enjoyed a remarkable vogue when it had lost all hold on the mind of the rest of Europe. Against this collective pessimism there was one Spaniard who reacted with vigor and devoted his life to the re-evaluation of those elements of the Hispanic past which showed promise of permanency. This man was Marcelino Menéndez y Pelayo, an extraordinary scholar, who died prematurely at the age of fifty-six, but whose writings fill a small library in the history of Spanish thought. Almost alone and unaided he set about a reconstruction of the Spanish past and achieved a monumental testimony to the fecundity and richness of the Hispanic genius. In volume after volume he sought to reassess Spain's past; point out the elements that had made her great in centuries gone by and evaluate in the light of scholarship the positive achievements of the Spanish mind. In his *Ciencia española,* Menéndez y Pelayo took up the cudgels against those who claimed Spain had no flair for the sciences and proceeded to demonstrate that Spanish science had attained an honorable place in a world which attaches so great an importance to the scientific. The sentiment was always present that Spain's mission in the world was not to be of this world, but to consist in sustaining, even alone and without help, the struggle against the world that was losing sight of those eternal values to which the Spanish people had unsparingly devoted their energies and their talents.

In Chapters 7 and 8 attention will be called to the extremist movements especially anarchism and socialism, as they have contributed to the social metamorphosis of Spain. While the intelligentsia concerned itself with the profounder issues of culture and transformation, the masses, especially in Catalonia and Andalucía, fell under the spell of doctrines which constituted an important part of the background to the events of the twentieth century. It would be a very grave mistake to assume that because attention has been paid to the political and intellectual trends of modern Spain that the social forces were less vital as a facet in the explanation of what led to the breakdown of the established order in 1936. The social aspect is so significant, indeed, that it seems preferable to detach it from the other currents and explain in considerable detail the origins of anarchism, communism, and socialism, in the light of their tremendous influence on contemporary Spanish thinking.

The intellectual struggle was posed between what Spanish writers have chosen to call "Spain and anti-Spain." The pessimism of the "Generation of '98" was by no means limited to literature. It was in the field of pedagogy that some of the most important results of this spiritual depression are to be found. Francisco Giner de los Ríos, professor of philosophy of law at the University of Madrid, embarked on a veritable crusade to reform the teaching methods and content of the Spanish schools. It was his conviction, shared by a considerable number of his contemporaries, that the youth of Spain was being drugged with a routine, uninspired, and uninspiring instruction that led to nothing and was not conducive to the titanic effort required to reject the errors of the past and rekindle the extinguished spark of the national genius. The idea of Giner de los Ríos was simple. He was eager to send the flower of Spanish youth abroad; inculcate the contemporary European attitudes; "modernize" the outlook of these students, and upon their return to Spain they would constitute the nucleus of a new generation which might in the course of time rise to power and begin the fundamental transformation of society which he believed necessary. The *Institutión Libre de Enseñanza* and the *Junta para Ampliación de Estudios e Investigaciones Científicas* became two of the most powerful institutions in modern Spain.

Giner de los Ríos, however, was dominated by the secularist idea and made no attempt to take advantage of the deep-rooted Catholic tradition of the country. His work gives the impression of either complete unawareness of this spiritual past or the deliberate effort to break with it and cast it into oblivion. With the idea of foreign contact and influence came the strong impact of the German thinker, Kraus. Menéndez y Pelayo, whose opinion must be taken with full consideration for his unrepentant traditionalism, described the work of Giner as leading to a kind of "lodge or mutual aid society, a tribe and a fraternity." The influence of the protégés of Giner de los Ríos can hardly be underestimated. They filled the school system and entered the universities; they gave the tone and note to the new reviews that appeared and set the pace for much of the intellectual production of Spain. The far-reaching consequences of this program can be seen during the Second Republic when so many of them came into positions of direction in public affairs.

The Catalan regionalist movement, too, formed a part of the rapidly developing new Spain that was the result of the Restoration and the events that led to the tragedy of 1898. While Catalanism was becoming more and more one of the major influences in Spain, in the heart of the peninsula, a political leader emerged who set about the difficult task of carrying out a reform of the static Cánovas regime. This man was Antonio Maura. He had first come into prominence in a liberal cabinet and had failed in his effort to work out a solution of the vexing Cuban question. He now inherited the leadership of the conservative party at a moment when it was regarded as a completely and insolubly fossilized institution, creaking and groaning with the demands of the modern age. In 1902 Maura delivered a speech in Valencia which was a shock to his audience. He cried out that disaster was very close and that the conservative party was far too apathetic under its present constitution to carry on as in the past. In synthesis his proposal was for a "revolution from above." Maura, a rare phenomenon in Spanish political life, was devoted to the monarchy and believed that no reform should be so sweeping as to endanger its stability. He made, at the same time, almost a fetish of "the popular will." He was convinced that the ills afflicting Spain came less from the ignorance, ill will, and perversity of the masses than from the egoism and immovable passivity of the leaders. The dilemma was clear; either the governing classes go about their own reform with the greatest possible diligence or they could expect ultimately the furious reaction of the masses, misled and misguided for so long.

Maura entered the government in 1902 as Minister of the Interior. The new Minister was fully conscious of the disastrous failure of his West Indian policy and he had no intention of exposing himself to the same result a second time. Catalonia was in the grip of agitation, an effervescence that bore certain similarities to the Cuban situation. Maura, therefore, in line with his conviction that reform must start at the top, undertook a policy of decentralization. His project as presented to parliament embodied the most advanced ideas regarding local autonomy. Maura was equally devoted to the idea that Spain was primarily a maritime nation and as such required a powerful fleet. He proposed to re-create this fleet after its defeat at the hands of the United States. In 1903 Maura became head of the government. He was definitely not lacking in courage. He accompanied King Alfonso XIII to Barcelona in a visit which was looked upon as practically suicidal by his colleagues. The strong Catalanist sentiment sweeping the city, together with the widespread republican sentiment, would seem to render inauspicious the visit of the monarch. The visit of the King, however, had one excellent effect in Catalonia. It brought about, thanks to the speech of Francisco Cambó, a split between the Catalanists and the Nationalists, the former remaining loyal to the regime while proposing reforms and the latter (a republican branch) expecting nothing from the monarchy.

Anarchism and Catalanism combined were fast becoming the plague of early twentieth-century Spain. Alfonso barely escaped assassination in Paris in 1905 at the hands of an anarchist. Maura was forced out and the government passed into the hands of the liberals under Canalejas. In eighteen months six changes of cabinet occurred and Spain was rapidly returning to the chronic chaos out of which Cánovas had once pulled it. The Catalan situation went from bad to worse. The virulence and animosity with which the extremist press in that area attacked everything — from the monarch, the flag, the national institution, down to the most insignificant ministry — was unbelievable. There was no restraint, no moderation, no sense of the proprieties.

This does not imply that Catalanism as such was responsible for these excesses. It signifies merely that within the general Catalanist movement there were elements allied with anarchism responsible for some of the more grotesque attacks on the central government and its representatives. Centralism had become an inflexible dogma of the traditional political parties. Anything that suggested a change or even a modification of this concentration of all powers in the national government was regarded as the rankest of heresy. Catalanism in general proposed a system of regional rights and autonomy. Only a tiny minority of the Catalanists believed in throwing bombs to achieve their ends. As a matter of fact both the Catalanists and the Basque traditionalists, who were at the opposite pole from the anarchists, held to essentially the same regional solution of the Spanish problem. We find the most eloquent expression of this point of view in one who can scarcely be suspected of sympathy for violence or for the extreme

Left, Vázquez de Mella, one of the outstanding spokesmen of traditionalism. In his speeches, particularly in 1906 and in the Cortes, he emphasized the difference between *nation* and *state* and urged that even if the regions of Spain became completely autonomous, the fact of the Spanish nation would still endure for historical, sentimental, and practical reasons. Vázquez de Mella was openly opposed to excessive centralism, and in this he coincided with innumerable moderate Catalans.[6]

Maura was in power from 1907 to 1909. One of his major achievements was the winning of the political collaboration of Francisco Cambó, the Catalan leader, a no mean accomplishment and one which among its many good results alienated the two extremes of the Catalan regional movement.

Despite the vision displayed by Maura, Spain was in the grip of a new era of confusion and irresponsibility. The pendulum which has so often swung from one extreme to the other was now in precipitate movement toward social and political anarchy. The revolution from above, of which Maura had been the chief advocate, was a failure; the revolution from below, which he had strained to prevent, was fast taking shape. The inspiration came from various sources: the Catalan extreme left with the anarchists, the bourgeois regionalists, the republican sentiment that cut across purely sectional lines, and was becoming a far more potent force than generally suspected. Spain was subject to the impact of influences from outside, and especially extremist experience elsewhere. One of the peculiarities of Spanish political life was that it was highly subject to alien influences with a marked tendency to adjust new political proposals to standards imported from abroad. It was paradoxical that the Spanish people who so bitterly resented foreign models were the victims of minority groups who reflected with rare faithfulness movements and trends that had arisen elsewhere. Socialism in imperial Germany, the trade union movement in Great Britain, extremism in France — all played a role in setting the pace for Spanish political development.

A word about republicanism. After the colossal failure of the First Republic, the movement had been broken and the remnants were ossified ideologists with little or no influence. It was some years before republicanism became coherent and articulate once more. In 1891 Vicente Blasco Ibáñez, better known to the English-speaking world

[6] Vázquez de Mella, *Obras completas,* Madrid, Vol. X, pp. 219–221; Osvaldo Lira, *Nostalgia de Vázquez de Mella,* Santiago, Chile, 1942, p. 119.

as the author of the *Four Horsemen of the Apocalypse,* founded a republican paper in Valencia, *El Pueblo.* This coastal city was the focus of a considerable republican sentiment. Barcelona and Madrid, despite their importance as dominant urban centers, were less addicted to this particular sentiment. It was not the inherent vitality of republicanism that managed a comeback in politics, but the ineptitude and the indirect collaboration of monarchism that produced this miracle. It would be no exaggeration to say that in many ways the monarchists were themselves responsible for the decreasing prestige of monarchical institutions. As early as 1904 the republicans demonstrated considerable strength, having obtained a majority in certain of the municipal elections, notably in Bilbao, Barcelona, Valencia, Seville, and Zaragoza.

The growth of socialism was not due fundamentally to the absence of social legislation or the improvement of the lot of the masses. In fact the conservatives were responsible for more effective legislation in this sense than the liberals, the latter having repeatedly invoked the suspension of the normal constitutional guarantees to bolster their position. If the monarchists were able to alleviate the situation of the urban workers, their policy was far less successful in the rural areas. Rural reform was paralyzed by the reluctance of the large landowners to make any concessions, and it was precisely this class that was entrenched around the throne. The inability of the conservative administrations to solve this problem, or even to begin the solution of it, contributed directly to the growth of extremist sentiment among the rural masses of Andalucía. The extraordinary combination under the banner of anarchism of the Barcelona proletariat and the Andalucian tenant farmers, which has puzzled so many observers of the Spanish scene, finds its explanation in the growth of a virulent Catalanism in the northeast and the unrest among the rural masses in the south.

Extremism had come to Spain in organized form in 1868 with the establishment of the Iberian branch of international Marxism. The split between Bakunin and Marx in 1872 produced a schism between the radical tendencies in the peninsula and henceforth there were to be two divisions: one libertarian under anarchist influence, and the other authoritarian under socialism. This conflict between two forms of extremism endured in Spain from that day clear down to the Second Republic. It was one of the major forces in the civil war and perhaps the fundamental cause for the ineffectiveness of so much of the republican effort between 1931 and 1939. Anarchism versus communism and socialism represented a permanent and apparently irreconcilable trilogy in the social and political annals of contemporary Spain. Lafargue, son-in-law of Marx, came to Spain after the collapse of the *Commune* in Paris. In close collaboration with the rising leader of Spanish socialism, Pablo Iglesias, the Spanish socialist party was founded in 1879. The intellectual influences on incipient Spanish socialism were many. In addition to simon-pure Marxism, filtered in through Lafargue, Iglesias drew a great deal from the French socialist, Jules Guesde. Further details of the development of socialism, communism, and anarchism will be found in Chapter 6.

It is highly important to remember that this period of the late nineteenth and early twentieth centuries is distinguished by the rising opposition to the established monarchy in the form, not of conventional republicanism, but extremism in its most violent form. The "tragic week" of Barcelona took place in 1909. This riot with its sequence of bloodshed and bitterness was caused by the decision of the war office to mobilize the recruits for service in Morocco against the Riffian rebellion. This decision was taken by the restless masses as a provocation. Pablo Iglesias, in a speech in Madrid, urged the troops to shoot into the air in protest against their forced service in Africa. On July 26, 1909, a general strike swept Barcelona. The outbreak of this social revolt was the signal for the burning of convents and outrages against the religious orders. Once again, with a monotonous regularity which was to become a pattern of Spanish life, the social upheavals were invariably accompanied by attacks on religion and especially on the clergy and the religious orders. In some parts of Catalonia a republic was proclaimed; the Civil Guard was attacked by the populace, or at least by that portion of the populace that was made bold by the constant incitement of the extremist leaders. It was necessary to send forces from Valencia and Madrid to put down the riots. In order to avoid an extension of the disorders to the entire country, the government made public the statement that it was forced to take action against a Catalan separatist attempt. This version was not true, but it served to circumscribe the rebellion to Catalonia. Francisco Ferrer y Guardia, anarchist leader, was arrested, tried, and executed. The case became a *cause célèbre*. In a strictly twentieth-century manner, left-wing organizations and sympathizers the world over deluged the press with protests and Ferrer was built up as a martyr to free thought and liberty. He was in a literal sense a forerunner of Sacco and Vanzetti as the rallying point of radicals everywhere. In another sense, the world-wide action taken on his behalf was a foretaste of the gigantic propaganda campaign against Spain after World War II.[7]

Political life became more and more confused. For a time the regime hoped for support against the rising tide of anarchism from the radicals now under the leadership of Alejandro Lerroux, destined to become a stormy petrel in Spanish life and one of its perennial political figures until the time of the civil war. The liberals were quite willing to ally themselves temporarily with the extreme Left, and in the Cortes they threw themselves into frenzies of denunciation of the government and all its works. The fall of Maura was the end of all hope for a constitution in Spain based on an intelligent, evolutionary conservatism. Social disorder was not curbed under Canalejas. The socialist strike of 1911, as well as the general railway strike a year later, revealed that the tactics of social revolution were rapidly making headway. The murder of Canalejas coincided with the definite liquidation of Maura as a political figure so that Spain was deprived of two talented leaders, both possessed of imagination and drive. The animosity against Maura was so profound and so overwhelming that Pablo Iglesias stated in the Cortes that anything was legitimate to prevent his return to office, "including physical aggression against his person." The liberals were beaten, morally and politically, in 1913 and Romanones, who headed the government, was ousted.

At this juncture the normal thing would have been the recall of Maura to take over the reins of administration. Faced by a desperate situation of irresponsibility, the King made efforts to create a kind of combination, a bicephalic thing, part monarchist and part republican. There was a tendency to turn to the intellectuals for guidance in this crisis. Among those interviewed by the King were Azcárate, a leading republican personality, Cossío, high priest of what has been called the secularist church of the *Institución Libre de Enseñaanza,* and Melquiades Alvarez, a reform leader who was to die in 1936, murdered in the Madrid prison by the extremists. Romanones, Dato, García Prieto — these are the names of alternating heads of the government,

[7] "There was an outcry all over Europe, and the mass movement had found a martyr. The habit of burning churches, followed occasionally in former risings, became a regular feature of every popular rising in Catalonia after the execution of Ferrer" (Borkenau, *Spanish Cockpit* [London: Faber and Faber, Ltd., 1937], p. 29).

none of whom gave it the stability or the continuity desired with such anxiety by the mass of people.

World War I plunged Spain into a new kind of crisis. The head of the Spanish government at that time was Eduardo Dato, an anachronistic sort of politician who believed with remarkable fervor that the methods of 1875 were perfectly applicable to the situation of 1914. Dato proclaimed Spain's neutrality. A greater man might conceivably have been led into dangerous adventures. Dato was so mediocre that activity was repugnant to him. He entrenched himself behind the rigid neutrality to which he had committed Spain, and refused to budge. This weakness was a source of strength. Spain remained neutral quite literally because the government was too inept to do anything about it. Sentiment was divided between the Central Powers and the Allies. Count Romanones and Alejandro Lerroux, the latter in the tradition of the Jacobins and the French Declaration of the Rights of Man, sought to pull Spain into the conflict on the allied side. Equally strong influences were at work to force Spain into a position favorable to the Central Powers. In some ways the two forces canceled each other, and Dato remained impassive in his insistence on neutrality. The Catalan problem became more and more acute. Gradually, thanks in large measure to the indifference of the central government, Catalonia was creating the instruments for a separate political, social, and cultural life.

One of the gravest problems of this epoch was the army. The story of the Spanish army is an important segment in the understanding of the evolution of the national institutions. There is a tendency at times to oversimplify the role and place of the army in the course of recent Spanish history. The outbreak of civil war in 1936 was often interpreted abroad, as the overweening ambition of army officers eager to replace civilians in the direction of public affairs. The real version is not quite so simple. Obviously the Spanish army was no longer the institution it had been in the glorious days of empire. During the nineteenth century it had vegetated up and through the Spanish-American War and, aside from the tiresome expeditions in Morocco and the ephemeral Mexican adventure, the army was never called upon to defend the nation against foreign attack or invasion. It was strongly influenced by the liberal and revolutionary ideas of the time. The notion that the army was a bulwark of conservatism and reaction against the inroads of new ideas does not give the accurate picture of the role of the institution. The absence of a specific function led to intervention in politics while Cánovas had eliminated politically minded generals and put the armed forces back in the barracks where he believed they belonged. But he failed to give them anything to do once they were in the barracks and this was a capital error. So bad did things become that the army officer and the schoolteacher were the natural objects of the mockery and popular humor of the masses. One of the monstrosities of the Spanish army after the defeat in 1898 was the utter lack of balance between the number of the men in the ranks and the officers. There were actually 499 generals, 578 colonels, and over 23,000 other officers for an armed force that was frequently less than 80,000.[8] This corps of officers was not immune to the trend of the times. If the Catalans, the trade unions, the industrial workers, and every other sector of the population could clamor for privileges and employ direct action to gain their ends, why should the army continue to tolerate official neglect? There developed unions within the ranks of the army, aimed at influencing affairs in their favor. A number of recalcitrant army officers were imprisoned; the public reaction was extraordinary and so discredited was the government that opinion was on the side of the military in their struggle with the civil authority. A newly formed revolutionary committee composed of Lerroux, Melquíades Alvarez, Largo Caballero, and Julián Besteiro declaimed against the government on behalf of the incarcerated military. Cambó, Catalan conservative leader, was bent on disrupting totally the present party order in order to re-create in its stead a new and more effective distribution of the parties.

The elections of 1918 were confusion worst confounded. The new parliament was completely unmanageable. About a hundred seats went to the government party and Maura's partisans had another twenty-five. There were twenty-three representatives of the Catalan *Lliga;* the Basque nationalists were there with seven members; there were socialists, Catalan republicans, and a variety of lesser breeds. The inchoate, insensate mass was an impossible legislative body lacking in every element of cohesion. The King intervened to urge the formation of a national government along the bipartisan lines then in vogue in wartime England and Maura consented to return from retirement to preside over the destinies of the cabinet. Internal strife made it impossible for this cabinet to achieve real harmony while regionalism flared up once more with terrific violence. The collapse of

---

[8] Aunós Pérez, *Itinerario histórico de la España contemporánea 1808–1936,* p. 333.

the Central Powers and the major reshuffling of the map of Europe motivated hopes in Spain that it was time to bring about the often proposed and never realized decentralization. The numerous Catalan parties joined in the demand for autonomy. Even Galicia, on the other side of Spain, was moved by the same sentiment. The Basque provinces played with the idea and formulated here and there, notably at Tolosa, a petition for autonomy. Of this more will be said in the chapter on regionalism, especially with reference to the Catalan situation where Cambó's *Lliga Regionalista* was split into two branches which became the *Esquerra catalana* and *Acció catalana.*

Barcelona once more was the scene of strikes, social unrest, and extreme violence with disorder reaching such a point that in 1920 some 394 citizens were killed in the streets. There was a dangerous tendency toward the creation of a state within a state; a system of disorder in which direct action was the rule. In that year there were 1316 strikes all over Spain. The local citizenry tried to meet the challenge by improvised organizations of one kind and another. Count Romanones was presiding over the central government at the moment and his method, in the good liberal tradition, was to send an emissary to Barcelona to treat with the extremists. The general strike was the reply to these gestures. Romanones fell and one weak, vacillating government succeeded another. The trade unions, in the grip of extremism, were met by the Employers Federation (*Federación Patronal*) seeking to counteract the spirit of unbridled violence. Between January 21 and 22, 1921, twenty-one residents of Barcelona were murdered. There was a disaster at Melilla in Morocco and, as usual in cases of grave crisis, Maura was invited to assume power once more. He returned on August 21, 1921, for the last time. Dato was assassinated and the parties combined to make Maura's life insufferable, in which task they succeeded admirably.

The Russian Revolution of 1917 had awakened faint echoes in Spain. For a time the anarchists welcomed the news of events in far-off Russia as a prelude to their type of emancipation. The formation of local Soviets seemed to strike a responsive chord in their minds. It was not long before Spanish anarchists were quite aware that the iron rule of Bolshevism was not the ideal toward which they were striving. The break became irreconcilable and it endured down to the civil war when a temporary coalition allowed the extreme forces to carry on together only to break again in the midst of war with calamitous results for the Republic's conduct of hostilities.

Demoralization was the order of the day. Civilians were sent out to Morocco to run affairs and an agreement was signed with Abd-el-Krim whereby he was bribed to cease hostilities. The funds thus acquired were used to purchase more war materials to kill more Spaniards. Terrorism was flourishing unabated all over Spain. A former governor of Vizcaya was murdered and the Archbishop of Zaragoza, Cardinal Soldevila, fell a victim to this nauseating wave of sheer, unmitigated terror.

In the midst of this chaos, a strong man appeared, the Captain General of Catalonia, Miguel Primo de Rivera. He was of the nobility, his family deeply rooted in the far south of Andalucía at Jerez de la Frontera. As the Marquis of Estella he had served in the Spanish forces for many years. On September 12, 1923, he signed the manifesto that constituted for all practical purposes a *coup d'état*. Everything had failed up to this time. The Morocco situation was an open, festering sore. The revolution in 1917 had been no solution. Constitutional government was moribund. The political parties were discredited. The army and police were suspected of intrigue and even connivance with the forces of disorder.

> Primo de Rivera started his job as a dictator under the most favorable auspices that ever inaugurated a dictatorship. His programme was contained in two sentences: destroy the old political parties, and reorganize the state by modernizing the country. In the six years of his dictatorship he did as much to achieve the second task as could possibly be expected. What elements of modern European life there are in Spain today mostly date from the time of Primo; the Republicans are loath to acknowledge it.[9]

Primo de Rivera was a remarkable man in many ways. His disdain of the shadowy government then in power was absolute, but, on the other hand, he was not a man of careful and thoughtful preparation. On the eve of the *coup,* he had made few plans, and almost no communications to other military commanders had been issued. He was impetuous, direct, completely sure of himself, and not at all given to theorizing about the duties and tasks of government. Within a few hours Primo de Rivera controlled Catalonia and Aragón while the liberal government made a vague gesture toward defense. The King, at San Sebastián, was urged to return to Madrid in the hope that his presence might turn aside this lightening that seemed certain to descend on the heads of the inept cabinet. Primo set out for Madrid on the fourteenth amid the acclamations of a citizenry that hoped for tranquillity if not peace and on the fifteenth he was invested with the

[9] Borkenau, *op. cit.,* p. 40.

supreme authority. The various shades of political opinion received the event with unexpected demonstrations of contentment, and Aniceto Alcalá Zamora, later first president of the Second Republic, expressed himself as willing to place no obstacles in the way of Primo. Count Romanones congratulated the country on the new regime which would liberate it from the "ineptitude of the civil governments."[10] Even the Catalinists saw Primo off from Barcelona station with every evidence of good will and support.

The inevitable question has been raised whether Primo de Rivera's dictatorship was fascist. Unfortunately we live in an era in which any regime we do not particularly like must by its nature be fascist, since the term is a general one of opprobrium. The loose fashion in which the word "fascist" has been bandied about to label innumerable governments and radically contradictory regimes, ought by this time to serve as a lesson in more careful semantics. But this, unhappily, is not the case. We are therefore faced by the contention that Primo de Rivera and General Franco are fascists and to be placed in the same debit column with Mussolini. Franz Borkenau states the difficulty very pungently:

> Primo's regime fascist? Has it, or could it gather the totalitarian powers' characteristic of fascism? By no means! Primo had no fascist movement, nor a large and enthusiastic party of all classes behind him. From the first to the last moment he was in power, he was passively tolerated by a population which, after all, appreciated good government, but saw no reason to help it.[11]

We can rid ourselves at once of the notion that Primo de Rivera was a precursor of the contemporaneous totalitarians. The fact that he coincided more or less with the march on Rome and the rise to power of Italian fascism was pure coincidence. His dictatorship was the typically Hispanic combination of vigor and softness, authority and weakness, competence and inertia. He ruled as a military man, with the limitations and the virtues of that state in life, totally unannoyed by the complexities of ideology and not concerned in the least about the customary fanfare and pageantry of some of the modern dictatorships. Spain wanted to be ruled; Spain had to be ruled if it were to subsist, and Primo proposed to rule it as long as necessary and as long as the Spanish people would tolerate it. Primo de Rivera himself was dominated by vaguely liberal ideas. His attack on the basic problems of Spain became then, not an extirpation of the evils

---

10 Aunós Pérez, *op. cit.*, p. 363.

11 *Op. cit.*, p. 41.

by their roots, but a careful pruning of the branches of the tree that produced those evils. He did not go to the essence of the thing or examine the validity of the whole structure of Spanish institutions, but preferred to think of the problem as one of men and not of ideas; as a matter of good administration and not the virtue or fault of the institution being administered.

That Primo de Rivera obtained action is beyond all question. Every visitor to Spain today remarks at the excellence of the paved highways running all over the peninsula. They were the work of the Primo de Rivera's dictatorship. Prisons, hospitals, schools, and public works came into being during the years he directed the destinies of Spain. The Moroccan question was solved in collaboration with the French. The social problem was met in part by the introduction of collective bargaining. The army was a problem, and Primo was forced to make concessions to it. He turned to the bourgeoisie for support and encouraged business interests, being supported in this enterprise by an extraordinary finance minister, José Calvo Sotelo. The Catalan question was met head on by decrees and restrictions with the result that Catalan sentiment was offended time and again by limitations on its expression.

Early in 1929 Primo de Rivera announced that this year would see the agrarian reform. The measure bearing the date of January 7, 1929, extended facilities to the farmer in peonage to acquire land by means of State loans, and the law was translated into practical terms by the extension of several million pesetas of credit, the rehabilitation of some 5000 farmers, and the breaking up into smaller farms of holdings representing many thousand acres. Provision was made for the proper organization of the farmers once the reform had been put into effect. Needless to say, there was strong opposition on the part of the landowners and the extreme Right.

The main political problem of the dictatorship was the party system. In rejecting the old party order, Primo de Rivera had simply gone ahead and governed without them although it was clear that something had to be substituted for their normal operation. The question was whether he could create a party or a political organization capable of bearing this responsibility. The so-called *Unión Patriótica* was created out of nothing and represented no real current of public opinion. The Consultative Assembly that was to take the place of the Cortes was not much better; an improvised affair that was very far from reflecting the opinion of the nation.

Opposition grew. The decline in the peseta shook confidence in the regime and in intellectual circles the hostility was violent. Primo de Rivera did not enjoy the support of the Church although there are writers who refer to it as though there were a secret conspiracy between the two authorities. The Concordat of 1851 was still in force and completely out of date. In the Basque country and Catalonia Catholic hostility became more and more pronounced and signs of rebellion had already appeared. In 1923 several generals, among them Weyler of the Cuban campaign, were condemned to the payment of heavy fines. On the fringes, other groups began to raise their heads including the various republican sectors. His regime did one very specific thing, however, it ruined the bourgeoisie through economic errors and unfortunate fiscal complications. The world economic crisis of 1929 was a very prominent factor in the liquidation of the dictatorship. In a statement prepared by Primo de Rivera on December 31, 1929, in which he examined the whole situation of the country and its regime, he complained bitterly that, "the aristocracy hates me for they find their privileges reduced, the conservatives refuse to join me . . . those closest to the Church do not believe the words and acts of the dictatorship conform to their best ideals; the industrial enterprises are opposed because in spite of greater profits, their taxes are collected; the civil servants object because in spite of better pay, they are obliged to work punctually. . . ."[12]

The intellectual ferment was unceasing. Miguel de Unamuno, from his refuge just across the border in France, shot dart after dart at the dictator and the Madrid Ateneo became a center of effervescence out of which the Second Republic was to come. In the universities and other teaching centers, restrictions had been insufficient to stifle the protest that was fast becoming articulate. In January, 1930, Primo de Rivera abandoned power; on March 16, 1930, he died in Paris while Alfonso XIII requested another general, Berenguer, to take office. In August, 1930, the Pact of San Sebastián was signed at a meeting of socialists, republicans, and left-wing Catalan groups with a *manifesto*

---

[12] Aunós Pérez, *op. cit.*, p. 392.

Under the makeshift arrangement of General Berenguer after the fall of Primo de Rivera, the makings of the future social revolution were already visible: "In the post-dictatorial period of Berenguer . . . there were symptoms. The most restless part of the student groups, which up to this time had been strongly in favor of Alfonso, began to demand the Republic and expressed complete disdain for the person of the monarch." Duque de Maura y Melchor Fernández Almagro, *Porqué cayó Alfonso XIII,* Madrid, 1948, 2 ed., p. 378.

in which the proposed republic was depicted as little short of the Promised Land. The signatures are among the best known of the leaders of the new Republic: Alejandro Lerroux, Alcalá Zamora, Fernando de los Ríos, Alvaro de Albornoz, Largo Caballero, Martínez Barrio, and Nicolau d'Olwer. On December 12, 1930, in a manner strongly reminiscent of the *pronunciamientos* of the mid-nineteenth century, Captain Galán and a comrade, García Hernández, led an uprising in Jaca, in the extreme north of Spain, for which the two officers were summarily shot. A day later a violent incident also contributed to creating martyrs for the Republic. At Cuatro Vientos, near Madrid, an incipient revolt was quashed and several of the seditious elements lost their lives. On April 8, 1931, the decree calling for elections was issued.

The intellectual antecedents of the Republic had already been achieved. At the Ateneo, opened and closed successively during the dictatorship, a new figure, Manuel Azaña had been elected president; an avowed republican and a writer of modest accomplishment. Dr. Gregorio Marañón, one of Spain's most distinguished physicians and a writer of distinction; Ramón Pérez de Ayala; and José Ortega y Gasset, all formed a part of the academic backdrop to the promised Republic. The republicans were unanimous in their refusal to have anything to do with elections or the constitution of a government as long as the King remained or the monarchy subsisted. Count Romanones managed a makeshift government under the leadership of an admiral, Juan B. Aznar. One of the important decisions of the government was to fix the elections for April 12. No general elections were involved and much less a referendum on monarchy versus republic, but simply the selection of the municipal authorities. The Revolutionary Committee that had issued the republican *manifesto* was jailed and condemned, only to have the sentence remitted. The republicans themselves hoped that the municipal consultations would show a trend to republicanism so that when the general parliamentary elections came in June the new regime would score a definite victory.

Professor E. Allison Peers has given us a graphic account of the elections and the atmosphere that prevailed on that decisive Sunday in April, 1931, when the course of Spanish history was radically and abruptly changed.

> At two o'clock in the afternoon, the figures received down to that hour, and published by the Home Secretary, showed that 22,150 seats had gone to the monarchists and only 5,875 to Republicans. The country districts had,

with few exceptions, supported the Monarchy; in Madrid, the numbers of seats gained by each group were exactly equal, and only in the principal provincial capitals and in the northern and eastern districts of Vizcaya, Logroño, Huesca, Lérida, Barcelona and Tarragona were there Republican majorities.[13]

The republicans were triumphant in the great cities and notably in Madrid and Barcelona. It is important to remember in connection with this historical election that even the republicans had never pretended that they were instituting a popular referendum on the question of retaining the monarchy or inaugurating the republic. The issue was not posed in specific terms, and the results showed that in the country at large the republicans did not obtain a majority of the municipal seats. Nevertheless, on April 13, the King was faced by a choice. The monarchists were unorganized and their strength lay primarily in the rural areas. Republican sentiment was growing by leaps and bounds. The abdication was demanded and it was demanded that the monarch leave Spain before nightfall of the same day. Refusing to resist, on the basis that no drop of Spanish blood must be shed, the King set out that night for Cartagena while Madrid went wild with excitement. Republican banners appeared everywhere and the Revolutionary Committee acting as the provisional government stood ready to take over authority, while in Barcelona the Catalan Republic was proclaimed. Here and there over Spain smaller communities had anticipated Madrid and Catalonia in announcing the end of the monarchy.

Spain was now embarked on the arduous and dramatic venture of the Second Republic.

---

[13] *The Spanish Tragedy* (London: Methuen & Co., 1936), p. 26.

Chapter 4. RELIGION AND THE CHURCH

THE problem of the Church in Spain was summarized by the brilliant Donoso Cortés in an address delivered on December 30, 1850:

> Spain has been a nation forged by the Church. The Church has served the poor. All the charitable foundations in Spain were for the poor. The revolution has changed all this. With the spoliation of the Church, the rents on land rose, and with the suppression of the tithes, a new and even more alarming rise took place.[1]

The question of the Catholic Church in Spain beyond doubt has caused more impassioned discussion than any other single issue, nor is it an easy topic to analyze. From the historical point of view, there is no adequate survey of the Church in Spain from the earliest times to the present. There is no good ecclesiastical history of the nineteenth and twentieth centuries with effective and complete information on such matters as Church properties and the consequences of the confiscation early in the past century. The absence of readily available information on this important matter leads inevitably to the vast amount of nonsense that is perpetrated in the name of "the Spanish question." This question arises in every debate regarding the Church, its doctrines, or its position in the world. The most inveterate enemies of the Faith insist on dragging Spain in, usually as the horrible example of clericalism, corruption, sloth, and spiritual decay. There is an almost irresistible tendency on the part of the detractors of the Church to do two things: first, to insist that all Catholics everywhere must, as a matter of faith and morals, defend everything in every so-called Catholic country. Hence, if the sewage-disposal system does not operate properly in Córdoba, Spain, a clinching argument against the Catholic Faith has been made. And second, there is an insistence on denouncing the Church for excessive meddling in such matters as charity, education,

[1] Donoso Cortés, *Obras escogidas,* Buenos Aires, 1943, p. 306.

and politics, and then simultaneously denouncing that same Church for not contributing more effectively to charity, education, and an improved political and social order.

The present analysis is not a history of the Church in Spain, but rather a series of comments on its place and its vicissitudes over the past century and a half. This brief summary may contribute something to understanding just how poor and important the Church often was in Spain, despite the long-repeated argument about its absolute control in "Catholic Spain." English-speaking readers, and especially those who are unacquainted with the nomenclature and trends on the continent of Europe, are confused by the notion that Spain is overwhelmingly Catholic and, therefore, its government, its institutions, its way of life, and its laws must of necessity be inspired by the strictest Catholic orthodoxy. This is frequently the very opposite of the truth. Spain has suffered from periodical outbreaks of anticlericalism, from government hostility to the Church, and from unfavorable legislation that has hampered and impeded much of its work. Under the dynasty of the Bourbons, Spain was infiltrated with many of the ideas then prevalent in France and elsewhere in Europe. Reforms of the type initiated by Pombal in Portugal were applied in Spain, and the religious orders were often the victims of savage repression and outright robbery of their properties. A facile liberalism found solace in its general sterility in aggression against the Church, the one institution least able to defend itself against violence. This sport was not limited to the two republics Spain knew, but to the monarchy as well. The partial and complete confiscation of the property of the Spanish Church was not the work of a single reign or a single person, but extended over most of the nineteenth century: 1812, 1820, 1837, 1868, and in the present century, 1931.

The problem of an impoverished Church supported by the government is fundamental in recent Spanish history. A Church possessing the necessary property for its work, both spiritual and material, independent of the State is perhaps a *desideratum*. This does not refer to the question of the relations between Church and State or even to the moot question of the union of Church and State. Cordial and harmonious relations between the temporal and the spiritual jurisdictions can hardly be conceived except as a very great blessing. The problem in Spain is not so much the *rapports* between the two, but rather the state of dependence to which the Church was reduced in the nineteenth century, as part of a policy of strengthening and enriching the State. This dependent station was responsible in a very direct way for the tension between the two authorities. The reader may be sure that this is no problem that has arisen under General Franco nor does it belong exclusively to the contemporary period. As long ago as 1840, Jaime Balmes, the gifted young Catalan priest, the centenary of whose death was celebrated in 1949, published his study, entitled *Observaciones sociales, políticas y económicas sobre los bienes del clero*. In this fundamental essay on the problem of the economic independence of the clergy, Father Balmes treated the whole question of spoliation by the State. He posed the one question that is at the basis of all discussions of the Church in Spain:

> What value can the guarantee by the public treasury have for so numerous a class [the clergy]? What is the value of such a promise in the light of the possibility of war, upheavals and other public calamities, and where the amount must depend on the will of a necessarily changing congress which may become very easily, not the expression of a generous and understanding people, but that of a narrow-minded party, or a turbulent, perverse and anti-religious faction?[2]

Here we have the essence of the problem. The State had taken Church property by force and now proposed, not a proper indemnity or compensation, to which the Church had every right, but simply a form of bribe to be made by annual grants of the crown or parliament. This lesser evil may have appealed to many Spaniards as the best solution of an extremely difficult situation. On the other hand, Father Balmes put his finger directly on the difficulty in pointing out that what might appear to be a gesture of good will and support could easily become the instrument of further spoliation and persecution. And this is exactly what happened in Spain up to the time of the civil war. The broad outline of the ecclesiastical history of the past century and a half may be suggested as follows:

1. The Catholic Church lost, in the course of the nineteenth century, most of its property and was reduced to a literal state of poverty.
2. Endemic anticlericalism dominated both the Spanish government and authorities long before the establishment of the Second Republic.
3. The Spanish Church, rather than determining the course of recent history, may be more accurately conceived as the victim of most of it.

---

[2] Jaime Balmes, *Obras completas,* Madrid, 1949, Vol. V, p. 720.

4. Despite these adversities and persecutions, the Spanish Church has managed to achieve notable success in the spiritual, intellectual, and moral order.

Before an examination of these general ideas, a word may be said about Spanish Catholicism as such. In the chapter on the Hispanic temperament some reference has been made to the spiritual attitude of the Spanish people, and the fact that all Spaniards, regardless of class or condition, are obsessed by the problem of God and of eternity. The most pious or the most profane are likely to be linked together by a common anxiety about human destiny and the hereafter. E. Allison Peers, that excellent mentor in things Hispanic, states quite simply that "the first in order of the conclusions which one draws about the Catholic Church in Spain is that it is the Church of the Spanish people."[3] It is perhaps this popular character of the Catholic Faith that disconcerts so many foreigners. Half measures in religion are as alien to the Spanish mind as in anything else. Unamuno has written of the profound impression made on the foreigner by the abundance of lacerated, bleeding, tragic figures of our Lord to be found in the churches and cathedrals all over Spain. "The Spanish Christ was born in Tangier," the Portuguese poet Guerra Junqueira was wont to say; meaning that the Christ who appears to us in wood and stone in Spain partakes of the force, the tragedy, and the agony derived from more primitive Africa, and which has been lost to refined and sophisticated Europe. Religion in Spain, like bullfighting, provides the Spaniard with strong emotions, demands that he give himself completely and draws him fully and entirely out of himself.[4]

As I have indicated before, the Spaniard is or he is not. There is no middle ground, no easy compromise, no detached indifference regarding the great problems of life, death, immortality, and eternity. Fallen-away Catholics in Spain become anticlericals, complete agnostics, or atheists. They rarely become members of one of the evangelical sects or give their allegiance to some other form of organized religion.[5] This

---

[3] E. Allison Peers, *Spain, the Church and the Orders* (London: Burns, Oates and Washbourne, 1939), p. 3.

[4] Miguel de Unamuno, *Ensayos,* Madrid, 1945, Vol. II, pp. 386–387. Essay entitled *"El Cristo español."*

[5] Salvador de Madariaga writes, "it is useless to offer the Spaniard that rationalism which, in the form of intelligent doubt, is such a 'soft cushion for the well-made head' of the Frenchman. The pendulum of the Spanish soul oscillates between the two extremes, self and the universe . . . either the religion of authority or that of the

Spanish Catholicism that merits the loyalty of so large a segment of the people and asserts its spiritual primacy over the almost entire population is not easy to reduce to simple terms. I would say that first of all, Spanish Catholicism is inflexible, not in the dogmatic or moral sense in which it conforms entirely to the body of Catholic belief, but in the sense of its adaptation to the *milieu*. The Spanish often say that French Catholicism is dominated by charity, in contrast to Spanish where the sense of justice is stronger. The French have a broader understanding of human frailty and weakness; they are more willing to make allowances. They seek to reach the indifferent and the negligent by presenting the Faith in the best possible form. The attractiveness of this presentation becomes the entering wedge. In the case of the Spanish adaptability is the least visible quality of its Catholicism, for there is an almost puritanical intrasigence that extends not merely to matters of faith and morals but penetrates the habits and attitudes of the people. The Spaniard in religion is a zealot — not a bigot. He is overwhelmingly devoted to the Holy See and extremely "Vaticanist" in his loyalty to the Church and often finds perplexing and dubious the religious position of his neighbors beyond the Pyrenees. He is disturbed and concerned by the evidences of compromise that have penetrated the thinking of Catholics in other parts of Europe. I recall vividly a visit some years ago to the then Cardinal-Archbishop of Tarragona. The first question posed to his American visitor was: "How do you explain this business of dances under parish auspices in the United States?" The problem of mixed marriage and the need for proper social activity under Catholic auspices had never occurred to His Eminence as the explanation of this phenomenon, for in Spain an arrangement of this nature would be inconceivable as well as unnecessary. In part religious unity explains the absence of some of the more pressing problems that beset the American Church and especially the American laity.

Spanish Catholicism is distinguished by a profound sobriety and an intensity that sometimes surpasses the imagination. A problem that puzzles the Spanish Catholic mind today is that spiritual revival in so many other countries is interpreted far too much in terms of humanitarianism and social service. The absence of evidence of emphasis on personal sanctification, of a more profound interior life, seem to the

---

solitary individual, the religion of absolute certainty or that of isolated search" (*Spain* [London: Jonathan Cape, 1943; New York: Creative Age Press, Inc., 1943], p. 128).

Spanish Catholic as a sign of superficiality and of inconsequence. To what end does the diffusion of social doctrine, of sound political principles, and the temporal policies of the Church lead, if there is not in the case of each individual soul a growing association with God; a more profound and enduring life in the sacraments? Side by side with this preoccupation is the subsidiary and closely related one: the disunion in the Catholic world that has come about through the clash of temporal interests. The contemporary Spanish Catholic is profoundly perturbed by the shocking evidence about him of division and discord.

There is, perhaps, an intimate conviction that the Spanish Catholic way comes closer to reflecting the intention of the Church than any other. This is a form of vanity shared by numerous other national Catholic groups. But in Spanish Catholic circles everywhere there is the constantly repeated anguish, best stated by Giovanni Papini in the alleged words of his fictitious Pope Celestine VI: "And now I say to you, with all the love that springs from your sorrow, that the only secret of salvation is the unity of all men reborn in Christ. Separation is the real sin against humanity."[6] Add to this the strong feeling that the world is a constant battleground and that the forces of evil must be routed, not once but repeatedly. Every relaxation, every refusal to look at the enemy clearly and unflinchingly, every retreat no matter how small, becomes a confession of impotence or of weakness. To the Spanish Catholic it is plainly Christ against anti-Christ. Although he tends to confuse sometimes Spain and anti-Spain with this conception of the forces in conflict he does see clearly that the modern world is irretrievably engaged in the conflict between the natural and the supernatural; between the light that emanates from God and the darkness that flows from confidence in the exclusive forces of mankind. The Spanish Catholic is pained that elsewhere he should be judged outmoded and archaic, and that his very fervor, so necessary today, is decried as a medieval survival which should give way to a more tractable attitude and he is prone to retreat before this accusation into the armor of even greater truculence.

That Spanish Catholicism has taken on a very strong national coloring admits of no doubt. The missionary activity of hundreds of Spanish religious the world over are invariably combined with an expansion of the cultural empire of Spain itself. Let it be noted, as it has been again and again in these pages, that this missionary sense, in which the

[6] Giovanni Papini, *Lettere agli uomini del Papa Celestino Sesto,* Florence, 1946, p. 259.

winning of souls is associated with the diffusion of the values of Hispanic culture, has never in the past and does not contain at the present time the slightest element of racism or that introvert quality of ethnic purity that distorted German thought for so long. Spanish nationalism tends to become synonymous with Catholicism.

Spanish Catholicism has been judged as external, ornate, showy, and mundane in its pageantry and splendor. Of course there is much in Spanish Catholicism that is spectacular. The great Corpus Christi procession at Toledo, for instance, has a great deal that is showy and mundane about it — highly decorated army officers, chatting officialdom, and very unpious groups of every kind. Side by side with that is the great silence of the average Spanish church, the invitation to meditation of the cathedrals, and the almost continuous presence of the ordinary citizenry at their prayers. There is a vivid and keen sense of the holy, a reverence for those things that deserve reverence. Let the Blessed Sacrament be carried along a street on the way to a sickroom, and well-dressed gentlemen along with waiters will drop to their knees in the presence of God. The fervor that permeated National Spain during the civil war has been admirably described by more than one writer.[7] Life in the towns and villages revolves around the Church and its liturgical calendar and retreats and pilgrimages have long played a very large part in the religious life of the Spanish.[8]

In synthesis, we may say that Spanish Catholicism, despite varying fortunes and periods of lassitude, has preserved consistently the essential elements of faith. True, there were moments of hiatus; epochs during which the Catholic tradition has become lax and obscure. Practice does not always accompany faith. But this Hispanic Catholicism is never a cold, intellectualized thing. Despite the brilliant theological tradition of Spain, which repeatedly won for it first place among the defenders of the faith, the remarkable fact of Spanish Catholicism is its tenacity among the ordinary mass of people. This is particularly true among the countryfolk. The peasantry has rarely been disturbed in its complacent faith. Political change, social upheaval, turmoil and revolution, even when anticlericalism has been at its worst, have had little effect on the country masses. In the cities, the story is entirely different. Homeless and uprooted workers have been subjected to enormous pressure toward secularism and extremism. Alien ideas

---

[7] Francis McCullagh, *In Franco's Spain,* London, 1937, p. 129.

[8] See the excellent description of Mass at the cathedral of Santiago de Compostela, in S. F. A. Coles, *Spain Everlasting,* London, 1946, pp. 197–199.

may, in individuals, have been allowed to take root and pervert the essence of faith as it has continued to be transmitted from generation to generation. But the real Spain — the peasants of Navarre, the Basque provinces, Castile, Extremadura, Catalonia, the Levant, and Andalucía — has retained its heritage with little change.

The reader will wonder, of course, how in this kind of country the exotic plant of anticlericalism has managed to flourish so persistently. The important fact to remember is that anticlericalism, and with it anti-Catholicism, grows and develops precisely because there is a very great Catholic tradition. It is a violent reaction to the general spiritual situation. The essential question is not puzzlement over the existence of anticlericalism, but a clear idea of how it has been produced and made effective. Obviously it is not sufficient to claim that the Church was wealthy and all powerful, which it was not, or that the people hated the clergy, which in general they did not. The ordinary Spanish clergy has always been extremely close to the people. To be sure, there has been what the Spanish call the *"clero de misa y olla,"* that is, the priest who limited his sacerdotal function to saying Mass and living well. This type has existed historically and exists today, but there are the thousands of ordinary parish priests, and especially the members of the religious orders, whose poverty has always been very real and who are indistinguishable from the mass whom they serve. The traditional picture of the unkempt, unshaven, and sometimes not very hygienic priest in the third-class coaches of the Spanish railways and in the little villages is not entirely inaccurate. It is necessary, nevertheless, to penetrate further and find if the absence of a clean-shaven face implies a like degree of spiritual slovenliness.

A later chapter on the course of events during the Second Republic and the civil war itself will reveal to what extent the outbreaks against clergy and hierarchy were not the spontaneous protests of an outraged people, but the carefully nurtured and organized determination to wipe out a force that stood in the way of the sovietization of Spain. The methodical, ruthless destruction of churches and wealth, the manner in which priests and religious were hounded to their death is not the picture of a people betrayed by their spiritual leaders, but of a minority so ruthless in its procedure that its reign of terror paralyzed reaction for a time. It is difficult to estimate how much of this horror was provoked by the encouragement, or at least the complacency, of a government that was quite willing for the uncontrolled mass to satiate its passions on nuns, religious, and works of art. The fact remains that anticlericalism as a natural process, unprompted by anything but a desire for vengeance, would be difficult to defend as a thesis.

Arnold Lunn has perhaps summarized the problem as well as anyone in saying that "The Church in Spain is hated not for its defects but for its virtues."[9]

The question of anticlericalism cannot be dismissed with a couple of irrelevancies or a spate of flippancies, to be sure. It is a serious matter and the complete exposition of its bases and antecedents would fill another volume. Wealth, luxury, and indolence, allegedly the attributes of the clergy and hierarchy, were not the causes. Aside from the fact that these qualities did not exist, if they were sufficient reason for outbreaks of violence, anticlericalism would be far more rife in more economically privileged nations where the financial status of the Church is infinitely better than it has ever been in Spain. The fundamental cause, insofar as there is a single, essential one, is the inevitable conflict between men who are bent on imposing the secular doctrine of our day on those who are willing to withstand any pressure to prevent this imposition. Secularism as a counterbalance to traditional religion has come perilously close to becoming a religion itself. The creed of laicism has consistently practiced an intolerance that far exceeds anything religion itself has carried out. Miguel de Unamuno has defined the threat of this force in saying: "There is something still more terrible . . . intolerant, fanatical, aggressive skepticism; a dogmatic skepticism in its very anti-dogmatism."[10]

This is precisely the root of the whole matter. The conflict with secularism in its varying forms presents difficulties of a very special nature in countries where a multiplicity of religions or no religion at all prevail. The resistance of the Catholic Church becomes in this case a minority bulwark, and sometimes an isolated one, in the path of the new doctrine. In countries like Spain, where the Catholic tradition is centuries old and forms part of the marrow of Spanish living, secularism under the guise of "enlightenment" runs up against an enormous barrier of unyielding resistance. This secularism is not simply a loose form of liberalism, as some have judged it, or a vague liberalization of certain customs, laws, and manners. It is an interpretation of the purpose of life and the destiny of man, as defined and precise as a religious creed. Those who have risen to power in the machinations

---

[9] From *Spanish Rehearsal* by Arnold Lunn, copyright Sheed & Ward, Inc. (London: Hutchinson & Co., Ltd., 1937), p. 237.

[10] Unamuno, *op. cit.*, Vol. II, p. 509. Essay entitled, "*Escepticismo fanático.*"

of elections and political maneuvering in certain of the traditionally Catholic countries have not been satisfied to limit their so-called "reforms" to the pure externals. If in Spain the liberals had restricted themselves severely to economics or even to the mechanism of government, the subsequent story might be very different. But they proposed agrarian reform — which was good in many ways — simultaneously with the expulsion of the Jesuits, the tearing down of crucifixes in the schools, and the absolute secularization of all instruction. These measures were proposed, voted upon, and carried out in an atmosphere of convent burning and priest killing which made the whole program repugnant and indefensible. English-speaking readers might meditate on the fact that the oversimplification so rampant in our own press, about the curbing of the power of the Church and the exclusion of the clergy from politics is not an answer to the demand for a real explanation of the phenomenon of anticlericalism. The puerile notion that everything has been said when one asserts that the State should govern and the Church should mind its own spiritual affairs does not clarify the intricate issues as they appear in Spain. Spanish leftism, liberalism, and reformism were almost invariably engaged in a fight not against the *influence* of the Church in those fields judged as outside its proper jurisdiction, but against the Church itself.

Much has been written, and, I daresay, much more will continue to be written, on the vexing problem of Church and State in Spain. There are those who speak of the dangers of a "political Catholicism" and the threat that flowed from the Royal Patronage and the subservience of the Church to the State in financial matters. This conception has been asserted in very plain language by Alfred Mendizábal: "The old system was not ideal for Catholicism. The concessions obtained from it were prejudicial to independence, sometimes even to that dignity so necessary to the Church."[11]

This problem of the relations of the Spanish Church and State in the period preceding the Second Republic dates, of course, from a very remote age. It was the result of a process of slow and gradual growth, in large measure the outgrowth of historical circumstances that were almost imperceptible in their development. The *Patronato Real,* or Royal Patronage, for example, has its origins in the period of the Christian reconquest of Spain, a time when the ordinary rules of

---

[11] *The Martyrdom of Spain* (London: Geoffrey Bles, Ltd., 1938; New York: Charles Scribner's Sons, 1938), p. 155.

ecclesiastical procedure were hardly in force and the State and Church were so closely allied as to give the impression of fusion. The State was, in fact, the "temporal arm" of the Church and collaborated step by step in the reoccupation and pacification of territory wrested from Islam. With the rise of the Spanish monarchy, certain privileges were granted by the Holy See. Patronage is defined as the authority to nominate or present a candidate for a vacant ecclesiastical benefice. Canonical institution obviously belongs only to the pope or in some cases to the bishop. It has often been contended that the privilege of patronage in the case of temporal rulers was a natural and logical consequence of their own intervention in the cases of churches or other benefices established by them. We discover that these "rights" go back far into history, as it is claimed that Pope Nicholas II in the sixth century was the first to make mention pontifically of the privilege.[12]

The early centuries of the Church in Spain witnessed frequent cases of the election of a bishop by the faithful and clergy. The conflict that arose often led the temporal rulers to intervene to prevent disorder, and in due time their own influence became a determinant in the designation.[13] During the subsequent period, and especially during the epoch of the Arian Church, there is considerable variation in the customs in this regard. After the reconquest had gotten under way the Patronage became better defined. The Castilian monarchs followed the Visigothic practice of designating and deposing bishops. Under Gregory VII and the Cluniac reform, efforts were made to restore relations between Rome and Spain to a more normal basis. Although universal patronage was abolished, particular patronage continued to be the rule. Whether the reconquest was the basic reason for the granting of the privilege of presentation is an historical point quite beyond the scope of this synthesis. The important fact is that the whole tradition is concomitant with almost the entire history of the Church in Spain. Alfonso X of Castile claimed in 1328 and 1348 that it was the custom for the monarchs to give consent to the elections of bishops. The royal power was extended during the succeeding centuries, especially during the fifteenth. In Aragón, Castile, León, Guipúzcoa, Vizcaya, and other parts of Spain the essential privileges of the Patronage in greater or lesser form were confirmed by specific papal grant. Under the Catholic kings the privilege was well established,

[12] Matías Gómez Zamora, *Regio Patronato español e indiano,* Madrid, 1897, p. 10.

[13] Rafael Altamira y Crevea, *Historia de España y de la civilización española,* Barcelona, 1913–1914, Vol. I, p. 123.

not as a universal, automatic rule, but as applying in particular although numerous cases. The centralization of power under Philip V complicated these relations. The Concordat of 1753 made possible an agreement between the Spanish crown and the Holy See, and it was this document basically that was incorporated in the Concordat of 1851, which still governs the relations of Spain with the Holy See. In a later chapter mention will be made of some of the contemporary complications that have arisen in view of the fact that the basic understanding regulating the relations under the Patronage is still the Concordat of nearly a century ago.

To the modern mind this confusing relation of Church and State makes little sense. In an atmosphere in which the function of the Church is totally removed from anything smacking of the civil, it is hard, perhaps, to understand how nebulous was the frontier between the two jurisdictions in traditionally Catholic Spain. The truth is that in many ways it was almost impossible to distinguish where one authority ended and the other began. The Catholic Majesties, for instance, asked Pope Alexander VI in 1494 for a Bull to the end that they might proceed to the reform of the religious orders in the country, and it was under the formidable Franciscan, Francisco Ximenez de Cisneros, that this reform was carried out at the royal command.[14]

The important thing in this dreary little disquisition on the juridical relations of Church and State is that the two authorities for centuries in Spain have collaborated intimately and that the unraveling of their respective functions and powers is no simple matter. Suffice it to insist that there is no place for an insistence on complete separation as the reply to all difficulties; for that solution, from the economic, social, legal, and every other point of view, is far easier said than accomplished.

But we may turn now to the problem of sketching summarily the story of the Church down through the past century, as a preamble to the present situation. There can be no reasonable doubt that at one time the Church was an extremely wealthy and undertaxed institution and the reasons for this wealth are entirely understandable. In the first place the orders and the hierarchy were the beneficiaries of innumerable gifts and inheritances which increased the lands and other forms of wealth forming their patrimony. The process of such accumulation was not fundamentally different from that of modern universities which gradually gather together stocks, bonds, and investments of various

[14] Marcelino Menéndez y Pelayo, *Historia de los heterodoxos españoles,* Vol. II, p. 31 sq.

kinds as the basis of endowment. The functions of the Church too were infinitely complex, going far beyond dispensing the sacraments or maintaining parishes. The Church was literally responsible for education — all of it, from the lowest to the highest — and for every form of charity and what would be called today social service. None of these tasks belonged to the State and when assumed by the Church — *faute de mieux* — the financial burden became very heavy indeed.[15]

In the sixteenth century it was estimated that half of the entire income of Spain belonged to the Church. There are ample descriptions of how the Church used its wealth for almsgiving, poor relief, orphanages, and the innumerable other social needs of the time. In the days of the generalized welfare State, we need not be particularly alarmed that an institution should dispose of sufficient riches to undertake these multiple tasks. If the State embarks on this sort of thing and far beyond it, we find it quite natural. The eighteenth-century Spaniard was not shocked by a Church that assumed the tasks just outlined as part of its natural and proper function. Moreover, the wealth of the Church has been acquired quite honestly, and there was no basic objection to its possession — except of course the covetousness of the State, that fast-rising and defiant institution that was to lay such broad claims in its own name.

The myth of the landowning Church dies hard. Even those who admit that the story about owning one third of the peninsula is naïve nonsense, still cling to the equally popular version that the Church is the proud owner of everything from the Madrid underground to cinema houses in Barcelona.[16] It is perhaps appropriate that the Society of Jesus should bear the stigma in this case as in so many others. The truth is that if competent observers are in agreement that the Church owns very little land in Spain ever since the confiscation of a century ago, the idea is still prevalent that other forms of wealth are held by the orders and the hierarchy. I would call attention to the effort made by E. Allison Peers to arrive at some conclusions regarding the

---

[15] I am indebted to the excellent volume of E. Allison Peers, *op. cit.*, for much of the source information on these points.

[16] Franz Borkenau says: "Never since [the spoliation of 1837] has the Spanish Church recovered its wealth in land. The story of the Church as the largest landed proprietor in Spain is a myth. Only a small part of its *landed* property has been regained. As a compensation, the Church and various orders accumulated an enormous amount of *mobile* property. The Church today is not the largest landowner, but the largest capitalist in Spain, particularly the Spanish Jesuits" (*Spanish Cockpit* [London: Faber and Faber, Ltd., 1937], pp. 8–9).

wealth of the Catholic Church in modern Spain.[17] With supreme patience the distinguished Hispanist has collected a large number of the claims that are advanced regarding Church wealth, and shows that not one iota of real evidence or proof has been produced to back up the estimates. Professor Peers cites, in one of his seven cases quoted to demonstrate the absence of proof, one author who wrote that "it was pointed out in the Cortes in 1931 that the Jesuits owned one-third of the total wealth of Spain." The Professor proceeded to pin the gentleman down as to who had pointed this figure out, when and under what circumstances. The reply was that it "had been heard in Bilbao." I might suggest that when it comes to claiming things have been said in parliament, that the source is easily available in the form of the *Diario de Sesiones*. I personally have gone through the *Diario* page by page for the entire year 1931 and have discovered nothing of the sort ever said, even at the height of the debate on the dissolution of the Society of Jesus.

No one need confuse the richness of the churches or even the wealth of certain cathedrals in art and other treasures with the real, effective wealth of the clergy or hierarchy. The possession of unique art objects by the Cathedral of Zaragoza, Toledo, or elsewhere does not mean that the average priest in that diocese is rolling in abundance. Obviously, too, if the total value, real or estimated of all churches — and every village has one — schools, seminaries, convents, and episcopal residences is taken, the Church has a reasonable amount of property. But the claim that it owns capital wealth, for investment purposes and derives from this source a vast income, is simply untrue and can be very easily demonstrated.

A word about how the spoliation came to take place. Excesses against the orders and the Church were no novelty in 1931. In 1835, there was a serious outbreak with the murder of a considerable number of religious. One historian has estimated that attacks on the Church follow a kind of cycle, the revolution of which requires about thirty to thirty-five years: 1835, 1869, 1909, and 1936.[18]

The Spain of the 1830's was a confused jungle of political passions and intrigue. The Carlist wars were in full swing and the reign of María Cristina was anything but brilliant. There were tragic incidents, revelatory of the low state of public affairs, such as the overthrow of the government of Martínez de la Rosa by a riot of soldiers in the

[17] Peers, *op. cit.*, Appendix, p. 199 sq.

[18] Aunós Pérez, *Itinerario histórico de la España contemporánea 1808–1936*, p. 91.

Puerta del Sol and the massacre of some eighty religious after public opinion had been inflamed by the absurd rumor that they had poisoned the public water supply and provoked a cholera epidemic. The new government included Juan Alvarez Mendizábal, a banker, who had lived long in London and passed for decidedly "progressive." A French writer has described him as "a Mason, very close to the British political circles and particularly the British ambassador in Madrid, George Villiers, in correspondence with the Duchess de Berry — a man with more contacts than culture; with more ideas than political experience."[19]

The Society of Jesus was suppressed on July 4, 1835. On July 25 of that year every convent in the country with less than a dozen members was dissolved. The month of July, 1835, may be compared to May, 1931, in the vast outbreak of violence all over Spain. In Zaragoza, Barcelona, Reus, Murcia, and elsewhere mobs burned convents and massacred religious. Mendizábal was supreme and the country looked to him to pacify the provinces and end the religious strife. His idea was an extremely simple one: settle the religious problem by eliminating the religious; pay for the war by confiscating their property; pay the public debt from funds raised from the property seizures. The fact was that a large number of the monasteries had already been despoiled in 1808 and 1820. By the decree of October 11, 1835, all convents were suppressed with the exception of about a dozen, notably among them Montserrat, Escorial, and Guadalupe. Even those unsuppressed, despite their brilliant role in the culture of Spain, were not allowed to admit anyone to their novitiates. On January 25, 1836, commissions supervised the transformation of the convents into military barracks and offices. The protest of the Holy See was met by a fatuous speech from Mendizábal in which he blandly announced that the "religious communities were no longer in harmony with the principles of civilization and ought to be suppressed."[20]

The effort to save Spain economically by the confiscation of Church property was a complete failure, for the whole business produced a hopeless confusion and fundamental disequilibrium in Spanish life. The treasury was left as bereft of funds as it was normally, despite the fanciful claims of Mendizábal and the wild estimates of great wealth that were aimed at assuring the country that its salvation depended on the extinction of the friars.

---

[19] Albert Mousset, *Histoire d'Espagne,* Paris, 1947, p. 447.

[20] *Ibid.,* p. 449.

The whole sorry business was conceived not merely to produce wealth, gratifying as that was, but to stabilize a hopeless political and social situation. The Carlist war had been exhausting and the clerical support of the pretender had been irritating to the groups in power. This was a form of exemplary chastisement in the mind of the liberal ministry. Much of the Church property was sold to the nobility, thus creating a new category of vested interests whose support could be counted upon for the dynasty:

> Among the conservative classes the sale of ecclesiastical property, which took place under conditions more favorable for the purchaser than for the State, created a network of interests, which necessarily thenceforth told in favor of the preservation of Isabel's throne, since Don Carlos could not be expected to respect these purchases. Thus the minister enlisted material interests as indirect support for the legitimate dynasty.[21]

The reason why Mendizábal's policy did not pay dividends is that the Church and the orders were already impoverished. If, indeed, during the century following the famous — or infamous — *desamortización,*[22] the Church has acquired some property, it was still far less than that which had been taken from it. The Church was largely a trustee of wealth and not a possessor of wealth itself and the funds acquired after its spoliation were spent for charitable and educational purposes. These funds came from endowments, gifts, and the dowries of women entering the religious life. "To describe the Church as rich, however, is misleading. A trustee is not regarded as rich merely because he administers the estate of a millionaire. The Spanish ecclesiastics were the underpaid trustees of national charity."[23] A Spanish critic of the Church, writing for Popular Front consumption, opines that "wealth has never been an obstacle which hinders the clergy from influencing the masses."[24]

The income of the Spanish hierarchy is another point about which it is easy to obtain precise figures. In recent times the Cardinal Primate of Toledo received an income roughly estimated at about $6,500 annually plus another thousand perhaps because of his rank as cardinal. The archbishops of Valencia and Seville received about $6,000 each, assuming the peseta to be at par. The ordinary Spanish bishop

[21] *Cambridge Modern History* (Cambridge University Press, 1907), Vol. X, p. 237.

[22] *Desamortización,* that is, the removal of property held in mortmain or the "dead hands."

[23] Lunn, *op. cit.*, p. 234.

[24] Enrique Moreno, *Catholics and the Spanish State,* London, 1937, p. 13.

received a salary that was approximately $4,500 to $5,000 — by no means a princely sum nor one that allowed for what might be called riotous living.[25] Prof. Peers has compared these figures with comparable incomes in the Church of England, in which the Archbishop of Canterbury receives £15,000 annually and the other bishops of the established Church amounts fluctuating between £5,000 and £10,000 per year. "One begins to see why the luxury of Lambeth is not to be found in Toledo."[26] The President of the Second Spanish Republic received a salary of a million pesetas a year, to be estimated according to the exchange of the day at about $160,000. Add to this another $200,000 for expenses, and it will be apparent that the "luxurious Church" was far less well provided for than the head of the allegedly democratic, people's Republic. The rest of the clergy received absurdly low stipends. A canon was lucky to have a salary of $600 a year, and some of the holders of lower benefices did not receive above $350 per annum. The parish clergy, needless to say, was still less well provided for. Some fifty priests in Spain received, before the civil war, over $500 a year while many received approximately $150 to $200. These stipends were paid by the State as compensation for the confiscation and property losses; in a word, the Church was robbed of its patrimony and in return was granted a niggardly income, quite insufficient for the ordinary expenses of living and administration. The splendor of the liturgy and the richness of the Church treasures contrasted mightily with the absolute poverty in which the great mass of hierarchy and clergy lived.

Along this line it may not be amiss to note than even today, when the Church is supposedly the recipient of the largess of a sympathetic government, even the hierarchy lives on an extremely modest scale. The great palaces are often cold and inhospitable, since there is no heating and no means provided for it. The table of the average Spanish bishop is much less generous than that of his colleagues in other countries.

The defects of Spanish Catholicism, in the sense of the human defects of churchmen, asserts Prof. Peers, "are not so much those of the Catholic Church as of Spaniards."[27] That is to say, the Church in Spain as elsewhere partakes of the national character and suffers or profits, as the case may be, from the national defects and virtues. The

---

[25] Peers, *op. cit.*, p. 28, and José Güenechea, S.J., *Pobreza del culto y clero en España,* Bilbao, 1916, p. 67 sq.

[26] Peers, *op. cit.*, p. 29.

[27] *Ibid.*, p. 39.

Irish and French, the American and the Mexican Church are influenced and colored by the nature of their human content. The Spanish Church has known periods of greatness and of decline; of brilliant achievement and great spiritual success, as well as frustration and temporary defeat, just as the Spaniards who make it up have suffered from the temperament with which God has endowed them. The Church as an abstraction or in a vacuum does not make sense; the Church as a living institution, whose revealed truths are applied and executed by men, helps us to understand the peculiarities and the vicissitudes of one of the most remarkable branches of the Church universal — the one which exists in Spain.[28]

---

[28] See Appendix 2, "Chronological Table of Via Crucis of the Spanish Church in the Nineteenth and Twentieth Centuries."

Chapter 5. THE SOCIAL BACKGROUND

NO REAL understanding of modern Spain is possible without some hint of the complex social and economic background on which the present structure of the nation rests. The Spain of 1939–1949 is not an arbitrary thing, conjured up in the mind of General Francisco Franco. It is not the creation of the civil war, for the simple reason that a large number of the more pressing difficulties of today are problems that Spain has grappled with for centuries and constitute a direct heritage from the past. Critics of the regime are prone to denounce the Franco government for deficiencies in the social order, some of which date from Visigothic times. One traveler was nonplused and irritated that Franco had not done something about the Gypsies who live in caves in and around Granada. This was to him quite obviously a sad failure of the regime which had not provided proper housing for this segment of the population. Needless to say the Gypsies have been there for generations and, oddly enough, show a marked preference for caves as places of residence.

Spain, let it be repeated again, is fundamentally an agrarian country; agriculture is the basis of its life and economic existence, with industry at best a secondary activity. Salvador de Madariaga has summed up the matter: "The existence of a vast agricultural population which the governing classes had proved unable to save from misery was perhaps the most serious evil in Spanish life."[1]

The agricultural situation has been and continues to be bad, for the forces of nature have not endowed the greater part of Spain with advantages of soil and fertility. This is demonstrated by the fact that two thirds of the population live on one third of the land, and this population is concentrated with considerable density around the coast. The interior offers the major challenge for cultivation and the proper utilization of the land. There are numerous hostile factors: aridity, long periods of drought, deficient transportation, and primitive methods

[1] *Spain* (London: Jonathan Cape, 1943; New York: Creative Age Press, Inc., 1943), p. 115.

of cultivation as well as an inadequate rural organization among farmers for the most effective development of the resources at hand:

> In short, 60 percent of our soil is not in cultivation! 40 percent of the land that is tilled is not utilized efficiently, and 70 percent of land that might be used is lacking in trees.[2]

Obviously, the rural and industrial economy of Spain is directly related to every other phase of the national life. As already observed, every Spanish government for centuries gives the impression that problems have been posed, but nothing actually advanced toward their solution. Nothing is perhaps more dangerous than to undertake to reduce the reality of Spain to figures and numbers, for statistics are neglected and the traditional *más o menos,* "more or less," covers most questions. There are, to be sure, notable exceptions. Thus in specialized economic circles today there is an increasing recognition of the importance of knowing with absolute precision the nature of any problem before attempting an effective and permanent solution. Parenthetically be it remarked that the growing attention to economics is one of the interesting intellectual developments in Spain since the civil war.

The Spanish peasant is a hard-working, long-suffering, obdurate individual who persists in preferring his own way of life to almost any other that either government or laws offer him. I have referred from time to time to the great capacity for work of the Spanish peasant and workingman. Laziness is not a trait among this stratum of society. The fact that life itself is hard makes devotion to the task at hand imperative. The *bon mot* to the effect that the secret aspiration of every Spaniard is to be able to get up at eleven o'clock in the morning applies, I am confident, to large sectors of the population of the cities and especially to the middle class, but definitely does not apply to the Extremaduran or Navarrese peasant.

The Spanish people — the mass of them — in the countryside and villages, give the impression of passivity and silent endurance in the face of hardship. Nevertheless it was this mass of people that time and again historically has determined the course of events in Spain. The expulsion of the Jews in the fifteenth century, the hostility against the Moors, the rising against the French in the early nineteenth century, all these were "mass" movements, and hence truly an expression of the popular feeling of the ordinary people.

---

[2] Pascual Carrión, *La reforma agraria, problemas fundamentales,* Madrid, 1931, p. 14.

This peasant mass, however, is by no means uniform. Regionalism, discussed in the following chapter, and the wide diversity of economic conditions breed a variety of land systems as well as differences in community life and rural outlook. These variations are reflected in the political attitudes, ideological influences, and relative degree of social stability of the different parts of Spain. Between the landless peasant of large sections of Andalucía and the conservative, deeply rooted small farmer of Navarre, there is an almost unbridgeable distance. This distance is reflected in the strong inclination toward anarchism of the one and the irreducible Carlism of the second.

The agrarian problem has been the preoccupation of every Spanish regime that has made any attempt at all to reorient the country along more stable economic lines. The Second Republic, in its avidity to make the nation over, included an advanced agrarian reform measure aimed at creating a type of peasant economy which existed in very few parts of the peninsula.

The present systems of land tenure may be summarized by a glance at the main areas of Spain. In Galicia, in the extreme northwest, the prevalent arrangement is that of the small holding, the predominant form of which is known as the *foro,* characterized by a lease extending for several generations of the holder, with a fixed payment and assurance of tenure. The system has its roots in the Middle Ages and springs directly from the encouragement given to peasants by the monastic orders to settle lands otherwise untilled. Much of the land was leased directly from the Church, the largest single owner of such domains. When Church properties were confiscated, the tenants became in many instances the owners, while in other cases the actual owners did not cultivate their lands but leased them out to *sub-forados.* Galicia is a classic land of much subsistence farming where tiny holdings are just sufficient for the maintenance of a single family, with nothing left over for export. It is not strange that one of the greatest centers of mass emigration abroad has been Galicia, for the *gallego* has always revealed himself as an enterprising type, capable of making a living under the most varying circumstances. Hispanic America is full of *gallegos* who have come out to work in industry, farm the land, or engage in commerce and so large has been their number that the term *gallego* has become the designation for all such Spanish immigrants regardless of their place of origin. Galicia has been a region of intense strife over land and of the endless legal complications arising out of the collection of the *foros* by absentee owners from peasants who, since they cannot be ejected, look upon the rent collector with the proverbially jaundiced eye. The system lends itself to political manipulation with the rise of local bosses who control blocs of peasants in the elections. The *forista,* or owner, has been the central figure in much of the social and political controversy in modern Galicia.

Small farms distinguish the rural economy of Asturias, the four Basque provinces, and part of Aragón where, generally, tenancy prevails on a family basis. One arrangement is that known as the *llar* or family communal farm, sometimes owned outright and disposed of by the head of the family, sometimes leased on what is virtually a permanent basis through successive generations. The prevalence of the family farm, accompanied by a very strong community spirit on the part of the farmers toward each other, has contributed to the high degree of stability in Navarre and to the extremely conservative character of its people. From the point of view of rural economy, it is one of the healthiest and traditionally deepest rooted areas in all Europe. In addition to the peasant, who owns his land outright, is the tenant who leases his land from the owner, tills it, and shares the crops with the proprietor. In all the Basque provinces this system is very common.[3]

Physical conditions are peculiarly favorable in this northland for such a type of farming. The abundant rainfall and the close-knit social order allow for a high degree of integration plus individuality. In Aragón there are two well-defined areas: one dry and parched, mountainous in character, south of Teruel where the peasantry live as agricultural workers under conditions of excessive poverty; the second, the Ebro Valley where farmers derive a reasonably good living from the land. In Catalonia, where general prosperity is the rule, agrarian conditions are appreciably more advanced. A double system prevails, strongly reminiscent of the north country, of small owners who lease the land to the peasants as well as peasant proprietors themselves. A form of the *foro,* or *censo,* as it is called in Castile, and a share-cropping arrangement as in the Basque country exist here. The cultivation of the vineyards, too, is an important agricultural activity in this area, and a special class, the *rabassaires* who have played an important role in Catalan politics and separatism, lease the land. The system provides for leases that are dependent on the life of the vine itself. In general, the entire north of Spain, from Galicia to Catalonia and with parts of Castile and León, is characterized by the

---

[3] Brenan, *The Spanish Labyrinth* (New York: The Macmillan Co., 1943), gives a careful and well-presented survey of the agrarian and labor situation in modern Spain.

small farmer under varying conditions, with a relatively good productivity and a strong tradition. It is to be noted that the most powerful Catholic tradition of Spain is to be found closely associated with the form of land tenure and especially with the type of land ownership and exploitation.

Down the coast from Catalonia is Valencia, Murcia, and the region of the *vegas,* which comprise one of the most productive lands of Spain devoted in large part to orange production. The irrigated lands are excellent, and the peasantry reasonably prosperous in contrast with those occupying the dry, sterile portions where poverty of an extreme sort is the rule. Around Granada and Murcia the peasants have been less favored with land of their own than elsewhere, despite the irrigation and the subsequent productivity of the soil. In general it will be noted that rural life in the north, although physically favorable, is austere, modest, and traditional, while in the Levant and on the Mediterranean coast the climate and favorable land conditions contrast completely with the adverse situation of Castile and the interior of Spain.

The agrarian problem in Andalucía presents special difficulties. It has become the classic example of *latifundismo,* that is, the concentration of land in the hands of the few. The situation is held up as a horrible case of impoverishment in the midst of potential wealth, of a peasantry ground down by misery under landowning conditions that have mistakenly been called *feudal.* In the province of Córdoba, as an illustration, the farms of more than 50 *hectáreas*[4] represent more than 27 per cent of the entire land surface. Farms of over 100 *hectáreas* constitute some 58 per cent of the total. In the province of Seville, farms over 100 *hectáreas* occupy some 71 per cent of the land area. It must be noted that this size farm is exceedingly large and far in excess of the small subsistence farms that prevail in other parts of Spain.[5] The dry, poor land of so much of Andalucía does not allow for intensive agriculture. The system of *al tercio* is common, whereby land is allowed to lie fallow or be plowed under and seeded only every third year. "This is the fundamental problem of Andalucía — how to support a large population on a dry soil."[6] The proportion of large estates rises in the province of

[4] One *hectárea* is equal to about two and a half acres.

[5] Carrión, *op. cit.,* pp. 14–17.

[6] Brenan, *The Spanish Labyrinth,* p. 116, copyright, 1943, by The Macmillan Company and used with their permission.

Cádiz to 58 per cent. In the single province of Seville, some 2340 landowners, or 5 per cent of the total number, control 72 per cent of the total agricultural wealth.[7] What type of agricultural worker does one find in this area? The totally landless kind, seasonal and subject to the infinite vagaries of rotating harvests. The situation in many parts of Andalucía is strikingly similar to that in the West Indies where sugar cane is the major crop; the same seasonal fluctuations, the same half year of unemployment, the same terrifying precariousness of living for men and their families. The utilization of land is frequently uneconomical. Cattle production, grazing, and pasture are often the form of exploitation on lands which could normally be turned to the production of food crops. Pascual Carrión states: "From the perspective of the city, it is impossible to see how the majority of our agricultural workers live with the loss of energy and the manpower that is wasted."[8]

The notion has long prevailed that if the peasant could only come into possession of the land his tribulation would be at an end. This, of course, would have to be done with justice to the owner. However, as the famous *ejido* in Mexico has amply demonstrated, the mere signing over of the land to the peasant does not solve the problem. The complex question of adequate machinery, seed, fertilizer, transportation, and marketing still remains. It is curious to note in this regard how the agrarian reform under the Second Republic conceived the spoliation of the landowning class and especially the *Grandeza* as the major objective of the campaign. The pages of the text of the reform are illustrative of the class consciousness that pervades every line. "Manuel Azaña, in the session of the Cortes of September 8, referred to the provision for expropriation without compensation of the rural lands belonging to the nobility."[9]

The more extreme left was by no means in accord with the solution of private ownership. We discover numerous writers prior to the Reform of 1932 who insisted that this was not the solution. "The private ownership of the land is contrary to nature and con-

---

[7] In Jesús R. Coloma, *El problema social de la tierra,* Madrid, n.d., pp. 24–25, we have a description of similar cases. The 16,000 *hectárea* properties of the Duke of Medinaceli in Cádiz included only 1000 devoted to food crops. In Seville there were farms of over 25,000 *hectáreas* for the raising of bulls.

[8] *Op. cit.,* p. 22.

[9] Francisco Arcaya, *La reforma agraria del 15 de septiembre de 1932,* Madrid, 1933, p. 7.

demned by natural law. In Spain the doctrine of agrarian collectivism has deep roots and has been explained and defended by such outstanding men as Fray Alonso de Castrillo, Juan Luis Vives, and Father Mariana."[10] Another commentator asserts that the results of subdivision or distribution of land would simply produce worse consequences than the present large concentration. "The excessive division of the land is the cause of more harm to the wealth of Spain than the large land ownings."[11]

The essential problems of agricultural organization, co-operatives, agricultural credit, and the like, have been woefully neglected. The scientific improvement of production to combat naturally adverse conditions is another element that has received only passing attention. Despite the much-vaunted republican program of land distribution and the demagogic tirades against the aristocracy, relatively little was actually carried out in this direction. In fact the very term "Agrarian Reform" became discredited to such an extent that under the present regime the expression *colonización* has been substituted. In a later chapter we shall treat on the constructive work of the present regime in the way of creating a more equitable agricultural order.

In Castile, especially in the south along the Tagus valley, the *censo* or *foro* system has prevailed, but with far less of the stability that exists in Galicia. Absentee landlordism has been rampant and with it innumerable deplorable conditions for the landless peasantry. In Extremadura and La Mancha, landlessness prevails as the soil is dry and sterile and the short-lease system rather than the long, as in the north, produces an endemic instability. Extremadura has been traditionally one of the poorest areas of Spain. Its estates have been large and its farmers ground down in poverty. Strife has been frequent and it is not strange that from this region came some of the chief extremists among republican representatives.

The study of the Spanish labor movement is no less important as a backdrop to recent events than that of the land systems. If there is variety and contradiction in the latter, there is no less of a problem in analyzing the nature and program of the numerous movements of an ideological character that have demanded the adhesion of the Spanish workingman. The converging of these various forces in 1936 is explained by the common sense of resistance to the National Movement.

[10] Emilio Palomo, *Uso y abuso de la tierra*, Valencia, 1930, p. 59.
[11] José Aragón, *La revancha del campo*, Madrid, 1929, p. 135.

The story of Spanish radicalism up to that time is one of profound divergence and open rivalry. It was not merely a question of jockeying for position, it was a matter of profound and vital differences in doctrine, theory, and approach to the solution of the social and economic difficulties of the country. It is important to grasp the difference because there is a widespread and dangerous tendency, especially outside of Spain, to lump all left-wing movements in Spain under the general title of "communists." Within Spain today the republican enemy during the civil war is indiscriminately referred to as the *Rojos,* or Reds, which might imply that all who were not with the Republic or its proposed social program were communists. Nothing could be further from the truth. There is a high degree of accuracy in the epithet during the civil war period for the reason that the moderates, almost without exception, abdicated their position and it was communism that ran the show for the major period of the hostilities. In the strictly limited sense, as used during the war to designate the enemy, it was justified. As a term to be applied to the numerous Left or center movements in pre-civil-war Spain, it is necessary to clarify the divergences and even the conflict between one movement and the other. For the purposes of this rapid survey, we shall consider the socialists, communists, anarchists, and the so-called anarcho-syndicalists. All of them play a significant role in Spanish affairs and all of them figure prominently in the period after 1931.

The general background of labor agitation extends much further back into the nineteenth century than the formation of the movements allegedly aiming at the betterment of the welfare of the worker. We need recall that the industrial centers of Spain are not numerous. Aside from Barcelona, Valencia, and Madrid — the three major cities — the foci of industry are to be found in Vizcaya, around Bilbao, and in scattered centers elsewhere in the peninsula. One of the major tasks of all radicalism was to co-ordinate in a single purpose the almost diametrically opposite interests of the steelworker in the Asturian mill (*Altos Hornos de Vizcaya*), with those of the transitory agricultural worker in Andalucía (*bracero*). The Spanish labor movement in this sense impresses one as singularly disjointed and lacking in universality. Another element which must be borne in mind is that, from the beginning, the labor movement was — with very limited exceptions — scarcely conceived of as anything but a branch of political action. The formation of trade unions and of political parties as the expression of the desire for betterment or change was almost simultaneous.

It is far too easy for non-Spaniards to judge the Spanish labor situation on the basis of a similar terminology when the reality is strikingly different. Just as in the case of liberalism, the expression loses meaning once it crosses the Pyrenees, so too when we speak of trade unions in Spain, they were very often something quite different from the A.F.L. or the C.I.O. or the trade unions of Great Britain. Spanish trade unions were basically ideological, that is, they stood for a doctrine and not merely for a course of action; their programs consisted not only of the improvement of labor standards, increased wages, and better living conditions; they included a conception of social reform and the transformation of the State and society. The transfer of the trade union's ideas into the arena of politics through parties in the Cortes was a phenomenon of first-rate importance and explains the vicissitudes of trade unionism in the peninsula after the civil war. The doctrinaire quality of the Spanish labor movement varies, of course, according to the pinkish or reddish hue of the organizations. There were, to be sure, moderate socialists who were very far from being proponents of the violent transformation of the social order. Men of the type of Julián Besteiro and Fernando de los Ríos were too academic in their socialism to satisfy the urge of those who came to the top in 1935, and it was precisely because of their moderation that spokesmen of this kind were submerged beneath the demands of the extremists.

Barcelona and Madrid were the two poles of the Spanish labor movement; the former distinguished for its individualism, separatism, and recalcitrance to discipline and, therefore, the natural center of anarchism; the latter, on the other hand, the focal point of socialism, more authoritarian and institutional, more in conformity in its attitude with the traditional Hispanic mentality.[12] The remote origins of Spanish socialism date back to Joaquín Abreu of Madrid, who introduced the ideas of Fourier into the peninsula. Fernando Garrido of the same city founded the first paper, *La Atracción,* in 1845. This was very shortly after Munts had formed the first association of weavers in Barcelona, the forerunner of the anarchist movement. It was entirely in line with the contrasting inspiration of the two movements that Barcelona should have taken by instinct to *action* while Madrid by the same logic produced a *newspaper.*

[12] Madariaga, *op. cit.,* p. 118.

It is curious to note how Spanish socialism and anarchism were inspired and promoted from movements abroad. In 1879 a small group formed the first socialist party in Spain under the name of the *Partido Democrático Socialista Obrero,* the leading figure being Pablo Iglesias, a typographer, destined to become the outstanding personality in Spanish socialism. Iglesias was influenced by such European socialists as Jules Guesde and Paul Lafargue, and by the developing French Marxist press. Jules Guesde was converted to Marxism in 1876 after a short period of anarchist conviction and after 1877 his paper, *L'Egalité,* became a leading organ on behalf of Marxist socialism. At the Marseilles congress in 1879 he expressed himself in favor of the formation of a working-class party, and in 1880 his program became the basis of the socialist workers' parties in France. It is not strange, then, that this activity should have repercussions across the Pyrenees, especially after freedom of association in 1881 permitted the Spanish socialists to regroup and reorganize their party. It was not until 1886, however, that they issued their paper, *El Socialista.* This was a period of formation and definition. Iglesias was singularly inflexible in his statement of the program, and in this sense followed the lead of Guesde. On the other hand, the party was weak in that it did not have trade-union strength. It proceeded, therefore, to devote attention to the task of picking up affiliations. Here we have the vitally important beginning of the socialist-anarchist rivalry which was to distinguish almost all Spanish labor history and, in general, it was anarchism that made the greatest headway in the campaign for working-class support.[13]

In 1888 the *Unión General de Trabajadores* was formed; a moderate and not at all revolutionary movement. Its membership was pathetically small and quite unable to compete with the anarchists and the combined party, the trade-union movement having almost all its adherents in Madrid and Bilbao. In the latter city, after the beginning of industrialization, the socialists began to make some headway to become a citadel of socialism, until the present century when Indalecio Prieto made the Vizcayan city and his own socialist leadership almost synonymous. In 1905 Iglesias and Largo Caballero (the latter rising to fame in the era of the Second Republic) were elected to the Madrid municipal council.

The socialists, up to the time of the Barcelona disorders of 1909,

[13] Elie Halévy, *Histoire du socialisme européen,* Paris, 1948, p. 195: "In Spain Marxism never managed to push anarchism back."

refrained from violence and looked with certain disdain even on the use of the general strike. They concentrated on the development of the *Casa del Pueblo,* the chain of club houses with library and other equipment that was destined to become one of the characteristic Spanish left-wing institutions. In 1909, however, they joined the anarchists and radicals in a strike. They fought the Maura government, and Iglesias managed to obtain a seat in the Cortes. In contrast with the anarchists, who were all for direct action and pulled no punches, the socialists clung tenaciously to the idea of parliamentary procedure and the ordinary electoral processes. By the time of World War I they had penetrated the mining and industrial north and were beginning to agitate among the workers in the Río Tinto area in the south. The electoral system and the long tradition of political control made it hazardous for them to expect to win power on the basis of ballots alone, so that socialism remained very much an opposition force until the Second Republic. Many socialist leaders — among them Besteiro, Largo Caballero, Iglesias, and others — suffered imprisonment and won the halo of martyrdom with the consequent increase in the socialist following throughout Spain. The aged Iglesias lingered on as leader until his death in 1925. The party then passed under the leadership of Francisco Largo Caballero and Julián Besteiro, two very different leaders of the same movement, for Largo Caballero had been a plasterer in the earlier days and Besteiro was a Madrid University professor.

Indalecio Prieto was coming to the fore at the same time. He had risen from humble origin in Bilbao to become a member of the Cortes. His name was to be reckoned with from this time on, and particularly during the hectic days of the Republic. The corpulent Prieto possessed a penetrating and caustic wit, a telling gift for repartee, and a very great parliamentary instinct. Among the republican leaders after 1931, he was undoubtedly one of the most talented and realistic. Even in exile, he has demonstrated a greater intelligence than the general run of his fellow expatriates. Prieto was less doctrinaire, more liberal — in the best sense of the word, and more addicted to feasible compromise than Largo Caballero. The overshadowing of the former and the rise to eminence of the latter is the most eloquent testimony to the transformation of Spain between 1931 and 1936.

Spanish socialism, like socialism everywhere, was split over the problem of communism. Just as in France, where the extreme Left had managed to divide socialist opinion and bring about the creation of the French communist party in 1920, so too in Spain there was a division of viewpoint over the matter. The Russian Revolution and the Third Internationale had posed an entirely new problem. Soviet insistence on taking the lead of all Marxist movements throughout the world forced each socialist party to examine its conscience to determine if it was willing to accept the terms laid down by the Third Internationale. In Spain the party split, and under Largo Caballero joined the revived Second Internationale. The Spanish communist party, founded by dissident socialists such as Francisco Mora, was joined by elements from anarcho-syndicalism such as Joaquin Maurín and Andrés Nin. In due time, a Left communist party appeared in Barcelona, representative of the Trotskyite current in Spain. The extremist movements of the Second Republican days were beginning to take shape by the opening of the decade of the twenties. In addition to the *Unión General de Trabajadores,* which had borne the brunt of early trade-union organization in the country, the more recent *Confederación General de Trabajo,* the C.G.T., was now increasing its strength. Largo Caballero, as U.G.T. leader, was deeply concerned with the advances of the rival trade union. He adhered tenaciously to the idea of the indispensable unity of the working class. Within the socialist ranks the old regional problem reared its customary head, for Catalonia was unimpressed by the austere socialism that was coming out of Madrid. The traditional resentment at "centralization" evidenced itself just as much in the socialist camp as among the middle class. Catalonia therefore produced its own *Unión socialista catalana,* which in general voted along the same lines as the *Esquerra catalana,* described briefly in the following chapter.

Socialism unquestionably appealed to great masses of the Spanish people. Despite its international connections, there was a tendency to operate within the national frontiers with preferential attention to national problems and in so far as it aimed at economic betterment, land distribution, decent wages, and conditions of work it was a novelty on the Spanish political scene where the traditional parties were largely unconcerned with social matters.

It has been argued that a weak and paternal socialist regime might prove the political panacea for Spain. I disagree with this because moderate socialism tends more and more to verge toward the immoderate, by the pressure of events. Whatever may be the intellectual virtues of a sane, balanced socialism, devoid of inflexible Marxist dogma, it would seem that this form is quite incapable of resisting the fierce onslaught of orthodox communism. Europe in the twentieth century has learned that communism is not to be met by adopting a whole series of semi-communistic measures. The insistence on going the whole way without compromise that distinguishes communism is precisely what made the capitulation of socialism in Spain inevitable. Although the Spanish temperament is in reality extremely egalitarian and quite disdainful of property and the profit motive, the kind of socialistic liberalism for which Prieto stood seems strangely out of place after the events of 1936–1939. I could well imagine Spain going communist if there were no co-ordinated counterforce to obstruct it, not because the Spanish are communistically inclined, but because if by chance they were to reject tradition and the spiritual heritage of centuries, they would in all probability seek the answer to their perplexities in the opposite extreme.

It is very clear that if the tendencies of 1936 had not been stopped short by the National Movement, the new republican phase toward which the Popular Front government was moving with breath-taking rapidity would not have been moderately socialist; it would have been increasingly and violently communist. In Appendix 3 this trend is traced in detail. In any analysis of Spanish history we always come back to the same point, that the Spanish mind is unadapted to elegant skepticism, cool objectivity, or dispassionate moderation. It is a pendulum that swings from the individual to the universal; from extremism to extremism. This type of mind makes the future of a diluted, watered-down socialism highly improbable.

Spain enjoys the dubious honor of having been the only European country in which anarchism really took root on a large scale. The doctrines of Michael Bakunin were relatively simple and completely out of keeping with the monolithic solidity of orthodox Marxism. During the critical years before 1872 Bakunin challenged Marx for control of the Internationale. The two protagonists were hopelessly divided. When Marxism protested against injustice and proposed to rectify things through the "capture" of the State, Bakunin rejected it. It was no injustice or inequality or anything of that sort that he protested against; it was against authority as such, which he interpreted as tyranny. Capitalism, the State, economy, and all that makes up the body politic would have to be swept aside before real liberty could prevail. He was anti-authoritarian, anti-State, and, above all, anti-God. This form of anarchism was the most completely optimistic thing that was ever perpetrated. Man is wicked not because of any fall or because of any inadequacy of his own nature, but simply because he is forced to live unnaturally in a tyrannical society that deprives him of the attributes which make for happiness. Bakunin was not in the least inclined to believe that the industrial workers of the more advanced capitalist countries were to constitute the vanguard of the revolution. His faith was pinned on the peasants and small-town workers of lands where mechanical progress was very limited.

Anarchism entered Spain in the person of Giuseppe Farinelli in the year 1868. Up to this time, as has been summarily indicated above, there was little in the way of organized activity in Spain. Up to 1862 small nuclei of workers existed here and there, and in that year some 15,000 presented a petition to the Cortes requesting recognition of the right of organization. Labor activity as such, while not always prohibited by law, was a vague thing, moving in a shadowy semi-illegal atmosphere. In 1840, Munts had founded the *Asociación de Tejedores,* and a confederation had been set up in 1854. In 1855 the first strike had occurred in Catalonia with 40,000 workers involved. That same year had witnessed outbreaks in Palencia, Valladolid, and Zamora. In 1859 there were cases of agitation and disorder in Badajoz and Olivenza. This was an indication that the ground was not entirely sterile when the first anarchist agents arrived in the country. There were peasant movements of more or less importance in the province of Granada, and Seville had been the scene of serious disturbances in 1857.

The trials and tribulations of anarchism in the initial period need not concern us here. Needless to say they were picturesque in the extreme. A little band of converts, without much knowledge of what it was all about, proposed to spread the libertarian doctrine among the workers and masses. The fact that the hazy ideas they preached and the hopelessly inadequate organization, or lack of it, on which they depended actually did produce results is testimony perhaps to the character of anarchism that makes it appeal to certain very definite elements of the population. The congress of 1870 led to the formation of a loose federation of more or less autonomous bodies. The Marx-Bakunin controversy, that reached a head in 1871, had repercussions in Spain. In 1872 another congress at Córdoba brought together an astonishing number of delegates from local groups and trade unions. The organization that emerged was strictly anarchist, uncomplicated by the ideological subtleties that had hampered previous activity and with tactics totally different from those of the Marxists. The whole idea of instructions from above, or action prepared by central committees, was repugnant to these absolute libertarians.

Obviously the anarchists believed in violence; it was, in fact, the very essence of their creed. Although they did not in fact come anywhere near gaining sufficient power to impose their system, the presence of a very large and fanatically devoted mass was one of the principal factors in the turbulence that came after 1931. The weakness, vacillation, and general inability of the Republic to maintain authority made it possible for the anarchists to prosper in an atmosphere that was highly congenial to them. It was confirmation of the well-known fact that Spanish society tends to break down under either a very weak regime or one that is lacking in sufficient historical continuity to impose its will through sheer tradition. That the monarchy has undoubtedly been Spain's best guarantee of relative stability is due to the fact that every Spaniard recognizes that the king is something quite apart from the rest of the population and, although every Spaniard may hopefully aspire to the presidency, none conceives of the kingship as anything but the prerogative of the royal family. The argument for monarchy gains force precisely because of this need to supply a unifying force that is above the mass and separated from it by heritage and family.

The revolutionary events of 1874, with the movement for federalism and the actual appearance of local authorities all over Spain acting without regard for the central government, seemed to give the anarchists a chance for the direct action they so constantly preached. The upshot was, however, that they did not succeed, and for a time appeared to have been wiped out. With the relaxation of restrictions in 1881, the anarchists, like the socialists, reformed their ranks and proceeded to re-create a party organization. There were splits and divergences in anarchist ranks, some of them the reflection of the changing ideas in anarchism abroad. In Catalonia there was a tendency to prefer trade-union action, while in Andalucía it was violence and direct action that prevailed. It was a period of rising conflict between the landless, miserable rural workers of the south and every agency of law and order. A long chapter might be written on the hostility between the famous *Guardia Civil* and the individualistic partisans of violence in the Andalucian countryside. Anarchist theory regarding collectivism and communism, and especially as concerns tactics, contributed to dividing the adherents of this tendency, and for a period of twenty years Spanish anarchism was split and divided. The general associations or federation no longer existed. Local groups maintained their doctrine without much regard for the activities of their partisans elsewhere. The period of the 1890's was filled with incidents of violence, and the action of the government to repress the anarchists extended to other bodies blamed for connivance in their activities.

The anarchists founded schools and sought to train children in the most completely libertarian ideas plus a fanatical hatred of the Church. The detailed study of this period, especially from 1890 on, demonstrates beyond any doubt how the atmosphere of Spain was poisoned systematically by the infiltration of extremism. The study of the events is convincing proof that the establishment of the Republic in 1931 was doomed to fail as a "liberal" institution, using the word in its British or American sense. The atmosphere of Spain had been vitiated by decades of undermining. Extremism was the order of the day and the Republic was like a dike through which a hole had been perforated, allowing the inundation of the nation by the most exotic and spectacular forms of radicalism. The Spanish monarchy up to 1931 was weak enough in its resistance to this contamination; the Spanish Republic operated under the naïve illusion that somehow these forces could be organized within the framework of a liberal, parliamentary regime.

Spanish anarchism was an austere, fanatical, almost puritanical movement, displaying a high degree of selflessness. It enjoyed popularity for a time and attracted the sympathy and interest of a number of the bourgeois. However, the advent of anarcho-syndicalism, whose role was to be of first-rate importance in the events that led to 1931, changed this panorama. The experience of the French syndicalists, the writing of George Sorel, the failure of the general strike in Spain in 1902, and the execution of Francisco Ferrer led to the formation of a new group, anarchist in thought and doctrine, syndicalist in organization. In 1910, the *Confederación Nacional del Trabajo* was formed at Seville so that syndicalism, the organization, became the instrument for the attainment of anarchism.

The doctrine of the new movement has been explained in numerous anarcho-syndicalist writings. We may take one of them as an example of this doctrinal content. Angel Pestaña in his *El sindicalismo, qué quiere y adonde va,*[14] explains the purposes of this "libertarian

---

[14] Barcelona, 1933.

communism." It is absolutely opposed to anything like the State communism of the Soviet variety. It rejects the whole idea of solving the problem of private property by having the State absorb it. The substitution of capitalism by the transfer of the means of production to a huge State organization is repugnant to the anarcho-syndicalists: "We are against the government whatever its political label may be. It is understood that we refer to a government that makes laws, and applies them, to a government that imposes rules and procedures."[15] The movement has no use for any of the procedures that are called parliamentary: "Anarchism and Syndicalism and all those who adhere to them are anti-electoral and anti-parliamentary, enemies on principle of all intervention or collaboration with the agencies of the State."[16] The definition of liberty of this Spanish anarcho-syndicalist summarizes as completely as any the doctrine of the movement: "The conclusion is logical. As long as there is authority or coercion which makes obligatory doing a thing, there is no liberty. The existence of any obstacle that nullifies, either partially or completely this liberty, implies a negation or a limitation of the principle."[17]

Pestaña describes in this book the program and methods of anarcho-syndicalism, with full details of how the new social order is to be brought about. Admittedly, when the writer comes to a description of just how some kind of order is going to be maintained after the liberation, the text becomes delightfully vague and general. Apparently it is anticipated that the intrinsic good nature of man will rise to the challenge once the evils of authority and tyranny are eliminated. For some years the new C.N.T. labored to increase its strength and engaged in many of the labor disputes that tore Catalonia and other areas. In 1913, the *Federación Nacional de Agricultores Españoles* was formed to reach the peasant masses in the name of libertarianism and was particularly successful in the area of Valencia and Murcia. Later the peasants' confederation was merged with the C.N.T.

The Bolshevik Revolution caused much soul searching among the anarcho-syndicalists. Some of them, like André Nin and Joaquín Maurín, wished to collaborate with the Bolsheviks while others, like Pestaña, refused to go along with the proposed affiliation of the C.N.T. to the Third Internationale. The Zaragoza Congress of 1922, under the Catalan anarchist, Joan Peyró, confirmed the decision to repudiate

[15] *Ibid.*, p. 23.
[16] *Ibid.*, p. 27.
[17] *Ibid.*, p. 71.

communism and maintain the C.N.T. as the anarchist stronghold. Under the Primo de Rivera dictatorship, the C.N.T. dissolved itself temporarily. The problem of the anarchists had long been whether to admit all workers to the C.N.T., although not convinced anarchists, or limit the membership to the partisans of the doctrine. The situation was solved in 1927 by the formation of the *Federación Anarquista Ibérica,* a secret organization made up exclusively of proved anarchists, all of them members of the C.N.T.[18] After the fall of the dictatorship, the anarchists reconstituted the C.N.T. and began definite plans for the social revolution. Every writer on the subject insists on the significance of the peculiar alliance of the Catalan city workers and the dispossessed Andalucian peasants, a combination of the greatest importance in the whole study of the social evolution of twentieth-century Spain. The anarchists had some strength in certain unions in Madrid, Zaragoza, among the fishermen and the steelworkers in Asturias. Anarchism created the revolutionary atmosphere and maintained the agitation. In terms of actual benefit to the workers, even from a limited point of view, anarcho-syndicalism has a poor record. Gerald Brenan insists that anarchism played its part in two respects: as an ascetic, revolutionary movement seeking to bring about a specific social order and as an atavistic movement, that in reality was a gigantic protest against everything prevalent in the modern world.

This Spanish anarchism was more than mere politics; it was a religion in the personal and collective sense of the word. It was not reform, or even the improvement that the trade unions sought, but a moral rehabilitation after the complete and total destruction of the existing social order. Anarchism in contrast to socialism was absolute — it admitted of no middle ground, and no compromise with what existed. The anarchists contrasted with the communists who were favorable to expediency and eager to take advantage of passing contingencies. They played very strongly on the innate sense of hostility of the Spanish masses to any government. The success of anarchism in channeling this sentiment during a given period is illustrative of a fact that must always be taken into account in any analysis of

---

[18] See Brenan, *op. cit.,* for the complete description of the movement. It is estimated the F.A.I. numbered 10,000 between 1934–1936 and their espionage system was very effective. Brenan cites the words of General Mola, head of the police forces between the dictatorship and Republic, who points out that the F.A.I. members in the postal and telegraph service made it possible for the anarchists to have full information on every measure taken for national and public security.

contemporary Spanish affairs; namely that there is a deep, ingrained instinct in the average Spaniard toward antagonism to the established authority. It may be Alfonso XIII, Primo de Rivera, Largo Caballero, or Franco, but the feeling that the only proper and decent position is against, sways thousands of the Spanish to criticism and enmity. Whether they are all prepared to act on that sentiment at a given moment is another thing. But this consideration of the rise of socialism, communism, anarchism, and anarcho-syndicalism serves one purpose; it reveals how the Spanish scene in 1936 was already heavily undermined by the elements of dissolution. The "plot" against Spain, of which the Nationalists have written so much, springs not only from specific preparations for the institution of the new order, but from the generally agitated peasants' and workers' *milieu* which made the radical leadership of a few so possible and which in the long run doomed the Republic, first to impotency and then to disaster.

Chapter 6. REGIONALISM

CATALONIA as a national entity embraces far more than its exclusively Spanish territory. "National Catalonia, the homeland of the Catalans, consists of three large geographical regions: Northern Catalonia, comprising the old Principality of Catalonia and the ancient counties of Rosselló and Sardinia, the little principality of Andorra and the Catalan-speaking zone of Aragón; southern Catalonia, the former kingdom of Valencia, and the third, insular Catalonia, the Balearic Islands."[1] Catalonia represents, like Portugal, one of the major divisions of the Iberian peninsula. It is a historical error to conceive of Catalonia as simply a Spanish province with a more or less autonomous history. Its national character derives from an important and influential place in history and from the possession of a separate language that is no mere dialect of Castilian, but as independent as Portuguese or Italian.

The point of departure for the proper understanding of Catalonia and of its place in the history of Spain is that it did not lose its peculiarly national character by union with the rest of the peninsula; that even today Catalan-speaking people inhabit Andorra, the south of France, a tiny area in Sardinia, and the whole coast line almost up to Alicante. Catalonia not only possesses a significant historical past, but a literature that at one time loomed very large in general European culture. The Catalan language, around which so much of the controversy over separatism and autonomy has raged, held a very high place in the Middle Ages as the instrument of refinement and of scholarship. Despite the decline of language and literature until the revival in the nineteenth century, pride in the past and attachment to the remnants of Catalan individuality persisted until rejuvenated under the impact of the Catalan renaissance of the nineteenth century.

---

[1] A. Rovira i Virgili, *Resum d'història del catalanisme,* Barcelona, 1936, p. 9.

Delving into history we find that most of Catalonia was overrun by the Moslems. A tiny corner up against the Pyrenees remained unconquered and became, just as Asturias in the west, the nucleus of the reassertion of Catalan nationalism. Barcelona was recaptured under the Franks and for two centuries after that Catalonia consisted of a series of *comtats,* or countries, under Frankish rule. By the end of the ninth century, independent Catalonia may be said to begin. Despite Moslem attacks, Norman marauders, and internal strife, Catalonia became increasingly a center of political and cultural importance; a crossroad of influences from all sides. Certain of its centers, such as Vich and Ripoll, were culture foci of importance. "Barcelona had maintained its importance through all historical vicissitudes, the Visigoths, the Saracens, the Franks . . . it had made the country of Barcelona the most powerful of all the Catalan counties. . . ."[2]

The Counts of Barcelona gradually assumed ascendancy over the rest of Catalonia. United with Aragón, Catalonia forged ahead as one of the most promising centers of the Mediterranean basin. Between the middle of the twelfth century until the beginning of the fourteenth century Catalonia grew in power and territory and the incorporation of the Balearic Islands, Valencia, and other areas gave the Catalan-Aragonese kingdom a place among the first powers of southern Europe. The period of maturity, as E. Allison Peers has called it, came between 1302 and 1479.[3] Catalan culture attained one of its highest points with the appearance of Ramón Llull, whose productive period extends from 1272 to 1315. This remarkable man whose works cover a wide range of subjects, including theology and mysticism, wrote in Latin and Catalan. His Catalan style has been praised as particularly colorful and pure, a demonstration that the language had already reached a high degree of perfection.[4]

Catalonia was blessed with capable and enlightened rulers; among whom Ramón Berenguer IV stands out most prominently. James the Conqueror extended Catalan influence and proved himself a wise and able administrator. The incorporation of Mallorca made Catalonia something besides a mere province of the Spanish mainland, becoming by virtue of this acquisition a Mediterranean state. James extended trade relations with North Africa, fortified the position of the country

---

[2] Ferran Soldevila, *Historia de Catalunya,* Barcelona, 1934, Vol. I, p. 68.

[3] *Catalonia Infelix* (London: Methuen & Co., Ltd., 1937).

[4] M. García Silvestre, *Història sumària de la literatura catalana,* Barcelona, 1932, p. 52 sq.

by marriage, and in general contributed to its prestige. Under James II (1291–1327) Catalan expansion in the Mediterranean reached its height. In 1303 began a century of heroic activity in the Near East and the Catalan contribution to the Crusades fills a great many decades of noble and colorful warfare against the infidel.[5] The marriage of Ferdinand with the Castilian princess Isabel in 1469 brought about the union of the two kingdoms, an event of the greatest significance for the future of Spain. The union was real in every way although Catalonia managed to retain much of its historical character, despite the contribution toward unification of the Catholic kings. However, "in the period of the Castilian dynasty, Catalonia was in political decline."[6]

The Catalonia that became a part of the Spanish kingdom had reached its full maturity. In literature, art, and architecture it occupied a worthy place among the peoples of the Middle Ages. Its troubadours and bards, its theologians and mystics made it a center of outstanding cultural achievement. The commencement of the political decline after the union was followed very soon by a similar spiritual decay. The union of Ferdinand and Isabel had been envisaged as one in which the rights and privileges of Catalonia and Aragón would be preserved and elaborate terms were drawn up to this end.[7]

Despite the theoretical guarantees, the process of Castilianization began in earnest. Castilian viceroys were appointed to Sicily and Sardinia; Castilian religious invaded the great monasteries of Montserrat and Poblet, and the Castilian language became the normal one in documents and official papers.[8] Catalonia was literally excluded from participation in the conquest and settlement of America, and the area was relegated to a secondary position at precisely the moment when the maritime greatness of Spain might have indicated a pre-eminent place for this outstandingly seafaring people. Under Charles V Barcelona enjoyed a certain prestige, since the monarch bore the title of Count of Barcelona. But Catalan influence was very meager. At the

[5] Ll. Nicolau d'Olwer, *L'Expansió de Catalunya a la Mediterrànea Oriental,* Barcelona, 1925. This study describes in detail the relations of Catalonia, commercial and military, with the entire Mediterranean basin. It is an extraordinary story of their presence in Cyprus, Egypt, Greece, the siege of Constantinople, and the entire Levant. R. Gay de Montella, *Catalunya, nació mediterrània,* Barcelona, 1933, emphasizes the close contact with the Mediterranean of historical Catalonia.

[6] Rovira i Virgili, *op. cit.*, p. 20.

[7] Soldevila, *op. cit.*, p. 126 sq. The Catalans were extremely zealous in preserving their own autonomy and especially their own administration.

[8] Peers, *op. cit.*, p. 71.

Council of Trent only one Catalan bishop was present among the numerous Spanish representatives. By the end of the sixteenth century Catalan had declined to such an extent that Castilian was used for almost every purpose except ordinary, everyday intercourse. Under the Bourbons, the language sank to the level of a rustic dialect, without literature nor encouragement from any official source.

Under the three Philips, the centralizing tendency became very marked. Portugal became a part of the common empire, and in Catalonia the language was further reduced. Now and again signs of opposition arose, notably against the Inquisition. Catalans were prominent in a great many fields of military and commercial activity, fighting valiantly at Lepanto and in Flanders in the wars against the Dutch insurrectionists. Under Philip III the light went out almost completely in Catalonia. There was tension under Philip IV, involving in this case the problem of taxation. The Catalans showed themselves to be loyal subjects in the French invasion of 1635 when this penetrated the Catalan territory of Roussillon, but the foreign invasion and the disregard of Madrid for the complaints of the Catalans led to rebellion. The popular movement of the year 1640 was commonly known as the War of the Segadors and with it gave birth to what became the national anthem of Catalonia, *Els Segadors* (The Reapers). The conflict lasted until 1652 when Barcelona was overcome, through sheer exhaustion, and the territory was reincorporated with Spain, retaining nevertheless its traditional liberties. Roussillon and Sardinia were lost to France. The common opposition to the French produced a temporary rapprochement between Catalans and Castilians, which was lost however in the separatist war that followed. Sixty years later Catalonia rebelled at the time of the weak and useless Charles II, and Catalonia was treated as a territory suitable for barter and was once ceded to France, to be returned to Spain at Ryswick. The struggle for the Spanish succession ended with the defeat of Catalonia once more and the loss of her remaining autonomy. The Catalans fought on the side of Charles of Austria against Philip of Anjou, grandson of Louis XIV. "It is possible that the Catalans of that time committed grave errors, and today many patriots consider it a mistake to have sided with the Austrian house against the Bourbons and to have shown a regional rather than a national spirit."[9]

The victory of Philip V ended the period of Catalan liberties. In 1716 the decree of Nueva Planta ended all idea of separatism and

[9] Rovira i Virgili, *op. cit.*, pp. 24–25.

introduced the unitary State with many of the features of the accord of 1640 eliminated. The Catalans appealed to Great Britain for aid and the case of Catalonia may be said to have been a matter of international disquietude during those turbulent years.

During the eighteenth century Catalonia became a region — a province in modern terminology — within the framework of uniformity so beloved of the Bourbons. This unity was in fact more political and ideal than administrative, for many of the local usages and customs in public administration subsisted.[10] The decline of Catalonia was in part due, not merely to the political pressure exerted by Castile, but to the decreasing significance of the Mediterranean as the center of the civilized world. The discovery of America and the opening of the routes to the Far East via Africa all conspired to reduce the economic significance of the region.

By the fifteenth century the Catalan language reached the peak of its expansion and henceforth it was rigidly limited to the small territory from which it had sprung. The prodigious capacity of Castilian to expand and absorb the most diverse peoples, as demonstrated in America, was a predominant factor in overrunning Catalonia and the flowering of Castilian literature on a universal plane tended to reduce the potentialities of Catalan. "Catalonia, poor, without trade, without industry; Catalonia without political autonomy, was destined to become subject to the culture of the Court, dependent on Castilian culture."[11] Catalans themselves began to use Castilian as their vehicle of expression to obtain a larger audience than the national tongue made possible. By the eighteenth century almost the only Catalan literature in existence were religious and devotional books, although a faint echo of the former grandeur of the Catalan language may be surmised in the government-supported publication in the eighteenth century of the *Gramática y apologia de la lengua catalana* of José Pablo Ballot. At the end of the century, with the first influences of the Encyclopedists, there were signs of a mediocre revival of Catalan although this is not to be confused with the development of nationalism in the modern sense. The latter phenomenon coincided with the collapse of the absolute monarchy and is closely associated with growing industrialization and the prosperity of the Catalan masses. It would be a grievous error to suppose that the national

---

10 Maximiano García Venero, *Historia del nacionalismo catalán (1793–1936)*, Madrid, 1944, p. 12.

11 Enrich Prat de la Riba, *La nacionalitat catalana*, Barcelona, 1910, p. 13.

sentiment in Catalonia was linked solely to the restoration of the language; it was intimately bound up with the superior economic position of the region over the rest of Spain and the inevitable resentment that this discrepancy produced. The French Revolution had considerable impact on Catalonia. During the war between Spain and revolutionary France, the French gave thought to a series of projects for the restoration of Catalan liberties and the establishment of a Catalan republic. Napoleon was no less zealous in the same direction. Marshal Augereau announced the intention of the French Emperor, in an address at Gerona, to restore the traditional liberties of Catalonia that Spain had wrested from them. Under the French occupation, the Catalan language together with French was used in the official publication, the *Diarí de Barcelona.* The official character of Catalan lasted only a few months. When the question of language was put to a vote, only one of the six members of the Catalan *junta* favored the continuance of the language; the rest preferred Castilian.[12] Catalonia fought as willingly and as ardently as any Spanish province against the French invader. There can be no question, as the reader may surmise from this cursory Catalan history, that the inhabitants of this region undertook at every opportunity to rebel against the Madrid government.

From the period of 1793–1795 to the war for independence that broke out in 1808, Catalonia ruled itself, thanks to the virtual disappearance of the central government. During the war against the French the Catalan *juntas* joined with those of the rest of Spain to form the network of local governments that took the place of the normal authority. The Catalan delegates to the Cádiz *Cortes,* the one symbol of Spanish sovereignty in a peninsula overrun by the French, were instructed to demand the re-establishment of the autonomy of Catalonia as it had existed before 1714. Cádiz was dominated, however, by unitary tendencies.

In 1822, Spain was divided into provinces, in imitation of the French departmental system, an arrangement abolished temporarily to be restored in 1833, shortly after the death of Ferdinand VII, when Catalonia was broken up into several administrative units.

At every point in the discussion of Catalan regionalism, the language assumes a place of the first importance. It was the literary language that gave Catalonia a tradition and outlet in the Middle Ages; it was the language that provoked much of the friction and hostility

[12] Soldevila, *op. cit.,* Vol. III, p. 890.

between Catalans and Castilians in the intervening period; and it was the restoration of the language that initiated the Catalan renaissance in the nineteenth century. By the early part of the past century, Catalan had fallen so badly into disuse that it had become the tongue of peasants and proletarians. "There was produced a corruption of Catalan and it was filled with Castilianisms, since it offered no resistance to infiltration as do other languages."[13]

The theater was one of the few instruments that served to keep the language alive with some claim to literary prestige, although the only survivals in the Catalan theater were a few miracle plays and a number of devotional pieces. A citizen by the name of José Robreño y Tort was enamored of the theater and took steps to assure the revival of the Catalan drama. The first productions were timid little pieces without literary value and couched in the popular speech. Some of them were bilingual, retaining both Catalan and Castilian, nor was Robreño's theater free of political motivation. His satires struck directly at many of the political conditions of the day and liberalism was reflected with rare fidelity in the plays produced both in Barcelona and all over Catalonia.

Catalonia was directly involved in the Carlist wars. The support of the Carlist cause by a number of Catalan bishops and many Catalan individuals led, among other things, to the reorganization of the system of justice, and the destruction of many of the local prerogatives to which the Catalans were most attached. The foundation of the University of Barcelona, in 1834, stimulated the revival of intellectual life and offset somewhat the new political restrictions.

A quickening interest in Catalan history became evident with the publication of numerous records from the Archives of Catalonia and Aragón. The faint stirrings of nationalism encouraged a new interest in the language, the history, and the culture of the region. The process whereby this apparently academic concern translated itself into political action is the story of Catalan nationalism.

It is apparent that the Catalan people of the past century belonged totally to the common stream of Spanish culture and history. Salvador de Madariaga has called the Catalan language "one of the Spanish tongues" and described the Catalans themselves as Spaniards who inhabit the Mediterranean coast. The genius of Catalonia formed an integral part of the larger mosaic of Hispania.

After 1850 the idea was launched of reviving the Floral Games, the

[13] García Venero, *op. cit.*, p. 40.

Jocs florals, as a means of encouraging poetical composition and interest in the regional language. There was a tendency to make the Floral Games the outward expression of a strong patriotic movement and Antoni de Bofarull and Víctor Balaguer, two of the promoters of the literary contests, emphasized the regional Catalanist character of the undertaking.

The Carlists and the republicans, the two extremist groups then existent in Catalonia, were the logical defenders of the new regionalism; the former because of their traditional defense of local autonomy, the regional laws and usages, and their general suspicion of the centralizing force of the monarchy in Madrid; the latter because they were against the monarchy as such and considered some form of federalism as the more adequate solution of the complex problem of Hispanic unity. It was, after all, a prominent republican and Catalan, Pi y Margall, who was president of the Republic in 1873. In fact there is a constant oscillation during these years of the mid-century between those who professed what may be called a "literary" Catalanism and those who sought to translate this revival into political terms. The figure of Manuel Milá y Fontanals, one of the greatest of Spain's literary critics and historians, fills a good portion of this period. Although invariably writing in Castilian, Milá worked over the raw materials of Catalan culture: its language, poetry, and literary potentialities. Víctor Balaguer operated in a different way. His thesis was the application of politics to literature; of converting the new Catalan expression into channels that would transform Catalan life. Francisco Romaní published his *El federalismo en España* in 1869, which was one of the first clear expositions of the problem of federal regionalism within the framework of national unity while Valentí Almirall contributed to the definition of the problem in his *Lo catalanisme,* published in Barcelona in 1886.

It is curious to note how Catalanist thinking moves gradually from a vague sentimental attachment to language and customs, to a sense of provincial difference, and ultimately to a well-defined, thought-out doctrine of federalism. "In 1879 Almirall was still using the word provincialism. In *Los fueros de Cataluña,* the word *regió* is applied to Catalonia."[14]

In 1869 the Pact of Tortosa was agreed upon by the Spanish republicans and this accord provided that Catalonia, Valencia, Aragón, and

[14] Enrich Prat de la Riba, in prologue to Lluis Duran y Ventosa, *Regionalisme y federalisme,* Barcelona, 1905, p. xiv.

the Balearic Islands should constitute a section or region of Spain, and that in terms of political action, these areas were to be considered as allied in the common cause. Tortosa was followed by similar agreements among other Spanish regions, notably Extremadura, Andalucía, and Murcia; the Basque provinces and Navarre and Asturias and Galicia. We have here, perhaps, a sort of forerunner of the regional statutes which were to play so large a part in the deliberations of the Second Republic and contribute so directly to the division of opinion in the period immediately preceding the civil war.

The First Republic seemed to be a heaven-sent chance for the Catalanists, for their intervention in its establishment had been decisive. Their presence in the cabinet made their influence a positive one with reference to the constitutional forms that the internal relations of the component elements of the peninsula were to take, and so strong was this influence that the Madrid press frequently charged the Catalans with taking over the Republic in anticipation of making Barcelona the capital of the new regime. In March, 1873, the Catalan deputies came extremely close to proclaiming the Catalan state, a step prevented by Pi y Margall, who felt it was premature and might gravely compromise the possibility of a federal constitution which would grant Catalonia everything it wished. It is not without significance that in July, 1873, the draft of the proposed federal constitution stated in Title I that the Spanish *nation* was composed of a number of *states,* among them Catalonia. Title VII provided that "The states are completely autonomous for economic and administrative purposes and shall enjoy the fullest political self-government in consonance with the existence of the nation."[15]

The collapse of the Republic and the restoration put an end temporarily to the Catalanist movement and stopped the trend toward a wider autonomy. "The great majority of the Catalans continued to function fully within Spanish politics. There was no Catalan politics; there was only Spanish politics in Catalonia."[16] The period was one of uncertainty and perplexity. Catalanism asserted itself in a plethora of journals and reviews, and in the improvement of the quality of the literary production. The absence of an effective Catalan theater had preoccupied many of those responsible for the renaissance, although the beginnings of a regional theater were perceptible toward the end of the nineteenth century. Many of the plays were full of political

[15] García Venero, *op. cit.*, pp. 139–150.
[16] A. Rovira i Virgili, *op. cit.*, p. 47.

innuendo, directed against the central authority and aimed at exalting local pride and loyalty. The number of associations, organizations, clubs, and the like, that came into being was phenomenal.

In 1880, Valentí Almirall brought the *Diarí Catalá* into existence, the first all-Catalan language daily paper. This was also the year of the first Catalanist congress whose purpose was to fix more precisely a program and at the same time create the instruments for the maintenance of close relations between the various Catalan-speaking sections of Spain. The 2200 delegates represented every conceivable tendency within Catalanism with the result that the congress was not free from controversy and violent dispute. Almirall expected the meeting to conclude with the formation of a political party consecrated to the task of realizing the Catalan ideals, but the practical results were far less spectacular. The decision was reached to establish a Catalan academy and exert vigilance for the preservation of Catalan civil law —relatively modest fruits after the first flush of high expectation.

Catalan regionalism was already beginning to show a threefold division; one sector on the left tending toward socialism and closer contacts with internationalism, a second that was profoundly regional and nationalistic in sentiment, and a third that was federalist within the Hispanic scheme of things. The conflict between the various points of view is no better illustrated than in the political literature of the time. Pi y Margall held firmly to the federalist idea; Almirall was more the separatist with a program that looked to the resurrection of Catalonia as a nation. The publication by the Bishop of Vich, Dr. Torras y Bages, of his *La tradició catalana* brought the spiritual and religious forces of Catalonia onto the scene. The spirit that animated this book may be judged from the vigorous defense of regionalism, the Christian tradition in Catalonia, and the perfect compatibility between universal Christianity and localism:

> Since the spirit of our region is essentially Christian as has been proved, we must now consider if the universal Christian religion of all humanity, destined to prevail among peoples of all races, can assume a regional character, become identified with a single area without losing any of its broader character. . . . The Church is regional because it is eternal. . . .[17]

A new organization, the *Centre Catalá,* which had been scrupulous in its determination to avoid politics, now became an expression

---

[17] Joseph Torras y Bages, *La tradició catalana. Estudi del valor étich y racional del regionalisme catalá,* Barcelona, 1892, p. 29.

of the political aspirations of the Catalans. In 1885 a memorial was addressed to the monarch, presumedly regarding purely economic matters, but which contained to some extent a statement of Catalan hopes. The Catalan commission which was dispatched to Madrid to present the memorial contained some of the most outstanding of the political and cultural leaders of Catalonia, among them, Valentí Almirall, Jacinto Verdaguer, Angel Guimerá, and others. The declaration contained a very definite reference to Catalan regional aspirations:

> We do not intend, Sire, to weaken and much less attack the glorious unity of the Spanish nation, but we do believe, that to achieve it, it is not good policy to destroy regional life, substituting that of the national capital. . . .[18]

The *Centre Catalá* split around the person of Almirall, and with the schism came the establishment of the new *Lliga de Catalunya.* It was not a party and made little effort to win mass support; it was a romantic, intellectual center for the cultivation of the Catalan tradition. The *Centre* formulated its political program in 1890, accusing the *Lliga* of separatism. The main points in the *Centre* plan were:

1. Catalonia shall form an autonomous entity within Spain.
2. Catalonia shall contribute to the general expenses of the nation without the central government's intervention in the collecting of taxes.
3. The region shall have legislative, executive, and judicial power.
4. The region shall contribute to the army in time of war on the basis of recruitment as determined by itself after fixing its contingent.
5. The Catalan language shall be official.

By this time a new voice had been raised in the chorus of Catalanists; that of Enrich Prat de la Riba. Recognizing that up to this time the whole Catalan question had been largely the product of Barcelona and that the provinces were scarcely touched by the propaganda, he proposed a new co-ordinated organization to bring together the numerous forces that were laboring for Catalanism. With the exception of the *Centre Catalá,* Prat de la Riba managed to pull the others into a new force called *Unió Catalanista.*

Prat de la Riba asserted that "the Catalan homeland, large or small, is our only country," and that it was the duty of Catalans to protest against the tyranny that maintained the "natural" nationalities

[18] A. Rovira i Virgili, *op. cit.,* p. 58.

in subjugation.[19] In the statement of principles adopted at Manresa in 1892, the new association rejected totally the idea of separatism, insisting that its first preoccupation was the determination of the bases of relations between the central power and the autonomous regions. With Prat de la Riba the first exposition of the idea of Catalonia as a nation begins. In his *Compendi de la doctrina catalanista,* published in 1894, he sets forth what for him is the doctrinal aspect of his stand.

Catalanism entered a period of open and avowed nationalism with Prat de la Riba. After 1896 militant regionalism penetrated organizations and circles which up to that time had been either mildly benevolent or indifferent toward the movement. Economic corporations of considerable prestige became a part of the fast-growing bloc and Catalanism was aided by the rise of a brilliant galaxy of writers, some of whom constitute the most eminent personalities in Catalan writing: Joan Maragall, Miguel Costa y Llobera, Santiago Rusiñol, Joaquin Ruyra, and a host of others.

The Catalans were generally opposed to the war against the United States and expressed this hostility in a manifesto in which the undertaking was denounced. Among other factors was the detrimental effect of the war on the business interests of Catalonia. The end of the century was distinguished by government hostility to some of the more active Catalanist propaganda and feeling ran high in Barcelona where every occasion was seized to manifest opposition to the Madrid government. It is hardly necessary to bore the reader with a detailed account of the numerous divisions, subdivisions, and schisms that appeared at the turn of the century in the various Catalanist groups. The *Centre Nacional Catalá* emerged, fused with the *Unió regionalista,* and ultimately ended in the *Lliga regionalista.* There were now strong currents against Catalanism on the part not only of the monarchists and partisans of the central authority but also on the part of the republicans, many of whom considered Catalanism as a romantic survival of medieval obscurantism with no real importance and only the slightest appreciation of the facts of contemporary Spanish politics.

The fusion in the *Lliga* had been made possible in large part after the striking electoral victory in 1901 and the organ of the new combination, *La Veu de Catalunya,* became one of the most famous newspapers in the cause of Catalan regionalism. A few months later the *Lliga* increased its prestige by winning the municipal elections in Barcelona,

---

[19] Prat de la Riba, *La nacionalitat catalana,* 1910, pp. 58–59.

ushering into politics two figures long destined to play a dominating role: Puig i Cadalfach and Francisco Cambó. The arrival in Barcelona of young Alejandro Lerroux, at the beginning of the century, and his rapid rise to political fame cannot be underestimated as another factor in the fast-changing Catalan political scene. Lerroux was an Andaluz, transplanted to Catalonia where his republicanism was to become a persuasive force during the entire twentieth century that culminated in the civil war.

The *Lliga* was split in 1904 at the time of the visit of Alfonso XIII to Barcelona. Some wished to abstain totally from all demonstration of good will; others felt that it was the occasion to present the legitimate claims of Catalonia. The fact that Cambó delivered an address to the monarch offended a considerable number of the members of the *Lliga*. On November 25, 1905, Catalonia was shaken by the first clashes between Catalanists and anti-Catalanists. The republicans were irritated and the military were outraged by what they considered to be an insulting caricature published in a humorous review. The result was an outbreak of violence with the destruction of property and particularly the *Veu de Catalunya*. Despite the airing of the incident in parliament on February 5 and 6, 1907, the outbreaks had served to bring the Catalanists together, for at Gerona, just one year before, the new *Solidaritat catalana* had been born.

The evolution of Catalan politics was such that it was no longer the so-called Right which had the monopoly on nationalism. The formation of the *Centre Nacionalista Republicá*, in 1906, revealed that republicanism was equally ready to combine with nationalism and regionalism to form a movement. The electoral victories of the *Solidaritat* were enormously encouraging to them, for in April, 1907, the group won 41 seats out of the 44 for the Cortes.

The *Solidaritat*, however, was quite incapable of hanging together. Divergences of opinion and the suspicion toward it of the Left tended to weaken its position, and by 1908 it was decisively defeated in the elections. In the municipal elections of 1909, the republican groups that had joined the *Solidaritat* broke away to establish a coalition of Catalan left-wing parties. The fact that the Left obtained more votes than the old *Lliga regionalista* and the Carlists together was a surprise and marks a new stage in the evolution of Catalanist sentiment. In 1909 the Left joined a new party under the name of *Unió Federal Nacionalista Republicana*.

Important as politics unquestionably are in the study of regionalism, it must not be forgotten that the cultural process was perhaps even more significant. The entrance of numerous parties under the banner of Catalanism tended to create the impression that regionalism was on the march toward certain victory. To the ardent Catalan nationalists this was quite insufficient. Catalonia must be re-Catalanized; this was the first and foremost problem and politics could never serve to revive the national spirit to whose resurrection they were devoted. It was on April 17, 1900, that the Catalan language was used for the first time in the Academy of Jurisprudence and Legislation in Barcelona. In 1901 members of the city council of Barcelona, elected as Catalanists, invoked their right to speak Catalan in the sessions. In 1902, in Tarragona, the mayor declared that Catalan could be used in the deliberations of the council, while a campaign was launched to introduce Catalan as the language in the courts of law justice. The crux of the whole problem was obviously the schools. As long as ordinary teaching was entirely in Castilian, it was hopeless to expect that a Catalan-speaking generation could be raised up capable of employing the language for cultivated and professional purposes. The program of the regionalists was fundamentally the complete Catalanization of everything, with Castilian a special subject only, necessary for communication with the rest of Spain. The *Associació protectora de l'Ensenyança catalana* was formed to defend the place of Catalan in the schools. In 1903 the first Catalan university congress was held to deal with the problem of Catalan in higher education. In 1906 facilities were created for the maintenance of chairs of Catalan language, letters, and history, at the University of Barcelona. The first congress of the Catalan language was held in October, 1906, at which an effort was made to assure the purity and the precision of the tongue. The *Institut d'Estudis Catalans,* founded in 1907, became the great research and scientific center of Catalan culture. Prat de la Riba, as president of the Barcelona council, devoted great energy to creating public libraries and advancing the cause of Catalan culture in general.

The disintegration of the *Solidaritat* and the culmination of violence in the Tragic Week of 1909 somewhat dampened the ardor of the Catalanists, for the twentieth century was showing a markedly different character from the nineteenth. Catalan nationalism up to this time had been primarily conservative, nurtured within the walls of normal, political conventionality. The new phenomenon that was appearing was extremism accompanied by direct action. Barcelona was to be torn very shortly by this novel force that seized nationalism insofar as it was a useful instrument of policy, and distorted it to social and political ends of an entirely different nature. The struggle for autonomy, toward which everything that has been said about Catalanism up to this point was headed, was now faced with the rise of revolutionary extremism. This extremism meant specifically two things: syndicalism and anarchism, both equally destructive of the established social order and equally consecrated to the methods of direct action and terrorism. By the end of the past century anarchism had already secured a tight grip on vast sectors of the Barcelona proletariat. The May Day disorders of 1890, the attempted assassination of Martínez Campos two years later, the Montjuich incident of 1896, the strikes of 1902, and the culminating tragedy in what was literally bloody civil war during a week in 1909 are all part of this growing picture of infiltration and destruction. The idea that Catalan nationalism or even separatism was from the beginning linked up with the extreme Left is a dangerous and confusing idea.[20]

By 1911 another idea regarding autonomy was developing. Instead of a series of isolated arrangements for the various Catalan provinces, it was proposed to fuse all of them into a single *Mancomunitat*. In addition to the Barcelona representatives, the deputies of Lérida, Tarragona, and Gerona, the other Catalan provinces were in agreement, and on December 8, 1911, a delegation presided over by Prat de la Riba waited on Minister Canalejas with the project. The proposal was well received and Canalejas promised to present it to the Cortes where it was introduced, approved in large part, and then suffered the vicissitudes of the rapidly changing governments of that period. Canalejas was assassinated, Count Romanones forced out of office, and Dato was reluctant to take effective action. Finally, late in 1913, by royal decree, the measure was put into effect and the various areas of Spain were authorized to join together for local administration. On April 6, 1914, the *Mancomunitat de Catalunya* was proclaimed under the presidency of Prat de la Riba.

The shifts and transformations in Catalan political parties became even more complicated after this decision. For a brief period between 1914 and 1916, the *Unió Federal Nacionalista Republicana* and the radical group of Alejandro Lerroux formed an alliance. The coalition was soundly trounced, since a great many of the members of the *Unió*

---

20 See E. Allison Peers, *op. cit.*, p. 158 sq.

were unwilling to see any sort of electoral combination with the Lerroux republicans, with the result that an effort was made to convert the *Unió Catalanista* into an authentic left-wing force with a nationalist tinge, advocating international socialism and the disestablishment of the Church, among other things. The *Lliga* continued to maintain its strength, with its conservative program and attitude. The year 1916 was one of electoral triumph for this movement. In 1917 the *Partit Republicá catalá* was formed with many elements that had belonged to the old U.F.N.R.

The problem of real autonomy was still very much in the forefront for the partial autonomy under the *Mancomunitat* did not satisfy the aspirations of the Catalans. On November 29, 1918, a petition was prepared by the *Mancomunitat* and the Catalan members of the Cortes to be presented to the Prime Minister, formulating the demands of the Catalans for regional autonomy. All parties were represented and the demand stated in the preamble that it was the expression of the fervent and unanimous will of the Catalan people:

> In theory the unity of the Spanish nation does not suppose the more or less absolute supremacy of the regions of Castilian origin over the others. In theory this unity is supposedly the result of the common action of all the regions. In practice, however, the unity represents an absorption in favor of the Castilians of all political life.[21]

The reception in Madrid was cold. Cambó, as a spokesman for Catalonia, raised the question in the Chamber, but was opposed by numerous other representatives who felt that all the concessions possible had been made to Catalonia. The atmosphere of 1918 outside Spain was one of jubilation over the end of the war and the feeling that new times were ahead. The Catalans were not exempt from the sentiment that in the reshuffling of the map of Europe they might be able to lay claim to full nationhood. It was becoming increasingly apparent, however, that under the monarchy, the transformation of Catalonia was impossible, for the present regime in Madrid had gone as far as it possibly could in granting local demands. Only a severe threat to the whole structure of the Spanish state could bring about a wider or more complete autonomy. The frustrating events of 1918 help to explain in large part the enthusiasm with which the Republic was welcomed in Catalonia and the joy with which the new dispensation was received, for only through a process of fundamental change could further progress in the way of autonomy be envisaged.

[21] Lluis Duran y Ventosa, *Regionalisme y federalisme,* p. 5.

Social agitation increased; tension in Barcelona tended to rise after 1919, and for the next few years the Catalan question remained very much in the foreground of thought and speculation. No steps of a tangible sort were taken to bring about a settlement. The emergence of Francisco Macià as the spokesman for the new state of mind became apparent. In 1919 the *Federació Democràtica Nacionalista* envisioned a very ample autonomy that would allow for the free entering into a pact for Iberian unity. In 1922, Macià made public his project of the *Estat catalá* or Catalan state. Separatism was now the order of the day and both the romantic stage as well as the purely nationalist was completely surpassed. A national congress held in July, 1922, fixed the basis of a concerted drive in this direction. New leaders were coming forward: Antoni Rovira i Virgili; Lluis Nicolau d'Olwer, later to join the First Republic cabinet in 1931; and Josep Ma. Pi i Sunyer. Out of this conference came a new organization, called the *Acció catalana.* With a new paper, *La Publicitat,* the movement set about diffusing its ideas and preparing the ground for action. Further, the new *Unió socialista de Catalunya* emerged as an attempt to wed the principles of international socialism with the nationalist aspirations of the Catalan people.

Then came the dictatorship of Primo de Rivera. The strong nationalism of Catalonia was already reaching out to join hands with the Basque provinces and Galicia:

> That night, in a theater located on the Paralelo, a nationalist meeting was to be held with the presence of delegates from the Basque provinces and Galicia. That meeting was the last that could be held by the nationalists, in a public way, before the dictatorship. With the advent of Primo de Rivera, a policy of violent repression against Catalonia was inaugurated. . . . All Catalan centers were closed, the display of the flag forbidden and the language harassed.[22]

In 1925 the *Mancomunitat* was suppressed and during the dictatorship the political parties were not allowed to operate. The only one was the *Unión Patriótica,* a fictitious organization that supported the regime. Many Catalans were reduced to purely cultural and literary pursuits during the period of Primo de Rivera, while others managed to get abroad and continue agitation for the Catalan cause. Macià carried on in Paris where the idea of his *Estat catalá* took root, and

---

[22] Aymamí i Baudina, *Macià. Trenta anys de política catalanista. Apunts per una biografia,* Barcelona, 1933, pp. 115–116.

there were rumors that he planned to use armed force if necessary to win Catalonia's freedom.

In October, 1926, preparations were made to invade Catalonia. They were foiled and the expedition came to an ignominious end. Macià was regarded a hero and retired to Belgium until such a time as Primo de Rivera's rule might end. The dictatorship proceeded to employ every method to extirpate Catalanism. The language was constantly hounded, shops were forbidden to advertise in Catalan; lectures or talks were forbidden and every effort undertaken to remove even the Catalan street signs in Barcelona. Primo de Rivera seemed convinced that the Catalan question was liquidated and would never arise again:

> Is it possible that in four years, a problem would be eliminated that had been agitated for a quarter of a century and which, before 1898, was already the product of a half century of gestation? . . . Of all those who proclaimed the death of Catalanism, and the definite liquidation of the Catalan problem, I believe no one was more sincerely convinced than General Primo de Rivera.[23]

Catalan politics followed their usual complex course after the fall of Primo de Rivera. In 1930, *Acció Republicana de Catalunya* was founded, separating from *Acció catalana* in the belief that the latter was insufficiently oriented to the Left. In March, 1931, the two organizations combined again under the title of *Partit catalanista republicà,* while the *Lliga regionalista* continued to hope for a transformation of Catalan institutions under the monarchy. Francisco Cambó preached harmony and good will up to the eve of the elections in 1931. He was in disagreement with the San Sebastián Pact which had assured autonomy to the different regions in the event the republic were triumphant. The political shifting became increasingly ideological. The Catalan republicans, the *Estat catalá,* and certain other elements came together to form the *Esquerra,* or Left, which came out on top in the critical elections of the spring of 1931 over the *Lliga.*

The advent of the Republic brought instant consequences in Barcelona, for the city was literally turned over to Luis Campanys, and on the balcony with him to fete the new regime was Macià, now the acknowledged leader of all Catalonia. The outburst of nationalist sentiment led to the display of Catalan flags and the immediate proclamation of the new Catalan state. However, it must be emphasized that this new "state" was not a full-fledged republic, even though the term was used. A little later the expression *Generalitat de Catalunya*

[23] Francisco Cambó, *Per la concòrdia,* Barcelona, 1930, pp. 19–20.

was to come in as the proper title for the new political entity. Macià was the new president and the hero of the day while Cambó was execrated and forced into exile in France. There was no chance of collaboration between Cambó and Macià and the former's followers became a minority opposition in the Catalan government.

An extremely important point to remember is that the movement for proletarian revolution and that of nationalism had been running along side by side for years in Catalonia without meeting except casually. The middle class was largely responsible for the nationalism. It was this class that was to feel the full brunt of the violence that was to sweep Barcelona and all Catalonia in 1936.

Everything had seemed hopeful for Catalonia in that spring of 1931. The Republic had come in without bloodshed. Macià had won an overwhelming victory for the *Esquerra* in the first elections in June. His triumph was so complete that everything seemed headed toward the happy consummation of the autonomous statute. President Alcalá Zamora was jubilantly received in Barcelona and no danger seemed to threaten from the other parties or from the monarchists. It was eighteen months later when the Statute for Catalan autonomy was finally passed in the Cortes, on September 9, 1932. There were rumblings, nevertheless, of the terrible storm that was brewing. Three times the peace of Catalonia was menaced by those who sought to provoke a "people's revolution." There were many in Catalonia who thought in terms of a revolution, and not merely of a statute: "Only the working class mentality can understand and solve the problem fully. . . . The revolution to come must be profound and reach the great mass of the workers."[24]

After an endless amount of debate and discussion, the Statute was finally passed, to the elation of Catalonia, although its provisions were not entirely satisfactory to certain sectors which hoped for an even more sweeping autonomy. The definition of the new status of Catalonia may be of interest as an example of the juridical regionalism now introduced into the republican institutions. Article I of the Statute reads:

> Catalonia is constituted as an autonomous region within the Spanish state, in conformity with the Constitution of the Republic and the present Statute. Its representative organism is the *Generalitat* and its territory that comprised in the provinces of Barcelona, Gerona, Lérida and Tarragona.[25]

---

[24] Jaume Aiguader i Miró, *Catalunya i la revolució,* Barcelona, n.d., pp. 149–150.
[25] C. Massó i Escofet and R. Gay de Montellà, *L'Estatut de Catalunya. Text*

Education was left largely to the new *Generalitat,* with the specification that Castilian should serve for all relations with the central government and as an obligatory subject for instruction in the schools. Catalonia would have wide control over its educational, juridical, and economic system, with the restoration of its own system of laws. Macià accepted the Statute although it was a compromise on many points and admitted publicly that he would have preferred another document.

The first three years of the Republic were relatively uneventful. Catalonia faced certain problems, however, of a serious nature. In the first place, there was the increasingly important realization that Barcelona and the rest of Catalonia are by no means the same thing. The migration of hundreds of thousands of workers from other parts of Spain, and very particularly from Murcia and the areas southward which are less favored economically, has changed the purely Catalan character of the major city. One of the problems of Catalanization is the very numerous minority of normally Castilian-speaking people in Barcelona. The man power of many of the extremist organizations came from the immigrants, and especially the Andalucians who were already strongly influenced by anarcho-syndicalism. Here too we find an explanation of the indifference of the extreme Left to the whole Catalan linguistic and cultural question and the fact that the brunt of the original campaign for the restoration of Catalan nationality was carried out by the middle class.

Despite a feeling that all was not attained, Catalans were still content that they were on the way toward the kind of autonomy they had always wanted:

> Catalonia wants to be the mistress of its own domestic life and if the roads toward that end are various, the end itself can only be one: liberty for Catalans in a fully autonomous Catalonia which in turn may form part of a voluntary federation.[26]

The Statute did not work automatically. As late as the elections of the autumn of 1933 many of the services promised to the *Generalitat* were still in Madrid. The swing to the Right observable all over Spain was evident in Catalonia in the comeback of the *Lliga* which gained a very considerable number of seats. With the death of Macià, Luis

---

oficial comentat, amb referencies legals i notes de la discussió parlamentària, Barcelona, 1933, p. 11.

[26] A. Rovira i Virgili, *Catalunya i la república,* Barcelona, 1931, p. 99.

Campanys, a relatively obscure lawyer but excellent organizer, governed supreme in the *Generalitat*.

As 1934 came in and the evidence that a crisis lay ahead was plain, the Catalans were torn between emotions. They wanted to keep the Statute, and if a dictatorship should be established it was obvious that the Statute would not survive, especially if the reign of Primo de Rivera had been any indication of the Spanish dictatorial mind. A triumphant republican Right might mean a diminution of their autonomy. On the other hand, the extreme Left was just as unpalatable, since in Catalonia itself this political and social element was totally uninterested in autonomy or statutes and completely wrapped up in revolution. The general drift, then, was toward the slightly left of center — to the form of republicanism represented by Manuel Azaña.

In addition, there was conflict between Barcelona and Madrid, as inevitable when two jurisdictions existed side by side and one of them still not entirely and carefully defined. The issue at hand was a law passed in Catalonia regarding lands. The landowners protested and the matter was taken before the Tribunal of Constitutional Guarantees, a sort of second chamber created under the Republic to pass, among other things, on laws alleged to be unconstitutional. The Tribunal rejected the law as one the Catalan parliament could not pass. There the matter stood and the Madrid government would make no concessions. The Catalan government was faced by capitulation or resistance. The latter could only take the form of armed rebellion and it is doubtful that anyone was willing to go to that extreme. Into this tense situation was tossed the far greater issue of the Asturias revolt in October, 1934. In the initial confusion that enveloped the rightist government in power and the serious uprising in the north, Campanys seized the occasion to proclaim the Catalan Republic. There was a brief flare of revolt, but Catalonia did not respond to the proclamation; for the Catalan people had striven loyally to abide by the Statute and work within the Spanish state. The audacity of their leaders — or rather some of their leaders — led them for a moment into a blind alley from which they were rescued only by the steadfastness of the military and the refusal of the masses to back up the ephemeral republic. It is assumed that Campanys was pulled into the plot by disillusioned extremists and ardent nationalists to whom the Statute was a straight jacket. The Statute was suspended and a governor general named from Madrid, although sober judgment prevailed in the Cortes and no precipitate action was taken to chastise all Catalonia for the folly of a few. By 1935 most of the practical provisions of the Statute had been restored and everything but the maintenance of public order was in local hands.

The critical elections of February, 1936, produced a great victory for the *Esquerra* in Catalonia. Luis Campanys and many of those who headed the electoral lists were in prison, but two weeks after the elections, President Campanys was back again with the blessing of the Popular Front Government and the forgiveness at least tacitly of the State against which he had rebelled. There was a considerable divergence between events in Catalonia and the rest of Spain during the five months between the elections and the outbreak of the National Movement.

There are certain conclusions to which this brief sally into Spanish regional history allows us to make. In the first place, the regional problem is not an artificial one. Catalonia is a nation, a people, and a culture, and is very definitely no mere subdivision of Castilian with no claim to autonomy. In the second place, the sense of history is lively among the Catalans and has provided them for generations with a keen perception of their own collective personality. Their role, on the other hand, is that of a Spanish people. Their greatness has been a part of the general Hispanic epic. Their fortunes at almost every critical moment have been bound to those of the rest of the peninsula. Economically, Catalonia cut off from the peninsula is inconceivable, for the hinterland has allowed Catalonia to become strong economically and develop industry. It is precisely this economic difference that also plays a very large part in the friction between Catalonia and the rest of Spain. Catalonia is richer, more industrious, sea-minded, and cosmopolitan as against Castile which is molded and guided entirely by its inland position. The centralization of the Spanish regime in Madrid and the insistence down through the monarchy on the greatest control from the capital has proved a source of irritation and annoyance to the Catalans who are eager to embark on economic projects on their own without the dead weight of bureaucracy and officialdom weighing them down.

THE BASQUE QUESTION

The problem of the Basque minority is often linked to that of Catalonia. There are, to be sure, certain points of analogy and at the same time certain very wide differences. In so far as the two are an expression of nationalism, the resemblance is considerable. Just as the

Catalan-speaking areas spill over into France and to a far less degree into Sardinia, so too is the Basque population concentrated not only in four of the provinces of Spain but in parts of Pyrenean France. A nationalism based on the inclusion in a definite territory of all those belonging to the same racial or linguistic group would, in both cases, involve separatism from France as well as Spain.

Catalan nationalism has never had the religious content that has distinguished the Basque. In the latter case, Catholicism has been taken almost as the common denominator for all that is authentically Basque. In Catalonia the language question loomed far larger than in the Basque provinces. It is notable that a great many of the major Basque centers, such as Bilbao, are not Basque speaking at all. In many cases the leaders of Basque nationalism express themselves in Spanish and are often only imperfectly acquainted with their so-called mother tongue. The last point of distinction between the two movements is that, in the case of the Basques, there is a very evident emphasis on racism while in Catalonia it is cultural tradition and provincial loyalty. The Basques have been the classic exponents of racism in the Iberian peninsula and the careful reading of their own nationalist literature proves eloquently that they conceive of themselves as a racial type quite apart from the rest of Europeans.

The Basque population of Spain inhabits four provinces: Navarre, Alava, Vizcaya, and Guipúzcoa. These provinces, despite their common Basque origin and the prevalence among them, especially in the countryside, of Basque speech, have never in their history formed a single state, and much less have they been tied in with the Basque departments of France. The incorporation of the Basque provinces into united Spain did not mean a simple annexation, but a form of association by which the provinces retained many of their traditional privileges and rights. The survival in the Basque country of systems of land and property ownership, taxation and economic organization, is one of the principal features of the region. This was accepted in the beginning, and Castile did not undertake to erase these elements of local autonomy that were historically deep rooted, and the *fueros* of the Basques were maintained consistently even in the face of considerable pressure. They managed to retain them even after 1714 when the Bourbon dynasty eliminated the local rights of Valencia, Catalonia, and Mallorca. This is not the place to record in detail the vicissitudes of the Basque local rights or trace the ups and downs of their fortunes. The vital thing to bear in mind is that we are dealing with a *people,* who are distinguished more by a social order and a traditional community organization than by the revival of a language or a literature as in the case of Catalonia.

The Basque provinces have been directly involved in the political turmoil of the past century in Spain. When the first Carlist war broke out in 1833 they declared for Don Carlos, defending this tradition against Isabel. Espartero, in ending the war, promised the Basques their traditional liberties. The Pact of Vergara, in 1837, included provision for this protection, and on October 25, 1839, the *fueros* were confirmed. One item was emphasized, however, which was of importance, and that was that the *fueros* were confirmed insofar as they did not contradict or conflict with the constitutional precepts of Spain as a whole. In 1841 the central government confirmed the establishment of a special economic regime for Navarre and the other three Basque areas.

Down to this time the Basques had enjoyed certain extraordinary privileges; they had their own parliament, law courts, and mint; they provided their own armed forces and administered their own affairs with remarkable competence and honesty. The land system and organization of the Basque provinces helps us to understand the fundamental conservatism of the people and the tenacity with which they have defended their traditions against very considerable odds. The prevailing agrarian system in Vizcaya, Guipúzcoa, and Alava is called the *aparcería*. This is a form of leasing land in which the owner leases a piece of land to a farmer, usually on the basis of an oral contract. These leases frequently pass from father to son and become a part of the tradition of the community. The relations of owner and leasee are usually excellent, and a great deal of social stability comes from the close relation of owner and tenant without the inconvenient features of the large landowning systems and complete separation of the two participants in the arrangement. The provinces have long functioned, then, on either small land holdings, or on leases that are handed down for so many generations as to become almost hereditary.

The Basque provinces are four in number, differing considerably one from the other. Guipúzcoa has as its chief city San Sebastián, one of the most sophisticated and cosmopolitan of the beach resorts of Europe. Vizcaya is distinguished by the importance of Bilbao, the great industrial and shipping center of modern Spain and a major channel for trade and business with the rest of Europe and the world. In contrast with Vizcaya and its bustling trade, Navarre and Alava are inland provinces; the former no longer Basque speaking except in certain of the remote valleys. It is an agrarian community, deeply attached to the soil and to its religion and is made up of an admirable population of hardy farmers and small merchants; a people that repeatedly have sacrificed everything for the traditionalist cause to which they are so addicted. Catholicism in the provinces differs considerably. In Vizcaya, the Church is excellently organized with a clergy that is enlightened and devoted to its duty. In Navarre, with a more agrarian atmosphere, the parish priest is a man of great influence and prestige, and the province has often been called the Ireland of Spain.

The story of the relations of Madrid with the provinces since the Carlist wars has been one of increasing restriction. By the law of July 21, 1876, conscription and taxation were imposed on the Basques, from which they had heretofore been exempt except as through local action they might choose to collaborate. On February 28, 1878, it was provided that they should pay certain taxes, although retaining a number of their privileges. After the budget accord of 1887 other changes and modifications were introduced, and in 1925 a law was passed providing for a global tax on the Basque provinces, fixed at forty million pesetas in 1927, and to increase gradually according to agreement. This was the state of affairs the Republic found when it came into existence in 1931. The ancient *fueros* had died in 1839 for all practical purposes, that is, as vital instruments for the maintenance of a high degree of independence. For the past hundred years the tendency has been to whittle down little by little the privileges granted the provinces in the name of a peninsular uniformity. Obviously to the rest of Spain the existence of special fiscal agreements with the Basque provinces seemed like favoritism of the worst kind.

The provinces represent a very small proportion of the entire nation; Navarre is sparsely populated, although the density rises to a very high figure in the concentrated population of Vizcaya and Guipúzcoa. The economic significance of the area cannot be underestimated. The Basque provinces revealed before the war the highest savings rate in Spain after Catalonia. The industrial strength of Vizcaya comes primarily from accessibility to the sea and the presence of mineral resources.

The origins of contemporary Basque nationalism are easy to trace. The major problem for the modern reader interested in the intricate subject of Spain is how did it come about that this virile, tenacious race, so devoted to the Church and so practical in compliance with its law, managed to find itself in 1936 on the side of the Republic? How does it happen that ten years after the victory of the nationalists, the Basque government in exile carries on in the name of the Republic with as ardent protestations of devotion to religion as ever?

In the first place one clarification is of supreme importance. Navarre and Alava did not, at any time, stand with the Republic, but were among the first to respond to the call to arms of the National Movement, sending some 30,000 men to the armed forces to fight against the Republic. In the second place, a great many Basques in Vizcaya and Guipúzcoa did not support the Republic, as is attested to by the large number of them executed or put to death either by republican tribunals or by mobs that blackened the name of the republican government during 1936 and 1937.

Basque nationalism was intimately bound up with the defense of the *fueros* and the traditions, and Carlism was the force that maintained this spirit during the nineteenth century. Up to the end of the past century, Carlism satisfied the desire for traditionalism, the defense of the local autonomy, and the repugnance for the innovations that had been introduced into the national administration, but the new nationalism which played its role in 1936 is a much later product. The Basque provinces were torn asunder by the conflict between the Carlist sentiment of traditionalism and the newer, more aggressive nationalism that was fomented by Sabino Arana de Goiri. This Basque had studied at Barcelona in the heyday of the Catalan renaissance and returned to his native province imbued with the idea of a national revival.[27] Under the motto, *Jaungoicoa eta Lagi-Zarra* (God and the old laws) he campaigned for the idea of Basque nationalism with a doctrine that was extremist, racist, and burningly anti-Spanish.

This new nationalism developed at the expense of Carlism. In the past century there was definite conflict between the Carlists and the liberals in the Basque provinces; in the present century it has been between the traditionalists and the nationalists. The two movements coincide in their profession of Catholicism and their defense of the *fueros*. The Carlists however have long operated under the slogan of "God, Spain, and the monarchy," with emphasis on the monarchy and the unity of Spain. The nationalists on the other hand have accentuated

[27] Arana de Goiri died in 1903. His book containing the exposition of the nationalist idea is entitled, *Biscaya por su independencia,* published, to be sure, in Spanish, not Basque.

the creation of a Basque country, based on the existence and reality of a Basque race.

In the republican Cortes there was a tendency on the part of the two groups to join together in resisting legislation hostile to the Church or the religious interests of the people. The granting of the Catalan Statute provoked a similar demand on the part of the Basques. In this connection, José Antonio Aguirre, leader of the nationalists, and Count Rodezno, Carlist spokesman, were in substantial agreement while the republican Left and the socialists were opposed to conceding an autonomy Statute.

The absence of any serious intention of satisfying the Basque nationalists by the Republic is best evidenced in the fact that the autonomy charter was passed on October 6, 1936, almost three months after the civil war had started. It was approved by a rump Cortes of some hundred deputies without the slightest debate.[28] No consideration was given Article 12 of the republican constitution that provided that the Statute should not come into effect until two thirds of the municipalities had approved it. The arrangement was made between the then republican leader Largo Caballero and the self-styled government of the Basque country, since only part of Vizcaya was in reality in the hands of the Basques of republican sympathies.

There is a very strong suspicion in the examination of the course of events that the Popular Front used the enticement of an autonomy charter as bait for the nationalists in the hope of dividing the Basque provinces, for it must be noted that in the crucial elections of February, 1936, the Popular Front did not come out at all well in this region. If this were the intention of the government — and its dilatoriness is no better shown than by the date of the granting of the Statute — it succeeded beyond expectations for the reason that not only within Spain but outside the peninsula the adherence of the Basque nationalists to the Republic has been the cause of endless speculation and confusion. The Popular Front in reality provoked a civil war between the Basques themselves — pitting Navarre and Alava against the other provinces and dividing Basque sentiment within the two provinces of Guipúzcoa and Vizcaya. It would seem that the Basques who preferred to stand with the Republic put autonomy and nationalism ahead of everything, even the integrity of Spain and the most succinct con-

---

[28] *Gaceta de la República,* Oct. 7, 1936.

clusion is that the Basque leaders "sacrificed the essential to the contingent."[29]

It is notable that extremely few Basque leaders, especially in the intellectual field, have been associated in the least with Basque nationalism. This contrasts with the Catalan movements in which the intellectual leadership has been much in evidence. The great Basque names of modern Spain: Miguel de Unamuno, Pío Baroja, Ramiro de Maeztu, Zuloaga, and a host of others, have invariably thought in peninsular terms. Narrow Basque nationalism did not attract them nor the many who have been prominent in almost every phase of Spanish life, especially in shipping, banking, and the technical professions.

Basque nationalism, whatever may be the degree of its sincerity and selflessness, is vitiated to a large degree by its anachronistic character. It is typical of the absolutism in politics which arose with the idea of self-determination and absolute independence in the past century. *Euzkadi,* as the Basque state was called, has never existed as a reality in the modern political sense of the term. Catalonia was wedded to the idea of autonomy; the Basque state to total independence. Racism played a very large part, as has been indicated, in the background of the latter movement. The most telling argument against this extremism is that a very large proportion of the Basque people themselves did not follow the government of *Euzkadi* nor evidence any sympathy for the separatist campaign.

There can be no question of the devotion of the Basques, of both tendencies, to the Church. There is, however, a slight note of religious superiority in the Basque position; a feeling that in some way their form of religious practice and conformism is better than that of the rest of Spain.

The most plausible explanation is simply that a small number of Basques, carried away by the mysticism of nationality and self-determination, preferred any arrangement and collaboration with anyone before sacrificing what was promised in the way of an autonomy charter. They were willing to pay the price of co-operation with the Popular Front to obtain the independence of *Euzkadi.* To their honor it must be admitted that during the civil war they allowed the churches to remain open and Mass was freely said in Bilbao even in the days when the nationalist advance threatened it with partial destruction.

[29] Anon., *La question basque et la guerre civile en Espagne,* Brussels, 1937, p. 21.

Chapter 7. DESCENT INTO ANARCHY

THE STORY OF THE SECOND REPUBLIC

THE centuries-old monarchy was scrapped in Spain as a result of the municipal elections of April 12, 1931, in which the republicans won only a minority vote. Technically the election of that spring was not a popular referendum on the form of government at all, for in normal circumstances the choice of municipal councilors did not constitute a major political event. It was plain, however, that this particular election was construed as an expression of opinion for the Republic or the Monarchy. The validity of the republican government has been contested on the grounds that this issue was never presented directly to the voters. This, of course, is true. On the other hand, both republicans and monarchists were perfectly aware that the municipal elections were enormously significant precisely because this interpretation had been given them. It was the showdown between the supporters of the traditional regime and the energetic and hopeful republicans. Thus it was that the great Catholic newspaper *El Debate* expressed its conviction that "Today is to be a great day for the expression of Monarchical sentiment" (April 12, 1931). On the other side, a manifesto to the Madrid electorate, signed by Gregorio Marañón, José Ortega y Gasset, and Pérez de Ayala, among others, stated that "the municipal elections of next Sunday are a first contact with the domestic enemies of the future of our country."[1] The monarchists looked forward to the elections as a vindication of their thesis that Spain was fundamentally monarchical despite the disillusionment of the dictatorship and the unfortunate experience of the past year under the ephemeral governments that had succeeded Primo de Rivera. The republicans, on the other hand, were hopeful that their strength would so increase as to make a bid for power possible in the near future. Even the most ardent of republicans

[1] *El Socialista,* Madrid, April 10, 1931.

did not expect that the result of the elections would mean the immediate installation of the new regime in office. The prudent Niceto Alcalá Zamora was convinced that the most to be hoped for was a step in the direction of a Republic.

In some sectors there was an effort to disparage the vote as signifying any fundamental change in the structure of the State. "The revolutionary Left persists in giving the municipal elections political character and they boast that the sum total of the votes will reveal the number of citizens who are in favor of the Revolution," wrote the Monarchical *A.B.C.* (April 11, 1931).

Elections are held in Spain on Sunday. No newspapers appear on Monday and only the *Hoja del Lunes,* a sort of composite of the entire press, is issued. Hence for a couple of days Spain was somewhat bewildered as to the results of the municipal elections. The figures released by the Home Office on April 14 showed that 22,150 municipal seats had been won by the monarchists and 5875 by the republicans.[2]

The popular vote was, to be sure, far larger than the number of seats won would indicate. It became clear within a very short time that the republicans had been unusually successful in the larger cities while the rural areas had remained monarchical.[3] It may be argued with a good deal of theoretical merit that the elections were never designed to test opinion regarding the regime; that they gave an overall majority to the monarchists and consequently could not be taken as proof of republican inclination. Moreover, by no logic could the triumph of the republicans in the larger cities be interpreted as the will of the entire Spanish nation. If this were the case, then the urban vote, by some strange superiority, would have an intrinsic superiority over the rural — a dubious basis for a judgment on elections. The fact was that the republicans were exuberant and the monarchists morally defeated. The latter had no will to resist; no conviction in the excellence of their cause. The republicans precipitated a revolution without awaiting the final returns or even assessing their real strength, since the

---

[2] *A.B.C.,* Madrid, April 14, 1931.

[3] An interesting side light is shown on the Republic by the fact that the full electoral figures were never published. E. Allison Peers recounts how the London *Times* correspondent applied months after the change to the Home Office for the records and was refused (Peers, *Spanish Tragedy,* Methuen & Co., London, p. 233 n.). Julio Alvarez del Vayo reports the same thing: "the counting of votes in the municipal elections of 1931 was never completed and no complete official and authentically detailed lists of results ever published. . ." (*The Last Optimist* [New York: The Viking Press, 1950], p. 216 n.).

enthusiastic demonstrations of their partisans everywhere created the necessary atmosphere that made action possible and inevitable.

Count Romanones, the outstanding figure in the last monarchical government, was opposed to resistance by force. By Monday night, Madrid was seething with excitement and the next day the Republic was actually proclaimed here and there, notably at Eibar in the province of Guipúzcoa. On Tuesday, at the meeting at Dr. Marañón's house between Alcalá Zamora and Count Romanones, the fateful decision was taken that the King must abdicate and leave Spain by nightfall of that same day.[4] In Barcelona the Republic had already been proclaimed and in Madrid the real government of Spain was the Revolutionary Committee, now the provisional government of the incipient Spanish Republic. Alcalá Zamora, designated president by his fellow committee members, an ex-monarchist and Catholic, proceeded to harangue the nation by radio as soon as he was installed. His address lauded the order with which the change had come about and praised the intentions of the new regime. He urged the citizenry to exercise the greatest vigilance over the government in its acts and ended with the promise of social justice. It must be remembered that the Republic in the opening days was not a government but a committee without a constitution or any of the normal instruments for carrying out all the tasks at hand.

The revolutionary fervor that had ushered in the Republic was interpreted by the republicans themselves as the wholesome enthusiasm of a people long deprived of their just participation in the affairs of State. The Republic was to remedy all that with full and modern parliamentary procedures, but even in days immediately following the proclamation of the Republic and before the initial zeal had had time to subside there were ominous signs that things were not to be as moderate and balanced as the optimistic Alcalá Zamora had anticipated. *El Debate* announced that "The number of Monarchical councilors is four times that of the Republicans. In Madrid and almost all of the large cities, the Republican Socialist combination has

[4] Dámaso Berenguer, in his book, *De la dictadura a la república,* Madrid, 1946, recounts this dramatic moment. Referring to the decision of Count Romanones to turn over the government to the republicans, Berenguer states: "I was astonished that this step had been taken for we had not been informed about it nor was it in the King's mind that morning when we were together. When I asked why this was done and who had authorized this interview with the revolutionists, Count Romanones answered that it had been agreed upon and that at six in the evening we would have to turn over the authority," p. 382.

won" (April 14, 1931). Four days later the same paper opined frankly that "We should be under no illusions. The Republic that has been proclaimed in Spain is definitely leftist and anti-clerical." On the same date *El Liberal,* Madrid daily, showed its convictions in the following comment: "We must be extremely careful. Every bit of tact is necessary in dealing with the religious problem for the enemy is supremely astute. . . . We do not want a Republic with celibates who dominate the minds of our women folk."

In reality there were two forces moving toward inevitable collision. The intellectuals who had fomented the Republic were convinced that its advent was their work and they visualized a sort of academic republicanism in which the problems of culture and the spirit would form the center of preoccupation. Side by side with that intellectual trend was the popular one, incubated by long decades of anarchism and extremism. The work of undermining the masses, both rural and urban, was to bear its fruit. The advocates of the total revolution were soon to face the partisans of the drawing-room revolution, typified by the members of the *Ateneo de Madrid*. Gregorio Marañón tells us of his own convictions in a little brochure issued by a communist publishing house in one of its series:

> The Spanish people felt themselves to be the masters of their destiny and this was a lot. This phenomenon was due to the long range intellectual propaganda, to books and their diffusion during the last years of the Monarchy. . . . The enthusiasm of the *Ateneo* was a symptom of the inevitable Revolution on the march.[5]

Reading and political thinking may have had something to do with the advent of the Republic, but it was far more probable that the fact that Spain had suffered thirty-two changes of government in the twenty years preceding 1923, and that from 1917 to 1923 no fewer than 3380 revolutionary strikes had taken place, plus 728 outbreaks that may be called social, contributed to the preparation of the ground for the new "revolutionary" rather than "intellectual" Republic that came in in April, 1931. Although socialism and anarcho-syndicalist extremism were rooted in Spain, there was little mass following for middle class, moderate republicanism. Where, then, were the republicans? There were so few that efforts had to be made to create them. The fundamental tragedy of the Republic was that it came in without real support from a convinced following, capable of giving it

[5] *Cuatro comentarios a la revolución española,* Madrid, 1931, p. 20.

the moderate orientation it promised. *Pravda* in Moscow was not entirely mistaken when it saluted the Spanish Republic on the day of its foundation with the remark that: "We salute the new regime, a necessary step for the liberation of the Spanish people." Salvador de Madariaga summed it up with the remark that "The Republican triumph of the 14th of April was no Republican victory at all."

The decree of the provisional government was a remarkable document, for it stated simply that it was acting because of the overwhelming popular support of the nation which had placed it in power. The composition of this government was a curious cross section of opinion: two radical republicans, two conservative republicans, two radical socialists, one nebulous republican in the person of Manuel Azaña, one Galician autonomist, one *Acció catalana,* and three socialists. The socialists had in reality been responsible for the large republican vote, and to them went several of the more desirable posts. It would be difficult to discover what particular sector of public opinion Manuel Azaña represented. An obscure public official and writer, Azaña had made his career on the fringes of the literary world and in the *Ateneo,* and Miguel de Unamuno once remarked that "one must be careful of Azaña. He is capable of setting the world on fire in order to secure readers." Azaña did in fact manage to set Spain on fire and came preciously close to committing an even wider act of political arson. Alejandro Lerroux was incorporated into the cabinet as a veteran republican and leader of the radicals, whose evolution was such that he was now regarded as fairly moderate. Diego Martínez Barrio, up to this time quite unknown outside Seville, was placed in charge of a new ministry, that of communications, while Marcelino Domingo and Alvaro de Albornoz, more leftist than some of the others, were placed in Education and Public Works respectively. An insignificant lawyer from Coruña, Santiago Casares Quiroga, whose name appears frequently in the last tragic chapter of the Republic, represented an equally obscure little party, the *Organization Republicana Gallega Autónoma* and was given charge of the Navy. Manuel Azaña, oddly enough, became war minister, a position for which it would have been difficult to conceive anyone with less aptitude. Lluis Nicolau d'Olwer represented the Catalans in the Economics Ministry. The socialists, Fernando de los Ríos, Indalecio Prieto, and Francisco Largo Caballero, were assigned Justice, Finance, Labor respectively.

All of these men figured among the *dramatis personae* when the play of the Second Republic opened; most of them were still involved to a varying degree when the tragedy ended. The last of the ministerial group was Miguel Maura for Home Affairs. Together with Alcalá Zamora he represented that vague antidynastic liberalism that animated so completely the first President. Both Alcalá Zamora and Maura were motivated by a very high idea of what the Republic should be and how it ought to operate and symbolized the allegedly conservative character the Republic was to take. The composition of the cabinet showed how little respect was paid to the actual electoral strength of the various representatives, for although Lerroux was probably the leader of the largest and most compact genuinely republican party his position in the cabinet was an isolated one.

The government was constituted on April 14, 1931. On June 4 the decree calling for elections for parliament was issued. These elections were set for June 28 and the Cortes was scheduled to meet on July 14. The provisional government was unencumbered by a program or commitments, for neither in the San Sebastián Pact nor in the electoral speeches nor in the Manifesto of the Revolutionary Committee to the country can one find much real content or a coherent, thoughtful program of action. The Republic came in under the rosy hue of screaming crowds and exultant oratory. The reading of the contemporary press gives the impression of absolute, awful vacuity, in which no one said anything although everyone talked constantly. It was not strange, then, that the first acts of the provisional government should have been negative, for there was a veritable mania to undo everything connected with the dictatorship. Miguel Maura, as Home Secretary, fired the employees of 7500 municipalities. By June 23, José Ortega y Gasset was already expressing his concern over the unfortunate turn the Republic had taken. The first decree of the provisional government had been amnesty for political prisoners. On April 15, declared a holiday by the new government, the common criminals in the Valencia prison rebelled at the notion that only those guilty of political offenses should go free. The Governor confessed that "when the authorities made an effort to pacify them, they were overcome. After some negotiations, and consultation with Madrid, they were liberated."[6]

The Republic was strong on holidays; April 15 was declared a free day and May Day was another occasion when a gigantic demonstration to the memory of Pablo Iglesias brought out the throngs and made the

[6] Quoted by Fernández Almagro, in *Historia de la república española,* p. 17, from official communication of the Governor of Valencia, dated April 15, 1931.

Republic essentially "popular." The provisional president, with a *naïveté* that is shocking in the light of the events of May 11, wrote that there was no need to guard anything: "bank, church or convent, for they are threatened neither by greed nor sectarian passion."[7] This sort of thing was repeated elsewhere. In Bilbao, where there were no political prisoners at all, in Barcelona, and in Seville, street mobs joined in exerting pressure to empty the prisons. Madrid was a model of good conduct compared with some of the other cities. In the Spanish capital the jubilant throngs paid homage to the Republic by lopping off the heads of statues, pulling down street signs reminiscent of the Monarchy, and destroying plaques of merchants who advertised the royal family among their clientele.

Two specific events showed that the socialist party considered itself the spinal cord of the Republic. The celebration in honor of Iglesias had not been merely a party affair but had assumed the proportions of a national and official commemoration. The cabinet had been present at the main festivities and the provisional president was handed the resolutions of the meeting which contained, among a large number of banalities, certain explosive features: reduction of the voting age to 21 years; a new agrarian law, and trade-union control of industry. The *Casa del Campo* was turned over to the socialists for their amusement and recreation. Provisional president Alcalá Zamora found no better solution to the whole difficulty than to shout from a balcony: *"Long live social justice!"* The first of May revealed even more eloquently the fact that the left-wing elements considered the Republic as their particular property. In Barcelona the communists made a bid for preferential consideration and would have assaulted the palace of the *Generalitat* if the assault guards had not interfered opportunely. In the Arenas Square the anarchists had already held a meeting frankly hostile to the Republic, and at Grenollers, in Catalonia, the municipal government found it helpful to express its adherence to the Republic of Alcalá Zamora by displaying the Catalan flag and the Red flag of Revolution.

The new electoral law paved the way for what the optimists called the "participation of the people" and what in reality was a form of mob rule. The old districts were suppressed and the electoral representation based on the province. Cities of over 100,000 inhabitants formed a special constituency and each 50,000 citizens were to have the right

[7] *El Sol,* May 3, 1931.

to a deputy. The age limit of electors was reduced to twenty-three years of age. To be elected the representative must obtain 30 per cent of the votes deposited. The Supreme Court was no longer authorized to pass on election cases. The remarkable thing is that the provisional government passed a law of such a fundamental character as this before the elections and without public sanction as the permanent and authentic administration of the Republic.

The provisional government, committed in theory to merely preparing the way for elections and a Cortes, undertook to initiate every conceivable form of change and transformation during its transition tenure. On April 28, it announced that the traditional flag of Spain was to be abandoned for a new tricolored insignia. This matter may seem trivial compared with the real problems that Spain faced, but the decision to scrap the emblem that Spain had employed for centuries was made by a makeshift government without the slightest opportunity for discussion in open parliament.

Alejandro Lerroux expressed himself in the days after the outbreak of the civil war as totally deceived by the new Republic:

> A Republic was organized with a fixed standard in mind which was the French Revolution. To give it an original aspect and make it a little more radical, the leaders fell into the error of not taking into account our geography or our character, our economy or the more recent experiences abroad. In this way the result was a Spanish republic which was as little Spanish as possible.[8]

In this un-Spanish Republic the fault did not lie with the conservative classes who presumedly had refused their support to it. A common opinion, especially diffused in the later republican propaganda, is that the Republic of 1931 was systematically sabotaged from the beginning by the Right and that the Catholics were particularly unwilling to give it their support. The very opposite is the case. The Catholics and conservatives were inclined to lean over backward to give the Republic every opportunity for success, and Alfonso XIII, in a letter to the monarchists, urged them to work within the Republic and support it by not placing obstacles in its way.[9]

El Debate, under the direction of the able and courageous Angel Herrera, today Bishop of Málaga, pronounced its verdict on April 14: "The Spanish Republic exists since yesterday. The Republic is the

---

[8] Alejandro Lerroux, *La pequeña historia. Apuntes para la historia grande vividos y redactados por el autor,* Buenos Aires, 1945, pp. 29–30.

[9] *A.B.C.*, May 5, 1931.

de facto form of government in our country. It is our duty, therefore, to accept it." It must be remembered that it was this newspaper and those associated with it who were primarily responsible for the formation of the new political group *Partido Acción Nacional*, later to be called *Acción Popular*, which persuaded great masses of Catholics to support the Republic. Under the later leadership of Gil Robles, this group made every effort, even to the sacrifice of its interests, to co-operate loyally with the institutions of the Republic. The Cardinal Primate of Toledo, Cardinal Segura, issued a statement to the effect that "it is the duty of Catholics to accept the duly constituted government. The obligation of Catholics under the Republic is to send representatives to the chambers who would defend the interests of the Church." Even the most convinced monarchists did not propose rebellion, but merely legal opposition within the framework of the new regime. The Republic chose to disdain these offers of collaboration, the acceptance of which might have saved Spain from the tragedy of civil war.

Twenty-six days after the Republic was installed the first clear-cut evidence was available of the unbelievable weakness and apathy which was to characterize it for five long years. On May 10 a group of monarchists decided to establish a center, protected, they supposed, by the laws and guarantees of the Republic, for the purpose of political propaganda. This was the *Círculo Monárquico Independiente*, the opening of which conformed entirely to the legal regulations. A mob gathered in front of the center and became so threatening that the officials called the Home Office for protection. No protection was given them and several were the victims of assault. The mob decided to move from the Calle de Alcalá to the office of *A.B.C.* A stand selling *El Debate* was burned and other acts of a similar nature carried out. The upshot was the closing of several newspapers, including *El Debate* and *A.B.C.*, the arrest of the latter's director, Luca de Tena, the closing of the monarchist center, and the taking over by the State of the *A.B.C.* premises.

These acts were the beginning of that deterioration in civil rights that was so characteristic of the Republic. If opposition newspapers could not function without threats and violence from mobs, none of whom were ever chastised by the government itself, there was little point in talking about democratic liberties. It may be well to remark here, for the point is of capital importance, that the number of newspapers and reviews forbidden by the Republic or arbitrarily closed reached into the hundreds. The honest examination of the Spanish Republic — not the rosy-hued appraisal that comes from the pages of *The Nation* or *The New Republic* or the oceans of propaganda issued by the Republic during the civil war — is more than convincing that whatever else it might be, this institution was definitely not democratic in any sense in which that term is understood abroad.

On May 11, one day after the above-mentioned events, convents and churches were burned everywhere in Spain. No one denies the fact of this widespread arson. It is astonishing — so astonishing in fact as to defy an explanation — that the convents and churches burned simultaneously as though a single will had condemned them to the flames. It is highly improbable that in Madrid and Málaga, in Barcelona and Seville, mobs should spring to life at the same moment, animated by the same desire, and carry out the same purpose, unless there was something of a co-ordinated plan behind it. Alejandro Lerroux expressed himself with bitterness over this wholesale destruction:

> The mobs did not allow the Republic to live without disgrace for more than twenty-six days. On May 10 the demagogues were in the street to carry out their Revolution. While God was being shot in the churches, the President attended Mass. . . . This time the murderers were rewarded with advancement in the government.[10]

The whole business was blamed on the modest little monarchical center whose meeting had been held on May 10. *El Liberal* opined that, "It is to be noted that during the forty-eight hours that the people of Madrid were in control at the time the Republic was proclaimed, nothing was done against religion. And this time, when a Monarchist plot is discovered in collaboration, with the extreme Left, the convents have burned without resistance on the part of the persons occupying them" (May 12, 1931).[11]

El Socialista explained to its gullible readers that the whole thing was a "senseless provocation on the part of the Monarchists" (May 12, 1931). The sentiments of this paper, the official organ of the socialist party, may be judged by the opinion expressed a few days later when it demanded that religion be eliminated from the schools so that "the teachers may work without these ghosts of the past hanging over them. This is an excellent Revolution to carry out" (May 23,

---

[10] *Op. cit.*, p. 33.

[11] This paper went beyond most of the press in suggesting that the monks and religious were themselves responsible for burning their convents in order to create animosity to the Republic.

1931). *El Sol* begged the public to be calm: "Order at all cost. This is our motto and outcry" (May 12, 1931). Oddly enough, the Captain General of Madrid, General Queipo de Llano, who in 1936 was to defend Seville for the National Movement, expressed himself publicly in a speech in the Puerta del Sol after the incidents: "The cause of all this is the infamous provocation of the Monarchists."[12]

A list of churches, chapels, convents, and works of art destroyed would fill pages of this book. In Madrid the Jesuit church, the Catholic Institute of Arts and Trades, the Carmelite convent, the Sacred Heart in Chamartín were all razed. In Alicante the Jesuits, Salesians, Augustinians, Capuchins, and Marists lost their convents. In Elda, Valencia, Cádiz, Seville, Córdoba, Murcia, and Granada, rightist centers were destroyed and convents given over to the flames. Of course, every rightist center that was entered and destroyed was labeled "reactionary" and a threat to the Republic. It was considered a criminal act to even protest against the excesses of the democratic government that stood calmly by on May 11 and did not interfere to stop the burning.

In his unpublished *Memorias* Manuel Azaña who, let it be said candidly, ought to have known what was going on, confirms a preknowledge of the outrages of May 11 as well as the later attacks on Church property and institutions. Under date of December 2, 1932, in the diary entry Azaña states:

> Casares arrived. The people in the Security office have just learned, by a confidential agent, that tomorrow there will be a disturbance at the University and, stimulated by this, the mob will try to destroy some convents. The agent is the same one who last year advised Maura of the proposed burnings. "Didn't you know," asked Casares, "that Maura was advised forty-eight hours before the event and did nothing about it?" I did not know it.

The facts were that the government did absolutely nothing to prevent the destruction. Every eyewitness concurs in the statement that the police and security forces did not lift a finger to prevent the mob from carrying out their intention. In the government at the time were such men as Alcalá Zamora, provisional president, a Catholic; Miguel Maura, Home Secretary and the Undersecretary of the same ministry; the Catholic, Ossorio y Florit, the Director of Security, the Catholic conservative, Carlos Blanco. If none of them were able to do anything to either prevent or curtail the wave of disorder, aimed exclusively at

[12] *El Sol,* Madrid, May 12, 1931.

convents, churches, artistic treasures, and similar institutions, the inevitable conclusion is that they were powerless and the government was in the hands of the more extreme elements in the cabinet. The files of the Home Ministry reveal that the police were perfectly aware of what was planned as early as May 10, and that Carlos Blanco reiterated his instructions that no steps were to be taken to break up suspicious crowds, even when they assembled in front of churches for reasons that were not difficult to surmise. In the archives of the Security office are to be found the record of the telephone communications from outlying posts regarding the development of the situation. In one case the police captain phoned in to say that two thousand persons, presumedly railroad workers, were gathered and that the firemen were completely passive in the face of the mob's obvious purpose. He asked for instructions which were never given. The fire-fighting forces made no effort to intervene until neighboring buildings were threatened by the flames. The existence of a perfectly coordinated program was visible in the efficiency with which gasoline was distributed, orders carried out by the incendiaries, and organized resistance to any attempt to interfere by onlookers cared for. There was, to be sure, some effort to cover the appearances and Carlos Blanco blamed the police commissars, later resigning himself, to be designated thereafter to other posts in the republican administration.

The provisional government acted at once against the monarchists, allegedly responsible for the excesses. Garrido Juaristi, Bernabeu, Cobián, and the Duke of Hornachuelos were arrested and several others were imprisoned. This initial period was distinguished by the expulsion of Cardinal Segura of Toledo, after a pastoral letter issued by him was construed by the government as hostile and seditious. The Bishop of Vitoria was similarly expelled for alleged political activity.[13]

The elections to the Constituent Assembly, which was to endow the turbulent Republic with a fundamental charter and regularly constituted institutions, were preceded by rising temperatures and orgies of extremist propaganda. *El Socialista* summed up the spirit of the times with the expression, "The real people must prevent by any means the return of the class of lepers whose sores we buried from sight on April 14" (June 2, 1931). *El Debate* and other conservative newspapers

[13] The Holy See demanded an explanation and protection for the faithful. Peers sums the situation up neatly by saying: "At that time it [the government] was incapable of safeguarding the lives or property of any group of citizens whatsoever" (Peers, *Spanish Tragedy,* Methuen & Co., London, p. 59).

were again suspended, and dozens of arrests were made of outstanding conservative leaders. The new electoral system was so arbitrary that some candidates needed nearly 100,000 electors to win their seat, while others could manage with as low as 19,000. A republican, Ciges Aparicio, admitted that the reform of the electoral law "was not the work of democracy, but of dictatorship."[14]

The election results gave the socialists about 120 seats, and the radical socialists and followers of Azaña another 50. The radicals, incidentally, headed by Lerroux, constituted some 90 members and in general were favored by the more conservative elements. It must be remembered that in Spanish politics as in France, the term *radical* often designates a political group more conservative than the straight socialists. Some 50 members of the *Esquerra Catalana* increased the government majority. The opposition was heterogeneous with small bodies of traditionalists and a few independents, whereas the older parties that had functioned under the monarchy were dazed, bewildered, and almost incapable of reacting to the socialist sweep. It was perfectly clear from the beginning that the socialists were the arbiters of the nation's destiny.

Julián Besteiro, Luis Jiménez de Asúa, and others were the moving spirits in what theoretically was a commission, composed of proportionate representation of all the parties, to draft the new constitution, marking the socialists the real architects of the new charter, as one of their more devoted partisans has affirmed.[15] The Assembly seemed to be interested in harassing the opposition or potential opposition in drafting the constitution, for one of its initial acts was to deprive José Calvo Sotelo of his seat as deputy for Orense. Although the brilliant ex-Minister of Finance of the Primo de Rivera period was living in Paris, his protest against the conduct of the Assembly was immediate and eloquent. He managed to enter Parliament in due time and for five years was to be a thorn in the side of the socialist and extremist majority, for no voice was comparable to his in his verbal flagellation of the weaknesses and conduct of the republican government. The Commission on Responsibilities, set up to look into the acts of collaborators with the dictatorship, had a field day with the arrest and incarceration of generals, civilians, and, above all, General Berenguer himself.

---

[14] *El Sol,* May 7, 1931.

[15] Luis Araquistain, in *El Sol,* Dec. 8, 1931.

The Constitution as finally presented is a remarkable document.[16] As a *tour de force* it probably merits some sort of record, for it was drafted and put in final shape in exactly twenty days, from July 23, to August 12, 1931. After this the Assembly proceeded to debate the text, and on December 1 it was approved. The opening phrases of the constitution are strictly orthodox socialist: "Spain is a democratic republic of workers of all classes, organized in a regime of liberty and justice." The preamble contains such items as a permanent renunciation of war as an instrument of policy, the expression of respect for international law, and the avowal that Spain has no official religion. The section on personal rights is almost lyrical: "No special privileges on account of sex, wealth, social class, political opinions, or religious beliefs"; freedom in the choice of a profession, and above all freedom "to express in any form their ideas and opinions, without previously being subjected to censorship." The franchise is extended to both sexes and the age of twenty-three set as that at which the citizen enters upon his duties as an elector.

The religious question played a very large role in the new constitution. The Republic was a strictly secularist institution under the laicism that did not mean simply separation from a particular religious body, but a very definite position against that body.

All payment of the clergy was to end two years after the promulgation of the Constitution and no religious institution was to be favored with financial support. Freedom of conscience was guaranteed and any religion could be practiced provided it was not contrary to public morals. Any public demonstration of religion had to have the sanction of the government. The religious orders were treated with extreme rigor. Any orders that required a vow — "besides the three canonical vows" — of obedience to an authority other than the legitimate authority of the State, were dissolved. Their property was to be nationalized and used for educational or charitable purposes. Any other orders could be dissolved under a special law, if, in the opinion of the public authority, they constituted a "peril to the safety of the State." No order could engage in education and one only guarantee was the promise that confiscation would be accompanied by an "adequate compensation." Needless to say, the term "adequate" was left vague and depended entirely on the will of the State itself.

[16] Allan Chase has made an original comment regarding "The Republican constitution patterned so closely on that of the United States" in his *Falange, The Axis Secret Enemy in the Americas,* New York, 1943, p. 7.

Divorce was introduced on the basis of mutual disagreement and just cause. Education became obligatory, and had to be *secular* and "inspired by ideals of human solidarity" (Article 48). Much attention was devoted to the mechanism of administration. The President of the Republic was to be chosen in a complicated way in which an electoral college, consisting of all the members of the Cortes and an equal number of outside electors chosen like deputies, selected the chief executive for a period of six years. The President could suspend the Cortes for a brief period and dissolve it entirely on no more than two occasions during his term of office, provided that on each dissolution he ordered new elections within sixty days. On the second dissolution the Cortes could censure his action. An absolute majority of the Cortes would automatically bring about the deposition of the President. This may sound very complex, but historically it is extremely important, since Alcalá Zamora was forced out of office in precisely this manner.

A number of points may be noted regarding the Constituent Assembly. First of all, its general level was not remarkably high. The intellectuals who had placed so much hope in this gathering of the representatives of the people were either silent or their words went unheeded. Such interventions as that of Miguel de Unamuno against the more rabid excesses of regionalism were literally voices crying in the wilderness. Many of them were profoundly disgusted at the antics of the Cortes. José Ortega y Gasset, writing in the paper *Luz* under the significant title, "These Republicans are not the Republic," described the constitution as "lamentable, without head nor feet nor the rest of the organic matter that is customarily found between the feet and the head" (June 16, 1932). The debate over the anticlerical articles is one of the most glaring examples of chicanery, parliamentary double talk, and unparalleled sophistry. Manuel Azaña calmly pronounced his conviction that Spain had ceased to be Catholic at all.[17] Fernando de los Ríos argued that the Church would be spiritually purified if it lost everything, and the State, quite incidentally, enriched. Azaña was particularly cynical in his treatment of the problem. When it was a question of freedom of conscience or the protection of the State — meaning specifically the Second Republic — the protection of the State must always come first. And indeed it did as later legislation showed.[18] It is astonishing how frequently the idea recurs

---

[17] *Diario de Sesiones,* Madrid, Oct. 13, 1931.
[18] *El Sol,* Madrid, Oct. 14, 1931.

throughout the history of the Second Republic that it must be protected, defended, and secured against those who would overturn it. The insistence on this defensive attitude gives one at times the impression that the Republic never really believed that there were enough republicans in Spain to justify its existence.

The upshot of the debate on religion was that the Society of Jesus was expelled and every Order ceased its teaching activities, since according to the "liberal" Manuel Azaña, everything they professed was contrary to the modern State. Admittedly illiberal though the proposal was, it was considered necessary to avoid anything that smacked of proselytizing in Spain. That is, the only proselytizing that was to be allowed was that engineered day in and day out by the Republic itself. In a word, the new Spanish democracy was going to make Spain republican and secularist by law, decree, and force, if need be, and all this quite obviously in the best democratic tradition. Never was the idea that the most incredibly intolerant are precisely those who propose to push their brand of tolerance down everyone's throat better illustrated than in the debates of the Spanish republican Cortes. The Prime Minister Alcalá Zamora, and Maura, the Home Secretary, both resigned — to their everlasting credit. Manuel Azaña was promptly ushered in as the new head of the government and demagoguery had taken one further step forward with the retirement of Alcalá Zamora temporarily from the scene.

How did the country receive this new constitutional dispensation? The masses were busily engaged making their own revolution. Strikes, disorders, and the like characterized every day in Spain. Grotesque incidents occurred constantly: at Uncastillo the lands were distributed without so much as the leave of parliament; at Corral de Almaguer the mob simply put the local mayor in jail and proceeded to social reform according to its own primitive conception; at Cúllar de Baza bloodshed took place as a result of violent encounters between clashing extremist factions. The strikes were one unbroken series of disorders, carried out by the naval construction workers in Gijón, the tramway employees in Seville, the peasants in Córdoba, and the gas and electric workers in Barcelona. Bombs and other weapons played a leading role in many of these disturbances, more political in character than economic. *El Socialista,* of Madrid, hardly an organ of moderate opinion, expressed its disquietude by saying: "Industry is in crisis. There is no work. In these difficult times for the national economy, the communists and syndicalists can find nothing better than to force workers into strikes . . . it is necessary that the working class be not misled by this empty agitation that leads only to unfortunate results" (Jan. 17, 1932). The extreme Left had already showed its claws with *Solidaridad Obrera* demanding the expulsion of Alcalá Zamora and Maura, the two more conservative elements in the first provisional cabinet: "The hour has come to kick the Alcalá-Maura combination out. They are pure Bourbons in blood. Down with the enemies of the Revolution and with the assassins. A Republic run by hangmen and murders interests no one" (July 2, 1931). The Home Secretary suggested at one point action against the syndicalists and communists which the socialists supported willingly, since anything that handicapped their rivals was desirable. But the Catalan government refused to accept the proposal, for Macià depended too much on the syndicalists to do anything against them. The civil governor of Catalonia, José Oriol Anguera de Sojo, supposedly the representative of the central government, was favorable to action curtailing the extremists. Macià demanded his resignation. Azaña — successor to Alcalá Zamora — acceded and Anguera de Sojo resigned.

The year 1932 opened with a constitution, a republic, a permanent government, and rising social and economic disorder over the entire country. The catalogue of disturbances would take a dozen pages merely to list. The communists launched movements against the civil guard and the police. In Castilblanco four civil guards were assassinated; in Jeresa, Valencia province, and in Calzada de Calatrava, Ciudad Real province, similar crimes took place. The classic comment of a leading socialist was that if in Castilblanco there had been no police, nothing would have happened. It was the period of jockeying between the socialists, who urged a gradual evolution toward socialism, and the anarcho-syndicalists who, now that the lid was off, were pushing the masses toward direct action. The tragedy in the government was that theoretical socialists had no idea of how to deal with the threat or no wish to deal with it, while the middle-class republican element, tied to the government by commitments, was helpless in the face of increasing anarchy.

One of the extraordinary acts of the Cortes was the passage of the "Law for the Defense of the Republic," approved a week after Azaña became Prime Minister. This law provided in essence that the Home Secretary, called in Spanish the *Ministro de Gobernación*, could suspend meetings, suppress associations, close centers, clubs, and other meeting places, and curtail newspapers. It presumed to empower the

Home Office with the authority to deal with strikes. As a matter of plain fact it was the instrument that allowed the Republic to violate with impunity every one of the personal guarantees contained in the Constitution. In a word, we have a written Constitution, in theory liberal and respectful of individual rights, followed within a matter of weeks by an all-embracing decree that gave the government power to violate legally every one of the constitutional precepts, and this is precisely what happened. The Republic became very quickly the principal persecutor of the Spanish people; the jails were filled with political prisoners, while the press — that is, the right-wing press — was hampered time and again in its legitimate task of criticizing the government. The Spanish Constitution, as an excellent expression of modern liberal thought, was inoperative from the start, for the Cortes deliberately provided itself with the full measure of authority to silence the opposition.

Meanwhile the disastrous religious policy was in full swing. The democratic Spanish Republic had declared everything that the Church or its ministers possessed to be the property of the State. Somewhat later the government decreed that the State might, in certain instances, consider these properties for ecclesiastical use, provided nothing given back to the Church was of artistic or historical value. The expulsion of the Jesuits and the elimination of the religious from teaching produced a body blow to the whole educational structure of the country.[19]

---

[19] Manuel Graña, *¿Que debe España a los religiosos?*, Madrid, 1932, points out in full detail exactly what the various orders and communities were doing when the Republic closed down on their activities. A few examples will suffice to show how much Spain owed the communities and of what it was deprived by the sectarian mania of the Republic. Augustinians: Center of Higher Studies at the Escorial, vast mission labor in the Far East, and Center of Historical Studies at San Millán de la Cogolla. Jesuits: social action, Catholic women's circles, credit unions, activity in reducing illiteracy, Colegio Máximo de Oña, reviews and publications, Colegio Máximo Sarriá with its brilliant work in science, and the Commercial University of Deusto in Bilbao. Salesians: administration of first printing school in Spain and care of over 17,000 poor children. Benedictines: the great monastery of Montserrat. Brothers of Saint John of God: administration of insane asylums, institutions for the blind, and care of 5000 feeble-minded. Franciscans: 42 schools in Spanish Morocco and 676 schools with 78,000 children in the peninsula. Capuchins: work in juvenile delinquency. Dominicans: missions in the Philippines and intellectual work in Spain.

The listing of the vast work of the women religious fills, as in the case of the book of Graña, an entire volume. All of this was to be eliminated because the Republic felt it could not survive with religious caring for the sick, the poor, and the needy.

From December, 1931, to November, 1933, the Republic lived under a government of the Left. The new cabinet was much the same as the provisional cabinet with a few shifts. Manuel Azaña, head of the government, left among his other possessions a personal diary, the text of which is a startling confirmation of the worst suspicions regarding the general incompetence of the ministers. Under date of December 9, 1932, Azaña speaks of himself as "surrounded by imbeciles." Marcelino Domingo, new Minister of Agriculture, was described by his superior as "totally ignorant of everything relating to rural life." The socialists continued as the dominant element, thanks to the fact that they had a large trade-union organization behind them, while the radicals and ordinary run of republicans, not represented in the new cabinet, were less fortunate, for their electoral force was nebulous and in some cases scarcely existent. The socialist party was prospering in power; from some 30,000 members in 1930, it now claimed 200,000 in 1932. A curious contradiction existed in the fact that socialist provincial and municipal officials saw no reason for checking social agitation merely because their party was in power. The civil governor of Córdoba reported the following: "I ordered a careful check of the dangerous elements in this province. My attention was called to the fact that the most dangerous were the mayor and municipal judge. There are many dangerous mayors. The majority of the city halls are in socialist hands and the socialist mayors are calamitous. Between mayors, judges and the commissions in charge of the rural police, you can easily imagine the state of affairs in this province."[20]

On January 18, 1932, an anarcho-syndicalist outbreak took place in the Llobregat basin, and at Cardoner, in Catalonia. The Madrid government acted in this case, largely because the uprising was not socialist inspired, although Macià in Barcelona opined that if the workers had received a just treatment this would never have occurred.

A further word regarding the essential liberties which the Republic was supposed to defend as the reason for its existence. This aspect is important because it forms the basis of the whole *apologia* for the Republic by its own partisans and sympathizers abroad. If the Spanish Republic was really democratic, respectful of individual rights, and scrupulous in its regard for the guarantees of the Constitution, that is one thing; if, on the other hand, it can be shown that the Republic, acting under the "Law for the Defense of the Republic,"

---

[20] *Informaciones,* Madrid, January 23, 1932.

paid not the slightest attention to the fundamental charter or to the most elementary rights of its citizens, then one of the essential bases of the whole structure collapses. We may divide this brief summary under the following items: (1) the right to work; (2) freedom of expression; (3) religious liberty; (4) public opinion and constitutional guarantees.

The Spanish Constitution, as already indicated, proclaimed the nation a Republic of workers. But it is necessary to point out that there were several special categories of workers. During the struggle to overturn the monarchy there had been some temporary evidence of solidarity among the various labor organizations, but under the Republic, the bitter rivalry of the U.G.T. (socialist) and C.G.T. (anarcho-syndicalist) became open and irreconcilable. The socialist federation was the apple of the government's eye, while the anarchists were treated with very great severity. Casas Viejas, Figueras, Sallent, and Figols are all names that figure in the repression of the anarchists. Strikes and layoffs became so common that Spain was literally in the grip of constant, implacable social warfare. Non-Marxist workers were often forced into unemployment, and to behold workers begging was a common sight on the streets of Spanish cities.

The socialists insisted on passing a law, known as the *"Ley de Términos municipales,"* a restrictive measure aimed at controlling migrant labor, especially in the rural areas. According to the law no laborer could be engaged who was not registered in the local municipality as a resident. In some areas the man power available was sufficient, in others it was necessary at harvest-time to contract additional workers from other districts. This was now prohibited by law with disastrous results to the agricultural communities. The measure was promulgated on April 28, 1932, and later abrogated. One of the main causes of the discontent and violence all over the countryside was this legislative measure so contrary to the nature and demands of Spanish agriculture and such a manifest restriction on the freedom of choice of residence and of movement. The freedom of work was seriously hampered by the constant use of the strike as a political weapon. In three years of the Republic, 15,000 strikes took place with a loss in wages estimated at over 230 million pesetas.

Article 34 of the Constitution could not be improved upon as a guarantee of the freedom of expression. The question is, was this article really applied, and especially did it ever apply to the legal, recognized opposition to the government? The "Law for the Defense of the Republic" had provided that any source of information might be curtailed that, in the opinion of the government itself, "might perturb public order and peace." This was an extraordinary weapon indeed in the hands of the socialist majority and the suspension of newspapers became a routine affair. *El Debate* was suspended so many times that it is difficult to keep count of them. Between May 11, 1931, and August, 1932, the opposition newspapers which were rigidly censored, fined, or suppressed reached such an enormous figure that to enumerate them would fill several pages.[21] One of the results, however, of the persecution of the large dailies such as *A.B.C.* and *El Debate* was the fantastic increase in their circulation as soon as the suspension was removed. The extremists then used other methods to undermine the opposition press. A strike was called in *A.B.C.* in 1934 because a single workman was not identified with the *Casa del Pueblo*. The upshot was a general strike in every printing establishment on March 12, 1934, with no papers appearing at all in Madrid except *El Socialista,* organ of the socialist party, which had the field clear for itself. Although the strike failed, it became a powerful weapon to make impossible the maintenance of a normal opposition press. *El Socialista* had this commentary to make on the situation: "The Revolution will come at the proper time. When it does come, it will not be for the purpose of new merit points for the government in power but to the end that the working class may seize power" (March 14, 1934).

In addition to the "Law for the Defense of the Republic," the government utilized the "*Ley de Orden Público,*" a handy arrangement to cover up whatever limitations were placed on free speech and assembly. The government was equally active in supervising the theater. It may

[21] Although the list is not complete, the extent of the measures may be judged from the following suspensions: Madrid: *A.B.C., El Debate, Informaciones, Diario Universal, El Siglo Futuro,* and *La Nación.* Alava: *Heraldo Alavés.* Albacete: *El Diario de Albacete.* Alicante: *El Día, La Gaceta de Levante, Patria, El Pueblo Obrero,* and *La Voz del Pueblo.* Almería: *La Independencia, Diario de Almería,* and *Heraldo de Almería.* Ávila: *El Diario de Ávila.* Balearic Islands: *El Luchador.* Barcelona: *El Correo Catalán.* Burgos: *El Castellano,* and *A.B.C.* Cáceres: *Extremadura,* and *El Faro de Extremadura.* Cádiz: *Nuestro Tiempo, Diario de Jérez, Claridad, La Información,* and *Regeneración.* Ciudad Real: *El Pueblo Manchego.* Córdoba: *El Defensor de Córdoba.* Granada: *El Ideal.* La Coruña: *El Ideal Gallego, La Verdad, El Compostelano.* León: *El Diario de León, La Luz de Astorga, El Pensamiento Astorgano.* Murcia: *La Verdad, El Eco de Cartagena, Cartagena Nueva.* Oviedo: *La Región.*

The list could be extended indefinitely, with Segovia, Seville, Valencia, Valladolid, Zamora, Zaragoza all represented by newspapers and reviews that were suppressed.

seem extraordinary that in the atmosphere of the Spanish Republic, where virtually anything seemed to be tolerated, there should be a severe censorship of the theater. But the secret is that the grounds were not moral; they were exclusively political. If the street vendors and corner kiosks were free to sell anything in the way of pornography, the field of politics was far more delicate. A play such as *La cartera de Marina,* at the Teatro Cervantes, with a number of ironical allusions to the government was broken up by the police. The review *Chungonia* was treated in like manner even though the impresarios had submitted the production to the Home Office and it had been cleared. A comedy by José Juan Cardenas was forbidden because it criticized some aspect of the socialist labor legislation. Jacinto Benavente suffered the humiliation of a positive scandal because in his play, *La melodia del jazz,* there was a slight reference to the Minister of Finance.[22] It is hardly necessary to add that the constitutional guarantee of the inviolability of correspondence was constantly mocked. The history of the Republic is one constant protest against the system of opening correspondence and exercising a literal censorship over every thought uttered even in private.

The religious persecution assumed gigantic proportions because the socialist government created a problem that had no basis in reality. The religious instruction imparted in the schools and the system of Catholic education from the primary to the university formed a part of the national cultural tradition and the efforts to destroy it represented from any point of view an outrage against education and a completely antidemocratic technique. It might be well for the defenders of the Republic — and their number is legion — to explain how a minority, such as the socialists, could possibly justify on a democratic basis a policy that ran directly counter to the sentiments of the overwhelming majority of the Spanish people. The republic put into effect the most dogmatic, tyrannical, and intolerant of all policies; the rigid secularism that brooked no opposition and no deviation. It imposed on a profoundly religious people an improvised, ill-digested, and ill-conceived laicism that in the minds of the socialist leaders passed for "democracy" and was simply a form of fatuous illiteracy. The elimina-

[22] As an item, amusing and absurd at the same time, the criminal phrase introduced by Benavente that merited the protest against the play was the following: "You act like a Finance Minister," one actor shouted. The second actor replied, "God made him that way!" The scandal was so great and the mob so violent in its threat to burn down the theater that Benavente was forced to appear and promise to exclude the phrase in future presentations. This was the "democratic" Republic.

tion of Catholic education did not mean that the State schools were going to improve overnight. The destruction of the former simply meant that thousands of children had no place to go at all and a new burden was added to the already heavy economic responsibility of the State. The Minister of Public Instruction, De los Ríos, announced blandly that the school population of 350,000 left without instruction by the law against the religious orders would promptly be absorbed by the opening of 7000 new schools. These figures, quite beyond the capacity of the government to carry out, merely confirm the thesis that the Spanish socialists lived in a dream world peculiarly their own, and with only the slightest relation to the real world of affairs.

The utter disregard for the will of those masses about whom the government talked so much may be seen in the reaction of the cabinet, and especially of Azaña, to the partial elections of 1933. Despite the fact that the vote had gone definitely against the government, which managed to obtain some 5000 seats out of 16,000. The problem to the Prime Minister was quite simple: "The only thing about the Sunday elections of any importance is that they were held in 2400 towns that would be called Rotten Boroughs in other countries."[23] The Prime Minister added that, "to say that the Spanish people have spoken in these elections is an exaggeration." With that flippancy the good democratic tradition was respected and the government remained in office.

In this short analysis of the absence of respect for personal liberty and the dignity of the individual, a word must be added regarding another very common practice in the Republic: the confiscation of personal property and the exiling of undesirable individuals to such dubious places as Bata and Villa Cisneros in Spanish Africa. Article 42 of the Constitution stated that: "In no case can the government exile or deport Spanish citizens a distance exceeding 250 kilometers from their place of residence." On February 11, 1932, the steamship *Buenos Aires* left Barcelona for Bata in Spanish Guinea with 104 deportees aboard. After the uprising of August 10, 1932, the deportations became almost a steady stream. It became common even in the Cortes for the government deputies, when an opposition speaker rose to challenge a socialist contention, to scream "To Bata, To Bata" at him. A long chapter could be written on the murderous policy of shipping political enemies off to vegetate in Africa in many cases after months in prison without trial and with no formal charges lodged against them.

[23] *Diario de Sesiones,* April 25, 1933.

The cases of the breaking up of meetings and the like are so frequent as to defy summary. To illustrate the technique of the socialist revolution: on January 17, 1932, 10,000 Catholics in Bilbao met in the Frontón Euskalduna. The socialists found no better way to break up the meeting than to shoot on them, with the result that three persons were killed. As a protest against this meeting and evidence of the pure democracy of which the socialists were advocates, the mob proceeded to burn the office of the newspaper *Gaceta del Norte,* destroy a convent, and the office of Catholic Action. The government met this situation by imposing a fine of 1,000 pesetas on the Sacred Heart College, on the basis that the nuns had fired from its roof.

The *Diario de Sesiones* for November 23, 1932, offers a remarkable bit of reading matter. Azaña was accused among other things of imposing the "Law for the Defense of the Republic" which some of the deputies claimed violated the Constitution. The Prime Minister responded airily: "What difference does it make what the Constitution says! I have no intention of departing an inch from this policy. When I drew up the Law for the Defense of the Republic, I stated that it was six months too late. The government merely regrets its generosity during the early stages." Here we have in splendid synthesis the spirit, the attitude, and the policy of the Second Spanish Republic. What difference if the Constitution did protect the individual, if this were inconvenient for the socialists? What if deportations are forbidden when exile to Africa is so handy to silence the irritating opposition? Moreover, the recognition and respect of these rights was merely "generosity."

It might have been tolerable if Spain were being well run, but even the blessing of efficiency was denied the unfortunate citizenry during those turbulent two years. The dollar was quoted at 9.09 pesetas on April 11, 1931; on January 16, 1932, it was at 11.86; and in May had reached 13.27. The increase of bureaucracy and the Catalan statute that left Catalonia to handle its own fiscal affairs had reduced the State's income with disastrous effects on the public administration.

Chapter 8. INFERNO LET LOOSE

THE disestablishment of the Church was not effected by a single law or an isolated act. It had its origin in the Constitution itself and was completed by the Law on Congregations, drafted in October, 1932, and promulgated some months later. The most drastic feature was that all teaching by religious must end by October 1, 1933, for the secondary schools and other institutions, and December 1 for the primary. There was some concrete progress made by the first Republican government in the educational field. Marcelino Domingo had set out to create the *escuela única,* that is a symmetrical organization of instruction from the primary to the university. In 1932 some 2500 new schools were opened and the salaries of teachers raised. Pedagogical missions were sent about in the country to bring culture to the unenlightened. Fernando de los Ríos, who succeeded Domingo in the post of Education Minister, could point to a certain number of activities as indicative of the effort of the Republic to produce results in this field. It is doubtful if the newly created schools, the teachers improvised in intensive short courses, and the various cultural enterprises on a university scale ever offset the ravages caused by the ousting of the religious and the consequent increase of the number of school children without instruction. Before the provisions of the law came into effect, the government fell and a new era of two years' duration began.

It may be useful to draw attention to the two fundamental documents on the religious situation of Spain during these critical two years. The basic one is, of course, the Encyclical Letter of His Holiness, Pius XI, *Dilectissima Nobis,* dated June 3, 1933. The text of this Encyclical is the most far-reaching condemnation of the policy of the Republic regarding religion that can be found, and the fact that His Holiness felt obliged to address the Spanish hierarchy and people in the most emphatic and unambiguous terms reveals the profound effect that the religious persecution had caused in the mind of the Church. "We have been astonished to learn that some, to justify the iniquitous procedures against the Church, have given as a reason the necessity of defending the Republic." The Holy Father refers to the "deplorable law on religious sects and congregations," and other expressions used in the Encyclical are equally strong. They refer to "the usurpation of the State" and assert that "while the Church is denied the right to dispose freely of what belongs to it, after it has been legitimately acquired or given to it by the faithful, the State assumes the power of disposing of this property for other ends entirely."

The Pope protested against the inhuman treatment of religious and the deliberate republican policy of submitting them to the maximum of vexations and annoyances. The insult to the Holy Father was patent in the law providing for the specific suppression of the Jesuits. In the Encyclical the Pontiff expressed his anxiety at this measure and in its concluding paragraphs urged Spanish Catholics to await the future with serenity, and above all to gather about their bishops and clergy in Catholic Action as the best means of defending their legitimate interests.[1]

The Encyclical had been preceded by the collective statement of the Spanish bishops, dated May 25, 1933, in which the list of complaints against the Republic is detailed, running from the seizure of cemeteries to the imposition of secularism in every school in the country. Catholic parents were urged to make very special efforts to preserve their children from the unfortunate influence of the aggressively secularist school that now prevailed. The reading of this solemn document is convincing evidence of the justice of the Church's position in the face of unwarranted attack and the careful examination of the Collective Letter is recommended to admirers of the "democratic" Republic as a prudent and thoughtful statement of the anguish of Spanish Catholics under constant pressure from the socialist minority.

The reader may well wonder why no reaction against the government was evident during these strenuous two years. There was a reaction, although it manifested itself in an unfortunate way. On August 10, 1932, a military uprising occurred in Seville. General Sanjurjo addressed a manifesto to the people of that city in which he said:

> In a year and a half of tyrannical sectarianism, the national economy has suffered losses running into millions. The sentiments of thousands of Spaniards have been outraged, the agencies of defense weakened and the armed forces

[1] Spanish text of Encyclical, Zaragoza, 1933; included in *Colección de Encíclicas y Cartas pontificias,* Madrid, 1942, p. 343 sq.

wantonly insulted. Criminality has increased and strikes are rampant. . . . We do not come to impose a regime contrary to the Republic but to liberate Spain from the oligarchy that in a year has caused the country such grave moral and material damage.[2]

The government was aware of the preparations for an uprising, and the failure to count on an element of surprise was undoubtedly the factor that doomed the movement to defeat. In Madrid the whole affair was liquidated in a couple of hours. I was in Madrid that morning of August 10, when, in the small hours, an attack was made on the Central Post Office and War Ministry and shooting took place in the Plaza de Cibeles. By dawn the evidence had been removed and the first news available to the Madrid public was that the uprising had been promptly repressed. In Seville the momentary success of the rebels was far greater and it seemed for a few hours that they would maintain control of the city with the support of a considerable sector of the civilian population.

The failure in Madrid had serious repercussions and was the cause of lack of support of other garrisons and cities. Manuel Azaña spoke to the Cortes on August 11 regarding the events of the previous day and, although his version may have to be rectified in its details, it is striking that the Prime Minister placed the greatest emphasis on the revolutionary conduct of the masses in resisting General Sanjurjo and who, in their excitement, proceeded to the classical destruction of property and churches. Azaña confided to the expectant chamber his impressions:

Masses of citizenry, of whose party affiliation I am ignorant, burned the following buildings: Círculo de Labradores, the newspaper *La Unión,* the residence of the Marquise de Esquivel, where General Sanjurjo had his headquarters, the residence of Luca de Tena, the Círculo Mercantil, the Blanco printing shop, the San Ildefonso Church, the offices of *A.B.C.,* a garage, and the home of José María Ibarra.[3]

The Republic took full advantage of the incident to bring some 80 accused before the bar of justice for conspiracy and plotting to restore the monarchy. There were 138 citizens, military and civilians, shipped off to Villa Cisneros without a trial of any kind. Sanjurjo himself was condemned and, as so often occurs in Spain in similar circumstances, later pardoned. EXILED IN PORTUGAL.

The story of bloodshed and violence during these two years of the

---

[2] Quoted in Fernández Almagro, *Historia de la república española,* p. 55.
[3] *Diario de Sesiones,* August 11, 1932.

Left domination did not end with August 10, for on January 12, 1933, one of the most famous incidents in republican history took place at Casas Viejas. The syndicalists and anarchists had planned a general attack on the garrisons and barracks all over Spain. In Lérida the attempt caused considerable confusion and loss of life; in Andalucía it was put down with greater difficulty; and at Casas Viejas fourteen individuals, forced to surrender and submit to arrest, were killed by their guards. Captain Rojas, the commander of the assault guards, was held responsible for the murders. The matter was wildly discussed in the Cortes and the government was accused of the most brutal methods in its attempt to suppress, not the spirit of revolution, to which it was wedded as strongly as the anarcho-syndicalists, but the successful revolutionary activity of these groups. The incident produced a clear-cut division in the Cortes; the Right criticizing unmercifully the methods of the Azaña government. The more moderate republicans, liberals, radicals, and, of course, the small monarchist and traditionalist sector in the chamber now formed a group irretrievably lost to the blandishments and machinations of the socialists in power. The Republic and the socialist party became virtually synonymous after Casas Viejas, and was forced very soon thereafter to face new elections.

The second anniversary of the Republic was celebrated on April 14, 1933. The extreme Left proclaimed the total failure of the revolution from above and even the republicans were disheartened by the course of events. The jurist, Sánchez Román, writing in *El Imparcial,* stated that the agrarian reform and the legislation that had followed it had contributed "to a still greater depression in agriculture and the same phenomenon is taking place in other branches of the public administration" (April 14, 1933). The tragic thing was, according to Sánchez Román, that "there is a tendency on the part of the government when circumstances get out of control — which is frequent — to by-pass the law and solve the immediate situation by arbitrary methods, abandoning each time this occurs a further part of its authority."

During 1933 a new word entered the Spanish language, *republicanizar.* The republican press popularized it, proclaiming that everything had to be "republicanized." The impression was that almost nothing in Spain was republican, even after two years of the regime. A new wave of petty persecution began. The careful reading of the *Gaceta de Madrid* for this period reveals an astonishing number of dismissals from public service. The Minister of Justice, Alvaro de

Albornoz, fired judges, magistrates, and public prosecutors for the most banal reasons. Among the more serious charges that could be leveled against a citizen occupying public office was that he belonged to a religious society, received religious in his home, or did not express his enthusiastic support of the Republic with sufficient vehemence. Miguel de Unamuno, never one to be blinded by partisan fury, irritatedly cried out that "Even the Inquisition was limited by the guarantee of rights. There is something worse than even that; the police Inquisition based on a general feeling of panic, and the invention of dangers for the purpose of getting authorization to proceed outside the law."[4] This "feeling of panic" was gradually creeping over Spain. *Vanguardia,* the Barcelona daily, expressed it in saying:

> It is useless to write or to protest. The Barcelona press is the recipient of thousands of complaints. The citizens are expressing their growing indignation in every tone. But all in vain. In Barcelona there are murder, attacks, the explosion of bombs, shooting frays in the streets, and every day innumerable crimes are committed. What do the authorities do about it? At times they meet solemnly and mysteriously and make long statements to the press. . . . In Catalonia anarchy is in control (July 6, 1933).

The government faced a crisis, but there was hesitation about dissolving the Cortes, for the partial elections of the spring of 1933, as already mentioned, showed a decided trend against the government and further evidence piled up that the government had lost the confidence of its electors. Elections were finally proclaimed for November 19, 1933.

In view of the fact that this was the beginning of the two-year interim of Right republican rule, it may be interesting at this point to indicate the composition and doctrine of those who were to assume the reins of government during this stormy middle period. José María Gil Robles had become the outstanding representative of the parliamentary opposition. On April 15, the day after the proclamation of the Republic, Angel Herrera, Director of *El Debate,* suggested to a group of young Catholic laymen in Chamartín de la Rosa the idea of forming a rightist group that would reflect traditionalist thought within the framework of the new Republic, and by the end of the month *Acción Nacional* was formed and duly registered with the Home Office. In its proclamation to the nation, the new group emphasized that it was not strictly a political party but a social movement for the defense of institutions not definitely identified with a particular political regime.

[4] Address delivered in the *Ateneo* of Madrid, November 28, 1932.

Little by little *Acción Nacional* became the firm redoubt of opposition to the socialist-dominated Republic. On May 18 the first central committee was formed with Angel Herrera as chairman. The movement very soon became a political party, and Gil Robles appeared at once as the most able and eloquent exponent of its doctrine. The party was forced to abandon the expression *nacional* in its title by virtue of a decree prohibiting its use for specific political parties and henceforth it was to be known as *Acción Popular.* By October 22 the first general congress was held with over 500 delegates representing a body of electors estimated at more than 600,000. The immediate result of this activity was an alliance with other rightist elements, under the general name of the *Confederación española de Derechas autónomas,* called in the alphabetical jargon of the day, the C.E.D.A. The main problem of this period was to reconcile the various rightist groups, some of whom were willing to seek a stable regime within the Republic, while others were frankly monarchist and did not go along with the Republic at all. Gil Robles established his own position quite clearly in his speech at Valencia in November, 1932, where he insisted that *Acción Popular* operate within the Republic. The problem then became one of determining if there was any possibility of a conservative transformation under the existing republican institutions. Could any rightist party really bring about changes that would stop the wild demagoguery that had distinguished the first two years? There was the possibility, too, of intelligence with the radical party, the one republican element that was passably conservative and willing to salvage as much as was possible from the wreck of the national institution under the 1931 Constitution. The final crisis of the Republic before the fateful elections of November, 1933, was a series of ephemeral ministries, responsibility for the last of which fell on Martínez Barrio, who formed a government on October 9, the very date on which President Alcalá Zamora dissolved the Cortes and called for new elections.

The elections of November 19, 1933, were of enormous significance for the future of Spain. Largo Caballero was particularly vociferous in the course of the campaign in emphasizing the nature of the issue at stake. In speeches against the conservative republicans, he harped constantly on the need for a complete revolution to achieve the ends for which the Republic had been established. The elections, nonetheless, were a landslide for the conservatives. The Home Secretary did not announce the final results until three weeks after the voting, and when the returns were tabulated it was plain that the socialists had suffered a severe beating. The Right won 207 seats, the Center 167, and the Left 99. A large number of the Right were avowed traditionalists and monarchists, and the majority of the Center were radicals of the Lerroux persuasion who now held the balance of power. If these members voted with the Right, it would be a decisive majority; if they chose to stand with the Left, the Right would be incapable of effective action. The largest single party was that of Alejandro Lerroux, a parliamentarian of vast experience and a seasoned republican, whereas most of the rightist leaders were complete novices and in politics for the first time.

The two ensuing years were destined to be ones of extreme frustration and disappointment. Professor Peers sums it up nicely in saying that "The two years of Left rule were years of high hope and crushing disappointments, but the two years of Center rule were years of monotonous depression."[5] There was no doubt, however, that the Spanish electorate had exploded in indignation in November, 1933. The rightist candidates in the various Madrid constituencies had polled some 30,000 votes in 1931; in 1933 they received 130,000. One candidate, a bitter enemy of the Republic and everything it stood for, Count Guadalhorce, a former Minister under Primo de Rivera, received twice as many votes as his leftist opponent in Zaragoza in a constituency that was notorious for its radicalism. The startling fact was not that the Right should win in Castile or Navarre, where it was expected, but in Granada, Córdoba, and Asturias, where socialism was firmly entrenched. One consoling feature of the elections was that Azaña's own party, *Acción Republicana,* won only five seats. The monarchists of the two branches were represented by some 43.

But Spain was not due to enjoy a normal shift in government. Largo Caballero had screamed rebellion all over the land during the tumultuous campaign and had talked loosely of elections on the eighteenth and riots in the streets when the returns were formally and officially announced. And it was precisely on the day the results were formally proclaimed that the C.N.T. and the F.A.I., the two anarcho-syndicalist organizations, provoked one of the most serious episodes of unrest in republican history. Initiated with bombs and grenades in Barcelona, the movement spread with incredible rapidity to the entire peninsula and for days, in countless towns, the red and black flag of anarchism was displayed from public edifices. Town criers made

[5] Peers, *Spanish Tragedy,* Methuen & Co., London, p. 144.

their way through the streets demanding that citizens give up their arms with the proclamation of libertarian communism all over Spain. Lands were seized, shops and warehouses destroyed, money declared abolished, and chaos spread everywhere. Some of the incidents were extraordinarily bloody. Trains were blown up at Puzol in Valencia province; at Villanueva de la Serena armed regulars fought for an entire night with the anarchist and communist bands who sought to usher in the social revolution. The reports from the rest of the country revealed that Zaragoza was one of the worst nuclei of rebellion. But there were many others, among them Huesca, Peraltasar, and Teruel. In Madrid the general strike did not materialize and there was little disturbance since the U.G.T. had ordered its members to continue work. In the Cortes a new government was formed under Alejandro Lerroux. It was in this atmosphere that on December 16, 1933, Spain began the experiment of a Center-Right regime.

Gil Robles preferred to remain aloof from the actual responsibilities of government until a more opportune moment. His whole policy has been designated in Spain as that of *"el mal menor"* (the lesser evil), that is, an acceptance of realities however unpleasant and a consistent effort to make the best of adversity even under an ungovernable Republic.

The problems facing the Lerroux ministry were almost insoluble and the Prime Minister himself fell into contradiction in presenting his program, for he suggested that the new policy would conciliate all Spaniards in peace and order and at the same time retain the achievements of the republican legislature to date. The impossibility of restoring peace and good will in Spain as long as the legislation of the former Cortes remained on the statute books was clearly evident — this was precisely the terrible dilemma. How could the esteem and the support of Catholics be obtained without an abandonment of the violently sectarian, anticlerical legislation that weighed so heavily on the country? From the beginning Lerroux was the victim of vacillation to which the municipal elections in Catalonia, the first under the Statute in 1934 and favorable to the Left, contributed a feeling of instability.

Dark clouds hung over the future. The socialists were temporarily silenced but by no means inactive. Largo Caballero delivered a speech on January 14, 1934, in which he stated that:

> If the working class wants political power the first thing to do is to arm. It is indispensable to establish firmly in the conscience of the working class

> that to win they must fight the bourgeoisie in the streets, and without this there is no way to win power. With this preparation, the thing to do is to wait for the psychological moment to start the struggle, when it is agreeable to us and not to the enemy. Definitely there will have to be street fighting.[6]

The idea of the social revolution was on the march. Prieto in parliament and Largo Caballero in the streets were the guarantees that this would come to pass. The strikes continued; every day saw a repetition of the same disorders, violence, and unrest. Obviously there was a reaction, although not from the government. Martínez Barrio, Home Secretary, simply ignored the disturbances and blandly announced that people were too much concerned with problems of public order. The reaction came outside the government and to a large extent outside the Cortes. The *Falange Española* had been born in the autumn of 1933, and by the spring of the following year it began to show signs of vigorous life. The Falange was quite aware that the threats of street action by the Left was no empty rhetoric. By February they were particularly aware that their own existence was a challenge to the will to power on the part of the Marxists.[7]

The Falange was not the only group that sought to form a front against the rising tide of anarchy; in monarchist circles the opposition took the shape of two organizations: *Comunión Tradicionalista* and *Renovación Española,* the latter group particularly alive to the intellectual challenge that monarchism must meet. The first represented the Carlists and their deep traditionalism, while the second presented monarchist doctrine in contemporary garb and with practical solutions of modern difficulties. Men of the caliber of José Calvo Sotelo, Ramiro de Maeztu, and others, gave it a new vigor and impetus. In 1931 the review *Acción Española* had appeared; in 1933 the fundamental volume of Ramiro de Maeztu, *Defensa de la Hispanidad,* saw the light of day; and by late 1934, after the terrible uprising in Asturias, Calvo Sotelo contributed to the formation of what is known as the *Bloque Nacional,* a sort of rally of all the rightist elements in a common antirevolutionary front. The components ran from the traditionalists under Rodezno and Pradera, to nationalists, Catalans unfavorable to separatism, Basques, and monarchist sympathizers in general.

---

[6] *Claridad,* Jan. 15, 1934.

[7] The Falangist, Francisco de Paula Sampol, was murdered on January 11, 1934, and on February 9 the Falangist student, Matías Montero, was shot down on a Madrid street.

All was not well in the Lerroux cabinet. Martínez Barrio, then Home Secretary and years later one of the moving figures of the so-called Republic in exile, stated in an interview that he would have no truck with the Right and that the purity of the Republic must be defended at all costs. The only thing that this declaration cost him was his job.[8]

A political crisis occurred over the proposed amnesty for political prisoners, first and foremost among whom was General Sanjurjo. President Alcalá Zamora was disinclined to go along with the amnesty proposal or give in to the Right on this issue, while Lerroux was constantly forced, on this matter as in others, to weave a tortuous course between the Left and the Right, without displeasing either or both. Lerroux himself was forced out of office and, despite the obvious prestige of Gil Robles, the President charged an obscure member of the government, Ricardo Samper, with the formation of a new government. Much of the vacillation this time was due to the character of President Alcalá Zamora, one of the really pathetic figures in this whole political maelstrom. A former monarchist, converted to republicanism, a Catholic who believed in the efficacy of the Left, a moderate who invariably turned to extremists for support, Alcalá Zamora was no strong swimmer in the tumultuous eddies that ebbed and flowed in Spain. Alejandro Lerroux has said of him that "he suffered from a legalistic mentality."[9] Lerroux himself was no personality to bring the Spanish ship back on an even keel; a radical turned moderate, he possessed a vast political experience and no doctrine, and as an old-time agitator in Barcelona he was quite empty of anything but good intentions when the moment of crisis came. Under Samper, ineptitude reached dizzy heights and the round of murders, bombs, and bloodshed went merrily on.

A common characteristic of Madrid life in that spring of 1934 was the Sunday excursions of the socialist youth organizations to the near-by Sierra de Guadarrama. Not all the time was devoted to breathing pure mountain air, for the socialists found it expedient for military exercises and not infrequently used this newly acquired knowledge, on returning to the capital, in breaking up what they chose to call a "fascist" newsstand or a rightist center. During the same spring there was an attempt at a general strike of all

---

[8] *Blanco y Negro,* Feb. 5, 1934.

[9] Lerroux, *La pequeña historia. Apuntes para la historia grande vividos y redactados por el autor,* p. 109.

Spanish peasants — an unusually difficult form of social agitation. It was sponsored by the Marxist *Federación de Trabajadores de la Tierra* and was dominated by exclusively political aims.

The strike failed by the middle of June, but not before vast destruction of property and countless lives had been lost. Catalonia was in a state of effervescence, thanks to the passage by the *Generalitat* of a new law called the *Ley de cultivos,* aimed at settling a dispute between landowners and the *rabassaires* or cultivators of the land. The details are not necessary, and suffice it to say that the law was submitted to the Tribunal of Constitutional Guarantees, the court of appeal under the Constitution. This tribunal rejected the law on the grounds that Catalonia was not competent to legislate in the matter. The members of the *Esquerra catalana* in the Cortes retired in protest and Luis Campanys made lurid speeches about taking up arms to defend Catalonia, while the Barcelona left-wing press went wild in denunciation of this outrageous imposition of the central government. The controversy lasted for four months, until the Cortes voted confidence in the government and the government requested Catalonia not to apply the law. After that came the holidays and nothing happened. In August the situation became grave in the Basque provinces, due to the problem of the elections of the municipal councils. Luis Campanys proclaimed Catalonia's solidarity with persecuted *Euzkadi,* and the whole affair was drowned in a rising chorus of protest and denunciation. There seemed to many Spaniards a definite intelligence between socialists, left-wing republicans, and the various breeds of separatists in Catalonia, the Basque country, and to a lesser degree in Galicia. The government delayed still further the long overdue municipal elections.

The atmosphere of tension was fast rising. Gil Robles had announced in April that his assumption of power would not be long retarded. In September he denounced the rebellious attitude of the Basque country and Catalonia, and again promised that a stop would be put to this descent into anarchy.[10] This speech was delivered at Covadonga, in Asturias, the cradle of the Spanish nation. The Asturian proletariat responded to what it considered a threat by a general strike. Returning to Madrid, Gil Robles withdrew the support of the C.E.D.A. from the government in power, toppling the radicals neatly into the street. The government fell, but instead of Gil Robles as Prime Minister, Alejandro Lerroux popped back into power. Three members of the

[10] *El Sol,* Madrid, Sept. 11, 1934.

C.E.D.A. were included in this revamped cabinet. This incensed the delicate democratic sentiments of the Left, who denounced President Alcalá Zamora for his perfidy. The President was the victim of hostility from both sides and, in the estimation of many, amply merited it.

October 5 witnessed a general strike throughout the country, with particularly disturbing aspects in Asturias, for it was the prelude to the great uprising of 1934, the first chapter in the bloody tragedy of Red Spain. The incredible, the monstrous thing is not that the Marxists should have attempted to seize control through terror and violence, for that after all is their program and their avowed purpose, but that the so-called moderate republicans were incapable of lifting a finger to stop this rush toward destruction. In the Spain of 1934 no one able to read could claim ignorance of the intentions of the Marxists, for their press screamed their purpose day in and day out and their speakers made no effort to conceal their revolutionary aims:

> Is it necessary for us to say now . . . that any retreat or any attempt to go back to political forms that have become obsolete will inevitably meet with the resistance of the socialists? And this is not because we feel any strong Republican sentiments for we are cured of that. . . . The Republic can count on us as its enemies — not the Republic itself obviously, but the kind of Republic we are asked to respect and which in turn has never respected us. . . . Our relations with the Republic can only be of one sort — to surpass it and control it.[11]

The outbreak of October was separatist and anarchist in Catalonia and revolutionary in Asturias. This was the real beginning of a concerted drive to bring about the complete social revolution toward with the communist miners' trade union. With the slogan of "carry-the Republic. It was the counterrevolution setting itself up against the legal or constitutional revolution of 1931:

> One must not forget how the Spanish Republic came in. The originality with which it was born was bound to produce other originalities. The pacific and festive change of regime was succeeded by a counter-Revolution which, defeated in the streets, very soon established itself in power.[12]

Luis Campanys was defeated in Barcelona by General Batet, as mentioned briefly in the chapter on regionalism. The conflict in Asturias was of a different nature and extremely complex. The center of hostilities was the mining country, inhabited by about 30,000

---

[11] Editorial in *El Socialista,* Sept. 30, 1934.

[12] Antonio Ramos Oliveira, *La revolución española de octubre,* Madrid, 1935, p. 11.

miners, many of them affiliated with the U.G.T., and about a third with the communist miners' trade union. With the slogan of "carrying out revolutionary justice," the miners proceeded to apply their principles. They operated along the lines suggested by the *El Socialista* on the eve of the events:

> The next month may be our October. Hard days await us. The responsibility of the Spanish proletariat and its leaders is enormous. We have an army awaiting mobilization and our plans for socialization (Sept. 27, 1934).

The full story of the Asturias uprising is yet to be written. In his book, *La revolución de octubre,* Marcelino Domingo claims that De los Ríos and Indalecio Prieto were informed fully of the details of the plot. The traffic in arms must have been very considerable to supply the rebels with such quantities of explosives and firearms. The Lerroux government took office under the shadow of a rapidly forming social revolution. *El Socialista* pronounced its verdict, reflecting the feeling of the party and masses in saying: "The workers await the inescapable crisis, the consequence of the forces ranged against each other: marxists and anti-marxists. If our advice were asked, we would say quite simply to the anti-marxists: surrender!" (Oct. 3, 1934.)

The atmosphere in Madrid was heavily charged and it was rumored everywhere that October 5 would bring the Revolution. By the following day it was clear that everywhere, except in Asturias, it had been put down. Oddly enough the October Revolution — the month itself was almost symbolic as a recollection of the Bolshevik venture in Russia — was limited in its actual scope for Catalonia and Asturias were, in fact, the only two focal points of revolt. Andalucía, normally effervescent with activity, was quiet. Extremadura, where outbreaks of this kind were almost monotonously common, was equally tranquil. And, above all, Madrid did not move on a large scale despite every evidence of the contrary, while the War Minister, Diego Hidalgo, accepted the advice of General Francisco Franco in everything relating to the operations against the rebellious Asturians. "I kept General Franco close by, sure of his loyalty, talent, youth and extraordinary qualities as a brave and intelligent Spaniard."[13]

The course of the Asturian revolt was somewhat as follows: The general strike was called on October 5, under socialist direction. By the next day, however, the socialists were overcome by the more extreme elements. The miners, well supplied with arms, munitions, and

---

[13] *Diario de Sesiones,* Nov. 7, 1934.

dynamite, marched on Oviedo, Gijón, and Avilés, the principal Asturian cities. The various left-wing organizations were united in Asturias, with the majority in the C.N.T. The technique of revolution itself was invariably the same. The miners attacked the civil guard and assault forces with ferocity, and after reducing them, took over the community. Shops were sacked and money abolished, giving way to a system of *vales,* as they were called, for purchases. The clergy was invariably murdered as well as persons in the community belonging to rightist groups. Oviedo was in the power of the extremists for nine days, and during that brief period suffered three revolutionary committees as its government: one socialist, the second socialist and communist combined, and the third communist entirely. The latter were numerically the smallest of the three participating elements, but very much the best organized and by far the most aggressive in their determination to stamp out every trace of opposition.

The mining region, from the geographical point of view, admirably lends itself to guerrilla fighting. Despite long months of agitation and excesses preceding the month of October, the republican government had taken no steps to defend it or even to provide the proper security forces for Asturias. For two days Oviedo was quite isolated from the rest of the country, and nothing was known of events within the Asturian capital until government planes flew over it. The excesses committed within the city constitute a veritable catalogue of crime and savagery; convents and churches burned, the cathedral badly damaged, the university blown up, the banks looted, and the main business street, Calle de Uría, devastated. The martyrdom of Oviedo began in October, 1934, and was destined to be repeated during the autumn of 1936 when General Aranda established its defense. The city was saved in 1935 from complete destruction, thanks to the arrival of General López Ochoa with troops. General Franco had urged the transfer of adequate forces from Africa, since the local soldiery was incapable of restraining the infuriated miners. The experience of the Asturias rebellion was a preview of still more serious things to come; a premature exposure of motives and tactics on the part of the extreme Left.

The situation, however, in the winter of 1934–1935 was excellent for the establishment of a strong central government with authority to suppress the innumerable threats to national stability, for the Left was temporarily discredited and defeated, the army had shown itself loyal to law and order, and the Cortes was so constituted that a majority favorable to a vigorous policy was attainable. Azaña, Campanys, and other socialist leaders were in prison; Prieto had fled and the socialist *Casas del Pueblo* were closed. The fiasco of the movement in Catalonia and the Basque provinces had left the separatists without prestige and the entire country rejoiced that order had returned. Lerroux was actually hailed as the "savior of Spain."

When the Cortes reconvened in November, the government was given the fullest vote of confidence. There were several roads open for it: it could be authoritarian and implacably severe; it could be generous and forgiving and turn the culprits loose once more, or it could also combine the two courses with sagacity and perhaps attain the kind of normalcy most Spaniards wanted. The tragedy was that the government did not follow any intelligent, logical course, but simply drifted along from day to day with no orientation or sense of continuity. One reflects, in retrospect, that Spain might have been saved the great bloodletting of 1936 if the Lerroux ministry had proceeded differently — in a word, if the government had really governed. Some indication of its policy was the fact that of the twenty-three sentences of death that reached the Council of Ministers in November, only two were upheld, and no action against Azaña and Largo Caballero was taken, since technically their names were not linked with the Asturian uprising. So, then, as the months wore on the rebellion began to take on the air of a glorious crusade; the Left hailing it as a significant step in the right direction. Fernando de los Ríos and Juan Negrín among other socialists visited Asturias in January of 1935, and the former expressed himself in *Le Populaire* of Paris as deeply impressed by the resemblance between the Asturian movement and the Paris commune of 1871. Lerroux did not seem particularly alarmed by this evidence of a trend of the extreme Left toward unity.

The spring of 1935 witnessed a series of ministerial changes. Gil Robles withdrew the C.E.D.A. representatives from the cabinet and for a time the only parties represented were the radical and a small one called the progressive, identified with President Alcalá Zamora. The systematic exclusion of the C.E.D.A. from power, despite its evident greater strength in the Cortes, was one of the extraordinary facts of the time. *El Debate* editorialized to this effect:

> People everywhere have demanded that the cabinet reflect the division of the Cortes. But the most numerous single group, with forty more members than any other, is not offered the direction of the government, nor even an equitable share in the cabinet posts. . . . The party never asked for anything,

did not overthrow governments, nor obstruct legislation, but always supported loyally the government in power. No one can explain the treatment that the party of Gil Robles has received (April 3, 1935).

The historical problem posed for the Right in parliament was simple: could it function as a representative majority within the Republic as then constituted? The conclusion seems to be that the fault lay in two directions: first, the inability of Gil Robles and his group to take the positive action needed at the psychological moment and, second, the weakness and impotence of the republican institutions to do more than temporize. There was a proposal for the reform of the constitution, backed, among others, by Alcalá Zamora himself, and a revision was called for of relations with the Church, the regional statutes, and a number of other basic points. The Left was unanimous in its opposition to such modification; the extreme Right, symbolized by Calvo Sotelo, wished to go much further: "If the proposed constitutional reform is to be immediate, partial, and parliamentary, I do not believe in it. The problem is one of total revision not substitution."[14]

Meanwhile, the government tried to carry on Gil Robles' undertaking to reorganize and strengthen the army. There was discussion of the Catalan question which had become urgent after the suspension of the Autonomy Charter as a result of the events of October and the agrarian question demanded immediate attention. From January to October, 1935, 254 armed assaults had taken place over the country, including one against the city hall in Madrid. In September another crisis occurred, forcing a reshuffling of the cabinet. Lerroux's fall from power was provoked by a scandal known as the *straperlo*. A Dutchman, Daniel Strauss, had undertaken to establish several gambling houses in Spain and had obtained, by means of discreet bribes, it was said, official authorization to this end despite the legal prohibition. He was to establish these centers in San Sebastián and Formentor, Mallorca. The enterprises failed and Strauss denounced the situation to the President. A number of the top figures in the radical party were involved, and Alcalá Zamora lost no time in eliminating Lerroux from the direction of the cabinet. In October a parliamentary committee looked into the matter and suggested the proper steps to be taken.

There were other minor scandals, and the most distressing feature for the C.E.D.A., which had no responsibility in the deals, was that it was linked in the government with the radicals. Under the guidance

[14] Speech delivered at *Renovación española,* Madrid, March 8, 1935.

of Chapaprieta, Finance Minister as well as chairman of the Council of Ministers, an attempt was made to revise the chaotic financial structure of the State. Alcalá Zamora was quite evidently unwilling to have recourse to Gil Robles, the logical candidate as Prime Minister. There were the usual endless consultations with the President as one politician after another paraded through the presidential office: Martínez de Velasco, Chapaprieta once more, Miguel Maura, and Portela Valladares until on December 14, the latter formed a government. The new Prime Minister had neither a party nor even a segment of public opinion behind him; he was not even a deputy and had served once as Home Secretary in one of the numerous Lerroux cabinets. The new government was about as sorry a spectacle as Spain had ever witnessed, a makeshift affair, totally without support and recognized by everyone as a rickety improvisation in the midst of crisis. The fact was that the Cortes as then constituted was quite incapable of offering an adequate solution, and may be compared with the strikingly similar situation in the France of the 1930's or in the France of the period after 1945. The whole technique of parliamentary rule became a long and tiresome juggling of politicians and positions, and the so-called "renovation" was nothing more than the replacing of one minister by another who heretofore had occupied another post.

Calvo Sotelo, with his usually rapierlike thrusts, pointed out the source of the whole difficulty: "At the end of 1935 the danger of revolution in Spain was never greater. No good can come from compromising with the lesser evils."[15] In the fifty-seven months of the Republic, there had been twenty-eight governments, that is, an average of about two months' tenure for each. On the first of the year, 1936, Alcalá Zamora suspended the sessions of the Cortes, and a few days later fixed the elections for February 16. This was to be the most fateful date in all modern Spanish history, comparable only to July 18 in historical significance. Manuel Azaña had remained aloof from party politics during these months, but he continued to grow in prestige among the Left and his speeches reflect the unceasing influence he exerted on politics. For the purposes of the approaching elections the Left, consisting of republican Left, republican union, socialists, syndicalists, anarchists, communists, and Marxists of every tinge and persuasion combined to form the Popular Front, the alliance that was to win the elections and preside over Spain's destinies for the five months before civil war swept the country.

[15] *A.B.C.*, Dec. 17, 1935.

The Popular Front waged a most active campaign, promising amnesty for the thousands of political prisoners still in jail; the reinstatement of employees who had been dismissed, no tampering with the sacrosanct Constitution, while the reforms envisaged since 1933 were expected to go forward under the impetus of the revolutionary ideologies. The *Bienio Negro,* or black two years of the Right, as the Left was wont to call it, was due to come to an end.

The whole business was a terrible confession of impotency and incapacity, for the truth was that the parliamentary system had broken down; Spain was ungoverned, misgoverned, and in the minds of some, literally ungovernable. It seemed the confirmation of the verdict of one historian:

> If this [a parliamentary regime] is as difficult in every country, as history and reason demonstrate, how can it be anything but difficult in ours which lacks a high degree of political education and the conditions of temperament and character, since, as Ramón y Cajal has remarked, one of the peculiarities of our people, as observed earlier by Humboldt and Sales y Ferré, is the absence of political sense and the weakness of a truly national patriotism.[16]

The ensuing campaign was one of the most lurid and unbridled in Spanish annals in which every conceivable device was used on both sides to attract the voters, for it was commonly recognized that the issue at stake was the future character of the Republic itself. Violence was a commonplace. Take any single day of the pre-electoral period, let us say, January 11, 1936. On that day the press records the following incidents:

> A masked band stole a truck in Barcelona and fired on those who gave chase.
>
> In the Puig station, an assault on the strong box with the death of a civil guard and a postman.
>
> In Málaga an attack on the box of the Compañía General de Carbones.
>
> In Lugo, destruction of the chapel of the Vírgen del Camino.

The tone of the Popular Front was unequivocal. On January 12, 1936, Francisco Largo Caballero stated at the meeting in the Cinema Europa, that "Before the Republic was established our duty was to bring about the Republic; but once that regime has been established, our duty is to bring about socialism. When we say socialism we mean Marxist, revolutionary socialism. One must be a Marxist with all that it implies. We will never give up the idea of transforming

---

[16] Manuel de Bofarull y Romaña, *Las antiguas Cortes, el moderno parlamento, el régimen representativo orgánico,* Alcalá de Henares, 1945, p. 118.

the bourgeois Republic into socialist and in allying ourselves with the republicans, we have not given up our Marxist ideology nor our liberty of action for the future. . . . After victory the working class will seize the right moment to impose the total victory of Marxism."[17]

After this frank statement of purpose and in view of the decisive role of Largo Caballero in the Popular Front government, how is it possible to assert that the victory of the Left in Spain was merely that of a moderate, reformist tendency, respectful of the Constitution and desirous of defending the best interests of a liberal Republic? Largo Caballero was not merely denunciatory of the Right; he threatened them with extermination, whether or not the results of the elections were favorable to the Left. Here is the absolute essence of the antidemocratic, antirepublican spirit that distinguished almost every act of the Popular Front from the time of its inception until its inglorious finish. On January 22 Largo Caballero said in Madrid:

> When things change, the Right need not ask for our benevolence. We will not respect the lives of our enemies as we did on April 14, 1931, when the Republic came in. If the Right is not defeated at the polls, we will find other means to beat them: means to obtain the total triumph of the Red flag, because, and I emphasize this, if the Right wins, we shall be forced to turn to civil war.[18]

Largo Caballero had finally captured the socialist party, split up to this time between two tendencies: one governmental and more moderate, the other frankly revolutionary. Under his leadership the party was openly committed to revolution and to communism, for the leader himself said, "I am a Marxian socialist. Communism is the natural evolution of socialism, its last and definitive stage."[19] The outlook for revolution was excellent in the winter of 1935–1936, and it may be remarked that it was not the army that threatened rebellion at that time but the leaders of the party combination engaged in campaigning for election. The evidence is overwhelming that the Popular Front was determined to seize power by any means, regardless of the outcome of the elections. In the magazine *Blanco y Negro,* Blanco Caro and Mauricio Karl published an article entitled "The Outlook for Revolution." On the basis of their investigations they were convinced that "the organizations we have visited do not possess real defenses against

---

[17] *El Socialista,* Jan. 13, 1936.

[18] *El Socialista,* Jan. 23, 1936. Often quoted in other papers as the most typical expression of Largo Caballero.

[19] *El Socialista,* Feb. 1, 1936.

revolution. Projects, ideas on paper, files are all they have" (Jan. 26, 1936).[20] The victory of the Popular Front, which in rightist circles was not anticipated at all, is attributed by that crafty old politician, Alejandro Lerroux, to the combination of excessive confidence, arrogance on the part of non-Marxists, and a lack of real unity among the rightist forces.[21]

There was some confusion about the actual number of deputies elected by the different groups on February 16. The independents were sufficiently numerous to make difficult the assessment of the relative strength of the two sides. The official figures of the Home Office were: Left, 240; Center, 46; and Right, 176. There was a good deal of second balloting, that is, second polling in the case of constituencies where no majority had been attained. On the evening of the sixteenth the returns had begun to come in from the larger cities, showing, as in 1931, considerable leftist advances. At the same time, the reports not infrequently showed that the Right was ahead in many provinces.[22] A distressing feature about the February elections was the manner in which the Popular Front seized control of the government even before the final returns were in, for the victors, or supposed victors wanted power without delay.

It can hardly be doubted that the elections of February, 1936, were accompanied by fraud and forgery. There is evidence to back up the contention that in a great many constituencies the results were destroyed or cleverly forged to convey the impression that the Popular Front had won.[23] In Cáceres and La Coruña the Popular Front obtained twelve seats that did not rightfully belong to it. There is the evidence of photostatic copies of the election returns showing, for instance, written certificates from towns many miles away from each other, written by the same hand and so attested by handwriting experts. In some districts in Málaga the returns were unanimous for the Popular Front, a most unlikely case, since many known rightists were in residence there. The explanation is the terrorism that was used to prevent electors from voting. The record exists of the provincial committee in Pontevedra, Galicia, in which it is stated as a perfectly

[20] Quoted by Alejandro Lerroux, *op. cit.*, p. 520.

[21] *Ibid.*, p. 504.

[22] Salamanca, Toledo, Granada, Léon, Palencia, Soria, Cuenca, Burgos, Navarre, Ciudad Real, Balearic Islands, La Coruña, Albacete, Zamora, Cáceres, Logroño, Segovia, Guadalajara, Alava, Santander, Ávila, and Valladolid.

[23] *Report of the Commission appointed to study the question of the illegitimacy of the government in power in Spain on the 18th July, 1936*, Madrid, 1946 (in English).

natural thing that the counting of votes had to be interrupted time and time again so that the police might quiet the mob in the streets seeking to impose their will.

The situation in Cuenca was particularly confused. It was decided to call special elections for May 3, and the second ballot, if that were necessary, for the seventeenth of that month.[24] It became known later that José Antonio Primo de Rivera, founder of the Falange, was a candidate for the Right. The chairman of the Cuenca provincial committee took the illegal and extraordinary step of declaring the election of May 3 the second balloting, thus making it impossible for Primo de Rivera to appear as a candidate at all. In the dossier on the case it appears that the Minister of Justice exerted pressure on the local authorities in Cuenca to prevent the candidacy of Primo de Rivera. There was a serious attempt to expel the opposition leader, Calvo Sotelo, from the Cortes by the delightful expedient of declaring false the elections in his constituency of Orense. The debates in the Cortes during the weeks after February 19, 1936, are taken up in large measure with disputes over electoral certificates. The Azaña government was formed so quickly, before the returns were either entirely in or had been certified as correct, that in many of the second elections the moral atmosphere was such as to make it difficult for the rightist candidates to have a chance. It was difficult, as one can imagine, for many electors to deliberately vote against the new, firmly entrenched government with every instrument of coercion in its hands. It would seem that the number of seats dubiously acquired was enough to assure the government of a precarious majority. The careful reading of the *Diario de Sesiones* for the months between February 19 and July 18 shows clearly that the government depended on a very slim majority to remain in office, and that the number of deputies present after elections of an allegedly fraudulent character was precisely enough to carry through government-sponsored measures.

There was no doubt that the elections of February 16 were understood by everyone as decisive. Even the rightists, who had felt strongly that victory would be theirs, were convinced that there was no probability now for anything except the descent straight toward communism. The electoral method itself was called into question by Alcalá Zamora. Writing at a later date, after his ignominious expulsion from the presidency, it is to be expected that the ex-President should harbor a certain resentment in his breast:

[24] *Gaceta de Madrid,* April 9, 1936.

> The Popular Front seized power on February 16, thanks to an absurd electoral method which gave the relative majority enormous advantages. In this way there were districts in which the Popular Front with 30,000 less votes than the opposition, managed, nevertheless, to get ten seats out of thirteen.[25]

The former President argued that the Popular Front had reached power by two steps: (1) on the night of February 16 to 17, without awaiting the final results of the polling, the Popular Front immediately began action in the streets; (2) the falsification of the electoral returns, whereby opposition candidates were declared defeated when in reality they had won.

The electoral law to which reference was made above favored decidedly the large coalitions against the splinter parties which so characterize Spanish politics normally. The law had been a socialist-republican invention in the 1933 days when they had lost precisely because of disunity. Indalecio Prieto did not hide the character of the law when he wrote: "We Republicans and socialists have made this law favorable to the large combinations and to the majority, and we have passed it primarily to favor the Left."[26] The result was that it was possible for the Right to get 4,633,905 votes in 1936 and have 213 seats, while the Left with 3,912,068 secured 265 seats.

The night of February 16 was an unforgettable experience for the Spanish people. As though the consequence of a concerted plan, mobs attacked dozens of political clubs and centers belonging to the opposition, entered and destroyed printing plants and newspaper offices, and committed countless acts of vandalism. Prisons were opened and even common criminals let loose. Convents and churches burned all over the peninsula. There is no space to list the churches and religious treasures wantonly sacrificed to the fury of the mob. The number ran well over a hundred. The initial excesses were dubbed "jubilation for the victory" by the cynics in power. After the first enthusiasm had passed, a more serious and concerted attack on the "reaction" was encouraged. In Cádiz, the Marianist College was seized and turned into a *Casa del Pueblo;* Granada fell victim to a general strike and for four days was completely in the hands of the mob. Julio Alvarez del Vayo, now a *colporteur* of Spanish republicanism in the United States and in United Nations' circles, expressed his conviction that the burning of *La Nación* and the San Ignacio and San Luis churches

---

[25] Alcalá Zamora in *Journal de Genève,* Geneva, Switzerland, Jan. 17, 1937.
[26] *El Liberal,* Bilbao, April 14, 1935.

meant that the people of Madrid protested against the slowness with which the Popular Front was in carrying out its program.

Crime became a normal thing and political murder a daily occurrence. Despite the rigorous censorship — a typical republican institution — it was widely known that prominent political figures as well as obscure citizens were being slain day after day. In Oviedo a former republican minister, Alfredo Martínez, was killed; in Bilbao, the businessman José María Maura; in Madrid, four workmen affiliated with the Falange were shot down while at work in the Plaza de Toros, and on March 13 the socialist Jimenéz de Asúa was attacked.

How did the government react to murder and arson carried on as a normal political system? Not merely by an embarrassed silence, but by the most extraordinary indifference and even defense on occasions. Day after day in the Cortes the voice of Calvo Sotelo was raised to condemn the depredations. Since the censorship would not allow a word of these happenings to reach the general public, Calvo Sotelo used the pages of the *Diario de Sesiones* to get the information out and his speeches were impassioned denunciations of the criminality that was going unpunished.

The Cortes during March and April was the scene of a violent, ill-tempered exchange of insults. The most abusive language was the rule and personal threats were so commonplace that scarcely a page of the printed text (undoubtedly softened in final printed form) fails to reveal some incident of this character. Dolores Ibarruri, communist deputy for Oviedo and commonly known as the "Pasionaria," expressed her "democratic" sentiments in the following genteel way:

> When I ask for the imprisonment of Gil Robles and friends, I am doing them an honor for they are going to contaminate with their presence the prison cells formerly occupied by the Asturian, Basque, and Catalan revolutionaries.[27]

When a deputy, Díaz Ramos, made the rhetorical remark in the course of a speech: "I have no idea how Gil Robles will die," the voice of another deputy was heard to cry out, "By hanging." This comment was duly recorded in the *Diario de Sesiones*.[28] Insolence reached its height when Calvo Sotelo asked Azaña point-blank if he could explain who had burned the Church of San Luis within two hundred feet of the Home Office itself. From among the other deputies came the explana-

---

[27] *Diario de Sesiones,* April 2, 1936.
[28] *Ibid.,* April 15, 1936.

tion, "The Bishop of Alcalá."[29] Azaña delivered in the session of the Cortes of April 3 a classic retort to the nationwide destruction that was going on; a reply that goes down in history as one of the really great expressions of fatuousness:

> The Republican government and the President do not undertake to justify anything or explain anything away. We must examine this situation like men and understand things in their broad human sense. I am scandalized that anyone should state how horrible that three churches have been burned. I also say, if not how horrible, what nonsense and what a pity.[30]

Rodolfo Llopis, then an obscure member of the Cortes and later to be an equally obscure member of the republican clique in exile, found it easy to explain everything away; the communist, socialist, anarcho-syndicalist violence and terror was all due to the sinister machinations of the monarchists. Churches were burned presumedly by their inmates in order to calumniate the Left; murders were engineered by the nobility and the "reactionaries" in order to cast discredit on the purity of republican motives. "On February 16 the Left won and nothing happened. Every single incident, everyone, has been provoked deliberately by the Right."[31]

The Azaña government was very far from satisfactory to the proponents of complete revolution. Comrade Maurín, communist minority member, pointed this out in the same memorable session from which the above extracts of speeches have been taken:

> In 1936, in a profoundly revolutionary moment, that terrifies the Right, the Azaña government is much less revolutionary. . . . Today the majority of the country is socialist and communist [*sic*] and nevertheless, the government is Republican in character.[32]

In a word, the communists were convinced that the Azaña government was but a step toward the new socialist order to which they aspired. The statement of Maurín is a clear definition of the fundamental dissatisfaction of the extreme Left with republican institutions and their determination to transform them to the ends of the social revolution. Calvo Sotelo and Gil Robles were outraged at this cynicism. The latter made it clear that the Spanish people could not endure indefinitely the state of anarchy to which they were being subjected. Calvo Sotelo denounced the apathy of the government day in and day

---

29 *Ibid.*
30 Manuel Azaña in Cortes, *Diario de Sesiones,* April 3, 1936, p. 222 sq.
31 *Ibid.,* April 15, 1936, p. 307.
32 Speech of Joaquín Maurín, *ibid.,* April 15, 1936, pp. 316–317.

out and his voice, silent in the greater part of the country because of press restrictions, nevertheless constituted the most vigorous indictment of the regime and the criminal negligence of the Azaña ministry. When the Prime Minister soothingly pronounced himself as not desiring civil war, Calvo Sotelo answered in ringing tones:

> If that were said on March 1, or 10, it might have passed without a retort, but to speak of tranquillity as the characteristic of the government six or eight weeks later when security of life in the street is nonexistent and social disintegration plainly evident, is too much. Or when the cry of Long Live Spain is met by the howl of Long Live Russia, you ask me seriously to believe that there is calm?[33]

Calvo Sotelo became famous for his frequent résumés of the destruction. In this same speech he indicated a detailed list of the churches, chapels, property, and lives that had been lost. It was an imposing monument to the "calmness and good will" of the Republic: 50 political centers razed; 36 churches partially destroyed, the burning of 106 more churches of which 50 were totally gutted — and all this in two months. Seventy-four murders and 345 wounded was the balance sheet of personal violence that had taken place within the few weeks preceding April 16, 1936, and when Calvo Sotelo reached his list of murders, Deputy Ibarruri called out, "How much did you pay the assassins?"

Manuel Azaña was ever ready with a quip or a *bon mot* to cover even the most terrifying situations: "I am persuaded that flames are endemic to Spain. In the past heretics were burned and today saints, even if in the form of statues or images. I see little point in this sort of thing."[34]

This elegant pose in the face of rising disorder may have satisfied the intellectual instincts of Azaña. Calvo Sotelo replied furiously a month later when the government bench made a statement praising the order in the Republic: "Authority! With three hundred churches burned since February 16!"[35]

In the meantime the position of President Alcalá Zamora was becoming untenable. His docility in the face of the Popular Front was beginning to waver and he was the victim of scruples in finding the state of anarchy the very contrary of what he had envisioned for the Republic. He vetoed a measure placing the rural lands of the country in the hands of arbitral boards with trade-union intervention, one of

[33] *Ibid.,* April 15, 1936, p. 290.
[34] *Ibid.,* April 16, 1936, p. 343.
[35] *Ibid.,* May 19, 1936, p. 705.

the last straws to break the patience of the Popular Front. The arrangement to oust Alcalá Zamora from the Presidency was evolved by Indalecio Prieto. The technical grounds were simple: it could be done according to Article 81 of the Constitution, providing that the President dissolve the parliament twice during his six-year term. After the second dissolution, the new Cortes could examine its necessity and an unfavorable vote of the absolute majority of the Cortes shall bring about the deposition of the President. The socialists went back into republican history and found to their satisfaction that Alcalá Zamora had not dissolved the Cortes for the elections with the sincere and pure motive of allowing the Spanish people to express their convictions, but from the unconfessable motive of wishing to bring parliament into harmony with his own views. The shallow sophistry of the whole proceeding was shocking. The socialists railroaded the measure through, and the C.E.D.A., having no love for Alcalá Zamora, abstained. On April 7 the President was deposed and by the time the new presidential elections rolled around, on May 10, Manuel Azaña was the only serious candidate. On May 13 the new President charged Casares Quiroga with the task of forming the new government.

Upon installation of Azaña in power unrest became incredibly violent. In the town of Tecla, landowners had been beheaded in the public square and religious services were impossible, since every one of the city's fifteen churches and chapels had been completely destroyed. In Yeste, in one bloody incident, 25 were killed and 118 wounded. On May 4, in Madrid, a mob of the worst elements of society lynched three nuns and two laywomen. Miguel de Unamuno describes the spectacle of mob action in Salamanca:

> A few days ago Salamanca was submitted to the shameful spectacle of mob action against one of the local courts. This mob of mad men and women, with a mass of children, all screaming and raising the clenched fist, wanted to lynch the judges, lawyers, and court officials. A large portion of this mob was made up of foul, evil faced, and dirty wenches with a placard on which was written, "Long live free love." This whole grotesque farce was protected by the public authority with orders not to interfere.[36]

The revolutionary fervor of the Marxists was rising constantly. Alvarez del Vayo talked in Toledo of "Spain converted into a socialist Republic in union with the Soviet Union." Largo Caballero claimed in Zaragoza that "the organized proletariat will carry everything be-

[36] Miguel de Unamuno in *Ahora,* Madrid, June 7, 1936.

fore it and destroy everything until we reach our goal." *Claridad,* the socialist paper, complained that "unfortunately in Spain there has been little civil war, little revolution and little disorder and chaos. We must see to it that this takes place in proportion to the reactionary resistance." The socialist and communist militia — estimated at some 150,000 at least — were training constantly. There is evidence that arms had been made available from the Soviet Union and even the socialist press made this clear in a veiled manner.[37] So desperate was the situation that a distinguished Catholic, who stood with the Republic and was in its diplomatic service, Angel Ossorio y Gallardo, cried out:

> We must speak clearly. Neither the government, nor parliament, nor the Popular Front mean anything in Spain. They are no longer in command. Those who do run the country are the organizers of unbelievable strikes, the hired assassins and those who pay them, the youngsters who pillage automobiles on the highways and those who use the pistol for persuasion.[38]

Indalecio Prieto himself was appalled at the vision of Spain in the late spring of 1936:

> We Spaniards have never seen so tragic a panorama or so great a collapse as Spain at this moment. Abroad, Spain is a country classified as insolvent. This is not the road to socialism or communism, but to desperate anarchism without even the advantage of libertarianism. The country is on the verge of economic liquidation.[39]

The only thing the Casares Quiroga government could find to say in the face of chaos and the rising strength of the Falange on the other side was that "In its relations with Fascism the government is a belligerent."[40] The prisons were filled with Falangists and persons suspected of fascism. Murders were mounting daily. On July 4, seven socialists were killed as a crowd left the *Casa del Pueblo.* On July 12, José Castillo, a lieutenant in the assault troops, was killed as he left his home. On July 13, José Calvo Sotelo was murdered by guards taking him to the Security Office for questioning.[41]

The full story of the official murder of Sotelo is worth repeating, for no single incident is so illustrative of the terrible state into which

---

[37] *El Socialista,* May 31, 1936.

[38] *Vanguardia,* Barcelona, June 2, 1936.

[39] Speech delivered in Cuenca, May 1, 1936, *El Socialista,* May 2.

[40] *Diario de Sesiones,* May 19, 1936.

[41] Regarding Calvo Sotelo, his ideas and influence on Spanish thought, see Aurelio Joaniquet, *Calvo Sotelo,* Madrid, 1939, and Carlos Cardell, *Antología de José Calvo Sotelo,* Madrid, 1942.

the republican institutions had fallen. World publicists who made much of nationalist violence, with reference to the death of García Lorca, are all too prone to forget that life under the Republic, and especially under the Popular Front, was most precarious, reaching extreme when a deputy to the Cortes was taken from his home and killed with impunity by official assassins. This is precisely what happened in the case of the opposition leader, Calvo Sotelo.

It was evident in the Cortes that Calvo Sotelo was looked upon as the most dangerous enemy of the extreme Left. He was not a fascist, nor did he advocate the totalitarian State. He was a monarchist, a member of *Renovación Española,* and a man of the very highest ideals and conduct. His conviction was profound and unwavering that the policy of the Popular Front was leading Spain directly to chaos and ruin and on this point he never hedged.

The full details of his murder are available in unimpeachable documents with the photographs of the autopsy and the testimony of a large number of the persons who participated.[42] On the morning of July 13, a station wagon, bearing the number 17 and used by the assault troops, left Pontejo barracks with a number of men under the command of Captain Fernando Condés. Another car followed, and the two sped toward No. 89, Calle Velazquez, the residence of José Calvo Sotelo. Condés, with José del Rey, Victoriano Cuenca, and several other members of the corps, demanded entrance. The house was searched and the telephone wires cut to prevent communication with the outside. Condés told Calvo Sotelo that the Security Office demanded his detention and presumedly his questioning. Calvo Sotelo entered the car with Condés and the others. At the corner of Ayala and Velazquez, Cuenca shot Calvo Sotelo twice in the back of the neck. The documents preserved in the School of Forensic Medicine leave absolutely no doubt that Calvo Sotelo was shot while unaware of the intention of his assassins and without self-defense. The murder car went on to the East cemetery where his body was left in the open. It may be added that the reception of unidentified corpses was so common an occurrence in the summer of 1936 that the cemetery employees were not in the least surprised to find an unknown body on their hands. Calvo Sotelo's family immediately notified friends and the search began, but his body was not found until the next day. The testimony

---

[42] *Causa General. La dominación roja en España,* Madrid, 1943, with full details of every aspect of the Calvo Sotelo murder and extensive photographs showing his body at the time it was discovered and the autopsy performed afterward.

of employees at the Security Office shows that the bureau made no attempt to learn of the fate of Calvo Sotelo even after his disappearance had been learned. In a word, the political figure who was being taken to the Security police for interrogation disappeared in the night, and for hours no one in that office made any effort to find out what had transpired. Under oath, another employee testified that news of the successful execution of Calvo Sotelo was transmitted to the Security Director, Alonso Mallol, but that the latter took no steps to verify the report, much less find out where Calvo Sotelo actually was. At noon the next day the cemetery reported to the city hall that the body of one presumed to be Calvo Sotelo had been discovered. The participants in this murder were protected by the government from testifying, and one of them, Lieutenant Máximo Moreno, was lodged in the Security Office to prevent his being interrogated. On July 25, after the civil war had started, the Calvo Sotelo files were seized in the Ministry of Justice by a group of armed men and have never been recovered.

On July 15 Count Vallellano, in the name of the members of the Cortes belonging to the traditionalist and monarchist factions, announced that his group was retiring from the Cortes: "We can no longer spend a moment in the company of those responsible for this criminal act. . . . Ever since February 16 we have been living in anarchy."[43]

The rightist deputies in the Cortes had lived for months under the threat of assassination and Casares Quiroga, in an exasperated speech, had denounced the Right as responsible for anything that might happen to Spain in the future, while the socialist deputy, Galarza, assured his fellow members of the Cortes that it would be no crime at all to commit violence against the leaders of the rightist groups.[44]

The death of Calvo Sotelo is proof that life under the Republic was no longer tolerable nor possible for men of good will. It was plain that no opposition could carry on its legitimate task in parliament in the face of threats of violent action. Even Indalecio Prieto found it necessary to say that "the death of Calvo Sotelo was regrettable."

What, then, was left? Nothing but opposition outside the Cortes, and this meant rebellion. The Spanish masses were frightened, tired, and

[43] *Diario de Sesiones,* July 15, 1936.
[44] *Ibid.,* June 16, 1936.

deceived by the farce they were living. It is small wonder that on July 18 the outburst occurred and that army and people rose to overthrow the travesty on government they had endured with singular patience for so long.

Alejandro Lerroux has listed six steps during the Popular Front government that led straight to the civil war:

1. The formation of the Popular Front;
2. The elections;
3. The crisis in the Portela Valladares cabinet;
4. The solution of the crisis by turning over authority to Manuel Azaña;
5. The legal destitution of the President of the Republic;
6. The murder of José Calvo Sotelo.[45]

---

[45] Lerroux, *op. cit.*, p. 524.

Chapter 9. THE EIGHTEENTH OF JULY

I HAVE tried to convey to the reader in the detailed chapter on the Republic something of the sense of frustration and impotence felt by the ordinary Spaniard in the spring and summer of 1936. This sense of whirling toward an abyss was felt not only by the so-called privileged classes but by the ordinary man in the street who realized that every guarantee of life and property was in abeyance as a result of the absence of any real authority of the State. I have attempted to describe in the previous chapter and in Appendix 3 the methods used to bring about this demoralization. In view of the decisive role played in 1936 by the army, a word may be in order with reference to the policy of disintegration employed against the armed forces of the nation.

The republican policy of systematic weakening of almost every organ of social stability extended to the army and the fact that General Franco was removed as head of the Military College at Zaragoza and later virtually exiled to the Canary Islands is evidence of the methods used to bring about the demoralization of the armed forces. If one asks what force still remained in 1936 that could possibly stop the descent into complete anarchy, the only possible answer is the army. It may be theoretically true that the army should be used only for purposes of national defense and should refrain from all intervention in domestic politics, but it is also necessary to consider the peculiar state of a nation doomed to chaos by the mismanagement and rashness of its government. The Spanish army, already badly weakened and with morale seriously jeopardized, was the only agency in 1936 capable of taking a determined stand on behalf of law and order. The so-called reforms of President Azaña as applied were invariably political, for they were part of a policy of "democratizing" or "republicanizing" the armed forces, so that everyone not addicted to the singular form of democracy professed by the Popular Front was either removed or sentenced to the particular form of elegant exile implied by service in such places as the Canaries, Ifni, or Spanish Guinea. Eight thousand officers were retired. General Mola complained bitterly that Azaña was tolerant of the most serious deficiencies, and the most grievous reflections of the discipline of the armed forces.[1] It is historically untrue that the army had displayed an attitude of systematic hostility toward the Republic. After April 14, 1931, the Spanish army had accepted the new state of affairs without protest; even the unsuccessful uprising of August 10, 1932, was not a military venture, since the majority of the participants were retired army officers or civilians. That the Spanish army was in grave danger of succumbing to the disintegrating influences of Marxism, may be judged from the exposé on this subject made in the Cortes in 1935.[2]

The letter addressed by General Francisco Franco to the then Prime Minister, Casares Quiroga, dated June 23, 1936, is evidence that the problem was the profound concern of the military leaders everywhere and that they had hoped that by opportune counsel the possibilities of further anarchy might be avoided. General Franco stated quite clearly to the Prime Minister that just as in 1917 the negligence and indifference of the public authority had undermined the morale and effectiveness of the armed forces, leading to the formation of groups among them for the defense of their interests, so in 1936 the situation was so grave as to threaten a repetition of the same thing. "I cannot fail to convey to you the danger that this sentiment on the part of everyone entails, not only from the strictly professional point of view but from that of all Spaniards in the face of the grave problems that threaten our country."[3]

It is quite clear that the Movement initiated by the army was a desperate step, taken at a moment when no other recourse seemed possible, nor can it be contended that patience had not been shown with the excesses of the Popular Front. The full story of the Republic's systematic attempt to weaken the armed forces through the shifting of commands and the infiltration of proved leftist elements has yet to be told in detail, although the virus of leftism had not, in 1936, affected more than a small part of the armed forces. Besides retiring officers of known anti-Left sentiments, there is other evidence to show how the trend of the times was permeating the army and other branches

---

1 Emilio Mola, *El pasado, Azaña y el porvenir,* quoted in Fernández Almagro, *Historia de la República Española,* pp. 219–220.

2 *Diario de Sesiones,* Feb. 15, 1935.

3 Fernández Almagro, *op. cit.,* p. 167.

of the military. Leftist agitation sought persistently to reach the army and air force, with notable effectiveness in the latter case. A single incident will indicate the rising spirit of antagonism between the army and the extreme Left. On March 14, 1936, a mob attacked and set fire to the building occupied by the *Diario de la Rioja* at Logroño. Assault troops were prevented from restoring order and the colonel in command, when he sought to get in touch with headquarters, was attacked by the mob and was obliged to take refuge in the city hall. The various officers who were with the commander then proceeded from the city hall to the barracks, protected by the mayor and a number of civilian employees. The irony of the whole situation was that the military had to be protected in their effort to prevent a disaster. At the barracks, the military still refused to react to the mob violence that by this time was becoming extremely acute. Officer Aguilar was hit, and the military responded with shots in the air. The riot that had been provoked was not instigated by the excesses of the military but by the organized depredations of the mob, which had already set several convents on fire. The civil authorities published an account of the incident in the paper *Izquierda Republicana,* lauding the fearlessness of the mob and lamenting the death of several distinguished citizens, without a word of mention of the role of the officers. This episode in the city of Logroño was typical of dozens of others all over Spain. It was clear that action was taken to provoke the military to countermeasures and thus justify punitive action against them.

In the late spring of 1936 it has been estimated that 90 per cent of the army officers were anti-Left; the air corps being the one arm that had suffered the penetration of extremism. At the Los Alcázares airfield, Commander Ortiz and a large number of his officers and men were of the left-wing persuasion. At Getafe, near Madrid, a goodly portion of officers and men were similarly contaminated. Commander Sandino of the Barcelona airfield was not only an active leftist but had been implicated in the events of October, 1934, and the rank and file in general reacted to the instructions and example of their officers. The investigations after the Asturias uprising in 1934 revealed the extraordinary fact that a large number of the soldiery participating against the rebellious miners were themselves former militants in leftist organizations and not infrequently Asturians from the same area as the rebels. The explanation of their conduct lay in the collective discipline that army life had developed among them.

Even before the Popular Front victory on February 16, 1936, during the period of the Portela government, the army barracks and centers had been subjected to a considerable amount of extremist propaganda, which established a concerted drive to discredit, humiliate, and infiltrate the armed forces by every possible means to the end that it might suffer demoralization in the face of the drive of the extreme Left for power.

The movement of July 18, 1936, was both improvised and premeditated. Obviously thought had been given to the possibility of insurrection to solve the apparently insoluble problems that faced Spain, although uprising was literally simultaneous in almost every part of the peninsula and Africa. On the morning of July 18 reports from as widely separated places as Seville, Zaragoza, Pamplona, and Barcelona showed that the commanders were undertaking to assure control of their particular jurisdictions. The charge is often made that the army was responsible for the whole rebellion and that the people were not behind it. Obviously there was an initial period during which the conflict was almost exclusively limited to the armed forces. Within a very short period, however, it became clear that the war was to be of considerable duration, the popular character of the nationalist support shown by the following facts, some of which are developed in greater details elsewhere in this book:

1. The nationalists were never faced by rebellion or even serious unrest in the territory behind their lines.

2. No large military force was ever necessary during the entire three years of the war to guard the lines of communication or protect the rear guard.

3. The loss of certain key points was the result of a false strategy rather than the absence of sympathizers. This was definitely the case of Barcelona, Madrid, Valencia, and other centers of importance.

4. Assuming that the nationalists could count only on those who had voted against the Popular Front in 1936, that is to say the traditionalists, monarchists, and rightists of various brands, this was sufficient to give the nationalist movement a majority.

5. The nationalists were never at a loss for recruits for the ranks during the entire period of struggle. The flow from the republican zone into nationalist territory to serve the colors was constant and numerous.

6. If there had been real popular indignation at the nationalists, a region such as Andalucía would have been impossible to control after

the first flush of occupation, when the bulk of the army was engaged in the Extremadura campaign and on the Córdoba front. Despite the socialist and communist militia and the long extremist tradition in the south, Andalucía did not constitute a problem of security for the nationalist government.

The character of the war was recognized from the start as a campaign for the restoration of the traditional values that had made Spain great. It was the explosive reaction to the horrible nightmare of Popular Frontism for so many months. Was it a crusade for Christian civilization? This has long been a moot point. There have been many highly reputable observers who have refused to accept the notion that Christian interests were involved in the nationalist movement of 1936. The most generous of these have considered that at best it was a movement for national liberation from the insensate regime that had tyrannized the country. I have no intention of examining here the subtle question, once so violently debated, of the Spanish civil war as a "holy war." The foremost critic of the holy war theory was Jacques Maritain. In his article in the *Nouvelle Revue Française* of July 1, 1937, he takes up this question in considerable detail.[4] We find, too, an extended treatment of the subject in the introduction by the same writer, published in French originally and later in English translation, to the book of Alfred Mendizábal, *The Martyrdom of Spain.*

Since the problem of what the Spanish civil war really was and how it can be interpreted is fundamental to every consideration of the results, it may be useful to summarize in a few lines the essential points advanced by M. Maritain. The prestige of the French philosopher makes it necessary that his observations be taken most seriously. M. Maritain considers such points as he feels contributed directly to the tragedy of Spain and gave meaning to any evaluation of the outbreak of July 18. He was pained that Moors collaborated with the movement and that destructive hooligans on the republican side should claim to be the protectors of culture and democracy. He was profoundly concerned about what he calls "religion confused with clerical power" with primary support for the clergy among the privileged classes. Obviously the question of the moral justification of July 18 poses a delicate problem for the foreigner. M. Maritain has hesitated to pass on the conformity of the insurrection to the principles pre-

[4] A French reply to the Maritain position is contained in Vice-Admiral H. Joubert, *La guerre d'Espagne et le catholicisme,* Paris, 1937.

scribed by moral theology, and on the question whether the insurrection did not cause more damage and ruin than the situation that had provoked it, he raises grave doubts.

Now it is clear that if the purely speculative aspects of the problem are left aside and a judgment formed exclusively on the basis of history and recorded experience, the Spanish problem becomes one of evaluating properly the long and confused epoch that I have undertaken to describe in Chapter 7. Was there any other solution in July, 1936, except armed rebellion? The facts seem to be reasonably clear. Spain was well advanced on the road to socialist totalitarianism with communism a growing factor in the life of the Spanish people. Ruthlessness prevailed in the imposition of the new standards and criteria regardless of the sentiments of a very large mass of the Spanish people. It may be a moot question whether a majority or a very large minority of the Spanish were opposed to the Popular Front. But whatever may be said it is unquestionable that even if the opposition were only 40 to 50 per cent — and certainly it was more — then the Popular Front could not democratically proceed in the fashion it did to stamp out every trace of opposition and destroy the traditions and social order to which so large a segment of the population gave its loyalty. Maritain is much moved, and properly so, by the perplexing problem of the Basque nationalists. Their situation was a very special one and continues to represent one of the delicate points in the story of the civil war. In Chapter 6 I have tried to explain some of the salient features of this complication.

> In the opinion of some people there is a question of this being a holy war. This notion of the holy war is worth examining. That the civil war — social war, political war, class war, a war of international interests and international intervention — has taken on yet another characteristic in Spain, that of a war of religion, is a fact which is explained by historical circumstance, both past and present, that can never be too much deplored. This characteristic naturally embitters the war, but it is not sufficient to transform it into a holy war, that is to say — for we must speak here with the most exact terminology — into a war itself raised to the order of sacred things and consecrated by God.[5]

It would seem that the main preoccupation of M. Maritain was that the name of God was invoked in a campaign in which the enemy was detested so bitterly that no sentiments of humanity or love were

---

[5] Introduction to Mendizábal, *The Martyrdom of Spain* (London: Geoffrey Bles, 1938; New York: Charles Scribner's Sons, 1938), p. 27.

held out to him. "We do not condemn the use of force itself," he claims, and then proceeds to argue that the crimes and evils of the Left were matched deed by deed with the outrages of the Right. It is unfortunate that many of the incidents claimed in 1937 as true have been revealed to be unfounded or grossly exaggerated, as is the case of Guernica and Badajoz. "Possibly in Spain all wars tend to become holy wars; in that sense the words 'holy war' no longer describe a certain thing of a determined objective nature; they refer to a disposition of the historic temperament of the Spanish people." It is clear that M. Maritain, like so many of his fellow countrymen, was unwilling to declare the national cause in Spain a holy war or a crusade, or even to extend to it their cordial support. In rejecting the collective letter of the Spanish bishops, he is obviously displeased that they took the nationalist side, and admonishes Catholics to remember that this sort of document is not binding in conscience.

I would be the last to underestimate the importance for Catholics abroad of the debate regarding the character and objectives of the civil war, for the conflict did pose a problem for the conscience of Catholics everywhere. It divided opinion so deeply that even to this day the wounds have not entirely healed and the present division in the temporal order between Catholics — those that consider themselves as "democratic" and those who incline more to what their critics call the "authoritarian point of view" — springs in large part from the Republic versus Franco controversy. The résumé of the central ideas expressed by Jacques Maritain represents more or less the stand taken by a very large body of Catholics in France, in the United States, and to a lesser degree elsewhere; they wanted to be neutral, to cry a plague on both your houses and refused to see the fortunes of the Church involved in the victory of either side. This, clearly, is a debatable matter and one which ought to be examined with far less heat and emotion that are commonly engendered the moment the name of General Francisco Franco enters the discussion. Winston Churchill gives us one of the sanest conclusions in this matter when he said that neither side could claim with justice the title deed of legality, and that Spaniards of all classes had to consider the life of Spain. "In this quarrel," he continued, "I was neutral. Naturally, I was not in favor of the communists. How could I be when if I had been a Spaniard, they would have murdered me, my family and my friends?"[6]

[6] Cf. Winston Churchill, *The Gathering Storm*, Vol. I (Boston: Houghton Mifflin Co., 1948; London, Cassell & Co., Ltd.), pp. 213–214.

The Republican propaganda during the civil war emphasized the "legitimacy" of the government and the illicit character of the rebellion. Perhaps no single point was stressed more consistently than this, despite the fact that the Republic itself had come into power by overthrowing the monarchy which in 1931 might easily have claimed — and did claim historically — to be the "legitimate" government of the Spanish people. A great deal of ink and no end of rhetoric were consumed in pleading this idea of legitimacy. Oddly enough, the left-wing partisans who defended the Republic invariably insisted on this aspect, a seeming contradiction to the idea of social revolution and the remaking of society. This notion of legitimacy played a very large role in delaying the proper international recognition of the Franco government. Regardless of the merits of one side or the other, the fact remained that after a certain period of time, the nationalists did hold the largest portion of the peninsula and their authority was predominant over the great majority of the citizens of Spain.[7] It would seem from every point of view, and especially from the Catholic conception of government and the State, that the argument about the legitimacy of the Republic is invalid and does not have any bearing on the case for or against the nationalists in the civil war. I do not believe that either the holy war debate, nor the question of legitimacy of the preceding government have an overwhelming bearing on the merits of the case, for the nationalists rose against a government that had ceased to perform the one function that behooves a government to perform, namely to govern. It was not a rebellion against a social order that merited the support of the people; it was clearly and plainly a rebellion to restore order and authority, abandoned totally by the Popular Front.

This point has been clarified by the address of the Cardinal Primate

---

[7] See the reasoning of John A. Ryan and Francis J. Boland: "Nor does it follow that one government can be deposed and another instantly substituted at the whim of the multitude. A will which does not follow the order of reason neither has nor can have validity. . . . Let us remember that changes of government, whether licit or illicit, are humanly unavoidable, and that this instability can never be eradicated by any force or any theory. . . . Hence at any time that the public good requires a new form of government and a new designation of rulers no pre-existing right of any person or any family can validly prohibit this change. The right to create the new legitimate government inheres in the community habitually or potentially . . . the necessity of constituting a new government exists whenever the preceding government has been destroyed, and there has been introduced a new government which cannot be abolished without detriment to peace" (*Catholic Principles of Politics,* p. 69 sq., copyright, 1940, by the National Catholic Welfare Conference and used with the permission of The Macmillan Co.).

of Spain at the cathedral of Santiago de Compostela in July, 1948. His Eminence reviewed for his listeners what communism had meant to Spain and the problem for the conscience of every Catholic regarding constituted authority. The republican government had declared its purpose of eradicating religion and had boasted quite publicly that this had been achieved. "Should we not also have been 'defenders of the city' not by taking up arms, but by exercising our doctrinal guidance and by striving, through our moral authority, to save religion and the country. This is what we did through our joint letter of 1937, which received a favorable response from Bishops all over the world."[8]

Even in the midst of the civil war and despite the grave anxiety he felt for the persecuted and the martyrs, the Holy Father took occasion, in his address to a group of Spanish pilgrims on September 14, 1936, to point out the havoc that communism had produced and the horrors it had left in its trail in Spain. With these words of warning, the Pontiff urged that compassion, patience, conciliation, and charity animate all Spaniards especially toward those responsible for the savagery and destruction that had sullied the name of the country.

Not only did a very large portion of the Spanish people support the nationalist movement, but it was striking the number of intellectuals and men of outstanding position in the world of letters, the arts, and sciences, who preferred the nationalist cause to the republican. This phenomenon is not limited to traditionalists or persons of known religious convictions. Even more remarkable is the fact that the younger generation was won over in large measure to the nationalist cause, to the extent that some of the sons of outstanding republicans were actively enrolled in the Franco forces.[9]

The sentiments of Dr. Gregorio Marañón serve to make this point clear. This brilliant physician and man of letters wrote in 1937:

> If one were to ask one hundred persons today — regardless of whether they are Spaniards or not — why they were for or against one or the other

---

[8] Part of text and comment in *The Tablet,* London, Aug. 14, 1948, p. 110.

[9] To mention but a few: Gregorio Marañón Moya, one of Dr. Gregorio Marañón's sons, was attached to the propaganda section of the nationalist forces during the war and later to the protocol division of the Falange. The sons of Pérez de Ayala, republican ambassador in London at one time, José Ortega y Gasset, and others, were all active in the war and have supported the regime since its inception. There were others who represent a complete break with the republican past of their fathers: José María Arreilza, Spanish ambassador in Argentina under Franco and son of a prominent Bilbao republican, and Joaquín Ruíz Giménez Cortés, presently Spanish ambassador to the Holy See, son of an outstanding liberal.

of the two parties which are fighting against each other in Spain, some would speak of their democratic principles, of their traditionalism, others of their militarism or anti-militarism, of their Catholicism or religion or of their neo-Catholicism, a curious species of the current ideological fauna, or perhaps even of their horror of the executions and air raids, or lastly of their personal approval or disapproval of the leaders of the respective parties. There are very few who base their stand on the true reason for the struggle which is this: "I defend the Reds because I am pro-communist," or "I sympathize with the Nationalists because I am anti-communist. That is the crux of the question."[10]

For the Catholic, the position was made irrevocably clear in the statement of the hierarchy, over the signature of the bishops, headed by His Eminence, the Cardinal Primate of Toledo, when they stated: "This most cruel war is, basically, a war of principles, of doctrine, of one conception of life and society against another, of one civilization against another."[11]

A final word regarding the atmosphere on July 18. In Madrid and the other cities, the government took the position that nothing of any importance had happened. The first reports, even in the rightist papers, were fragmentary and inconclusive. *A.B.C.* informed its readers on July 19 that "The government of the Republic had issued an official bulletin regarding the military movements." It then proceeded to devote most of its space to expressions of bereavement for Calvo Sotelo as they poured in from all over the country. The only news disseminated by the government was that "a group of rebels in possession of the Seville Radio are giving the public fantastic news items." As regards other points, it was stated that "In Málaga the assault troops have successfully resisted the attacks of the seditious groups." It was not until July 25 that the change came. On that date, *A.B.C.* appeared with the flaming letters across the front, "VIVA LA REPUBLICA!" for during the previous day its monarchist directors had been expelled and the paper taken over by the republicans. It now spoke in the new edition of the rebellion as "the Fascist movement." During the first week the government refused to accept it as

[10] Gregorio Marañón in *Revue de Paris,* Paris, Dec. 15, 1937.

[11] Cardinal Gomá, *Por Dios y por España,* Barcelona, 1940, p. 23: "Spain was at the bottom of the abyss and its only salvation was by the sword" (p. 24). "The country and religion — *arae et foci* — were in the gravest danger, the responsibility for which belongs to those who carried out a policy totally repugnant to the national sentiment and our history" (p. 25). All the pertinent episcopal texts are to be found in the collection, *La Iglesia y la guerra civil española* (*documentos eclesiásticos*), Buenos Aires, 1947.

a rebellion, considering it merely a series of more or less spectacular uprisings, which would be put down as easily as that of Sanjurjo in 1932. The fact that the Cuartel de la Montaña in Madrid and General Goded in Barcelona were suppressed with alacrity contributed to this optimism. However it was Indalecio Prieto who, on July 25, stated his conviction that: "We are faced with the greatest uprising in the history of Spain." He was, needless to say, very right.

The national movement of July 18 was linked from the moment of its inception with the name of General Francisco Franco Bahamonde. Although during those first days, especially in the Castilian and Navarrese press, it was General Emilio Mola who loomed the largest. In Andalucía, General Queipo de Llano captured the popular imagination. General Franco, as has been indicated, was in the Canary Islands at the time the first movements broke out. It was after his arrival in Morocco, followed by the successful crossing of the straits, that his name became the most prominent. In addition to this, his potential rivals, General Sanjurjo and General Mola, were both killed in the early stages of the war. It has sometimes been said that General Franco has been extraordinarily successful in the manner in which potential challengers to his position were eliminated. Among the civilians, Calvo Sotelo would unquestionably have commanded the very greatest prestige and respect.

General Franco was born in El Ferrol in Galicia, the son of a commandant of the naval port and dockyard. The General was one of three sons. The eldest, Nicolás, played an important role during the war and has been ambassador to Portugal for many years while Ramón Franco achieved fame as an aviator, crossing the Atlantic in 1926. Both Ramón Franco and General Queipo de Llano were looked upon as left-wing officers, attested by the latter's devotion to the Republic in the days of its foundation. They joined unhesitatingly the revolt in 1936 against the kind of Republic neither of them had ever envisaged. Francisco Franco entered the Alcázar at Toledo in 1907, obtained a commission a few years later, and was dispatched to Morocco in 1912. At the age of twenty he was already a captain, after distinguished service in Africa. The Morocco experience was a powerful influence on his entire career and thinking, for here he became deeply attached to Africa and its Moslem inhabitants. At twenty-three he was a *comandante,* that is, major, and in 1920 was back in Morocco collaborating with the picturesque General Millán Astray in the organization of the Foreign Legion. The Legion, made up of Spaniards as well as foreigners, won fame for its conduct in the Riffian wars and later during the civil war, in which it was one of the fundamental units in the nationalist offensive up through the peninsula. In 1923 Franco was a lieutenant colonel in the Legion and rose to the rank of colonel under General Primo de Rivera. When thirty-three, he was a brigadier general as a result of his outstanding service in the Morocco campaigns that ended in 1926. It was Primo de Rivera who designated General Franco as head of the new military academy at Zaragoza where he remained until 1931, with one interval during which he pursued higher studies in military science in France.

General Franco had not taken part in politics and when the Republic came he refused to participate actively in the political movements that were taking shape. It may be of interest to note that General Franco took the position that it was the nation that counted and not the form of government. The first manifestos in 1936 after the nationalist movement had started were all signed in the name of the Republic, proof that there was originally no idea of a fundamental change, but merely the restoration of order. He was removed from the Zaragoza Academy and given a less prominent position at La Coruña until 1933 when he became military governor of the Balearic Islands. General Franco was called to Madrid at the time of the Asturian revolt in 1934 and directed the operations leading to the successful repression, later becoming commander in chief in Morocco for a brief period and chief of staff under Gil Robles, then Minister of War. Under the Popular Front he was exiled to the Canary Islands from which unpromising spot it was anticipated that he could do no damage. On July 19, 1936, General Franco reappeared in Morocco to begin the slow climb toward victory and power.[12]

---

[12] There are numerous biographies of General Franco in Spanish, some good and some mediocre. One of the standard works is Joaquín Arrarás, *Francisco Franco,* first published at Seville in 1937, and in English translation, *Francisco Franco: The Times and the Man,* Milwaukee, 1938. There are others: Emilio Diez, *General Franco,* Seville, 1940; Fernando de Valdesoto, *Francisco Franco,* Madrid, 1943; and Franco's own book, *Marruecos, diario de una bandera,* Madrid, 1922.

Chapter 10. THE CIVIL WAR

1. THE MILITARY OPERATIONS

THE military aspects of the civil war began immediately, since the lines were closely drawn between those who would no longer tolerate the prevailing anarchy and those who were bent on defending the Republic even at the cost of chaos. Two phases distinguished the nationalist uprising: the first was what a competent writer has called the "technique of the coup d'état," that is, the seizure of control and authority in numerous cities and places by the army; second, the formal decision of the armed forces of the nation to enter the arena against the government then installed in Madrid.[1] On the republican side two measures were envisaged to forestall the possible reaction long contemplated: first, the weakening of the army through the shuffling of commands and the virtual exile of its leaders; and second, the wholesale arming of the masses, particularly the representatives of the trade unions and syndicates. The clash of these diverse tactics produced a short period of confusion until the sporadic conflict became a full-fledged civil war.

It is clear that neither side anticipated that July 18, 1936, was to be the commencement of a long, bloody, and formal war. Those who took the awful responsibility of restoring Spain to law and order as well as those who were driving implacably toward the extremism of the Left, conceived the events of that July as a temporary crisis; a passing moment of high tension, to be solved quickly and neatly at the risk of little more than a wave of rioting. It was construed very much as a repetition on a wider scale of the abortive effort of General Sanjurjo in August, 1932. Consequently, there was an almost total absence of formal preparation for war. Much that was done on both

[1] Luis María de Lojendío, *Operaciones militares de la guerra de España, 1936–39,* Barcelona, 1940.

sides was the result of improvisation. It was not until well into the autumn that the two sides settled down to the serious work of waging what promised to be a protracted struggle.

The first successes on the nationalist side, and which in large measure determined the preliminary course of the struggle, were due to the audacity and vigor of the leadership. It must be remembered that if the republicans put into effect immediately the policy of arming the masses, the nationalists had had no opportunity to prepare the rank and file of the people for participation in a war. There were, on both sides, certain elements of the population ready and willing to take their place instantly in the defense of their respective causes. The republicans could count on the various extremist groups: anarchists, communists, socialists, and the politically inclined trade unions. This proletariat responded with alacrity to the call to arms. On the nationalist side there was evidence of a strong popular support of the cause over which General Francisco Franco was shortly to assume supreme leadership.

The notion that the nationalists were dependent entirely on mercenaries, Moors, and professional soldiers has long since been blasted. Thousands upon thousands of men, young and old, flocked to the colors, scarcely had the proclamation of war been issued. The public square of Pamplona was filled as soon as the news of the events in Africa reached that capital, with thousands of Navarrese eager to join once more in the defense of the traditional values without which they could conceive of no Spanish greatness. These Basques from Navarre, with their red berets and in many cases antiquated firearms, formed the nucleus of the famous *Requetés*. In connection with this problem of the degree of popular support of the two causes in conflict, a British observer has remarked that it was a notable fact that in the entire territory under nationalist control, there was no need for coercion of any kind or even for a police force of any serious size.[2]

There is considerable discrepancy regarding the relative strength of the two sides. One view is that the nationalists had "at

[2] Arthur F. Loveday, *Spain, 1923–1948* (London: Boswell Publishing Co., Ltd., 1949), p. 56. An extraordinary statement is made by Dr. de Azpilikoeta in his *Le problème basque,* Paris, 1938, p. 17, when he says that "the insurgent military attacked them (the Basque provinces), invaded the territory of Guipuzcoa, coming from Navarre which they had overcome by surprise during the first moment of the outbreak." The notion that Navarre was "surprised" and "overcome" by the nationalists when the Navarrese were the first to rise in support of the movement, is too amazing for comment.

their disposal the greater part of the armed forces of the country — the Civil Guard, the Foreign Legion, a division of Moorish troops from Spanish Morocco, four fifths of the infantry and artillery officers and a certain number of regiments recruited in the north and therefore reliable. They also had the Carlist levées or Requetés which for some time had been drilling secretly and the promise of Italian and German tanks and aeroplanes if necessary." Against this formidable array, the same author tells us, the Republic had only "the Republican Assault Guards and a small and badly armed air force. But the plans of the rebels were defeated by the tremendous courage and enthusiasm with which the people rose to defend themselves, and by the loyalty of the naval ratings who at a critical moment deprived them of the command of the sea."[3]

Another writer, who does not see the republicans in the light of defenders of law and order, affirms that "the situation between the two opposing forces of Right and Left at that moment was one which told heavily in favour of the Left. They not only had control of the unions but had succeeded in dominating, if not terrorizing, the administration."[4]

It is true that the nationalists had a well-trained, tough nucleus of troops in the Foreign Legion, the Moorish units, and the regular army that was with them. They were strong in officers, but weak, on the other hand, in certain important respects which were of very considerable significance to success in the war. The republicans had most of the navy and a small air force and the well-knit, audacious trade unions which they armed immediately.

It is not accurate that the nationalists began with everything in their favor. The great urban centers of Madrid, Barcelona, and Valencia were in republican hands and the mere existence of an organized government gave the Republic certain definite advantages. It had the machinery of administration at its disposal and possessed — an enormous asset — the gold reserves of the Banco de España. The embassies, legations, and consulates of foreign powers were accredited to it and it therefore had available ready means for contact with other countries. The possession of the heavy industry centered about Bilbao cannot be underestimated. The Republic enjoyed still another asset that cannot be overlooked; it had land communication with France

[3] Brenan, *The Spanish Labyrinth,* p. 316, copyright, 1943, by The Macmillan Co. and used with their permission.

[4] Cf. R. Sencourt, *Spain's Ordeal,* Longmans, Green and Co., p. 97.

and easy access to the sea via the Mediterranean and the northern coast and the principal airfields were in republican hands. Finally, the nationalists had a far more difficult task of defending their zone than the republicans, for General Mola in Navarre and General Franco in Africa were hundreds of miles apart with the major nationalist center of strength sandwiched in between republican territory. In striking the balance sheet it may be said that the republicans held the material advantages while the nationalists had a marked superiority in discipline, order, and leadership.[5]

The civil war started by the uprising of the garrison commanders in many parts of Spain. Broadly speaking it may be said that in Galicia, part of Asturias, part of León, two of the Basque provinces (Alava and Navarre), part of Castile, Aragón, Cádiz, and Algeciras the revolt was successful from the very beginning and these areas were never subjected to reconquest by the republicans. On the other hand, the failure of the rebellion in Barcelona, Valencia, and Madrid represented a most serious setback. Had these three cities fallen at once there would have been no war or at the most a very short period of struggle.

At the time the struggle began the nationalists were very far from effectively organized. Aside from the troops in Spanish Morocco, the

---

[5] The contention that the nationalists possessed all the advantages in the conflict is completely refuted by the statements of Indalecio Prieto himself. In two speeches Prieto advanced the claim that the Republic was destined to win because of its overwhelming superiority in men, money, materials, and ideology. "In my opinion the subversive movement is lost from the moment that it failed to win a fundamental element, the navy. The army in Africa can do nothing; it cannot cross the Straits and will remain pinned down there" (*A.B.C.,* July 25, 1936).

On August 9, 1936, Indalecio Prieto delivered a far more important and precise speech: "A war is primarily a matter of means of resistance. Who possesses the greatest possibility of winning a war? The one who has the most materials." Prieto then stressed the three elements he claimed favored the Republic: money, industry, and morale. "All the financial resources, all the gold reserve of Spain are in the hands of the government" (*El Socialista,* Madrid, Aug. 9, 1936). He emphasized that the industrial power of the country was almost exclusively in republican hands; and finally that all of these factors contributed to the high morale of the defenders. Prieto pointed optimistically to the so-called republican victories: Alto de León, Alto de Navacerrada, Somosierra, Zaragoza, Oviedo virtually reduced, and finally, "the absence of military talent on the rebel side." This was Prieto's summing up of the prospects within a few weeks after the outbreak of hostilities.

The idea that the rebellion was a "fascist movement" was implicitly denied by none other than Indalecio Prieto himself in the third of his radio speeches in which he avowed quite openly that the "extensive and complex insurrection does not have a purpose at all clear to us" (Campoamor, *La révolution espagnole vue par une républicaine,* p. 55).

Foreign Legion, the army was not in ideal condition for war operations; the 1935 recruits had been dismissed and those of the 1936 class had not yet been called into service. General Mola in Pamplona had approximately 400 soldiers at his command, while General Queipo de Llano in Seville, who performed miracles with his tiny force, did not have more than 185. The figures prove that the army was not long prepared for revolt, nor had the military commanders much chance to organize their forces. The military uprising had all the earmarks of a desperate move at a moment when there was no possibility of further endurance of the misgovernment and anarchy of the Republic. The known threat of a communist coup d'état probably brought about the decision to rise when conditions were not yet entirely favorable.

There was scarcely any ideology involved in the movement at the beginning. General Franco did not denounce the Republic as an institution, but rather spoke in the name of a republicanism that had been outraged and degraded. There was no elaborate program, no *Mein Kampf* ready at hand to provide the ideological trimmings of a regime. There was no idea even of a regime as such. The movement was for one purpose: to make life tolerable after the months of savage misrule of the republican government that had abdicated every principle for which it had been created. The famous *Falange Española,* which joined the revolt from the time it began, did not constitute the equivalent in Spanish affairs of the National Socialist Party in Germany. In the latter case the party brought the movement into power. In the former, the Falange was merely one of the numerous forces, and not the most important, that had joined the nationalist movement. Later, after the establishment of the movement as a government at Burgos on October 1, 1936, the Falange along with the other political groups involved were merged into a single political force. But this came later and very pragmatically, as part of the needs of war and the effective conduct of it and there was nothing to foreshadow it on July 18 when the hostilities began.

The Spanish army in Morocco was the first to rise up in arms against the government. The maneuvers then taking place at the *Llano Amarillo* military quarters in Africa brought together a number of the commanders: Colonel Solans, Lieutenant Colonel Seguí, and others, who forced the commander of the Melilla area, General Romerales, to capitulate. On the night of July 17, after a brief exchange of shots with the leftists, Melilla was taken over. Colonel Yague in Ceuta and

Colonel Sáenz de Buruaga in Tetuán immediately joined. On July 19, after a flight from the Canaries, General Franco landed in Morocco where the situation was already under control and reports coming in from the peninsula. With Morocco firmly established as a basis of operations, the new conquest of Spain was about to begin.

Even in as simple a matter as the voyage of General Franco from the Canaries to Morocco truth has not prevailed. When the subcommittee of the Security Council was considering the "Spanish case" in 1946, it was stated that the first evidence of German intervention in the Spanish civil war was the fact that General Franco had been transported to Morocco in a German plane. *The New York Times* made mention of this version:

> The first German intervention took place toward the middle of July, 1936, at the moment when Hitler placed at Franco's disposal an airplane belonging to the Deutsche Lufthansa for the historic flight from the Canaries to Tetuán, which was the opening signal of the revolt. As soon as the war started Franco sent the same plane on to Germany to request aid.[6]

There was no German plane involved in the flight of General Franco to Africa; the one transporting him being British, and the pilot, Captain Beeb, has himself recounted the episode. It was on July 11 that the plane left Croydon. Among its passengers were a commander who had belonged to Scotland Yard, B. C. Pollard; his daughter, Diana; and a friend, Dorothea Watson. The plane stopped in Biarritz, Lisbon, and Casablanca on route to the Canaries. There it picked up General Franco and returned to Africa, stopping at French Morocco on the way to Tetuán.

General Franco reached Tetuán at about seven in the morning of July 19. The news that reached him in his Moroccan headquarters was confused; Seville had been the scene of an uprising on the afternoon of the eighteenth and General Queipo de Llano almost singlehanded had turned the tide in favor of the movement. The Battle of Seville, as it is sometimes called, was won in the barracks where General Queipo de Llano presented himself with two other commanders. In line with the strictly revolutionary character of these early days, Queipo de Llano utilized the radio to the fullest extent, taking a leaf from the Marxist handbook in his clever and effective propaganda. With only a handful of devoted adherents he won the city and suppressed the attempts of the Left to get control. The inherent drama of the

---

[6] *The New York Times,* Nov. 7, 1945.

situation passed into the heroic story of the uprising and Queipo de Llano overnight became a legendary figure, and his contribution at a crucial point on the Spanish mainland may well have assured ultimate victory. Without Seville and the south of Spain there would have been no landing from Morocco, and without this landing no campaign northward. The simultaneous uprisings elsewhere in the peninsula might easily have died away of inertia.

In Zaragoza, capital of Aragón, the rebellious forces were equally successful. The problem was to act with rapidity to prevent control of the city by armed mobs, whose arming had been sanctioned by Madrid. The swift action of the military commanders assured nationalist control of Zaragoza, Jaca, Huesca, Calatayud, and Teruel. The basis of operations on what was to become the famous Aragón front was thus assured. In Valladolid, magnificent city in the heart of Castile, the rapid action of General Saliquet brought it into the nationalist camp. Córdoba, Jerez de la Frontera, Cádiz, and other places in the extreme south joined the revolt on the eighteenth, as soon as the news from Africa made it clear that the movement was something more than a sporadic uprising of the military. Zamora, Burgos, and Pamplona represented no problem, for the strength of nationalist sentiment in the north was very great. With control assured in that area, the nationalists could count on an extremely important source of recruits. General Aranda in Oviedo sought to overcome the miners who were in arms for the Republic, but serious defections in that city brought about the celebrated siege which constituted one of the stirring episodes of the civil war. In Toledo, Colonel Moscardó transferred his command to the Alcázar, the military academy located in the immense building constructed under Charles V. There was sharp fighting in Granada and La Coruña before nationalist control was complete. In El Ferrol, the naval base, fighting took place with the sailors of the *España* and the *Almirante Cervera*. In Cáceres, Segovia, Ávila, and in the island territories of the Baleares and the Canaries, the nationalists prevailed after some skirmishing. This was, then, as of July 22, the nucleus of nationalist Spain. The areas under control were isolated one from the other.

In Barcelona, a key center, General Goded did not make the mistake that occurred in other places, of shutting himself up with his troops in the barracks, but so deployed his troops as to effect a junction after controlling the two main thoroughfares of the city. The armed mob, far superior in number, prevented this consummation and the revolt was put down piecemeal. The rest of Catalonia followed the lead of Barcelona.

In Madrid, the control of the streets was soon in republican hands. The main center of nationalist opposition was the Montaña barracks. The fall of this defense post and the massacre of the surviving defenders ended for all practical purposes resistance within the Spanish capital. On July 21 and 22 the republicans overcame Guadalajara and Alcalá de Henares. Isolation was the cause of the collapse of the movement in Málaga, Almería, and Albacete. In San Sebastián, close to the French frontier, the nationalists were defeated on July 23. In Valencia, indecision and hesitation wrecked the nationalist hopes of a quick victory although the garrison resisted for several weeks until early in August, when the situation had begun to jell and the initial confusion had ended.

The map of Spain at this moment was divided into three clear-cut zones. There was nationalist Spain comprising Old Castile and León, connected with Navarre and Aragón on the east and toward the west with Galicia and part of Extremadura, around Cáceres. On both sides of this nucleus was territory under republican control with the entire north, from the French frontier to Asturias in their hands. In the south and east, the Mediterranean coast, from Port Bou on the border of France to Algeciras, was republican. New Castile and the largest part of Extremadura was similarly under the control of the Madrid government. Here and there within that territory were foci of resistance: Toledo, Oviedo, the garrison in Gijón, and in the far south the thin line of Córdoba, Granada, Seville, Cádiz, Jerez, and Algeciras. The republicans had every advantage of compactness and facile communications. A great deal of the initial vacillation was due largely to the inability to communicate speedily the plans and action of the different sectors and the absence of a well-thought-out and co-ordinated plan of action to be applied simultaneously cost the nationalists an early victory.

There is another basic difference between the two sides in conflict which should be emphasized. The nationalists were an army, well drilled, disciplined, and responsive to the demands of the technique of war; the republicans in the initial stages were a mass, more devoted to the implantation of revolution than to the exigencies of warfare. During precious weeks the Republic lost time in aimless destruction, the rooting out of alleged antirepublicans, and the exacerbation of a class consciousness which might have been very well for the future revolution but was not likely to produce tangible results against the technically superior plans of the nationalists. It was inevitable that on both sides the first days and even weeks of the conflict should have been revolutionary in character. Only in August did the situation acquire the proportions of organized warfare.

The two major problems faced by the nationalist command in this initial period were: the transport of forces from Africa to the mainland against the overwhelming naval superiority of the republicans, and stabilization of the lines of defense in territory already held. The second task depended in a large degree on the achievement of the first, since it was necessary to gain a foothold on peninsular Spain before defense, and much less, advances, could be realized. The republicans based in Barcelona were already pouring forces toward Aragón, and there was real danger that this line could not be held. If it collapsed the northern sector would be lost with irreparable damage to the incipient strategy of the nationalist command.

The full story of the crossing of the Straits of Gibraltar from August 5 onward is one of the stirring events in this epic of heroism and devotion. The situation of the republican fleet constituted a virtual blockade of the entire coast line. The Madrid government gave orders on July 18 that the cruisers anchored in El Ferrol and the destroyer *Jaime I* set out at once for the Straits of Gibraltar. Other war vessels were immediately ordered to Melilla in Africa. In a number of cases the officers of the ships were massacred *en masse,* as was the case on the *Jaime I,* for the vessels at sea were a reflection in miniature of the revolutionary ardor that dominated Madrid and Barcelona. It has been claimed that the innumerable crimes and acts of violence committed aboard the warships were the result of direct and specific instructions from the Navy Ministry in Madrid. There is evidence to support this contention. The consequence was that a large portion of the available fleet was stationed in the Straits to prevent the crossing of the nationalist forces. The destroyer *Churruca,* temporarily under nationalist control, managed to get one contingent across to Cádiz before the rebellious sailors rose against their officers, and small vessels, under cover of night, carried reduced forces day after day. A few ships under nationalist command slipped by despite republican vigilance. On July 19 air transportation was used for a limited number of the best units.

The republican fleet was concentrated at Tangier and from this point, incursions were organized against Morocco. The fleet bombarded and harassed the bases of Ceuta and Melilla and rained shells on Cádiz. The republicans were responsible for the violation of the neutrality of Tangier, guaranteed by international statute. General Franco protested energetically to the International Zone Commission against this flagrant infraction of the arrangement. The presence of vessels of other nationalities in Tangier threatened to convert the port into a center of hostilities. On July 23 the republican fleet retired and henceforth operated out of Cartagena and Málaga.

By early August it was clear that the peninsula could not be saved by driblets; that a large force must get across despite the blockade. It was due to the ingenuity of General Franco that the details of this astonishing operation were worked out and effected. With the two vessels at its disposal, a very small number of lesser craft and the few planes available for protection, a convoy was organized between Ceuta and Algeciras. In an audacious move that involved fighting against the larger republican unit, the *Alcalá Galiano,* the blockade was broken and three thousand troops with abundant war material landed on the peninsula. By the end of September the Straits were completely clear of republican war vessels. The only explanation of this extraordinary situation in which the Republic had every conceivable advantage, was that revolutionary ardor is not enough to win battles. Crews without adequate officers, and the indiscipline that comes from mutiny, were not assets in the struggle against an organized and properly disciplined force.

The stabilization of the various fronts could now be undertaken, although limited resources of the nationalists made it impossible for them to launch powerful offensives against each of the major republican sectors. The war tended from the beginning to become one of fixed position, with concentrated advances according to the material and human resources available. The holding of certain fundamental positions was by no means easy. The ousting of the republicans from the Sierra de Guadarrama near Madrid represented a very considerable operation, and the severe fighting on the Alto de León constituted one of the initial encounters of major proportions of the war. Under the supreme direction of General Mola, every effort was made to assure control of the mountains north of Madrid so as to assure proper support of the hoped-for uprising in Madrid itself. The occupation of the heights of Somosierra represented an important step in the advance toward the capital from the north. A portion of the late summer and autumn of 1936 was devoted to a series of local operations, destined to assure the control of positions favorable for more ambitious advances. The conquest of Sigüenza represented an achievement of the nationalist forces in this preliminary period where fighting against the republicans, consisting of anarchist units made up of railroad workers and a women's battalion called "La pasionaria," caused the city to suffer enormous destruction. With its fall on October 15, the northern front was stabilized.

The Aragón front presented difficulties of a very special nature, for the persistence of the republicans in attacking in that sector and the accessibility of Barcelona as their basis made the stabilization considerably more difficult. It was not until February of 1937 that this front may be said to have assumed its more or less permanent character until the end of the hostilities. The aggressive operations in these first days by the republican forces from Barcelona shows more eloquently perhaps than any other single episode the revolutionary and Marxist character of the armies at the service of the Republic. One column preparing to attack Zaragoza was composed of anarchist elements of the *Confederación Nacional de Trabajo,* together with other extremists organized in groups the names of which are testimony to the ideology motivating their adherents: Lenin, Karl Marx, and Pi Suñer. A second column was directed by Buenaventura Durruti, the well-known anarchist leader. A third column, aimed at Teruel, was formed of improvised troops from Valencia. One of its divisions was called Pancho Villa, another "Liberating Eagles"; a portion of its components were prisoners from the penal institutions of Chinchilla and San Miguel de los Reyes. A fourth column of recruits from Madrid and Cuenca under the command of the communist, Uribe.

Thousands of the most violent and extremist elements of Barcelona and Valencia poured into the towns and villages of Aragón and there was no limit to the rapacity, brutality, and orgy of murder and violations that accompanied this so-called liberating force. It was months before this line could be made firm at the cost of countless lives. Aragón was saved, however, from the extremist avalanche, and Zaragoza, its capital, played the same role in the civil war as during the Napoleonic invasions, for it is the natural center of communications between Madrid and Catalonia, and its control represented a very promising advantage against an enemy. The fact that the Balearic Islands were occupied early by the nationalist forces, with the support of the civil population, added another element of stability and served as important bases for air raids on republican-held objectives along the mainland coast.

During the entire end of July and well into August, small army units, especially the Legion, undertook to consolidate and extend the territory under nationalist control in Andalucía. From Seville and Granada, mopping-up operations tended to widen the areas controlled and bring about more effective communication between them. After the memorable August 5, with the breaking of the blockade, the war became more regular. There were some local successes; the break in the siege of Córdoba, penetration into the province of Málaga by the forces under General Varela. There were numerous other advances, and the larger offensive by General Queipo de Llano, in January of 1937, completed the first chapter in the stabilization of the Andalucian front. Perhaps the most important single event in the story of hostilities in the south of Spain was the offensive against Málaga, between January 14 and February 13, 1937, and its conquest was the last of what may be termed the minor operations. The moment had arrived for the larger movements aimed at liquidating sector by sector the republican front.

The major military aspects of the civil war may be divided into the following main chapters or major operations:

1. The initial struggle for Madrid. The advance through Extremadura. The conquest of the Tagus valley and Toledo. The Guadalajara offensive. Stabilization of the Madrid front.

2. The conquest of northern Spain. The campaign in Guipúzcoa. Siege of Oviedo. The offensive in Vizcaya, the march on Santander, and the conquest of Asturias.

3. The republican initiative. Battle of Brunete. The Aragón front. The epic of Teruel. The battle of the Ebro.

4. The nationalist offensives. The offensive from Aragón to the sea. The offensives in Andalucía. The advance to Castellón. The conquest of Catalonia. The final victory.

The operations against Madrid riveted the attention of the world on the Spanish capital during the great days of November, 1936. Two aspects distinguish this phase of the war: the first, the employment of mobile forces and rapid marches such as that which captured Badajoz and connected the two parts of nationalist Spain; the second, the steady, hard pressure of highly organized troops against an objective. This was the characteristic of the siege of Madrid of such long duration. From August through November, the nationalist army marched northward to effect the junction so indispensable for the later operations. This army was exclusively Spanish — there can be no question of "foreign" aid. It was composed of the flower of the African forces, largely the Legionnaires and the Moors.

It may be opportune at this point to mention the role of the Moorish troops in the conflict. One of the accusations made against the nationalists was the use of African troops, from Spanish Morocco and Ifni. This was interpreted as vitiating the contention that Franco and his forces were fighting for Christianity or that the war was anything but a military conspiracy fought with mercenary troops. First of all, the Spanish scarcely look upon the Moors as "foreigners." They had been under Spanish influence and control for centuries. Ever since the remote days when the Cid Campeador had used Moorish soldiers to capture Valencia against Islam, the tradition of close comradeship was built up. It was no more startling for a Spanish army to contain Moors than for the French to have Senegalese or troops from other parts of the African empire, nor more extraordinary than for the United States army to include Negroes. There was in many respects far more affinity between the Moslem Moors, firm believers in God, and the nationalist movement, than between the latter and such sacrilegious hordes as were fighting for "democracy." The Republic itself had employed Moorish troops twice. The first time was by Azaña against the Sanjurjo uprising in Seville and the second by Lerroux in 1934 in Asturias. The argument regarding Moorish troops used by the nationalists collapses when it is observed that Manuel Azaña utilized them for the defense of the republic.

The campaign for Extremadura, which was to lead to the gates of Madrid, was initiated on August 3, when Commander Castejón left Seville with troops brought from Africa by air. This, perhaps, is the best example of the high confidence of the nationalists in their cause, for this advance movement was undertaken even before the assurance of the possibility of the Ceuta-Algeciras crossing was absolute. On August 7, General Franco himself transferred his headquarters to Seville and took supreme command of the peninsular operations, while General Yagüe was given command of the troops engaged in the Extremaduran drive. Later General Varela succeeded him, and it was the latter who delivered Toledo and arrived within sight of Madrid. As the convoys across the Straits became more regular and the number of troops swelled to appreciable numbers, the campaign was planned in various directions, all converging ultimately on Madrid. The bulk of these forces, and the detail is important in order to establish that they were Spanish, consisted of army regulars, *Requeté* militia, regiments of Falangists, and what was known as the *Cuerpo de Voluntarios de Sevilla.* The advance was so successful that on October 1 General Franco was confirmed as supreme commander of the armed forces and *Caudillo* of Spain in a ceremony at Burgos, with headquarters set up at Salamanca.

By August 10 the forces were at Mérida in a remarkably rapid movement that was preliminary to the battle of Badajoz. The nationalists were in territory where they might reasonably expect a sympathetic reception. The old Roman town of Mérida fell and the Madrid government hastened to send reinforcements to Badajoz, a point of supreme importance, for once Extremadura fell the link between the north and south would be established. To be sure it was not an ideal link, for communication would be tortuous and complicated because of the roundabout routes, but no single achievement would so hearten the nationalist partisans as the achievement of this hoped-for linkage.

Extremadura in summer is hot beyond all description. Its dry, arid countryside, its poverty-stricken villages and towns, the hot wind from the south, the *solano,* blowing across it, are not conducive to easy living. In that late summer of 1936 Badajoz became the crucial encounter of the two forces. It was not the first of the engagements, but certainly one of the bloodiest and most decisive. Readers horrified at the violence of the Spanish civil war and the numerous bloody byproducts that accompanied it may well be reminded that civil wars, our own War between the States included, bring out the strongest and often the basest of feelings. Hatred and ferocity combined at Badajoz to make that battle a high point in an already bloodstained record of impetuosity, savagery, and barbarity. The news of the execution of General Goded in Barcelona and of General Fanjul in Madrid produced a reaction of bitterness on the part of the nationalists. The republican defenders were no less savagely determined to stop what they chose to call "the fascist beast."

Mérida was the fragile point at which the link of North and South was established. It was necessary to defend it at all costs. Lieutenant Colonel Tella remained in that city to organize the defenses against the expected counterattack, while Yagüe, Catejón, and Asensio set out for Badajoz. Assault guards and civil guards had been rushed up from

Madrid in the meantime to buttress the republican defenses. Lieutenant Colonel Tella opened the battle on a front some five miles long on the afternoon of August 13 against defenders three times more numerous. The nationalists before the city were only 3000 strong and in a far more exposed position than their adversaries.

The city is protected in part by the Guadiana River. It was a fortified city in the ancient sense of the word with heavy, thick walls, bastions, bulwarks, and fortifications of the Vauban type. Lieutenant Colonel Asensio occupied the extreme right; on the left, surrounding the southern and southeast section of the city, was Castejón, from which position he launched the attack on the Menacho barracks. The nationalists were at a distinct disadvantage. They managed to approach the city walls from which a mortiferous fire was directed against them by the local garrison, which had gone over to the republicans, and by the newly arrived militiamen from Madrid under Puigdendolas. The Puerta de la Trinidad was chosen as the most vulnerable spot for the assault, and against it was directed the fire of the few nationalist cannons. The republican aviation, in turn, was extremely active, and all day, August 14, the battle raged with unabated fury, the republicans resisting savagely from the hospital after the walls had been breached in several places. It was the Legion that assumed the responsibility for the attack through the Puerta de la Trinidad, where they met a murderous cross fire that decimated their number. The first wave fell almost to a man. The second came forward totally unprotected, tossing hand grenades and singing the Legion song. Of the Sixteenth Company, only the captain, a corporal, and fourteen men got through to the square beyond, opening the way for their comrades who swarmed through the breach. The fate of Badajoz had been decided. In the afternoon Castejón took Menacho by storm.

The rest of the day street fighting went on fiercely while the juncture of the nationalist forces made it possible to extinguish the focus of resistance in the cathedral. By nightfall Badajoz was in nationalist hands. The city was literally covered with corpses. This aftermath of the bloody fighting gave rise to the legend which has since been known to the civilized world as the "Massacre of Badajoz." To this day this story persists with all that impenitent tenacity which seems to accompany everything connected with Spain; with the tenacity that attaches to the Inquisition, to the expulsion of the Jews, and to all the unspeakable tales of the cruel and bloody Spaniard. The world will probably continue to believe that nationalist fury made of Badajoz an even more terrifying place than it was on that evening of August 14, 1936. Together with Guernica, of which we shall speak later, Badajoz remains as one of the major blots on the escutcheon of the nationalist cause and any defense of the movement led by General Franco is likely to turn on an explanation of Badajoz and Guernica. Do we really know what happened at Badajoz?

The reports spread abroad stated that the conquerors shot two militiamen on the steps of the high altar at the cathedral and that from 1500 to 2000 of the defeated were killed in cold blood after the capitulation. Badajoz became the theme song, so to speak, of the anti-Franco propaganda, tending to show that the nationalists were guilty of the most unconfessable atrocities. The Paris edition of the *New York Herald Tribune* and the French Havas Agency reported that 2000 victims had fallen to the nationalists in an unprecedented massacre. The American correspondent, Reynolds Packard, was indicated as the writer of the first story. He later repudiated it as a fake, was in Portugal at the time, and did not write anything of the kind. Another American correspondent, John Elliot, of the same paper, was in Badajoz as probably the first non-Spanish newsman to visit the city and he saw no evidence of a massacre and reported none. The Havas man was in Portugal and could not possibly have reported on events in Badajoz from an eyewitness point of view. The evidence regarding the two militiamen shot in the cathedral is that they were killed while using the interior of the cathedral as a base of attack, a not unlikely thing, since churches were used throughout the war as the center of the fighting. Two British officers, Captain Nangle and Lieutenant Skeffington Smith, entered Badajoz very soon after it was captured and denied the story of a massacre, nor is there sound evidence that men were shot without trial.[7]

The armies of Castile and Andalucía were now able to combine. The expeditionary force from the south moved quickly to Cáceres, which was in nationalist hands, and then on to Trujillo, from which point the shrine of Guadalupe was saved by the swift action of

---

[7] The legend was exploded in Major Geoffrey McNeill-Moss's book, *The Epic of the Alcazar* (London, 1937). This volume contains the false reports and the disclaimers that followed it. It is interesting to note that *Time* also exploded it by a description of how the figures had gotten into the world press and, once lodged there, could not be easily removed. See also *Bulletin of Spanish Studies,* University of Liverpool, Oct., 1937, p. 215. A good account of the battle and subsequent legend is contained in Sencourt, *op. cit.,* pp. 142–146. Arnold Lunn destroys the legend in his book of impressions of the civil war, *Spanish Rehearsal,* pp. 228–230.

Castejón. Five thousand persons bottled up in the monastery were liberated and the rich treasures of that most splendid religious monument saved from destruction or spoliation.

On August 26 General Franco established his headquarters in Cáceres. The way was now open for an advance up the Tagus valley. This new stage in the operations took about a month. Navalmoral de la Mata was taken by the advance forces of Yagüe. The rolling country in this area lies between the Tagus river on one side and the Gredos mountains on the other and was ideal for an advancing army. The objective was Talavera, which was looked upon by Madrid as one of the outer defenses of the city, and therefore intended to be held at all costs. Some 10,000 republicans defended this vital point and were well supplied with materials of war, as is attested to by the rich booty the nationalists took after the capture of the town. The city was surrounded, the airfield captured, and the railway station occupied. Despite numerical superiority, the republicans were quickly overcome. Among those distinguishing themselves in this action was one of the nationalist commanders, Mohamed Ben Mizzian, a Moor. The second stage in the advance of Madrid began, which was crowned with the taking of Maqueda and its castle, properly considered as directly linked with the defenses of the capital.

No engagement revealed more clearly the different technique of warfare of the two sides than Talavera. On September 5 and 6 plans had been made for a republican counterattack on Talavera and a column of some four thousand men had been formed in Madrid. The nationalists met this attempt some seven miles from the town in the open country where Lieutenant Colonel Asensio met them head on while Castejón crossed the Tagus and attacked the enemy from the flank and rear. The latter retreated as best they could in wild disorder, leaving behind them in their precipitation three armored cars and three complete batteries. After some days of mopping-up operations, the decision was made to advance and relieve the defenders of the Alcazar of Toledo.

It has long been a question whether the decision of General Franco to come to the aid of the defenders of the Alcazar did not delay him in the attack on Madrid, and perhaps give the Republic the necessary time to erect the defenses of the city. A distinguished Spanish commentator on military aspects of the war, Luis María de Lojendío, devotes several pages to an explanation of the decision and the importance of considering the relief of Toledo, not only of supreme sentimental or moral value, but also the wisest military decision, in order to give the advancing forces a wider and more secure base.[8]

The epic of the Alcazar has often been related, for it was unquestionably the culminating point of heroism in this war which was filled with instances of individual and collective valor. The Alcazar became the symbol of the nationalist spirit and to a very real degree of the spirit of Spain. Toledo lies some fifty miles south of Madrid, and rises on its hill above the Tagus river. From the bridge over which one enters the city can be seen the high walls of what was once the military college of the Alcazar. It was one of those typically Spanish constructions, massive, heavy, with towers on each corner. It dominated the panorama of pre-civil war Toledo. Today the pilgrim to the Alcazar relives another story: the unbelievable resistance of Colonel Moscardó and his men for long weeks before relief came in late September. The Alcazar stands today just as it was when relief came: ruins and desolation, the deep tunnels and underground room, the passages and the offices, are all filled with relics of the siege. A plaque in Colonel Moscardó's office commemorates his celebrated reply over the telephone to those who threatened to kill his son if he did not capitulate. A small museum holds many of the objects which survived the siege, including copies of the mimeographed newssheet, laboriously put together from radio reports picked up. The reading of the files of this little paper is a moving, pathetic experience. Nothing perhaps reveals more completely the peculiarly Spanish capacity for irony and for the sardonic in the midst of the most grueling trials than the caustic and often flippant humor of this sheet.

When the news came out of Africa in mid-July, the cadets were on leave. Colonel Moscardó, military governor of the province, threw in his lot with the nationalists and retired into the Alcazar with the civil guard and others then in the city. About 1100 men were assembled for the defense, and with them were members of their families, children, and others, making the total number of persons within the walls, 1996. There were difficulties in the way of bringing the scattered civil guard together from all over the province, since Toledo itself was in republican hands.

On July 24 this small group openly espoused the nationalist cause, without the slightest anticipation of relief from anyone, for at that early date General Franco was still concerned with preparations for getting the first troops across the Straits. Taking into consideration

[8] Luis María de Lojendío, *op. cit.*, pp. 150–152.

their isolation in purely republican territory close to Madrid, which facilitated the increase and relief of the besiegers, the decision to defend themselves in the Alcazar was an act of the sheerest heroism. The siege lasted for sixty-seven days of unrelieved bombardment, shelling, mines, and underground explosives, and constant attack. Huge floodlights were used at night to show the Alcazar up as in bright daylight. The garrison and their families lived far down within the great construction, deprived of any contact with the outside world except over the wireless from which they derived a vague idea of how the campaign was really developing. On August 22 nationalist planes dropped letters to them from General Franco and later, thanks to an accumulator, they managed to hear the Portuguese stations.[9] The feeding of the two thousand people, despite good supplies, was a most difficult problem. Ammunition was abundant, since it was a garrison. The defenders managed to obtain grain from time to time from a near-by granary through rapid sorties under cover of night. Fuel was provided from the timber that came crashing in after each bombardment. Three doctors and a minimum of medical supplies were available to take care of the sick and wounded while operations were performed without recourse to anesthetics. Nearly 60 per cent of the defenders were killed or wounded in the course of the siege. Colonel Moscardó could communicate by a telephone that continued to function. It was over this tenuous connection with the outside world that he was told by the republican besiegers that if he continued to resist his son would be shot. His refusal was instantaneous with the recommendation to the boy that he reconcile himself with God and cry: *"Viva España!"*

On August 4 their loss was twelve dead and sixty-five wounded from sorties; on the eighth sixteen bombs fell on the common rooms of the college and rendered them useless; on the fourteenth the garrison was attacked, with the whole scene lighted up by searchlights. The enemy sought to set the stables aflame and poured a withering fire against the defenders. Radio Madrid announced that night that the garrison had surrendered. Far to the southwest Badajoz was relieved on that same date, but this, however, the defenders did not know. On the twenty-fourth the sound of mining was heard, and it became apparent

[9] See a remarkable description of this whole episode in Eleonora Tennant, *Spanish Journey*, London, 1936, pp. 39–61. The classical account is by Geoffrey McNeill-Moss, *op. cit.* The Spanish accounts are legion and vary from the extremely documented to the purely impressionistic.

that the enemy was tunneling under the building to blow it up. This mining was being accomplished with pneumatic drills which vibrated to such an extent that the defenders were able to follow the progress closely. The probable area of explosion was marked off and the garrison took turns in watching. The boring was accompanied by constant bombardment and surprise attacks from time to time. More than once the republicans managed to pour gasoline over part of the defenses, setting them on fire.

There was no priest in the beleaguered fortress but only an altar before which the defenders prayed and offered up their sacrifices to the Blessed Virgin. Geoffrey McNeill-Moss tells us how they endured the agony of these long weeks with faith in their hearts: "We believe; we have Faith. They do not believe. They would stamp out the Faith."[10] This admirably summarizes the simple faith of the civil guard, Falangists, seven cadets, and the workers and farmers who crowded the Alcazar. On September 11, a Madrid-priest, Father Vázquez Camarasa, visited the garrison. He came as an emissary of the republicans, one of the few priests in sympathy with the Republic left in Madrid. He baptized the two children born during the siege, said Mass, and distributed Holy Communion, remaining to urge their surrender. The depression of this visit must have been profound on the harassed, weary, and filthy denizens of the battered Alcazar. A republican officer proposed in parley that the women leave, but they themselves on consultation indicated they would not leave, nor surrender, and if the men capitulated they would fight on alone.

On September 18 the long-awaited explosion took place; a tremendous blast that tossed one of the towers meters into the air. One whole wall was gone and the attackers confidently expected to press forward unobstructed to finish off the few remaining survivors. The mass of debris was so vast as to almost entomb the defenders and acts of heroism were necessary to counter the ensuing attack. With a rapidity that was breathless they threw up barricades where formerly walls had protected them; they manned the breaches with machine guns and within a few moments were ready to receive the invaders. Grenades, bombs, armored cars, all were employed by hundreds of republicans against the much-depleted garrison. The attack was made from all sides of the building, the survivors multiplying themselves to meet the onslaught. The first wave of invaders, anticipating only the

[10] Geoffrey McNeill-Moss, *op. cit.*, p. 257.

slightest resistance, was mowed down, but more came on until nightfall. The day ended with no decision for the attackers. The explosion had killed very few, but had forced a reorganization of the defenses. On the twenty-fifth the first signs of deliverance came with nationalist airplanes circulating overhead.

The troops fresh from Talavera were on their way. General Varela, who had captured Loja and Antequera, was reinforcing them. They overcame the triple trenches at Maqueda and on September 26 penetrated Toledo. The forlorn remnants that had been men welcomed General Franco with fervid enthusiasm. In their exhaustion they had written one of the glorious pages of history — and a refutation that in the twentieth century men can no longer give all for what they believe to be right.[11]

After the relief of Toledo the advance continued toward Madrid, to reach its logical culmination. It took a full month for the nationalist forces to get from Toledo to the outskirts of Madrid. Other columns were advancing from other directions threatening from Vavalperal on the north and moving down from the Sigüenza side. By late October the encirclement of Madrid was well nigh complete. It was a long period of weeks of capturing village after village, fighting against the first inroads of winter, from which the Moorish troops suffered severely. By October 29 Soviet tanks had appeared to support the counterattacks around Madrid.

The siege of Madrid became a process of slow attrition. The defenders were protected by the complicated geography of a great urban center in which every building, every street, and every corner became a parapet for defense. This sort of defense, as was proved later in World War II, made it possible for a smaller number of men to ward off a very much larger attacking force. Within Madrid the councils were divided. Largo Caballero urged resistance to the end, while Indalecio Prieto preferred a more moderate policy. The upshot was the flight of the government to Valencia over the one road still open for an exit from the capital. The great number of militia in

[11] The absurdities which certain left-wing writers have attained is no better illustrated than in the description of the siege of the Alcazar in the pages of Jellinek, Frank, *The Civil War in Spain,* London, 1938. The republican militia was so tender-hearted that they insisted on mediation with the defenders "for they could not bring themselves to destroy a work of art and seriously endanger the lives of women and children" (p. 428). Every incident of the heroic defense is submitted by this writer to relentless irony. When Colonel Moscardó received General Varela at the end and announced that there was nothing to report, Mr. Jellinek finds no better comment than, "Somehow, somewhere, one seems to have heard the story before" (p. 432).

Madrid plus reinforcements from Valencia and Barcelona increased the defenders to a very appreciable force. In addition the International Brigades appeared for the first time and about which a word is said in the section of this chapter on foreign intervention. Let it be observed too that as Madrid became endangered the political scene in republican Spain became more definitely tinged with red, for extremism came more pronouncedly into power with each nationalist success. Azaña had long since vanished into the obscurities of Montserrat monastery. It was communist, Soviet-dominated Spain that was fast emerging.

Until well into the spring of 1937, the Madrid front absorbed the attention of the world. While by all odds the most dramatic of the engagements, it was not the only one, nor even for that matter the most significant in the total picture of the war, although defense of the city undoubtedly changed the technical aspect of the war. The rapid nationalist advance had not led to the formation of a hard, resistant line in the territory already overrun, and the fluidity of the Madrid defenses made it possible for the defenders to conceive their action in terms of counterattack and even minor offensives. The war around Madrid became an interminable jockeying for position, thrusts and rectifications of the lines, occasional sharp encounters between republicans and nationalists when the former left the security of their prepared positions to engage in open fighting; it was a war of nerves and of patience.

The first wartime Christmas found the Madrid front strangely quiet. Interest was beginning to develop in some of the other sectors: the Coruña highway, the advances in Córdoba and Jaén provinces, and the heavy fighting at Teruel. The month of February was largely occupied with the battle of Jarama close to Madrid. This prolonged engagement was singularly bloody and fought with ferocious pugnacity on both sides. In March came the battle of Guadalajara, which has passed into the popular memory as the classic defeat of the Italians. It is true that the Italian volunteers on one side and the International Brigades on the other were in the front line of the fighting, but the battle was by no means decisive nor did it occupy that position of enormous significance which has been attributed to it in the total history of the military operations of the war.

The Guadalajara campaign represented a slight rectification of the front by a considerable advance over a wide area. One of the novelties of the action was the appearance of highly motorized columns, in sharp contrast with the magnificent improvisation of the early stages when the advancing troops requisitioned buses and private cars. The center of the operation was the village of Algora, less than a hundred miles from Madrid. The Italian divisions *Penne Nere* and *Fiamme Nere* participated in this action. The enemy was entrenched with troops composed of the Sixty-Fifth Brigade and the Thaelmann, Garibaldi, Dombrowski, Dimitrov, and Madrid columns. Once the battle was ended, the line was stabilized and remained so until the final offensive of the war. Guadalajara had a further importance unrelated to the military events, for it was the basis of one of the most remarkable cases of republican propaganda. After the encounter, there was a literal deluge of propaganda, reports, petitions, and protests, based on the presence of Italian units in the engagement. The republican government — then at Valencia — protested to the United Kingdom on March 13 and 29; to France on March 29; to the League of Nations on the thirteenth; and to the Soviet Union on the twenty-ninth. A White Book was issued, called "The Italian Aggression" in which documentation was rather limited although the presence of Italians was exploited as a sort of invasion of the peninsula. It was undoubtedly a serious mistake on the part of the Italians to publicize, with considerable brazenness, the happy outcome of the first days of the battle, for when it became clear that the results were meager and that Guadalajara was not a nationalist victory, the propaganda boomeranged to the discomfiture both of the Italians and the nationalists.

At this point a word may be introduced concerning the remarkably honest military reporting on the nationalist side. Lojendío, who was responsible for many of the public statements on operations, confesses that he was often annoyed that General Franco's headquarters was so reticent in releasing the story of battles in actual progress. There was a very real effort to make the reports conform strictly to what was happening, with an absence of boasting or gratuitous prediction which is so disastrous from the propaganda point of view.[12] It was often the case that foreign correspondents were not allowed to communicate the news until 24 or even 48 hours later, when full confirmation could be obtained of what had transpired. The Italians depicted Guadalajara as a great triumph almost before the engagement started. Mussolini's celebrated telegram from the vessel *Pola* on his way to Libia represented the height of a propaganda based on inadequate facts.

---

[12] Lojendío, *op. cit.*, pp. 220–221.

On the Madrid front, the *Casa del Campo* and the Ciudad Universitaria were the centers of attraction. The latter, built in the days of Alfonso XVII was a huge affair where the Faculties of Medicine, Sciences, Philosophy, and Letters and innumerable special schools and institutes, formed in their ensemble the University of Madrid. The Casa de Velázquez was one of the most attractive of the centers, dedicated to French students and researchers and it was in the midst of the ruins of this academic building that the nationalists maintained their lines for long months as a sort of *enclave* toward the heart of the great city. The worst of the fighting took place there during the first months of 1937, and during the entire course of the war, until the final entry into the city, the Ciudad Universitaria was the advance guard against which attack after attack was systematically launched.

The Northern Campaigns

The campaign in the north, of no less importance than those already described, coincided in time with the advance on Madrid. There is a constant overlapping of events and operations, especially after the stabilization of the lines.

The north represented a supreme importance for the nationalist command, for Santander, Bilbao, and the coast line to Irún on the French border included some of the most important industrial areas of modern Spain. The Asturian mines, the shipyards, and factories of the Basque country, and the connection with France overland were all significant regions which in republican hands gave them an advantage. This summary of the operations may be divided for the sake of clarity into five major parts or episodes, about which the most general observations may be made: (1) the campaign in Guipúzcoa; (2) the liberation of Oviedo; (3) the offensive in Vizcaya; (4) the conquest of Santander; (5) the conquest of Asturias.

The political and social factors in the north of Spain were considerably different from those in other areas and affected directly the reaction to the uprising and the course of events. In the Basque country, aside from Alava and Navarre where there was unanimity of sentiment, there was the strong separatist and nationalist sentiment which has been described in an earlier chapter and complicated the panorama to an incredible degree. In Asturias, the social problem was aggravated by the existence of a very old revolutionary tradition among the miners, whose participation in the bloody events of 1934 have already been mentioned and among whom communist influence was strong. Santander was crushed between the Basque provinces on one side and Asturias on the other and its relief was impossible until one or both of the other regions had been brought under nationalist authority. There were heroic episodes in this region as in other parts of Spain, and at Gijón, Simancas, and elsewhere, tiny nuclei of resisters held out against republican pressure for a long period.

The formal advance for the conquest of the frontier province of Guipúzcoa came in 1937. The area of San Sebastián and Irún was of the greatest importance because of the proximity of France and the need for cutting off a vital route leading into the neighboring country. The basis of the advance was Navarre itself. The topography led to a type of guerrilla warfare which had long since been abandoned elsewhere. The total force involved was very small and was probably never more than six thousand, almost entirely Navarrese — *Requetés* and Falangists, whereas the republican forces were composed almost exclusively of the well-known militia, extremist elements from Bilbao and other urban groups, totally unadapted to the exigencies of mountain warfare. The conquest of Irún was the next strategic achievement of importance to the nationalists — strategic in the international sense after the domination of the Straits of Gibraltar. By late September nationalist control extended over the entire province of Guipúzcoa.

If Badajoz represented a high point in the normally high emotion of the Spanish civil war, the siege of Oviedo is no less moving as a spectacle and as an example of devotion to an ideal. The visitor to Oviedo today finds ample evidence of the terrible destruction rained down on the Asturian city for weeks. Despite the miracle of reconstruction, the wounds are visible to the most casual eye.

Colonel Aranda had decided for the movement on July 19, but his position and that of the troops faithful to him was made difficult by the literal invasion of the city by miners belonging to the various extremist organizations. After a state of war was proclaimed, a large number of the extremists fled the city and by the twentieth Oviedo itself was in nationalist hands. Its tragedy was that of an almost defenseless city, for the mountains surrounding it on all sides were in republican hands, and the urban population was at the mercy of the fire from enemy positions. From the date of the initiation of the uprising until October 4, the main character of the siege of Oviedo was the relentless and unceasing bombardment of the population. Let it be said that in the long story of propaganda — so much of it palpably dishonest — regarding the atrocities of the nationalists against Badajoz, the destruction of Guernica, or the shelling of Madrid, rarely is a word said regarding the republican siege of Oviedo. If ever there was a ruthless destruction of a civilian population and mass bombardment against military and nonmilitary objectives alike, that was the case at Oviedo. The evidence is overwhelming that the intention was the total and absolute obliteration of the city. It was no casual bombardment, but a systematic, organized, and co-ordinated effort to reduce the city to rubble.[13] On October 4, the anniversary of the Asturian revolt of 1934, the republicans prepared a general attack against Oviedo. The following week was one of unmitigated martyrdom for the besieged city. It had withstood a siege of two and a half months already, with no outlet, no communication of importance with the rest of the country, and almost no source of supply or munitions; water was lacking, food rationed to the point of invisibility, the sanitary facilities were beginning to give out, and the constant losses could not be replaced by fresh recruits. On October 12, the outlying sections of Oviedo were in republican hands, and in San Lázaro street the fighting was at such close quarters that the row of houses on one side was in the hands of the nationalists; on the other, the republicans.

The need for relieving Oviedo became as imperative as that of the Alcazar at Toledo, both for reasons of sentiment and national morale. The first columns from Galicia, under the command of Colonel Teijeiro, reached the periphery of the beleaguered city on October 17 and, on penetrating, discovered that of the original five thousand defenders, scarcely seven hundred remained at their posts. For a moment in the fast-moving history of the war attention was riveted on the desperate, super-human resistance of this handful of men in the Asturian capital, whose relief had come after the conquest of some of the most difficult terrain in all Spain. As the nationalist troops moved toward Oviedo, they had been forced again and again to restrain the natural impetus of their forward movement by the need of cleaning out isolated pockets of republicans and pacify areas behind them where extremist influence was still rampant.

From September 22 to the end of March, 1937, the front in this area was more or less stabilized with only minor action occurring

---

13 The republicans were not above bombing other open cities as is attested by an eyewitness in Granada who speaks of the constant bombardments of that city through July and August, 1936. Helen Nicholson, *Death in the Morning*, London, 1937.

from time to time. The third great advance of importance was the conquest of Vizcaya. The Vizcayan campaign revealed how profound and thorough the reorganization of the nationalist fighting forces had become. One of the main preoccupations of General Franco during the early months of 1937 had been the revamping of his forces to bring them up to par technically and reduce losses. The romantic army that had begun the war — what writers have sometimes called the typical revolutionary period of the hostilities — had been superseded by a modern, mechanized, and efficient force, with a maximum of discipline, arms, and direction. This reform was evident in the campaign for the liberation of Vizcaya. The stalemate on the Madrid front convinced the nationalist commanders that the most urgent step was the removal of the pressure on the nationalist zone lying between republican territory; the relief of the north and the incorporation of those provinces with the rest of Spain would eliminate one of the most serious obstacles as well as supply materials of war and industrial plants for the successful prosecution of the conflict elsewhere.

The topography of Vizcaya is complex and difficult for the movement of troops and the damp, rainy, and muddy climate, constituted another obstacle to the penetration of its territory. The offensive of General Mola, commenced on March 31, 1937, against the outer defenses of Bilbao, formed by an intricate pattern of trenches, barbed-wire entanglements, underground passages, and pillboxes. In early June these fortifications were submitted to the most intense bombardment preparatory to the advance on the great port city, and two months and twenty days after the beginning of the offensive Bilbao was in nationalist hands in one of the most intricate operations heretofore realized in the war with the exception of the investment of Madrid.

The town of Guernica was occupied on April 28, after it had been bombed two days earlier. Just as Badajoz had loosed a wave of propaganda, so the bombing of Guernica takes its place as one of the celebrated episodes around which much fanciful legendry has accumulated. It was depicted as the ruthless, inhumane bombing of an unprotected city, with the aggravating feature that it was revered by the Basques. Guernica was a town of some five thousand people with a garrison of two battalions quartered to the north. Since the beginning of the war it possessed a factory devoted to the manufacture of small arms and munitions. Although the arms factory, the barracks, and the railway station all constituted legitimate objectives in wartime, the real difficulty is to determine just what took place at Guernica on April 26, 1937. The newsman who gave the world the story that was so played up for its propaganda value was George Lowther Steer, a free-lance correspondent who frequently sent in material to the London *Times*.[14]

The accounts of this correspondent appeared in the *Times* of April 28 and May 6; in the *Spectator* of July 30; and in an article in the *London Mercury* of August, 1937. The first report in the London *Star* stated that General Mola had ordered the town razed to the ground and German planes were reported to have accomplished the strafing with unheard-of ferocity. For three hours, it was said, high explosives and incendiary bombs were dropped on the civilian population. The *Star* reporter claimed that he had arrived at Guernica at five in the afternoon and had talked with President Euzkadi, who opined that it was the "war's worst atrocity with no military justification." Reuter informed the world that the bombardment had lasted for three and a half hours, commencing at 4:30 in the afternoon. "Hundreds of men, women, and children were roasted alive." The Basque parliament meeting in this ancient capital, and the historic oak tree of Guernica were reported to have escaped.

Other reporters visited Guernica later and stated that whole streets were untouched by bombs. There is no such person as "President Euzkadi," since the name was Aguirre, and *Euzkadi* was Basque for *Basque*. Reuter's dispatch said that airmen leaned out of their planes to toss hand grenades against the defenseless town. Robert Sencourt suggests that airmen do *not* lean out of planes and that hand grenades are not used for this type of bombing. No mention is made of an arms factory or station as obvious military objectives. The *Times* contribution by Steer came the next day after this preliminary report. The raid began at 4:30 and was made with half-ton bombs, and a highly combustible substance that was dropped in tubes. These tubes of incendiaries were tossed down in street after street to produce raging and uncontrollable fires. Machine guns were used to mow down defenseless citizens. The oak tree of Guernica under which Their Catholic Majesties had promised to respect the rights of the Basques was untouched as was the parliament house, the *Casa de Juntas*. Steer quoted President Aguirre to the effect that the raid

[14] A full account of this controversial subject is given in Sencourt, *op. cit.*, pp. 237–249, with a careful analysis of the evidence and the contradictory reports on the subject.

had for its purpose the wounding of the Basques in their sensitivity to tradition. He argued, too, that in all probability it was aimed at demoralizing the civilian population in connection with the drive on Bilbao. Steer does not write as an eyewitness. There are numerous internal discrepancies, including the time of his arrival in the town. This is variously stated as at midnight, and at two in the morning. In the May 6 article he speaks of being in Guernica until one in the morning. In the *Spectator* article, he tells of wandering around Guernica between eleven in the evening and one in the morning.

He speaks of Mass being celebrated all day in the local churches — a most improbable practice even in wartime. He tells of "sniffing for petrol," when he has already assured us that the fires were caused by incendiary bombs and not by petrol tossed into houses to burn them. In his article of April 27 he states that "the whole town of 7000 population, plus 3000 refugees, was systematically pounded to pieces." Yet hours later he refers to houses still falling and to others standing. He describes a mad automobile drive along the highway to Guernica, and almost in the same breath explains how the roads were clogged with refugees with their household effects. The several articles cited are full of the most glaring contradictions. A telegram dated May 4 refers to the Mayor of Guernica, referred to as a priest named Aronategui, having spoken over the radio in Bilbao. The dispatch of April 28 reports that "an elderly priest named Aronategui was killed by a bomb." A third priest by the name of Aronategui appears as broadcasting but *not* as mayor. The probability that there were three different priests of the same name in a town of 5000 taxes the credulity of even the most sympathetic to the classic version of the destruction of Guernica. The fact is that there were no competent foreign witnesses, and the stories as they have been woven are the result in every case of accounts and versions given after the event.

There are admitted discrepancies on the other side. The first nationalist reaction was to deny that planes had gone up at all that day because of unfavorable weather conditions. Later it was admitted that Guernica had been bombed. That there were probably excesses in the attack admits of very little doubt. Afterward, the Guernica question was examined with considerable care, especially the fires that did so much damage. The *Times* of May 5 reported the consensus:

> It has been asserted that Guernica was subjected to bombing of exceptional intensity, but the distinctive marks of an aerial bombardment are not numerous, few fragments of bombs have been discovered, the façades of buildings

standing are unmarked and the few craters were larger than anything hitherto made by a bomb in Spain. From their position it is a fair inference that these craters were caused by exploding mines which were unscientifically laid to cut roads.

On May 1 a group of foreign correspondents visited Guernica and, like the *Times* account, they testified that the indications of heavy bombardment were not visible and the walls still upright bore no traces of bomb damage, but showed every sign of fire.[15] In many of the houses the correspondents saw the clear evidence that gasoline had been spread to provoke the flames.

The *Echo de Paris* of May 3 speaks of deliberate arson in the town. The testimony in favor of deliberate destruction and not a spectacularly heavy air raid comes from a number of experienced British officers, one of whom was a distinguished airman and especially competent to judge the results of heavy bombing on cities: Sir Arnold Wilson, Brigadier Page-Croft, Major Yeats-Brown, and Wing Commander James, the latter well known for his observations on the use of incendiary bombs in Madrid. The report of these officers showed that the number of bombs actually dropped was extremely small, perhaps a dozen and all were light weight. There were no signs of incendiary bombs in any of the streets of the town and it seems reasonable that it would have been almost impossible to achieve such a degree of precision as never once in a three and a half hour raid to have hit the street a single time. In a photograph taken on October 6 the famous oak and municipal building were quite intact. Everything pointed to destruction *on the ground,* that is, deliberate arson by desperate defenders shortly before they were forced to abandon their position. This is entirely in line with other republican actions of a similar nature. They burned Irún and Eibar and made every effort to destroy San Sebastián before it was occupied by the victors. They sought to destroy as much as they could of Bilbao, and on October 12, 1937, at the Cangas de Onís in Asturias they undertook to repeat the same destruction, against historical monuments or sites which when the story got out would unquestionably shock the civilized world and create a propaganda disadvantage for the nationalists.

In this connection we may take the word of war correspondent, Harold G. Cardozo, whose account of the entire Spanish war is

---

[15] Dispatch of Havas agency in *Le Temps,* Paris, May 3, 1937.

singularly sane and balanced. Having received numerous accounts of the Guernica incident from other correspondents who had carefully examined the scene, he said that none of them saw the number of dead who would have been lying in the streets had even one tenth of the stories told been true. The correspondents entered Guernica a few hours after the first Nationalist patrols, giving the Nationalists no time to fake the situation. They did see bombed houses in ruins, but they were unscathed by fire. There were houses burned out, but they were not pitted by bomb fragments and the roadways showed no scars.

> As a result I can state that it seemed to me — I am not an expert — that undoubtedly the fires were entirely apart from the destruction caused by air bombs. The majority of the burned houses — whole streets of them — showed not the slightest signs of damage by bombing.[16]

The Guernica incident, then, is at least open to serious debate as to exactly what happened. It may be stated on the basis of all the evidence we have that there was an air raid; that German planes may very likely have done the bombing, but that the destruction of the city and its civilian population by air raids does not stand up to close scrutiny. The evidence points to destruction on the ground by the retiring republicans who sensed — and in this they were right — that they had in this spot a made to order propaganda appeal to the world, ready to swallow almost any tale that came out of Spain, provided it reflected no credit on the nationalists.

The attack on Vizcaya had been distinguished by two armies face to face, with a slow, gradual advance forward on the part of the nationalists. The Santander campaign in the late summer of 1937, on the other hand, was a campaign of movement, and although there was considerable sharp fighting, there was an absence of the fierce frontal attacks that characterized the Vizcaya chapter. The republican forces had suffered severely after the fall of Bilbao where some 15,000 prisoners had been taken in the course of the campaign, and when Santander was invested the enemy had neither the time to reform its units nor to reorganize adequate defenses. There was, therefore, a strong element of surprise and rapidity which proved psychologically advantageous to the nationalists as well as a demoralization of the republican forces produced by the failure at Brunete. The republican govern-

---

[16] Cf. Cardozo, *The March of a Nation* (New York: Medill McBride Co., 1937; London: Eyre & Spottiswoode, Ltd., 1937), p. 282.

ment, faced by the steadily increasing pressure in the north and the prospect of a complete evacuation, attempted to distract the nationalist attention by staging a number of attacks on other fronts. Teruel became a flaming war front once more, Toledo was attacked, and in June a number of thrusts were launched against the nationalist forces in the León mountains. The Brunete encounter from July 6 to 27 represented one of the more considerable republican efforts to break through the nationalist lines. The principal effect of the critical fighting at Brunete was to force a number of units in the north to be shifted and thus slow down the advance along the coast. The Santander campaign was of such importance that General Franco himself made daily visits to the battle front to observe the progress.

The attack was so well planned and so brilliantly carried out that twenty republican battalions were cut off and rendered useless. One of the features of the Santander operations was the surrender *en masse* of whole units of the republican forces. On August 26, General Dávila entered Santander.

The conquest of Asturias was the logical sequel to the capture of Santander, for this region was now entirely surrounded by the nationalists. The operations were carried out by the close blockade of the coast on the part of nationalist vessels, the movement along the coast itself by the advancing armies, and a slower penetration through the mountain passes of the rough interior. General Aranda, the hero of the siege of Oviedo, was in command of the forces that were gradually uprooting the republicans in the mountainous interior of León. It was typical mountain warfare, with precarious roads blasted by mines, remote passes savagely defended, and every movement complicated by the difficulties of the terrain. It may be noted that in this phase of the campaign the destruction of towns and hamlets by the retreating republicans was often complete. Tiny shepherd villages such as Tarna were left in absolute ruin; Isoba, Villamanin, Santa Lucía, La Vid, and innumerable other Leónese hamlets were left lifeless and in ruins as the retreating forces retired before Aranda's advance.

General Solchaga, in the meantime, made steady progress along the Asturian coast, operating in some of the most magnificent scenic areas in all Europe, the splendid *Picos de Europa*. Early in October the celebrated sanctuary of Our Lady of Covadonga was occupied. The details of the conquest of this glorious monument to the greatness of Spain, the humble spot from which the heroic reconquest of the peninsula against Islam had its beginnings, are as moving as anything in the entire chronicle of the civil war. From the peaks and heights overlooking the sanctuary, the nationalist forces could look down on the basilica. There was fear that it might be destroyed before they could reach it. It was the night of October 1, 1937. Darkness had already set in, and the rain was falling steadily, covering the mountainsides with mud and making the descent extremely perilous. The Fifth Navarrese Brigade undertook the audacious task of moving down into the valley and assuring the security of the church. Despite sporadic fire of the retreating militiamen and the inclemency of the weather which soaked them to the skin, they reached their objective despite considerable losses. Before another day dawned they had placed the national flag over the basilica and its bells pealed forth to reveal that Covadonga was in the hands of the traditionalists.

On October 21, the general headquarters in Salamanca announced that the northern front had ceased to exist; the war in Asturias, Santander, and the Basque provinces was over.

The Period of Republican Initiative

The three main episodes in the period of the civil war designated as that of republican initiative are: Brunete, Teruel, and the battle of the Ebro. These are the three moments during which the Republic took the initiative and made a serious effort to accomplish more than passive defense. It has been noted that from the very beginning of the hostilities General Franco had set the pace in terms of strategy and had forced the enemy to meet him in large measure on his own terms. Moreover, the technical superiority of the nationalist armies made it possible for them to choose the conditions and moment for decisive action. The republican forces from the very beginning had conceived of the war in terms of revolutionary action. Throughout the struggle there was a strange and obsessing persistence in confusing military action with politics, where as in nationalist Spain politics played no part at all and every attention was devoted to the purely technical aspect of war. This difference can hardly be overestimated in examining the story of the course of the hostilities. After the political crisis of May, 1937, within the Republic, a serious attempt was made to reorganize the fighting forces. The anarchists were restrained, since their method of battle was anything but orthodox. The result of this determination was the series of vigorous republican counterattacks.

The battle of Brunete, to which passing reference has already been made, took place during the month of July, 1937. At first the nationalists were disoriented by the rapidity and strength of the offensive which took them by surprise, and it was some days before the full implications became evident. General Franco placed General Varela in charge of the defense of the Brunete pocket, where the heaviest pressure was being exerted. It appeared very soon that the offensive aimed at a general break-through all along the line and not a limited local incursion. As has been suggested, political considerations played a very large part in the attack, for the loss of Bilbao despite its superb defenses had seriously demoralized the republicans. Indalecio Prieto, reputed a moderate within government circles, was forced on the defensive and a very definite turn toward a more extreme policy emerged. There was a rising demand for action, aimed at three definite objectives:

1. As a diversion from the campaign in the north and force the nationalists to withdraw forces to meet the attack.
2. Consolidate through a brilliant victory the position of the newly established government. This was a matter of prestige value.
3. Increase influence and confidence abroad.

The battle was concentrated almost entirely in the area around Brunete. Here, in a sector about ten miles long, the republicans penetrated a distance of perhaps eight miles. On the eve of the battle, July 5, Indalecio Prieto and the Pasionaria visited the front, where the most detailed preparations had been made for the attack. The offensive was described as the relief of Madrid and vengeance for the defeats suffered in the north. In many ways the surprise element on which the republicans counted did not result favorably for them, although in the initial breach opened in the nationalist lines, the enemy poured in brigade after brigade which has been described as confused milling about of hundreds of troops in an area far too small for effective operation. The break-through was complete and the republicans might easily have reached Navalcarnero in a single morning if the impetus had been retained or a more orderly advance effected. The major danger consisted of the nationalist units on either side of the breach, who endangered the long arrowlike penetration of the republicans. By July 11 the republican advance had been stopped, and the line gradually became more rigid. The battle was characterized also by a larger participation of aircraft and during the first four days over fifty republican planes were downed. Six days later, the second phase commenced. From fortified positions the republicans undertook to defend their slight advance and consolidate it. By July 24 the national counteroffensive was in full swing and on the twenty-sixth the whole nationalist line had advanced perhaps a mile; the republicans were definitely checked.

With the conclusion of the battle of Brunete, the center of attraction shifted to Aragón, while the silence that hung over the Madrid front was a curious hiatus in the long siege of the capital. It had been anticipated that Brunete would be the beginning of the definite liquidation of the Madrid front in one sense or the other, but the contrary was the case and it was Aragón that flared up as the center of operations once more.

The Aragón front was long, extending from Teruel through Belchite close to Zaragoza itself and northward to Huesca and ending near Jaca almost on the frontier of France. The offensive against this line was rather a series of thrusts and not a single, massive drive, lasting from late August until almost the middle of November, 1937. The republicans were faced by the same political necessities as in the past; the League of Nations was due to meet shortly and it was hoped that a military victory would assure a wider degree of support from abroad than the dreary series of defeats the Republic had suffered to date. The republican forces were estimated at some 85,000, including the International Brigades, now incorporated with militiamen after the terrific pounding they had taken at Brunete. The offensive was planned minutely. The propaganda effects were not overlooked and the command had taken the precaution of assuring the foreign correspondents that once Zaragoza was captured the shrine of Our Lady of Pillar, so venerated all over Spain, would be respected. On August 24 the offensive started on an extremely long front. The nationalists were especially hard pressed in the area of Quinto and Belchite, where no natural features of the terrain exist to make defense feasible. Belchite will long be remembered as one of the most heroic defenses of a handful of men against tremendous odds. A little pocket of nationalist troops, isolated behind the republican lines, held out with rare courage and sacrifice against impossible odds.

On a much smaller scale than at Toledo, the besieged in Belchite became the symbol of the breaking of the republican offensive. The air force dropped food and munitions for the resisters until on September 6 it was no longer possible to hold out and the last remnants of the gallant little band succumbed to overwhelming force.

The offensive moved northward, near Jaca and within sight of the higher Pyrenees. At no place was success more than temporary and the attempted diversion from the defeats in Asturias failed in its purpose.

Late in 1937 and early in 1938 the Teruel sector flared up; on December 15 a new offensive started along lines that were almost identical with those that had prevailed in the previous operations. The pressure on Teruel became very strong and General Franco was forced to give up the preparations for the offensive against Madrid to take care of the new threat that was developing in Aragón. The offensive was soon converted to a counterattack by the nationalists, although the subzero weather seriously retarded the advance and Teruel itself was converted into one of those last stands which occurred with almost monotonous frequency throughout the course of the war. Another epic of heroism was written by the defenders in this city who, reduced to the seminary building, held out in the face of every privation and want. The Red Cross was approached to aid evacuation, and even when the resisters were preparing to depart, the republicans invaded the city, seized hundreds of prisoners, and retained Teruel as a major prize. It was not retaken until February, after a number of important engagements such as the battle of Alfambra had taken place.

The battle of the Ebro was a prolonged affair, lasting from July 25 to the middle of November, 1938. This battle, which was decisive for the future of the nationalist cause and particularly for the proposed penetration of Catalonia, had four major aspects: (1) republican pressure and infiltration; (2) the consolidation of the lines and the stopping of the advance; (3) the prolonged period of trench warfare; (4) the nationalist offensive.

The republicans managed to cross the Ebro on July 25 and effect a number of important incursions in enemy territory. The Valencia propaganda machine gave the world ample information regarding the objectives of the attack. It was realized by nationalist headquarters that a full-dress offensive was under way and not simply a series of sharp thrusts. After the beginning of August the Ebro battle front became little more than trench warfare with heavy firing and shelling, but no decisive action.

The various republican offensives had all been seized by General Franco as an opportunity to destroy the enemy. At Brunete, Teruel, and the Ebro front, the advances had led to a counteraction which culminated in the virtual elimination of important segments of the enemy force. The balance of the war was now definitely on the nationalist side and after the battle of the Ebro the issue was no longer in doubt. Henceforth there were to be a series of great advances, by which republican territory was narrowed more and more until the final remains of the broken and discredited troops were pushed across the frontier into France. The first of these was the push down toward the Mediterranean from Aragón, and the march to the sea, an essential part of the policy of hacking republican territory into strips; the second thrust was toward Castellón and Sagunto; the third in Andalucía; the fourth in Catalonia; and the final movement the one that sealed the victory.

The successful conclusion of the battle of Teruel meant that nationalist forces were now prepared to move down the Ebro valley to the sea. In week after week of steady progress southeastward, the combined nationalist armies under the direct command of General Franco, now installed in the Pedrola estate near Zaragoza, advanced toward the Mediterranean. The details of the push add nothing to the already stirring argosy of achievement and victory. On April 15 the troops reached Vinaroz on the seacoast, and republican Spain was split.

The Galician corps that reached the sea set out at once to take over the coast. With a rhythm that was not to decrease until final victory, in 1939, the armies moved straight from Teruel to Castellón in a segment of the coast that lies just above Valencia. The advance now was characterized by larger and larger numbers of prisoners, captured in every town through which the victorious armies passed. On June 15, 1938, Castellón was taken and another point on the seacoast came into nationalist hands. During June the interest in the push to the sea was somewhat diminished by the activity of General Queipo de Llano in the south, and certain engagements in the far north, in the Pyrenean area. In the far south, on the frontiers of the provinces of Badajoz and Córdoba, where ever since the beginning of the war very little change had taken place, the nationalist forces were now on the move, cutting off slices of republican territory, reducing constantly and methodically the ever narrowing space within which the Republic still managed to move.

The conquest of Catalonia (December 23, 1938, to February 10, 1939) was the great episode that closed the war and assured the final victory. Once Catalonia had been taken, Madrid could no longer hold out. The nationalists were not even obliged to operate against Alicante,

Murcia, Valencia, and the other parts of Spain that up to the last moment remained in republican hands.

On December 23, four breaches were opened in the enemy lines. The most difficult sector in the republican front, the Montsech heights, were stormed successfully in midwinter. From all sides and directions, divisions of the advancing army pushed down into Catalonia; the great names of the civil war were all there, Moscardó, Solchaga, Kinderlán, Vigón, and many others. By January, 1939, the onrush was irresistible; Tarragona fell, and late that month Barcelona was invested. It was anticipated that the Catalan capital would offer a long and terrible resistance and might be destroyed in the fierce fighting that would ensue. The city was subjected to bombardment on January 22 when General Yagüe with his Moors camped within striking distance of the port, although the only real resistance was a desultory cannonading from the heights of Montjuich. Barcelona fell and the remnants of the republicans fled northward toward Gerona and the frontier of France.

In Madrid there was chaos. Fighting took place between extremist elements within the city. The government was gone and there was no authority. The Defense Council of Madrid had come into existence after the disappearance of all government. On March 28, Madrid was open wide to the entrance of the nationalists.[17] This was followed shortly by the collapse of Valencia, Cuenca, Ciudad Real, Murcia, Jaén, and the other regions that had been under the Republic up to the end. On April 1, 1939, General Franco announced to the world that the war was over.

2. FOREIGN INTERVENTION

No single problem connected with the civil war has aroused more controversy than that of foreign intervention. Everyone knows that there was intervention on both sides. Unfortunately the exact figures are impossible to present. The very nature of the war and the conscious efforts to confuse public opinion led to considerable inexactitude regarding the volunteers.

The quest for foreign intervention on the part of the republican government coincides almost exactly with the outbreak of the war

[17] The last weeks in Madrid were tumultuous. Colonel Casado had seized control and the communists were forced to seek refuge or flee. "Colonel Casado addressed the people to condemn the shameful flight of Jesús Hernández and the 'Pasionaria' " (*A.B.C.*, March 8, 1939). On March 12 the same paper announced the "communist sedition is fast being liquidated."

itself. The Madrid government dispatched Captains Ismael Warleta de la Quintana and Juan Abola to Paris to conclude large purchases of war materials. Fernando de los Ríos, then in London, was ordered to Paris on July 23, to "assist" the Spanish ambassador in his negotiations for material aid from France.[18] De los Ríos visited Pierre Cot, Edouard Daladier, and Jules Moch in search of assistance to the Republic. The letter of the De los Ríos to José Giral, dated July 25, 1936, throws considerable light on the beginnings of foreign intervention in Spain. After a discussion of the Spanish situation and French interest in supporting the Republic, De los Ríos states:

> A new question arose, that of Spanish aviators coming to Paris for the planes. I explained the impossibility of doing this, in view of the few aviators we have and our intention to retain the French pilots. I was told — by one who knew — that the planes and bombs were ready and could leave the next morning.[19]

The difficulty seemed to be that the Ministry of Foreign Affairs in Paris was reluctant to have French aviators take the planes to Madrid, although there was never any question whatever about delivering planes for combat purposes in the Spanish war.

One of the initial sources of republican man power was the presence in Barcelona during the summer of 1936 of some 15,000 men of various nationalities who had come for a sports festival. A large number of these "sportsmen" immediately joined the fight and participated in the initial action against the nationalists in Barcelona and formed the nucleus of the later International Brigades. By August the French leftist press was vociferous in its demands for recruitment for intervention in Spain:

> The French government authorizes the formation of groups of volunteers to go to the aid of the Spanish workers. We are confident that the volunteers for liberty will come, not only from France but from other countries.[20]

---

[18] The fullest information on these points is available in the documents and files of the Foreign Office in Madrid.

[19] *Garibaldini in Ispagna,* Madrid, 1937, p. 3, contains an account of the participation in this action during the first days of the civil war. In *I accuse France,* by "A Barrister," London, n.d., page 3, we find the comment that on July 20, 1936, the Spanish Ambassador in Paris, under express orders of the Spanish Foreign Minister, visited the French Prime Minister, M. Blum, and asked him to supply immediately abundant supplies of war material which would include 13 bombing planes, to be delivered that afternoon in the airdrome of Prat del Llobregat, Barcelona; 50 light machine guns; 2 million machine-gun cartridges; 1 million Lebel cartridges; 8 75-cm. guns with appropriate shells, and 20,000 gas bombs.

[20] *L'Humanité,* Paris, Aug. 7, 1936.

The national command at Burgos, in its communiqués of August 27 and 28, 1936, pointed out the presence of Frenchmen in the republican forces and the fact that French army officers had been observed in combat. In the engagements at Behovia and San Marcos foreign troops had been identified among the enemy forces. On July 30, 1936, the republican government transferred 1500 kilos of gold by plane to France in payment of war materials and for expenses for encouraging recruits for the fighting front.

The French trade unions took upon themselves the job of recruiting volunteers. Lieutenant Colonel Luque and Commander Prado of the republican forces reached Paris to enlist technicians and officers. The Spanish archives contain the originals of the contracts made with those who agreed to service in Spain. Another commission flourished in Paris under Professor Jiménez de Asúa, offering the rank of captain and an inducement of 10,000 francs to those joining up. On August 14, 1936, the first contingent crossed the frontier into Spain.

The French pilots who left Paris on August 5 with six planes were taken into the republican army at once, with a salary of 150,000 francs a month, and another 35,000 on taking off for Madrid. The facts and figures on the growing French aid during the late summer of 1936 are perfectly clear. The facts are the following: August 7, 15 Devoitine planes; August 9, 6 Potez-54; August 16, 2 bimotor planes, Dragon; August 22, 4 bimotors Croyton and 1 Airspeed.

French aid continued in increasing quantities, despite the adherence of France to the Non-Intervention Committee, and the sources of information regarding French assistance are abundant: the capture of French material by the advancing nationalists, and the various accounts that have appeared since that day to confirm in detail the exact degree of aid given the Republic by France.[21]

On the basis of personal observation, Pierre Héricourt recounts that in the months of May and June, 1937, he counted among the loot, captured by the nationalists, 318 machine guns, 1358 automatic rifles, 2,600,000 cartridges, 53 37-mm. guns; 32 75-mm., and 155 16-mm. guns of foreign origin. During the summer of 1937 the actual list of war material of French origin included such items as 12,500 gas masks, which could not have been released except by the expressed authorization of the French War Ministry; 172 Hotchkiss machine guns, 122 Saint Etienne machine guns, and over 25 million Lebel

[21] See Pierre Héricourt, *Pourquoi mentir,* Paris, 1937, and *Les Soviets et la France, fournisseurs de la révolution espagnole,* Paris, 1938.

cartridges. During the final campaign in Catalonia, the quantities of war material captured as the republican armies collapsed demonstrated the monumental character of the war supplies that had come from France. It is a melancholy reflection that this same material of war, made available to Spain in such gigantic quantities for the defense of the republican cause, might well have been one of the elements in the French unpreparedness a year later in the war against Germany.

The decision to support the Spanish Republic through communist channels is no longer open to the slightest discussion. Although Soviet aid in the beginning of the war was indirect and it was only at a later date that vessels proceeding from Soviet ports delivered war materials to the Republic.

On July 26, 1936, under the chairmanship of Gaston Mommousseau, French communist leader, a committee met in Prague to examine the bases of aid to the Spanish Republic. The main points in this intervention were to be:

1. Create a fund of a billion francs to support the Republic.
2. The Soviet trade unions to raise the major portion of this amount.
3. The Soviet banking agencies to arrange for the transfer of this money.
4. The administration of the fund to be in the hands of a committee of five: Thorez, Ercoli, Dolores Ibarruri, Largo Caballero, and José Díaz.
5. The formation of a brigade of 5000 men, to be recruited from the working class.

Soviet intervention was less evident during the first months of hostilities, but when Largo Caballero took over the reins of government, the Soviet Union intervened far more directly. As early as October 16, 1936, Stalin telegraphed José Díaz, general secretary of the Spanish Communist Party:

> The Soviet workers in aiding the revolutionary working masses of Spain are merely doing their duty. They are aware that the liberation of Spain from reactionary Fascist oppression is not a private Spanish affair but the common cause of all advanced and progressive humanity.

The supreme director of Soviet supplies to Spain was Yagoda, the O.G.P.U. head and later victim of the great purge and a Captain Oulansky was sent to Odessa to take charge of the shipments destined for the Spanish Republic. Supplies began to arrive in increasing quantities at Barcelona, Valencia, Alicante, and Cartagena. So great was this initial Soviet aid, in the autumn of 1936, that Largo Caballero was moved to exultation in his address to the republican forces on October 28, 1936: "At this moment we have in our hands a formidable amount of mechanized equipment, tanks, and a powerful air force."[22]

The nationalist communiqué of October 29 called attention to some forty tanks with Soviet personnel, protecting the advance of the republican militia at Seseña, and after that date Soviet supplies moved with increasing precision. The first definite information regarding direct Soviet aid is the arrival of the Mexican vessel *América* in Barcelona, on August 14, 1936, with a cargo of chloride of soda "Made in the U.S.S.R."

The list of Soviet vessels and their supplies would take pages to enumerate. The facts are there to prove that this aid was very far from being exclusively symbolic. On October 11, the *Kilimin* discharged war materials at Alicante; on the nineteenth the Soviet merchant ship, *Chrustchew,* unloaded 42 trucks and 200 tons of munitions; on October 23, the *G. Dimotrov* brought 6 planes, 48 military trucks, and 1106 tons of munitions. The republican press, especially that of the port cities, saluted the arrival of these supplies as evidence of the solidarity of the democratic states.[23] On October 31, the *Transbalt,* of some 12,000 tons, reached Barcelona with eighty Soviet airmen while fifteen other Soviet vessels arrived in Spanish ports with every conceivable variety of war material: special airplane parts, 16 light tanks, machine guns, and light artillery. On November 1, 50 Soviet tanks were unloaded in Alicante, fully equipped down to the last detail, and the Soviet ship *Kursk,* from Odessa, unloaded hand grenades, small bombs, 2000 tons of rifles, and other war materials. The frequency of the arrivals increased and by February, 1937, the average was two a day while other vessels, flying the flag of Greece, Norway, Mexico, and various countries also carried Soviet war materials.

If Soviet aid in war materials was enormous and sustained, the presence of representatives and agents on Spanish soil was no less important, comprising in the main technicians, directors, and in-

---

[22] See Madrid press for Oct. 28, 1936. See also, Toynbee and Boulter, *Survey of International Affairs, 1936–1937,* London, 1938, Vol. II, p. 198 sq., with descriptions of the levies on wages and other evidences of Soviet collaboration with the republican government.

[23] Valencia press, end of Oct., 1936.

structors. Rarely did Soviet citizens engage in combat. It was the International Brigades that bore the brunt of the actual fighting at the fronts.

The first Soviet technicians of whom we have precise knowledge arrived in Cartagena during September, 1936, on the ship *Rostok* and belonged to the tank corps and various air services.[24] Early in October, 1936, Soviet agents were observed in the International Zone of Tangier whose purpose was apparently to foment trouble for the nationalists in Morocco.[25] Near Cartagena, at a point named San Javier, Soviet technicians organized a seaplane base staffed exclusively by Soviet citizens. At Los Alcázares, elaborate repair and construction shops were set up under the direction of Soviet pilot, Michael Kirigin and a pilot-training school under Soviet direction functioned at Alcantarilla. Soviet technicians ran the hangers at La Rabassa and Salou.

The supreme technical direction of the Soviet aid to Spain was in the hands of General Berzim, onetime head of the Red Army Intelligence Service and a veteran of many years in the Soviet army. Arthur Stashevsky, as commercial representative of the U.S.S.R. in Barcelona, occupied a key position in the delivery of the stream of supplies for the republicans. Ambassador Rosenberg, who came to Madrid upon the establishment of diplomatic relations between republican Spain and the Soviet Union, brought with him the usual inflated personnel and was accompanied by a number of specialists in Soviet penetration.

The Soviet Consul General in Barcelona was Vladimir Antonov Ovshenko who had served in the Red army in the Ukraine and had been in charge of its political propaganda services. The Consul General was by no means of a retiring disposition, for from the balcony of the *Generalitat* of Catalonia, he announced to the expectant inhabitants of the great port city, that "Russia is with you. The Russian communists will not tolerate a Fascist victory. To prevent it we shall stop at nothing."

Intervention was not limited to a few technicians, or to the supervision of the entry of supplies, for the Soviets literally took over a number of administrative functions of the republican government.

---

[24] There are numerous accounts of how Madrid was filled with foreign — and Soviet — technicians, aviators, and other personnel. Clara Campoamor, *La révolution espagnole vue par une républicaine,* p. 174, and Louis Fischer, *Men and Politics,* p. 387.

[25] Abraham Mennowich, Ernest Mulier, Bruno Weil, Willie Neumann, and others.

Aside from the military operations, Radio Barcelona was run by one Kolzow-Ginsburg. The detective service in the Catalan city was under A. Wronski. The office of one Stashevsky was the center for all matters relating to commercial or business transactions. Armaments came under the direction of Vladimir Bischitzki. In Bilbao, one Toumanov was almost dictator. In Madrid, the names of Gorev, Skoblewsky, and Aralink figured among the most prominent agents. The Soviet ambassador attended the republican cabinet meetings and took part in their deliberations.[26]

France and the Soviet Union were by no means the exclusive sources of aid for republican Spain. Various countries of central Europe, and especially Czechoslovakia, contributed to the assistance, and Greece served as a base for the reshipment of material from the eastern Mediterranean. We find in a letter dated October 30, 1936, from F. F. Guardiola, to Colonel Jiménez de la Bereza in Barcelona, specific reference to the war materials available for importation and the indication that certain materials from Great Britain and supposedly destined for China are available to Spain. The writer lists the various items which can be obtained: from France, tear-gas bombs in huge quantities, numerous types of planes with the authorization of the French air ministry; from London, 10,000 light machine guns of the Hotchkiss type and munitions; from Czechoslovakia it was proposed to receive planes of various types and purposes, motors, machine guns, Mauser rifles, munitions, and military vehicles of various descriptions. Curiously enough, it was proposed during October, 1936, to accept the offer of Jacques Risler of the Pasteur Institute in Paris to set up a factory in Barcelona for the manufacture of gases.[27]

Czech material went through the Polish port of Gdynia and attained ample proportions during the early months. The figures on exportations

---

[26] An extremely interesting account of the whole civil war period is given by the former Minister of the Interior in the republican cabinet, Julián Zugazagoitía, *Historia de la guerra en España,* Buenos Aires, 1940. Among other things he states: "The Spanish republic had not become communist overnight. The instinct of self-preservation pushed it inevitably toward the Soviet Union. . . . Russia was, on the establishment of relations, our one hope. It was a life preserver" (p. 111).

[27] The statistics of the war material that actually entered Spain between October 20 and November 20, 1936, at a time when the nationalists were receiving no aid from anyone and were dependent on their own resources, show the fabulous character of foreign aid to the Spanish Republic. The list for this period of a month includes: 100,000 rifles, 300,000,000 cartridges, 15,000 machine guns, 200 field guns, 75 anti-aircraft guns, 300 bombers.

through that port were actually published in a report to the local Chamber of Commerce. They included munitions, machine guns, rifles, planes, and various artillery pieces. Documents taken from the republican army show the amount of such deliveries through the port of Santander, shipped from Gdynia. Obviously much of the aid was purchased by the republican government directly. In other cases, the aid was part of the ideological common front that the extreme Left was attempting to create around the Spanish issue.

One of the astonishing features of this whole turgid history of foreign intervention in the Spanish civil war is that Germany figures prominently among the suppliers of arms and munitions to the republican forces. We have been led to believe that the forces engaged in mortal combat were nicely divided between Right and Left; good and bad, heroes and traitors. The Republic was supposed to be fighting for democracy and the nationalists for the imposition of military rule under the aegis of Hitler and Mussolini. This ludicrous *reductio ad absurdum* of the issues is seriously shaken when we discover that German ports were important as the point of embarkation for considerable supplies to the republican armies. The Spanish archives reveal how this traffic operated, for in its files may be found a communication from the embassy in Berlin to the effect that one Catsuropulos, an Athens' industrialist and intermediary, offered Fokker planes, German powder, and other war materials obtainable in Germany to the Spanish republicans.[28] Apparently German munitions concerns and even the German government were quite willing to allow war materials to leave Germany destined for Barcelona, under the flimsy pretext that Greece was the point of destination. The nationalist government of Spain protested to Berlin on July 23, 1938, on the basis of the information mentioned above. The German embassy replied, in

[28] Note of July 22, 1938. The fact that the German government was far from enthusiastic over the quick triumph of the nationalist movement is revealed in the following quotation: "From the German point of view, a hundred percent victory by Franco is not desirable. We are more interested in a continuation of the war and the preservation of tension in the Mediterranean. . . . Nevertheless the fortifying of the Italian positions in the Balearic Islands cannot be tolerated by France or Great Britain and might lead to war against Italy, in which case Spain, if entirely in Nationalist hands, would take part on the side of Italy's enemies. . . . In view of the information given the Führer by Generaloberst Goering, it is considered imperative to reduce or abandon all aid to Spain. The Führer is in agreement with this." (Report of meeting, Nov. 5, 1937, of Hitler, Goering, von Neurath, Blomberg, Fritsch, and Admiral Raeder. Quoted in *Nazi Conspiracy and Aggression,* Vol. III, pp. 303 and 305. Document 386-PS.)

a note dated in San Sebastián, October 21, 1938, to the effect that these materials had reached Greece from the Hirtemberg Munitionsfabrik, near Vienna, and that the sales had been suspended after the incorporation of Austria into the Reich. On December 6, 1938, the Spanish ambassador again urged that the German government put an end to this traffic so detrimental to the interests of nationalist Spain. The whole business was hopelessly complicated by the intervention of Greek and Turkish agents, and the entire mechanism of international intrigue, for which the Spanish civil war was an ideal stage.

The International Brigades

The most spectacular form of foreign intervention was, of course, the International Brigades. In line with the agreement reached at Prague, it was proposed that a small brigade be organized especially in view of the ease with which the nationalists defeated the so-called "People's Army." After General Varela took Talavera de la Reina and the threat against Madrid became menacing, a far larger effort was envisaged. Maurice Thorez visited Barcelona and Madrid and dealt directly with Largo Caballero, now in control, and proposed in late September, 1936, a far more ambitious program of action, including the formation of the volunteer groups, under the designation of International Brigades. The French Communist Party was the logical agency to carry out the organization and operation of the scheme, since Thorez could function under the cloak of parliamentary immunity and since the communist minority in the French Chamber of Deputies was indispensable to the Popular Front cabinet. The number of the agents of French communism dispatched to Spain reveals the importance of this activity to the extreme Left. André Marty was placed in general charge of the program in Spain and André Malraux, today a fervent supporter of General de Gaulle, directed the organization of the air arm. The French leftist press began one of those noisy, synchronized campaigns such as only the communists are capable of producing — and of stomaching. The central committee for the recruiting of the Brigades was located in the Rue Lafayette in Paris with Thorez, Marty, Klement Gottwald, Palmiro Togilatti, and Luigi Longo as members. The military adviser was the Soviet General Karol Swierczewski, whose *nom de guerre* became General Walter. Although a Pole by origin, General Walter had been for many years in the service of the Red army. Other recruiting centers were scattered all over Paris and in the French provincial cities. The communists, with their socialist and radical collaborators, created with great rapidity a complex system of enlistment, transportation, and entry into Spain with Perpignan the focal point for this movement toward Spain. It was estimated that at the end of 1936, some 600 recruits came through Perpignan each day.

The functioning of the system was perfect. After a brief stay at Figueras near the French frontier, an appropriate number was transferred to Albacete,[29] where the serious organization of the Brigades began after the arrival of Marty at the end of October. The first order for the organization and concentration of the Brigades bears the date of October 29. Marty was accompanied by a considerable staff with numerous nationalities represented: the Belgian Van der Bosch; Lieutenant Colonel Hans Kahle, German; Ludwig Renn, the German novelist, and many others. The political side of the Brigades was represented more by the Italians and the French. Albacete became, in fact, a formation center for the republican resistance, with churches, schools, and other buildings taken over by the Brigade organization. There were centers for training in the reading of maps, for aircraft observation, and the preparation of political commissars. The Brigade Cheka was presided over by Marty, and its sinister activities provided him with the somber name of the "Butcher of Albacete." The Brigades were notable for the excellent organization of their hygienic and health facilities, a large portion of the medical aid, both in personnel and money, coming from Jewish sources, notably from America. Their uniforms were made in France; small arms were imported from Mexico and later from Poland and Belgium, while heavy weapons were mostly Soviet.

The rapidity with which the nationalists advanced on Madrid made the use of the Brigades indispensable before their training was complete. In November, 1936, the Brigades were sent to the defense of Madrid under the direction of General Kleber, whose real name was Lazar Fakete, of Hungarian origin. He had served in the Austro-Hungarian army in World War I, fell prisoner to the Russians, and was released by the victorious revolution in 1917, from which date

---

[29] The accounts by former members of the Brigades are numerous. One anonymous record, from a British member, entitled, *In Spain With the International Brigade: A Personal Narrative,* London, 1938, p. 7, gives this impression of entrance into republican Spain: "The red flag was flying everywhere with the hammer and sickle of the Soviets, while the smallest children seemed to be able to sing the Internationale and give the clenched fist salute. . . . I began to think I had come to a Bolshevik state instead of a democratic one."

on his career was that of a Soviet officer. On November 7, when it seemed evident that Madrid would fall, the Eleventh Brigade was ordered to the Madrid front.

In Albacete new formations were rushed, André Marty combining his military activities with the most rigorous elimination of all non-communist elements or suspected Trotskyites. In Madrid, the picture of life has been drawn by Ernest Hemingway in his description of the Gaylord Hotel in Madrid, center and focal point of this strange, unreal, and extremely un-Spanish gentry that had in some devious way managed to become the spokesmen and defenders of the Republic.[30]

---

[30] An extremely curious footnote on the role of the International Brigades is the large number of participants who have since risen to positions of prominence in the countries east of the Iron Curtain. Many of the leaders also occupy posts of importance in the communist movements in western Europe. The initiative in the formation of the Brigades was taken by George Dimitrov, then general secretary of the Komintern, and André Marty, French communist leader who had been responsible in large measure for the naval mutiny in 1919 of the French fleet in the Black Sea. The military adviser of Marty in the organization of the Brigades was "General Walter," who later became Minister of National Defense in the provisional government of Poland. Klement Gottwald, now President of Czechoslovakia was political adviser, and with him was Luigi Longo, vice-chairman of the Italian communist party who served in Spain under the name of Luigi Gallo. Many of those who have achieved fame were in Spain as political commissars, in other words, as men in the confidence of the communist parties to supervise the political reliability of the armed forces. Ludwig Renn, German writer and an ex-communist, was attached to the Thaelmann Brigade. Marty's lieutenant in Spain was Auguste Lecouer, subsecretary in the Ministry of Industry in Paris for a time after the war. General Vincet, member of the General Staff in Spain and a regular French army officer, as well as Colonel Roy Tanguy, former political commissar of the Fourteenth Brigade "La Marseillaise," also returned to his post in the French army. Charles Tillon, prominent French communist and member of the government during the period after the liberation when the communists formed a part of the government, served as a commissar.

Pietro Nenni, although a socialist, at least in name, was commissar for the Garibaldi Brigade; a number of other Italian personalities, such as Randolfo Pacciardi, Giuseppe di Vittorio, Giulano Payeta, Francesco Scotti, Illio Borontini, Giovanni Pesco, Clemente Maglietta, Velio Spani, and Eduardo d'Onofrio, all active in communist circles or in the communist-controlled Italian trade unions, served their dubious apprenticeship in Spain. Ivo Rukasinov, a general in the Yugoslav army, was an officer in the Brigades and other Yugoslav military of high rank who served are Slatic, Branko Ribkar, Bore Naksov, and Janko Gregov. Bohumil Lastovicek, a battery commander in the Gottwald Brigade, has been director of the Czech National Radio under the "popular democracy." Lace Holdos, political commissar of the Brigade, became afterward vice-president of the National Slovak Council. The commander of the Masaryk battalion, Milos Nekvasil, was later head of the Czech censorship and Joska Spirk became in time president of the Czech Metallurgical Workers. Ilya Bart, a Czech writer, headed in due time the Czech writers' guild. Jirzi Horsky became a lieutenant colonel in the Czech army, after serving

The unsuccessful offensive against Segovia and La Granja led to a break between Largo Caballero and the Soviet direction of the Brigades.

Soviet intervention played a large role in the political as well as military aspects of the war. After it became apparent that the La Granja offensive was useless for the relief of Bilbao, the Soviet technicians turned to Brunete as the most plausible solution of the difficulties and it was proposed to break through to Navalcarnero and smash the nationalist encirclement of the capital. All the Brigades except the Fourteenth participated in this action and suffered grievously from the resultant defeat. Moreover the iron rule of communism was not to the liking of many of the volunteers who were not all moved by the fervent devotion to Stalinism that animated Comrade Marty. There were desertions and escapes, executions, and a lowering morale so that the activity of the Brigades was becoming an international scandal. Officers and highly placed directors fell into disgrace or were liquidated and the Brigades became the sordid, frightening repetition of the communist will to crush all who deviate. General Kleber, who had disappeared, returned at the head of the Brigades during the Aragón campaign, but the losses had become so heavy that it was necessary to introduce Spaniards into the ranks.[31]

---

as colonel in the Fifteenth Brigade. Leopold Horrman, a captain in the Dimitrov Brigade, became head of the Czech security police.

Colonel Szyr, political commissar of the Palafox Brigade, turned up as undersecretary of industry in the Polish provisional government. Mietowski, of the Dombrowski Brigade, became undersecretary of police in Poland. Colonel Torunczyk, a political commissar, was transformed into undersecretary for annexed territories in the Polish government. Former Colonel Tadeusz Oppman, of the Dombrowski Brigade, was assistant military attaché in Paris. Ksiezarezyk, former battalion commander in Spain, became military commander of Cracow. Mieczyslaw Szleyen, a political commissar, became director of political education of an officers' center in Lodz.

The director of the Varna Radio in Bulgaria, Karanov, was a captain attached to the Information Section of the general staff of the International Brigades. Georgi Tochev, a tank officer in Spain, directed tank instruction in Plovdiv.

Walter Roman, former political commissar, became a colonel and director of propaganda in the Defense Ministry in Budapest. Ladislas Rajk, recently executed by the Rakosi government, was assistant chief of information on the Brigade general staff. Ferenc Munnich, also a political commissar, became prefect of Hungarian police. Miklos Szalvoi, another Brigade officer, became a general and chief of the security service of the Hungarian army.

[31] An excellent source on the International Brigades is their own publications. A reproduction of those in English may be found in *Volunteer for Liberty. Publication of the International Brigades during the Spanish Civil War, 1937–38,* New York, 1949. This is a commemorative volume issued by the members of the Abraham

The variety of nationalities represented by the Brigades is revealed in the prisoners that fell to the nationalists during the Catalan campaign, among whom were 141 British, 70 Americans, 42 Germans, 42 French, 31 Poles, 24 Australians, 24 Portuguese, 12 Swiss, 9 Italians, and a host of other nationalities.[32]

To avoid the necessity for retiring the volunteers under the non-intervention arrangement, wholesale naturalizations were authorized and documentary proof is abundant, showing innumerable cases of foreigners who were given Spanish citizenship to allow them to remain.

There were also volunteers and outside aid on the nationalist side, with a number of units formed by foreigners, notably the Portuguese volunteers under the name of *Viriatos,* the White Russians, the French forming the Joan of Arc unit, and the Irish who constituted a small group within the nationalist ranks. The major aid from the point of view of fighting personnel was the Italian. It must be remembered that at this time, General Franco had been denied the status of belligerent by other nations and was not bound, therefore, by any international agreements, since the rest of the world refused to treat him as anything but a vulgar rebel with no rights and therefore no responsibilities. In contrast, the Madrid government was still held in esteem as the legitimate, official government of Spain and the only one with which the other powers maintained normal diplomatic relations. The disparity in position and especially the totally different juridical position of the two forces in conflict is an important element in appraising the significance of foreign aid in the war.

The first period of Italian participation, on the basis of a few volunteers, was the Málaga campaign in early 1937. These volunteers were generally ill prepared, unaware of the treacherous nature of the war, and convinced that the relatively easy conquest of Málaga repre-

---

Lincoln Brigade and gives numerous facsimiles of the Brigade journals during the period of the war.

I have gone through dozens of these journals now preserved in the Municipal Library of Madrid. The astonishing thing is that in addition to the common languages such as Italian, German, French, English, and Polish, there was a journal published for Albanian members of the Brigades called *Vulnetari i Lirisë,* indicating how even the obscure nationalities were marshaled for the fight against Spain.

The totally communist character of the Brigades is revealed on every page. The *Volunteer for Liberty* in English, Vol. I, No. 23, Nov. 15, 1937, published a large photograph of the Plaza de Independencia in Madrid with huge pictures of Stalin, Voroshilov, Litvinov, Molotov, Kalinin, and Lenin. The issue of Dec. 13, 1937, reported the visit of Major Clement Attlee, who "led the assembly in a loyalist salute."

[32] *Le Matin,* Paris, Aug. 17, 1938.

sented the most severe trial of the conflict.[33] Guadalajara was a lesson of the first order and ended this initial period of joyous and easy optimism. The Italians participated in the conquest of Santander. Some 30,000 took part in this operation, organized in three purely Italian divisions and two mixed Brigades, part Spanish and part Italian, and there was Italian participation on the Aragón front. After that there was a marked tendency for it to decline. In the Catalan campaign, for example, only one Italian division operated, the *Littorio,* by the side of several of mixed composition. The nationalists never employed the Italians as shock troops in the same manner as the republicans their International Brigades. In general the brunt of the advances and the opening of breaches in the enemy positions was carried out by the Legion, the Navarrese units, and the Moors from Spanish Morocco and Ifni.

The strict chronology of the foreign participation is important. There were International Brigades in Madrid in late October and early November, 1936. The first Italian volunteers arrived at Cádiz and Seville for incorporation in the fighting forces at the very end of 1936, with General Roata in charge at the beginning. Colonels Piazzoni and Guassardo began the development of the mixed units which bore the name *Flechas.*[34]

German support of the nationalists took a variety of forms. There were a considerable number of "volunteers" in the nationalist armies, as is attested by articles in the German press, and German aircraft

---

[33] On this point we have the testimony of Franz Borkenau, who was at Málaga and observed the events of the nationalist advance from the republican side: "Naturally there were the usual German and Italian planes and pilots. But the press, both Spanish and foreign, was full of news about the intervention of Italian infantry units since the beginning of the offensive; actually no such units participated. My companions and I, who visited all the important sectors of the Málaga front in the first days of February, invariably inquired about the enemy troops holding the positions opposite the Republican lines. Invariably the answer was that there were Moors . . . foreign Legion, and Falange. We consistently inquired about Italians; every commander of a subsector replied that in his sector there were no Italians; there might be in other subsectors. Prisoners had been taken; there were no Italians among them. . . . Had German infantry units participated in the taking of Málaga they would probably have continued to appear in the following fights at Motril. They did not, however. . . . It is moreover a fact that no German or Italian prisoners had been made for many months (with the exception of pilots) either at Málaga or elsewhere; this changed soon after Málaga" (*The Spanish Cockpit* [London: Faber and Faber, Ltd., 1937], p. 223).

[34] A good account of the intervention from the Italian side is contained in Francesco Belforte, *La guerra civile in Spagna. Gli interventi stranieri nella Spagna rossa,* Rome, 1938. Beginning of Red intervention, p. 43 sq.

played an important role in the fighting. Germans actually at the fighting front were organized as the Condor Legion, a relatively small force compared with the Italians:

> According to the information at the disposal of the British government the number of Italians who left was approximately 22,000 and the number of Germans about 6,000 (Mr. Butler in the House of Commons on the 5th of June, 1939, in answer to a parliamentary question).[35]

Although the Condor Legion, dispatched in November, 1936, was distinguished by its extreme mobility and technical perfection, it was largely in the field of training that the Germans lent an effective aid to the nationalists: in the use of tanks and antitank defense and flame throwing as well as in engineering and artillery tactics, signal and communications services, and many other specialized branches. Not until after November 18, when the impetus of the first attack on Madrid had worn itself out, did the German and Italian governments break relations with the Azaña regime and recognize the new state with headquarters in Burgos.

---

[35] Toynbee, A. J., and Boulter, V. M., *Survey of International Affairs, 1938,* Royal Institute of International Affairs, 1942, Vol. I, p. 358.

Chapter 11. THE CIVIL WAR:

THE SCENE BEHIND THE LINES

THE impact of the rising in Africa produced an almost immediate reaction in the Spain under republican control, although it is impossible to generalize with reference to all republican territory. The tragedy was that the central government in Madrid, weak and vacillating, was both unable and unwilling to exert control over the lawless elements that surged to the surface as soon as it became evident that the country faced war. The ample autonomy of Catalonia made Barcelona an almost independent area under influences that were not always the same as in Madrid. For one thing, the political trends tended to be different in the two centers. Madrid never knew the preponderance of Anarchists such as dominated Barcelona in the early weeks.

The executive power of the Madrid government in Barcelona had virtually disappeared after the suppression of the military uprising of General Goded and the Catalan regional government reigned supreme. Every reporter who has written of his impressions of the Spain of the first weeks of the war refers to the confusion in authority that prevailed. Franz Borkenau writes of having to get a sort of *laissez passer* from an anarchist committee at the frontier before proceeding on his journey.[1] The American newsman, H. Edward Knoblaugh, writes of having four more or less autonomous committees stamp his papers on entering Catalan territory.[2] It must be emphasized that the reaction in Catalonia was far more social than military while in Madrid, correspondents were in agreement that the atmosphere was that of a city in wartime, and later of a capital under siege. Barcelona

---

[1] Borkenau, *The Spanish Cockpit*, p. 68.

[2] H. Edward Knoblaugh, *Correspondent in Spain* (New York: Sheed and Ward, 1937), p. 31.

and the Catalan provinces gave the impression of a region in the grip of social revolution. This fundamental difference is essential to the understanding of republican Spain during the entire course of the war.

Barcelona in the first days of the civil war presented a picture of revolution in full swing. The churches that had escaped the destruction of previous years, and especially of February, 1936, were burned and pillaged. H. Edward Knoblaugh reports the burial vaults torn open, the remains of religious placed in full public view in grotesque postures, and other scenes equally repugnant.[3] Armed workers in civilian dress roamed the streets and confiscated automobiles were filled with the representatives of the innumerable committees and revolutionary groups that were in control, their sides painted with the letters of their organizations: CNT, FAI, UGT, PSUC (The United Socialist-Communist Party of Catalonia). Others bore the letters POUM of the Trotskyite deviationists and at times the letters all appeared together as a sort of assurance of proletarian solidarity in the struggle against the insurrection. The letters UHP covered walls and other cars — the letters that were to become one of the famous slogans of the republican revolution: *Uníos, Hermanos Proletarios,* "Unite Proletarian Brothers." The ominous flag of anarchism flew everywhere; there was no police control and no effort to guarantee the protection of either the individual or property. Requisitioning had gone to incredible lengths, including hotels, factories, and shops.[4] The approaching campaign against Zaragoza seemed to dominate the thought of the masses in Barcelona and it was anticipated that the Aragonese capital would fall quickly and that a successful expedition would be led against Mallorca.

Madrid, with perhaps an atmosphere less proletarian or at least less completely revolutionary and certainly less anarchist than Barcelona, was nevertheless in the hands of the comrades and especially of the *Milicianos.* This improvised military organization conformed entirely to the general pattern of confusion and disorder and it was common knowledge that in the early days the militia often fought or rested as the mood dictated. Numerous militiamen went up to the Alto de León front for an afternoon and returned to Madrid to the more comfortable life of the requisitioned hotels and cafés. Innumerable

---

[3] *Ibid.,* p. 32.
[4] Borkenau, *op. cit.,* p. 71.

young women, of the working class, donned the famous *mono*[5] and became a part of the defense machinery of the Republic. The militia represented the various political sectors of the Republic: the Left republicans, anarchists, socialists, and communists and political considerations weighed heavily in the choice of officers; the customary thing was for complete improvisation in which purely military considerations had small part.

The republican government at the moment of the outbreak of the war was under the leadership of José Giral Pereira as Prime Minister. The shift toward extremism is no more aptly shown than in the decree of September 4, 1936, proclaiming the reorganization of the government. The new Prime Minister, who combined his functions as head of the cabinet with that of War Minister, was Francisco Largo Caballero. The Minister for Foreign Affairs was Julio Alvarez del Vayo. Juan Negrín held the portfolio of finance. Communist influence was most evident in the designation of Jesús Hernández as Minister of Education, a prominent member of the party.

One of the major tasks of the new government was to bring some sort of order into military affairs. The Largo Caballero cabinet decreed that purely voluntary service must be dispensed with and henceforth men would be conscripted into the army. Moreover, voluntary retirement from the front when the spirit moved was severely discouraged by summary executions. The methods for lifting morale were numerous, including rigorous censorship so that newspapers refrained from publishing reports of such events as the fall of Irún or San Sebastián or even the successful relief of the Alcazar.[6]

Wireless sets were rounded up and Radio Madrid did everything possible to maintain constant interference with the nationalist broadcasts. The whole story of the nationalist advance up through Extremadura, to Talavera, Toledo, and the gates of Madrid was kept from the public, to such an extent that the Madrid population was literally shocked to hear the first far-off boom of enemy cannon.

The fall of Irún precipitated the fall of the government on September 4. The Cortes was now no more than a shadow; of its 430 members, only some 100 of the extreme Left were still available. This rump organization met occasionally, but ceased to be a force of any kind in the destinies of Spain. The Republic was distinguished after the out-

[5] *Mono* — a sort of overseas cap much in use by the "People's Army."

[6] *A.B.C.*, Madrid, July 28, 1936, jubilantly reported the Alcazar as about to surrender.

break of the war by the complete suspension of all the ordinary constitutional forms and even the most elementary operation of representative government. On November 5, 1936, the government was reshuffled again, and on November 7 the cabinet, accompanied interestingly enough by the Soviet ambassador, left Madrid for Valencia. In May, 1937, the government suffered another fundamental change in which the socialist-communist group emerged against the anarchists; Juan Negrín became Prime Minister with Indalecio Prieto as Minister of Defense, and two communists, Jesús Hernández as Minister of Education and Health, and Vicente Uribe Galdeano of Agriculture.

The transfer of the government to Valencia included the gold reserves of the Bank of Spain. Indalecio Prieto declared to newsman Knoblaugh that the republican government had reserves amounting to the equivalent of $700,000,000 and therefore did not hesitate to use it to induce volunteers and especially airmen to join the republican forces.[7] The problem of the gold reserves is one of the most fabulous chapters in this whole nightmarish period.[8] There is absolutely no doubt of the gigantic plundering by the republican government of the national reserve, and especially the use, both public and private, of this wealth for purposes which were inimical to the interests of the nation. There is first of all the story, backed by documentary proof, of the transfer to the Soviet Union of what never belonged to the Republic itself as a regime, but to Spain as a nation. Much has been written, and often quite vaguely, about the

---

[7] Knoblaugh, *op. cit.*, p. 43.

[8] The full story of the plundering by the republican government of public and private wealth is a shocking thing. By the decree of September 13, 1936, the government ordered the Bank of Spain to turn over its gold reserves, some 21,964,444 pounds sterling of which were transferred to France. On September 14, the Bank was literally assaulted and over two billion pesetas taken. On September 26, 250 cases of gold were sent to Marseilles on the vessel *Tromontana,* and on October 2, 250 more cases were dispatched to the same destination. Late in October several hundred more cases of gold were sent to France and in January, 1937, some cases were sent by air to Toulouse. Private deposits were taken by force, for the decrees of October 3, 10, and 16, 1936, simply impounded private wealth in banks. The banks delivered 5,026,613,320 pesetas in this manner. Two more decrees of October 20 and 29, 1936, opened up the boxes containing other forms of wealth: jewels, heirlooms, etc. The treasures of numerous churches were seized. Aside from the incalculable destruction of religious treasures, much of this artistic wealth was simply seized by the government for its own purposes. Needless to say a goodly number of the republican leaders managed to store away in the Chase Bank, Midland Bank in Britain, and other foreign banking houses very appreciable wealth. The full documentary proof with photostatic copies of the incriminating evidence has been published, a large part of it in the volume entitled, *Causa General. La Dominación roja en España,* Madrid, 1940.

gold that found its way to the Soviet Union and presumedly remained there for uses which one may easily suspect.

On October 25, 1936, 7800 cases of gold were shipped out of Cartagena on the Soviet vessels, *Kine, Neve,* and *Volgoles*. Evidence shows the intimate financial tie-up with Russia. On February 16, 1937, the republican government arranged with the People's Finance Commissar of the Soviet Union for the sale of gold to the amount of $51,160,888. At the same time the equivalent of this gold was to be transferred to the Delegate of the Foreign Trade Commissariat of the Soviet Union in Spain in payment for goods sold to the Spanish government. There is evidence that Dr. Negrín had accumulated a tremendous fortune, estimated at over $50,000,000, in a villa at Beuville and in February, 1939, this sum was shipped to Mexico on the yacht *Vita*.[9] The controversy between Indalecio Prieto and Juan Negrín over this fortune became a major issue within exiled republican government circles. Under the direction of Martínez Barrio, late president of the Cortes in Madrid, a remnant of this body proclaimed the formation of a committee to take charge of this booty in the name of the Spanish nation and as a part of the national patrimony. These funds and others spirited out of Spain have maintained the Republic since its collapse and have made possible the creation of a republican government and the very considerable propaganda carried on abroad against the Franco regime.

The record of the exiled republicans regarding the reserve has been consistently bad, for at no time has any rendering of accounts ever been made nor a public statement with precise details clarified the mystery. No one outside those directly responsible has any idea of the total amount, or the precise use that has been made of these funds which, we must repeat, were not *republican* but *Spanish*. There are some ugly angles of this whole sordid story as in the case of the collections of the Toledo Cathedral which were wantonly plundered and

[9] An amusing aspect of this controversy, still shrouded in considerable mystery, occurred in Mexico, when Indalecio Prieto became a columnist in the daily *Novedades*. The well-known Mexican writer, Alfonso Junco, suggested that Prieto explain the mystery of the *Vita* and the use of the funds that had reached Mexico. If the United Nations was privileged to interfere in Spanish affairs it seemed logical that Mexico and especially Mexican public opinion might be interested in the kidnaped treasury (Alfonso Junco, *El Gran Teatro del mundo,* Madrid, 1937, p. 360 sq.).

Julio Alvarez del Vayo, a strong critic of Indalecio Prieto, proposes his version of the *Vita* incident and the transfer of Spanish wealth to Mexico in *The Last Optimist* (New York: Viking Press, Inc., 1950), p. 292 sq. The sum total of this account places Prieto in an extremely unfavorable light.

the artistic treasures of centuries taken away by the government. The complete list of this spoliation exists in documentary form, showing that on September 4, 1936, José Giral ordered the provincial authorities in Toledo to transfer these riches to Madrid, allegedly for protection. These objects and treasures were never returned nor have they been located. The presumption is that they form part of the "national patrimony" now in the hands of the exiled republicans. Since the end of the war there has been a sad story of rivalry between Prieto and his *Junta de Auxilio a los Republicanos Españoles* and Negrín's rival organization, the *Servicio de Emigración para Republicanos Españoles.* This sterile wrangling of a group of defeated exiles has little importance for the future of Spain, although it is a tragedy that such a large portion of the wealth of the nation found its way illegally into their hands when the government collapsed, for under no conceivable law can the seizure of the gold reserve of a country be justified as part of its legitimate defense.

After the departure of the government to Valencia, a *Junta de Defensa* remained behind to defend Madrid; its composition following the exact lines of the government as to the distribution of political influence. General Sebastián Pozas, commander of the Guardia civil, now on the republican side, was in charge of the defense.

The rapid advance of the nationalists undoubtedly redoubled the effort of those devoted to ferreting out reactionaries and other dubious elements. The whole, painful story of persecution and murder of those not 100 per cent loyal to the Republic will some day be told, for it is an account which will run to hundreds of pages, as no province, city, town, or village of Spain within the republican zone escaped it. It is a hideous, horrifying repetition of sadistic torture and inhuman treatment of the innocent. Rare is the Spanish family that lived within the republican zone that did not suffer directly from the fear, terror, and constant activities of the murderous *Chekas.* The custom of taking persons out at night to shoot them in some near-by spot became a national institution under the name of the *paseo.* No authority intervened — none could; and the government accepted this sort of thing as one of the exigencies of war.

The tumultuous days of July, 1936, when the mobs were armed, represented a literal bloodbath for all Spain. Prisoners were murdered in cold blood; pedestrians shot on the streets; members of the middle or upper class hounded and assassinated. The prisons overflowed and theaters were utilized to house the large number of persons constantly being rounded up. The institution of the *Cheka* made life in republican Spain a nightmare. It is estimated that some 225 of these instruments of terror existed in Madrid alone. The Government supported them as is evidenced by the fact that the representatives serving on them were cloaked in the authority of public agents. A little later these same members were enrolled in the official police, when it became necessary to fill the gaps in that body due to the participation of many of the regulars in the armed forces. Knoblaugh describes the method of work in this way:

> Cars labelled CHEKA and carrying red and black flags patroled everywhere, loaded with armed men on the lookout for Quinta Columna suspects. Their work was simplified by the fact that Spanish law requires citizens to carry identification cards giving age, description of bearer and place of residence. These could be checked against the political credentials supplied to Leftists in good standing with their respective parties. The raiders entered cafés, some standing guard in the doorway, while the rest passed from table to table demanding to see everyone's credentials. . . . Many of them, like the guards stationed on the highways every few kilometers apart, could not read the writing on the passes. Some of them looked at the cards upside down. Those Spaniards who could not show membership in one or other of the Front parties were dragged off and generally were heard of no more.[10]

The Casa del Campo, the wooded park near the Royal Palace, was one of the favorite spots for this macabre sport. There was nothing clandestine about it, for the somber nightly routine was known to everyone. The bodies were collected the next day and displayed in the morgues where relatives and friends were allowed to search for the missing among them. It was not only Madrid; it was everywhere in republican Spain. One can visit any city today and without exception there is a spot where the extreme Left carried out this sinister work. In Santander it was the spot overlooking the sea, where bodies were hurled from high rocks into the water. In Valencia, it was outside the city on one of the main highways. I know personally several persons in Valencia who lived in the suburbs and came in daily to their work. They recount how for weeks and even months, not a morning failed to reveal its grisly quota of victims — all presumedly "vile reactionaries." The number of victims will never be established, although it is

---

[10] *Op. cit.*, p. 70. Of the innumerable accounts of the agonizing life led in republican Madrid after July 18, 1936, I find none more absorbing than the final chapters of the book of Rodolfo Reyes, *De mi vida: La bi-Revolución española,* Mexico, 1948, p. 455 sq. This Mexican of long residence in Spain recounts the horrors of his plight and that of many other foreigners, without mentioning nationals, during the months when authority was in the hands of the mob (New York: Sheed and Ward, 1937).

estimated as 60,000 for Madrid, 30,000 for Valencia, and 50,000 for Barcelona, and these figures are taken as extremely conservative. Did the victims include only violent enemies of the Republic or persons who were potentially collaborators with the advancing nationalists? The answer is an emphatic "no." The murders were carried out on an unprecedented scale and included persons from the extreme Right to republicans and even known leftists; noblemen and workers; intellectuals and children.

The whole horrible picture cannot be attributed exclusively to irresponsible mobs. While many of the executions were doubtless the result of the panic and confusion of the first weeks, and many due to personal feuds rather than political reasons, the duration of the murders pointed to a system rather than sporadic violence. During the period José Giral was Prime Minister, his Director General of Public Security presided at a meeting at the Fine Arts Club in Madrid at which a central Cheka was established, endowed with the widest authority and charged with the task of condemning the victims without trial or formalities. This Cheka received the name of the "Provincial Committee for Public Investigation," and was popularly known as the "Fine Arts Cheka," also as the Fomento Cheka because of the Madrid street on which it was located. The committee was made up of the representatives of all the political parties and of the trade-union organizations, a fact which refutes the idea that it was merely the instrument of the more extreme of the political factions. This Cheka sent thousands of persons to their deaths; authorized innumerable depredations, and was responsible for the mass murder of prisoners, to which reference will be made shortly. Among other things, it turned over to the republican government 472 cases of gold and silver objects and jewels, including many sacred vessels stolen from churches. The organization was dissolved in November, 1936, when the Nationalist advance came dangerously close.

The full responsibility of the government for this frightful state of affairs is amply proved by the documents available. One of them, signed by Angel Galarza Gago, republican Minister of the Interior and dated Valencia, May 14, 1937, refers to the need for protecting the members of the extinct committee, one of whom, Leopoldo Carrillo Gómez, had been arrested. "Since the Provincial Committee for Public Investigation has functioned under the direction and the responsibility of the Government of the Republic and of all the organisms of the Popular Front which compose it, we are all of us bound to avoid, by all the means at our disposal, the repetition of such arrests when due to causes connected with the affairs of the aforementioned Committee of Investigation."[11]

The militia, on its own, held courts anywhere that might be convenient, in cafés, garages, or the back rooms of a vacant building. The judges were self-constituted, the defendant was deprived of all right to speak and often had no idea of what he was accused. The deliberations took perhaps five minutes and the wholesale executions followed immediately. The "Popular Tribunals" that succeeded these improvised courts were not much better and expedited matters with almost the same alacrity. Evidence was dispensed with and the normal rules of examination and cross examination became a tragic farce. One of the most monstrous of the crimes committed in the name of democracy and common decency was the attempt to arrest the entire panel of 122 lawyers who had protested, just before war broke out, against the lawless killings and especially the official murder of Calvo Sotelo. They were ordered arrested and tried for sympathy with the hated Right. Most had fled; others had already been executed. Of the 69 who were located all managed to establish their innocence. Many of these were executed without further investigation, an eloquent and terrible example of popular justice.

The real victim of the months of violence was order and law. All ordinary legal processes were abandoned and juridical precepts so indispensable to organized society were thrown overboard. The Spanish Republic became a dictatorship, with justice or the travesty of it that bore its name exclusively in the hands of the mob.

One of the most abominable crimes was that perpetrated on August 23, 1936, in the Madrid Model Prison. The press had carried on a campaign of incitement against some of the Model Prison inmates and Minister Giral's own paper, *Política,* in its edition of August 8, 1936, called upon the masses to wreak vengeance on several of them. Let it be noted that the crimes were not directed against Falangists and

---

[11] Letter of Minister Galarza to the Director General de Seguridad, Madrid, May 14, 1937. The documents on the Chekas are to be found in the *Causa General,* p. 83 sq. There were 226 of these institutions in Madrid alone, a list of which is given in this work, pp. 86–92. The Fine Arts Cheka was responsible for about 1000 murders. The government granted the Chekas the right to distribute the booty resulting from the robbery of private dwellings. Another horrible organization was the so-called *Escuadrilla del amanecer,* or dawn squad, devoted to arrests, prefabricated trials, and murder. *Heraldo de Madrid,* for August 13, 1936, praised the efficiency of their bloody work.

known Franco sympathizers, but also against those who were either suspect in the eyes of the rabble or in some way deemed as not 100 per cent sympathetic to the particular authorities in control. Militiamen and women stationed in the prison were responsible for the murder of Melquiades Alvarez, a senior member of the Madrid bar, a leader of the Democratic Liberal Republican Party, and at one time Prime Minister. Other victims of this horror were Ramón Alvarez Valdés, José Martínez de Velasco, Manuel Rico Avello, a former Minister of the Interior, who had served in 1933 in the cabinet of Diego Martínez Barrio. The Minister of Interior and the Director General of Public Security cannot be exonerated of responsibility, for they were personally at the prison when the bloody events took place. The republican press, instead of deploring the bloodshed and demanding the chastisement of the culprits, praised them for their "proven courage and discipline."[12] The massacre of August 23 was directed by one Enrique Puente, a baker by trade and a militia leader. Even after the crime had taken place the government left the prison in the hands of the local Cheka supported by a few militiamen belonging to the republican Left, José Giral's own party. It is a commentary on republican justice that the new commander in the prison was henceforth Felipe Emilio Sandoval, who himself had been incarcerated for murder shortly before. For months the Model Prison, which belied its name, was the scene of mysterious disappearances and of prisoners spirited away, never to reappear.

When the nationalist threat became more imminent, the government authorized by written order the removal of thousands of political prisoners who, without trial or investigation, were executed by machine guns in Paracuellos del Jarama and other places near Madrid by the Public Security militia. Huge trenches dug for the purpose accommodated their bodies as they were mowed down. These mass graves may be found not only in Paracuellos de Jarama, near the Barajas airport, but at Torrejón de Ardoz, and Ribas de Vaciamadrid.

It was tragic irony that despite the countless efforts of the diplomatic missions in Madrid, the government paid scant attention to their requests for humanitarian conduct. Let it be stressed that many of the diplomatic missions, and not least among them those of the Hispanic American republics, saved hundreds of lives at very considerable risk, for the embassies and legations of those nations, recognizing

[12] *El Liberal,* Madrid, August 27, 1936.

the right of asylum, were thrown open to the unfortunates who had no recourse to the courts or to the authorities, and who were in the greatest danger of death. A few days before the mass murder, Julio Alvarez del Vayo, Minister of Foreign Affairs, addressed a note to the British Chargé d'Affaires in response to a humanitarian *démarche,* in which he guaranteed that the lives of prisoners would not be placed in jeopardy and that they would receive fair and open trials. A few days later one of the greatest mass executions in the history of the civil war took place.[13]

In the Porlier Prison of Madrid the militia, designated as guards by the government, assassinated two radical republican members of the Cortes: Gerardo Abad Conde and Fernando Rey Mora. Prisoners were often executed arbitrarily without any reference to who they were or what they had done. Lists were sometimes made up by random selection from an index of those imprisoned.

It is necessary to insist that this was not the work of isolated individuals or the rabid bursting of popular indignation quickly to subside. The republic was permeated with the new conception of "people's justice." The statements to be found in republican sources of the period reflect almost the precise terminology employed in Yugoslavia at the time of the trial of Archbishop Stepinac, in which every appeal was made to the "people's law" as against the statutes or written provisions. We find such an appeal in Spain to the various prosecutors of the lower courts in which it is stated that "the republic is a system of Justice and Justice emanates from the people. The administration of justice must be inspired on this basic principle, and since that noble and great people is now giving its life-blood for a system of freedom and justice, let us give it the justice it wants at the pace and in the way set by itself."[14]

It is not to be supposed that this persecution was directed solely against Spaniards, for the republican government was guilty of some very grave violations of international law. The murder which took place on the outskirts of Madrid of Baron Jacques de Borchgrave, attaché of the Belgian embassy in Madrid, who was seeking to aid some of his compatriots who had been inveigled into the International Brigades, is an example. Evidence of the crime was made public, but no action was ever taken. The sisters of the Uruguayan consul in

---

[13] Madrid press, Oct. 25, 26, 1936. Also, Nov. 14, 1946. It was denied that illegal executions were taking place.

[14] *El Liberal,* Madrid, Sept. 3, 1936.

Madrid, Dolores and Consuelo Aguiar Della Días, were arrested by the communist militia and their bodies later found on the Andalucía highway. The Uruguayan government responded by breaking off diplomatic relations with Madrid. Efforts were made through diplomatic intervention to save the life of the descendant of Columbus, the aged Duke of Vergara, who had never engaged in politics, but he was murdered by socialist militiamen.[15]

When the government decided to convert the prison at Ocaña into a hospital, it was informed by Red Cross officials that it could accommodate five hundred beds. The 189 prisoners there, instead of being transferred, were simply lined up and shot.[16] There was a considerable flurry abroad regarding the execution in Andalucía of the great poet García Lorca, by the nationalists. It would be the height of folly to suppose that the nationalists were innocent of acts of violence or of offenses against justice. There are authenticated cases of arbitrary imprisonment and the execution of several priests in the Basque country. But there was nothing of the widespread, systematic, organized, and officially approved reign of murder that was so shocking in the Republic. The figures put forward as authentic reached such a colossally high level that public opinion abroad found it difficult to credit them. The world in general was sold on the idea that the Spanish republic was a democratic institution fighting for its life and had little notion of the degeneracy that had occurred prior to July 18, or the increasingly Marxist complexion of things. They were unaware that two wars were going on simultaneously in Spain; the war against the nationalists and the war for the sovietization of Spain. The moderate republicans, devoted to the rule of law and order, were either out of the country, exterminated, or incapacitated for action. The republic of 1936–1939 was no longer the institution of Gregorio Marañon, Aniceto Alcalá Zamora, or José Ortega y Gasset, for their classical republic, under liberal principles and with parliamentary procedures was now a police state, ruled by ruthless doctrinarians and administered by mob rule. It must be remembered, too, that nothing is quite as useless when dealing with a struggle of this kind as the listing of this, that, or the other distinguished name as evidence of the perfidy of one side. The world was treated to a tremendous propaganda onslaught with the death of García Lorca. The equally regrettable dis-

---

[15] Other foreigners killed included Bridget Boland, Irish, in Bilbao, June 16, 1937, two Swiss, and several Argentines.

[16] Knoblaugh, *op. cit.*, p. 88.

appearance of Ramiro de Maeztu, for which the republicans were responsible, could be used to prove the hostility of the Republic to culture.

The death of José Primo de Rivera in Alicante prison was another case of murder without due process of any kind. The leader of the *Falange* had been imprisoned before the civil war started, a victim of the numerous restrictions on freedom of speech for which the Republic was responsible and details of which have been offered in a previous chapter. It is reported that Minister Largo Caballero was anxious to avoid his death, since the nationalists held his own son, but the anarchists insisted he be tried. The trial was of such a nature that after one day correspondents were refused admission and no cabled stories could be sent abroad. He was executed on November 20, 1936, and Largo Caballero's son was shot in retaliation by the nationalists.

There can be no serious question that the accounts of the murders, amounting to thousands, are not a question of "fascist propaganda." The evidence is there for anyone to see. As serious a student of Hispanic affairs as E. Allison Peers devotes a chapter in his book, *Catalonia Infelix,* to the tragic record of murder, arson, and spoliation in that area.[17] Another observer, Clara Campoamor, estimates fifty to a hundred corpses a day in Madrid alone.[18] Competent foreign correspondents were agreed that this wave of terror was part and parcel of the revolution and the prosecution of the war. The London *Times* told week after week, on the basis of firsthand observation, the terror that reigned over the land.[19]

The Church and its clergy were the primary targets of this persecution. The record of the Republic in this regard has already been examined in synthesis, but there remains the partial story of the years between 1936 and 1939 when, by comparison, 1931–1936 seemed a paradise indeed. This new era of persecution was distinguished by the wholesale murder of priests and religious, men and women; destruction of what remained of Church property and churches themselves, and the elimination of every sign of religion or of religious

---

[17] Methuen & Co., London, 1937, Chapter XIII, "Proletarian Revolution and Civil War."

[18] *La révolution espagnole vue par une républicaine,* Paris, 1937, p. 98.

[19] Sir Edward Griggs writes in the *Times* (Oct. 9, 1936) that "there has been undisputable evidence that massacres on a revolting scale were being practiced in Madrid and Barcelona. Not only murder but the torture and mutilation of old men, women, girls and children. . . ."

influence in the country. The number of clergy actually killed reached the thousands. In addition to these persecutions, it would be unbearable to describe in detail the outrage, sacrilege, and destruction that accompanied this hounding of religion. To arson was added the destruction of vestments and vessels, the morbid opening of ancient cemeteries, the display in sacrilegious and grotesque poses of those who were responsible for the wanton destruction — all this forms a part of the horror that hung over republican Spain. There is no chance whatever that all of this can be chalked up to exaggeration or that the priests and religious were simply nationalist agents who ought to have been shot for their pains. A simplification of this sort is nothing short of monstrous, for the evidence is plain that the clergy were murdered because they were clerical; that opinion or political tendency had nothing to do with it. The revolution, as I have already pointed out, was not merely anticlerical, but was profoundly antireligious in inspiration.

The testimony of an unquestionably unbiased body, a group of Protestant churchmen who visited Spain in the winter of 1937, confirms this statement: "Many certainly have been killed . . . unless the parish priest was actively unpopular, he was not killed by his own people."[20] In short, the most that the average priest could hope for was not to be shot by his own parishioners. As to his chances of not getting shot at all, that, it would appear, was extremely dubious. Mr. Loveday in his *Spain, 1923–1948* quotes the *Manchester Guardian,* sympathetic to the republican cause, as stating that "the attack on religion has been more radical in loyalist Spain than anywhere else in the world, even Mexico and Russia. All Roman Catholic churches have been closed down as places of worship and nearly all have been completely destroyed. . . . In loyalist Spain there is nothing left to persecute."[21]

Space makes it impossible to do more than skin the surface of this important problem. Every corner of the republican jurisdiction was affected by the persecution. In Catalonia alone, 21 Capuchin Fathers, 9 lay Brothers, and 7 seminarians were murdered between July, 1936, and April, 1937. In the period ending November, 1936, 28 Jesuits of the province of Aragón lost their lives. Thirty members of the religious

---

[20] *Report of a Group of Anglican and Free Churchmen Who Visited Spain, January 29 to February 9, 1937,* quoted in Peers, *op. cit.,* p. 254.

[21] Boswell Publishing Co., London, 1949, p. 119.

community at the great monastery of Montserrat were executed.[22]

The full moral weight of condemnation comes from the hierarchy of Spain which, in the collective pastoral of July 1, 1937, stated that some 2000 churches had been totally destroyed or plundered and some 6000 secular priests killed up to that date.[23] Even the Anglican chapels in republican Spain were closed and several of the Anglican bishops who visited the country could not appear in clerical garb.

---

[22] A full account is contained in the volume *La persécution religieuse en Espagne,* Paris, 1937. It was published anonymously but is known to be the work of Dr. Juan Estelrich, a Catalan writer and member of the Spanish parliament since 1931, as well as a close collaborator with the Catalan regional government. Peers gives this personal information, and states that, "I know personally of the care with which his statistics have been collected," *Spain, the Church and the Orders,* Burns, Oates & Washbourne, London, 1945, p. 170. The existence of a co-ordinated plan for the destruction of the Church can admit of no doubt.

The Barcelona newspaper, *Solidaridad Obrera* (July 26, 1936), stated bluntly that "religion is not yet dead. This must be borne in mind in connection with future activity." Every form of sacrilege and vicious antireligious usage was tolerated. *Mundo Gráfico* (Madrid, Dec. 30, 1936) published pictures of confessionals out on the sidewalks used as collection centers for the contributions to the republican armed forces.

[23] Also see discourse of the Holy Father to Spanish pilgrims in September, 1936, *Acta Apostolicae Sedis,* Vol. XXVIII.

The bishops who suffered martyrdom at the hands of the republicans are: Eustaquio Nieto, Bishop of Sigüenza, 72 years old, judged by street mob, executed July 27, 1936, and body burned. Silvio Ruiz, Bishop of Lérida, placed himself in government custody, and was turned over to militiamen. Shot before cemetery wall, Aug. 5, 1936. Cruz Laplana Laguna, Bishop of Cuenca, 71 years old, killed on a highway, Aug. 8, 1936. Florencio Asensio Barroso, Titular Bishop of Urea and Apostolic Administrator of Barbastro, murdered, mutilated, and tossed into common grave, Aug. 9, 1936. Miguel Serra Sucarrate, Bishop of Segorbe, 79 years old, killed on Aug. 9, 1936, by a band of Left republican supporters of President Azaña. Manuel Basulto Jiménez, Bishop of Jaén, taken from a prison train on way to Madrid. Murdered at Vallecas on Aug. 12, 1936, together with 200 other prisoners. Manuel Borrás, Auxiliary Bishop of Tarragona, executed Aug. 12, 1936. His body was examined by witnesses who reported mutilations and partial burning with gasoline. Narciso de Esténaga Echevarría, Bishop of Cuidad Real, taken from his house, escorted outside the city, and murdered on Aug. 22, 1936. Diego Ventaja Milán, Bishop of Almería, murdered Aug. 28, 1936, and body exposed to the profanations of the mob. Manuel Medina Olmos, Bishop of Guadix, murdered with the Bishop of Almería. Manuel Irurita Almandoz, Bishop of Barcelona, seized after flight from palace and taken before San Elías Cheka, murdered, Dec. 3, 1936. Anselmo Polanco y Fontecha, Bishop of Teruel, murdered near Figueras, Feb. 7, 1939, body left unburied. Juan de Dios Ponce, Apostolic Administrator of Orihuela.

Republican propaganda claimed that these murders were the work of the first few weeks of popular indignation. It may be observed that the Bishop of Teruel was murdered just before the final collapse of the Republic, in its last stronghold in Catalonia.

But it is useful, in order to make the account of the persecution and the terror in republican Spain more accurate, to pick out two given localities far removed one from the other, and where circumstances were quite diverse, socially and politically: Bilbao and Andalucía. The record of violence against men and women, clergy and laity alike, in the two areas is overwhelming.

During August, 1936, the prison of Larrínaga in Bilbao and smaller jails connected with the prefectures of police were insufficient to hold the growing number of persons incarcerated for political reasons. It was therefore decided to utilize two vessels, the *Altuna-Mendi* and the *Cabo Quilates,* as prison ships. Later the *Arántzazu-Mendi,* with prisoners from Guipúzcoa and a number of *Requetés,* was drafted into this service. These floating prisons in the harbor of Bilbao became one of the great horrors of the civil war, where hundreds of persons were cruelly and barbarously treated, many sent to their deaths after the most refined tortures, flagellation, beating with burning sticks, and the like had been applied.[24] The priests aboard were subjected to the most revolting and unprintable chastisements. A French bishop had occasion to visit Bilbao during that period and his statement reflected the absolute horror of what he had seen: "On leaving the Spanish hell," is the title of his remarks. "In the fetid holds of the vessels anchored in the Bilbao channel, 3000 hostages await their liberation or death. What I have seen is too horrible and cruel for words."[25] As a commentary on the technique of illusion, the Bilbao newspaper *Euzkadi,* organ of President Aguirre, pronounced itself as satisfied at the visit of the French prelate who had left Bilbao with the best impressions of the state of the prisons.[26] The Bishop commented publicly on the fact that the 3000 prisoners were under arrest and detention in large part because they were subscribers to *A.B.C.,* the Madrid monarchist daily. A list of subscribers in the Bilbao area had been dispatched from Madrid and this had served as a basis for the arrest of the victims.

On September 25, 1936, the executions began. Groups were selected from among the prisoners, and those who were spared for the moment

[24] José Echeandia, *La persecución roja en el país vasco,* Barcelona, 1945. This is a firsthand account of prison conditions in Bilbao and the Basque country. It proves beyond a doubt that a large number of Basques were not in sympathy with the so-called autonomous government nor with the Republic.

[25] Statement of Mons. Mathieu, Bishop of Dax, in *La Petite Gironde,* Bordeaux, Sept. 26, 1936.

[26] Edition of Sept. 23, 1936.

awaited in terror the massacre of their comrades. On the near-by docks mobs of militiamen and women screamed invectives and hurled insults at the prisoners, demanding raucously that they be put to death. All through the night the groans of the dying merged with the oaths of the militia as they rolled over bodies in search of valuables. On one of the vessels a daily practice was to force the seventeen imprisoned priests to sing the Internationale. Fifteen of them were lined up in one group and shot down in the midst of their simple farewell: "Good-by, Brother. Until we meet in Eternity." The story of the priests assassinated in Bilbao is one of the minor chapters in the glorious martyrdom of thousands all over Spain. There was no pleading, no vacillating, no apostasy.

On land, the prisons were packed with unfortunates. A partial list includes individuals of every profession and condition: captains in the army, machinists, members of the Falange, the consul of Paraguay, and Carlists. The prison, *Los Angeles Custodios,* was reserved for the aged and the infirm, none of whom were spared the brutalities to which all political prisoners were subjected. José Luis de Goyoaga, president of the council of Vizcaya, has left an account of the hideous January 4 in the prison when it was stormed by a frenzied mob under the direction of the militiamen. The prisoners were shot in groups of five. The list of the victims in this case included a wide range: Carlists, priests, members of *Acción Popular,* and others. The reports on mass assassinations in Guipúzcoa conform in all details to the account just given in abbreviated form of what transpired in Vizcaya. It is impossible to assume that in this area the Basque separatist government was totally unaware of what took place or was incapable of a minimum action against the excesses of the mobs, the militia, and the various branches of the armed forces. Ignorance obviously was not the reason; complicity is the only explanation of how these horrors could continue in a region where the Basque republicans claimed to be fighting for religion and independence on the side of the Republic.

It was not only in the larger centers, but in the villages and countryside all over the Basque country that men and women were murdered for political reasons. In the province of Vizcaya, in towns such as Algorta, Abadiano, Amorebieta, Baracaldo, Berriz, Corranza, and Elorrio, the rhythm of murder went on unabated. The incomplete list of the victims in the single city of Bilbao occupies a dozen closely printed pages. The majority of those who fell before this fury were Carlists, the stanch traditionalists of the Basque mountains.

The story in the south of Spain is a dreary repetition of what occurred elsewhere in the peninsula. A British observer, Arthur Bryant, wrote the preface to a lengthy report on communist atrocities in southern Spain.[27] Some of the accounts in the volume to which he writes the introduction are unspeakably foul. There was the infamous case of the women of San Martín de Valdeiglesias, who were each forced to submit to violation by 25 ruffians before they were mercifully liberated by death. This documentary study is not a piece of propaganda, but an eyewitness account with the most careful sifting of evidence of those who were present and in many cases were themselves the victims of the communist tyranny. Bryant states from his own experience in republican Spain:

> I spent some time wandering through the remoter parts of Spain . . . what I saw astonished and appalled me. Over the land lay a sense of brooding terror and tragedy. For many months past the apostles of Communism had been sowing the seeds of a creed of hatred in a rich soil of ignorance and destitution . . . every sort of outrage has been committed.[28]

This, incidentally, was before the civil war actually started. Let us take some examples of the pathetic and moving story contained in these pages. At Almendralejo, Badajoz province, the list of the murdered runs to the dozens, draws not only from the middle class, but from humble laborers, such as the López Cabeza brothers, Manuel Nieto Marín, Manuel Guillén Ramos, and José Jiménez Marcos. In the village of Azuaga, in Badajoz, 105 murders were committed by the communists. Seven friars and an equal number of secular priests were brought from Fuenteovejuna and thrown into jail where they remained for 48 hours without food or drink. The list of killed in this single locality fills three printed pages. At Castro del Río in the province of Córdoba, whole families were wiped out including the Menéndez family of nine men. In Espejo, Córdoba province, the Red orgy lasted from July 22 to the end of September:

> Antonio Luque Reyes was arrested in his house and while he was being led away handcuffed, a communist attacked him with a hatchet; he managed to flee and hide in a drug store, but the Reds followed him, bound him to an iron rail and shot him in the legs, cut off his hands, finally dragged him to the square and killed him.[29]

---

[27] See, *Second and Third Reports on the Communist Atrocities Committed in Southern Spain From July to October 1936* (London: Eyre & Spottiswoode, Ltd., 1937).

[28] *Ibid.*, p. x.

[29] *Ibid.*, p. 33.

The medical reports on unburied bodies in the village of Granja de Torrehermosa are gruesome beyond all description. A delegation of physicians was ordered to make the most careful survey of the situation and determine exactly what had taken place. Their report tells of a five-year-old girl killed with an ax; a woman of 60 whose skull was crushed, another with hatchet wounds all over her body, and others all showing the most violent forms of assault. At Mérida in Badajoz province, some 100 citizens, whose politics the communists did not like, were forced in the heat of the day to dig their own graves and were summarily shot. At Ronda, in Málaga province, over 600 murders were committed that have been verified and authenticated. At Calera y Chozas, in Toledo province, Bonifacio Resino Avila and his wife Fidela Gómez, an aged couple, were attacked; the man's legs were cut off and he was then murdered in his wife's presence. A typical demonstration at this village was to force the children to assemble at the church and witness the most revolting profanation of the sacred vessels and altar. At Maqueda, Toledo province, the detailed report shows that the excesses commenced days before the civil war started, an important fact since it is argued from time to time that the violence was due to nationalist bombardments and in retaliation for nationalist excesses elsewhere. Aside from the fact that the chronology does not bear this out, the close censorship exerted by the republican government would have made it extremely unlikely that reports of this kind could have reached all Spain simultaneously.

At San Martín de Valdeiglesias, province of Madrid, the cruelty reached incredibly fiendish heights and the rape of women in the presence of their fathers and husbands was common. A communist from Madrid who had come to take over the post of municipal secretary opposed the excesses and was himself immediately tortured and put to death. These accounts, as has been indicated, represent the most scrupulous investigation with sworn affidavits by the surviving victims and witnesses. If the central government was impotent to assure order and reasonable safety, then it had virtually abdicated its authority as a government and clearly had no right to parade before the world its claim to represent the authentic will of the Spanish people. There is no supposition necessarily that the government *ordered* these murders and savagery; the assumption is that they were known, tolerated, and, if deplored, the measures taken to assure a moderating influence were extremely unproductive of results.

The story of the internal evolution of the Republic during the war years is of secondary importance to the gradual shrinking of its territory and the clarity with which its final defeat was heralded by continuing nationalist successes. It may be said in general, however, that the characteristic features of the politics of the Republic was an increase in the sternness with which the central government repressed all deviation and discrepancy; the improved discipline in the military forces; and the gradual usurpation by communists or communist sympathizers of a predominant position in the affairs of State. Strife was constant in republican Spain between the extremist organizations. The government in a certain sense was no longer the master of its own life. The trade unions, so intimately bound up with politics and split and subdivided by ideological conflict, had become the only real power in the nation. The P.O.U.M. or Trotskyite communists were liquidated or expelled; the anarchists in the C.N.T. were likewise reduced to considerable impotence, giving way to the socialist-communist combination, which was to direct republican affairs until the collapse.

The disappearance of Indalecio Prieto as the major force in the republican government was due in large measure to his refusal to accept subservience to Soviet intervention. His departure meant the almost complete control by the communists or their adherents of the key positions. The reshuffling of the cabinet on April 5, 1938, placed Juan Negrín in power, with Alvarez del Vayo once more as Foreign Minister.[30]

Parliamentary conditions in the Republic scarcely improved during 1938. The Cortes met on September 30 near Barcelona and, after the usual speeches, adjourned *sine die* until such a time as it might again be summoned by the government. It was the most complete abdication of any kind of control over the activities of the executive branch. In late October the P.O.U.M. leaders were sentenced to long terms of imprisonment, a very clear indication that Stalinist communism was on top. The League of Nations commission that visited Spain informed the world that the food situation was extremely bad and appealed for aid. The proclamation of a return to religious freedom

---

[30] Alvarez del Vayo's pro-communist sentiments may be judged from a speech reported in the International Brigade paper, *Le Volontaire de la Liberté,* No. 30, July 2, 1937, published in Italian originally: "Democratic centralism, ideological unity, auto-criticism, adherence to and defense of the Soviet Union and international proletarianism . . . let every left wing socialist ask himself what point among these he cannot accept?" This quotation contains all the classical pro-Soviet expressions.

on December 9 was largely a façade, since almost every church was destroyed and the few remaining priests quite unable to appear publicly. At the end of the war the communists insisted on carrying on the struggle and Negrín and his group, bound as they were to the Soviet Union, would hear nothing of peace or of capitulation.[31]

On February 4, 1939, after Gerona was captured, Azaña, President of Spain and who for most of the war had remained at Montserrat near Barcelona with no active participation in public affairs, Luis Campanys, President of the *Generalitat* of Catalonia, and Aguirre of the Basque government crossed into France. The communists were the only ones bent on continuing the fight.

One of the most interesting aspects of the republican defense was propaganda. It is perfectly evident that the Republic devoted the greatest efforts to convincing public opinion abroad of the justice of its cause and there is no doubt that it succeeded admirably. The success of republican propaganda was so great that to this day it is literally impossible to get a hearing in many circles for a fair and impartial statement of the Spanish case. The Republic sold the world the idea that it was a democratic, duly elected representative form of government, to which the great majority of the Spanish people adhered and it managed to create the impression that the opposite side was exclusively fascist, foreign supported, and made up of an ambitious military clique bent on seizing power for the most unidealistic reasons.

The working of this propaganda machine is worth noting. H. Edward Knoblaugh, as a newsman in Madrid and Valencia, has described it for us with special mention of the censorship: "from my conversations with many foreign correspondents who have been covering the war from General Franco's side, I can say with assurance that the Nationalists have not even remotely approximated the degree of efficiency the Loyalists have achieved in this direction [censorship]."[32] The propaganda was so organized that every report out of Spain fitted, according to this experienced newsman, into the "intricate pattern of Popular Front policies." In his account of the restrictions on the free flow of news we discover that reporters in Madrid were forbidden to touch certain subjects, and the listing of them is a revelation of the state of affairs: (1) foreigners and foreign equipment on the republican

---

[31] Salvador de Madariaga, *Spain* (London: Jonathan Cape, 1943; New York: Creative Age Press, Inc., 1943), p. 407: "Dr. Negrín was not free. He was attached to Moscow by a chain of gold."

[32] *Op. cit.*, p. 131.

side, (2) references to interparty strife in the Republic, (3) any reflection on the efficiency of the military leadership of the Republic, and (4) anything that might indicate civilian demoralization.[33]

The republican propaganda machine was as complete and as effective as the nationalist was not. There was an elaborate Ministry of Propaganda set up, with large sections devoted to publicity abroad and through it tons of news material, articles, pictures, reports, and every conceivable form of propaganda were slipped out. Knoblaugh remarks that even editors in small cities abroad received their share of the packages of material dispatched with regularity. Foreign reporters in republican Spain had very small chance of remaining if their stories as published abroad revealed anything unfavorable to the republican cause. Atrocity stories were diligently fabricated and hatred against the Moors was worked up to fever pitch. The wave of propaganda reached such proportions that very soon nothing that the Franco forces did could possibly be the accomplishment of Spaniards; it was always the work of foreign mercenaries. The republican propaganda machine managed to convince the world that it was not really hostile to religion; one of the points most emphasized was that the Basque Catholics remained loyal to the Republic. The flaw in this was never mentioned: that an enormous number of Basques were enrolled with the *Requetés* and that those who were for the republicans obviously were inclined to place first emphasis on political separatism rather than on religion, which may have been comprehensible, but should not be attributed to religious motivation.

The internal political situation in the nationalist zone during the war largely revolved about the problem of creating the machinery of administration, since the movement forward and the conquest of province after province posed invariably difficult problems in this order. The movement in 1936 had not begun, as had already been said, as a form of government or even a preference for a form of government. The emergence of the outlines of such a state was the product of developing events. The nationalists were faced from the beginning with a series of problems. First of all, what form to give the new Spain that was appearing? Second, was General Franco, the supreme military leader to be necessarily the artisan of the new state? Third, could the various elements that went to make up the nationalist cause be effectively co-ordinated within the structure of this state?

---

[33] *Ibid.*, pp. 138–139.

General Franco was not the only leader in the struggle against the Republic, although he was certainly the outstanding figure and by common consent it was felt that he was destined to see the conflict through and Spain restored.

The party situation was also complex. Between the Carlists with their firm support of traditionalism, the *Renovación Española* in favor of the successor of Alfonso XIII, and the Falange which was neither monarchical nor conservative but with a radical social program, there was not entire harmony. The decision of General Franco to merge them had as its motive the avoidance of internal friction during the critical period of the war. None of the parties possessed either the force, the *élan,* or the personalities to assume the single and supreme direction of political life. There was a very marked tendency of a large segment of the movement in favor of the restoration of the monarchy as a consequence of the war. The differences between the Falange and the *Requetés* was deep; the former was a recent movement, audacious, energetic, and with a program of action designed to transform Spain. The latter was rooted in the profound traditionalism of the Basque country, deeply religious, devoted to the monarchical idea, desirous that Spain seek its place in the world by its own unaided efforts. The traditionalists thought in terms of Spain's glorious past and the inexhaustible resources of its own spiritual tradition; the Falange envisaged a radically new solution. The Falange was strong in Castile and Extremadura; traditionalism in Navarre and the Basque provinces. One of the major problems was the rapid increase of the size of the army which brought in large masses of men who were not politically minded. The Falange had lost some of its outstanding leaders with the deaths of José Antonio Primo de Rivera and Onésimo Redondo. Ramón Serrano Suñer, Franco's brother-in-law and later Foreign Minister, recounts the confusion of the early days and the manner in which politics suddenly came to the fore as a pressing problem in the midst of the demands of the military operations.[34]

The nationalist movement had begun as a negative action aimed at rectifying the policy of the Republic. It could not, obviously, appeal to the country simply on the basis of a return to the *status quo* before 1936 or even 1931. The decision for unity was slowly maturing in the minds of General Franco and his collaborators. A violent conflict be-

---

[34] Serrano Suñer, *Entre Hendaya y Gibraltar,* Madrid, 1947.

tween the various tendencies within the Falange indicated the urgency of a solution and the impossibility to deal with the progress of the war as though politics did not exist and the decree on unification was issued April 19, 1937. The Falange unquestionably secured a major place in the new dispensation. It was generally felt that, despite its heroism and aura of romanticism, traditionalism had little to say in the modern world, or at least in the face of the urgent social and political questions that this world poses.

The idea that the new regime, whose bare outline began to emerge in the spring of 1937, was the work of foreign pressure or even of foreign models does not stand up under close examination. In the accusations brought against the Spanish government in the Security Council, it was stated as one of the major points that the Franco regime had come into being as the result of the direct aid of Germany and Italy. The chronology of events reveals that this is open to the most serious question. For one thing, when the nationalist government was created, on October 1, 1936, at Burgos, there were almost no foreign volunteers in its armed forces. The movement was entirely Spanish at that time with no influence from abroad of any appreciable kind. It must be remembered, too, that the total army under arms throughout the civil war, on the nationalist side, reached about 1,200,-000, The number of foreign volunteers even at the highest point was infinitesimal compared with the far superior efforts of the Spanish themselves. In a word, the structure of the new regime was beginning to take shape before any foreign participants appeared. Certainly if military aid was not yet apparent, it is extremely doubtful that political intervention was already taking place, especially in the light of the slowness with which General Franco got around to working out a political solution. Moreover, the republican government failed in its efforts to convince the League of Nations that Spain was the object of foreign intervention. A more striking testimony to the fact that the creation of the nationalist government was not considered at the time a foreign imposition, but a Spanish affair, comes from the recognition extended to it as early as November 8, 1936, by a number of countries.

By April 5, 1939, almost every nation in the world with the exception of Mexico and the Soviet Union had recognized the Franco regime as the legitimate government of Spain. We may add that this recognition implied nothing as to approval or disapproval of the form of that government, but merely recognized Franco as the head of the legitimate government of Spain at the moment and that the Republic had ceased to exist. This recognition was extended without discussion and without conditions. If it were true that the regime was nothing but a prolongation of the Rome-Berlin Axis and the puppet of Hitler, why then in 1939 did nations such as Great Britain, France, and the United States not call attention to this before recognition or as the basis for not recognizing it at all? In 1946 the Spanish government was discovered to be the creation of the Axis without national roots and unresponsive to the will of the Spanish people. In 1939, it was recognized normally and no question was raised to withholding permanent recognition from it. Since the Axis was engaged in war and defeated between these years, nothing surely could have happened between 1939 and 1946 to change the essential *nature* of the regime. It is therefore a curious contradiction that an argument should be brought forward six and seven years after recognition which was not applied at the time that recognition was extended.

The note of the French government — then under the Popular Front — at the time of the exchange of diplomatic representatives, is eloquent in its testimony to the attitude prevailing at that moment:

> At the moment when the French government, desirous of continuing friendly relations with Spain, proposes to establish diplomatic relations with the government of General Franco, the two governments believe it necessary to define the principles that inspire this action.
>
> The French government, convinced that the National government of Spain combines all the conditions necessary to guarantee the independence and integrity of Spain, takes note, as a result of the conversations at Burgos, that the repeated statements of General Franco and his government express faithfully the principles that determine the foreign policy of the Spanish government.
>
> As a result the two governments affirm their will to maintain friendly relations, live in neighborly terms and carry out in Morocco a policy of loyal and open co-operation.
>
> Signed in Burgos, February 25, 1939.

The political outlook for Spain in those early days was not brilliant. Various solutions presented themselves as theoretically possible. The experience of the republic was such that it was highly improbable that the victorious movement would re-establish the institutions and form of government of the defeated element. The restoration of the republic in Spain, as an act of the Franco regime, was as inconceivable as the maintenance of the Confederacy would have been in the United States at the conclusion of the civil war. The loser loses; this is fundamental in war. The Republic was liquidated as an idea. There was no chance of its resurrection, no matter what theoretical merits it may have had. Practically speaking, "Republic" in Spain was associated with the particular Republic of 1931–1936, not with the republican idea in the abstract. The word conjured up the disorders, frustration, chaos, and powerlessness of those five years. It recalled the terrible contrast between the republic as conceived by its initial liberal proponents and the later development that contradicted so completely these high ideals. Liberal democracy was impossible, for innumerable Spaniards were quite convinced that this form of government was unworkable in the country.

The decree of unification was opposed by certain sectors of the Falange. One of the Falangist leaders, Manuel Hedilla, was suspected of subversive activity and it was known that he had dispatched a telegram to certain of the provincial leaders which was deemed dangerously close to sedition. Hedilla himself was arrested and condemned to death, although the execution was not carried out. Numerous other Falangist leaders were imprisoned. The reaction of the traditionalists was somewhat different, sometimes described as skeptical, unconvinced of the virtues of union, and with no illusions about attaining power in an immediate future. The army was pleased because it represented an element of discipline over the Falangist militia which, because of the party connection, was frequently insubordinate.

Another phase was the diplomatic. Among the first nations to recognize nationalist Spain were Guatemala and Salvador, and on November 18 Germany and Italy extended this recognition. Sir Robert Hodgson was named on November 16, 1936, as diplomatic agent of Great Britain in nationalist Spain, and a few days later the Duke of Alba received a similar designation in London. This was not recognition, but simply contact. Other countries, even those most hostile to the regime, sent agents of one kind or another, and a great many newspapermen. The German representatives included such well-known figures as General Faupel, long known for his activities in the Hispanic and Hispanic-American world, and later Von Stohrer. Serrano Suñer insists that Faupel was responsible for all sorts of local intrigue at Salamanca and for encouragement of Hedilla and the more Germanophile of the Falangists.[35]

[35] *Ibid.*, p. 48. There is evidence to show the hostility of the Italians to the Germans in Spain and especially of the bitterness of the latter toward General Franco, and

On January 30, 1938, the government published the names of the ministers and the decision to transfer the center of activities to Burgos, and the improvised, provisional structure that had served in Salamanca was abandoned. The new government undertook to bring together the various elements in the situation, a kind of "all party government," if the term can be used. Count Jordana was designated Minister of Foreign Affairs. He had served under Primo de Rivera in the days of the dictatorship and had been High Commissioner in Morocco until the advent of the republic. Other members were Count Rodezno; General Dávila, as War Minister; Andrés Amado, a former collaborator of Calvo Sotelo, the Finance Ministry. Strictly Falangist influence was almost entirely absent from the cabinet with the exception of Pedro González Bueno, who was in charge of what would normally be the Labor Ministry, called the Ministry of Trade Union Organization and Action. Serrano Suñer was designated Minister of the Interior.

The two years of the regime in Burgos had as its principal purpose the winning of the war, and the modicum of internal stability through institutional life that the advent of a new Spain demanded.

It is a curious side light to the history of this period that at one moment Indalecio Prieto undertook to organize a counter-Falange movement under the name of F.E.A. (*Falange Española Auténtica*). It was based on the assumption that the Falange was not keen about union with other parties and that its social program represented a very

---

their earnest desire to strengthen the position of the Falange. "The Falange is fascism without organic doctrine and with a pronounced left-wing tendency" (Cantalupo, *Fu la Spagna,* p. 118).

"The outstanding enemies of Franco were the German agents, beginning with General Faupel. . . . The Germans supported the Falange and not Franco, or rather the Falange against Franco. . . . The German agents with whom I spoke did not hide their hatred of Franco who was considered reactionary and a friend of the clergy, a supporter of the monarchy and the aristocracy" (*ibid.,* p. 165).

General Faupel was so strong in his conviction that he proposed to the Italian ambassador the elimination of Franco. "On the morning of the 21 he [Faupel] came to see me and stated that Franco must be eliminated. The supreme military and political control could not be left in his hands, and that the Falange was determined that he should not be the head of the state after the war" (Cantalupo, *op. cit.,* p. 198). Cantalupo's book is one of the most brilliant and suggestive studies to appear on Spain during the civil war. An old time, pre-fascist diplomat, Cantalupo analyzes the conflict of German and Italian interests and shows that internally the extreme element in the Falange was far from convinced of Franco's leadership. The merger of the political parties may be taken as a move to eliminate this hostile sector among the forces supporting the nationalists.

close counterpart to the socialist, therefore making of it the left-wing expression of the nationalist movement. The maneuver did not succeed, but it is an interesting commentary on the fact that moderate socialism in republican Spain saw in the Falange a kindred program to its own. After the battle of the Ebro, the French government, apparently convinced that the Republic was doomed, dispatched an agent to Burgos in the person of M. Bérard. This was the preliminary to the presence of Marshal Pétain as French ambassador. The war was then at an end and the new regime faced the difficult and arduous problems of reconstruction to which we shall allude in another chapter.

Chapter 12. THE NEW REGIME EMERGES

THE victory parade in Madrid on March 18, 1939, followed a few days later by the conclusion of the Catalan campaign, brought the nationalists face to face with the problem of normal government and internal reconstruction. Before examining the emergence of the new regime and the political institutions with which it was endowed, it may be well to consider briefly the mood and temper of the Spanish nation immediately after the conclusion of hostilities. The civil war had lasted nearly three years, during which approximately a million lives had been lost. While considerable areas of the country had been fortunate in escaping destruction, notably Galicia and a large part of Andalucía, the rest of Spain had suffered terribly, from the total loss of cities like Teruel and Brunete to the minor damage done to Barcelona and Valencia. The worst feature, however, was moral and psychological. Spaniard was pitted against Spaniard, and in many families members were divided in sympathy and not infrequently fought on opposite sides. A French reporter described movingly the profound moral division that prevailed in Spain and regarding which our facile, superficial advocates of "democratization" and "liberalization" seem totally ignorant:

> In Spain, in contrast with the international war, the enemy was within the country. Families have fought against families; brothers against brothers, and fathers against sons. To heal so deep a wound an orderly regime was necessary. . . . Moreover the bitterness is still very much alive. I have heard persons mention the name of their family's murderer and speak of possible future vengeance.[1]

The first thing to remember about Spain after 1939 is that one section of the population had defeated another section. It was not a regional struggle, as was the American civil war; it was a profound social cleavage, affecting every part of the country. The violence and

[1] Gilbert Ganne, "Quatre semaines en Espagne," *La France Catholique,* Paris, Aug. 19, 1949.

bloodshed that preceded the actual outbreak of war and the fury of sadism that distinguished the period of the war itself left a deep and enduring mark on the spirit of the Spanish people. Today in Spain the visitor will hear from almost everyone with whom he comes in contact authentic tales of the terror and murder through which they lived. I know few Spanish families in which at least one member was not assassinated and everyone recalls vividly cases of *paseos* or nightly murder parties in which an uncle, a father, a son, or a mother were taken from the home and found later, a corpse on some road outside the city. In a great many cases the murderer is suspected or actually known. In other cases it was due to betrayal by the servants, information passed on by a waiter or by someone who saw in this a chance for revenge. The members of the various *Chekas* that passed the perfunctory sentences of death are equally known. It must be remembered that a large number of those who were responsible for this violence are still in Spain living out their lives side by side with the victors, for only a very small proportion of the republicans actually managed to escape abroad. The Spanish tragedy is the slow process of reconciliation between those who won and those who lost. Civil war leaves this trail of bitter recollection which only time — and perhaps generations — can entirely eradicate.

I know of individual Spaniards who recount how from time to time they come across in the course of their business or professional activities persons who in the days of the terror were members of *Chekas* that condemned them or were personally responsible for informing the authorities of their whereabouts. The reader can well imagine the state of mind of a citizen who unexpectedly finds himself face to face with a former porter or domestic whom he knows was directly responsible for passing a death sentence on his father. This does not happen once but a thousand times in Spain today, producing tension and rekindling old hates. It makes the restoration of cordiality among the various sectors of the population infinitely difficult. It is as though the soldiery of Sherman's army had settled down side by side with the citizens of Columbia, South Carolina, after 1865, to work out together the reconstruction of that battered city. Is it conceivable that there would not have been an explosion of hostility between the two? Apply this analogy to modern Spain and a correct appreciation of the present-day state of mind is possible.

It was inevitable, too, that when victory was achieved there should be repression. The Spanish jails were filled to bursting with the defeated. This is the natural accompaniment of the triumph of one side over the other. Denazification filled the compounds and prisons of Germany as the process of weeding out went on. Why, then, should it be surprising that after the holocaust of the Spanish civil war the same thing should transpire? The accounts of the final months of the war during the late winter and spring of 1939 reveal how this took place. In town after town everyone who had collaborated actively with the Republic and especially who had been guilty of violence against persons, was rounded up. In most cases every republican functionary or petty official gave himself up as the best guarantee of his life. Every available place was packed with prisoners until it was feasible to sort out the technically guilty from those who had actually committed crimes. Thousands of republican army men went over en masse to the nationalists as the collapse approached and were detained until the necessary machinery could be put to work to return them to civil life.

We must remember that for the victorious nationalists the defeated Republic under the Largo Caballero-Negrín domination had meant communism, and that they had saved Spain not merely from the Popular Front but from effective communization. Therefore, the active convinced enemies of the national movement — not necessarily the rank and file — were assumed to be in sympathy with a doctrine totally destructive of the essence of Spain. This profound conviction led the victorious movement to scrutinize with considerable care the character of the prisoners brought into camp. Apply the reasoning to defeated Germany and the allied attitude toward it and one gets, perhaps, the perspective of the situation. The western occupying powers had a fear that in some way the partisans of the former German order would filter back into administration and places of confidence. The Spanish nationalists felt exactly the same about the defeated republicans. Unfortunately, the whole thing has been confused by the use of the term "democratic" as applied to the Republic. Whatever it might have been in origin, one may be absolutely assured that by 1936, and particularly during the course of the civil war, the Spanish Republic was about as republican in sentiment, devotion to democracy, and respect for the ordinary processes of representative government, as, let us say, Gottwald's Czechoslovakia.

The Spanish civil war brought to the surface the most violent emotions. Many of the complexities of the contemporary Spanish scene spring directly from this emotional carrousel that lasted for three years.

There was strong dislike of France for the attitude of the French government during the civil war and the open partisanship on behalf of the Republic and there were grave reservations regarding the United States and Great Britain for the same reason. On top of victory, the bittersweet fruit of the savagely exhausting civil war, World War II closed in on Spain like a vise. Barely able to begin the process of reconstruction, the nation was forced to play a delicate and infinitely patient game to avoid involvement in the greater hostilities. These, had Spain participated in them, would have been the finish of the country.

The conclusion of World War II left the Spanish isolated within the encirclement of ill will and universal disdain. Is it any wonder, then, that the natural consequences of the civil war have endured longer than would have been normal, if Spain had had any real chance to rehabilitate herself in a balanced world? The atmosphere of 1939 was inevitable and its prolongation many years later is explained. There is a feeling in Spain that, were the government to relax, a situation not unlike that of the Greece of 1949 might follow, for there is no lack of willingness on the part of the exiles to provoke border incidents along the Pyrenees and one can well imagine the consequences were Spain to neglect her defenses or relinquish too much the present rigid control.

This is not an *apologia* for Spain. It is an expression of hope that in the future the Spanish problem will be approached with a greater sense of realism and a willingness to understand how Spaniards felt in 1939 when the civil war terminated. If the United States, in 1949, felt that its national integrity required that eleven communist leaders be tried and convicted for their program of political action, is it any wonder that Spain, which knew communism in violent action as well as in thought, should be chary of any concessions that might bring it back again? We may profitably reflect on the fact that the only western European country where communism actually obtained a toe hold and was on the way to victory was in Spain. Had the civil war not come, judging from the actual state of affairs in June and July, 1936, it is no exaggeration that within a year or two a dictatorship of the proletariat with complete sovietization would have come. The Spanish today are quite aware that their country escaped this debacle almost miraculously. Convinced that anything is worth while to prevent a recurrence of the nightmare of 1936, is it small wonder that the Spaniard is likely to be overvigilant and overrigid in his attitude toward anything smacking of communism or

Marxist infiltration? Let the contemporary American contrast the modest experience of his own country regarding communism in the years since 1945 with the far greater experience of Spain in 1936. If vigilance in the United States against infiltration is justified, I submit that the attitude of the Spanish government is no less comprehensible.

In the first days of the civil war, the press in nationalist Spain made almost no reference to the form of government or even to the political problem as such. The publication, *El Norte de Castilla,* of Valladolid, to take one example, in its issue of July 22, refers simply to the proclamation of the *Junta suprema militar,* and of General Mola. The same journal on July 23 condemned left-wing socialism in definite terms but not the Republic as an institution and spoke of "the dictatorship of the Popular Front and the farce of socialism."

We have a definite hint of the character of the new regime in one of the early speeches of General Franco in which authoritarianism is indicated as the guiding principle:

> Spain will be organized according to a totalitarian concept, with full respect for its traditions, and with consideration for its historical nationality, unity, and continuity. All this with the establishment of a severe principle of authority.[2]

It was evident that the war years were devoted largely to the immediate problem of winning the armed conflict. Political policies, despite their pressing importance, were improvised, and enough of a national government was created to carry on the larger tasks of conducting the war.[3] On September 29, 1936, General Franco was named Head of the Spanish State. It is not without importance that for a long time, the term "Spanish State" was employed, a significant phrase indicating the fundamentally provisional nature of the national institutions.

This preliminary groping for a solution of the institutional life of Spain has remained the basic problem of Spanish life today. The division between the Falange and the monarchists, to take one discrepancy as an example, is inspired by the fear of the latter that Spain is too much a personal affair and its government far too uninstitutionalized, that is, without the guarantees of continuity and permanence that the monarchists believe indispensable

---

[2] *El Norte de Castilla,* Valladolid, Oct. 2, 1936.

[3] Serrano Suñer, *Entre Hendaya y Gibraltar,* Madrid, 1947. This book describes the halting first steps toward a stable government.

for the survival of the nation in the event of the disappearance of the *Caudillo*. The concentration of government in the hands of a single leader, without the necessary superstructure, is the basic point that concerns them and not opposition to General Franco as a leader, although in some monarchist circles that feeling is strong. On the other hand, the defenders of the present regime insist that steps have already been taken to assure permanency even in the event of the *Caudillo's* death; a great deal of the contemporary discussion in Spain is concentrated around this issue. The monarchists are convinced — that is, those who are critics of the Franco regime — that the real power is personally his and that even the cabinet is pretty much a rubber-stamp organization without authority and without prestige except as the Generalissimo delegates it.

On October 1, 1936, as has been indicated, the provisional government was set up. On January 30, 1938, and August 8, 1939, various ministries were created and the full mechanism of the State restored. Civilian participation became a fact in the course of the war, and the creation of these various agencies made it possible for the nationalists to claim that they were something more than a mere movement, that they were a duly constituted government with all of the powers and authority that goes with that status. The fundamental steps in the organization of the new Spain may be summarized as follows:

1. Formation of the *Junta de Defensa Nacional* (July 24, 1936).
2. Decree providing for the unification of the various parties supporting the National Movement (April 19, 1937).
3. Decree of April 19, 1937, with changes of July 31, 1939, establishing the bases of the *Falange Española Tradicionalista* and the J.O.N.S. (*Juventudes de Ofensiva Nacional Sindicalista*).
4. Bases of *sindical* organization and social legislation promulgated and *Fuero del Trabajo* (March 9, 1938 and December 6, 1940).
5. Creation of the Spanish Cortes, July 17, 1942, with modifications of March 9 and July 15, 1946.
6. Basic laws of local administration, elections, and the like approved (November 25, 1944).
7. *Fuero de los Españoles* (July 17, 1945).
8. The Succession Law (June 8, 1947).

Here we have in synthesis, without elaboration or detail, the main steps that led from the improvised machinery of government in 1936 to the present structure. Whether it is sufficient to guarantee a normal, peaceful transition from the dictatorship to the regular monarchy is, of course, still problematical, but to claim that no structure at all exists is a palpable exaggeration. It is not without interest to observe that in many respects nothing that functions in Spain today is particularly new. The idea that all precedents were scrapped and the structure of Franco Spain was erected *ab avo* is quite erroneous. In fact there still prevails in Spain an incredible amount of legislation and practice dating from the nineteenth century and even from the republican period. The legislation regarding public works, to take a single case, dates from 1877 and the judicial system is not basically different from that of the Restoration in the past century.[4]

The principal documents that merit more detailed examination are the Falange program, the *Fuero de los Españoles,* and the constitution of the Cortes with the provisions for the monarchical restoration. In this chapter we shall examine the *Fuero,* the Cortes, and the general mechanism of the State. In the following chapter, devoted to the Falange, the details of the program of that party will be noted.

The *Fuero* is basic to an understanding of the functioning of the present Spanish State, for it constitutes what may be loosely called the Bill of Rights and defines the rights and duties of Spanish citizens. It was drawn up and debated by the Cortes and was promulgated by General Franco as "a fundamental law, regulating the rights and duties of the citizens."[5] In synthesis, this document provides the following:

ARTICLE 1. The Spanish State proclaims as its directing principle respect for the dignity, integrity, and liberty of the human person, as a member of the national community, and subject to the common good.

ARTICLE 2. Spaniards owe faithful service to the country, loyalty to the Chief of State, and obedience to the laws.

ARTICLE 3. The law protects all Spaniards alike regardless of class or condition.

---

[4] Some of the legislation still in effect in Spain without any modification includes (1) law of civil procedure of February 3, 1881, (2) law of criminal procedure of September 14, 1882, (3) the Civil Code of 1888, (4) the laws on administrative procedure of 1889, regulations and laws on public order, dating from the republican period. A whole body of fundamental legislation in effect in contemporary Spain dates either from the monarchy or from laws passed by the Republican Cortes.

[5] *Fuero de los Españoles,* Madrid, 1945. Published as a pamphlet by the Under-Secretariate of Popular Education.

Article 4. Spaniards have the right to respect for their personal and family honor. Whoever violates it shall suffer the penalty of the law.

Article 5. All Spaniards have the obligation to education and the duty of obtaining it. The State shall see to it that no one of ability shall be deprived of instruction because of economic difficulties.

Article 6. The profession and practice of the Catholic religion, which is that of the Spanish State, shall enjoy official protection.

No one shall be molested for his religious beliefs nor private worship. No external ceremonies or manifestations shall be allowed but the Catholic.

Article 10. All Spaniards have the right to participate in public affairs of a representative character through the family, municipality, or trade union. . . .

Article 12. All Spaniards may express their ideas freely as long as they do not run contrary to the fundamental principles of the State.

Article 17. Spaniards shall enjoy legal security. All the organs of the State shall function in conformity with pre-established law which cannot be either arbitrarily interpreted or changed.

Article 18. No Spaniard can be detained under arrest except according to law. Within seventy-two hours after arrest, he must either be freed or turned over to the proper judicial authority.

Article 19. No one can be condemned except under a law existing prior to the commission of the act and in accord with a proper court decision.

Article 22. The State recognizes and protects the family as the natural unit of society and with rights and duties above positive human law.

Article 24. All Spaniards have the right to work.

Article 25. Work, because of its essential human character, cannot be considered as a purely material thing but only in accord with the element of human dignity.

Article 27. All workers shall be protected by the State in their rightful claim to a just wage, sufficient for themselves and their family.

Article 28. The Spanish State recognizes the right of the worker to security and protection against misfortune.

Article 30. Private property as a natural means for the fulfillment of the end of the individual, family, and community, shall be protected.

Only the more significant articles are given here in translation. The reader will obviously ask whether this statement of human rights is respected in practice. Spain is one of those countries where the distance between the letter of the law and the reality is frequently very great. It is not always proper to assume that what the statute book says exists, is necessarily the reality.

The answer to the question whether the fundamental guarantees are respected is not easy to answer. In the section of this chapter devoted to the prison system and the problem of political prisoners an effort is made to examine this much debated question. One of the best definitions of contemporary Spain I have heard is that it is, to give the Spanish text, *un absolutismo teórico, distinguido por la inobservancia* — "a theoretical absolutism, characterized by inobservance." If we mean by absolutism the complete control by a single person with no flexibility whatever, we are wrong. If we assume that the ordinary processes we call democracy — that is, the free play of institutions, of ideas, and of men — works in Spain, we are equally wrong. Spain is a curiously provoking sort of place, because theory and fact never seem quite to coincide. Elaborate laws often do not work, for no body puts them into effect. Custom and tradition time and again win out over the formal proposals of either the State or the lawmaking authority. The resources of the Spanish people for avoiding the observance of an unpopular law are infinite, and this fecundity very often makes mockery of the best conceived statutes. But even in this complex situation there can be no doubt that the regime has become softer and more flexible in the course of the years. Halting and inadequate as many of the steps may be, there is concrete evidence that evolution in the Spanish system has taken place. True, it is still rigid, top heavy, complicated, and in many ways outmoded. Foreign pressure and the high tension of world war years and international ostracism have contributed to making that evolution much slower than it might normally have been. Had Spain been left to its own devices after 1939, there can be little doubt that the institutions of the dictatorship would have become far more "liberal" than they are at present. I believe one of the most effective summaries of the state of affairs has been given by Constantine Brown, whose virtue consists in having visited Spain on several occasions over a period of years and not being taken in by the superficial appearance of things:

> There is no question that General Franco is a dictator. But during the ten years that he has been chief of state, he has greatly softened the rules

under which the Spanish people live. To casual observers there is no more indication that there is a dictatorship here than in many western countries.[6]

The Cortes is supposedly the legislative branch of the Spanish State. The term "deputy" is no longer used, having been replaced by that of *procurador*. The present Cortes, according to the law of July 17, 1942, contrasts strikingly with the old Cortes or parliament in that the free play of party politics has disappeared. A profound distaste existed after 1939 for the operation of parliamentary government as it had been known under the Republic and the eternal crises, meteoric shifts and changes, and the endless consultations for the formation of a new government became a relic of history that cannot be artificially resurrected even if the will to do so were present. The present Cortes today consists of functional representation. The following are the permanent, *ex officio* members of the legislature: (1) ministers of State; (2) national councilors of Falange; (3) chairmen of the State Council, Supreme Court, and the highest military tribunals; (4) representatives of the national trade unions, to number no more than a third of the entire body; (5) mayors of the 50 provincial capitals and one representative of the remaining provincial cities; (6) university rectors; (7) president of the Spanish Institute and representatives of the royal academies and the Council of the Scientific Investigation; (8) representatives of the Bar, the physicians, engineers, architects, pharmacists, veterinarians, and similar professional groups; (9) outstanding persons, who, because of "their ecclesiastical, military, social, professional, or administrative stature" may be designated directly by the Chief of State in a number not to exceed fifty.[7]

The Cortes, in the organic act creating it, is defined as the "superior agency for the participation of the Spanish people in the work of the State." The justification of this professional representation, so alien to ordinary parliamentary tradition and inherent in the corporate state theory, reposes on the basic theory that governs the Spanish state expressed by José Antonio Primo de Rivera: "Every man is born in a family, belongs to a township, and has a trade or profession" with the conclusion that the most authentic representation of the mass of people is through the family, the municipality, and the trade union.[8]

[6] *Evening Star,* Washington, D. C., Nov. 20, 1949.

[7] A useful small manual on the functioning of the Spanish government is Manuel Fraga Iribarne, *Así se gobierna España,* Madrid, 1949.

[8] Roberto Reyes, "Representación orgánica de la nación española," published in *Arriba,* July 18, 1947.

The members of the Cortes are of two varieties: elected and permanent. The designated members are either *ex officio,* because of the post occupied, or in the case of not more than 50, may be named directly by the Chief of State, an arrangement somewhat like that of a certain number of senators in Italy who are drawn from the artistic, intellectual, or scientific world and named by the President. The term of office is three years with frequent partial elections to cover vacancies.

The jurisdiction of the Cortes covers a wide field: the budget, taxation, economic policy, international treaties, civil legislation, social problems, public administration, public instruction, and the judicial organization. The Cortes may either initiate legislation or it may receive proposals from the Chief of State and Council of Ministers. Does the Cortes really function or is it a façade to create the fiction of a legislature? It is clearly not a completely sovereign parliament with supreme jurisdiction, for the simple reason that Spain today has abandoned the idea of legislative supremacy nor does not have comparable powers either to initiate or to reject legislation as, let us say, to the French parliament or the British House of Commons. It would perhaps be far more accurate to say that the Cortes, as organized in 1942, is the beginning of a parliament. An apologist of the system has stated that "the law establishing the Cortes is fundamental and a revision requires an absolute majority of the Cortes itself and a national referendum. . . . But even if it were desired to work toward a still more representative system, it would not be necessary to modify basically the present law."[9] There are cases in which the Cortes has taken a position contrary to the Chief of State and ministers; a proposed statute regarding urban rent controls was held up for a year in the Judicial Commission, and when it was returned to the executive was scarcely recognizable after the amendments and changes, and a law regarding tax reform was obstructed by the opposition of nearly half the members of the Cortes. In a word, it would be inaccurate to describe the Spanish parliament as a totally subordinate, parrotlike body, comparable to the Hitlerite Reichstag, brought together to cheer the Chief of State when he addressed it, nor, on the other hand, would it be historically exact to present it as a full-fledged independent parliament. It is the beginning of a legislature, a quasi parliament, if one may call it that, with the possibility of development.

---

[9] *Ibid.*

Spanish administration is highly centralized, the outgrowth of an historic trend going back to the union of the peninsula. In economic and social matters Madrid has absorbed almost everything, while the provincial jurisdictions have steadily diminished. This unfortunate tendency is by no means a Spanish monopoly, for every western nation suffers from the same tendency. In Spain it reaches incredible heights, and businessmen are prone to state that whereas twenty years ago a great many operations could be performed locally, today it is invariably the rule that one must go to Madrid for action.

The provincial administration is not, however, without importance. The 50 Spanish provinces are headed by a governor named from Madrid and comparable in many ways to the prefects of French Departments. There exists the *Diputación provincial* to represent the strictly provincial interests, under a president and a representative for each division within the province and these local representatives are chosen on both a territorial and corporate basis, along lines somewhat similar to the national Cortes. In a great many local matters the provincial authorities have considerable latitude. The municipal government is headed by a mayor, designated from above, under conditions that are quite similar to those that apply to the provincial governors. The city and town councils are elected in a rather complicated way: one third chosen by direct vote of the heads of families, another third by the trade unions, and the final third elected by the other two thirds already chosen.

The judicial system is headed by the Supreme Court, with several divisions according to the subject matter of litigation submitted to it: civil criminal, two devoted to administrative matters, and one assigned for everything relating to social legislation. Below the Supreme Court are the *audiencias territoriales,* equivalent roughly to a district court, and finally the local tribunals, extending down to the municipal. The ecclesiastical courts are completely separate, culminating in the Rota, re-established in Spain in 1947 by agreement between the Spanish government and the Holy See. There are special military courts, tribunals for fiscal matters outside the ordinary jurisdiction of the regular system, and certain very specialized ones such as the *Tribunal de las Aguas* in Valencia where, for centuries, water for irrigation has been distributed and assigned without appeal to any other court. The judges are without exception careerists. Spanish law still retains a great many survivals of local usage and custom, particularly in Aragón, Catalonia, and Navarre.

The most important effort to restore Spain to a normal regime was the promulgation of the Succession Law and with it the referendum of 1947. The Cortes drafted and approved the fundamental law reestablishing the monarchy and created the special council to determine the royal succession. In Article 3 of the Succession Law it is provided that:

> In the event of a vacancy in the headship of the State, a Council of Regency will assume the supreme authority, to be formed by the President of the Cortes, the prelate of highest rank, and the Captain General of the armed forces.[10]

The *Consejo del Reino,* or Royal Council, is designed to collaborate with the Head of the State and is composed of the following members, in addition to the President of the Cortes: Captain General of the armed forces; Chief of the General Staff; President of the Council of State; Chief Justice of the Supreme Court; President of the *Instituto de España;* one member for the Cortes, the trade unions, local administration, university rectors, and professional groups; three members designated directly by the Head of the State.

Among the important functions of the Council is the proposal of a successor to General Franco before the Cortes. The law provides that General Franco may propose at any time to the Cortes the person who is to succeed him as king or regent. The Council of Regency is to rule in the event of a lapse between Franco and whoever succeeds him. In the case of the death or incapacity of General Franco, with no successor chosen, the Council of Regency shall assume the direction of public affairs and within three days convoke the Royal Council, to decide on such a successor. The details of just how this system is to operate are not fundamental; what is important is that the law requires that whoever becomes king shall be a Spaniard, at least thirty years old, a Catholic, and shall "be loyal to the principles of the National Movement," that is, the Falange.

As an indication of the possibility that General Franco would abandon power before either death or incapacity, it is noteworthy that in the original text which the *Caudillo* drafted, he included the word "resignation." This expression was struck out at the urgent suggestion of certain of his collaborators because of the impression it might give of a decision already germinating in the General's mind. It is significant, though, that this was definitely one of the possibilities animating

---

[10] The most detailed text treating of this problem and the results of the referendum is *El Refrendo popular de la Ley española de Sucesión,* Madrid, 1948.

General Franco in proposing that the succession be guaranteed by the present law.

The Succession Law envisages, then, the restoration of the monarchy and that General Franco in his own good time shall choose the occupant of the throne. There is no possibility, as some have claimed, that the *Caudillo* himself expected to become the head of a dynasty, since the law specifically provides that the succession shall be guaranteed only in a person of royal blood. The fact that the law prescribes the age of thirty as necessary for the occupation of the throne has led some critics to assume that General Franco proposes to sidetrack Don Juan entirely in favor of his son until the latter reaches the statutory age. Some hint of the General's intentions may be gained from his speech to the Cortes in May, 1949, in which the problem of continuity is posed:

> What greater guarantee for the continuity of the regime can be asked? Have the elective republics or constitutional monarchies before us revealed any greater? It is useless to pretend any greater security for the future. . . .[11]

After defending the Succession Law in these terms as a sufficient guarantee for the future, General Franco gave a broad hint that he does not anticipate retiring in the immediate future, by adding: "And even in that future which, thank God, still seems distant, when my vigor declines or my life ends."

The Cortes approved the Succession Law on June 7, 1947; on July 6 it was submitted to a popular referendum and on July 26 was promulgated as law. Prior to the popular consultation, the text of the law was submitted to widest publicity in the press and over the radio networks. The Electoral Law of 1907 was utilized, curiously enough, as the basis for the polling and every Spaniard over twenty was obliged to cast his ballot. The elections were secret; of this there can be no serious doubt, nor was there corruption at the polls or coercion of the voters.[12] Foreign criticism was quick to seize on the referendum as another totalitarian trick. One British paper claimed that the number of electors was materially reduced since all who had relatives abroad or out on conditional liberty, were excluded.[13] As a matter of fact, the number of persons excluded for reason of

[11] *A.B.C.*, May 19, 1949.

[12] "According to the press and British eye-witnesses the ballot was secret, fair, and orderly throughout Spain" (Loveday, *Spain, 1923–1948*, Boswell Publishing Co., London, 1949, p. 238).

[13] *The Observer*, London, June 22, 1947.

crimes or political imprisonment did not exceed 1.62 of the total voting population.

The problem posed a difficulty of an entirely different order. Although the elections were secret and no evidence appeared that either fraud or coercion had been employed, there is no doubt that opposition to the Succession Law and to General Franco did not have a chance to speak out; it was the pre-electoral campaign that was restricted. The press, the radio, the government, and the other official organs joined in a tremendous chorus of praise of the law, and of the necessity of demonstrating Spanish approval of the Franco regime by an affirmative vote.

There was a division of opinion among the monarchists, for it must always be remembered that the number of the monarchical faction makes impossible easy generalization. The legitimists of the Don Juan persuasion represent probably the bulk of those who favor the return of the King and the normalization of the state, while the Carlists are divided between Count Rodezno, who accepts Don Juan with certain reservations, and Manuel Falconde, leader of another traditionalist group who place their hopes in Javier of Bourbon Parma. A third Carlist group prefers Carlos of Habsburg-Bourbon, grandson of Carlos VII, last Carlist pretender in the third civil war. A small group of partisans of the Alphonsine tradition are inclined to Alfonso Carlos, son of Don Jaime, himself the eldest son of Alfonso XIII. Don Juan issued a statement shortly after General Franco had submitted the Succession Law to the Cortes in which he explained that he could only accept a normal and unconditional transfer of authority. Despite the fact that the Succession Law did not satisfy, and could not satisfy the hopes of many of the supporters of Don Juan, the monarchist newspaper, *A.B.C.*, distinguished clearly between its reservations and its more general support of the Franco regime, pointing out that there could be no serious basis for doubting the legitimacy of General Franco's authority.[14] Manuel Falconde insisted that his traditionalist group abstain completely from voting, as a sign of protest against the Succession Law. Other traditionalists, especially the Navarrese of Count Rodezno, went along with the measure.[15]

---

[14] *A.B.C.*, July 18, 1947.

[15] A note on Carlism may be useful. It began in 1833 with the death of Ferdinand VII. The Carlist dynasty runs as follows: Carlos V, during the period of the seven years' war to 1840; Carlos VI, during second war to 1849; Carlos VII, from April, 1872, to March, 1876; Alfonso Carlos.

Javier de Borbón: head of the *Comunión tradicionalista,* direct descendant of

The activity on the part of the exiles was extraordinary. In view of their contention that the election was a farce and could not possibly be taken seriously, the amount of attention devoted to it was disproportionate. The republican government in exile denounced it all, of course, as a nefarious scheme to prove that Franco was popular when they knew perfectly well that 90 per cent of the Spanish people were against him. The United Nations was favored with one of the innumerable petitions from the exiles denouncing the referendum, and President Aguirre of the Basque government in exile expressed his conviction that no decent Basque would go near the polls. The clandestine organizations inside Spain, the U.G.T.-C.N.T. liaison committee and the leaders of the *Alianza Nacional de Fuerzas Democráticas* all joined in urging their partisans to abstain, while the communists clamored for an anti-Franco manifestation. *Mundo Obrero* stated that "No anti-Franquist will cast his ballot on July 6."[16]

Radio Moscow and the Spanish republican network from France bombarded Spain before the election with instructions to abstain rigidly from the polls and demonstrate hostility to the regime by positive action against it. In one case the instructions were that the guerrilla fighters inside Spain were to attack the polling places, destroy communications, and convert the roadways into impassable barriers for traffic. The result of this activity was practically nil either because there were so few opponents of the regime in Spain willing to employ violence that the method did not work, or the propaganda from the outside had lost its vitality and, above all, actuality.

During the election, foreign newsmen were free to visit any of the polling places and examine the procedure in any part of Spain. A member of the British House of Commons visited a number of the electoral colleges in Barcelona, and two American newsmen in Gerona and two British journalists in Bilbao circulated about with restraint. As is well known, foreign comment in general was not particularly laudatory. The Spanish press published in full the statements issued in Washington and London regarding the referendum — revealing in this particular that the Spanish people do not live completely in dark-

---

Philip V and brother of ex-Empress Zita of Austria. Don Javier studied in France and Vienna, fought in the Belgian army. In World War II he was imprisoned by the Germans, condemned to death by Vichy, and saved by the intervention of Marshal Pétain. He was in Dachau and Natzweiler concentration camps. He claims the succession of his uncle, Alfonso Carlos.

[16] *Mundo Obrero,* Toulouse, June 19, 1947.

ness regarding the outside world. *Arriba* notes that Norman Armour stated from the Department of State that "there is no proof that the press restrictions before the voting were relaxed, or that the Spanish people had a chance to discuss the Law freely."[17] The Reuter dispatch from London was published in full to the effect that in Foreign Office circles the feeling was that the wording of the Succession Law left the Spanish people little chance to really express its views on the regime, and "the voters could only choose between the Regime or abstention, and in this case abstention was interpreted as support of the regime."[18]

The official results showed that of the 17,178,812 voters, 15,219,563 actually cast their ballot, and of this number there were 14,145,163 pros and 722,656 cons and 351,744 ballots were thrown out as spoiled. On the basis of the official figures, then, one may presume that between the cons and the spoiled ballots there were well over a million, while some two million others refrained from going to the polls at all. The published results in the daily papers did not give the exact number of abstentions and it was generally understood that the publication of these figures was forbidden.[19]

Toward the end of 1948 the long anticipated municipal elections were held on a number of successive Sundays. This was carried out along the lines described earlier in this chapter and represented the second time Spaniards have gone to the polls under the present regime.

There is no problem more complicated in connection with the emergence of the new Spanish regime than that of political prisoners. It is impossible to treat of the contemporary Spanish scene, and particularly of the form and policy of the Franco regime, without considering the question of political crimes and the number of individuals incarcerated for such activities. Observations range from those that claim there are no political prisoners at all in Spain to the most complete condemnation of the penal organization of the country, as a survival of total barbarism. It is extremely hard to come to absolute conclusions on this point, because for one thing there is a great deal of confusion between common and political criminals. It frequently

---

[17] July 10, 1947.

[18] *Ibid.*

[19] *A.B.C.*, July 8, 1947. The British member of the House of Commons, Edward Carson, visited the polling places in Barcelona freely and gave his impressions in the London *Star* (July 11, 1947): "I am convinced the voting was absolutely secret and in my opinion the elections were fair. I believe, moreover, that the falsifying of the results would have been unnecessary for the majority was undoubtedly affirmative."

happens that a common housebreaker or highwayman claims to be acting in the underground and consequently depicts himself as motivated by political ideology. In other cases the type of activity engaged in by the clandestine opposition becomes for all practical effects common criminal action. A so-called guerrilla fighter who seizes the funds of a bank may, in a most liberal interpretation, be considered a political criminal, when in fact the act for which he was imprisoned was ordinary lawbreaking. Certain basic facts may however be presented as borne out by adequate evidence. They were the following: (1) Spanish penal legislation and the prison system are fairly good by any standard; (2) the number of political prisoners has been exaggerated far beyond the realities; (3) an enormous work of rehabilitation of prisoners and of care for their families has been carried out in a spirit of great humanity and charity.

Even as severe a critic as C. L. Sulzberger in *The New York Times* is in agreement that "although the system as a whole is rotten and the people are frequently condemned to prison for no good reason the prisons themselves are relatively good" (Nov. 30, 1948). The most complete analysis in English of the Spanish penal system is that of Halliday Sutherland, a British physician, who came to Spain recently and visited a large number of the penal establishments quite unescorted and unannounced. His conclusions are of significance because he is a particularly competent judge. He quite rightly calls attention to the fact that the western world is prone to pass hasty judgment on the so-called "political prisons" of General Franco, and ignore the equally important fact that elsewhere the victor has proceeded with far greater severity. The penalties given many former Nazis in Germany surpass in severity anything dreamed of in Spain.[20]

Another fundamental thing about the Spanish situation, and it bears constant repetition, is that the theory and the reality are not always the same. Sulzberger expressed it in saying that "Spanish laws are frequently well thought out, if badly executed."

Not only that, but even the most severe Spanish law is softened and even ignored in innumerable cases. I personally know of more than a half dozen cases of persons tried and convicted for murder with sentences of thirty or more years' imprisonment who, after two or three years, were on the street. I know, too, of one prison whose warden allowed even his worst cases to make frequent visits to their

---

[20] Halliday Sutherland, *Spanish Journey*, London, 1948.

homes, on condition that they re-enter the institution once their errand was completed. It would take pages to cite cases of individuals who have been political prisoners and are now back in ordinary life without the slightest handicap. There are literally thousands of socialists now in the trade unions who make no attempt to conceal their affiliation and there are the ex-republican army officers in official positions and individuals condemned to death who work freely and normally as though nothing had happened. Allow me to cite one specific case simply as an illustration. At the editorial office of *Mundo Hispánico,* one Juan Antonio Cabezas is employed. This particular individual, now closely connected with the well-known review, was a former editor of *Avance* in Oviedo, one of the most violently left-wing papers in the peninsula. He was a fervent and active supporter of the Republic and a pronounced anticlerical. His activities were far from passive. In the course of time he was condemned to death — not once but twice — under bizarre conditions; was pardoned and is living out his life tranquilly in a magazine office, with a son who is now a Jesuit novice. The story is not complete without mentioning the fact that Cabezas was the recipient of a literary prize under the present regime, while in prison. This sort of thing happens constantly; the case cited is not a rare exception and, therefore, every judgment on the Spanish prison system and severity of measures taken against the political enemies of the regime must be tempered by the discrepancy between the theory and the reality.[21]

It is probable that during the period, 1939–1940, there were upward of 300,000 political prisoners awaiting trial or examination. This figure has been dropping steadily ever since that date. The estimates of the present prison population vary and are subject to elastic estimates; Sulzberger quotes the figure of 120,000; Constantine Brown writes that Spain's jails hold a maximum of 200,000 and that, once the normal prison population is eliminated, there are perhaps 50,000 political prisoners.[22] The claim is frequently advanced that even outside prison

---

[21] Angel Ganivet remarked this anomaly long ago: "The punishment of criminals is regulated in Spain, apparently, by a code, and, in fact, by a code accompanied by the systematic application of the pardon. In other countries the normal procedure would be to modify the code and bring it into line with sentiments of moderation. In Spain the code remains absolutely rigid and its effects are nullified by constant violation of its provisions." *Idearium Español* in *Obras completas,* Vol. I, p. 146.

[22] Constantine Brown, *Evening Star,* Washington, D. C., Feb. 6, 1947. This excellent correspondent adds: "Even in France where the purge is said to have ended at least 50,000 persons are being held as collaborationists or friends of the Vichy government.

the thousands of individuals under "conditional liberty" form a part of the great army of the politically contaminated. We find the following statement: "While, as with political prisoners, there is no means of verifying the numbers of watched liberty, it is estimated that hundreds of thousands of Spaniards are thus withdrawn from productive activity and live an uncertain existence." In a footnote to this same comment, it is said that "opposition sources estimated the number of such parolees at 1,750,000 in July, 1947, the government contended there were only 300,000."[23] On the other hand, a very competent observer, the I.N.S. representative in Madrid, Edward Knoblaugh, who has been on the ground of Spain for years, puts the figure for political prisoners at about 33,000, and adds the pungent comment that under the Republic there were 35,000 political prisoners when Spain had a population of only 23,000,000. In comparative terms, the number today is proportionately less than in 1934.[24]

The statement that under "watched liberty" the ex-prisoner is deprived of his opportunity for economic reintegration in the community is misleading, for the Spanish State provided by its establishment in May, 1943, for a division in the Ministry of Justice to deal with the problem and to facilitate work for the parolee in whatever enterprise suited his capacities.

The list of pardons and remission of penalties by statutory action is remarkably long. Beginning with the complete revision of all sentences for political offenses, ordered on January 25, 1940, the successive legislation aimed at reducing the number of persons held for political crimes is as follows:

June 4, 1940, granting freedom to all prisoners with sentences up to 6 years, and half time off for those up to 12;

October 1, 1941, the benefits of the pardons of the year before were extended to all prisoners with sentences up to 12 years;

October 16, 1942, extending to those under sentence up to 14 years 8 months;

March 13, 1943, up to 20 years;

The Fresnes prison in Paris . . . is said to hold some 5000 such persons, many of whom have not yet been brought to trial. . . . The 50,000 political prisoners in Spain, which has a population of 28,000,000 appears small in comparison with other countries."

[23] *Foreign Policy Reports.* Foreign Policy Association, Vol. XXV, No. 4, May 1, 1949, p. 43.

[24] H. Edward Knoblaugh, *Peoria Register,* Peoria, Ill., April 11, 1949.

December 17, 1943, benefits extended to those under sentence of 20 to 30 years.

The actual number of prisoners released during the course of the first eight years after the civil war are as follows:

1939	981	1944	24,721
1940	10,336	1945	9,860
1941	47,244	1946	13,109
1942	29,375	1947	4,258
1943	57,549	1948	4,701

The official figures have it that on September 1, 1949, the total prison population of Spain was 37,576. Those condemned and incarcerated for crimes of rebellion were announced as follows: central prisons, 875 men and 57 women; in provincial and military prisons, 1371 men and 33 women.[25] Obviously exact figures are literally impossible to get. I have seen a large number of the *dossiers* in the files of the agencies charged with pardons and have been astonished at the large number of cases of individuals of socialist, communist, and anarchist background who have been released and reinstated in society. Moreover it may be confidently said that the system of concentration camps does not exist in Spain today. Here again the testimony of Constantine Brown, who has written abundantly on the subject, may be of interest: "It has been definitely established that, with the exception of one detention area for aliens who cross the border without identity papers, there are no concentration camps in Spain."[26]

---

[25] The official position in the matter may be ascertained in the publication, *Cárceles Españolas,* published by the *Oficina Informativa Española,* Madrid, 1948. Count Ciano speaks of the situation in 1939: "One of the gravest questions is the liquidation of the so-called Red problem. There are some 200,000 prisoners in Spain today [July, 1939]. . . . Condemnations are based on these criteria: those responsible for crimes are executed; the organizers and leaders of the Republican forces and government, if not guilty of shedding blood, receive prison terms of from ten to twenty years; the ordinary soldiers who were conscripted are returned to their homes and remain under police surveillance for a time. The prisoners can reduce their sentences by work and each day's work counts for two days' imprisonment. . . . The treatment of prisoners is good and the proof of it is that almost none of them try to escape. The children of condemned Reds are treated with a great humanitarian spirit. Within the Falange youth organizations they are received without question. Executions are still numerous. In Madrid alone 200 to 250 a day; in Barcelona 150." *L'Europa verso la catastrofe,* pp. 443–444.

[26] Constantine Brown, *Evening Star,* Washington, D. C., Feb. 27, 1947. In September, 1950, General Franco explained in an interview to the Italian publication *Roma* that the number of prisoners in Spain had declined markedly in recent years. A num-

The Spanish penal system provides for remission of sentence by means of voluntary labor. In the second place, if he works, his earnings are saved for him, so that on leaving the institution he has a fund with which to begin again. In 1944, for example, some 71 per cent of all prisoners were engaged in productive work inside or outside the prison walls. The prisoner's earnings are administered by the *Patronato de Nuestra Señora de la Merced,* a prisoner's aid society, established in 1944. In 1945 the prisoners earned a total of over twenty million pesetas. Moreover, the society takes care of a vast number of children, and particularly those whose parents have suffered imprisonment. There is vocational and professional training for prisoners with aptitudes and in farm prisons.[27] It is not without interest to observe, too, that, as a case in attitudes, the reaction of the former political prisoners released for return to civil life during the incident in 1944, when armed bands crossed the Pyrenees, is worth recording. There were 8500 such ex-prisoners in the four frontier provinces. Exactly 14 joined the invaders.[28]

In short, the actual examination of the penal system and the working of the prisons reveals that there is an extraordinary effort being made in contemporary Spain to re-educate the criminal and restore him to a useful place in society. A great deal of work is being done to eliminate illiteracy, encourage the knowledge of trades and crafts, foment artistic interests, and bring about a return to religious practice of the prisoner. The reduction of sentence by virtue of voluntary work, with the profits retained exclusively for the prisoner, is an innovation of the first importance in the country and reveals a particular concern for the future stability of the prisoner once he leaves the prison.

This chapter on the institutional life of the modern Spanish state would be incomplete if attention were not directed to the extraordinary work of Count Marsal and his National Trust of St. Paul,

---

ber of foreign visitors confirm the optimistic assertion of the Spanish government. A group of Norwegian journalists, Sinding Larsen, Leif Borthen, and Odd Medboe, visited the Spanish prisons in detail and reported their impressions of the excellent organization and humane treatment of prisoners. Two American visitors, both specialists in prison administration, praised the hygienic conditions and advanced methods of the Spanish penal establishments. In a signed statement Miss Isabel Margaret Smith, of the United States Department of Justice, attested to the fact that Spanish prisons were not the hideous concentration camps that have been depicted (statements published in *Ya,* Madrid, September 22, 1950).

[27] For a description in detail of a Spanish prison I would recommend Sutherland, *op. cit.,* Chap. V, p. 56 sq.

[28] *Ibid.,* p. 53.

the existence of which is one of the most striking examples of humanity and Christian charity to be found anywhere in the world. This nobleman, who is a businessman at the same time, has given of his fortune and time to organize a group to alleviate the misery of those who have been imprisoned.[29] The high degree of human understanding, the direct contact with the prisoner or his family, the absence of all trappings of bureaucracy, and the anonymity with which the Trust works are all part of a wholly admirable undertaking to relieve the sufferings that are the heritage of the civil war. This Trust, called originally the National Trust for Prisoners and Convicts, was created on July 26, 1943, and General Franco requested on March 2, 1944, that Tomás de Boada y Flaquer, Count Marsal, should head this new institution, with the widest possible autonomy and freedom of action. The tasks were enormous: visit penal establishments; establish contacts between prisoners and their families; train prisoners for useful work after release; care of the prisoner's family while confinement lasted.

General Franco himself laid down the broad rules under which this humanitarian job was to be accomplished:

> In order to perform your task well, do your best to ensure two things: first, that the prisoners' letters and indeed all their messages reach you directly, without the interference of anyone or anything, and secondly, make every assurance that in the work of the Trust, between your recognition of a real need to be remedied and its effective remedying, as little time as possible should pass.[30]

The Trust deals with an infinite number of requests. It receives thousands of direct charity appeals, especially for family allowances, and is constantly beset with requests to obtain the conditional release of prisoners. One of the very common activities of the Trust is to aid ex-prisoners in changing their place of residence. It has also done a yeoman's job in the education and care of prisoners' children. No separate schools have been created. The children are entered into regular institutions and the best of training given them without the slightest information ever revealed that they are the sons or daughters of prisoners.

---

29 The work of the Trust, which is described very succinctly in these pages, is explained in an English booklet entitled, *Chronicle of the National Trust of St. Paul,* Madrid, 1948.

30 *Chronicle,* p. 24.

Chapter 13. THE FALANGE

THE great stumbling block to an understanding of contemporary Spain is the *Falange Española,* the so-called single party with which the present regime is intimately linked. Even men with the best of good will fail to understand the Falange; it looks like a fascist party, it prescribes a fascist uniform, it is intensely nationalistic, and it operates without competition. It requires, therefore, careful analysis, not merely as to what it stands for but what it actually means in present-day Spanish life. A few preliminary observations will aid us to appraise properly the past role and the present status of the Falange. First of all, it was merely one of the many groups that supported the nationalist cause in the civil war; second, it was merged for better or for worse with the other organizations that gave their support to General Franco; third, General Franco himself was not a Falangist when the war began; fourth, it has been maintained since 1939 by State support, with a definite decrease in its influence and prestige; and fifth, a very great number of Spaniards in high position, as well as among the rank and file, do not subscribe to the Falange at all and consider it in a certain respect as outside their field of interest.

The Spanish are not, as one may have surmised from previous remarks, a people capable of great regimentation. There has never been the same kind of mass adherence to the Falange that distinguished the national socialist party in Germany or the fascist party in Italy. The major fact is that the Falange did not provide the environment for the rise to power of the present regime, but rather that the regime raised the Falange to its privileged position. This is a fundamental distinction because fascism elsewhere was a mass movement that carried its leaders to power in a wave of great popular enthusiasm. In Spain the regime was brought into existence and solidly established during the war, the Falange being only one element in the political structure. The origins of the Franco government were not rooted in fascism in the ordinary sense of the word. I have tried repeatedly to make clear that the regime was built piece by piece, as an experiment in improvisation, and that the Falange formed one of the segments. Its position would have been very different had the victorious sweep of the war and the will of the leadership not integrated it in the common cause and erected it as the ideological basis for the New Spain.

The formation of the Falange dates from the republican period when there was a vast stirring among many of the younger men, discontented with the prevailing demagoguery and eager to bring about a return to a creed that would emphasize the eternal values of Spain. The intellectual sources of the movement are numerous: Vázquez de Mella with his vigorous traditionalism; Ramiro de Maeztu, whose writings captured the imagination of many who yearned for tradition and authority; Víctor Pradera, whose *El Estado Nuevo,* published in 1934, sapped confidence in the conventional parliamentarianism to which the nation seemed wedded; and Ernesto Giménez Caballero, whose *La Nueva Catolicidad* sounded a strong authoritarian note.

The actual organization was undertaken by Ramiro Ledesma Ramos, and the small group issued in the spring of 1931 a statement called *La conquista del Estado.* This was the beginning of the J.O.N.S., that is, the *Juntas de Ofensiva Nacional-Sindicalista.* In Valladolid another group came into existence under the leadership of Onésimo Redondo, with a marked Catholic tone infused. Many of the J.O.N.S. founders were anything but ardent Catholics and several were tainted with communism and anarchism. The development of the movement in Valladolid was somewhat along different lines, but before long the two met and fused and out of this came the use of the yoke and five arrows which has remained as one of the most visible external symbols of present-day Spain. These were in reality nothing but minor movements, grouping a few dozen young men without real leadership and no claim on public attention. The republican period was peculiarly favorable to political groups of every color and persuasion and they were somewhat lost in the general confusion.

The appearance of José Antonio Primo de Rivera on the public scene and his ultimate leadership of the new party to be called Falange gave it a different orientation. In 1933 a movement was launched under the name of the *Falange Española.* It was formally presented on October 29, 1933, at the Teatro de la Comedia in Madrid. The speakers were Alfonso García Valdecasas, a professor who had organized previously the *Frente español;* Julio Ruíz de Alda, a man of science; José Antonio Prima de Rivera, son of the dictator; and Marqués de Estella in his own right. The Falange in its beginnings was not the work of a collection of street ruffians, but the culmination of the enthusiasm and ardor of young men disgusted with the eternal struggle of Right and Left and eager to restore Spain to its greatness. This point is of some importance, since there is a tendency to assume that the Spanish Falange was quite divorced from anything but a fanatical desire to attain power. Onésimo Redondo came over to the Falange after considerable activity in Catholic Action, and perhaps contributed as much as any one to assuring that the movement would remain within the Catholic tradition.

In 1934 the J.O.N.S. and the Falange were united and a directing board of Primo de Rivera, Ledesma, and Ruíz de Alba formed at Valladolid. There was friction between José Antonio and Ledesma. Even though the latter was made head of the syndicates, there was ultimately a falling out. At this stage of development, José Antonio was preaching a complete revolution, as thorough in its way as that of the extreme Left. He was in parliament for a time, only to be defeated in 1936. The triumph of the Popular Front increased the Falange membership, but led to the arrest of José Antonio, who was first lodged in Madrid and then transferred to Alicante, where he was executed by the Republic on November 20, 1936. Onésimo Redondo was killed during the opening days of the civil war, so that it appeared the Falange was doomed to languish for lack of leadership. It was destined, however, to come through as the principal instrument for the political conduct of the war, and ultimately to form a part of the new united front under the more elaborate name still of *Falange Tradicionalista Española y de la J.O.N.S.*, with Francisco Franco as the *Caudillo*.

What specifically did this organization propose? The celebrated 26 points summarize the aims of the movement and can be given here in their essence:[1]

1. Belief in the supreme reality of Spain. To strengthen it, elevate it, and improve it, is the urgent collective task of all Spaniards.
2. Spain is a predestined unity in the world. Any conspiracy against this unity is abhorrent. Any form of separatism is a crime. The existing constitution, insofar as it encourages disunity, is a crime against the destiny of Spain. For this reason, we demand its abrogation.

---

[1] The official English text is reproduced in Arthur F. Loveday, *Spain, 1923–1948* (London: Boswell Publishing Co., Ltd., 1949), p. 258 sq.

3. We have a will to empire. We demand for Spain a pre-eminent place in Europe. We will not put up with international isolation or with foreign interference. With regard to the Hispanic American world we aim at unification of culture, economic interests. . . .

4. Spain's armed forces must be adequate to assure this position.

5. Spain must aspire to become a great maritime power.

6. Our State will be a totalitarian instrument in the service of National integrity. The family, municipal and syndical channels are to be the means for participation in the life of the State. Political parties are to be abolished.

7. Human dignity, the integrity of man and his liberty are eternal and untouchable values.

8. The National Syndicalist State will permit every initiative compatible with the collective interest of all.

9. In the economic sphere Spain will be organized along corporate lines in a system of vertical syndicates.

10. We repudiate a capitalist system that ignores the needs of people, dehumanizes property, and condemns workers to misery. Our spiritual and national convictions repudiate Marxism.

11. We condemn class war and the domination of one class over another.

12. The primary object of wealth is to improve the conditions of life of the people.

13. The State recognizes private property and protects it against great finance, speculators, and usurers.

14. We are in favor of nationalization of the banks and the corporate organization of public services.

15. Every Spaniard has the right to work.

16. Every able-bodied Spaniard has the duty of working. The Nationalist Syndicalist State condemns those who live without working.

17. The standard of living of the Spanish people must be raised. We are committed to the reform of agriculture.

18. Agricultural production will be increased by a number of specific measures: national credit system, irrigation projects, and so forth.

19. Agricultural society will be organized along new lines, with a redistribution of cultivatable lands, the organization of rural workers.

20. We shall undertake a campaign to increase cattle production, reforestation.

21. The State shall be empowered to confiscate any property unjustly acquired and enjoyed.

22. The reconstruction of the village communal lands will be one of the first tasks of the National Syndicalist government.

23. Every citizen will receive pre-military training.

24. Persons with talent but without means shall be aided in their education and have access to the universities.

25. Our movement will incorporate the Catholic spirit in the national reconstruction. The Church and the State will arrange a Concordat defining their respective jurisdictions. The State will tolerate no interference with its own dignity or the national integrity.

26. The Falange desires a new order of things; its methods are direct,

ardent, and aggressive. Life is a battle and must be lived in a spirit of sacrifice and service.

The program is an odd combination of social reform, a passion for justice, strong, heady nationalism, and the "strenuous life" once preached for another clime and people by Theodore Roosevelt.

Was the Falange fascist in the ordinary sense of the word and does it remain so? The question is not out of place and can best be answered by a careful examination of the writings and statements of the Falangist leaders, particularly José Antonio. The evolution of the Falange may be divided into three stages: (1) from its foundation to the outbreak of the civil war; (2) from July 18 to the conclusion of the civil war; (3) from 1939 to the present.

Obviously the Falange had been launched shortly before its leader was executed and there was in reality no time for the mature, solid, and enduring movement of which José Antonio had probably caught a glimpse but about which he was still in the process of thinking through when he was imprisoned. There is something improvised and ill digested about much of the Falange writing; it is the odd case of a movement in its beginning being suddenly catapulted into a decisive position of power and authority, with its ranks bloated with new members and without the necessary time for normal evolution. I am inclined to think that this is the basic reason why the Falange has always been to a large degree an artificial sort of thing, for its roots were not down deep enough in 1936 to grow on its own strength; vigor and life were infused from outside, by circumstances and by the desire to utilize it as one of the necessary instruments for the conduct of the war. When the work of reconstruction and rehabilitation came, the Falange was expected to respond to a task for which its personnel and experience could scarcely equip it. It was always a minority movement — a handful of zealous and courageous young men. José Antonio, whose place in Spanish life today is that almost of a hero of antiquity and spiritual guide to the New Spain, has probably been elevated to a pedestal that would amaze him were he to return to this world. There is, nevertheless, a great deal that is contagiously attractive about him; his speeches in the Cortes; his adamant defense of the memory of his father; his tireless effort, despite his own title of nobility, to preach social justice; and his sometimes effective, sometimes superficial writings, all belonging to a young man who promised much and who in time might well have achieved a solid structure of thought.

It has been denied that either José Antonio or the interpreters of his thought preached totalitarianism. Here again much depends on the definition of terms. If we accept the Mussolini definition of the "totalitarian" State, then certainly neither José Antonio nor the Falange ever indulged in that completely pagan version of the all-powerful State. In the Cortes during 1934 José Antonio replied to the charge of fostering fascism in Spain with the following observation:

> Fascism has a certain number of external and interchangeable traits which we have no desire to take on. People are little prone to careful definition and charge us with the characteristics of Fascism without realizing that we have taken from Fascism more or less what you have taken. You — the Azaña government — have a conception of the State which you are vigorously imposing. This sense or concept of the State, this belief that the State has a mission and something in which to believe, is one of the important elements of Fascism which can easily be separated from a great many other aspects — some of which I like and others I find impossible.[2]

A Falangist commentator has remarked that "José Antonio managed to separate from fascism its temporal and contingent elements, and place whatever it possessed of permanent value at the service of a Christian ideal."[3] The careful reading of José Antonio's writings and speeches show that for years he devoted an excessive amount of time to explaining that the movement he headed was not an imitation of the Italian or German fascism, but a strictly Spanish undertaking, with some characteristics that resembled fascism but not modeled on anything but the experience and aspirations of the Spanish themselves. To the charge of being imitators, José Antonio replied:

> We answer that if being Fascist means that we have faith and belief in our capacities and have a faith and belief in our country, as something superior to the individuals that compose it, as something with a life of its own and a mission in the world, then we are. But we reject this expression if it means that to be a Fascist the externals are enough: parades, uniform, and activities that are more or less spectacular and decorative.[4]

There was a great deal of emphasis on the individual, on the human person, which was not fascist in its implication. "The construction of the new order must begin with man, with the individual. We must operate as members of the western community, as Spaniards

---

[2] José Antonio Primo de Rivera, *Diario de Sesiones,* July 3, 1934, p. 4394.

[3] José Luis de Arrese, *El Estado totalitario en el pensamiento de José Antonio,* Madrid, 1945, p. 30.

[4] *Obras completas de José Antonio,* Madrid, 1942, p. 211.

and as Christians."[5] In 1933 Onésimo Redondo had asserted that "to adopt the systems of Hitler or Mussolini in Spain is to fall into the same errors as our adversary. . . . We must be careful to avoid what outside of Spain is called communism and Fascism."[6]

In 1934 José Antonio was invited to a fascist congress at Montreux and refused:

> The information that José Antonio Primo de Rivera, chief of the *Falange Española de las J.O.N.S.*, planned to attend a Fascist congress in Montreux is completely false. The Chief of the Falange was invited but categorically refused because of the conviction that the genuinely national character of the Movement precludes any such international attachments. Moreover, the Falange is not a Fascist movement. It coincides with Fascism on some points, but each day its own peculiar character becomes more clear.[7]

In Valladolid, José Antonio repudiated completely what he called "the pantheism of the State" and insisted that: "We consider the individual fundamental because this is the essence of Spain where man has always been the bearer of eternal values."[8]

García Valdecasas, a founder of the Falange, wrote in 1942, when the Axis was at its height and it might be expected that Spanish Falangism would be desirous of attaching its chariot to that particular star:

> The state is not an end in itself for us. The State must be an instrument for the salvation of sacred values. These are, for us, liberty, the integrity and dignity of man, and therefore it is the duty of the State to respect them. Furthermore, the most authentic spirit of Spain refuses to recognize a supreme value in the State . . . above the State there is a moral order, of truth and precepts to which the State must submit.[9]

The integration of the various political groups and tendencies in 1937 was not aimed at creating a single totalitarian party, but rather to co-ordinate all currents of opinion favorable to the nationalist cause for the achievement of victory.

In this defense of the individual, the thought of José Antonio is perfectly clear, for whatever may be said about the imperialistic exuber-

---

[5] *Ibid.*, pp. 92–93. Speech at Cine Madrid, May 19, 1935.

[6] *Libertad,* Valladolid, Nov. 20, 1933.

[7] *A.B.C.*, Dec. 19, 1934. Charles Foltz in his book, *The Masquerade in Spain,* p. 71, among other inaccuracies, states that Primo de Rivera attended this congress where he met Degrelle, Mosley, Codreanu, and the other budding fascist leaders of Europe. Primo de Rivera was never there, as his own communication to the press demonstrates.

[8] Speech delivered in Valladolid, March 3, 1935.

[9] *Revista de Estudios Politicos,* Madrid, Jan., 1942, pp. 26–27.

ance, the fervent nationalism and the ardent hope for the revival of Spain's greatness, it cannot, on the basis of his writings, be argued that José Antonio was a partisan of a collectivist State, in which the individual would be a mere cog.[10]

It is quite true, as José Luis de Arrese admits, that in the early days the Falange used the expression "totalitarian," and this term was later dropped precisely because José Antonio considered that it was confusing to use the same word that in Germany and Italy, to his way of thinking, meant something entirely different. Arrese insists that when José Antonio spoke of totalitarianism, he meant what might be more appropriately called in Spanish *totalidad,* that is, he urged a social and political order that would recognize the needs and rights of the total population and not merely of certain sectors, classes, or categories; an argument against the policy of the Republic which he considered as favoring one class against the rest of the nation.[11]

José Antonio strove constantly to explain that the movement did not mean the deification of the State, nor a pantheistic submission to its blind forces. His famous debate in the Cortes with Gil Robles did not end the controversy on this point. There is unquestionably confusion in the thinking of the founders of the Falange on many points, and it is probable that had José Antonio lived beyond 1936 he would have achieved a doctrinal statement far more compact and unified. It is interesting, nevertheless, in discussing the Spanish Falange, to indicate these currents and the effort on the part of the founders to forge an ideology that was Spanish, Catholic, and at the same time the opposite of parliamentarianism in which they saw the destruction of Spain as a nation.

Spain today is a dictatorship; a centralized authoritarian regime in which the Falange is not the equivalent, in an exact sense, of certain single parties that existed or still exist in other European countries. One does not find in the literature of what is called in Spain simply, "The Movement," the rigidity of the Marxists or the almost mystical attitude toward the party of the Nazis. It would appear that in contemporary Spain far more lip service is paid to the Falange than its actual influence warrants.

---

[10] The writings of José Antonio abound in the defense of the individual. "Falange considers man the combination of body and soul, with an eternal destiny" (*Obras completas,* p. 560). "The reorganization of Europe must begin with the individual, for it is he who has suffered the most in this destruction" (*ibid.,* p. 82).

[11] *Op. cit.,* p. 52.

The Chief of the State was made the National Chief of the *Falange Espoñola Tradicionalista y de las J.O.N.S.* by the unification decree of April 19, 1937, and, according to Article 47 of the statutes, the control by the Chief is absolute and he is responsible to no one within the movement. The National Council of the Falange consists of a certain number of elected members as well as a smaller group of ex officio participants; these elective councilors drawn from Spanish public life and representing a wide variety of interests. The actual administration of the Falange is under the control of the *Junta Politica,* the permanent organ of the National Council of which the *Caudillo* is also president. The General Secretariate at Alcalá 42 in Madrid is in charge of the practical operation of the movement. An interesting section of Falange is the *Instituto de Estudios Políticos,* created in September, 1939, and whose function is doctrinal, that is, to supply the intellectual content of the movement. Its publication, *Revista de Estudios Políticos* is, in fact, a mine of useful information regarding Spanish politics, economics, and international relations. The Undersecretariate consists of a number of "delegations" of dependencies, the chief of which are the *Delegación Nacional de Provincias,* the *Delegación Nacional de la Sección Feminina,* the *Delegación Nacional del Frente de Juventudes,* and finally the section having to do with relations abroad.

Of these unquestionably the women's section and that of the youth are the more important. The women's branch was established in 1939 and is at present under the direction of José Antonio's sister, Pilar Primo de Rivera, who has devoted her life to carrying out the political and social ideas of her brother. The function of the women's branch is extremely wide and includes not only political education within the movement itself, but civic training in general. One of the important phases of this branch is the supervision of the Social Service system, based on the obligatory participation by women, under conditions laid down by the decree of May 31, 1940. Spanish women, if they are single or childless widows, must devote a certain time to social service under the direction of the movement. This service is obligatory for obtaining positions in the State, in the movement itself, and in many agencies connected with the State. The women's branch has extended its activities to a very wide field including sports, health and sanitation, and cultural activities. Among the latter the well-known dance and musical groups of the women's section have appeared throughout Spain, and in the autumn of 1949 made a most successful tour of several South

American countries. Its activities, through *Auxilio Social,* reach into every Spanish town and community.

The youth organizations are of considerable interest in that they are aimed at capturing the imagination and loyalty of the young people, and particularly of those in the educational institutions. The *Frente de Juventudes* was created in 1940 with two purposes in mind: first, to prepare good party members, and second, to diffuse a knowledge of the movement's doctrine among the members of the new generation. The *Frente* is divided into two sections, masculine and feminine. Within the boy's organization are four groups, according to the age of the participants: seven to eleven, eleven to fifteen, fifteen to eighteen, and eighteen until military service. Among girls, the period of training and active participation in the movement runs from seven to seventeen years. The concrete purposes of the *Frente* are the following:

1. Political education in the doctrine and spirit of the Falange,
2. Physical education,
3. Premilitary training for boys,
4. Co-operation with the Church in religious education,
5. Supplement the work of the State in certain fields: health, education, etc.,
6. Home training in the case of young women,
7. Organization and conduct of camps, and special courses.[12]

The *Frente* intervenes in the political guidance of young people who are not affiliated officially with it, and controls to a considerable extent such specialized institutions as trade schools. In the field of higher education, the Falange exerts its control through the *Sindicato Español Universitario,* popularly known as the S.E.U. This elaborate organization follows almost point by point the structure of the Falange itself, with its supreme direction, council, provincial groups, and organizations within the faculties and specialized divisions of the institutions of higher education of the country. It is a trade union for the universities, and groups its members in a professional organization comparable to the unions for arts and trades affiliated with the Falange.

It is almost impossible, as is evident even from this summary account of the activities of the Falange, to distinguish sharply between

[12] *Guía de la vida social de España,* Madrid, 1946, p. 385.

the social work of the State as such and of the Falange as its instrument or agency. The characteristic of contemporary Spain is a certain overlapping and above all an effort to make the Falange a vital part of the structure of the State, an effective working arm for carrying out the national program in certain designated fields. Up to 1946 the Undersecretariate for Popular Education included a number of activities later transferred to the regular Ministry of Education such as the national office for the press, with particular attention to censorship. Under the direction of Tomás Cerro Corrochano, this bureau has been in charge of censorship, control of the foreign press, and relations with correspondents stationed in Spain. There was a propaganda division under Pedro Rocamora, the purpose of which was evident, while radio, the theater, the cinema, had special divisions devoted to that field of activity. Health and sports also have their own secretariates.

The Falange possesses its own chain of newspapers. In every provincial capital and, of course, in Madrid, one finds the regular press plus the "Party Press." In Madrid the two pages are *Arriba* and *Pueblo*. In the provinces there are some 30 morning papers and about six or seven afternoon dailies, giving the Falange a very great intervention in almost every phase of Spanish life.

The Falange was unquestionably an important element in fighting the civil war and very particularly was it indispensable for the ordinary administrative work that the National Movement required after 1936. It is easy to conceive the real difficulties of the nationalists, as they advanced victoriously, to find competent persons for the local governments, municipalities, and civilian administration in the conquered territory. The Falange supplied many of these, and when the movement became national in fact as well as in theory with the establishment of the Burgos regime, the Falange again was a compact organization with personnel available for a great many of the necessary functions. In addition, the Falange absorbed an enormous army of persons as soon as it became the dominant force in the New Spain and there flocked to it thousands of persons who presumedly had been affiliated heretofore with organizations of a very different political and ideological tinge. It is no exaggeration to say that the Falange exists through the will of General Franco and, it would seem, with all due reservations, that he could exist without the Falange, but the latter would enjoy a doubtful vitality without the *Caudillo*. This produces in the Falange a loyalty to the present regime without which it would have no possibility of existence or probably even of survival. Any change or even considerable shift in the Spanish regime today might prejudice the special position Falange occupies.

There is no doubt either that its position has become less decisive than it was in the heyday of the civil war or in the years immediately following it. It is notable that as World War II progressed the Falange became less and less the sole spokesman of the New Spain, and an interesting evolution to trace would be the descending role of the Falange and the gradually increasing one of the Church in contemporary Spain. It is not an easy matter about which to generalize, but it is perfectly plain that Falange declined as the medium of expression after 1942, and that the Church and Catholic thought in general have appeared as a far more significant ingredient in this complex thing called contemporary Spain.[13]

The Falange experienced internal strife and conflict with the other elements that had been fused with it in 1937, for there was always a "radical" branch within the movement that pushed for a total social revolution; in some cases based more or less on the model of the Portuguese *Estado Novo*. The traditionalists, whom one suspects of discomfort in the double harness with the Falange, stood out for a social transformation along strictly Christian lines. There was a period when certain wings of Falange were loudly anticlerical and impatient of the deep-rooted attachment of the traditionalists to the usages and norms of the past. Much of this was eliminated at the unification by the strength of will of General Franco. Ledesma himself bolted the movement and denounced José Antonio Primo de Rivera for having truck with monarchists and other assorted rightists. The Marqués de Eliseda, a Falangist deputy in the Cortes, at one time abandoned the movement because as a Catholic he could not accept parts of its program. It must be remembered that the Falange in the closing days of the Republic was a revolutionary movement in every sense of the word; unfavorable to the monarchical restoration, con-

[13] "I found a few Falangists in Spain. Only three Falangists still remain in the government. . . . Only a very few still wear the five arrows and yoke symbol in their button hole. Strictly speaking they are not pro-Franco at all, for they do not approve the political fluctuations and compromises of the Caudillo. In foreign affairs they refuse to accept the restoration of the monarchy except under a form which might be called elective. They are passionate advocates of authoritarianism and militarism and collective discipline. . . . The Falange is in state of decomposition. Moreover it must not be forgotten that it encountered a strong resistance from the Church that had no confidence in its secularism and materialism" (Jacques Blondeau, *L'Aube,* Paris, June 2, 1949).

sidering that the monarchy had been liquidated in April, 1931, and that its carcass could not be revived, thus alienating a large sector of Catholics who were monarchists in conviction and inclined to think that the parliamentary tactics of the C.E.D.A. were the most appropriate for the circumstances. Against this attitude in the Cortes and the hope of a restoration, the Falange was resolutely opposed.

It is a very great error, then, to assume that the Falange is a sort of refuge for all rightists, reactionaries, die-hard conservatives, and royalists to whom the Republic was anathema. The Falange attracted revolutionaries as did the extreme Left, and it was this spirit that gave it the initial impetus. The only real point of contact between the Falange and the Right was that both were opposed to Marxism in whatever form it might rear its head. When the Popular Front triumphed in the February, 1936, elections, the Falange was outspoken in its criticism of Gil Robles and what it deemed the catastrophic policy he had followed. Moreover, the provincial leaders of Falange were advised to avoid commitment with the military in the uprising of 1936, and Primo de Rivera himself was adamant in his initial refusal to become tied to any "reactionary movement."[14] It would seem that the Falange envisioned itself as the standard-bearer of the revolt against both capitalism and Marxism, and as the foundation of the New Spain. Events got out of hand and the rebellion of 1936 was taken in charge by experienced and able army men. Falange was a useful and necessary thing and within a few days after July 18, it had taken its place within the mosaic of movements and sentiments that made up the National Crusade. Henceforth it was to be dominated by the personality of the *Caudillo*.

Elsewhere in this book reference has been made to the hostile attitude of the Falangist leader, Manuel Hedilla, in the period immediately following the unification, for fear that the Falange's revolutionary content might be sacrificed.

Unification did not mean that everyone within the composite organization was content with the arrangement or able to fuse their separate aims in this rather unwieldy superstructure. Hints and even incidents of considerable moment reveal from time to time that within the Falange there is a considerable amount of discrepancy. For the past ten years it has been the old story: the revolutionary-

[14] Felipe Ximenez de Sandoval, *José Antonio, una biografía apasionada,* Madrid, p. 521. Francisco Bravo, *Historia de la Falange española tradicionalista y de las J.O.N.S.,* Madrid, 1940, contains documentary information on these points.

minded Falangists, and especially the younger group as opposed to those who wish to return to some form of stable conservatism, are dropping the insistence on the revolutionary aims at the movement.

In the middle of February, 1949, a controversy developed after the publication in *Arriba* of an article, signed José Viver, which criticized the *Sindicato Español Universitario* for its excessive revolutionary attitude and tenets and opined that too much revolution has been talked to the university students and at the wrong time. The S.E.U. review, *La Hora,* retorted (February 18) by stating that since the writer of the critical article was a monarchist, "his views on the social and political problems of Spain, and particularly on the need for a social revolution must, logically, be very different from that of the Falangists."[15] The analysis of the two trends, that is, monarchist and Falangist, is admirably summed up in this paper and is useful as indicating that, despite fusion, there are still profound discrepancies within the official party structure:

> The Monarchists were reactionaries in politics and mildly progressive in social questions. They only aspired to a Spain where their religion and their conception of a Motherland would not be exposed to constant danger. Their position was not at all revolutionary; on the contrary, it was always defined as counterrevolutionary. On the other hand, the Falange group was revolutionary in politics and in social questions — profoundly revolutionary.[16]

The criticism of *La Hora* goes much further, claiming that the monarchists have been satisfied in their main demands; the Succession Law has given them the guarantee of the royal return and the social legislation has been more than enough to fulfill the ideal of betterment on that score. The Falangist program is the one that has been sidetracked and ignored. Almost none of the salient points in the Falangist program have been realized: oust capitalism, establish national syndicalism, nationalize the Bank, bring about the agrarian revolution, profit-sharing in industry, create a national people's army, and bring about a concordat between Church and State. None of these have been carried out, and one of the responsible causes is that the present regime still operates on much legislation and practice that antedates the civil war. The old Civil Code remains fully in force, and with this sort of survival the full realization of the Falangist program is out of the question. *La Hora* states boldly that the present regime "no longer

---

[15] An account of this controversy and its significance can be found in *The Tablet,* London, March 19, 1949.

[16] *Ibid.*

supports the Falangist idea of social revolution. . . . The Conservative revolution has triumphed over that of the real revolutionaries. . . . The truth has been stated, that the State has reached the peak of its revolutionary ambitions and has now become Conservative."

This statement of position, without equivocation or ambiguity, frankly critical of the regime and even denunciatory of its deficiencies in the revolutionary order, comes from Falangist sources. It reveals several things: (1) that criticism is not totally obsolete in Spain; (2) that the old guard of the Falange is afraid that the regime has forgotten the vital revolutionary content of its program and does nothing toward realizing the syndicalist state; and (3) that the Franco regime, while preserving the form and the symbols of Falangism, is very far from impregnated with the original ideology that was launched in 1933.

In short, important as the Falange is as an instrument of government and administration and despite the fact that it retains its theoretical position as the guiding thought of the New Spain, the actual vigor of its work is mitigated by a very wide indifference of the Spanish people and a feeling that in many ways the machinery of the movement as well as its program has been surpassed by events and circumstances.

Chapter 14. ECONOMIC AND SOCIAL PROBLEMS OF CONTEMPORARY SPAIN

THE best introduction to the complex social and economic situation of contemporary Spain is the statement of a thesis which, in the case of this author, is a profound conviction; that the Spanish problem as it is so frequently called, is not only political, but very definitely economic. Far too much attention is given to the externals of regime, form of government, or political expediency. I am equally convinced that the Spanish people are more concerned with an orderly and productive economic system than with the particular governmental structure that prevails. The positive issue in Spain since the end of World War II has been the search for economic stability. Politics has become an issue more prominent in the minds of foreign governments and the press than in Spain itself. The average Spaniard is more vitally concerned with a workable economy that will provide him with the necessities of life than with the debate about the present regime, the restoration of the monarchy, or the improbable return of the republic. The old passions and divisions subsist, to be sure, and there are unquestionably sectors of public opinion interested fundamentally in a political transformation, but the rank and file are faced by the one great issue that overshadows everything else — the restoration of a national economy that works, that produces, and that will provide the minimum of security to which they have a right.

Life is extraordinarily difficult in modern Spain for all classes. The peasant is faced with the basic sterility of so much of the Spanish land and often lacks sufficient use of that land itself while the urban worker is reduced to the necessity of subsisting on a pittance, since one of the curious phenomena of Spain is that wages have risen relatively less than in other countries. The essence of the problem for the individual Spaniard is to stretch a very small and stable wage to cover a cost of living that in reality has become ten times higher than in pre-civil-war days. It would be no exaggeration to say that the wage of the worker in the cities and towns of the peninsula fluctuates in a very general average between 12 and 25 pesetas a day and with this is obliged to maintain himself and his family. The result is that it is an almost impossible task, and that illogically in many ways the standard of living is perceptibly higher than before the civil war.[1] A number of factors which contribute to the state of affairs today may be summarized as follows:

1. The isolation of Spain and the impossibility over a period of years of developing normal trade abroad, with the subsequent importation of those articles of consumption which the country either does not produce or produces at too heavy a cost.

2. The reduction of effective export trade, small as it is, to food products, such as fruit, olive oil, and the like, all of which are not produced at present in sufficient abundance to satisfy even the domestic market.

3. The three-year drought that has burned and shriveled the Spanish countryside and reduced production incalculably.

4. The limitations and restrictions on the free development of new economic enterprises.

While real wages are clearly insufficient, the working class has managed to survive through two means: the first are the subsidies and grants from the State, or by State action through the enterprises for which the worker labors which help to increase his income; the second aid is the very common custom of gainful employment by more than one member of the family. In the larger cities it is quite common for working-class families to have several members employed and this employment may extend to women in the factories, which is common in Catalonia, especially until marriage, and in the employment of minors in a variety of occupations such as the sale of newspapers and lottery tickets.

The lot of the middle class is no less grave, although the enormous bureaucracy absorbs a disproportionate number of employees, and it is no exaggeration to say that the State itself is the largest Spanish industry and the national budget the largest income source for thousands of people. The average salary of countless employees certainly does not exceed 750 to 1000 pesetas a month, which is inadequate to

---

[1] The standard of living has increased in the sense of demands by people for more goods. The increase in such things as radios, travel, cinemas, the consumption of wine, is one of the extraordinary features of Spanish life today.

maintain a family in decent living conditions. The cost of living in a city like Madrid today for a family of several members, under desirable conditions with a minimum of well-being, would probably be 3000 to 5000 pesetas a month. The result is frequently that persons are forced to occupy more than one job, and so distribute their time and energies as to piece out the insufficient basic salary. This applies not only to employees but to many of the professional group. University professors and teachers are so underpaid as to be forced to engage in subsidiary activities to make living possible. There is a very clear tendency toward the gradual proletarization of the middle class, a phenomenon that is slow and painful but nevertheless perceptible. In certain of the administrative branches this situation leads to inevitable corruption, for it is hardly to be expected that members of the civil guard or of other agencies will live at a starvation level when the possibility exists under the innumerable forms of economic control to obtain certain extras without which they cannot subsist.

The only classes more or less immune at present to the growing pressure of economic strangulation are such as find themselves highly placed in the administrative scheme of things and thus have a sufficient income, or the speculators and profiteers who operate outside the legal restrictions on the black market and consequently become rich.[2]

It may be useful in this survey of the social and economic status of Spain to emphasize certain fundamentals that give a broad picture of the state of affairs and of the possibilities of a solution. Obviously it would be unfair to assume that the economic evils that beset contemporary Spain are exclusively the fruit of internal ineptitude, mistaken policy, or sheer impotency to do anything about it. Spain belongs to the world even if the world does not wish her to share a small place on the planet. The circumstances of the times have conspired viciously to throttle the revival of the nation. It must always be remembered that for some fifteen years Spain has lived a completely abnormal existence. The closing years of the Republic with its chaos and instability were followed by the crippling civil war. World War II hampered Spanish recovery precisely at the moment when the will to reconstruct was at its peak and great accomplishment might have been possible. The ostracism of the years since the end of the war have accentuated the economic predicament and slowed down the

---

[2] The landowners, or those deriving their income from rents, are in a most critical situation because of the freezing of such rents. Many religious communities are in dire straits because of the decreased income obtainable from their lands.

impetus toward recovery. Spain has received absolutely nothing from abroad in loans or economic aid, and the various commercial treaties signed after 1945 have been in large part limited in scope and of small value for the total rehabilitation of the country.

Honesty obliges one to acknowledge that the economic policy of the present Spanish government represents another serious factor in the situation. There is, to be sure, more than one school of thought on this matter. To the partisan of statism and heavy controls it may seem the right direction, but to those who still believe, old fashioned and outmoded as it may seem, in the virtue of a large degree of private initiative, this policy does not make sense. But even with controls and restrictions extending to every department of economic life, Spanish policy does not reveal a clear-cut tendency. The difficulty is that the Spanish are not gifted in the way of controls and it may almost be asserted that even when controls are imposed they frequently do not work in the manner anticipated, and their violation becomes to some extent the normal thing. There is not the rigidity of, let us say, the Germany of the autarchical days, nor is there the resignation that so characterizes the British people when faced with the forces of economic destiny. On the other hand, Spain does have one asset which is of incalculable value; the diligence and imagination of its people. If economy is to be something besides mere impersonal production and consumption, the intrinsic character of the mass of Spaniards becomes an asset of the first importance. The Spanish worker is a peculiar creature; proud, able, hard working, and disposed to make the best of adverse circumstances. He can be incited to rebellion and to unrest, as in the past, and he can be oriented toward the most fantastic of social utopias. He can also be encouraged and directed wisely to the end of first class workmanship and productivity.

The problem before us is to examine the economic situation of Spain realistically and honestly and suggest some of the major difficulties in the way of its reconstruction. It is not in the spirit of carping criticism or of political *parti pris* that this description is conceived. Observation leads to certain conclusions, and those conclusions seem to the writer inevitable and clear.

First, a word about the structure of Spanish economy. Spain is, as the reader knows, primarily an agricultural country. Neither resources, nor sufficiently developed water power, transportation facilities, or other factors have up to now provided the peninsula with the elements for great industrial development. Industrialism is possible, of course, on a modest scale, but not in terms of effective competition with the more highly favored nations of the world. Since agriculture is the basis of livelihood and the source of almost all economic production, it is equally important to note that this agriculture has been and continues to be extremely primitive. Productivity is limited by the nature of both the soil and the methods applied to its cultivation and in most of Spain the technical equipment for the exploitation of the land is lacking, particularly tools, mechanized procedures, and fertilizers. The result is that in the countryside of Spain there exists what the Spanish economists call the *paro ensubierto,* that is, concealed stoppage of work. Vast armies of peasants are required for the simple tasks of the farm. The transition to modern methods, were it to come, would obviously pose a tremendous problem of unemployment and exodus to the urban centers with the consequent dislocation of the population and the increase of unemployment and even unemployability on a very large scale. This means that the mere improvement of agricultural methods *per se* is not the answer to the economic problem. It is one of the facets in this general policy of improvement to be necessarily taken into account, but others are further required to achieve the balance and stability desired. The product of the soil in terms of farm income is equally low with a resultant subsistence farming and negligible purchasing power of the peasant.

Faced by the real problem of the excess of man power, to be absorbed elsewhere, the only solution is industry. We arrive again at something of a vicious circle. Industrial production on a large scale cannot develop without a foreign market, and this market implies the ability to compete effectively against more favored nations. The domestic market alone could not possibly maintain large-scale industry for the simple reason that the purchasing ability of the mass of people is so small that such industrial activity could not maintain itself with profit. To achieve even a measure of such purchasing capacity at home poses the first and fundamental question of all social and economic reform in Spain: the complete rehabilitation of the rural areas and the placing of the peasant in a position to become a consumer. No program of social reform can possibly overlook this axiomatic statement, for without the rejuvenation of the country and the transformation of the peasant economically and socially, the possibility of a real evolution in Spain is out of the question.

There is a very marked tendency at the present time to begin, not at the bottom, but at the top. The work of the *Instituto Nacional de Industria* reflects this inverted thinking. This organization, under State direction, proposes establishment of new industries in Spain. This may seem a praiseworthy proposition, but the difficulty lies in the fact that the process of industrialization has been encouraged in many cases as a *technical* and not an economic achievement. Let us observe exactly what we mean by this. An industry may come into existence, produce certain materials, and demonstrate that it is possible with the resources and raw materials available to accomplish it. But this does not mean that the technical achievement will prove necessarily a good undertaking economically. To assure its economic value, the industry must be able to produce in such a way that it can stand on its own feet, open its markets, and effectively compete with similar products from elsewhere. An excellent case in point is the production of trucks in Spain. Normally the country is not equipped to produce trucks or automobiles on a large scale either for home or foreign consumption. The *Pegaso* truck, which I daresay is a very good one, has come onto the Spanish home market. It is estimated that the total capacity of production does not extend much beyond a very small number a month. This shows that the technique is there. What is lacking is the economic justification for the effort put into the making of trucks. It may be said then that Spain shows many signs of a very good technical ability, unaccompanied by an equally clear and common sense economic intelligence. With the frontiers virtually sealed off, there is no domestic market capable of taking local products that represent in their manufacture something of a *tour de force.*

Another factor of supreme importance in the understanding of the present Spanish economy is the existence of monopolies. The contemporary economic order is distinguished by a curiously hybrid arrangement of private property and strict monopolistic control. The whole elaborate system of licensing for the establishment of industries and for the purchase of the raw materials forms a part of this panorama. A striking example is the case of cotton. Priced at 8 cents the kilo in America, the fixed price in Spain is 60 pesetas. This price is almost a standing inducement to less scrupulous industrialists to arrange for the purchase of pesetas in the free market abroad and especially in Tangier where the rate is approximately 40 to 45 pesetas for the dollar, contrasting with the long established quotation of 11 pesetas at the banks. Importing licenses are hard to get and the restriction is so severe that manufacturers undertake to work outside the official limitations and thus build up a black market which has been one of the plagues of the country. A recent case was that of an apparently small Catalan textile industry with a capitalization of some 100,000 pesetas. It was able, nevertheless, through the type of operation just described, to prepare textiles for export to the amount of some million pesetas.

Textile goods manufactured in Spain are unquestionably one of the standard articles which would find a ready market abroad. The policy has been heretofore to depend on bilateral treaties and commercial agreements. This is palpably a false procedure. Spain can never function economically on the basis of a trade balance exclusively with the United States or on the dollar basis. The United States can operate, plainly enough, as if Spain did not exist. The only possibility is a freer market in which Spain could sell to a wide variety of countries and particularly Hispanic America, which would indirectly produce dollars and a balance of foreign currencies of which the country stands in the greatest need. The mind of Spain today is that dollars are essential for the revival of industry and commerce. The methods invoked to bring about this happy consummation are dubious in the extreme, for numerous discouragements are placed in the way of those who individually and on the basis of private initiative are eager to open up markets for Spanish goods. The same applies to the currency. The pegging of the peseta at 11 to the dollar when the real exchange was about 40 presented a temptation to deal in the clandestine market. It may be interesting to note that the reason why a run-away inflation has not occurred in Spain is the rigid control of wages, kept at a minimum regardless of the rising cost of living.

Another element in the complicated economic policy of Spain is the absence of co-ordination between the various agencies of the State empowered to control economic affairs. One could devote pages to the contradictory policies frequently undertaken by the various agencies. The Ministry of Labor functions as though the Ministry of Social Security did not exist, and so on down the line. The arbitrary fixing of prices may be justified in part, but it has the effect of stimulating what may be called a "hidden production" that operates outside the controls and does not form a part of the normal transaction that produces taxes and revenue for the State. The black market is caused in large measure by the price schedule, arbitrarily fixed at too low a figure which in turn either discourages production completely or forces goods into illicit channels. Scarcity is provoked in large measure by this monopoly arrangement. It has been suggested that Spain might well adopt the Belgian system of flooding the market with consumers' goods and thus eliminating the black market simply because the free play of prices and production went to work and the speculator found no role to play. The speculator, needless to say, does not form a productive element of society from the point of view of the State. The burden of taxation, the support of the innumerable social services, and the armed forces fall, then, on the visible solvent gentry, and it is this small group who bear the brunt of a very heavy and increasingly intolerable system of taxation. The absence of a curtailment of this state of things means that the State loses a considerable revenue and the poor, for whom many of the services are maintained as well as the benefits of a more favorable price level and abundance of goods, suffer the direct effects of the restriction.

The essential problem, let it be emphasized once more, is not the creation of the present regime. Spain has suffered for centuries from economic maladjustment. Many of the capital errors that now appear in their aggravated form were inherited from the regimes that existed before the civil war. The main criticism of the regime today is that it is so completely wedded to the notion of rigidity in control that its own inflexibility hampers the real recovery of the Spanish economy. To be sure, it may be argued with considerable force that this anomalous state of affairs also prevails in other countries. But judging the Spanish economic order in the abstract and regardless of complicity or responsibility, it may be asserted that it is the positive example of control that does not control, of stimulation that discourages, and of recovery that impoverishes.

What, then, is the solution? The first suggestion is a direct loan from government to government; a second possibility, which does not exclude the first, is the encouragement of private capital investment, assuming of course that certain obstacles are removed and some of the more onerous controls eliminated. Spain offers a rich field for investment. The Spanish worker, as already indicated, is industrious and capable; what he needs is the tools with which to work and the stimulus of profit. Perhaps a combination of foreign investment with local capital, limited as the latter is, would go far toward stimulating economic recovery, for this would avoid the political onus, restore Spanish confidence, and relieve the State of its crushing burden.

The whole field of social reform in Spain must be treated, although very briefly. The main conclusion to which the careful observer arrives in this regard falls into two categories: first, that legislation has far outrun performance and, second, that the social legislation is far too elaborate for the actual economic possibilities of the country. The same error has been committed that has been noted before: the social program has exceeded the economic and this inversion of procedure has produced a most erratic result.

Obviously the small increase in salaries and the real devaluation of the peseta with reference to goods available have forced the State to take energetic measures to succor the vast number of the population who otherwise could not make ends meet. There is also a political purpose involved. The working class in general had supported the Republic and the present regime has found it necessary to seek to win over this sector of the populace through extensive aids and social services. Both the State and the Falange combined to give the worker innumerable guarantees, some of which strike the observer as excessive. It is virtually impossible today to dismiss a worker no matter what his deficiency or fault may be, for the protection is such that the worker has more and enjoys more security than at any time in Spanish history. The Republic in the heyday of its demagoguery offered nothing like the security held out to the ordinary worker at the present time with the limitation that he cannot strike nor agitate as in the old days. The State-controlled trade union, called the *Sindicato único* or *vertical,* proposes to protect him and satisfy his demands before they even arise. It may be said, and I admit that documentary evidence for this is not easy, that the Spanish worker accepts, enjoys, and utilizes these benefits, but has not given his wholehearted allegiance to the regime in return. Many workers retain their old convictions and feel that they are the beneficiaries of so many attentions because of the potential danger they represent to the social peace of Spain.

The general economic situation in contemporary Spain may be summarized, from the internal point of view, in this manner: (1) relatively low increase in wages; (2) very large increase in prices; (3) consequent lower purchasing power of the peseta; (4) absence of investment capital; (5) outmoded character of machinery, transportation, and other aspects of the productive process; (6) heavy burden of the social legislation; (7) severe restrictions on production imposed by the deficiencies in electric power; (8) absence of adequate commercial exchange with other countries.

A certain number of statistics, taken from official publications and reports of economic groups unrelated to the government, reveal graphically the decline in agricultural production, despite considerable State aid and encouragement. Reference to this production in terms of pesetas is unenlightening in view of the depreciated nature of the monetary unit. Therefore these facts are depicted in terms of an index, taking 1929 as 100. The results show:

Year	*Index*	*Year*	*Index*
1929	100	1939	74.70
1931	92	1942	75.10
1932	109.50	1944	73.90
1934	108.90	1945	52.10
1935	97.30	1947	71.70

The fluctuating decline in agricultural production is visible from these index figures, despite the commonly heard accusation that the State deliberately favors agriculture to the detriment of industry. The industrial index shows that, taking 1929 as 100, industrial production had reached 122.7 in 1947. Obviously both the agricultural and industrial estimates must be taken in full relation to the growth of population over the period of nearly twenty years, which tends to demonstrate that the Spanish economy has either declined or, in the case of slight improvement, has not grown in proportion to the increase of the number of inhabitants.[3]

No single problem is quite so grave as the absence of sufficient electric power. From the practical point of view, this insufficiency signifies not only a diminution of industrial activity, but countless difficulties in everyday life. In Madrid, for instance, electric power must be cut off periodically even for the most essential purposes; elevators are run on certain days or between certain hours and electricity for domestic use is restricted to definite hours. Street lighting and illumination for display purposes is reduced to a minimum, and in Catalonia, where the problem is equally grave, industrial plants are restricted to part time with the consequent partial unemployment and reduction of production. Although the natural conditions are not favorable for the production of electrical energy, it is significant that a number of electrification projects have been carried out beyond the available energy for their maintenance. The tragedy of scarce electric power is no better illustrated than in the fact that in Catalonia restrictions

[3] The population of Spain in 1930 was 23,563,867, and in 1947, 27,374,401.

were imposed five days a week, and in December, 1948, only 18 per cent of the total normal electric power was available.

A subject of considerable importance is the disposition of public funds as revealed in the budget. The figures for 1949 are available and help to throw considerable light on the distribution of public revenues. The total budget was estimated at 16,628,672,000 pesetas for expenditures with revenue at 16,070,569,000, representing an estimated deficit of 558,103,000 pesetas. In 1947 the deficit stood at 1,130,292,000, and in 1948 at 191,200,000. The sum 5,494,257,000 pesetas is earmarked for the army, navy, air force, and security units in general, that is, 31 per cent of the entire budget, while education received the sum of 1,189,747,000 pesetas. The public debt is estimated in round numbers at 54 billion pesetas. It may not be out of place to indicate certain comparative figures regarding national expenditures for different purposes, keeping in mind that the figures are not in themselves a sufficient key to the realities in view of inflation. The rise in expenditures for all branches of the armed forces has been steady, from 1,329,000,000 pesetas in 1940 to 3,969,000,000 in 1947. Education has experienced a similar rise, from 360,000,000 pesetas in 1940 to 987,000,000 in 1947, and public works represent another heavy expenditure.

The very high percentage of the budget devoted to the armed forces finds its explanation in a number of factors, especially in view of the fact that Spain has been in a certain sense in a state of war, open or potential, since 1936. The entire period of the world war was one of an armed expectancy, and fear that any radical reduction in the forces might invite disaster. The political and international isolation of Spain has influenced very directly the maintenance of such a considerable army, navy, and air force. The question whether the amount devoted to this purpose is justified by the circumstances is, of course, impossible to determine. It would not be correct, however, to assume that the Spanish armed forces are maintained at an absurdly high figure when the tendency everywhere is toward fantastic expenditures for the same end. The examination of the Swiss, British, or United States budgets reveal the same trend toward a higher proportion, not to mention the carefully concealed proportional expenditures of the lands beyond the Iron Curtain.

The situation of the peseta in terms of the economic advancement of the country and especially with relation to foreign trade merits a word. It must be constantly borne in mind that Spain lost virtually its entire gold reserve during the civil war. This scandalous operation, carried out by the Republic for the benefit of the Soviet Union and the republican leaders, left the nation bereft of one of the major guarantees of its own solvency. This absence was severely felt during the first decade of reconstruction and readjustment. Imports are necessary to cover innumerable products that are either not produced locally or cannot be produced within reasonable economic limits. To discourage excessive importation, the State has followed a policy of rigid restriction. The peseta could not leave Spain except under the authorization of the *Instituto Español de Moneda.* This restriction applies to purchases abroad, travel by Spanish citizens outside the country, and all the necessary operations for contact and exchange with other nations. The first substantial modification of this policy occurred with the new regulations providing for a minimum importation and exportation of currency (August 1, 1950). During almost every year of the present century, the balance of international trade has shown a considerably higher percentage in imports than in exports.

It has been evident that a devaluation of the peseta is a necessary step for the stimulation of Spanish foreign trade. The contradiction in Spanish economic life is that the national income as a whole has declined, the value of the peseta has been inflated, and the cost of living has soared to something like nine times what it was in 1922–1926. At the same time a vast and extraordinarily effective program of public works, improvements, and economic development has been carried out. Spain is living on its own flesh and has achieved a precarious although skillful balance which has allowed the country to carry on despite its isolation and the total absence of every form of outside aid. This is accompanied by a very heavy increase in the money in circulation: in round numbers five billion pesetas in 1930, ten billion in 1940, and 26 billion in 1949.

The decline in the national income as a whole is a phenomenon to which passing attention may be given. The following table illustrates in terms of the normal 1929 peseta the situation since 1929:[4]

---

[4] The Spanish press makes available the figures on this point. "The National Economic Council has made public the fact that the National income has increased slightly in 1948, from 200,693,000,000 pesetas in 1947 to 208,517,000,000 pesetas in 1948. On the basis of the 1929 pesetas, the National income is less in 1948 than in 1947," *El Correo Catalán,* Barcelona, Nov. 24, 1949.

			Per inhabitant	
Year	*Peseta, 1949*	*Peseta, 1929*	*Peseta, 1949*	*Peseta, 1929*
1929	25,213,000	25,213	1,092	1,092
1932	25,566,000	25,742	1,075	1,083
1935	24,759,000	25,289	1,012	1,033
1940	36,130,000	20,977	1,049	819
1944	63,133,000	23,499	2,372	883
1947	102,693,000	24,457	3,751	893

The essence of the Spanish problem is increased production. Everything else: standard of living, foreign trade, social welfare, and the security of the national currency depends upon this. In agriculture this implies an increase in the total area in cultivation, which presupposes in turn improved methods, mechanization, improved production in areas now under cultivation, and a rational importation of food products. From the larger point of view, the opening up of a freer market with better opportunity for industrialists in investment and production, together with greater co-operation abroad, would be an enormous step forward in the present closed economy of Spain. It would not be honest to attribute this experiment in autarchy entirely to the will of the Spanish to be exclusive. The Spanish situation has been dubbed by one writer "a tightly controlled little experiment in unimaginative nationalism."[5] That it is semiautarchical admits of little doubt, but that it is entirely voluntary is another thing entirely. The Spanish did not seek to close the French frontier in 1946 nor were they responsible for the slowing down of trade relations elsewhere. They have been consistently forced back on their own meager resources and have had to learn to live alone and like it. Nationalism in economics is not, I suggest, an exclusively Spanish trait. Even its control system which strikes the visitor so often as hopeless in its complexities is no worse than that of Great Britain.[6]

Industrial production has receded in some instances, and this is especially true of such items as iron. For example, taking the index of iron production in 1929 at 100, we find that it ran along the following lines in the succeeding years:

---

[5] George Shuster, article, "The Catholic Controversy," in *Harpers Magazine,* Nov., 1949, p. 29.

[6] *Round the World,* Glasgow, Sept., 1949, article, "A Look at Spain," p. 135: "Spain is the most 'controlled' country in Europe outside Britain — or Germany."

Year	*Tons*	*Index*
1929	748,936	100
1932	296,481	39.6
1935	341,114	45.5
1940	579,386	77.4
1944	550,830	73.5
1947	503,384	67.2

This table shows that the total iron production is less than in 1929, but it reveals a very steady climb over the disastrous decrease of the republican era. Whatever may be said for the blessings of libertarianism under the Republic, the augmentation of economic production was not one of its great achievements.[7]

Real investment, that is in productive enterprises, has decreased between 1929 and 1947 from an index figure of 100 to 88.8. This is explainable in large part by the terrible devastation of the civil war and the need to rehabilitate enormous areas for production. The loss of real capital during the three years of war has been estimated at 66,916,000,000 pesetas at their 1929 value. The increase of real capital in the seven-year period from 1940 to 1947 represents about 17,419,000,000, leaving a deficit with reference to 1936 of 49,497,000,000 pesetas at the old prewar value. It is impossible to emphasize enough the fact that the Franco regime was faced in 1939 with this reality. The process of raising itself by its own boot straps has been an arduous and painful one. The tragic loss has not been entirely overcome and cannot be overcome in a single ten-year period. The severe critics of Spanish accomplishment during the first decade are prone to forget this point of departure, overlooking the almost impossibly tight restrictions that have forced the Spanish government to seek economic salvation in unorthodox and often faulty methods. If the economic rehabilitation of France has been difficult after World War II, in which she suffered far less than Spain in destruction and the loss of human

[7] Franco himself had been perfectly frank about the situation. In an interview with C. L. Sulzberger, of *The New York Times* (Nov. 12, 1948), the *Caudillo* stated: "Spain has certain special needs. One is to replace dilapidated and outmoded industrial equipment. Not only is much of our machinery worn out, but for example, in our mines, we could greatly expand our mineral production if we had modern mining equipment. Our railroad and transportation system must be transformed. . . . It is a vicious circle. Our production is limited because we have not the means to augment it and we cannot buy these means because we cannot export sufficiently to obtain the necessary dollars."

The Generalissimo stated bluntly to the Cortes that, "The gravest problem that Spain has found in the way of its economic recovery has been the disproportionate balance of payments" (*A.B.C.*, May 19, 1949).

life, it is small wonder that the Iberian peninsula has had an uphill row to hoe.[8] The civil war loss of 1,150,000 dead, a half million émigrés, among them some 40,000 children taken to the Soviet Union of whom no news has ever been obtained, was a most serious drain on man power. Despite this, the inherent vitality of the Spanish people evidences itself. The rise in population since the war despite difficulties and even misery attests to the fecundity and splendid natural youthfulness of the Spanish people.

Some of the external appearances of the Spanish economy are irritating. There is every evidence of luxury among many of the governing groups. The splendid cars parked on city streets cause a great deal of adverse criticism among the mass of people who see in the plethora of imported cars a luxury that is not in keeping with the modest resources of the nation. The black market thrives lustily, and *estraperlo* has long since entered the Spanish language as a permanent word. White bread was for a long time technically forbidden, but in none of the better clubs or cafés was it ever lacking. Gasoline and its by-products have to be obtained very frequently on the black market. Even the severest critics of the regime recognize that General Franco himself is totally incorruptible; they wish that those around him were sometimes less inclined toward personal profiteering.

Spain has tried to operate on the basis of a series of bilateral trade agreements with specific countries. Despite the pressure of the United Nations and the atmosphere of hostility that has enshrouded Spain for so long, positive progress has been made in this direction. The list of such agreements is a startlingly long one. Some of them are minor in their importance as a source of indispensable imports, but others are of real significance for the future of Spain. With Argentina a number of treaties have been drawn up since 1939, and in 1946 an elaborate arrangement was worked out for Hispano-Argentine exchange and for loans from Argentina to Spain. From incomplete information available in Madrid it would not seem that the operation of the agreements has been entirely satisfactory nor have the results been as large as anticipated, partly, no doubt, owing to the peculiar economic policy evolved by the Argentine government itself.

---

[8] An admirable study of the economic situation is contained in the review, *Les Etudes Américaines,* published by the Institut des Hautes Etudes Américaines in Paris, Cahier XIII, 1949, article, "Conjoncture Espagnole," by M. A. Dauphin-Meunier, p. 5 sq.

Trade agreements have been also signed at various dates in 1946 and 1947 with Belgium, Chile, Denmark (France suspended in 1945 because of closing of the frontier), Great Britain, Ireland, Italy, Netherlands, Portugal, Sweden, Switzerland, Turkey, and Uruguay. Two of the most important countries with which Spain has carried on trade have traditionally been France and Great Britain. With the latter, an agreement was reached in 1948. Anglo-Spanish trade represented some forty million pounds sterling per annum, a not negligible amount indeed. There is an inordinate amount of price juggling, special features, discounts, premia, and the like, attached to this agreement which is definitely a little out of line with British free-trade ideas in the past. But the fact remains that the Labor government has not stood in the way of a trade arrangement which is mutually advantageous. The Spanish Foreign Minister spoke of it as one of the most important trade agreements yet signed with the British empire.[9] The most attractive item in the arrangement was 750,000 tons of British coal for Spanish industry. Since the opening of the Franco-Spanish frontier, trade has developed normally with France. New agreements have stimulated it and, oddly enough, without a French or British ambassador in Madrid relations are as near normal as one could wish. The technical diplomatic tension between Spain and these two countries has not hindered the increase of trade relations or the profitable exchange now going on across the border and over the sea.

In this connection it may be noted that American trade was never shut off even in the midst of the United Nations fulminations and the withdrawal of ambassadors. "In 1947 and 1948 the major part of Spanish foreign trade was with the United States."[10] Spain carries on trade with all sixteen members of the Marshall Plan bloc, especially foodstuffs such as oranges and canned fish. A more recent agreement with Italy, replacing that of 1947, opened up new opportunities for Spanish trade and it is anticipated that some 275 million pesetas in commerce will be carried out with Italy, the latter supplying electrical equipment, mining machinery, tractors, automobiles, and similar materials, in exchange for foodstuffs.[11]

The prospect for a relaxation of the rigid attitude heretofore officially preserved would seem to be indicated in the address of Chargé

---

[9] *The Tablet*, London, Aug. 7, 1948.

[10] *Les Etudes Américaines, op. cit.*, p. 17.

[11] *A.B.C.*, Nov. 19, 1949. Dispatch from Rome of correspondent Julián Cortés Vanillas.

d'Affaires Culberton, in Barcelona, March, 1948, in which he stated that the only change in the American attitude toward Spain was in placing no obstacles in the way of loans by private American banks to Spain.[12]

There can be no doubt that, despite its errors and shortcomings, at the basis of the efforts of the Spanish regime are three things: (1) improvement of the conditions of the working classes; (2) limitation of the abuses of capitalism; (3) more equal distribution of wealth.

The year 1950 opened with forebodings of another dark period for the national economy. Transportation services, cotton mills, fertilizer, and tractors still were the most pressing needs for the Spanish economy. Following on the devaluation of sterling, the decision of the Spanish government to rely on the differential rate system to bring Spanish into line with world prices put fresh obstacles in the way of foreign trade, upon which depends the acquisition of currencies with which to purchase machinery and raw materials. The continuance of restrictions eleven years after the successful conclusion of the civil war prompted *The Tablet* correspondent in Madrid to speak of a bureaucracy in *delirium tremens*.[13] Despite the limitations, commerce showed exceptional vitality to the extent that imports actually rose for the period ending June, 1949, while exports showed an increase of 18 per cent in quantity and 30 per cent in value. One of the reasons for this gratifying improvement was a soaring trade between Spain and France; the latter country ousting the United States from the second place it had long held in trade with the peninsula. There has been a narrowing of the gap between the relative values of exports and imports, with emphasis on the fact that the nation has been increasing manufacturing in its interests. This is to be observed in the fact that over the past ten years the purchases of manufactured goods have been increased very slowly while those of raw materials are greater than in 1936; on the export side more manufactured articles and less raw materials have been sold abroad.

The present Spanish government has been accused of seeking theoretical autarchy as the solution of its economic problems. The personality of Juan Suances, Minister of Industry and Commerce, has long figured in the discussions of the economic outlook, for it is he

---

12 Discussion of this point and future of Spanish international economic relations in *Problèmes et relations internationales: l'Espagne,* Brussels, 1948, p. 19.

13 London, January 28, 1950.

who has been primarily responsible for the superhuman efforts of the nation to create an industrial order that would sever the traditional dependence on the so-called "advanced" economic areas of the world. On March 7, 1950, the Minister released the details of a two-year plan to industrialize Spain with the prediction that within two years sufficient progress would be made to transform the economic structure of the nation. It was estimated that by 1956 the basic industrialization of Spain would be completed.[14] This ambitious plan calls for the intensive development of the mineral resources of the country in the hope that 300,000 tons of soft coal may be obtained in mines in the Gijón area and 150,000 tons of lignite in the Pyrenees. In regard to transportation, Spain has made great efforts to decrease dependence on foreign manufacture of aircraft and automobiles. In May, 1950, the government launched a 400 million peseta loan to start the railway program. The production of Fiat cars with Italian technical aid is envisaged and six of the leading Spanish banks concluded arrangements with the Fiat works to build a new Fiat model. The necessity for improving the railway system, essential not only for ordinary traffic but for defense, led to the floating of a loan for the purchase of 14,000 tons of rails in Belgium, 100 passenger coaches in France, and sufficient raw materials for the construction of another hundred.[15]

High hopes were entertained for a foreign loan in dollars to allow for the reorganization of the economy. The adverse vote in the United States Senate on April 27, 1950, in which Spain was excluded from possible E.R.P. benefits, killed temporarily any idea of Washington as a source of this much-needed assistance. "The rejection does not mean disaster for Spain but it does mean hard sledding."[16] Obviously the full success of the proposed industrialization program makes a loan almost indispensable. But there remains the very pressing question of increasing agricultural production for the reason that population is rising faster than the quantity of food necessary for its support. Despite the real increase in the production of coal and electricity since 1939, wheat has actually decreased, and olive oil, a staple of the Spanish diet, totaled 270 thousand metric tons in 1949 as against 209 in 1939 and 660 in 1929.

The government has not been discouraged by the somewhat bleek

[14] *The New York Times,* March 8, 1950, "Spain blueprints industrial gains."
[15] *Ibid.,* Dispatch of Sam Pope Brewer, May 10, 1950.
[16] *Ibid.,* May 13, 1950.

outlook caused by droughts and a struggling economy. In a speech to the National Agricultural Fair in May, 1950, General Franco insisted that Spain can modernize her agriculture and overcome the serious deficiencies now being endured. There has been a tendency in recent years, with an eye on industrialization, to neglect agriculture. "His speech and the great emphasis laid on the Fair support the belief that the government has decided to give a greater share of its attention to agriculture and try to restore the balance between it and industry."[17]

A very serious problem has been the extraordinary power of the National Institute of Industry which has been accused of hampering the expansion of private industrial concerns. By the end of May, 1950, some of the restrictions on the free operation of the market were removed, especially with reference to certain foodstuffs, and there was a surmisal in Madrid circles that perhaps the large control of the Institute over commerce might be relaxed. The major economic question continues to be the degree of State control over both industry and commerce. Reports in June, 1950, indicated that the government anticipated entering the steel industry, and this was widely interpreted as a victory for Minister Suances, a partisan of increased State control over industrial life.[18]

In addition to the declaration of a free market in certain food products in the late spring of 1950, the Spanish government took a decisive step on August 1, in establishing a relatively free currency exchange. From the practical point of view the new policy is fundamental in its implications: The United States dollar is quoted at 39.50 instead of the arbitrary 11 pesetas before, and 25 pesetas for tourists. For the first time since pre-civil-war days, pesetas can be exported within limits and the visitor may take into the country up to 10,000. "In almost every country, currency control has tended to freeze the exchange of money without reference to the causes that produced fluctuations and without reference to the steps that should be taken to make a currency sound. The results have been extremely mediocre."[19] All of these innovations constitute a sign that the rigidity of the Spanish economy is beginning to give way in the face of the very great need of encouraging a greater degree of free play in foreign trade and domestic commerce.

---

[17] *Ibid.*, May 27, 1950.
[18] *Ibid.*, June 9, 1950.
[19] *A.B.C.*, Madrid, Aug. 17, 1950.

Obviously the decision of the United States Congress in August, 1950, approving a loan of some 100 million dollars to Spain, aroused the greatest interest in Madrid, despite the fact that the possibility of aiding Spain's economy was now directly linked with the worsening international situation, and it was evident that the proposal was made as part of the broader purpose of assuring Spanish participation in the common defense of western Europe. Whatever the motive may have been, the signs of the time, as of the late summer of 1950, pointed definitely to an increasing interest in American circles to guarantee the economic stability and future of the peninsula. It would seem that the Spanish authorities are willing to let events take their course, confident that common sense will ultimately dictate the need for this form of action.[20]

In September, 1950, the Congress of the United States approved a proposal for a loan of $62,500,000 to Spain, despite President Truman's known opposition to the measure, and his reluctance to carry out the mandate of the legislative branch of the government. This was tangible evidence that sentiment both in Congress and outside had moved a long way toward the re-establishment of normal relations with the Madrid government.

The system of social legislation in vogue within contemporary Spain is nothing short of formidable. Earlier in this chapter it was suggested that the legislation has perhaps outrun the economic possibilities of the country. It has been criticized too as excessively paternalistic, distinguished by a veritable passion for security, and concentrated administratively in the State. This defect — if it is a defect — is shared by Spain with a large number of other countries where the welfare state conception predominates.

The point of departure for the study of Spain's social legislation is the *Fuero del Trabajo*,[21] promulgated on March 9, 1938. This Labor Charter affirms in its preamble that Spain is Catholic, social, and indivisible, and that its program must conform to these ideas. Work is recognized as the supreme dignity and every protection must be given it with guarantees against social instability. Under the chapter on capital it is noted that "after allotting a fair interest to capital, the profits of the enterprise shall be applied first to the reserves neces-

---

[20] *Gazette de Lausanne*, Switzerland, May 23, 1950, "Madrid insists on its independence but wants an American loan."

[21] The complete English text of the Charter is contained in Loveday, *Spain. 1923–1948*, Boswell Publishing Co., London, p. 263 sq.

sary for a sound position, the improvement of production, and betterment of working conditions and the living of the workers." Under Article XIII, the vertical trade union is established: "All factors of economy will be incorporated, by branches of production or service, in vertical guilds."

His Excellency, Mon. Angel Herrera, Bishop of Málaga, has praised this document for its recognition of the place of labor in the social order: "What does the *Fuero del Trabajo* mean? This admirable document elevates the status of work. It is in line with the Encyclicals . . . the entire Charter is profoundly Christian."[22] The Labor Charter was included in the later *Fuero de los Españoles,* to which reference has already been made. These documents fixing the duties and privileges of Spanish citizens were praised by the Cardinal Primate of Toledo as "fortunately marking a step in the direction of Christian liberty as opposed to State totalitarianism."[23]

Obviously, social legislation was no complete novelty for Spain. From the time of Cánovas steps had been taken in this direction and the name of Azcárate is particularly linked with social reform in the peninsula. The Institute of Social Reform of 1903 was the concrete result of the preliminary studies and the *Instituto Nacional de Previsión,* created in 1908, was concerned primarily with social security in various forms. The dictatorship of Primo de Rivera was productive of a number of important social measures. Under the Republic, despite a number of positive advances in social legislation, the predominant characteristic was the intimate connection between labor and politics. Under the present nationalist government, the Ministry of Labor is the principal agency for social reform, together with three other major organizations: *Instituto Nacional de Previsión,* in charge of every form of insurance on behalf of the working class; *Instituto Social de la Marina,* for the protection of those who make their livelihood from the sea and a source of aid to the fishermen; and the *Instituto Nacional de la Vivienda,* engaged in a wide housing program.[24]

It is impossible to give an exhaustive treatment of this question in these brief pages. Some idea may be useful of how the Spanish regime

---

22 Lecture of Bishop Angel Herrera, published by *Consejo Superior de Hombres de Acción Católica,* Madrid, 1947, pp. 25–26.

23 Pastoral letter of the Cardinal Archbishop of Toledo, August, 1945.

24 The most complete and handy survey of Spanish social legislation is contained in Florentino del Valle, *Las reformas sociales en España,* 2 ed., Madrid, 1948.

has devoted very special attention to the social problem and the character of its legislation. Up to the end of 1947, for which detailed figures are available, the expenditures for social purposes attained the sum of nearly 800 million pesetas. The major investment was in cheap housing, for which purpose almost half of the total amount indicated was expended. A fundamental feature of the present social legislation is the family allowance. Up to the present regime nothing as complete or all embracing existed, although in a few cases under private initiative, some attempt had been made to meet the economic problem of the large family. The system is obligatory for all employers and applies to all persons employed for wages. In 1943 the scale was such that allowances ran from 40 pesetas a month beyond wages for two children to 1,080 pesetas for a family of twelve. In 1939 some 158,036 enterprises were operating the family allowance, with 787,707 workers benefiting from it. In 1947, 306,285 enterprises were involved with 4,276,969 workers as beneficiaries. In addition to the allowances, there are several subsidiary laws for direct aid of a similar kind. Widows and orphans are cared for by special legislation. School children incapable of continuing their studies because of financial difficulties are aided by small grants. A system of aid for the newly married allows a non-interest-bearing loan of 2,500 pesetas for the man and 5,000 for the woman, repayable in easy installments. The large families are further protected by reduction of taxes, preferential treatment in schools, hospitals, and public institutions, and special reductions for railway and bus travel.

The insurance system embraces maternity, sickness, work accidents, illness contracted in the line of professional duty, old age and incapacity, and special protection in the case of seamen and fishermen. From the point of view of social security, the following abbreviated table gives a general idea of the progress in modern Spain.

1938 — Reorganization of social security service. Family-allowance system inaugurated.

1939 — Allowances for widows, orphans, and old age. Extension of family allowances to the rural areas.

1940 — Regulations revised for security and hygiene in factories and shops. Increased protection to mothers and children.

1941 — Special aid to large families. Loans for the newly married. National fund for work accidents and temporarily incapacitated. Protection of miners against silicosis. Family allowances doubled.

1942 — Maternity aid expanded, with special attention to working women and workers' wives. Sickness insurance extended.

1943 — New increase of family allowances. Special provision for social security among farmers and farm workers. Increased subsidy for accident insurance. Regulations laid down for social security for fishermen.

1944 — Increase in old-age pensions. Sickness insurance on large scale becomes effective. Domestic servants included in social security.

1945 — Family allowances worked out for those under sickness relief, or temporarily without work.

1946 — Extension of silicosis protection. Increase of payments for accident and sickness insurance.

1947 — Insurance for diseases contracted in line of duty.

In the field of labor efforts have been made to convert the worker into an active participant in the productive process, and the regulation of work and labor relations is the object of some one hundred statutes governing this aspect of economic life. An important beginning has been made in the field of profit sharing by workers in industrial enterprises. As early as June, 1943, the first steps had been taken, and by 1948 certain conditions were laid down to assure the proportionate participation of workers in the profits of the establishments in which they were engaged.[25]

Bishop Herrera called attention to the importance of this development when he stated that "It would raise the mass of workers to the position of real factors in the industrial life of the country," citing at the same time the beneficial results of the innovation at the Alfa Sewing Machine Company in Eibar where a system had been worked out of labor participation in the enterprise by converting the employees into share holders.[26]

Advance along these lines was indicated by Manuel Martínez Pereiro, official of the Ministry of Labor, in pointing out the growing participation of workers in the factory boards concerned with advancement

---

[25] *Boletín oficial del Ministerio del Trabajo,* May 2, 1949, with ministerial order of April 9, 1949, establishing bases for profit sharing.

[26] *Op. cit.,* p. 29.

and employment. In the construction trade some progress toward profit sharing has also been made.[27] Space forbids a detailed account of the trade schools, institutes for professional training, and one particular establishment which is extraordinarily interesting, known as the *Escuela de Capacitación social.* The latter, which I had occasion to visit in Madrid, is an institution created to provide short intensive courses for workers in the general social, economic, and cultural fields. During the 40-day courses the worker lives in the institution. The groups come from a given industry or trade and are chosen within their own localities. I examined carefully the entrance papers and in no case was mention made of political affiliation or religion and the worker is free to attend religious services if he chooses. Many of those who have passed through the Madrid center, one of the largest in the country, have been known communists or socialists and, despite the fact that their convictions were known before entering, no effort was made to coerce them. The purpose is to provide a cultural and professional leaven among the ordinary workers, with an opportunity for contact with the broader currents of Spanish life, and with a great deal of attention devoted to visits to historical sites, museums, art galleries, and the like.

Much space could be given to the complex legislation on salaries and the multiple efforts to increase the workers' purchasing power in terms of the rising cost of living through paid vacations, Sunday rest with salary, and overtime wages. In the chapter on the Falange, reference has been made to the *Auxilio Social* and its work on behalf of children, maternity cases, and free soup kitchens for the hungry.

Unemployment, both seasonal and permanent, has been a blight on the Spanish economy. During republican days it reached fantastic heights with almost constant disorders, and in 1936 alone there were 829,389 classified as unemployed. This number has been vastly reduced with efforts to provide subsidies for those who do not obtain work. The *Caja de compensación del Paro,* as it is called, was inaugurated in 1945 to deal with this problem.

The housing projects form a part of the general program of reconstruction after the civil war and new construction initiated by the present government. The full story of reconstruction in Spain, from the material point of view, is fabulous; whole cities that were literally wiped out have been rebuilt in their entirety: Teruel, Brunete, the

[27] Manuel Martínez Pereiro, lecture to *Hermandad Obrera de Acción Católica. Primera semana nacional,* Madrid, 1946, p. 46.

many small towns of the areas around Madrid and in Aragón. The evidences of war are very few today, and in some localities where the fighting was particularly destructive it is virtually impossible to discover more than occasional traces of the hostilities. The *Instituto Nacional de la Vivienda,* or National Housing Institute, has contributed to the expansion of cheap housing for workers and farmers. In 1948 the actual results of the housing program showed that in the previous seven years, 30,117 units had been built; 610,522 in the process of construction, and another 118,773 in prospect for the immediate future. The homes that have actually been turned over to the purchasers represent an investment of some 250 million pesetas. The law of November 25, 1944, established favorable bases for modest-priced homes for the middle class, with long-term payments and exoneration from taxes for a given period. In the larger cities, workers' homes have been constructed in the most modern style, with several hundred families per building. Special provision has been made for farm homes, and in the first legislation approved in 1939 it was proposed that some 80 per cent of all funds invested in housing be allotted to the rural zone.

The development of public works is another striking achievement of the present regime. With limited resources, scanty importations from abroad, and unfavorable natural conditions at times, the Spanish State has accomplished wonders in this field. Reservoirs and the development of water power have been pushed with particular interest in view of the very real need in Spain of increased electrical power. About 28 large dams and water deposits have been built, and some 20 other reservoirs have already been completed and are in service. Irrigation has progressed definitely despite the devastating consequences of the three years' drought, and some 250,000 acres in the Ebro and Guadalquivir valleys have been made available to productive agriculture. Swamp drainage has progressed and work has gone forward on the dredging of the Ebro to make it navigable. Bridge and road reconstruction after the war with new extensions to meet an increasing population have made encouraging progress and over 3600 kilometers of new railway have been envisaged, with over 2500 already under construction. The program for electrification calls for 4500 kilometers of electrified railroads of which a few have actually been put into operation, notably the Madrid-Segovia and the Madrid-Ávila runs which have already been completely electrified. Shipbuilding has been encouraged and in the single year 1945, despite the pressure of wartime conditions abroad, 21 large vessels were built in Spanish shipyards. During 1946 some two hundred craft were built, among them passenger and freight vessels of considerable dimensions. The Spanish fleet of both small and large craft is about 1300 at the present time, as against 995 in 1936 when the civil war began.

Land reform is a particularly interesting topic in modern Spain. The organization charged with the important task of dealing with land reform and redistribution is called the *Instituto Nacional de Colonización.* The main task of this Institute is the acquisition of lands for the settlement of landless farmers and farm workers, and eighteen regional or local bodies are specifically charged with responsibility for carrying out the measures. The project involves not merely the rehabilitation of the farmer or the conversion of the rural worker into a landowner, but the encouragement of a return to the land on the part of those who left it or who evince a desire to establish themselves and families on the land. A whole series of "preferred zones" have been set up, in which agricultural conditions have been improved to allow for a better rural life. In some cases new towns and villages have been created as is the case of La Vid y Guma in Burgos, Foncastín in Valladolid, El Temple in Huesca, and many others. These farm towns and villages are provided with modern housing, favorable conditions for the exploitation of the land, and every inducement for settlement. This is the basic reason why the program is called "colonization" and not simply "Agrarian reform" as in the past. The decree called *Ley de Parcelaciones* of July, 1942, provided for the acquisition of lands and their redistribution to farmers. Between 1942 and 1947, 18,612 landless farmers were provided with property under conditions laid down by the agency.[28] In addition to land as such which is far from sufficient to solve the complex rural problem, progress has been made in irrigation, appropriate construction for the development of certain crops, farm machinery, seed and stock, and defense against insect pests and other natural factors.

The last point to be considered in this survey of the social and economic background of modern Spain is the trade unions. The object of the new trade-unions, envisaged in the Labor Charter, was to abolish organizations along strictly class lines and bring the State into the movement. By virtue of the legislation of 1940, the

---

[28] An excellent survey of the status of the farm question is contained in the newspaper *Arriba,* Madrid, July 18, 1947.

Delegación Nacional de Sindicatos was authorized to direct the whole trade-union movement, and many heretofore independent or autonomous groups were absorbed, among them the *Confederación Nacional Católico-Agraria,* with some 2726 local branches.

The vertical unions are divided into the following categories: water, gas, and electricity; food and food products; sugar products; bank and stock exchange; grain products; fuel products; construction; amusement industry; fruit and truck garden; cattle products; hotel and affiliated branches; chemical industries; wood and cork industries; metal trades; olive production; paper, press, and graphic arts; fishing industry; fur industry; insurance branches; textile industries; wine, beer, and beverage production.

Within each of these trade or professional branches are grouped all workers; affiliation with the union is obligatory for the worker and the employer. The "verticality," if the word may be used, consists of the fact that all those working in the same branch, be they in labor, the technical sphere, or management, belong to the same union.

The *Sindicato único,* or single trade union as it is called, poses a number of serious difficulties for the outside observer. In the first place, it destroys completely the idea of labor, government, and management as three separate agencies and places them together within the same union. In the second place, State control becomes complete for all practical purposes. There is no doubt that the Spanish workers have profited from the present trade unions in the sense that innumerable demands have been met; in fact, one of the real dangers of the present situation is that too much is conceded regardless of intrinsic merit in order to avoid demands by labor. Moreover, within the unions today are innumerable socialists and other former trade-union militants who have not changed their basic ideas and have simply transferred their place of operation from the old ideologically inclined unions of the pre-civil-war days, to the new, monolithic system that now prevails. It would seem to be true that the workers are skeptical of the present state of affairs and participate in the unions, not in the spirit of something that belongs to them, but as an obligatory arrangement out of which they can obtain a considerable benefit. This is stated by Father Del Valle in his excellent summary of the social program: "Perhaps a more active worker participation in the functioning of the unions would win over more of them than is the case today."[29]

---

[29] Del Valle, *op. cit.,* pp. 132–133.

There are many other subsidiary organizations that have been created by the unions or in connection with them, and so numerous are they that one of the most frequent complaints in Spain today is that much of the ordinary business life, especially the industrial, is controlled by the unions, their immense bureaucracy becoming another obstacle in the way of the freer and more fluid economic life of the country. I have found great resentment among large sectors of the Spanish workers against the unions as they exist. They are charged primarily with being "totalitarian," as run from the top down, as lacking in real worker participation, as being a strait jacket within which a luxuriant bureaucracy has developed and flourishes, and as failing to win the real consent of the workers to collaboration.

These criticisms seem to me in many ways to be well founded. One recognizes naturally that after 1939 Spain could not go back to the old trade-union system, with the U.G.T. and C.N.T., and its socialist and anarchist infiltration. The trade unions had fought the civil war as much as the left-wing political parties and it was not to be expected that these foci of agitation and disruption would be allowed to become re-established. In this sense the refusal to revert to the "class struggle" is entirely justified. The question is whether the present organization satisfies either the demands of a rational trade-union movement or even the ultimate aim of the system itself, namely, the reconciliation of the working masses with the other agents of production in a harmonious whole. Even the most optimistic cannot hold that the latter objective has been achieved in modern Spain.[30]

[30] An opinion of considerable value is that of Bernard Sullivan, since 1909 a member of the National Union of Tailors and Garment Workers in England and a representative of the Labor Party on the London County Council since 1937, who states, with reference to a recent visit to Spain: "The workers' stewards at the engineering firm protested to me about the British conception of the workers having no freedom and claimed that they had not got workers control which seemed to be supported by some of the employers who claimed they still had ownership but not managerial powers. . . . There seems to have been a transfer to the workers of wealth which has given them an air of independence and confidence in the future, while their participation in the building of workers' homes and hospitals, and the welfare services they help to manage, is giving them an experience that will fit them one day to share in a democratic government of their own country" (*The Catholic Herald,* London, Sept. 30, 1949).

Chapter 15. THE CHURCH IN CONTEMPORARY SPAIN

THE account of the Church since the nationalist victory in 1939 is not an easy task, for the situation is full of subtleties and the ever present danger of oversimplification. Almost all of the stock assertions regarding the status and attitude of the Church today in Spain are open to qualification. Does the Church support the present regime? One school of thought tells us that the Church is largely an instrument of politics, devoted to combating any current of thought that runs counter to it and completely wedded to the present regime. Expressed in its crudest form the position of the Church is characterized by opinion as: "an overriding dedication to institutional self-interest; a tough, prideful imperviousness to criticism; a profound suspicion of any intellectual inquisitiveness; a contempt for any kind of education not synonymous with indoctrination; a sharp distrust and hostility toward any political or social movement that could be called radical, leftist or liberal and a respect that approaches reverence for power in any form."[1]

It would be easy to dismiss these statements as sheer exaggeration, their utterance revealing a singularly impervious mind to the nature and character both of the Spanish people and their environment. That the Spanish are impatient of criticism is unquestionably true, for few nations have been subjected to so much criticism that is sweeping, inaccurate, dishonest, and prejudiced. Resistance to social change may best be judged by a statement of exactly what is being done in Spain today in the direction of the social betterment of the masses.

The whole history of Spain in the first decade after the civil war

---

[1] Emmet John Hughes, *Report From Spain* (New York: Henry Holt and Co., Inc., 1947), p. 75. This book constitutes one of the very few reports on the Church in modern Spain. Written by a Catholic it has been considered as a dispassionate judgment on the Spanish Church and its status. Unfortunately it is marred again and again by categorical statements that are inaccurate, and reveals serious defects regarding the facts.

is one vast social transformation. Whatever may be said about the regime, it has been more than merely "radical" in its social program; it has been positively revolutionary. There is a strong current of thought in Spain that things have gone too far in the social order and that a bit of conservatism is in order. Intellectual curiosity, I think, is best evidenced in the cultural production under Catholic auspices. Certainly a dispassionate examination of the work being done, scientific, literary, and theological, will confirm the fact that there is a very lively intellectual life in Catholic circles.

To one who thinks the Catholic atmosphere is stifling of all inquisitiveness, I would urge attendance at such gatherings as those organized by the *Asociación Nacional de Propagandistas Católicos* (Alfonso XI, 4, Madrid), at the Pontifical University of Comillas, or at any one of the Spanish universities. I recall with particular pleasure meetings at Valencia, Murcia, Oviedo, and Barcelona with members of the clergy, university students, and representatives of Catholic Action, whose intellectual curiosity was sharp — in fact far sharper — than one would find among comparable groups in almost any other European country. I have found no evidence at any of the institutions run by either the orders or by the diocesan clergy that intellectual uniformity is the rule and in many cases the bishops themselves are directly responsible for stimulating active intellectual life. It would be extraordinary to accuse the Bishop of Salamanca, promotor of the Pontifical University, of lack of inquisitiveness, or the Bishop of Vitoria, sponsor of the famous *Conversaciones Católicas* at San Sebastián for intellectual lethargy.

But the main problem is not a refutation of these generalizations about Spain; our interest is to examine the status of the Church today, vis-à-vis the State, and something of the work being done by the hierarchy, clergy, and laity within the country for its spiritual rehabilitation. As has been mentioned, the Concordat of 1851 has continued to remain in force, despite the fact that it is not satisfactory and that the circumstances obviously require a new agreement between the Spanish State and the Holy See. One of the main points in the 1851 agreement was the recognition by the Holy See of the validity of the sales of the expropriated properties of the Church, for which in return the Spanish State was to make payments on a regular basis for the maintenance of the Church. The major difficulty in the Concordat was obvious; it placed the clergy on the basis of state employees and made their stipends comparable to those of civil functionaries.

It did establish firmly, what was afterward all too often forgotten, that the clergy was compensated on a regular basis as a right and not as a gift or concession on the part of the State. In any event the meager stipends were not just compensation for the expropriations, and to this day, despite the considerable aid in reconstruction given by the Franco government, the State is far from liquidating its debt to the Church — debt is perhaps hardly the word, for it was unmitigated confiscation, accompanied by violence.

As far as the Orders were concerned, no offer was made for compensation although the Concordat did guarantee them a certain basic tranquillity. Heretofore they had been the easy victims of predatory Finance Ministers, bent on filling the treasury in the most painless way, and the Concordat granted them a period of about eighty years of reasonable peace and quiet for recovery from the disaster precipitated by Mendizábal. The Orders have been accused of using the Concordat as a cloak to increase their numbers and on this point the document was vague, providing expressly in Article 29 that "religious congregations and houses of St. Vincent de Paul, St. Philip Neri, and another Order from among those approved by the Holy See" would be admitted as necessary to carry out certain specific tasks in which the State was to collaborate. The fact was that the Orders in general stabilized their existence, expanded their work, and performed great service all over the country. In 1860 a *convenio* was entered into, that is, a special agreement, by which the State confirmed its recognition of the status embodied in the Concordat and recognized without limitation the right of the Church to acquire property.

That the Concordat of 1851 is outmoded is probably true, although it contributed to the normalization of the relations of Church and State for almost a century. There is real need for a revamping to bring it into line with the realities of today and the new needs of the Church in Spain. In this case, as in so many others, the present regime has coasted along on legislation and agreements that often antedate not only the Second Republic but even the First. There has been a great deal of discussion in Spain regarding a new concordat or a revision at least of the old and it is generally understood that a difference of opinion exists between the State and the Holy See regarding the present validity of the Concordat of 1851; this divergence of views on the matter complicates a new arrangement.

The relations between the two jurisdictions have been settled by partial agreements entered into by the State and the Holy See and is possible that these *convenios* may form the basis of a new concordat. One of the most significant was that of July 16, 1946, signed between the government and the Holy See and treating of a large number of ecclesiastical designations. Without going into all the details, a few examples will suffice to indicate the *modus operandi* of the agreement and how both State and Church function jointly in many of the appointments.[2]

Article III provides that the designation of cathedral deans shall be made after the Ordinary has presented a list of three candidates to the Chief of State who shall, in turn, choose one, whose name will then be given first place on the list sent to the Holy See. Article IV defines the conditions under which canons shall be designated. The provision is very similar to that prevailing for chairs in the Spanish universities, that is, the proper academic title and *oposiciones* or competitive examinations. In Article X, the Spanish government commits itself expressly to "the observation of the first four articles of the Concordat of 1851 . . . and in no case to legislate in any matter of interest to the Church without previous agreement with the Holy See."

Ecclesia, official organ of Spanish Catholic Action, comments editorially on the agreement in these terms:

> The Spanish State moves gradually toward a Concordat with the Holy See on the basis of partial agreements which later may be incorporated into a new document. The new agreement just signed . . . is drafted in most cordial terms and reveals great understanding on the part of both contracting parties. It is far removed from the regalist mentality that dominated so many of our statesmen in the past.[3]

The designation of bishops has probably caused more widespread interest than any other single aspect of the Church-State problem in Spain. There is a curious notion in the Anglo-American world that in some odd way, the Spanish government literally designates and probably actually co-operates in the consecration of bishops. The process of designation is quite simple and forms a part of a very long Hispanic tradition. When a see is vacant it is customary for the State and the Nunciature in Madrid to exchange views regarding the proper person to fill it. The list drawn up usually contains six names, and is dispatched to the Holy See where it may be rejected outright or three preferences may be indicated. This list of three is then returned to Madrid and the head of the State chooses one which he then

---

[2] Full text of this partial agreement in *Ecclesia,* Madrid, July 20, 1946, No. 262, p. 7.
[3] *Ibid.,* p. 3.

proposes to Rome for formal designation as bishop. This process is known as the "Right of Presentation." It will be observed that from the beginning the State neither selects nor much less imposes a candidate against the will of the Holy See or as an arbitrary gesture toward the Spanish Church. The whole procedure forms a part, let it be emphasized once again, of a very ancient tradition, and while it may not be desirable in many other countries, in Spain it represents a fundamental part of the *mores* of Church-State relations. In general relations under the present regime have been most cordial and little friction has been encountered in the designation of the occupants of vacant sees and, in point of fact, by the time the list actually reaches the head of the State and the Holy See, the preliminary discussions have ironed out possible difficulties. The direction of negotiations with the ecclesiastical authorities rests with the Department of Ecclesiastical Affairs of the Foreign Office.

A very delicate problem arises regarding the degree to which the Spanish Church supports the present regime, or, to use the phrase of its critics, how far the Spanish Church is committed to a particular temporal order, which, no matter how well intentioned, is not eternal, and may be followed by other regimes which will seek to saddle the Church with responsibility for the defects of the present system. There are many opinions and not a few facts in conflict that make anything like a rash judgment or conclusion out of the question. These opinions run along three general lines and may be summarized as follows:

1. The present regime is favorable to the Church, supports it generously, and recognizes in it a collaborator in the reconstruction of Spain. There is no sound reason why the Church should refuse this collaboration since it can hardly prefer antagonism to full understanding and hearty co-operation from the civil authority.

2. The Church is undoubtedly the recipient of grants and aid of all kind from the State. Many of its bishops and clergy have gone too far, however, in committing themselves to support of this particular regime. It would be better to maintain a greater independence so that in the event of a change in the nature of the State the Church would be less exposed.

3. The Church has sold out completely and is a subservient and blind instrument of the present regime. Bishops and clergy are nothing more than the lackeys of the regime and are at the best state officials, subject to the whims and caprices of the system. The Church has completely lost its hold on the masses because of this policy, and in the event of a change it will be the first to suffer the consequences of its too intimate association with the dictatorship.

Here we have, I believe, the main positions taken by those within Spain who give thought to the problem of the Church. One discovers that those favorable to the present regime extol without fail the enormous religious revival in Spain; the crowded churches, the hundreds of young men at Mass and at the sacraments; and the countless manifestations of Catholic fervor. Vocations have increased enormously, to such an extent that the seminaries are packed and many aspirants have to be refused. Religious orders are flourishing as never before, and Catholic culture is manifest in a hundred reviews, magazines, and publications of every sort and religious culture is evident in splendid centers for religious study and in the pontifical universities. While all of this is true, the critics insist that it is largely fictitious and that this upsurge of religious fervor does not affect the great mass of people, for it is largely limited to the middle class and the younger generation of professional men and women. The late vocations are so frequent that rare is the day one does not find the announcement in the public press of the ordination of someone who has been an architect, physician, or lawyer. Does this revival reach the great mass of the population? The critics claim that the working class has been virtually untouched by the advance of Catholicism and that despite social legislation, the diffusion of Catholic doctrine, and the work of Catholic Action, only the smallest segments of the working class have been converted. I am inclined to think this is largely true. The Spanish working classes have for generations been alien to the Church and all it stands for and their conversion *en masse* cannot, of course, be expected within a few years. There is reason for discouragement in the resistance of the industrial proletariat to the penetration of religious ideas although obviously there are notable exceptions.

The Spanish hierarchy, as a whole, has made its own understanding of the situation clear from the beginning of the war. In the *Collective Letter* of July 1, 1937, the bishops accepted the war as the inevitable result of the insufferable tension under which Spain had been living. In later communications of a similar nature, the hierarchy has reiterated its stand at the beginning of the civil war and its faith that the contest of arms was a necessary purging of a Spain wracked by disorder and impiety. Now it must be plain to any Catholic that the expression of the hierarchy in this solemn fashion must be taken in all seriousness, despite an extraordinary tendency on the part of foreign Catholics — and not a few reporters among them — to assume that anything the Spanish hierarchy says must be tainted with self-interest and not reflect the real Catholic thought of the country.

The acceptance of the tragedy of civil war and its aftermath as the supreme sacrifice to cleanse the nation does not mean that since that date the hierarchy has been solid in support of every purely temporal policy. There are differences of opinion among the bishops, clergy, and laity regarding the Franco regime. Within such organizations as the *Asociación Nacional de Propagandistas Católicos,* made up of an unusually brilliant and competent group of professional men, there are those who have taken their stand firmly with the present regime, while others have preferred to retain their reservations, and in many cases are partisans of the immediate monarchical restoration with the return of Don Juan. There are discrepancies here as elsewhere as to how much politics should play their part in purely religious organizations.

One of the issues on which there was a clear divergence of viewpoint was the referendum of July 6, 1947, regarding the succession. Here was a practical political problem, of great interest to the Spanish people and of undoubted importance for the future of the Church. It is probable that practically all Spanish Catholics, with the exception of a very small minority, prefer the monarchy and are in favor of its restoration. The question of when that restoration is to come about, and in whose person, is another problem entirely. In this temporal order, it was not unnatural that the hierarchy should vary in its judgment. Nine Spanish bishops[4] issued pastorals or circular letters regarding the referendum; eighteen others reproduced the letter of the Cardinal Primate with commentary or a recommendation that it be taken into consideration by the faithful,[5] and a few simply reproduced the text with no comment of any kind;[6] while the rest said nothing at all. On this issue the Archbishop of Valladolid expressed himself in favor of an affirmative vote on the succession law as proposed by the government and the Archbishop of Valencia expressed his views to the priests of the archdiocese in the following words:

[4] Toledo, Valencia, Valladolid, Burgos, Orense, Salamanca, Tortosa, Badajoz, and Murcia.

[5] Ciudad Rodrigo, Jaén, Astorga Santander, Cádiz, Barbastro, Zamora, Orihuela, Vitoria, Mallorca, Menorca, Lugo, Ávila, Sigüenza, Lérida, Huesca, Cuenca, Madrid, León, and Palencia.

[6] Zaragoza, Granada, Barcelona, and Soria.

> You should be far removed and appear to be so removed from all worldly currents, from anything that divides the souls that God has confided to you. The Church is not political. The Church will never be political. May you never have the sorrow of knowing that souls have drifted away because of your temporal preferences. . . .

Regarding the Falange, it is well known that there are discrepancies among the hierarchy. The Bishop of Madrid-Alcalá, Dr. Leopoldo Eijo Garay, appears as an adviser of the National Council of the *Falange Española Tradicionalista y de la J.O.N.S.*[7]

The Cardinal Archbishop of Seville, His Eminence Pedro Segura Sáenz, forbade absolutely the customary inscription found in churches everywhere in Spain to José Antonio Primo de Rivera, founder of the Falange, and there have been cases of conflict within the archdiocese because of the Cardinal's dislike of the movement and its activities.

An extremely delicate point refers to the freedom of expression on the part of the hierarchy and clergy within the framework of the existing censorship. Technically all strictly Catholic publications are exempt from censorship; *Ecclesia,* official organ of Catholic Action, publishes what it pleases and does not follow the general press line laid down for the secular papers. Unfortunately there are cases of suppression, such as newspaper *Tu,* organ of the Young Catholic Workers Association, which was doing a first-class job in the field of social action among the working class.[8] In 1939, a pastoral letter of the Cardinal Primate, entitled *Lecciones de la guerra y deberes de la paz,* was forbidden to circulate by the censorship and His Eminence protested against this restriction in the name of the liberty of the Church:[9] "A Catholic State, by government authority, has prohibited rigorously and totally the publication of a pastoral letter of a prelate of the Church." Cardinal Segura announced, in 1949, that "as regards this Archdiocese, we have, in our files, irrefutable proof to show that repeatedly the same abuse has been perpetrated of refusing proper publicity to pastoral documents, not only outside the Archdiocese, but what is even worse, within it."[10]

The occasions on which the censorship was exercised is not without interest and is contained in the pages of the *Boletín* in the text of the Cardinal's admonition to the clergy and faithful:

---

[7] Fomento Social, *Guía de la vida social de España,* 1946, Madrid, p. 375.

[8] This suppression took place in November, 1949.

[9] *Boletín oficial eclesiástico del Arzobispado de Toledo,* Oct. 15, 1939, p. 309.

[10] *Boletín oficial eclesiástico del Arzobispado de Sevilla,* March 15, 1949, No. 1,554, pp. 212–213.

1. On September 8, 1947, a pastoral on the danger of Protestant propaganda. The General Press Office forbade its reproduction.

2. On December 14, 1948, a pastoral letter entitled "Alerta católicos! Peligro de contagio en el alma" was not allowed to be reproduced in the Spanish press or even in the local press of Seville. This was done by telephonic communication from the National Press Office. The National Radio was forbidden to mention it.

"These facts show in all clarity, a mistaken principle that cannot continue and which, in conscience, We must denounce: that of attributing to the State the right to prohibit, when it judges prudent, the publications of the pastorals of the prelates and the Holy See."[11]

The various attempts to interfere with the freedom of expression of the Catholic press and hierarchy have not meant that the principal pronouncements of the Holy Father failed to reach the Spanish public. It has commonly been stated that many of the major messages of the Supreme Pontiff have either been mutilated or passed over in silence.[12] To keep the record straight, it may be mentioned that the outstanding pontifical documents have all been made available to Spanish readers with the largest possible diffusion.

The conclusion is that there are diverse currents of thought on temporal matters within the Spanish Catholic Church although, in general, it is not inaccurate to say that the Church as a whole recognized that the National Movement was a necessary reaction to the chaos of the Republic and the descent into anarchy. The feeling of gratitude for the favorable policy of the State is tempered by a feeling of concern over certain cases of obstructionism and the overzealous desire of some of those in authority to curb the freedom of expression of the Church and her hierarchy. This does not necessarily mean opposi-

---

[11] *Ibid.*, pp. 213–214. His Eminence Enrique Cardinal Pla y Daniel, Archbishop of Toledo and Primate of Spain, stated in a pastoral letter on the eve of Catholic Press Day, June 29, 1950, that the Church had the right to an uncensored press. The Cardinal asserted: "If the Church is recognized as a perfect society, such as acknowledged by the Spanish state, she cannot be denied the right to have her own press; not only the ecclesiastic press (such as diocesan bulletins) . . . but also its apostolate of the press of doctrine and information, since in this epoch the manner in which information is presented has an important influence on readers . . . often practically more than doctrinal explanation itself. . . . He who defames or fails to acknowledge the legitimacy of the Catholic press, specifically as such, or who arbitrarily wishes to subject it to the state under a totalitarianism condemned by His Holiness Pope Pius XII in his recent discourse before the International Congress of Catholic journalists, is not in accord with the Church, though he may call himself a Catholic" (N.C.W.C. News Service, June 30, 1950).

[12] Francis McMahon, "Report on Spain," *New York Post,* Nov. 30, 1946.

tion to the regime or a desire for a drastic change now and at once. There is concern over the close connection between the two, inevitable perhaps in the circumstances, and the idea that if a breakdown should come the Church will suffer once more the vagaries of persecution. We find this best expressed in a letter of Don Juan to the Holy Father, dated July 9, 1947, in which the King states:

> On behalf of the true ends and spiritual interests of the Church, I would wish that the government of the Monarchy could work out with the Holy See a greater administrative separation between State and Church to the end, that for its own well being, the latter might be removed from political conflict.[13]

Spanish political affairs tend to operate in the same manner as a pendulum; from the extreme of persecution and confiscation, the trend reached the opposite extreme of an overzealous concern for the Church and a protection of its interests which often in the past became a form of dependency on the State. The Franco regime has unquestionably given full support to the reconstruction of the Spanish Church; the rehabilitation of churches, chapels, seminaries, and schools all over the country is one of the most remarkable features of this gigantic effort to efface the consequences of the burning and destruction of the period beginning in 1931. In Valencia alone, of the fourteen churches razed to the ground, thirteen have been rebuilt. In every town and village of the peninsula the evidence is there of the contribution of the State to the replacement of the edifices that had been eliminated. The State has spared no effort or expense to provide the Church with the resources necessary for its labor, although the financial arrangement now in existence provides only the most modest existence for the clergy.

The religious problem of modern Spain cannot be solved by the oversimplified contention that Church and State should separate, for it must be remembered that in human relations centuries of history are a positive and definite influence. It is easy to say that it would be better for the Church to go its own way, free of all State influence, interference, or control, although arrangement, which seems so ideally suited to the conditions in the United States or other countries similarly situated, cannot be created out of nothing. Tradition weighs very heavily on the Spanish Church and the Spanish mind and the fine distinction between the Church and politics, so easy to establish in theory, becomes hopelessly bogged down in the realities of Spanish

[13] Unpublished text of letter dated July 9, 1947.

life. The elements of temperament, to which we have referred so frequently in these pages, play a very large part in this problem.

The fear of a return to disorder, and the natural repugnance for a revival of the tragic days of destruction and incendiarism contribute to the preference for a slow, natural evolution, unmarked by hysteria and verbal pyrotechnics which might easily provoke a serious cleavage in contemporary Spain. There are mixed emotions too, such as the natural loyalty of the Spanish Church to the nation and the refusal to hamper its work in the midst of the perilous international situation through which it has traversed.

The Franco regime has made a definite play for Catholic support and one of the firmest supports in its program is its Catholic — or as its enemies say — its allegedly Catholic character. The commonly held idea that the Church needs Franco might more exactly be stated by asserting that the Franco regime needs the understanding of the Church. A French writer, dealing with this specific subject, comments: "Finally, it is not the Church that is attached to the Franco regime but the reverse, although it would seem that the Church has abandoned Franco and is moving gradually in another direction, undoubtedly toward a monarchy of the British type, to be introduced at some time hence."[14] The American newsman, Constantine Brown, states that the more conservative elements of the Church are against concessions to the religious minorities beyond those already in existence, since there is no evidence that these concessions would change United States policy toward the regime: "The Franco government, which cannot count on any friends among the principal western European governments, needs the support of even the most conservative members of the national Church. Its position might become seriously jeopardized if it does not yield to these elements without a counterpart of good will from America."[15]

The degree to which the Franco regime is Catholic is a moot point, for it is dangerous, obviously, to proclaim any single temporal regime as embodying all that the Church stands for as the ideal Christian society. There are vital elements within the regime which are strongly Catholic and nothing in the theory of the State is inherently opposed to Catholic teaching and this is accompanied by a respect for the Church and her beliefs which sets the tone for

---

[14] Georges Suffert, "L'Eglise, soutient-elle Franco?" in *Témoignage Chrétien,* Paris, No. 259, June 24, 1949.

[15] Constantine Brown in *Evening Star,* Washington, D. C., Nov. 28, 1949.

Spanish life. There are, on the other hand, elements which are less in consonance with the principles laid down by the pontiff's system of trade unions, which are not the *ideal* type of organization envisaged by the social teachings of the Church.

It may be well at this point to dwell on the social action of the Church. A very ancient bromide has it that the Spanish Church has always been a reactionary, obscurantist institution, devoid of the slightest impulse toward the social betterment of the masses. Emmet Hughes expresses it by speaking of the "failings and blindness of the Spanish Church in the last fifty years."[16] There is a long and dreary legend about a Spanish clergy belonging to the privileged classes and consequently unable to understand the yearnings and aspirations of the mass of people: "The Spanish clergy had made a political mistake understandable when we remember that they belong to the political oligarchy."[17] As a matter of fact, both in the past and at present, the bulk of the clergy springs from the peasant masses. One of the complaints of the Spaniards themselves is that too many of the clergy belong to the lower classes and are consequently intellectually unprepared for the task of social betterment. "That the clergy derive largely from the ranks of the people is one of the glories of the Church in Spain, for by the closeness of their contact with those whom they serve they are able to enter into their lives much more intimately than if they were drawn from the leisured classes and the aristocracy."[18]

The Spanish clergy has a long tradition of earthiness that would do credit to any country in the world. It is not the absence of understanding of the social question, but the precarious position under which the Church has lived for the past 150 years that has severely hampered it in this field. How would it have been possible to develop active and dynamic social programs under the conditions of persecution and ill will that prevailed from the end of the eighteenth century when the Church was barely able to keep alive and in operation, much less concern itself on a large scale with labor, the peasantry, the problems of industrialism, and the myriad other questions that the gradual economic transformation of the nation demanded? Moreover, the prevalence of a strong anticlericalism in the government during the critical nineteenth century was not conducive to a courageous and

---

[16] *Op. cit.*, p. 72.

[17] Charles Foltz, *The Masquerade in Spain* (Boston: Houghton Mifflin Co., 1948), p. 23.

[18] E. Allison Peers, *Spanish Tragedy*, Methuen & Co., Ltd., London, p. 41.

energetic social program which would have brought down on its head a still more severe condemnation and increased persecution.

The Church in the centuries before the persecution did not fail in this important task. "In the sixteenth and seventeenth centuries the Spanish Church had been, as I have said, a levelling institution. Its close connection with the State had given it an interest in social and political questions such as the Church in other Christian countries had never possessed."[19] The Spanish Liberal, Salvador de Madariaga, speaks of the Church at that time as "a great, noble and creative institution."[20] Acquaintance with the social legislation of the centuries preceding the late eighteenth reveals eloquently the constant and untiring effort of the Church to improve the social and economic status of those in misery or poverty.[21] There is a vast social literature in the eighteenth century which writers have either forgotten or never knew about, concerning the *cofradías* or brotherhoods, the *gremios,* and the variety of social action agencies and organizations which, in the spirit of the time, contributed to the alleviation of need and the reform of the social institutions that made that poverty possible.[22] The traditions of brotherhoods and primitive trade unions date back to the time of the *Siete Partidas* in Spain and it is estimated that some 26,000 of these voluntary associations flourished in Castile alone in 1770.[23] It was during the eighteenth century that Campoamor and Jovellanos attacked the *gremios* and weakened them in the name of industrial liberalism.

Space does not permit of an elaborate account of the historical development of Catholic social action. Both in the rural and industrial field there was considerable activity in the nineteenth century and up to the time of the civil war. In such areas as León and Valencia and many others — these two were particularly well developed — social organizations and unions flourished with very considerable results. The system of credit unions displayed striking vitality:

> Early in the century some enlightened members of the clergy realized the

---

[19] Brenan, *The Spanish Labyrinth,* p. 45, copyright, 1943, by The Macmillan Co. and used with their permission.

[20] Madariaga, *The Rise of the Spanish American Empire,* London, 1947, p. 143.

[21] A splendid collection of the social measures through the centuries is contained in the book of Luis Curiel, *Indice histórico de disposiciones sociales,* Madrid, 1946.

[22] Antonio Rumeu de Armas, *Historia de la previsión social en España Cofradías, gremios, hermandades montepíos,* Madrid, 1944. Especially Chapter XV sq., p. 275 sq.

[23] Madariaga, *Spain* (London: Jonathan Cape, 1943; New York: Creative Age Press, Inc., 1943), pp. 119–120.

social and political possibilities of this field. A campaign of propaganda, fostered by bishops and priests, led to the creation of not a few rural associations termed 'syndicates,' having for their main object the organization of rural credit. This was achieved by means of banks based on joint and unlimited liability, a system which, in the small area of the village, seems to work satisfactorily. The movement met with considerable success, and the sketch of a federation was first attempted in 1912, when the federation of Old Castile and León syndicates came into being. Others followed, until the whole country was covered by the *Confederación Nacional Católico-Agraria.*[24]

The influence of this organization may be judged by the fact that its deposits and loans reached 250 and 200 million pesetas respectively in 1926. The vigor of these Catholic rural life associations and the elaborate network of credit unions and other forms of rural aid can hardly be overestimated and one of the tragedies of today is that all of them have been forced out of existence. The civil war and the tendency toward centralization of the present government made it impossible for them to subsist. The consequence was that they either languished and disappeared, or were taken over by the official State agencies set up to care for the problem. It is a pity, for their vitality derived from their local, spontaneous character, rooted as they were in the soil of the provinces and frequently around the parish as the center. It was the perfect illustration of the principle of subsidiarity to which the Holy Father has so frequently referred in his pronouncements on social doctrine.

In the labor field, Catholic activity historically is not negligible despite imposing obstacles. During the middle of the nineteenth century, a number of Catholic trade unions came into existence along modern lines and in some of the provinces such as Navarre, Old Castile, and the Basque country they were extremely successful. A Jesuit priest, Father Vicent, was responsible as early as 1861 for the formation of Catholic unions, as the *Centros Católicos de Obreros* in Valencia, but it was not until 1910, with its main basis in the northern provinces that the *Consejo Nacional de las Corporaciones Católicas obreras* was formed, a more mutualist than orthodox trade union. In 1912 the *Federación Nacional de Sindicatos Católicos Libres* was established under the directions of Fathers Gerard and Gafo and up to 1923 their economic action was of the greatest importance as they represented genuine trade unions in the fullest sense of the word.

---

[24] *Ibid.*, pp. 116–117.

Needless to say the civil war ended all this, and with the new regime the vertical union was introduced with the abolition of all other forms.

But against this historical background, geared quite obviously to other conditions and times, the social thought of the Church today is by no means without interest. In the field of theory and doctrine Spanish production is very respectable. Such centers as *Fomento Social,* under Jesuit auspices, with its splendid review of the same name, represents one of the most significant contributions to social thinking in contemporary Spain and it provides a platform of the first importance for the airing of views and conceptions regarding current social problems.

It is absurd, of course, to summarize in a few brief lines the vast field of Catholic social thinking in Spain. One thing, however, is obvious, namely that there is a great deal of debate and discussion of these problems, both in theory and in practice. The questions of planned or directed economy, of liberalism and statism, of the participation of workers in the benefits of industry — all these are actively and sometimes violently thrashed out. I have experienced personally some of the gatherings at which the whole question of worker participation in the management and profits of the industrial enterprise was discussed with considerable vehemence and an astonishingly wide knowledge of trends abroad and the current literature on the subject.[25]

In a survey of this kind it is imperative to be selective, as these notes are not an examination of Catholic social action all over Spain.

---

[25] The bibliography is so extensive that only a few titles can be mentioned to indicate the variety of contemporary Spanish social writing. There are fundamental texts such as that by Severino Aznar, *Estudios económico-sociales,* Madrid, 1946; or that by José Larraz, *La meta de dos revoluciones,* Madrid, 1946, an excellent statement by a former finance minister, in which he condemns the two extremes of economic liberalism and super-State control. It is amusing to note that Dr. Larraz did not hesitate to condemn the prevalent doctrine of statism in vogue in Spain, and, as finance minister, he excluded from the budget the entire appropriation for the *Falange.* Needless to say he did not long remain in his post. Add to this the large number of works from the pen of Father Joaquín Azpiazu, S.J., all of them of first-rate value. Incidentally it may be mentioned that one of the most admirably complete editions of the Encyclicals, both social and others, is that of Spanish Catholic Action, Madrid, 1942. The full index and superb organization of the texts makes it almost unique among the collections in any language. Parenthetically it may be said that the idea that *Mit Brennender Sorge* was never allowed to be published in Spain is disproved by its inclusion in full in this collection under the prologue of the Cardinal Archbishop of Toledo, dated July 11, 1942, when the Axis was still very far from defeated. The text in 1937, the year of its appearance (March 14), was published in Spain in various newspapers in the nationalist zone, including the *Diario de Navarra,* Pamplona, and *El Norte de Castilla,* Valladolid.

In every Spanish city and particularly in the larger ones there are a number of corporations and organizations devoted to social action in one form or another. In Barcelona one finds an excellent center for clerks and employees engaged in shops and business houses; in Madrid a workers' center where a form of extension training is offered to members of the working class. In Santander, Oviedo, Zaragoza, and elsewhere there are other enterprises of the same nature. It would be tedious to outline the function and operation of each of them. Suffice it to note several specific projects now going on, which will illustrate the kind of work that is being accomplished under Catholic auspices.

The social and economic organization of the Archdiocese of Valencia is one of the most remarkable achievements in Spain. It may be due in part to the fact that the present Archbishop is a Salesian and is himself of the most humble origin. The situation in this archdiocese at the end of the civil war was particularly difficult, for the destruction had been widespread and the life of the community badly disorganized. With authorization of the Holy See the Archbishop launched a campaign for a loan of ten million pesetas with a bond issue. The enterprise has functioned so effectively that today the archdiocesan bonds are quoted on a par with those of the province and municipality of Valencia. The idea was to channel off for spiritual purposes funds which otherwise would have gone into public or some form of private investment. The archdiocese has established the *Banco de Nuestra Señora de los Desamparados* for the effective and equitable distribution of alms, aid to the needy, and for the numerous projects for which the funds from the loan are to be utilized. A special branch of the bank has been set up to carry out a housing project, in which the Archbishop is particularly interested. In June, 1948, the first stone was laid in the initial construction project located in the Patraix suburb of Valencia and which will include at completion 276 low-priced houses for workers and lower middle-class families. In a single year half of these proposed houses were already constructed, and with this success a second group in the Tendetes suburb was started to include 160 houses of a similar type. More than a hundred of these are partially completed. On November 27, 1949, the first two hundred houses ready for occupancy were turned over to the most needy on the basis of a drawing. On this same date, the first stone was laid for two new housing projects, in San Marcelino and Nuestra Señora del Puig, the former of these two to embrace 500 houses, with parish and school. The intention is that this fund will, within two years, be used to construct over a thousand houses at an investment of fifty million pesetas. The total financing scheme is extremely complex and depends on donations, reduced payments from the beneficiaries, and loans negotiated both privately and through public agencies by the archdiocesan office created for that purpose. One of the features is that the Archbishop has created a regular office of economic affairs to put the entire archdiocese on a completely self-supporting, businesslike basis. On March 8, 1948, the Archbishop established the *Instituto social del Arzobispado* for the diffusion of a knowledge of social doctrine and to seek the most effective means within the archdiocese for its application.[26]

Bishop Angel Herrera of Málaga has received more publicity possibly than any other prelate, for his career lends itself particularly to public interest. As a former lawyer and director of the great Catholic daily, *El Debate,* Herrera was one of the most influential laymen in republican Spain. In 1935 he retired to Fribourg in Switzerland to study for the priesthood and was ordained in 1940, taking up his work afterward in Santander, his native city. In 1947 he was consecrated Bishop of Málaga. He could not have been appointed to a more miserable and poverty-stricken diocese with spiritual and social needs of the most acute sort. This extraordinarily vital and dynamic prelate has created a number of important projects. Perhaps the most significant is his *Escuela Social Sacerdotal.*[27]

On October 12, 1947, when he took possession of the diocese, Bishop Herrera announced the establishment of the Priests' School as one of the main points in his program, for he was bent on forming a socially conscious clergy. The founder of *El Debate,* former President of Spanish Catholic Action, founder of the *Editorial Católica* and the *Asociación Nacional de Propagandistas Católicos* was no visionary. He was long trained in practical matters and quite aware of the difficulties in the way of success. On January 11, 1948, the school began its work in Málaga.[28]

The course of study embraces three principal divisions: economics, sociology, and law; emphasis is placed on modern languages, and it is interesting to observe in the articles of foundation that "English is so obvious a necessity for those engaged in the social field as to require

[26] *Ecclesia,* April 24, 1948, No. 354, p. 8, with the full text of the announcement of the Institute.

[27] See account, under heading "Religion," of Bishop Herrera in *Time,* March 28, 1949.

[28] *Ecclesia,* March 6, 1948, No. 347, pp. 5–6, with full details of the project, courses, and decree setting up the institution.

no defense." The Bishop wishes his priests to be fully cognizant not only of the general nature of communism, but the methods, procedures, and *modus operandi* of left-wing extremism.

The entire course lasts two years, divided into four semesters of four months each as a minimum. The purpose is to prepare priests specifically for social action and it is anticipated that after the conclusion of their courses they will serve as advisers, directors of social centers, workers' institutes, and the like. Their studies are envisaged as the preparation of specialists, both in theory and practice for future leadership in the Catholic social movement in Spain.

The initiative taken in the diocese of Málaga promises to start a whole chain of similar projects in the country. The special blessing of the Holy Father was extended to this effort, in a letter from the Papal Nuncio, Mons. Cayetano Cicognani to Bishop Herrera, on June 18, 1948. In the diocese of Vitoria a Social School for Priests has been set up in direct contact with Málaga.[29] In Oviedo, on a slightly more limited basis, a similar school has been instituted for recently ordained priests. The Spanish cardinals in conference approved a statement urging the creation of schools of this type along the lines of Bishop Herrera's initiative. This statement is of importance since there is an idea that Bishop Herrera stands alone, condemned in his enterprise by his fellow bishops, and quite definitely a *vox clamantis in deserto.* The Pontifical University of Comillas, near Santander, organized a special institute on social matters for priests during 1949, and in September of the same year the Pontifical University of Salamanca held a similar institute on social and economic problems, attended by some hundred clergy and religious from all over Spain. The conclusion of these efforts was the creation of a special Episcopal Commission for Social Action, whose purpose is to encourage institutes, congresses, social weeks, training schools, and the general effective participation of the Church in the social betterment of the Spanish people.

Were there sufficient space for the detailed description of other enterprises, mention might be made of the remarkable housing project undertaken by the Bishop of Córdoba, along lines similar to those mentioned in the case of Valencia. The practical results in Córdoba have been excellent, with a large number of dwellings actually in the hands of their tenants. In Santander, in the north of Spain, one of the

[29] *Ecclesia,* July 3, 1948, No. 364, p. 6, describing the establishment of the new school in Vitoria with a program identical with that of Málaga.

most interesting Catholic social experiments is that of an entire fishermen's village, created under circumstances that will permit the moral and social rehabilitation of one of the most neglected sectors of the Spanish population. I visited this village in 1947. It is a complete community along the most modern lines with every facility for the protection of the family, the education of the children, and the stable life which under circumstances heretofore prevailing has been an impossibility. In Santander also is to be found the *Escuela Oficial de Aprendices,* or trade school. The Young People's Catholic organization of Santander conceived the need in 1942 for a night school for workers and in conjunction with other bodies similarly interested, the school was actually inaugurated in December of 1943 with 103 students. Since then it has become one of the most effective professional and spiritual agencies among the working class in Santander.

Mention might be made, too, of the movement of workers attached to Catholic Action. An enthusiastic and eager group of young men has made possible a movement known as the *Hermandad Obrera de Acción Católica.* Although only recently formed, the organization has made considerable impact on the working class, especially the younger workers. Unhappily, as indicated elsewhere, its energetic and outspoken newspaper *Tu* has been suppressed. The reason of its suppression is one of the delicate points in the present-day Spanish situation, because the various social action branches of Falange have long conceived all social action as pre-eminently their task. In Chapter 13 reference was made to the structure and actual accomplishment of the organization in this field. Since it is entirely State supported and forms a part of the system of State aid, there is a tendency to look upon anything initiated under Catholic auspices, outside Falange, as trespassing on a field already marked off for the latter.

The Catholic employers have organized a movement known as *Acción Patronal,* and publish an active paper of the same name. In thumbing through numerous issues, it is remarkable to observe the frank manner in which the social question is dealt with by bishops and members of the clergy. This particular section of Catholic Action insists on the need for facing the social problem openly and courageously. It reveals a remarkable high degree of social consciousness in its approval of the various study weeks of the workers' movement; its applause in every case of an industrial enterprise which conforms in its management and treatment of workers to Christian social principles. In the issue of *Acción Patronal* of June, 1947, we find a detailed article in which the *Industria Española del Jabón,* operating in Navalcarnero, is singled out for praise for the enlightened way it operates with lunchrooms, clinic, sports field, and circulating library for its employees.

Many of the publications of these various Catholic social action groups are the most outspoken expression of dissatisfaction with existing conditions to be found anywhere. I would suggest that those who believe that no criticism of any kind is permitted in Spain not limit themselves to the daily press but seek out the more specialized journals, reviews, and magazines, and particularly those that concern themselves with social and economic problems. *Acción Patronal* denounces in large headlines in its issue of July, 1947, that "The unfortunate masses are suffering in complete neglect in miserable hovels in the suburban areas." This publication unhesitatingly denounces the Latas sector of Madrid where it is claimed infant mortality reaches 45 per cent, and almost every resident lives under subnormal conditions.

There is a pronounced social trend in Spain as indicated by the above cases and is the answer to the eternal skeptics who see nothing in Spain but impenetrable medievalism. The Cardinal Primate expressed himself as convinced that "a Church restricting itself to liturgical functions, a silent Church such as its enemies would like to see, cannot accomplish the mission entrusted to her," repeating the words of the Holy Father.[30] The voice of the Church has been raised against the land system, particularly in Andalucía, urging that steps be taken to alleviate the misery of the landless.[31]

A word as to Catholic Action, for Spain is one of the countries in which official Catholic Action is most highly developed in organization. Its structure is clear and logical, its branches well defined, and its functions capably mapped out. Its function as the lay apostolate has come in recently for considerable attack. Emmet Hughes seems obsessed by the idea that Catholic Action is the legitimate and direct heir of *Acción Popular,* and the C.E.D.A.[32] The broad purpose of Catholic

---

[30] Quoted in dispatch of Francisco Luis to N.C.W.C. News Service, June 6, 1949, and delivered at the Ninth Social Week in Spain.

[31] Canon Juan Font del Riego of the *Patronato de la Sagrada Familia* in Córdoba attacked the problem of the large landholdings with vigor and clarity during the social week. Bishop Herrera proposed a solution to the land problem in an address to twenty-five landowners at Antequera. His conclusion was, "I find it very difficult to think, and I am using a soft word, that the present system of large estates can endure in Andalucía" (*Boletín oficial del Obispado de Málaga,* May–June, 1948).

[32] Hughes, *op. cit.,* pp. 60–61. He develops the idea further that the designation of

Action, in Spain as elsewhere, clearly does not need to be restated, for in essence it is simply the lay apostolate at the service of the hierarchy for the attainment of the end for which the hierarchy itself exists; the spiritual conquest of men for Christ.[33] The Spanish hierarchy in numerous pronouncements has emphasized its importance and urged affiliation with it by every Catholic capable of doing so.

The history of contemporary Spanish Catholic Action dates roughly to 1876 in the days of Cardinal Moreno of Toledo, whose purpose was to repair the moral ruin provoked by the civil strife of the nineteenth century and organize all Catholics into a solid bloc that would rise above the political differences that separated them in the temporal order. On January 29, 1881, the statutes of the *Unión de los Católicos de España* was promulgated. The organization was duly constituted and received the blessing of His Holiness Leo XIII. Unfortunately the movement did not endure, divided primarily by the political differences between the Catholics themselves, as there was a marked tendency to identify Catholic interests with a particular political group.[34] Pope Leo XIII, in the Encyclical *Cum Multa* (December 8, 1882), urged that religion and politics be kept distinct and that great care be taken to avoid the danger of "considering as virtually separated from Catholicism everyone who belongs to another party."

The failure of the *Unión* led to further efforts; in 1889 the first national Catholic congress was held in Madrid under the aegis of the then Bishop Sancha of Madrid-Alcalá and in succeeding years congresses were held in various parts of Spain, notably in Zaragoza (1890), Seville (1892), Tarragona (1894), Burgos (1899), and Santiago de Compostela (1902). On April 22, 1903, Pope Leo XIII addressed his *Quos Nuper* to Cardinal Sancha in which he reiterated his fervent desire for the unity of Spanish Catholics and the stimulation of concerted action on their part.[35] After the Tarragona congress in 1894, the

---

Alberto Martín Artajo as Foreign Minister was a clever move to bring Catholic Action into camp and make it the principal support of the Franco regime. Hughes stresses the same point in his report to *Time* (June 23, 1947) in which he speaks of the "supposedly nonpolitical Catholic Action group."

33 The most complete treatise on Catholic Action in general and Spanish Catholic Action in particular is Zacarías de Vizcarra, *Curso de Acción Católica,* 3 ed., Madrid, 1947.

34 Cardinal Reig, *Principios y bases de reorganización de la Acción Católica española,* Toledo, 1926, p. 64: "For many people it was difficult, in the concrete circumstances of the country, not to identify Catholic unity and Spanish tradition with specific political parties."

35 *Actes de Léon XIII,* Paris, n.d., Vol. VII, pp. 162–164.

Junta Central of Catholic Action was set up with members designated by the bishops of Spain. The leading personality in this effort was the famous Marqués de Comillas, Claudio López, who directed its destinies for over thirty years. The year 1894 was also the date of the formation of the labor and rural groups to which passing reference has already been made. Cardinal Aguirre, in 1910, laid down the general rules that were to guide the action of the Catholic groups. Catholic Action at this time was somewhat ambiguous, since it was apparent from the criteria of the Cardinal that he had in mind primarily social action rather than the broader field of the lay apostolate with which modern Catholic Action has become identified.

Under Cardinal Guisasola the modern form of Catholic Action began to take shape. He founded the *Acción Católica de la Mujer* (1919) and the two major labor or social action groups. Cardinal Almaraz founded the *Juventud Católica* (1924). The Marqués de Comillas was eager to reform the whole organization and insisted on the need for an institution similar to that which had been created in the Netherlands and for a social action comparable to the one recently formed in Italy. It was the Marqués who urged that the proper diocesan and parochial groups be constituted under the national body or general direction. Under Cardinal Reig the contemporary form of Catholic Action was set up; the men's division took the name of the *Junta Central de Acción Católica masculina;* the women's, *Junta Central de Acción Católica feminina,* and a national board was set up to represent both organizations. The new form was based not on individual members designated by the hierarchy, but on the representatives of Catholic associations or organizations in existence which were affiliated with Catholic Action. It was under Cardinal Segura, during the brief period that he occupied the see of Toledo, that Spanish Catholic Action became a strong and well-integrated organization. As soon as the civil war was concluded, Cardinal Gomá undertook the reorganization of Catholic Action in a series of meetings held at Toledo in May, 1939, and the result was the establishment of the general directing board, the *Junta Técnica Nacional,* or executive secretariate, and the four classic branches of contemporary Catholic Action: men and women, young men and young women. The main feature of the new orientation is the insistence on strong parochial and diocesan organization, without obstruction to the development of a sound national entity. The men's branch of Catholic Action was the last to be formed, although its absence had been covered in part by the *Asociaciones de Padres de Familia,* an active and important group whose primary aim was the defense of the family.

The structure of Catholic Action today represents a nice balance between a thoroughly national organization, yet with roots in the diocesan and parochial life of the country. The mechanism is the following:

Junta Suprema: Under the presidency of the Cardinal Primate with representatives of the Conference of Bishops. The Cardinal is the representative of the other Bishops in the supreme direction of Catholic Action.

Dirección Central: This is defined as the superior directing and coordinating agency of Catholic Action on a national scale. It is charged with the execution of the decisions of the *Junta Suprema.* The membership under the chairmanship of the Cardinal Primate consists of the ecclesiastical advisor, a priest secretary, a law executive director and two other members named by the Primate.

Junta Técnica Nacional: The executive activity of the whole organization depends on the Supreme Council of each of the four branches and the technical or executive secretariate, under the name of the *Junta Técnica.* It is the law body essentially and concerns itself with those tasks that do not specifically fall under the jurisdiction of each of the four branches. It brings together a large number of laymen and women and the representatives of numerous specialized branches within the general framework of Catholic Action.

Los Consejos Superiores de Rama: These are the governing bodies of each of the four branches.

Junta diocesana: Each diocese has its own directing board and secretariate. Under this comes the parochial organization.

There are numerous other Catholic bodies either affiliated with Catholic Action or co-operating with it. It is impossible to list their numerous activities or even the names of all of them. They include, by way of example, the *Confederación Católica Nacional de Padres de Familia; Federación Católica de Maestros Españoles* (Teachers' Association); *Confederación de Congregaciones Marianas; Conferencias de S. Vicente de Paúl* (St. Vincent de Paul societies); *Hermandades profesionales católicas* (the numerous professional associations such as physicians, pharmacists, architects, and the like), and numerous others.

A striking form of religious revival in Spain has been the formation of such institutes as the *Opus Dei.* This lay organization, whose full title is "Sacerdotal Society of the Holy Cross and the Work of God," was founded in Madrid in 1928 by Mons. José María Escriva de Balaguer. Since the conclusion of the civil war it has made great strides in the country and was formally approved by the Holy See on June 16, 1950. One of the major undertakings of this lay apostolate has been to penetrate Spanish university life and restore spiritual and traditional values within the classroom and in the laboratory. The institute has attracted a large number of outstanding intellectuals whose influence is becoming extremely important within the academic life of the country.

The history of Spanish Catholic Action does not reveal at any stage the slightest inclination to become involved in partisan politics. In the regulations it is stated that:

> The Association excludes all political action from the field of its activities, without neglecting because of that the rights of God and His Church wherever they may be attacked.
>
> To avoid confusion, the directors and active workers of the Association cannot at the same time participate actively in political life, even on a personal basis.[36]

When Alberto Martín Artajo, president of Spanish Catholic Action, was designated as Minister of Foreign Affairs, he resigned immediately from Catholic Action and since then has not engaged in any activity connected with the organization and so careful were the directors of Catholic Action to avoid the accusation of politics, that Alfredo López, the president, did not attend the ceremony when Martín Artajo took office. There was considerable discrepancy within Catholic Action regarding the acceptance by its former president of a high government position, a difference of opinion that sprang precisely from the fear of many that it would be interpreted as a political move and might involve Catholic Action in active support of the present regime. On the nonpolitical nature of Catholic Action I can speak with considerable personal knowledge, for in the spring and early summer of 1947 I visited every corner of Spain for the purpose of lecturing under the auspices of Spanish Catholic Action. In the course of three months of constant travel and contact with perhaps fifty to sixty local and diocesan bodies, I had the opportunity of learning something of the sentiments of the members of the various groups. Two conclusions became clear in the course of this sojourn; the first that everyone in Catholic Action was leaning over backward to avoid anything that touched politics and never once, in dozens of public lectures, did the

---

36 *Reglamento general de la Asociación de los hombres de la Acción Católica,* Toledo, 1945, 3 ed., Chap. I, art. 2, p. 4.

presiding officer or anyone else ever make the slightest mention of the regime, of General Franco, or of the possible support by Catholic Action of the *status quo;* the second conclusion, from innumerable conversations with members of every conceivable variety, was that there was no meeting of minds whatever among them on the question of the regime. There were some who were ardently pro-Franco; others indifferent; others who were opposed to the regime. There were monarchists of the Don Juan persuasion, others of the Carlist, and still others who preferred the present state of affairs. There were critics of Franco who did not conceal their antagonism. There were others to whom he was the savior of Spain from the anarchy of Marxism. The general conclusion is that Spanish Catholic Action is seeking primarily to do the job for which it was created, namely, collaboration with the hierarchy on the part of the laity in winning souls for Christ. I must confess that instead of political interference and instead of serving as a kind of party façade for the regime, my own conviction is that Catholic Action is doing everything in its power to avoid this contingency and to date has succeeded remarkably well.

Chapter 16. RELIGIOUS MINORITIES

1. THE PROTESTANTS

THE Spaniard who may discover this book will undoubtedly be surprised that attention is devoted to a problem which to him scarcely exists: Protestantism in Spain. Protestantism is as alien to Spain as Buddhism or Islam to England and the United States. It never penetrated the peninsula to an appreciable degree, never became rooted, and remains an experience quite outside the normal experience of the Spaniard. There is reason to believe that this problem has been whipped up in part because it strikes a sensitive chord in the Anglo-American conscience and serves as a very useful instrument for the promotion of the consistent campaign against Spain. For some years, before the Protestant "persecution" was discovered, it was the alleged mistreatment of good "democrats" which evoked scandalized protests from all over the world. Now that the majority of these democratic stalwarts have been shown to respond to the dictates of the exiled Spanish Communist Party and its front organizations, it seems wise to place the emphasis on another matter, and one which, if true, is capable of arousing considerable sympathy abroad.

There is no real Protestant problem in Spain and there never has been. A Protestant writer, Stanley I. Stuber, writing in *The Christian Advocate,* relates some of his impressions of the situation in the country: "It was impressed upon me strongly, especially as I viewed the famous cathedral in comparison with our little Protestant chapels, that in Spain, the Protestant faith is an alien religion, living at the very mercy of the Roman Catholic hierarchy and the Franco dictatorship."[1] That Protestantism is an alien religion in Spain is absolutely true. The full truth of this observation is perhaps not realized by the Protestant minister who made the statement. It is precisely this alien quality

[1] *The Christian Advocate,* Chicago, Ill., Vol. 124, No. 26, June 30, 1949.

of Protestantism that is the cause of so much of the friction that comes from the persistent effort of evangelical missionaries to obtain a foothold in the land. The number of active Protestants in all Spain is so small as to be negligible. If one eliminates the Protestants of foreign origin, with their own chapels such as the one attached to the British embassy in Madrid or the Swiss community in Barcelona, the number of Spanish Protestants who work at their religion is a mere handful. Granted that this mere handful has rights which the majority must respect, it is not strange that the Spanish State and the dominant Catholic Church have failed to operate in terms of the problem posed by the existence of this infinitesimal minority. Governments and institutions legislate for and concern themselves with those whose presence is at least visible. No one insists that the United States government take special cognizance of the Moslem minority in the country, or make special concessions to the end that Islam may not be hampered in its free expression, for the retort of anyone to such a proposal would be that the number of Moslems does not warrant any such attention.

One finds disconcerting the literal army of American observers, who visit Spain and discover that the Protestants are forced to live as second-rate citizens under virtual ghetto conditions. The American journalist, Homer Bigart, a Pulitzer prize winner, has given us the alleged story of Protestants in Spain in the most lurid language. To him, the Spanish Protestant is a second-rate citizen, deprived of almost all the ordinary liberties of humankind: "He cannot hold official position in the Government, nor can he rise to an officer's rank in the army, unless he conceals his religious beliefs. He is not allowed to practice his faith in public. The chapel he attends must not display any exterior evidence that it is a place of worship. It cannot advertise its existence, not even with a bulletin board. It cannot be listed in the public directories." To this litany of misery is added the statement that the Protestant clergy in Spain suffer much the same type of persecution that the Catholic clergy undergoes in communist Hungary. Not only that, but Bigart assures us that "the same fear motivates both oppressions. As in Hungary, where the Catholic Church is regarded as the most dangerous enemy of the Red dictatorship, so in Spain the Protestants are looked upon as an evil force bent on disrupting the existing order, the Spanish way of life."[2]

---

[2] *Report on Spain,* as published in the *St. Louis Post Dispatch,* Feb. 23, 1949.

It is inconceivable, indeed, that a penetrating and conscientious observer should discover an exact analogy between the situation of Protestants in Spain and the massive, ruthless persecution to which the Catholic hierarchy, clergy, and faithful in Hungary have been submitted. We have yet to learn of fake treason trials of Protestant leaders in Spain nor does one find evidence that Protestant clergy are imprisoned for alleged sedition. The fact that there have been a number of *popular* manifestations of anti-Protestant feeling in Spain is very far from evidence that there is a concerted, conscious, intentional persecution with the full weight of the State behind it. Let it be remembered, too, that Protestants are not entirely without responsibility on this score. The attitude expressed in almost every piece of evangelical writing on the subject is that of hostility and loathing of the government in Spain and of the Catholic Church. So-called Protestant missionary activity is carried on with hatred of Spanish institutions and of the faith that has been that of the Spanish people for centuries. It is a repetition of the same thing that Catholics in Hispanic America have found so tiresome: blatant charges of idolatry and superstition; aspersions on the devotion to our Blessed Lady; attacks on the clergy and the "reactionary" hierarchy. How then is it surprising that Spain, having come through a civil war during which the existence of its religious institutions were threatened, should not find this new annoyance from outside a source of irritation? With an estimated 15 per cent of the British people churchgoers and perhaps 50 per cent of the Americans with no religious affiliation at all, it seems strange indeed that Protestant money, energy, and time should be spent to bring so-called enlightenment to Spain.

The whole issue is cluttered up with wild accusations and assumptions which show the crassest ignorance of the facts of Catholic life. In Stuber's article, from which I have quoted, it is contended that "The Roman Catholic position in Spain (as it is everywhere else, when Catholics are in the majority) is that this Church is the only true church and is, therefore, the only one entitled to liberty. Freedom of religion is a necessary evil which must be tolerated for the time being only when it prevents greater evils." This extraordinary contention errs on several counts. In the first place, it is high time that Spain as the absolute synonym of Catholicism be discarded. This writer, as well as others who devote so much time and hysteria to beating the drums in the so-called Church-State issue, might examine the situation of countries like French Canada, Eire, or the Catholic cantons of

Switzerland, where Catholic majorities are so absolute that if they willed — in a perfectly democratic fashion — they could rule absolutely. Protestants are undisturbed in each instance and enjoy not only a tolerance as minorities but actual proportional — and sometimes more than proportional — representation in government and public administration.

The charge that Protestants in Spain are second-class citizens and that a world issue ought to be made of it sounds very strange from writers and journalists in the United States who have at home some of the most flagrant cases of second-class citizenry. By the same logic used to denounce the Spanish for the restrictions on their handful of Protestants, Spanish journalists might insist that diplomatic ties with Washington be further curtailed because of the iniquitous restrictions on Negroes in plain violation of the constitution. In practice we have second-class citizens all over the land. Negroes certainly cannot aspire to any number of places in our society. And a Catholic — as we learned in 1928 — had best not seek the presidency. A Catholic in politics in any number of our states has an exceedingly rough time of it as popular *mores* and attitudes make it impossible for him, for religious reasons, to make a success of such a career. I venture, too, that in the public school systems of numerous American states, a Catholic teacher, who pronounces himself as such, would not be particularly favored by the local school boards. The talk of "second-class citizens" and the like becomes in this as in so many cases, sheer hypocrisy and the shoddiest of reasoning.

There is another aspect of this problem, more difficult perhaps to explain but which is essential if an understanding of Spain is to be attained. The present Spanish regime, as well as many of those that preceded it, construes religion as one of the great unifying forces of the nation. At the risk of repetition, the importance of this conception must be restated. The economic inequalities, the regionalism, the violent temperament of the Hispanic people, all of these are curbed and softened by the influence of a common faith and practice, reaching far back to the beginnings of Spanish history. This common heritage is looked upon — for good or for ill — as a very precious thing and one that must be preserved. The horrible experience of the Second Republic with its grotesque secularism and violent anticlericalism demonstrated that if wide religious differences became prevalent, one new element of clash and of conflict would be added to the caldron of vitriolic peninsular life. Moreover, if Spain possesses today a relative unity on the religious issue, what positive advantage is there to introduce doctrinal confusion and denominational squabbling? If the evangelicals who are so bent on converting Spain do not believe that Catholicism is necessarily wrong, then they have no justification for messing about in the religious life of the Spanish people. If, on the other hand, they believe Catholicism wrong and propose to make an issue of it, certainly the Spanish Church is fully and completely justified in resisting and making it clear that it does not intend to allow the challenge to go unanswered. The Protestant churches in Spain have always been largely the handiwork of foreigners. So great was foreign influence — which is another way of saying how un-Spanish evangelical Christianity is — that in the early days of the Second Republic when it was decreed that foreigners should not be ministers of churches or heads of congregations, Protestantism suffered very greatly from this restriction.[3]

The modern mind, and very singularly the American mind, finds it impossible to grasp the desirability even of religious unity. Political conformism has become so ingrained in the thinking of our people that anything else appears as subsidiary and inconsequential. It seems to Americans quite proper to spend 36 weeks trying before the courts the leaders of the American Communist Party for proposing to overthrow the existing government. Denazification of the defeated Germans became a moral obligation. They had to be purged of the improper political thinking that had led to the catastrophe and re-educated in the acceptable democratic spirit and ideas. Democracy becomes, then, a form of unity and a rallying cry for the nation. We have a congressional commission whose diligence is widely recognized in ferreting out un-American and undemocratic movements, activities, and incidents. What precisely constitutes this "un-American" activity? It means a deviation of proportions from the standard of political conduct we have set up as a nation. I am not arguing here, obviously, whether this is good or bad. I merely suggest that a nation — any nation — has to have some criteria for its national unity. In some cases it may be political institutions; in others it may be in part, at least, religion. It happens that the unifying force in Spain, more than politics, economics, or social institutions, is religion, and in this case it means specifically the Holy, Roman, Catholic, and Apostolic Church. Conformity to

[3] Araujo, García, and Grubb, Kenneth, *Religion in the Republic of Spain,* London, 1933, p. 51. This survey of the Protestant situation in Spain emphasizes how hard hit the evangelicals were by this restriction on the ministry of non-nationals.

tradition in the spiritual field may therefore be conceived as fundamental to the common good of Spain as devotion to democracy in the defense of the American way of life. This sense of religious unity is to the Spanish as vital and significant as that of unity about a commonly recognized manner of living together politically to us.

On this score, it would seem that the major responsibility of the American approaching the Spanish situation is a willingness to consider the possibility of different values from those that we set up in this country as the *sine qua non* of national well-being. The Spanish have never been wedded to a constitution, to a form of government, or to a political arrangement in the same manner as Americans. The place of religion is an entirely different thing in the Hispanic scheme of things from that prevalent in many other western countries. Is this insistence that religion does have a place in national life something bizarre and queer?

Now the assumption seems to be on the part of many of these non-Catholic critics, that unless Protestantism has full and absolute freedom for any activity it proposes, there is no real freedom of religion. By the same logic, Catholics might insist that steps be taken to protect Catholic minorities in certain of the predominantly Protestant countries from the horrors of second-rate citizenship and restrictions on their absolute freedom of action. If the treatment of Protestants in Spain is to be deplored then I insist that the case of the Catholics in Sweden ought to merit a word.[4] Sweden passes, quite properly, for one of the reasonably advanced countries of the West. Its institutions are generally accepted as democratic and the conduct of its government has never left it open to severe criticism from abroad. Certainly no one — Catholic or otherwise — has ever suggested that the American diplomatic representative in Stockholm be removed. However the facts are there for anyone to see. No Catholic can teach in the public primary school of the nation. No Catholic may become a member of the Council of State of the kingdom. If two Swedish Catholics marry, they must have the banns read the customary number of times in a Lutheran parish. If a Swedish Catholic goes abroad he must have a certificate of good conduct from a Lutheran pastor. If a Swede decides to enter the Catholic Church, he must announce this intention

[4] An excellent account of this situation is contained in *La Croix,* Paris, Nov. 7, 1947, from the observation of M. Benoit Braun who made a protracted visit to the Scandinavian countries. See also *L'Eglise Catholique en Suède,* Malines (Belgium), 1937.

in the Lutheran parish. The Catholic Church cannot, without specific approval, acquire property. Convents and monasteries are prohibited by law. It will be said that, after all, the number of Swedish Catholics is so small that it really makes little difference. The Swedish Catholics are more or less as numerous as the Spanish Protestants. How, then, can the critics of Spain become so incensed by the terrible sufferings of their coreligionists there and have no concern, if they are interested in religious liberty, in the status of Catholics in Sweden? It may be submitted that the present situation of Swedish Catholics is not the most completely democratic or in accordance with the precepts of the fullest religious liberty. There is, of course, an explanation for this state of affairs. The Protestant reform in Sweden brought with it repressive measures. Many of them have been abolished and those subsisting probably will be. Some of them, such as those mentioned, subsist and form a part of the Swedish legislation of today. There is the common notion that Catholicism is an alien thing, out of step with the Swedish way of life, and quite foreign to the spirit and temper of the people. In part this is true. It is the reverse of the Spanish situation.

In democratic Switzerland, where the reign of law and the will of the majority are hailed as almost perfect, there are serious restrictions on Catholics. Article 50 of the Federal Constitution provides that no diocese shall be erected without the consent of the Confederation. Article 51 stipulates that "the Jesuit Order and groups affiliated with it cannot exist in any part of Switzerland and all activity inside the Church as well as in teaching, is forbidden." This restriction can be extended to any religious community judged by the State to be dangerous or to contribute to unrest among the various religious groups. Article 52 states that no new religious communities shall be established nor shall those once suppressed be re-established. These are very precise limitations on one particular religious group, and the one, incidentally, representing 40 per cent of the Swiss people.

It may be added too that the disquietude felt in some circles about the close union of Church and State is no better exemplified than in countries like Sweden, Norway, Denmark, and Great Britain. The close association of the Church and State in Spain has often been pointed out as a threat to the freedom of the Church. Needless to say, real union of Church and State does not exist in Spain at all and cannot exist in a Catholic country. The fact that in Sweden the head of the State and of the Lutheran Church is the same person represents a far more complete fusion of the two authorities than anything existent in Spain.

How do the Spanish themselves look on this problem? A fairly adequate statement comes from the pen of the Spanish Jesuit, Father Constantino Bayle, who writes in reply to a Scandinavian criticism that Protestants are persecuted in the peninsula. This criticism is characterized by a contention that, in order to achieve a place of some prominence in the present administration, daily Communion is almost a requisite. Father Bayle deals with the absurdity of any religious condition for office. Spanish legislation, says this well-known priest, cannot be expected to take into account every tiny minority within the national frontiers, any more than in Iceland Catholics are considered an important element of the population. It is untrue that the Spanish State requires any proof of Catholicism for the holding of a public post. It is true that a militant Protestant could probably not rise very high in the public service. Nor could a militant Catholic in Norway for the same reasons.

The accusation that it is legally impossible to publish the Protestant version of the Bible or to meet for worship even in private is quite untrue. These statements were given wide publicity in the United States through the articles of William H. Newton on religion in Spain.[5] He would have discovered any number of copies of the Holy Scriptures at the Editorial Española, No. 2 Calle Zurbarán, Madrid, under the direction of Isidro Aguilar Caballer. The Protestant editions of the Bible were very far from eliminated. The figures, provided by the Protestants themselves, confirm this activity. The figures are as follows:

1944:	Bibles	984	
	The New Testament	991	
	Parts of the Bible	4050	*Total* 6025
1945:	Bibles	1488	
	New Testament	1807	
	Parts of the Bible	4286	*Total* 7581
1946:	Bibles	773	
	New Testament	2668	
	Parts of the Bible	3710	*Total* 7151

In addition there were some 4993 volumes distributed by private persons in 1946, and 3467 in 1947.[6] There is absolutely no restriction

[5] William Newton, series for the Scripps-Howard papers. Article in *The Washington Post,* May 24, 1949.

[6] *De Linie,* Amsterdam, Oct. 31, 1947.

on meetings. Protestant chapels hold meetings regularly, and in private homes there is nothing to stop any number of prayer meetings or religious conferences anyone may want to hold.

H. Edward Knoblaugh, a competent observer who has been in Spain from long before the civil war and is head of the Madrid bureau of the International News Service, comments:

> All recent stories from Spain tending to give the impression that non-Catholics are persecuted, are greatly exaggerated. There have been some fanatic outbursts against Protestant chapels, but they were more political than religious. They were committed when England was blocking every Spanish effort to enter the Marshall Plan and the mobs attacked the British embassy at the same time (*The Peoria Register,* April 11, 1949).

What is the position of Protestants in Spain? The exact figures are hard to get because of the somewhat nebulous character of membership in the various Protestant churches. The problem has been examined by two Protestant missionaries, Araujo and Grubb, whose survey of religion in Spain was cited above. It was believed in many Evangelical circles that the advent of the Republic in 1931 would throw the doors wide open for the penetration of Protestantism. There was a change in the legislation and considerable opportunities were given to the various denominations which had heretofore been denied them. The progress recorded during the five years of the Republic did not indicate that there was any great anxiety on the part of the rank and file of the Spanish to change their religion. The book by Araujo and Grubb provides a number of statistics of value in appraising the situation in Spain at the time. The total population of Spain in 1933 was estimated at 23,500,000, and the Evangelical community numbered some 21,900, of whom only 6259 were classified by the different sects themselves as communicants. Twenty-five societies cared for this Evangelical activity in the country and there were missions maintained by groups in the United States, Britain, Northern Ireland, Holland, Germany, Sweden, and France. There were an estimated 166 local churches with 265 workers, of whom 142 were Spaniards.

The report includes many illuminating observations on the status of Protestantism during the period from 1910 to 1930. "During these years there has hardly been noted any progress in Evangelical work in Spain." The work of the various Protestant churches was spoken of by the authors as "exotic," since most of the ministers were paid by foreign committees. In listing the various geographical areas of the country, the report comes up with the conclusion that outside the Mediterranean coast, in almost every other region: Catalonia, León, Andalucía, and Galicia, "much of the work has been very disappointing." Despite this disappointment, it is not without importance to note that the Protestant churches held property to the value of well over five and a half million pesetas in 1933 — at a time when the peseta far exceeded its present depreciated value.

The present situation of Protestants in Spain must be examined somewhat in the light of their status over the past century, and especially with reference to the evolution of legislation in Spain on the religious problem. The idea of religious toleration was introduced into the Constitution of 1856, Article 14 of which stated that "No Spaniard or foreigner shall be persecuted for his religious beliefs as long as he does not give expression to them through acts against religion itself." This somewhat curiously worded precept is in itself typically Spanish. Just how it was to be applied was never determined, since the Constitution of that year did not go into effect. The Constitution of 1869 was another thing entirely. This provision was the cause for the unleashing of an enormous anti-Catholic persecution, the importance of which will be suggested in a moment. The exact text of this article is as follows:

> Public and private worship by foreigners belonging to other religious denominations is guaranteed with no other limitations than those imposed by the universal rules of morality and law. If there are any Spanish citizens who profess a faith other than the Catholic, the provisions of this paragraph are applicable to them.

This law implies quite plainly that almost all the Protestants in Spain at the time were foreigners, for the very existence of non-Catholic Spaniards, at least as an organized group, was looked upon as a rarity.

During the period of the First Republic, as well as afterward, the Church lived through a most difficult time and the story of the persecution has been described in another chapter. The story is important, of course, because it is a necessary part of the rectification of the idea that Spain was a country closed to all ideas not Catholic and totally in the grip of a fanatical and ruthless clergy and hierarchy. The very opposite was the case. The persecution of the Orders, the dissolution of the Society of Jesus, the confiscation of Church properties were all carried out long before the Revolution of 1931 and before the advent of Franco. In other words, the notion sometimes expressed that Protestantism is the first challenge, so to speak, to the hegemony of Catholicism in Spain is sheer nonsense. The Church was having an extremely rough time of it from the day that Ferdinand VII returned to the throne, and the unpleasantness of 1931–1936 was merely the culmination of this painful process.[7]

The Constitution of 1869 was short lived. With the return of the monarchy, the new fundamental law was drawn up in the form of the Constitution of 1876 which was destined to endure for the next sixty years. Catholicism was declared the official religion of the State, but liberty of conscience and the right to private worship were guaranteed. Article 11 of this document reads textually:

> No one shall be molested on Spanish territory because of his religious opinions nor because of the private practice of his beliefs as long as respect for Christian morality is maintained. Public ceremonies or demonstrations will not be allowed except those of the official religion of the State.

The problem of this article is identical to that which arises under the present Spanish regime. Precisely what is understood by "private worship" and what does the expression forbidding public worship really mean? The royal ordinance of October 23, 1876, clarifies the idea to some extent. Public manifestations of religion were taken to mean street processions, the display of the emblems or insignia of a religion in public places, posters and publicity material, or acts of worship taking place outside the buildings or temples destined for that purpose. These provisions remained in force until the fall of the monarchy in 1931, despite innumerable efforts to modify them.

Among the first acts of the new republican government in 1931 was the abrogation of all of the laws heretofore in force regarding the Church. The Concordat was denounced and entirely new legislation introduced. The new Constitution in Article 27 stated that:

> Liberty of conscience and the right to practice freely any religion is guaranteed in Spanish territory. . . . All religious groups may carry on worship in private. The public manifestations of religion must be authorized in each case by the Government.

The legislation passed by the Cortes during the turbulent months of 1931 was almost without exception unfavorable to the Catholic Church. In general the Protestants in Spain had no reason to complain of the new legislation, for it went far beyond anything that had pre-

[7] See *Cambridge Modern History*, Vol. XI, for reference to the mid-century controversy over ecclesiastical properties, and the increasing restrictions on the Church.

viously prevailed. For the first time there was a chance for obtaining something like public acknowledgment of their beliefs. There was unquestionably a certain degree of support, by the Evangelical bodies in Spain, of the left-wing parties that had been responsible for the legislation just mentioned. As late as 1936, on the eve of the decisive elections of February of that year, the President of the Alliance of Evangelical Churches in Spain, in the official publication of that group, *España Evangélica* (Jan. 30, 1936), recommended that Spanish Protestants vote for the Left because "from the temporal point of view, this is our only hope for freedom to proselytize." The fact that many of the Protestant bodies in Spain did support the Left so solidly led to the melancholy reflection contained in the *Carta Circular a los Evangélicos Españoles* in 1945 that "many of the Churches and many of our brethren have had to pay dearly and continue to pay for this close association with Leftist elements who could not fail, in the long run, to do injury to our cause."

But the impression must not be given that Protestantism flourished in Spain during the Second Republic or that the various forces that contributed to the collapse of constituted government were in any sense sympathetic to Protestantism as against Catholicism. The evidence is absolutely overwhelming that the major forces in the Spain of the Republic were simply antireligious, and included Catholics, Protestants, and Moslems in more or less the same category. There were cases of anti-Protestant violence. Araujo and Grubb, the two Evangelical observers already quoted, observe that in October, 1932, there was an attack on the Protestant Church at Marín in Galicia, the largest Evangelical community in the nation. The attempt to destroy this church was resisted not only by the members of the congregation, but with the aid of many of their Catholic fellow townsmen.[8]

With the close of the civil war and the advent of the new regime, it was expected that the whole religious problem would be re-examined carefully. There were indications of this in the decision of June 7, 1941, with the Holy See to maintain a number of the articles contained in the Concordat of 1851. During the war itself, the nationalists had given an assurance that their proposed regime was not to be one of intolerance and persecution. The statement of the Duke of Alba in November, 1937, emphasized this point, although the situation was somewhat vague prior to the drafting and approval of the *Fuero de*

[8] Araujo and Grubb, *op. cit.*, p. 46.

los Españoles, to be translated loosely as the "Spaniard's Charter." This document was unanimously passed by the Cortes on July 13, 1945, and contains, in 36 articles, a statement as to the rights of the citizenry as well as their duties. It is not a Constitution, since it does not provide specifically for the structure and organization of the State. Article 6 of the Charter reads as follows:

> The profession and practice of the Catholic religion, which is that of the Spanish State, shall enjoy official protection. None shall be molested for their religious beliefs or their private practice. No other ceremonies or external demonstrations than those of the Catholic religion shall be permitted.

This text does not depart in any notable degree from those that had prevailed during the past century. The expression is the same and fundamentally the intention is the same. Nothing in the *Fuero de los Españoles* proposes the persecution or the elimination of whatever religious minorities may exist in the country, nor can this article possibly be construed as reflecting the intention of extirpating by violence other religious persuasions. The one substantial restriction is that concerning public demonstrations of religion. Protestants in Spain under this law may not, it is true, organize street processions or engage publicly, on the street and in the market place, in worship. In part this provision is simply a reflection of the kind of society one finds in Spain. Prudence would dictate that Protestant demonstrations be restricted in communities where 98 per cent of the people are Catholic. It is the same logic whereby Catholics in the United States do not propose to organize monster religious processions in communities in this country, where the number of Catholics is very small or where the attitude of the public is such that acts of this kind would be profoundly unwise, productive in all probability of tension and even friction.

The justification of the Charter and its specifically religious terms appears in the following form in the pages of the official journal of the Cortes:

> The Charter presents a formula, which, without persecution, affirms, and without violence, protects, that religious unity which is the heart and soul of our history, the creation of a hundred generations, the supreme ideal for which the heroes and martyrs of our Crusade shed their blood and laid down their lives.[9]

In general Article 6 of the Charter was well received in Spain. Contrary to the provision of 1876 which was protested by His Holiness

[9] *Boletín oficial de las Cortes españolas,* No. 111, julio 13 de 1947, p. 2303.

Pius IX and by the Spanish hierarchy, the new law received the blessing of the bishops and was accepted by the Holy See. Some reservations were expressed by a very small minority of Catholics, particularly the Carlists who found it a bit too liberal for their liking. The Protestants themselves found it satisfactory. Apparently there was the general expectation that the new legislation would virtually exclude Protestantism from the country. The provision of the Charter was acclaimed therefore as eminently satisfactory even though not as completely favorable as would be ideally desirable. In the bulletin of the Spanish Evangelical Churches, the new law was received under the heading "A Great Opportunity."[10] The Article notes that from reports received from the provinces the effect of the new law on the Evangelical denominations was entirely favorable:

> In reality, the fact that we can now count on a legal and constitutional basis for our activity will allow us to restore the life of our congregations in many of the more important Spanish cities. It means that after a long and painful period of suffocation, a wide and effective door is now opened for us. We realize that it is still not entirely open and we hope for other concessions to the end that we can preach the Gospel with full liberty.

Once again the expression "private worship" was the cause of considerable discrepancy. One school of thought, headed by the Carlists, interpreted it most restrictedly as meaning worship within the home, with none of the trappings of a church, chapel, or temple, and without any activity such as collecting funds or carrying on propaganda. The Protestants themselves went to the other extreme and insisted that "private" was to be taken as meaning nonofficial or non-national, that is unsupported in public as signifying the State.

As a matter of fact this question was decided for all practical purposes in 1945 by the ministerial decree of November 12, which allowed the reopening of Protestant churches. The text of this document is not without significance and may be useful to indicate the state of mind and point of view of the Spanish government:

> At the beginning of the National Movement, it was found necessary to suspend the freedom of worship and consequently close the chapels of non-Catholic groups in Spanish territory, in part because of the hostility of many of the pastors of these churches and secondly to safeguard the essential spiritual unity of the people.
>
> Since the causes for these measures no longer exist and in view of the need to restore normality in this respect, the removal of the legal restrictions

[10] *Carta Circular a los Evangélicos Españoles,* 1945, Nos. 8–9.

on these dissident groups is authorized by the *Fuero de los Españoles.* Article 6 of this Charter establishes that no one shall be disturbed because of his religious beliefs nor shall there be public demonstrations by other religions than the Catholic. Within these limitations, the dissident groups enjoy tolerance. The Ministry, therefore, after discussion by the Council of Ministers, establishes the following conditions for such worship:

1. Non-Catholic religious groups may worship freely anywhere in Spanish territory, provided this worship is conducted inside their respective churches, with no public manifestation. The directors of these denominations or the persons in charge of the worship are free to organize religious ceremonies on condition that any ulterior purpose or end is avoided; that is, political relations with illegal groups or anything that is not purely pious or liturgical.

2. Authorization to open such a church should be made in each individual case to the provincial governor, such authorization to be accorded on the basis of the present provisions. The governor in turn will inform this Ministry. The authorization will be communicated to the person requesting it.

3. The provincial governors shall protect the worship thus authorized and shall not interfere in the work of the churches nor in their private ceremonies.

4. The provincial governors shall inform this Ministry of any abuses or violations of the law in this regard.

Madrid, November 12, 1945[11]

The annual meeting of the Evangelical churches of Spain in Madrid during June of 1945, expressed great optimism for the future, which optimism seemed justified by the ministerial decree just quoted.

The growth of Protestantism in Spain, thanks to this policy, has undoubtedly been considerable over the past three years. The Protestant review, *Life of Faith* (Aug. 20, 1947), contains certain information on how the protestants have not merely rebuilt the churches destroyed during the civil war or limited themselves to the congregations already in existence, but have gone out actively to win conversions. The following paragraph refers to a single community in Spain, which may be taken as more or less typical: "There was not a single Protestant in the town when the first place or worship was opened last November [1946]. At present [August, 1947] the congregation consists of about fifty people, among whom twenty have announced their conversion. The same situation prevails more or less in most parts of Spain and the authorities seem entirely favorable."

It could not be said that the Spanish government or anyone else did anything that could be construed as persecution of the Protestants. The number of churches has vastly increased. Conservative estimates indicate that there are 165 chapels and churches; seventeen of

---

[11] See *La situación del protestantismo en España,* Madrid, 1948.

which are in and around Barcelona, eleven in Madrid, and the rest distributed over the country. It is not the existence of Protestant chapels in Spain that has bothered Spaniards, nor is it a will to persecute that animates them; it is rather the extraordinarily aggressive methods and procedures put into effect over the past few years by Protestants which have aroused the antagonism of many Catholics. The proof that persecution was never either intended or carried out rests not only on the facts already presented, but on such things as the allocation of paper for Protestant reviews and news-sheets. *Notas de la Obra Bíblica, Constancia,* and *El Eco de la Verdad* were being published freely in Spain during the years when paper was extremely scarce.

There is little doubt that Protestants in Spain have gone far beyond the limits laid down by the *Fuero* and the decree cited above. In innumerable cases, Protestant services have been held in such a manner as to be clearly visible from the street and serve to attract crowds. There has been a considerable tendency to publish Evangelical literature with a distinctly Catholic cachet, to catch the unwary. The statement of the Archbishop of Zaragoza, published in *Ecclesia* under date of January 17, 1948, points out that "it is known to us with certainty that the Protestant sects have renewed their activity in this city by distributing books, pamphlets, and Bibles. November 23, the day we had set aside for encouraging among the faithful the knowledge and diffusion of the Sacred Books, was taken advantage of by them to intensify their propaganda openly and without discretion." The previous year, on the same occasion when the reading of the Bible was encouraged by the hierarchy, Protestant editions had been distributed at the doors of the Catholic churches. The Cardinal Archbishop of Seville, in a pastoral of September 8, spoke of the dangers among the humble of Evangelical propaganda, especially the campaign to discredit the belief in the doctrine of Mary Mediatrix. During November and December of 1945 six new Protestant chapels were erected in the archdiocese of Seville, and 26 in 1946.[12] Other activities equally deplored were the publication of magazines imitating in format and appearance parish publications, and the insistence on selling or distributing such literature at the entrance to Catholic churches. At the gathering in Barcelona of the delegates to the congress of Marianist Congregations, such literature was distributed at the entrance of the building where the meetings were being held.

[12] *Gaceta oficial del Arzobispado de Sevilla,* Sept. 10, 1947, p. 578 sq.

An important element in the whole situation is that many of the more aggressive groups do not represent the older Evangelical tradition. Seventh-Day Adventists and the Pentecostal Church have invaded Spain to some extent and the voices of not a few Evangelical ministers have been raised in order that these activities be not confused with what might be called the more normal Protestant bodies.

It may be forgiven the Spanish people if they find it difficult to make a clear distinction between Protestantism *vieille école* and the newer sects that have sprung up, for the tendency is to put them all in the same category and label them collectively Protestant. It is clear from abundant testimony that many of the old-line Evangelicals, especially the Anglicans and Lutherans, look upon these more novel bodies as anarchical and irresponsible. There is no doubt that the intransigent, solid attachment to the Church, and above all the deep devotion to the Blessed Virgin have provoked many attacks by Protestants in Spain on the faith of the majority. It would be absurd to deny the essentially anti-Catholic nature of the Evangelical movement; that is that sector of Protestantism in Spain which is not strictly tied in with a foreign legation or embassy or forms a part of a definitely foreign colony resident there.

The Protestants themselves have acknowledged the strong element of anti-Catholicism in their activities. Pastor Brutsch, in his *L'Evangile du Christ: l'Espagne meurtrie et nous,* published at Geneva in 1937, states frankly that: "one of the characteristics of Spanish Protestantism is that it is anti-Catholic." Or, if one prefers a more substantial testimony, one may read the following statement in the bulletin of the Spanish Evangelicals, published in 1946: "That Protestantism constitutes a threat to 'Roman peace' we are the first to admit as a solid fact and an honor for the Evangelical churches." Further evidence is found in such publications of Spanish Protestantism as the *Escudriñador Bíblico,* issued in Madrid. In the issue for October, 1947, this review, now in its fourth year, contains an article in which the following comments are made regarding Catholicism:

1. The indulgences sold by the priests to the people are simply a trick of the Devil.
2. God never sent saints in order that people adore them.
3. The practice of clerical celibacy is spoken of as a Satanical institution and perversion.
4. Bishops and priests should be free to marry like anyone else.

5. These are but a few of the false doctrines of what the review in question calls the "Apostate Catholic Church."
6. The Bible is full of this apostasy and that God insists that men to be saved abandon Catholicism.

This publication was issued immediately after the inauguration of a new chapel on the Calle Trafalgar in Madrid. On October 31 a body of students demonstrated against the chapel, denouncing the insults proffered to the Blessed Virgin, the Church, and the saints.

There is deep resentment in Spanish Catholic circles at the pretended evangelization of their country by Protestants, for whatever may be the deficiencies of Spanish Catholics and whatever may be the present miseries in the social and economic order, the overwhelming majority clings fiercely to the traditional religion, so intimately bound up with their history and glories. Much of this resentment springs from the conviction that when Spain was suffering its martyrdom during the Republic and the Civil War, few Protestant voices were raised to protest the bloody outrages. *La Civiltá Cattolica* of Rome, in 1937, devoted attention to the Protestant reaction to the wild persecution of Catholicism in Spain. Long before the war Protestant statements were frequent that the time had come for the Christianizing of Spain. At an Evangelical congress in Utrecht, in 1927, it was proposed that a Faculty of Protestant Theology be set up in Madrid and translations into Spanish of the lives of Luther and Calvin made ready for distribution. In May, 1936, the Lausanne Committee for the Evangelization of Spain announced that its purpose was to set Spain free of the yoke of Rome. A little bulletin called *Tidings from Spain,* the organ of the Spanish Evangelical Missions, in the issue for September and October, 1944, has this to say about the state of affairs in Spain: "In 1935 the number of illiterates — who in 1907 had formed 60 per cent of the population — had been reduced practically to half. Under Franco's regime it is not likely that things are getting better because it is a rule of the Catholic Church to keep people illiterate." This comment did not tend to endear Protestantism to the Spanish people.

A word on the school situation. It is commonly stated that Protestants have no right to the education of their children according to their religious beliefs. The Elementary Education Act of July 17, 1945, is perfectly clear on this point. Article 28 provides for the confessional education of non-Catholic foreigners. Articles 5, 28, 56, 57, and 63 are binding on children of Spanish nationality and provide only for Catholic instruction. This, in reality, is not in the least surprising in view of the nature of the State and its relations to the Church. Protestant schools existed prior to the present regime. They were, as admitted by Protestant writers, almost exclusively devoted to propaganda purposes. Nor was their standard particularly high. Araujo and Grubb point out the grave deficiencies of these establishments.[13] If Protestant schools were to be provided for the Protestant children alone, the number would be infinitesimal. The calculation is easy. Assuming that there are some seven thousand Protestants, that is, native Spaniards and not members of a foreign community, and if this seven thousand had one thousand children of school age, it would seem absurd to establish a school system exclusively for this microscopic minority, much less secondary and institutions of higher learning.

Nowhere does one find, for instance, that the Swedish State concerns itself in the slightest with the several hundred Catholics that live in Sweden and who must bear a number of disabilities more severe than anything existing in Spain for Protestants. Although no formal institution of instruction, registered according to the law, there are Protestant schools in Spain, and they exist among the very tiny communities to afford religious instruction to children of this persuasion who frequent the State schools.[14]

There has been some considerable Protestant protest over the matter of marriage. The charge has been made that in Spain a valid marriage must be performed by a priest. The outcry has been principally against the Act of March 12, 1938, which, in fact, did nothing but repeal the republican legislation of June 28, 1932, which recognized civil marriages alone as valid. A return has been made to the former use of the canonical form as obligatory for Catholics and the civil form for non-Catholics. The latter, after the civil ceremony, might appear before their own pastor, on the condition that at least one of the contracting parties declare expressly not to profess the Catholic Faith. In general, nonbaptized persons or those baptized as Protestants have no difficulty at all. There are certain complications in the case of mixed marriages, and especially of lapsed Catholics.

The notion that Catholic practice is required for official positions or that proof of Catholicity is demanded for government posts is sheer nonsense. There are cases such as that of a professor at the University

---

[13] *Op. cit.*, pp. 75–76.

[14] Henry Smith Leiper, *Christianity Today. A Survey of the State of the Churches*, New York, 1947, p. 90.

of Zaragoza who teaches mathematics and is a Protestant. The university is State maintained, yet no obstacle was placed in the way of this particular professor. The restrictions are far less rigid than in Sweden where only members of the State Lutheran Church can be schoolmasters and where other denominations cannot maintain schools of their own.

We come now to the so-called anti-Protestant demonstrations and incidents which have been seized upon so avidly to show that Spain is a land of persecution and intolerance. The facts concerning the incidents have been ascertained with the maximum of care: some on the spot in Spain itself and others through discreet correspondence with Spanish priests and others who are well informed regarding the problem.

After the assault on the Protestant chapel on Calle Trafalgar, a considerable number of mimeographed tracts of the very greatest violence were distributed. The British Embassy used them as the basis of its protest. However, the fact that they were not printed and were unsigned indicates that they were not approved by the State. As a matter of fact, this case and the others to which reference will be made, were largely protests *against* the Franco government and not solely against Protestants. That is to say, the extreme Right, if one may use the conventional term, used this anti-Protestant agitation as a means for criticizing the regime for its liberalism and leniency toward the minority groups.

The actual incidents that have taken place, as near as one can ascertain, include the following: (1) Grenollers, Catalonia, September 21, 1947; (2) Barcelona, October 11, 1947; (3) Madrid, October 31, 1947; (4) minor incidents in Parets and Manresa, both in Catalonia, exact dates not available.

The press comments abroad on these incidents exaggerated them out of all proportion. Thus the French paper, *Midi-Libre* of Montpelier (Nov. 6, 1947), stated that Protestant churches in Barcelona, Grenollers, Madrid, and Seville had been reduced to ashes by frenzied mobs. The statement is untrue, in general and in the details. Spain is a country where the destruction of churches became something of an art in the days of the persecution. Nothing of that sort has taken place against the Protestants.

Grenollers, a small Catalan city of about 17,000 inhabitants, has something of a reputation for violent political feeling. During the Republic and the civil war a number of Carlists were assassinated in the town, its Catholic churches burned, and its entire clergy murdered.

The Baptist chapel occupies the ground floor of a private house at Number 20, Calle Elisabet, and consists of two adjoining rooms, the furnishings consisting of some forty chairs, a rostrum for the reading of the Bible, and a bookcase. The rooms had been used before the civil war as the headquarters of the local unit of the Carlist *Requetés* — a detail — but an important one in the light of the subsequent events. Since the *Requeté* as well as his son had been killed during the war, his widow rented the rooms to an innkeeper for his surplus trade. He, in turn, in May, 1947, leased the rooms to the Baptists. Up to that time there had been no Protestant church in Grenollers. The widow as well as the local traditionalists protested loudly and long against this profanation of the rooms once used for quite different purposes by their martyred comrade, and there was a popular feeling that this was no way to honor the memory of those who had given their lives to God and country. On Sunday afternoon, September 21, a number of Carlists, returning from a meeting, stopped several persons seeking entry to the "temple." The Evangelical gathering had begun under the guidance of a young man from Tarrasa with about 30 persons present. The Carlists interrupted the meeting and discovered among the pamphlets and books in the room several that seemed to them insulting to the Blessed Virgin. One of the books was entitled, *Pepa y la Virgen.* It was a story of a young girl named Josefina, the nickname for whom in Spanish is *Pepa* who prayed to the Blessed Virgin for a favor. An Evangelical is depicted as approaching her to say that this prayer is worthless since she must address God directly and through no intermediary. They proceeded to slap the pastor, break up the furniture, and toss the literature out of the window. The neighbors attracted by the noise gathered and in general expressed disapproval of what seemed to them misplaced zeal. The police arrived shortly and order was restored. Protestant services have resumed in this locality and no further disturbances have been reported. It is to be noted that the pastor and the 30-odd persons gathered in the chapel were all Spaniards and no outrage to a foreigner was involved.

The second incident of some importance took place in Barcelona. Some thirty *Requetés* in uniform, on leaving the Cathedral where they had attended a Mass commemorative of the battle of Lepanto, made their way toward the local Methodist chapel, located on the Calle Ripoll. They entered the building and proceeded to wreck the furniture, including a piano. The ecclesiastical authority strongly disapproved of this act of vandalism, and the responsible *Requetés* were arrested.

The third incident occurred in Madrid, in a large building on the Calle Trafalgar, which was British property and which contained a chapel of considerable size. This chapel, with a seating capacity of 700, was by far the largest in Spain and had been inaugurated on October 17, 1947. After certain attacks on the Blessed Virgin, as reported widely, a group of students decided to visit the chapel to sing the *Salve Regina.* When their entrance was obstructed they proceeded to break in, throw the chairs out the windows, and destroy some of the other furniture. They wrote "Viva la Virgen" on the walls of the chapel.

These are the principal incidents. There may have been others of less significance. But even with every concession to their importance, none of the three incidents listed above constitutes a flagrant or violent case of anti-Protestantism. What is most important is that these acts were condemned by the proper ecclesiastical authority, the responsible persons arrested, and in every case those who engaged in the acts belonged to the *Requetés*. In no instance were the ordinary members of Spanish Catholic Action involved. Rather the contrary. The members of Catholic Action deplored this recourse to violence. A personal letter to the present writer from a distinguished Barcelona priest, under date of December 15, 1947, states:

> On October 31, the Requetés distributed leaflets in Barcelona in which they declared the growth of Protestantism and accused the Franco government of leniency toward the sects. Several members of Catholic Action undertook to prevent the distribution of this inflammatory literature which called for the suppression of Protestantism. It was considered by every responsible person as a direct and willful incitement to violence. I myself witnessed a most acrimonious discussion between Requetés and members of Catholic Action, the latter seeking to prevent the former from handing out their leaflets at the entrance of the Church of Santa María del Mar.

In these cases, as in many others, the foreign press had insisted on generalizations that are not supported by the facts. It is the conviction of a great many well-informed persons that the political enemies of the Franco government have taken full advantage of these incidents to whip up passion against Franco, especially in the English-speaking world.

The best statement on the attitude of the Church is that contained in the first joint pastoral of the Spanish bishops, issued in June, 1948, which devoted considerable attention to the problem of the religious minorities in the country.

> Blessed be the hour — and may God hasten it — in which attacks against the Catholic Church on the part of all religious confessions which acknowledge Christ may cease, and in which the efforts of all who believe in Jesus and in the values of the spirit against materialism and its consequences in the social and political order may be joined together.

The introduction of this first joint pastoral since 1936 is devoted to doctrinal considerations and reminds that the duty of bishops is to be vigilant for the preservation and purity of the Faith. Questions of religious freedom and toleration are not merely political and social, but also dogmatic, involving the right of the Church to protect the integrity of the Faith. "Jesus Christ founded only one Church," the pastoral states. "A Church born centuries later could not be founded by Him, just as a church which does not remain united with the successors of Peter cannot be true.

"For this reason, the faithful are not free to adhere to any church. It is first of all a sacred duty to belong to the only true Church founded by Christ, which vividly stands out and is known for its qualities of being One, Holy, Catholic, and Apostolic.

"Human society must acknowledge God as Father and revere His power. Thus justice and reason repel the atheistic state."

Turning to the particular circumstances of the Spanish people today, the pastoral points out that non-Catholic Spaniards are in such insignificant number that a public law concerning their position would hardly be necessary, but that there are also in Spain a goodly number of foreigners from predominantly Protestant countries or countries with large Protestant minorities. To protect their rights, as well as those of non-Catholic Spaniards, Article 6 was placed in the Spanish Charter.

The Spanish bishops express surprise that in some instances Catholics in other countries have misconstrued this guarantee of freedom of conscience by the Spanish Charter, and the pastoral expresses special appreciation to the Jesuit magazine *La Civiltá Cattolica* in Rome for its presentation of the situation of Protestants in Spain.

These bishops lament the splitting up of Christianity by the multiplication of Protestant denominations and groups, and deplore the manner in which these divisions have interfered with the efficacy of the mission of Christianity in the world.

While expressing confidence that the people of Spain will remain true to the Catholic Faith, its teachings, and practices, the archbishops and bishops observe that this does not mean "that a public campaign of Protestant proselytism and of attack against the Catholic Faith might not endanger certain incautious persons," and that this exigency is to be avoided, not by acts of violence, but by bringing such abuses to attention of public authority and "by strict enforcement of regulations following the fundamental law of the State."

"Faith must never be forced upon people through violence," the pastoral declares. "Charity paves the way and always requires the efficacy of divine Grace."

While intransigence with respect to the revealed truths of Christ is an essential mark of Catholicism, the bishops aver this protection of the integrity of the Faith is not "incompatible with serenity, understanding, gentleness, and the true charity that Christ teaches us to practice even with respect to our enemies."[15]

Paul P. Kennedy, writing from Madrid in December, 1948, for the special roundup of religious news the world over published by *The New York Times,* makes the following statement:

> There is no available evidence that these cases of vandalism followed a pattern or had been instigated by governmental or religious organizations. To investigators they appeared to be the result of outbreaks of fanaticism that in some cases had been inspired by violently anti-Protestant pastoral [*sic*] letters. In nearly all instances, the Government provided indemnity for the damaged churches and in some instances placed effective guards around various chapels for added protection.[16]

2. THE JEWS

The Protestant question has received world-wide publicity and has aroused considerable interest particularly in the English-speaking countries. The problem of the Jews in Spain is less well known. It merits, however, special attention, in the light of the record of the Spanish government during the crucial years when European Jewry was threatened with persecution and literal extinction.

On May 16, 1949, the Israeli delegate to the United Nations expressed the viewpoint of his government regarding Spain. Although Israel had not taken part in the preliminary discussions of the Spanish case, Eban felt called upon to express his concern that "even though the Spanish regime was not responsible directly for this policy of extermination, it was an active ally and sympathizer with the government responsible

---

15 Carried under date of June 19, 1948, by N.C.W.C. News Service.

16 *The New York Times,* Dec. 25, 1948.

for that policy and as such contributed to the effectiveness of the alliance. . . . For us the essential point is the association of this regime with the Nazi-Fascist alliance which corrupted the moral foundations of civilized life."[17]

The Israeli delegate made perfectly clear that he was not attacking the Spanish regime nor criticizing the Spanish people; he was perturbed by what appeared to be connivance in the frightful persecution for which Hitlerite Germany had been responsible. The statement of the Israeli delegate may be taken as an appropriate point of departure for a cursory examination of the policy of Spain toward the Jews both during and after the war.

Spain can indeed be proud of this page in her contemporary history, for the evidence reveals that the Madrid government utilized every avenue and took advantage of every channel to render aid to the Jews. The existence of normal relations with the German government were used to the limit to favor the persecuted. The Spanish diplomatic representatives exploited the relative good will of the German authorities to defend the interests of the persecuted both in Germany and in the occupied territories. Within Spain, the religious, military, and civil authorities were generous to a fault in offering a sanctuary to those fleeing the concentration camps of Nazi Europe.

There is abundant evidence of the gratitude of Jewish leadership for the aid extended during those difficult years. Maurice L. Perlzweig, president of the World Jewish Congress, meeting in Atlantic City in late November, 1944, addressed a letter of appreciation to the then Spanish ambassador in Washington, Juan Cárdenas, in which, in the name of the executive committee of the World Congress of Jews, he requested him to thank the Spanish government for the "refuge given Jews from the territories under the military occupation of Germany. We understand perfectly the difficulties of the situation and realize the great effort the present war represents for the economy of Spain. Therefore we are doubly grateful that the refugees have been allowed to remain in Spain until a permanent residence could be obtained. . . . The Jews have a long memory and they will not easily forget the opportunity given thousands of their brethren to save their lives."[18]

In the mass of accusations launched against the present Spanish

---

[17] *United Nations. General Assembly,* Two Hundred and Fourteenth Plenary Meeting, May 16, 1949, pp. 116–117.

[18] Photostatic copy of letter to Ambassador Cárdenas in archives of *Oficina de Información Diplomática,* Madrid.

government, racism does not generally figure among the more prominent. There is no lack of evidence, however, that this charge is now and again utilized to discredit the Franco regime, linking it ideologically with Berlin. A minor instance of this character involved the refusal of the censorship in Madrid to allow the film, "Gentlemen's Agreement," to be shown in the peninsula, and this decision was taken immediately as evidence of anti-Semitism. The basis for the rejection had nothing to do with the essential argument of the film, but involved certain emphases and a number of distortions that contained a double meaning in the Spanish language. If these were corrected, the film could be shown without objection. The foreign press seized the case as clear and irrefutable evidence that Spain was dominated by anti-Semitism.[19] The reply to this gratuitous assertion was made by Gabriel García Espina, General Director of Cinemas and Theaters, who insisted that "In Spain, no racial problem exists and we are entirely free from all anti-Semitism."

The film, incidentally, was shown at the *Kursaal* in Barcelona, *Palacio de la Prensa* in Madrid, and at other theaters in the peninsula. The basic difficulty in the whole incident was that the Spanish censors were reluctant to include in the showings some of the more flagrant instances of anti-Semitism which would shock the Spanish public, without knowledge of the rabid feeling against Jews that prevails in some parts of the world.

Spain itself has a long and honorable Hebraic tradition. The expulsion at the end of the fifteenth century, for religious motives, did not eliminate the Semitic injection that plays so important a part in the character and the psychology of the Iberian people. The descendants of the Spanish Jews — the Sephardim — are to be found scattered all over the world, with large concentrations in the Near East and North Africa, while within Spanish territory itself there are some 14,000 Jews in Morocco and perhaps 8000 in the peninsula itself. The Spanish government has traditionally been interested in the lot of this curious branch of the Jewish family, which has retained with rare tenacity an archaic Spanish and the recollection of the Iberian homeland. General Primo de Rivera decreed on December 20, 1924, that Sephardi Jews might obtain Spanish citizenship if they so desired by a very simple process and proof of their remote Spanish origin. When World War II broke out, the Spanish government interpreted the exist-

[19] *The New York Times,* Oct. 2, 1948. It was suggested that the Spanish position was that brotherly love did not extend to Jews.

ing legislation regarding the Sephardim in the most generous way possible and invariably extended protection and aid to them whenever they solicited it. A brief description of the steps taken by the Madrid government in different areas will serve as evidence of the pro-Jewish policy followed consistently during the tragic period from 1940 to 1945.

The persecution of the Jews began in France with the Nazi occupation and the creation of the Vichy regime and restrictive measures began with the obligation to register as a Jew, culminating in the obligatory use of special insignia. The Spanish government concerned itself immediately with the 2000-odd Sephardim in Paris, for the consulate in the French capital, under date of September 17, 1940, informed Madrid that the Sephardim were subject to exactly the same measures as all other Jews regardless of nationality or citizenship. In November, 1940, the Spanish Foreign Office instructed the embassy in Vichy "to inform the Sephardim that they testify to their character as Spanish nationals so that they may be defended when necessary."[20]

On March 7, 1942, the Ministry of Foreign Affairs issued definite instructions to its diplomatic mission in France to "defend the interests of the Sephardi Jews and demand of the French authorities strict compliance with the Franco-Spanish agreement of 1862."

The embassy in Vichy and the consulate in Paris exerted every effort to protect the Sephardim who were, after all, the particular sector of the Jewish community over which the Spanish government could claim some responsibility. During the spring of 1942 the demands of the Spanish authorities were granted so that Sephardi property was exempted from certain restrictions imposed by the German occupation forces. In July, 1942, the Spanish consulate informed Madrid that the Sephardim were not obliged to wear the Star of David insignia and were allowed to frequent public places despite the statutory prohibition. The Jews who sought the protection of the Spanish consular authorities were invariably aided to the best of their ability and means at their disposal. Those who wished to leave France and find refuge in Spain itself were aided in this intent. Numerous Sephardi leaders, Edgardo Hassid, Fernández, Nik Alberto Saporta, Enrique Saporta y Bajá, Mauricio Carasso y Asser, and other representatives of the Sephardi community, addressed the Spanish Foreign Minister in October, 1941, to express their gratitude for the

[20] Archives of the Foreign Office, Madrid.

defense of their interests. "Spanish legislation in this regard is inspired in the best Catholic principles and admits of no distinction between Spaniards because of racial origin. . . . Thanks to the efforts of our diplomatic representatives, the German laws against our Sephardi brethren have been stopped." It has been conservatively estimated that Spanish intervention in occupied France saved some 3000 Jews from extermination; with the members of their families and relatives, this number is much larger.

The lot of the Sephardi community in occupied Rumania was not a particularly happy one. Many of these Jews were descendants of exiles from Spain, but their juridical status was, to say the least, in very grave doubt. Proof of their Spanish citizenship, lost in the course of four and a half centuries, was difficult. The Spanish government exerted every effort to rescue and protect them, although, in strict international usage, it could easily have paid no attention at all to these long separated and almost forgotten fellow citizens, more or less assimilated with the nationalities among whom they had lived for generations. The Spanish minister in Bucharest, in Dispatch No. 58, April, 1941, states: "As a result of my personal intervention, we have stopped the application of a decree expelling our Sephardim and we have obtained the formal promise that henceforth no Spanish subject will be expelled without consultation with the Legation. This result is not entirely satisfactory, since it is not only important that the Sephardim be allowed to remain here but that they be allowed to make a living."

The Spanish government made use of the Hispano-Rumanian agreement of April 30, 1930, regarding the protection of Spanish property rights in Rumania and the Legation was instructed to insist that the Sephardim be included under the provisions of this protection. The diplomatic mission was able to communicate on August 23, 1943, Dispatch No. 410, an agreement of the Rumanian government to exclude from the loss of their property all those who claimed Spanish citizenship, "even if of Israelite origin."

The numerous Sephardi colonies in Greece were the object of the greatest solicitude on the part of the Spanish authorities during the difficult period of Nazi occupation. Isaac Weisman, former delegate in Lisbon of the World Congress of Jews, reported at the Atlantic City meeting in 1944 that the Spanish government had intervened immediately and effectively to aid the distressed Jews of occupied Greece. Four hundred Sephardi Jews in the Hairadi concentration camp were saved from deportation to Poland by the prompt action of the Spanish authorities. The Madrid government made known its decision to assume the protection of all Sephardi Jews who sought its aid regardless of whether they were in possession of the proper papers or not. This protection was extended to Bulgaria, Hungary, and other parts of occupied Europe where there were Jewish colonies of remote Spanish origin.

The Spanish authorities in Tetuán and the consulate in Rabat made particular efforts to secure the exemption of Jews from the rigors of the anti-Semitic legislation in force in French North Africa, although the results of the efforts were not as successful as elsewhere. The dilatory tactics of the French foreign ministry, despite repeated communications, led to the recognition of certain exceptions to the general laws and, among others, significantly enough, of "those Jews who were serving as honorary Spanish vice-consuls."

Despite every effort, numerous Jews of Spanish origin were interned in concentration camps. The endless red tape that dealings with the German authorities involved was no obstacle to the determination of the Spanish government to obtain the liberation and repatriation of these unfortunate victims. Recognition of this effort is clear from the letter of the American Relief Organization to Director Baraibar of the European section of the Spanish foreign office, dated October 15, 1943, which states textually: "Allow me to assure you, Mr. Baraibar, that the efforts of the Spanish government and your own to help these unfortunate victims of persecution, are highly appreciated and our intention is to co-operate in every way possible."

On December 14, 1943, the foreign office instructed the embassy in Berlin to undertake negotiations at once for the liberation from Belsen of the Sephardi prisoners, and that provision for their repatriation via Port Bou would be made. On January 18, 1944, the German embassy in Madrid replied to the Spanish note, regretting this insistence on protection for the Jews and asserting that in most cases it was impossible to separate Spanish Jews from the rest. The German government was willing, however, to allow Jews in the south of France to seek refuge in Spain. On February 9, the first contingent of Sephardi refugees, numbering 259, reached the Spanish frontier. Of these Jews, 162 had been in Belsen. On February 13 a group of 983 who had left Belsen on the seventh entered Spain and went on to Barcelona. The refugees had suffered the loss of almost all their valuables, and their money had been taken from them by the German authorities. The Spanish government, on February 28, directed the embassy in Berlin to insist that the German government return the money taken from the refugees and after some months it was possible to restore these funds to the Jews newly established in Spain.

Numerous Sephardi Jews resident in Paris took advantage of the facilities to enter Spain. Those with documentary evidence of citizenship constituted no problem, and those who lacked such evidence were placed under the protection of the Spanish authority, and in many cases the attempts of the Germans to deport them to forced labor were forestalled. The fortunes of many Jews were placed under official Spanish custody in the Paris banks. The Spanish Chamber of Commerce was instrumental in obtaining a relaxation of certain German restrictions which in consequence permitted many Jews to carry with them articles of valuable and convertible documents for their livelihood after reaching Spain.

The Spanish government collaborated fully with Jews who had taken refuge in its territory and were anxious to allow them to join families and relatives in their normal places of residence. The government actually offered the use of its own vessels to transport Jews to Palestine, under a neutral flag, although British opposition to any arrangement for the transportation of Jews from Greece to Palestine, as proposed by Spain, made impossible the carrying out of this humanitarian act. It is the Spanish government, nevertheless, that bore the blame for ill will and lack of co-operation in the furthering of effective aid to the persecuted. After the war Spain continued to aid those Jews who were eager to find permanent homes in the Near East. On July 19, 1945, the Spanish vessel, *Plus Ultra,* reached Haifa with 400 Jews who had been residing temporarily in Switzerland, and 150 orphans from Barcelona.

The status of the Jews in Spain belongs to the general subject of the situation of the religious minorities. The world is led to believe that small religious groups in Spain are the object of a barbarous and sanguinary suppression. If the case of the Protestants is of interest as evidence of distortion and exaggeration, attention should be drawn to the position of Jews in Spain today. On January 2, 1949, a number of Jews gathered together at the new synagogue, located at Cardenal Cisnerros, No. 62, in Madrid. The opening of the new temple was in entire accordance with Spanish legislation and enjoyed the full approval of the public authorities. The responsibility for the construction of the new synagogue belonged to Moisés Lawenda, a Jew of Polish origin whose family had been wiped out in Poland; Ignacio Bauer, a very prominent Spanish Jewish historian and man of letters as well as lawyer; and José Cuby, of British origin, at present a resident of Spain. The Jewish community in Madrid has its own cemetery, next to the civil one. During the period of republican rule, when Pedro Rico was mayor of Madrid, the attempt was made to secularize this cemetery as all others. Under the present regime the fullest liberty has been restored for the Jewish burying ground. Two synagogues have also been opened in Barcelona for the Jewish community since the end of the civil war.

From the cultural point of view, there is a lively interest in Spain regarding the Hebrew language, literature, and tradition, especially as related to the long-separated Sephardim. The *Consejo Superior de Investigaciones Científicas* established a special section for Hebrew studies in 1940. This organization, under the name of Institute of Hebrew Studies, began to operate in 1940, at the precise moment when the Nazi forces overran France and German pressure was strongest on Spain. The Association of Friends of the University of Jerusalem concerns itself with active exchange between Israel and the learned institutions in the new Jewish homeland. We find, for instance, in the Jerusalem publication, *Hed ha-Mizrah,* of March 17, 1944, an article devoted to the progress of Hebrew studies in Spain under the suggestive title of "A Christian institute for Hebraic research in Franco Spain":

> It is impossible to speak of anti-Semitism in Spain. There is no anti-Semitic legislation in Spain, contrary to the idea that the government of that country is not favorable to Jews. . . . Imagine my amazement to find an institution under Christian auspices where priests and laymen gathered to carry on Hebrew research . . . my visit was the source of enormous satisfaction . . . and for the first time in my life I was received with the greatest cordiality precisely because I was a Jew, and in this country which is supposedly anti-Semitic.

An important sector of the Jewish community in Spain is that resident in Morocco. The 14,000 Jews settled there are scattered among the towns and cities of the Protectorate. By special law, promulgated on August 20, 1941, the normal functioning of Jewish life in Morocco is guaranteed, not only for those of Spanish nationality but for foreigners as well. Each community is autonomous and is authorized to send representatives to the public boards to treat of questions of specific interest to the Jewish community. In the social field, the Spanish authorities have been spending upward of a million pesetas a year on behalf of the Jewish communities for such things as free school lunchrooms, clothing for those in distress, medical aid, and special donations for Jewish religious festivities. The budget of the Protectorate of Morocco includes every year a sum for the maintenance of a special section of the Ministry of Justice devoted to the application of Jewish law and in the administration of which a number of rabbis intervene directly. These rabbinical magistrates function normally all over Spanish territory; to a far greater degree, let it be said, than in French Morocco. In the market place of the Spanish zone, the Jews are allowed a special section for the preparation of their foods, as are the Moslems. The number of synagogues in Spanish Morocco is large: 15 in Tetuán, 8 in Larache, three in Villa Nador, and others scattered about the territory.

In the educational system of Morocco, the education and cultural division of the High Commissioner's Office includes a special branch called the *Asesoría de Enseñanza Israelita,* under the immediate direction of a number of the Jewish community. The Jews are provided in Tetuán with the institute Maimónides for secondary instruction, where the fullest instruction is provided for specifically Jewish careers: teachers of religion, Hebrew language, synagogue officials, and the like. Jews attending the strictly Spanish institutions are provided with special religious instruction apart from the Christians. The Spanish government subsidizes these centers exactly as it does those in which the Catholic religion is taught. Moreover, scholarships for advanced study in the peninsular universities and technical centers include invariably representatives of the Jewish interests in Morocco. The same applies, of course, to the Moslem communities, provision for whose education and general participation in the life of the Protectorate is along the same general lines.

In view of the large number of displaced Jews over the world and the frequent complications that arise to determine nationality, the Spanish government by the law of December 29, 1948, extends Spanish citizenship to a large number of Sephardim abroad. By special accord with Egypt and Greece, the Spanish State extended its protection to those Jews who claimed Spanish origin and who wished to take advantage of its citizenship. It is interesting to observe that despite the statement in Article 23 of the republican constitution, approved in 1931, regarding the extension of Spanish nationality to the Sephardim, no action was ever taken in the matter by the republican Cortes. The profound concern for the Jews manifested by the present regime is no more eloquently illustrated than in the fact that the entrance examinations to the Spanish foreign service include a whole section devoted to the Sephardim, their culture, and Spanish policy toward them.

Whatever may be the valid objections to the Spanish system of government or to its legislation, it cannot be accused of racism, anti-Semitism, or social, economic, and political distinctions based on ethnic condition. Few nations of Europe have been so totally free of this stigma. The passionate devotion of the Spanish to their traditional Christianity has not led to persecution and extermination of those who hold to other ideas. The evidence on the conduct of Spain toward the Jews during and since World War II is ample in demonstrating the high humanity and profound respect for human dignity that guided the Spanish authorities in the treatment of this problem.

Chapter 17. HISPANIC CULTURE

THE term culture is used in a very broad sense to describe what may be more accurately called the "intellectual atmosphere of contemporary Spain." One of the remarkable blind spots in many foreign visitors to the peninsula is the complete inability to see what is very plain and I suspect that many of those who make a rush tour of Spain to write about it afterward are painfully ill equipped in language and knowledge of Hispanic culture to pass judgment on this somewhat specialized point. Therefore we are submitted to a deluge of commentary regarding the cultural desert that is Spain by observers who do not seem to have made the effort to visit a bookshop or drop in on one of the numerous institutes forming the *Consejo Superior de Investigaciones Científicas.* A casual visit to such an excellent shop as the Casa del Libro in Barcelona or the same establishment in Madrid on the Avenida José Antonio, would serve to show what is being produced and printed in Spain.

"Well aware that his most dangerous enemies are people who think, Franco has waged a quiet all-out campaign against Spain's intellectuals, with the result that today all originality has gone out of Spanish letters, true scholarship is well nigh dead and Spain's once famous universities have become well regulated parrot houses."[1] This comment is followed by the assertion that funds are withdrawn for cultural purposes, books restricted, and that professors are weeded out for their anti-Franco views. It is not merely Americans who find no sign of intellectual life in Spain. Georges Suffert, writing in the pages of the French *Témoignage Chrétien,* states emphatically that "the second characteristic is the silence of the people. Spain keeps still. There are no more writers. . . . There is a global collapse of culture. The name of Lorca means nothing to the young people of twenty; nor does

---

[1] Ernest O. Hauser, "Should We Shake Hands With Franco?" *The Saturday Evening Post,* Philadelphia, Feb. 26, 1949, p. 139.

that of Picasso. All social studies are the work of priests. Foreign papers are rare."[2]

Practically every line in this statement is inaccurate. There are numerous writers, some good, some bad, and many mediocre; the name of García Lorca not only is widely known, but his work is still read. In almost any bookshop one of the first things that catches the eye is the collection of García Lorca, either in the cheap *Austral* texts of Espasa Calpe, or in fine editions, and re-editions have been constant ever since the end of the civil war. Marcelle Auclair, writing in the Paris *Nouvelles Littéraires* (April 6, 1950) reports the wide interest in García Lorca in Spain today. Social studies abound by laymen as well as priests. Foreign journals are readily obtainable in the large cities. M. Suffert is annoyed that the communist *L'Humanité* is not on sale. This perhaps is a sign of the fact that the line has to be drawn some place. *The New York Times,* overseas edition; *The New York Herald Tribune,* Paris edition; the *Parisien Liberé; Le Monde; Le Figaro; Combat; L'Epoque; Le Populaire;* and *L'Aube,* to mention a few of the leading French papers, are all available in Barcelona, Madrid, and elsewhere. It is to be noted that *L'Aube* and *Le Populaire,* to single out only two of the journals named, have been highly critical of Spain and very far from sympathetic to the present regime. The leading London papers are there: *Times, Daily Mail,* and many others. Portuguese, Italian, and even an Austrian paper were on sale in the kiosks in the streets of Madrid in November, 1949. Magazines such as *The Saturday Evening Post, Colliers, Time, Life,* and many others, can all be purchased readily anywhere in Spain.

Currency problems account in large part for the difficulties of wider cultural exchange with other nations, and particularly with the United States. This restriction is not peculiar to Spain. Frenchmen, Italians, and British are severely hampered in their desire to secure American publications and books by the barrier of currency. One may find, however, a reasonable number of learned and scientific publications from the United States in Spanish bookshops. In 1947, under the auspices of the Casa Americana, a successful exhibit of American scientific publications and reviews was held.

Not only has Spain produced a host of new writers, but many of its best known names have returned, encouraged by the regime to take up

---

[2] Georges Suffert, "Impressions of d'Espagne," *Témoignage Chrétien,* June 24, 1949.

their residence once more in the country and carry on their literary and scientific work. Perhaps the most famous among these names are those of José Ortega y Gasset, one of the intellectual founders of the Republic; Dr. Gregorio Marañón, in whose house the deliberations with Count Romanones took place to bring about the departure of the King in April, 1931; Ramón Menéndez Pidal, the octogenarian philologist and literary historian, whose enormous writing is still going on. Ortega y Gasset, honored by an invitation in the summer of 1949 to the Goethe festival in Colorado, is not a Catholic, nor does his philosophy conform to the traditionalist pattern. He has returned to Spain, published his collected works, prepared new essays and books, lectured at the *Ateneo,* and, as he himself stated, "the government pays no attention whatever to me and does not interfere in the least." He created the *Instituto de Humanidades* in Madrid, of which he is the present director.[3]

Dr. Gregorio Marañón, another founder of the Republic, continues to enjoy his wide reputation as a physician and writer in Madrid, without the slightest impediment to his movements or activity. Dr. Teófilo Hernández, the personal physician of Manuel Azaña, resides in Madrid unmolested by the authorities. Benjamín Jarnés, a violent enemy of the regime, returned from Mexico to live in Spain, where he died shortly afterward. Gregorio Martínez Sierra, the well-known dramatist, returned to Spain a few years after the end of the civil war. Gregorio Prieto, the painter, Catalina Bárcenas and Margarita Xirgú, the distinguished actresses, and Salvador Dali have all returned under normal conditions to live and work in Spain and it is reported that Agustín Millares Carlo, who has spent some ten years in America, is returning shortly. Alejandro Lerroux, the outstanding republican leader, died in Madrid in 1948, after returning from residence in Portugal. Numerous other political figures of the republican period, including deputies and ministers, have returned to Spain with no obstruction in the way of their residence, among them Agustín Viñales and Gonzalo Figueroa O'Neill.

LITERATURE

Spanish history of the first decade of the present regime has been rich in the production of new evaluations and appraisals of the Hispanic past and the historical destiny of the country. In a certain

[3] Article in *A.B.C.*, Madrid, Nov. 22, 1949, entitled "Segundo año del Instituto de Humanidades de Ortega y Gasset."

sense, the major intellectual effort has gone into scholarship rather than pure literature. José María Pemán, former president of the Spanish Academy and himself a distinguished literary figure, has expressed the opinion that not only in Spain but in the entire Hispanic world there is an emphasis on "erudition as against creative literature which seems to be dominated by the social consciousness of our time."[4]

This does not exclude the rise of a younger generation of writers, who give great promise for the future of Spanish letters. In the field of the novel, the names of Ignacio Agustí, Camilo José Cela, and Juan Antonio Zunzunegui are frequently mentioned among the most outstanding. One of the popular forms of stimulating literary production is through attractive prizes and awards the number of which is legion. Fine reviews such as *Mundo Hispánico* encourage writing in the field of specific Hispanic interest and the Nadal prize for the novel is a much appreciated encouragement to rising novelists. The Ministry of Education offers a National Novel Award and the Spanish Academy makes available its "Fastenrath award," principally in the field of poetry.

The Nadal award in 1944 brought to light one of the most promising younger novelists in Spain, Carmen Laforet, for her novel *Nada*. The national prize for the novel was given in 1948 to a humorous work, *La Ulcera,* of the Bilbao writer, Juan Antonio Zunzunegui. In fact, the novel had fallen off considerably in Spain prior to the civil war. The essay became the popular form of literary expression. Since the war the popularity of the novel has begun to recover. It is too early to judge, to be sure, the enduring quality of many of the novels that have been published. Some of them are from the pens of men and women in their twenties. It is astonishing that the civil war has not colored more completely the contemporary expression in literature. Among the leading names that come to mind in connection with the present literary trend are several the influence on whom comes direct from Pío Baroja, including Camilo José Cela and Carmen Laforet. Several others have devoted themselves particularly to the evocation of the past or of the regional qualities of Spain. In this category are to be found Juan Antonio Zunzunegui, Bartolomé Soler, Ignacio Agustí, Eulalia Galvarriato, and José Antonio Muñoz Rojas, with his *Historias de familia*. Among those who contributed something before the immediate present, but must be considered as contemporaries, are Ramón Ledesma Miranda, the short-story

[4] Chávez Camacho, *Misión de prensa en España,* Mexico, 1948, p. 249.

writer, Tomás Borrás, Pablo Cavestany, and Manuel Halcón. Oddly enough the humorist school of writers is represented by a number of most promising younger men. Antonio de Obregón, with his *Hermes en la vía pública;* Edgar Neville, *Don Clorato de Potasa;* Alvaro de Laiglesia, *Un naúfrago en la sopa* and *El baúl de los cadáveres.*

The experience of the war left its imprint inevitably on the modern generation of writers. Rafael García Serrano, *La fiel infantería, Eugenio o la proclamación de la primavera;* Manuel Pombo Angulo, *La juventud no vuelve,* and *Hospital general* are indications that this current has produced some works which may have permanent value.

Obviously these superficial comments on the Spanish literary scene do not take into account the continued productivity of the older and better known writers. Dr. Gregorio Marañón has now reached a bibliography of fifty volumes and continues to produce regularly. Azorin, whose sensitive essay has long been the joy of the unhurried and who is dear to the lover of the minutiae of life in unspectacular detail, continues to write with amazing fecundity. There is an outstanding production also of fine editions of both the classics and contemporaries and the famous *Colección Aguilar* is one of a half-dozen enterprises of this sort. A most remarkable undertaking is that of the Editorial Católica, under the name of *Biblioteca de Autores Cristianos.* This enterprise, which edits the newspaper *Ya* and the review *Criterio,* has been publishing a vast collection of the basic works of Christian culture. Its dozens of titles include such items as the Bible, the works of St. Francis of Assisi, St. Augustine, St. Thomas Aquinas, St. Ignatius, the complete works of the remarkable Jaime Balmes, St. Bonaventure, the Spanish religious theater, the great Spanish mystics, and a host of others. At a price of 30 to 50 pesetas a volume, the collection has sold extraordinarily well, revealing the real interest in solid literature of this kind.

The Spanish tradition in poetry is more difficult to judge, for the past ten years have been dominated by those who rose to fame during the period preceding 1936: Antonio Machado, Juan Ramón Jiménez, Pedro Salinas, Jorge Guillén, Rafael Alberti, García Lorca, Gerardo Diego, Vicente Aleixandre, Luis Cernuda, and Manuel Altolaguirre.

Poetry at the present time is in the throes of a crisis; not so much because of the absence of poets as of readers. Poetic creation has become somewhat formalistic, with far less of the personal and human that distinguished the previous production. There are a number of outstanding names, however, who maintain the tradition of Castilian verse. José García Nieto, founder and director of the review *Garcilaso,* became one of the leaders of the postwar movement in poetry. His books, *Víspera hacia él* and *Del campo y soledad,* reveal that effort to return to the form and style of the Golden Age. The influence of the style of Garcilaso has been considerable. José Luis Cano, in *Sonetos de la bahía* and *Voz de la muerte,* has been responsible for the poetical collection *Adonais.* Eugenio de Nora and Victoriano Cremer have edited the review *Espadaña* in the provincial city of León, and represent a tendency opposed to the Garcilasan tradition. Rafael Morales, *Poemas del toro,* is a promising post-civil-war writer. José Antonio Muñoz Rojas, whose prose has achieved some fame, is also a poet in *Abril de almas.* José Suarez Carreño, in *La tierra amenazada,* is an independent and very personal writer. Carlos Bousoño is regarded as one of the outstanding newer poets, José Hierro and Julio Maruri edit the review *Proel* in Santander, revealing once again that the Spanish provinces are not lacking in literary creativeness. José Luis Hildago, whose premature death deprived Hispanic letters of a most promising figure, has left his *Los muertos.* José María Valverde represents in Spain the Catholic tradition which has become so accentuated in France. Rafael Montesinos, in *Incredulidades,* and Ricardo Molina, in *Elegías de Sandúa,* emphasize a very personal note, the latter editing a literary review, *Cántico,* in Córdoba. Manuel Gil, a native of Aragón, is distinguished as a critic and a poet of great potentialities, *Poemas del dolor antiguo.* Alicante, on the Mediterranean coast, has a review in *Verbo,* further evidence of the strongly regional character of Spanish letters. José Albi directs it, and one of his collaborators is Carmen Conde, considered as one of the Spanish women writers with a keener personal note in contemporary poetry. Among the women is Concha Zardoya, translator of Whitman. Catalonia is reasonably strong in modern verse. Félix Ros, *Doce sonetos de la muerte;* Manuel Segalá, *Elegías;* Juan Eduardo Cirlot, Fernando Gutiérrez, and others, form the Catalan school, all writing, incidentally, in Castilian. Madrid, traditional literary center of the peninsula, is not lacking in promising names. The most prominent are Carlos Rodríguez Spiteri, Alfonso Moreno, Leopoldo de Luis, Juan Guerrero Zamora, and a host of others. Even in the faraway Canary Islands, whose isolation often causes it to be overlooked in any survey of Spanish letters, there is a flourishing group of poets, with Agustín Millares, Pedro Lezcano, and Ventura Doreste. José María Millares, *Canto a la tierra,* as well as Manuel Pillares in continental Spain reflect the social anxieties of the times. In the Basque country, at San Sebastián, one of the most notable of the contemporaries is Gabriel Celaya, who directs the poetry series *Norte* and has produced an abundance of prose and poetry of his own.

A number of the younger Spanish poets reside abroad. Among them are Francisco Giner de los Ríos, Antonio Aparicio, Lorenzo Varela, Rafael Dieste, and others.

Spain has always been distinguished in the field of the essay. The casual piece, the short reflection, the type of thing that finds its way more readily into the columns of the newspaper or the review, has been easier than the book or the larger compilation. The essay at present reflects the same tendency I have mentioned with respect to much of Spanish thinking. The civil war produced a severe examination of conscience, a retaking of stock of the past, and an inquiry regarding the future. Spanish essayists tend to look in upon themselves and in many cases appear to take as their central theme the problem and the anguish of Spain itself. Pedro Laín Entralgo, professor of the history of medicine, has followed in the tradition of so many of the great medical figures of the peninsula. Like Gregorio Marañón, he has delved into history and philosophy and has made literarily accessible a great deal concerning the history of his own science. Typical of his production is *España como problema*. Salvador Lissarague, contributor to the famous *Revista de Occidente*, has written in the field of law and history. José Antonio Maravall has concerned himself with the seventeenth century and the eternal problems of the *Quijote*. Ramiro Ledesma Ramos, later to become active in politics, has written works of philosophy and political theory. In this field there are numerous writers of importance who promise much for the future: Leopoldo Palacios, José María Sánchez de Munaín, Manuel Granell, Julán Marías, and Emiliano Aguado. Manuel García Pelayo has specialized in political and international questions. Luis Díez del Corral has translated from the German and is the author of a voluminous study of liberalism as a doctrine. There is a marked preference in Spain today for artistic and historical topics. Melchor Fernández Almagro, Federico Sopeña, Enrique Azcoaga, María Luis Caturia, and Luis Santa Marina belong to this particular trend.

The purely literary essay, so popular in modern Spain, is represented among others by José María de Cossío, Antonio Marichalar, Guillermo Díaz Plaja, Ricardo Gullón, Guillermo de Torre, and others. Joaquín de Entrambasaguas, professor at the University of Madrid, is one of the outstanding figures of the younger school of literary historians.

This extremely brief listing of names excludes almost without exception the large number who still produce abroad and who form the not unimportant group of Spaniards in exile. Obviously the purpose here is to indicate that, despite the tremendous convulsion of the civil war and the disorientation of the present century, Spain continues to be productive in literary efforts, with a new generation at home developing. The provinces are singularly rich in literary effort, itself a happy sign of emancipation from the hegemony of the capital. Spanish letters may not be as exciting today as in the days of the first two or three decades of the century. It would be impossible, however, to assert that there is no intellectual curiosity, no production, and no signs of a renewal of creative letters.[5]

Translations from foreign languages vary greatly. Contemporary and classical novels from the English, French, and German abound in every variety of edition and in the field of thought, it would be impossible to cite the vast army of foreign thinkers and writers represented in Spanish translation. It may be interesting to note that Jacques Maritain, whose sympathy for the Franco regime is extremely limited, is represented by all his principal works. Despite the general rejection among Spanish Catholics of Maritain's position, his *Humanisme intégral* and other well-known works are all available in the original or in Spanish translation.

Book production is generally high, the statistics revealing that in 1948, despite the paper shortage, over 5000 titles were issued in the country. Of these, 170 were philosophical in character, 700 were in the field of jurisprudence. Pure science counted 240; applied science, 600; the fine arts, 200; and over 2000 works of poetry, novel, biography, and short stories were produced. Should the reader suppose that the Spanish read only theology and devotional works, it may be noted that of the 5000 titles, only 290 were strictly religious or theological.[6]

It has been stated from time to time that the Catalan language is no longer tolerated as an instrument of literary expression. It may be

---

[5] An excellent brief introduction may be obtained in the *Diccionario de Literatura española,* Madrid, 1949. A handy volume for contemporary poetry is *Poseía española actual,* Madrid, 1946. On the conflict within Spanish intellectual circles provoked by the civil war and its literary effects, see Del Río, Angel, *Historia de la literatura española,* New York, Vol. II, p. 267 sq.

[6] *España, 1948,* p. 113, issued by the *Oficina de Información Española,* Madrid. The list of Spanish cultural, scientific, and learned reviews occupies 204 pages of the *Catálogo de Revistas Españolas, Ediciones Cultural Hispánica,* Madrid, 1948.

well to examine in a cursory fashion the status of Catalan and the way the problem presents itself today. In the first place, the Catalan language as such is not prohibited and any visitor to Barcelona will soon discover that he hears far more Catalan on the streets than Castilian. If he goes inland to the various provincial cities of Catalonia, he will hear no Castilian at all. With the civil war, the discouragement of the Catalan language as a vehicle of expression in the press, government, and schools was definitely a part of policy. The reasons are multiple. In the first place, the Republic had allowed the language to take precedence so completely over Castilian as to drive out the latter — the national tongue. In the second place, the primacy of Catalan became closely associated with separatism and Catalan extremism. The reaction — inevitable if deplorable — was to discourage Catalan as much as possible. After the conclusion of the civil war, with its centralizing effect both in administration and culture, Catalan was not used for public purposes.

During the course of the past ten years this situation has changed considerably. Catalan has always been used by the Church in those areas where it predominates, for sermons, confession, and religious instruction, continuing today as vigorously as ever. In Tarragona, during 1939, authorization was given for the publication of the catechism in Catalan. More remarkable yet is the revival of Catalan publishing, and although political subjects and newspapers are still not encouraged, the State has allowed a large variety of Catalan books to be published, over forty editions having been issued in 1946. The *Editorial Selecta* in Barcelona has undertaken the publication, in de luxe and in cheaper editions, of most of the great Catalan writers: Victor Catalá, Joan Maragall, Eugenio d'Ors, Santiago Rusiñol, Jacinto Verdaguer, and others. In 1946 the work of J. Gibert, entitled *Girona. Petita historia de la ciutat i de les seves tradicions i folklore,* was awarded the first prize by the National Book Institute for the best edited book during that year. I cite the year 1946 because since that time more and more Catalan books have been issued to such an extent that any Barcelona bookshop has its windows full of them.[7]

---

[7] I can attest personally to the fact that Catalan publishing is flourishing by the fact that I purchased in November, 1949, some thirty volumes of Catalan writing, classic and modern, in Barcelona.

"The Catalan literary movement has continued limited production. Again the censorship has clamped down . . . and many authors have been denied the right

THE PRESS

The press in Spain today is controlled and censorship is applied to almost everything that intimates in the least serious criticism of the regime. Without quoting names, I know for certain that the number of abstentions in the referendum of July 6, 1947, was carefully suppressed for a time. The declarations of prominent figures is likely to be softened, as was the case of former ambassador Hayes in his statement regarding the policy of the United States toward Spain in which the portion of the statement that expressed the hope that the Spanish regime might become more like the Portuguese was simply cut out. Criticism of economic and social matters is guarded and discrete while outward criticism of political affairs is completely forbidden.

Spanish press censorship, however, is very much like Spanish administration in general in that it is neither consistent nor subordinated to a very clear idea. A Mexican journalist has spoken of it as a "directed press without direction."[8] In all honesty it must be said that ideology is the one commodity most lacking in contemporary Spain with reference to the press, although there is healthy censorship of the scandalous and the immoral. To one who knew Spain in the days of the Republic, the deluge of pornography that cluttered up the stands and news racks is well out of the way. Spain today is far more moral in this external fashion than in 1931. One of the remarkable characteristics of the censorship is the benevolence with which the government endures certain foreign journalists who have remained in the country for the sole purpose of discrediting it. Their number, unfortunately, is legion, and Americans figure very large among them. There have been American journalists who have accused the Foreign Minister of pilfering the public coffers; there was a Frenchman who reported to his Parisian readers two murders in a convent as gospel truth; and a Portuguese writing for British papers who informed his public of the almost complete control by the maquis of the area of Ávila and Segovia, and who would not retract even when offered an official car to visit this region and see for himself. These characters were politely invited

---

to publish their works. . . . It is out of the question to think of a daily press. . . . In spite of everything Catalan writers continue to produce" ("Des de Barcelona," *Bulletin of Spanish Studies,* University of Liverpool, Vol. XXV, No. 100, October, 1948, p. 279).

[8] Armando Chávez Camacho, *Misión de Prensa en España,* pp. 395–396.

to cease their journalistic activities. Many of them came for one purpose: to "expose" the regime and bring it into discredit abroad.

An amusing incident characteristic of the somewhat complex way censorship works in Spain, and added proof of the fact that in this contradictory country one can never take the law for the reality, is told by the Madrid correspondent of *The Tablet* of London. In October, 1948, a musical comedy, *Las Leandras,* popular during republican days, was revived in Madrid and played to full houses. Normally productions of this kind must be approved by the Theatrical Council, a subordinate body to the Subsecretariate of Popular Education of the Ministry of National Education. The Council turned the play down three times on moral grounds — and its decision would seem to have been justified since the play offers ample room for censorship. Somehow, strings were pulled, and the show was put on. Catholic Action protested and two prelates handed in a written protest. Nothing happened since it was now the duty of the public authority to defend its own action in permitting the show to go on.[9]

The problem of freedom of speech and expression is also complicated by innumerable nuances. Americans are singularly conditioned to the idea that the only source of criticism of government or policy is the newspaper. In Spain, as in other Mediterranean countries, freedom of speech may be vocal as well as printed. We have the testimony of the newsman Constantine Brown, who, visiting Spain in 1947, reported:

> Unlike Hitler's Germany and Mussolini's Italy — the only two other dictatorships I have visited personally — there appears to be no fear among the Spanish people, in Madrid at least, of expressing themselves freely.[10]

Constantine Brown calls attention in the same article to the fact that the Spanish working day runs from 10 a.m. to 2 p.m. and from 4:30 p.m. to 8:30 p.m. The hours in between are often passed in cafés and other public places, affording rare opportunity for the freest and sometimes most caustic criticism of the government. I can add to his testimony that outside Madrid, as well, there is no dearth of criticism of the government and its policies. I have traveled about Spain from end to end, on trains and other conveyances and have yet to discover a single Spaniard encountered in this casual fashion who has refused to discuss the regime or its policies. Some have been critical, some denunciatory, some inclined to skepticism; all, however, were

---

[9] *The Tablet,* London, March 19, 1949.

[10] *Evening Star,* Washington, D. C., Feb. 25, 1947.

completely uninhibited in their expression, either by the fact of speaking to a stranger or for fear that they might be overheard. I have actually heard the severest criticism of the government in the presence of a policeman, and no one seemed to be disturbed in the least.

> I attended a coffee party in a large café here and heard the most biting and sarcastic remarks about certain officials who were alleged to be grafting heavily, and about Franco who was said to be shutting his eyes because he was afraid to fire them. . . . Persons in public places speak their minds frankly and without fear of arrest as long as they do not incite to revolt, a crime which is punishable by a long prison term or death.[11]

The atmosphere of Spain in this sense is not at all that of a police State — or at least of a properly managed police State. Freedom of movement within the country is absolute, with the traveler going where he pleases and seeing what he wants. He may visit anyone and in the many times I have been in Spain since the end of the civil war never have I seen the slightest sign that my movements interested anyone at all.[12]

Even though the coverage of the average Spanish paper with reference to the world at large is good, and Constantine Brown remarks that it is better than the French papers, nevertheless, Spaniards are woefully ill informed of what is said abroad about their own country. Even though the foreign press is admitted freely, there are occasions when certain papers are forbidden for a brief period of time. *The New York Herald Tribune,* of June 22, 1949, complains of this state of affairs and calls attention to the suppression in Spain of news regarding that country before the United Nations, the bomb outrage in Barcelona of that month, and Secretary Acheson's disparaging remarks concerning Spain as a credit risk. All of this is quite true. There is an extraordinary sensitivity in Spain, both in government circles and without, regarding foreign comments on Spain. There is the strong feeling — amply backed up by the facts — that the world press gives Spain an extremely bad coverage. The superficialities of innumerable writers, correspondents, and observers irritate and annoy the Spanish. They are in constant wonderment that visitors who are given every chance to see for themselves turn up with the most outlandish commentaries on

---

[11] *Ibid.*

[12] In 1947, 127,682 foreigners visited Spain. In 1949, 822,220 persons crossed the frontier at Hendaye into Spain. Between January 1 and June 30, of this year (1950) 871,717 tourists crossed at the Hendaye-Irún frontier (*A.B.C.*, Madrid, Aug. 10, 1950, p. 19).

things which can easily be verified. The isolation, the hostility of so much of the world, and the violence with which the country has been denounced, all conspire to make the Spanish sensitive and irritable in these matters.

THE SCHOOL SYSTEM

Primary and secondary education have received a considerable impulse during the past decade. Spanish commentators claim that the new laws governing public instruction come close to faithful conformity with the principles laid down in the Encyclical, *Divini Illius Magistri.* Present legislation makes attendance at school obligatory.[13] Provision is made for aid to those who are too poor to send their children or provide for the school materials once they are matriculated. The teachers are obliged to receive training in the *Escuelas del Magisterio* for a period of three years. To combat illiteracy, the new legislation provides for one school for every 250 inhabitants as against one for every 500 established by previous laws. The effort to increase the number of schools, still woefully inferior to the needs, has been consistent. In 1940, as soon as normality returned to Spain, the program was launched. The results in terms of new schools is the following:

	New schools created
1940	481
1941	519
1942	492
1943	599
1944	497
1945	580
1946	1499
Total	4667

The estimate for 1948 was a total of 2000 new school buildings.

It is difficult to calculate the exact increases in salary for primary school teachers because of the fluctuations of the peseta and the present inflationary trend. In 1942, 53 million pesetas was earmarked for in-

[13] It is true, of course, that there are insufficient schools and that it will be a very long time before proper provision is made for the entire school population. This is true of Spain — after a civil war — as it is true of the United States or Great Britain. It is lamentable to discover misplaced irony in the comment of the reporter in Spain who describes the pitifully inadequate conditions of many schools and concludes: "Many of the country's bosses think, as Spaniards have for centuries, that education of the poor is not desirable" (*The Chicago Tribune,* Aug. 25, 1947, article by Arthur Veysey).

creases in teachers' salaries added to a total amount spent for the salaries of the teachers of over 312 million pesetas a year. In 1944, another 67 million pesetas in round numbers was allotted for the same purpose. In June, 1947, the Cortes approved a bill, retroactive in character as of January 1, with another increase of 50 million pesetas.

Almost the only criterion for judging the progress of education since the Republic is the number of schools and teachers in active service; the number of teachers in 1935 was 47,674, and in 1948, 56,121. The State has aided private schools to a very large degree, most of them run by the religious orders. Nearly eight million pesetas were destined in 1948 for this purpose. A similar improvement has been noted in specialized education for the blind, deaf-mutes, and mentally defective pupils. Technical education, long abandoned in Spain, has received special attention from the present regime. Since 1940, specialized engineering schools, veterinary institutes, and other comparable institutions have been either restored, amplified, or newly constructed. In Madrid, Córdoba, León, and Zaragoza, new veterinary schools have been erected. Industrial trades and arts have been encouraged by the erection of appropriate buildings in Gijón, Valencia, Valladolid, and Zaragoza. In Vigo, Tarrasa, Las Palmas, and Santander the old constructions have been modernized. Between 1940 and 1942 the Ministry of Public Instruction spent nearly 20 million pesetas in this field. On March 2, 1945, the *Enseñanzas Profesionales de la Mujer* was created to care for technical and trade education of women. Commercial schools have been erected in La Coruña, Vigo, Pamplona, Lugo, Logroño, Sabadell, Huelva, and Jaén, in addition to notable improvement in those already in existence. Over three million pesetas are set aside in the current budget for workers' education and technical training.

Even before the conclusion of the civil war, the new regime had concerned itself with education. The decree of September 20, 1938, changed the general orientation of secondary education and made provision for a thoroughgoing reform. The secondary institutes, as they have been called in Spain since their creation in 1847, were subjected to fundamental improvement. Their number in 1949 was 120. Case after case could be cited of how these institutes, equivalent, let it be said, to the ordinary college training of the United States, have been favored. Such centers as Lope de Vega and San Isidro in Madrid have been reformed at an expense of some three million pesetas; entirely new institutes have been erected in Algeciras, Alicante, Barcelona,

Cartagena, Castellón, Cuenca, Cueta, El Ferrol, Huesca, Jérez de la Frontera, La Coruña, Lérida, Lorca, Lugo, Melilla, Murcia, Oviedo, Pamplona, Reus, Salamanca, Santa Cruz, Santiago, Tenerife, and Teruel. The Statute of 1938 re-established the principle of free education, abolished by the Second Republic, that is, the full freedom of private initiative in the establishment and administration of schools. Nearly 700 *Colegios,* or secondary colleges in the European sense of the word, exist in Spain today.

There can be no serious doubt that, despite its backwardness in providing popular education for everyone and, in the face of financial and material difficulties of a very real character, contemporary Spain has forged ahead with notable success. The observer who visits these institutions or concerns himself with educational matters is struck by the vitality and energy with which the problem of primary, secondary, and technical education is being faced.

HIGHER EDUCATION

University education in Spain has received a considerable impetus since the end of the civil war. Aside from the material destruction so common all over the zones involved in the war, a new orientation was given the universities, and within them was re-established the traditional "colleges" along the English university lines, long since abolished in Spain. These residences form an integral part of the university and contribute to the type of community life which had all but disappeared in the Spanish institution of higher learning. I have visited many of these centers, in Valladolid, Murcia, and elsewhere and can testify that they are slowly transforming the internal life of the institutions, giving them a personal, comradely flavor entirely lacking in the former Spanish university.

The figures speak in part for themselves. In 1935–1936, the last year of the Republic, there were 29,249 students in institutions of higher learning; in 1940–1941, the first year of the Franco regime, this number had increased to 33,763. In the brief space available, it is impossible to review the revival of education and research all over Spain, but few examples will indicate the degree to which the work of learning and scholarship has been encouraged in contemporary Spain. The existence of the research centers in almost every field of the humanities and the sciences is the most conclusive reply to those who have described Spain as an intellectual desert. The most impressive — almost too impressive indeed — example of university construction, is the University City just outside Madrid. Started under Alfonso XIII, part of it was in use when the civil war broke out. It became one of the principal fronts, and nothing escaped destruction. The reconstruction of this gigantic campus with its innumerable faculties and research facilities has progressed to the point that all of the faculties except law are now housed there. Dormitories, residences, assembly halls, laboratories — all have come into being over the years between 1941 and 1949 and in 1942 the sum of 39 million pesetas was spent on the city. Late in that year arrangements were made by law to provide a fund of 225 million pesetas in government bonds from which the University City could draw for its maintenance and progress and in October, 1943, the solemn inauguration was held of the reconstructed city. Within three years after total destruction one of the largest university centers in Europe was back on its feet and in more effective operation than when the Republic ended in 1936.

The most ambitious research undertaking in Spain today is unquestionably the Higher Council for Scientific Research, created in November, 1939, and destined to co-ordinate the entire research program of the Spanish universities and specialized institutes. It may be of interest to observe that the document setting up this foundation expressed the conviction that "the divorce existing between speculative and experimental science must be terminated." Although the tradition of Spain has been largely in the domain of the moral sciences and with great emphasis on the speculative, the first decade witnessed a very considerable upsurge in the experimental and applied sciences. Work in the field of economics, for instance, a long neglected discipline in Spain, has made remarkable strides. The range, too, of the work envisaged by the Council is vast; each discipline or branch is organized as a separate institute, with its own facilities, libraries, and other aids to research. There are the José de Acosta Institute of Natural Science, the splendid San José de Calasanz Pedagogical Institute, the Bernardino de Sahagún Institute of Anthropology and Ethnography, and institutes for geophysics, entomology, medieval studies, parasitology, musicology, biology, chemistry, Arabic and Hebrew studies, engineering, veterinary sciences, and the Fine Arts. There is the outstanding Institute of Political Studies which has done significant work in the social and political sciences.

One of the characteristics of the Council is decentralization. The work is not concentrated in Madrid alone. In every university city there are local branches of the Council's institutes and sections of the medical research centers; the Institute of Musicology functions in Barcelona, along with a center for applied biology; Granada has become the first Spanish center for Arabic studies and has developed first class facilities for the language, literature, and culture of the Arab world, and this city also houses an Institute of Parasitology. In Oviedo, the chemical institute flourishes; in Toledo, the Institute of Church History; in Salamanca, that of Canon Law; in Santander, the Menéndez Pelayo University, frequented by large numbers of students and intellectuals as one of the major summer centers in the country. In Seville the school of Spanish-American studies is situated next to the great Archive of the Indies and at La Rábida, made famous by Columbus, there exists a center for historical research of the New World. In Jaca, near the French frontier, an institute flourishes for work in the field of natural studies of that area. Specialized area studies in the Canary Islands, Galacia, and other regions have been encouraged.

The enrichment of the specialized libraries has been fundamental in this enormous program aimed at endowing Spain with the most modern equipment of scholarship. The lists of such acquisitions would read like a library catalogue; the Institute of Hebrew Studies, to which very great attention is devoted, possesses ten thousand volumes today; the Gonzalo Fernández de Oviedo Institute of Spanish-American Studies has developed from the most modest beginnings to a center with some 5000 books and several hundred reviews; the specialized Jerónimo Zurita Institute of History has brought together nearly 10,000 volumes and innumerable reviews.

Every institute has its own official review for the publication of the results of its own research and some of them issue several, as is the case of the Antonio de Nebrija Institute of Philology and the Diego de Velázquez Institute of Art and Archeology. Nothing is more extraordinary in the intellectual life of contemporary Spain than the array of learned and scientific journals and reviews that are in circulation and never has she offered to the world the results of so much fruitful work in fields that had often been neglected in the past. The most important result perhaps has been that the great men of science have been able to find encouragement and facilities for their research. Ramón Menéndez Pidal in philology, Ramón y Cajal in medicine, and innumerable others have been allowed to achieve important work with the maximum of facilities.

I have suggested that there is considerable development in the field of the economic sciences. The number of reviews is fast increasing. There are important contributions in *Anales de Economía, Moneda y Crédito, El Economista, Boletín de Estudios Económicos,* and others. A technical bibliographical institute for economics has come into existence recently to provide information regarding publications and research in this field.

The sums expended in the field of scientific research reach very respectable totals. In 1940 the Council spent only 4,000,000 pesetas. The next year the amount reached 11,000,000. In 1943 it was 31,000,000, and in 1945, 36,000,000.[14]

No survey, no matter how superficial, of Spain's intellectual life today would be complete without reference to the *Instituto de Cultura Hispánica,* at Alcalá 95 in Madrid. This was the former *Consejo de la Hispanidad,* reorganized to serve as the nucleus of Spain's cultural program abroad and the stimulation of contacts and exchange with the rest of the world. Under the direction of Joaquín Ruiz Giménez for some years a professor at Seville, now Spanish ambassador to the Holy See, the Institute received a great impulse, which has been continued under Alfredo Sánchez Bella and a corps of competent and specialized collaborators. Its work embraces a whole galaxy of activities: summer schools, publications, and cultural exchanges abroad.

The field of art has by no means been neglected. The world-famous Prado museum has been enlarged and enriched during the past few years and was reopened in July, 1939, shortly after the civil war ended. The facilities have been increased and several new rooms opened with new paintings and sculpture, including a museum of modern art with a remarkably complete collection. A Museum of the Spanish People, a Romantic Museum, the Cerralbo, Sorolla museums, and others, constitute a passing commentary on the effort that has been made in the first decade to organize more effectively the artistic treasures of Spain, present them to the public, and encourage their study.

Side by side with the university centers already described, it is impossible to omit mention of the celebrated ecclesiastical universities that are in the midst of a particularly brilliant period of development. Without mentioning all, perhaps the most famous are the Pontifical University of Salamanca and the University of Comillas, near Santander, under Jesuit direction. These two centers are rendering an in-

[14] See *The Higher Council for Scientific Research, Publicaciones Españolas,* Madrid, 1946.

estimable service to the Church and to science in modern Spain. At Comillas, magnificently located on a promontory overlooking the Cantabrian Sea, a large number of Hispanic American seminarians study. At both centers — Salamanca and Comillas — there is the atmosphere of a return to the theological and philosophical spirit of the Middle Ages. The production in these fields, as well as in that of biblical exegesis, is astounding. The examination of the index of publications reveals the vast variety of subjects and topics that have been published during the past few years. It would be impossible to list the numerous houses of study and seminaries that are maintained all over the country. Some of them are housed in ancient monasteries, redolent of the centuries; others, like the Jesuit house in San Cugat near Barcelona, still smell of paint and plaster. The energy that is going into the intellectual and cultural life of Spain strikes the interested observer as a feverish anxiety to catch up, to surpass the sluggish past, to vitalize work in the sciences, arts, and humanities.[15] There is an eagerness to transform Spanish intellectual life, with more direct reference to the needs and spirit of our century.

---

[15] A general survey of intellectual conditions is contained in Octavio Nicolás Derisi's "La investigación científica y la cultura en la España actual," published in *Ortodoxia,* Buenos Aires, No. 15, 1947.

Chapter 18. SPAIN AND WORLD WAR II

THE full story of Spain during World War II has yet to be told. The publication of a considerable body of material taken from the German Foreign Office has shed some light on that complex period, but even the documentary evidence now available does not clarify many aspects of the situation nor has a full account been rendered in any of the standard volumes that have appeared during the past few years.[1] Until the Spanish archives are fully available as well as those of other interested governments, we shall not be aware of all the implications of the incomplete account made available from documents seized in Berlin. Moreover, one suspects that the wish was often father to the thought and that those items that seemed especially damning to the Franco government were published with singular alacrity. Felix Morley calls attention to this when he writes, "The Department of State, on March 4 of this year, released to the press a most tendentious selection of documents carefully culled to prove Franco's wartime subserviency to the Axis. The Soviet Union promptly cited these in support of the resolution demanding collective intervention in Spain, which the Polish delegate introduced in the Security Council on April 17."[2]

There is, first of all, considerable doubt whether we are as

[1] Aside from the mountain of official material issuing from the United Nations, there are a certain number of standard works that deal with the question: Sir Samuel Hoare, *Complacent Dictator,* New York, 1947; Carlton J. H. Hayes, *Wartime Mission in Spain,* New York, 1945; Herbert Feis, *The Spanish Story,* New York, 1948; François Mirandet, *L'Espagne de Franco,* Paris, 1948; José María de Areilza, *Embajadores sobre España,* 3 ed.; Ramón Serrano Suñer, *Entre Hendaya y Gibraltar,* Madrid, 1947; Thomas J. Hamilton, *Appeasement's Child. The Franco Regime in Spain,* London, 1944. There is a lurid literature that has helped to titillate palates avid for sensationalism, such as Allan Chase, *Falange. The Axis Secret Enemy in the Americas,* New York, 1943.

[2] *Human Events,* Washington, D. C., July 3, 1946.

yet in a position to pass final judgment on the foreign policy of Spain between 1939–1945, because of insufficient evidence. Secondly, even what evidence is available is not complete, nor has it been organized so as to create an impression. In the United States particularly, policy in this regard has been guided by so complete an anti-Franco phobia that real objectivity in the presentation of the documents is not absolutely certain. We find even the actors in the drama itself in profound disagreement. Sir Samuel Hoare stresses the negative side of the Franco policy and lists with precision what he terms the Allied charges against the Spanish government.[3] Carlton Hayes, on the other hand, has expressed the conviction that "General Franco, unlike Mussolini, was determined in 1940 not to enter the war."[4]

The basic problem of Spain's attitude during the war is extremely important because it is unquestionably the source of much of the antagonism that the name of Franco has evoked since 1945 in international circles. One of the really significant tasks that remains to be done before a clear panorama of this situation can be attained is the detailed study from sources as to the precise evolution of Spanish policy during those difficult years. Obviously we must be a bit wary of quoting mere pro-Axis statements of General Franco and his press during the period of the war. One can form a veritable anthology of such quotations which give the impression that the *Caudillo* was on the brink of entering the war. Despite these statements, and some of them quite effusive, Spain did not enter the war and showed no intention at any time of entering it. The acts, it would seem to me, far outweigh the statements.

It is amazing that we are still convinced that a speech delivered in 1942 *proves* a permanent state of sentiment. If this were true, every American statesman of the war period would be subject to the un-American Activities Committee surveillance and probably brought before a tribunal for pro-Soviet statements during the war. General Eisenhower was entirely correct when he pointed out once that during the war years no American in high position was innocent of strong pro-Soviet utterances. Obviously in 1949 this would not seem to condemn them as active sympathizers of the Kremlin. When the shoe is on the other foot, there are always apologists to find that what is "criminal" in the case of Franco is "ex-

[3] *Complacent Dictator* (New York: Alfred A. Knopf, Inc., 1947), pp. 190–197.

[4] *Wartime Mission in Spain*, p. 65, copyright, 1945, by The Macmillan Co. and used with their permission.

peditious" in the case of Roosevelt.[5] Would it be proper to accuse Roosevelt of selling out to the Falange and committing himself to a continuation of friendship "in the best sense of the word"? To a large sector of American opinion it was understandable and defensible that Roosevelt should employ the soft phrase to turn away the possible wrath of the Madrid government because the success of the North African invasion was at stake. Suppose we apply the same logic to General Franco's position. He, too, used honeyed phrases to turn away a possible German invasion, a very real threat for years.

Spain's position when World War II broke out was clearly an unenviable one. The nation was torn and devastated; in the throes of setting up the new regime, liquidating the remnants of the defeated army, and providing for the civil population. It was exhausted, poor, and weary. The victorious Spain had no particular reason to feel gratitude to the forces arrayed against the Axis. Great Britain, France, and the United States — all of whom were later to enter the hostilities — had treated the nationalist cause with either marked hostility or indifference. Aid had come, or had been made available, from Italy and Germany and there was a natural feeling of gratitude for this support. Fundamentally it was no more inconsistent than for the incipient United States to feel warmly toward monarchical France that had given it needed aid in the struggle for independence.

As a neutral during the war, Spain's position was undoubtedly uncomfortable. With the war swirling and ebbing about her frontiers, Spain was perhaps only slightly more advantageously located geographically than Sweden or Switzerland. An important element in the judgment of Spain's relations to the Allies during the war is that the virtual domination of Europe by the Germans forced every neutral to follow a policy that was not to its liking and which, if judged abstractly, constituted a violation, technically at least, of the very neutrality it professed. Sweden was forced to depend almost entirely on Germany for its economic existence during those years. German

---

[5] *Foreign Policy Reports,* "Spain in the Post War World," Robert Okin, Aug. 1, 1947, Note 12, p. 124. "For the sake of the North African invasion, President Roosevelt was forced into a more expedient cordiality. On November 8, 1942, he wrote to Franco, 'Your nation and mine are friends in the best sense of the word. . . . You and I are sincerely desirous of the continuation of that friendship for our mutual good. . . . I am, Dear General, your sincere friend' " (quoted in Hayes, *op. cit.*, p. 91).

troops moved back and forth across Swedish territory and lines of communication were maintained with occupied Norway. Yet Sweden is a member of the United Nations in good standing, and no reservations are held against her because of acts which aided the German cause during the war. The case of Turkey is even more interesting. For years the Turkish government played a cautious game of balancing one interest against the other and there was a time when it seemed that Franz von Papen might swing Turkey into the Axis camp; there were other times when the pressure of the Allies was greater. It was not until the very end of the war, when the result could no longer be in doubt, that Turkey finally took its stand. Yet Turkey enjoys the full privilege of United Nations' membership and is the grateful recipient of American aid and support.

The Spanish were in a very similar situation with German pressure strong against them. The importance of the western Mediterranean was obvious, and the strategic significance of Gibraltar very great indeed, and the wonder is that the Germans did not overrun Spain and occupy the Straits. A few pro-Axis speeches in Madrid and even a definite pro-Axis policy by Serrano Suñer — verbal more than material — was a cheap way to avoid commitment, hold off the Germans, and preserve the neutrality of Spain which was needed for its own recovery and which contributed, in the long run, very greatly to the Allied cause.

The menace of German invasion hung over Spain from the collapse of France to the year 1943. Every utterance, every step, and every act of the Madrid government had to be measured in terms of the reaction on the force that stood ready at the Pyrenees to push across the peninsula. This is the overwhelming reality within which every decision of the Spanish government must be considered during those critical years. As suggested a complete anthology of pro-Axis speeches can be compiled as well as all kinds of felicitations on the part of General Franco and his foreign ministers to the Axis powers. But the question is, what did all this add up to? An effusive telegram to the Führer might have been annoying to the public opinion of the Allied powers, but the fact remains that such telegrams were never followed up by action in favor of the Axis. Let it be repeated again, that Spain's neutral conduct, responding exclusively to Spanish self-interest, in itself was an extremely favorable factor to the Allied cause. It is very easy to point out the innumerable acts which Spain might have performed which would have hindered the Allies in the African invasion, in the Mediterranean operations, and in the whole conduct of the war.[6]

The Spanish government had signed the Anti-Comintern Pact in April, 1939. This apparent entry into the growing combination dominated by Germany did not impede an agreement with France on the eve of the outbreak of the war. M. Georges Bonnet, Foreign Minister of France at the time, has written:

> Toward the end of August, 1939, M. Lequerica (Spanish ambassador in Paris) confirmed Spanish neutrality in the event of a European war. A few days later it was proclaimed officially. The Madrid government observed it completely during 1939–1940. Spanish factories made arms and planes for our use. . . . French Morocco could be left entirely without defenses and without the least danger and the material and men sent to the continent where they were so desperately needed. In June, 1940, there was only one French regiment in Morocco and Algiers. The Jordana-Bérard agreement was rigidly respected.[7]

General Jordana, Spanish Minister of Foreign Affairs, had promised Léon Bérard, French diplomatic representative at Burgos, that Spain would remain neutral if hostilities broke out. The part of the agreement of most significance concerned Morocco, and the two powers agreed to maintain a policy of frank and loyal co-operation in North Africa:

> From September, 1939, to June, 1940, our government could bring all the troops and materials it wanted from Morocco, Algiers, and Tunis without the slightest qualm.[8]

During the months of suspended animation that distinguished the winter of 1939–1940, Spain adhered scrupulously to its declaration of neutrality, reiterated in April when the Low Countries were invaded. British Minister Butler declared in the House on the occasion of the Anglo-Spanish trade agreement in March, 1940, that "we have no

---

[6] The most vitriolic condemnations of Spanish policy are to be found in the "Case against the admission of Franco Spain to the world security organization," a memorandum submitted by The Friends of the Spanish Republic to the United Nations, San Francisco, April 25, 1945. It is a curious document full of unproved assertions, statistics, and figures, and, among others, Walter Winchell as an authority for information on Spain. The second is "The Problem of Franco Spain," by Oscar Lange, Library of the Polish Embassy, Washington, D. C., 1946, the diatribe that set off the discussions on the Spanish question in the Security Council. Both memoranda form a synthesis of the main accusations against Spanish conduct during the war.

[7] Georges Bonnet, *Fin d'une Europe. De Munich à la guerre,* Paris, 1947, p. 82.

[8] *Ibid.,* p. 380.

cause to complain of the Spanish government's attitude which has been one of strict neutrality."[9]

The relations between the Spanish government and the Axis powers is a long series of messages, interviews, and exchanges of one sort or another, the total sterility of which is their most remarkable feature. Every act of Spanish diplomacy, including the visits of Minister Serrano Suñer to Germany and Italy, seem to revolve around one thing: Spain's willingness to join the war on certain conditions, and these conditions are invariably such that it is known beforehand they cannot be met either by Germany and much less Italy. The careful reading of much of this correspondence does not show that Franco was collaborating with the Axis; it shows that he was postponing by every conceivable means a showdown. Fortunately for Spain, Germany was sufficiently occupied elsewhere not to take direct action across the Pyrenees regardless of Spanish hesitation.

The gap between expression and reality is revealed in every important document that has come to light. At the interview of Serrano Suñer with Hitler, on September 17, 1940, a great deal of attention is devoted to the problem of reducing Gibraltar and of Spain's African ambitions.[10] The Spanish Foreign Minister speaks of Morocco as Spain's *Lebensraum* and "the natural expansion objective." Gibraltar is described as "definitely less capable of resistance than in the west." The curious thing is that all of these discussions — and this is merely the first of a great many — go over and over the same ground, with new objections and evasions and lead to absolutely nothing. If Spain were convinced that French Morocco belonged to its own natural sphere of influence and must be included, it would have been relatively easy in June, 1940, to simply push into that territory where, as Foreign Minister Bonnet admitted, there was scarcely a French soldier to defend it. Spain could have followed the same tactics as Italy in declaring war on France in the moment of the latter's collapse. Spain did not do so and continued to respect the agreements with France despite the facility and even the immunity with which they could have been violated or scrapped, on the basis that the Vichy government was no longer the same French government with which the original Jordana-Bérard understanding had been negotiated. One of the

---

[9] Cited in Loveday, *Spain, 1923–1948* (London: Boswell Publishing Co., 1949), p. 171.

[10] *The Spanish Government and the Axis: Official German Documents,* published by the Department of State, Washington, D. C., 1946, pp. 9–13.

strongest arguments to support the contention that Spain gave lip service to Axis co-operation and did nothing, is that if she had really wanted to enter the war, 1940 would have been the ideal moment. Yet 1940 and 1941 are the beginning of irritated recriminations on the part of the Axis leaders regarding Spain's evasiveness. The criticism leveled against Spain by the Axis itself does not come in 1944 or 1945, when the cause was lost, but at the very height of Axis prestige and power. An element of annoyance creeps into the interview between Hitler and Mussolini at the Brenner, on October 4, 1940. Spain entered the discussion and the Führer expressed his fear at accepting the Spanish claim to French Morocco, especially since Germany herself had her eye on certain bases there in the light of the reconstructed German colonial empire. The Duce opined that one of the major difficulties was that the Spanish themselves failed "to state what they needed and in what proportions."[11]

The Führer's impression of Spain as an ally was not encouraging. "The main impression of the Führer is that Spain is in complete disorder. . . . The Spanish have no idea of their own possibilities and aim at objectives far beyond their strength."[12] By the end of 1940 Hitler was expressing himself in still less flattering terms of the Spanish: "Spain has refused to collaborate with the Axis and I am afraid that Franco is going to do the most foolish thing he has ever done in his life. I deplore all this, for we had completed plans to cross the frontier on January 10 and attack Gibraltar early in February."[13] Count Ciano reports that in a conversation with Hitler, the latter dealt specifically with Spain, expressing himself as follows:

> If Spain had acted loyally toward the Axis (the Führer expressed himself in harsh terms regarding Franco) the British position in Gibraltar would no longer exist and the attack on the British positions in North Africa would be easy. This did not happen and there is no sign it will happen in the near future.[14]

On August 25, 1941, at the Führer's headquarters, the Spanish question was on the agenda for discussion with the Duce. The German leader was outspoken in his irritation:

> The Führer expressed himself in bitter terms toward Spain and asserted

[11] *L'Europa verso la catastrofe* (interviews, documents, and papers of Count Ciano), Milan, 1947, pp. 595–597.

[12] *Ibid.*, p. 603, Oct. 28, 1940.

[13] Hitler to Mussolini, *Les lettres secrètes échangées par Hitler et Mussolini*, Paris, 1946, pp. 105–106.

[14] *L'Europa verso la catastrofe*, p. 650.

> that this country had been for him a real disillusion. . . . The Duce . . . observed . . . that it was useless to exert pressure to get the Spanish to intervene.[15]

The refusal of the Spanish to actually intervene when every circumstance pointed to a German victory, illustrates the careful, cautious policy of the Madrid government and its delicate playing off of the Axis against the best national interests. Captain Liddel Hart, the distinguished British military commentator, noted that "we were saved from an attack on Gibraltar, thanks to the obstinacy of Franco."[16] Numerous letters and reports of interviews could be cited to demonstrate the anxiety and deception of the Axis leaders regarding the policy of the Madrid government. Even in the documentary evidence so assiduously collected by the Department of State to blacken the Spanish record, we are informed that Ambassador Dieckhoff was forced to admit that Spain was out of hand: "I could only point with the greatest emphasis — and I was speaking on the order of my Government which was taking a very serious interest in these matters — to the fact that it would be a very dangerous policy for Spain to make concession after concession to the English and Americans; Spain would thereby find herself on the down-grade. . . . "[17] The Spanish government was perfectly aware of the course of the hostilities and was perhaps persuaded even that the Axis was destined to win. Ramón Serrano Suñer makes no effort to disguise his own conviction at that time: "For my part I must honestly confess that I believed firmly in the Axis victory after seeing the astonishing success of the campaign in France. . . . "[18] The caution with which the Spanish foreign office proceeded is all the more extraordinary in view of this sentiment. Foreign Minister Serrano Suñer made several visits to Berlin and Berchtesgaden (September and November, 1940).

General Franco had apparently always insisted on making certain distinctions between the Axis powers, and whatever sentiment was involved was for Italy far more than for Germany. In every page of

---

[15] *Ibid.*, p. 672. Admiral Leahy, speaking of the Italo-Spanish discussions, said that when General Franco arrived in Rome he told Mussolini that the Spanish people would never allow the Germans to pass through Spain, even should he wish to authorize such a movement. Leahy opined that General Franco himself was opposed to such a proposition and, from similar evidence which appeared from time to time, it seemed that Franco, while desiring to appear neutral in the war, really was on the side of the Allies (cf. Leahy, W., *I Was There* [New York: Whittlesey House, 1950; London: Victor Gollancz], p. 19).

[16] ***Sunday Dispatch,*** London, Sept. 22, 1946.

[17] ***The Spanish Government and the Axis,*** p. 36. [18] Serrano Suñer, ***op. cit.***, p. 139.

Serrano Suñer's remarkable book it is plain that he felt a very great warmth for Italy and its culture, while Germany was an alien quantity with which it was necessary to deal, but for which there was no element of affection.[19]

On October 20, 1940, Colonel Beigbeder was replaced as Foreign Minister by Serrano Suñer and three days later General Franco met Hitler at Hendaye on the Franco-Spanish frontier. We must remember that October, 1940, was the darkest hour for the British, and if there was ever a moment when the Axis victory seemed absolutely sure it was then. Despite the significance of the meeting, the results were nil and Hitler obtained nothing from the Spanish despite the rosy future he described within the New Order that was being created in Europe. The Spanish government was in a position literally to determine the course of the war in those grim days, for entry in the war with German forces in the peninsula would have meant the capture of Gibraltar and the closing of the Mediterranean. It would have meant the collapse of French North Africa and very probably Spanish occupation of the territories belonging to France. It was obviously a temptation for any government eager to expand its possessions and range itself on the side of the triumphant coalition. But General Franco did not take that step. Certainly retaliation on the part of Britain would have been negligible. A blockade was of no importance since Hispano German trade relations were overland. The only possible explanation is that General Franco was animated by an intense desire to remain neutral and did not wish to hitch the destinies of his country to Germany.[20]

The meeting of General Franco and Hitler at Hendaye was an historic occasion. For one thing Franco had held off from any of the protocol visits to the Axis capitals.[21] Prof. William L. Langer has commented on this famous meeting:

[19] *L'Europa verso la catastrofe,* p. 440, Ciano speaks of his visit in 1939 to the *Caudillo,* who often spoke of Italy and never of the Axis, "because the Spanish want to emphasize the clear-cut difference in their sentiments for Italy and for Germany."

[20] Herbert Feis has written, "The Spanish government seemed possessed of the power to decide whether Britain could continue to resist outside her own island" (*Foreign Affairs,* January, 1948, p. 378).

[21] Salvador de Madariaga has commented on this meeting: "The Caudillo met the Führer at the Spanish frontier, the longest distance from Berlin Hitler ever travelled to see anyone; and though the visit took place after a three day stay of Himmler in Madrid, and although both Ribbentrop and Señor Serrano Suñer were present, no very material results were seen to come out of the meeting up to the end of 1941" (*Spain* [London: Jonathan Cape, 1943; New York: Creative Age Press, Inc., 1943], pp. 437–438).

> Hitler expounded the military situation as it was and as it would be after Britain's defeat, which was not far distant. If Spain would cooperate, Africa could be shut off against England and, once Gibraltar had been taken, the Mediterranean too would be closed. He therefore proposed an immediate alliance between Germany and Spain and the latter's entry into the war in 1941. . . . Now this was not at all to Franco's liking — he began to hedge and evade — Hitler tried to reassure him — but Franco remained dubious.[22]

The same writer insists that "Hitler was furious for meeting such resistance and never forgave Franco for his unwillingness to be persuaded and is said to have remarked frequently that he would not name such a fellow as a Kreisleiter in his government."[23] Herbert Feis, whose volume on this period is by no means a eulogy of the Franco regime, points out that "late in the night Franco broke off on the plea of fatigue. But his lavalike outpouring of talk left its mark upon Hitler. When a few days later in Florence, Hitler told Mussolini of the pact that had been completed, he said that the exertion of reaching a conclusion had been so great that rather than have the conversation over again, he would prefer to have three or four teeth pulled out."[24] It is not improbable that the Spanish were quite desirous of making precisely this impression. Obviously nothing irritated the Germans quite so much as insubordination and loquaciousness in getting to the point. Combine this with the splendid Spanish disregard for statistics and precise facts and it is comprehensible that the German leaders were perhaps fast cooling toward the idea of tying Spain in with the Axis on the march.

In November, 1940, General Yuste entered Tangier and occupied the city. This act has constituted one of the main accusations against the Franco regime. "The incident, which constituted aggrandizement up to the limit of possibility, proves that the Spanish dictator's program of neo-imperialism was to be taken seriously."[25] The city of Tangier was ruled by a form of international control dating from 1923. The fact that this government was composed of the representatives of a number of governments worked passably well in peacetime. In war it was impossible. In 1940 France was overrun and had sought an armistice; the Low Countries were virtually incorporated territory, and Great Britain and Italy were enemies after the Italian declaration

---

22 *Our Vichy Gamble* (New York: Alfred Knopf, 1947), pp. 91–92.

23 *Ibid.*, p. 93.

24 *The Spanish Story* (New York: Alfred Knopf, 1948), p. 95.

25 The Friends of the Spanish Republic, *op. cit.*, p. 11.

of war on June 10, 1940. There was danger that all North Africa would speedily fall under German control. The only nations that were outside the conflict were Portugal and Spain. Spain was the only one that had signed the statutes of 1923 and 1928 regarding Tangier. In this document the neutrality of Tangier was proclaimed.

What power, then, was in a position to maintain even a semblance of neutrality in the situation? The Spanish colony in Tangier was some 20,000. Spanish control extended over a portion of Morocco. It seemed desirable to include Tangier in this administration in the name of the Sultan. The Spanish government decided to extend the neutrality of the Spanish zone in Morocco to Tangier, now that its normal institutions had completely broken down under the impact of the war. Moreover, everything seemed to point to an early Axis occupation of North Africa, especially that portion under French sovereignty and it was improbable that an Italian and German advance across Algiers and Morocco would deliberately respect the tiny Tangier enclave.[26] The occupation forces of Tangier were not Spanish troops at all, but those of the Caliph, that is, native troops from the Morocco territory. The Spanish communicated the decision to the Control Commission in Tangier and the appropriate foreign representatives at once and at no time did the new authority refrain from active co-operation with the foreign interests. On December 31, 1940, Spain and Great Britain exchanged notes with reference to the protection of British interests. The Spanish administration cannot be accused of an abuse of power, for it respected to the end the neutral character of the zone. That no change was made in the mixed courts or in the legal system prevalent in Tangier is evidence that no permanent incorporation was intended. By February, 1941, an agreement had been worked out with the principal powers.

It would be absurd to claim that the Spanish press in general was favorable to the Axis cause and that from the propaganda angle the Germans up to 1942 were very much on top of the pile. I have gone

---

[26] See letter of President Roosevelt to General Franco, Nov. 8, 1942, quoted in full in Hayes, *op. cit.*, p. 91. E. Allison Peers has commented on the question of Tangier: "That, so soon as three of the four guaranteeing Powers were at war with each other, the fourth should assume sole control was clearly a perfectly correct and non-provocative step which in fact was taken with the knowledge and acquiescence of Britain and France and met with no criticism in either country. Nor, in the Spanish Government's bald official announcement of what had been done, was there the slightest suggestion of the contrary" (Peers, *The Spanish Dilemma* [London: Methuen & Co., 1940], p. 79).

through most of the Spanish papers for the period 1939–1945. The strident propagandistic note is not particularly evident in the non-Falangist newssheets. *A.B.C.*, for example, reported with singular objectivity the entire course of the Pacific campaign of the United States and the gradual throwing back of the Japanese. There was much talk of the New Europe and one could cull countless statements that give a decided pro-Axis impression of events. On December 2, 1941, for instance, Serrano Suñer was quoted as hoping that Spain might participate fully in the tasks of the new constitution of Europe.[27] In an article in *A.B.C.*, taken from the German review *Wille und Macht,* the Foreign Minister insisted that:

> We can assert that ideologically we form, with our own individual character, a part of the national revolutionary bloc opposed to the democracies and communism. Historically we belong to the bloc of those nations who claim a place in the sun, in the face of injustice and spoliation (Aug. 15, 1942).

Dozens of similar utterances could be brought forth to show that Spain was fervently pro-German and there unquestionably was a very strong pro-Axis sector of public opinion and in government circles. On the other hand, the slow development of Allied propaganda, and its effectiveness as time went on, showed that much of what the press and the radio said was more in the way of a counterpropaganda, designed to persuade the Axis of Spanish collaboration even though the concrete evidences of that co-operation were sometimes eloquent in their absence. There were, undoubtedly, some definite contributions to the Axis cause, such as the dispatch of laborers to Germany, the daily press reporting the departure of workers for Germany, a second group of six hundred leaving late in 1941.[28]

One of the main charges in the Security Council indictment against the Franco regime was the dispatch of the Blue Division to fight on the Russian front. This coincides with a number of outstandingly pro-Axis speeches of Serrano Suñer, particularly one delivered on March 14, 1941. On July 17, commemorating the National Movement, General Franco addressed the Falange, saying that the Allies had already lost the war.

The *División Azul* was a token force sent against the Soviet armies and as a symbol of the profound anticommunism of the Spanish people.

---

[27] *A.B.C.*, Dec. 2, 1941.
[28] *Ibid.*, Dec. 4, 1941.

In Spain it was explained as a gesture against the Soviet Union rather than in favor of Germany — a situation comparable somewhat to the Finnish action against the Soviet Union which was more anti-Soviet than pro-German in its implications. The Spanish government conceived of it as a response to the Soviet influence on the International Brigades of the civil war days.[29] A large number of these volunteers under General Muñoz Grande were the same ardent young men who had taken up arms in 1936 against the Republic, and their motive was to retaliate for the unutterable damage the Soviet Union had done to Spain in the civil war period. A French writer has described what he claims to have been the methods of recruitment and the frenzy with which the division was organized to fight in Russia: "It is just that we recognize that many of those who joined did so voluntarily, moved by various sentiments. Among the convinced Falangists, hatred of Russia was the main reason. Many young men joined to revenge a father or a brother who had fallen in Spain, a victim of the Reds."[30] Obviously to the Allies any opposition to the Soviet Union in 1942 seemed nothing short of treason. To the Spanish — who had no particular reason to feel profoundly grateful to the United States or Britain — the Soviet Union meant Soviet technical aides at the Hotel Gaylord in 1936; the Soviet Ambassador sitting in on republican cabinet meetings; and Soviet vessels landing munitions and guns at Barcelona and Valencia. The presence of the Blue Division on the eastern front was in part a matter to be interpreted against this background and experience and obviously the same visual angle did not exist for the Americans as for the Spanish.

By the end of August, 1942, Serrano Suñer was replaced as Foreign Minister by General Jordana and this was taken as a shift in the orientation of Spanish foreign policy. From then on a perceptible change in the atmosphere began to occur. The Allied landing in North Africa in November, 1942, was the severest test to date of Spain's neutrality. The slightest deviation could have provoked a disaster for the Allied cause. An attack on Gibraltar, a hostile demonstration in

---

[29] Hoare, *Complacent Dictator* (New York: Alfred Knopf, 1947), p. 139. In referring to the Blue Division, the former British ambassador writes, "The report circulated in the Allied press that the division was composed of criminals from the prisons was not accurate, nor was it true to suggest that the men fought badly when they reached the front . . . it would be unjust to suggest that the misguided young men who composed this unfortunate unit were cowards or ex-criminals. They were nothing of the kind."

[30] François Mirandet, *L'Espagne de Franco,* Paris, 1948, p. 109.

Spanish Morocco, or a secret combination unknown to the Allied command could have precipitated a very grave situation. This did not take place. The testimony is overwhelming that Spanish neutrality was of the greatest importance in assuring the success of the undertaking.[31] It is perhaps useful to recall that the political problem faced by the Allies in North Africa and the entrance to the Mediterranean was not Spanish but French. It was Giraud, not Franco, who posed the delicate question of relations. The Spanish attitude was entirely correct and there was considerable contact between the American and Spanish commanders. On January 4, 1943, General Patton visited Larache in Spanish Morocco, and in June, General Ordaz, the Spanish commander in Morocco, visited the American headquarters to receive an expression of recognition for the correct conduct of the Spanish authorities.

General Eisenhower himself has testified to the importance of the Spanish position of neutrality in making possible the African invasion: "The operation offered more than an ordinary chance of success, if Spain remained neutral."[32] Former Secretary of State Cordell Hull was equally persuaded that Spanish neutrality was a fundamental asset in this connection, and spoke of its maintenance "in the interest of Allied strategy."[33] Spain was threatened obviously not only by the Germans hovering on her northern frontier but by the possibility that the Allied powers might choose the peninsula or at least the Canary Islands as a basis of operations.[34]

The tone of Spanish declarations began to diminish in pro-Axis intensity as 1943 wore on. On May 12, 1943, General Franco delivered an address at Almería in which he urged that peace negotiations be undertaken. This was interpreted at once as an Axis feeler for conversations and produced a bad impression in both camps. The fall of Mussolini in July of that year had a deep repercussion in Spain and unquestionably brought forth a pro-Allied opinion that had heretofore

---

[31] Harry C. Butcher indicated the importance of Spanish neutrality: "All depends on the accuracy with which our political leaders can foresee correctly the reactions of French and Spanish forces in North Africa to the landings . . . the whole campaign had to be considered as depending on political factors" (reprinted from *My Three Years With Eisenhower* by permission of Simon and Shuster, publishers. Copyright, 1946, by Harry C. Butcher).

[32] General Eisenhower, *Crusade in Europe* (New York: Doubleday, 1948), p. 93.

[33] Cordell Hull, *Memoirs* (New York: Macmillan, 1948), Vol. II, p. 1326.

[34] Eisenhower, *op. cit.*, p. 43, in which the General speaks of the study of given plans for possible invasion through Norway or the Iberian peninsula.

judged it prudent to remain more silent. In August the British ambassador, Sir Samuel Hoare, urged General Franco to take steps to withdraw the Blue Division from Russia as an indication of good will.

No single incident has stuck in the mind of the American public as much as the alleged cablegram of felicitation sent by General Franco to José Laurel, puppet head of the Japanese inspired government in the Philippines. The facts are as follows: On October 14, 1943, Laurel dispatched a cable to the Madrid Foreign Ministry announcing the establishment of the independent republican government. For years the Japanese minister in Madrid, Suma, had urged that the respective diplomatic missions be raised to the category of embassies without a favorable response on the part of the Spanish authorities. The Japanese minister suggested that acceptance of this proposal would serve as a guarantee of the protection of Spanish interests in the Philippines. This veiled threat did not influence the Madrid government. The Spanish consul in Manila, José del Castaño, was under strict surveillance by the Japanese, and Spanish businessmen suffered very considerably from the occupation. General Jordana, the Foreign Minister, felt that perhaps a message to the Filipino people and not their fictitious government, would serve to evidence Spanish interest in the former possession. On October 18 such a message was sent, the text of which was as follows:

> No country has had so close relations for so many centuries with the Philippines as Spain, and these links of history, blood and affection are indestructible and will endure whatever the circumstances may be. Expressing the feeling of the Head of the State, Generalissimo Franco and of the Government and Ministry of Foreign Affairs as well as that of the Spanish people, I may say that relations between the Philippines and Spain will always be conducted on the basis of understanding and good will.[35]

Uppermost in all of this was the so-called "wolfram battle," described in detail by Ambassador Hayes: "In October, 1943, with the tide running so generally favorable for us in Spain, it naturally occurred alike to the State Department and to the Embassy that the time was auspicious for persuading the Spanish Government to halt wolfram

---

[35] Doussinague, José M., *España tenía razón (1939–45)*, Madrid, 1950, pp. 281–290. Carlton J. H. Hayes, in his *Wartime Mission in Spain,* discusses the agitation of the American embassy with reference to the Laurel incident.

exports to Germany altogether and thus give the *coup de grâce* to our adversary in economic warfare."[36]

Former Ambassador Hayes also has told the story of the aid that Spain gave directly and indirectly to the Allied cause. Much of the indirect aid was passive; it was the refusal of the Spanish government to do anything at all that was helpful. The positive aid took a number of forms, some of them of very great utility for the common cause against the Axis. Hayes mentions, among other things, the "16,000 Frenchmen, with Spain's active help, who were transported to Africa"; the stout resistance of Minister Jordana to German pressure during a difficult time; the Jews liberated from Nazi tyranny by the efforts of the Spanish government; the noninternment and release of many American and allied airmen; and the relative freedom for the work of the American and Allied intelligence services.[37]

The various forms of aid may be summarized as follows:

1. Refusal to renounce extraterritoriality as proposed by the Nanking puppet government in China.
2. Friendly relations and support of Portugal during the conversations leading to the cession of bases to the Allies in the Azores.
3. The refusal to raise the Spanish legation in Tokyo to the status of an embassy.[38]
4. De facto recognition of the French provisional government in Algiers.
5. Permission to French combatants to cross Spain to join Free French forces in North Africa despite repeated German protests.[39]

---

[36] Hayes, *op. cit.*, p. 183.

[37] Hayes, *op. cit.*, pp. 119–128. "It could easily have stopped, or at any rate gravely handicapped, our espionage against the Germans, and if the Spanish government had been committed to the serving of Axis interests it would have done so." Secretary Hull lists 18 specific ways in which Spain aided the Allies (Hull, *op. cit.*, Vol. II, pp. 1333–1334).

[38] See *German Documents; Conversations With Japanese Representatives, The Department of State Bulletin,* Sept. 15, 1946, p. 485. "With regard to Spain the ambassador [Oshima] declared that his government has had some unsatisfactory relations with the Spanish government lately. In the hesitation to raise the Japanese legation in Madrid to an embassy Tokio perceived a lack of confidence which indicated that Spain estimated the prospects of the powers in the Three Power pact somewhat skeptically" (May 19, 1943).

[39] A French testimony on this point states: "The Spanish government showed itself relatively tolerant and gave the refugees resident permits to remain in Spain. Some 30,000 took advantage of this policy" (Ippécourt, *Les chemins d'Espagne. Mémoires et documents sur la guerre secrète à travers les Pyrénées, 1940–1945,* Paris, 1948, p. 169).

6. Refusal to recognize Mussolini's republican government in Italy.
7. Refusal to designate a minister to the Hungarian government of Szalazy.
8. Facilities offered by Spain to refugees and particularly Jews.
9. Release of American fliers after crashing or forced landings in Spain.
10. Permission to Air Transport Command to use Spanish airfields.
11. Granted Allied claims to Italian ships interned in Spanish ports and purchased from Italian government by Spain.
12. Breaking of diplomatic relations with Japan, April 12, 1945.
13. Far greater commercial relations with Allies than with Axis during the war period despite German protests.

On May 25, 1944, Winston Churchill delivered a speech to the Commons. He dealt with the Spanish problem in a way which sums up the historically sound attitude. There are a number of phrases of great significance in this statement: "There is no doubt that if Spain had yielded to German blandishments and pressure at that juncture our burden would have been much heavier. . . . But the main credit is due to the Spanish resolve to keep out of the war." With reference to the African landings, the Prime Minister added, "I can assure the House that the passage of these critical days was very anxious indeed. However, the Spaniards continued absolutely friendly and tranquil. They asked no questions; they raised no inconveniences." He referred to the enormous number of ships anchored near Algeciras in range of Spanish shore guns and nothing was ever done to hinder them. "I must say that I shall always consider a service was rendered at this time by Spain, not only to the United Kingdom and to the British Empire and Commonwealth, but to the cause of the United Nations. I have, therefore, no sympathy with those who think it clever and even funny, to insult and abuse the government of Spain whenever occasion arises."[40]

There is a vast amount to say about policy during this critical period. As I suggested at the beginning of this painfully inadequate résumé of some of the high points in Spanish relations with the world during the war years, there is a mass of documents to go through, much productive research to be done, and a great deal of careful evaluation before the full story of Spain and World War II can be considered as

[40] Loveday, *op. cit.*, Boswell Publishing Co., London, p. 208 sq.

fully clarified. It is a subject about which we are still ill informed although the broad shape of the explanation is gradually becoming clear.[41]

---

[41] An interesting interpretation of the situation of the exiled republicans abroad during World War II is given by the journalist, Manuel Penella de Silva. The thesis of this writer is that the exiled republicans were the real allies of the Axis, and not the Franco regime. Their one purpose in life was to force Spain into war on the side of the Axis at any cost. These exiles saw the war from the narrow point of view of their own interests. They wanted one single thing — the collapse of Franco, and they were willing to do anything to force Spain into war against the Allies. In this sense they worked against the best interests of the Allies, for had Hitler established himself at Gibraltar, the results, as we have seen, for the Allied cause would have been disastrous. Moreover, a great many of the republican exiles were not at all badly treated by the German occupiers. Aside from Largo Caballero, none of the leaders in occupied France were even jailed. "In Hitler's Germany not a single Spaniard was annoyed for being an enemy of Franco" (see, Penella de Silva, "Escándalo en América," *Mundo Hispánico,* Madrid, No. 19, Oct., 1949).

Chapter 19. SPAIN AND THE WORLD SINCE 1945

As WORLD WAR II came to an end and the first vague pattern of the approaching postwar world began to take shape, it was generally felt that Spain as a problem must be dealt with. The general sentiment may be summarized in saying that Spain was a problem that had been by-passed and overlooked in the gigantic task of bringing the Axis to heel. Now that the clash and noise of battle was over, Spain, as an island of reaction and Fascism in a Europe that had seen this institution crumble, must be dealt with in effective and exemplary terms. It is quite possible that a good portion of the public opinion abroad, especially in the United States and Great Britain, was persuaded that the Franco regime would topple of its own weight, unable to stand up any longer against the massive opposition of the outraged Spanish people. The idea was deep rooted that General Franco occupied power solely through the good will of the Axis and that, once the support was gone, no human power could keep the structure from collapsing.

This did not happen in the late spring of 1945. The reasons are, of course, multiple. For one thing, as has been stressed repeatedly in the preceding pages, the civil war was primarily a Spanish affair and was won in large measure by the Spanish themselves. This simple fact has never sunk in upon the consciousness of many observers and commentators. The expectation of the prompt collapse of the regime was, in a very large measure, mere wishful thinking. Former Ambassador Hayes comments on how reporters and publicists loudly proclaimed the imminent fall of the regime after every important advance in the road toward Allied victory: after the North African invasion, after the ousting of Mussolini in Italy, after the occupation of Rome, and after the successful Normandy landing. None of these events seemed to produce the slightest effect on the Franco government in terms of its permanency in power. The expectation that the Spanish people would rise up in arms to throw off a government that all of them heartily detested did not materialize. Here, too, the reasons why such a movement did not materialize are quite simple and require only the most general knowledge of the civil war, the character of the regime, and the reactions of the mass of the Spanish people. With the advent of peace the hopes of those who were intent on getting rid of Franco soared anew. With the Axis gone, what possible chance did Franco have? This was the lighthearted reasoning of the gullible and the starry eyed who believed everything they read about Spain and were persuaded that Franco's days were definitely numbered. Despite the widespread optimism that Franco could not endure, instead of waiting for this happy consummation to take place in the normal evolution of things, agitation began for pressure to be brought to bear to give the inevitable trend a slight but effective shove. This pressure was particularly noticeable at the Conference of the United Nations in San Francisco in the late spring of 1945.

From April 25, when the spectacular performance opened at the San Francisco Opera House, until the United Nations became what may charitably be called a going concern, the "Spanish case" was a hardy perennial. Month after month the serious business of the world was shelved to devote attention to the Spanish case; it became something of a *cause célèbre,* and each September meeting of the General Assembly was almost certain to be ushered in with an attack on the Franco regime in Spain and the proposal that something be done about this outrageous menace to the peace of all mankind.

Prior to the convocation of the San Francisco conference there were signs to indicate that perhaps common sense might prevail with reference both to Spain and to other similar problems. The whole issue — leaving aside the fundamentally explosive nature of anything concerning Spain — was the degree to which the victorious alliance of Allied powers were going to make it their business to intervene in the affairs of peoples who for one reason or another had not participated in the war. The ardent desire to "do something" about Spain was accompanied by an equally potent perplexity as to how to go about it. If the Spanish people had done nothing for themselves for six solid years, how were they to be moved to action? Internal revolution, repugnant to even the most violent enemies of Franco within the country, did not seem to offer much perspective and the return of the so-called republican government in exile by the ordinary processes of law or recourse to the tribunals obviously offered no solution. The only remaining possibility was to pose the Spanish problem before an international body and perhaps through concerted international pressure bring about the ousting of General Franco. The intrigues in this direction early in 1945 were very considerable; exiled republicans flocked to San Francisco; the corridors of the Palace Hotel and the Opera House were darkened by the figures of Indalecio Prieto and Alvarez del Vayo, and there could be no question that the former rulers of Spain were determined to exert every influence toward the undermining of the Franco government.

With reference to the delicate question of interference in the domestic affairs of other peoples, President Roosevelt contributed to the hope that perhaps nonintervention would really become the rule of conduct of the new international society. On January 6, 1945, in his message to Congress, the Chief Executive presented the essential points of the Atlantic Charter and the principles that were to be incorporated in the Dumbarton Oaks agreement. There was pointed and meaningful reference to an international society *juridically organized* and based on mutual respect for sovereignty. The President emphasized that normal international relations could only be achieved within the framework of juridical norms in which political and partisan passion must be subordinated to the end that these relations might not be poisoned. Unfortunately, these lofty juridical principles and the respect for sovereignty were completely abandoned. The rawest and crudest of political pressures were employed for ends that had nothing to do with the progress and welfare of the nations.

No occasion prior to San Francisco was lost to push the case of Spain. At the meeting of American states in Mexico City, known as the Chapultepec Conference (February, 1945), there were efforts to introduce the Spanish problem, and the principle of nonintervention and sovereignty were restated in the same terms as they had been in the previous conferences. It was asserted that the American states are juridically equal, that intervention in the domestic or external affairs of a state is condemned, and that recognition of the respect for the personality, sovereignty, and independence of each state forms the basis of international order. This expression definitely eliminated any chance for favorable action on the demand that the American states approve collective pressure on Spain.

On June 19, 1945, Luis Quintanilla, member of the Mexican delegation and former ambassador of that nation to Moscow, proposed that a resolution be adopted declaring that Spain would not be admitted as a member of the United Nations. The statement was approved and incorporated in the Protocol of the Commission. The text read:

> The Mexican delegation considers that paragraph 2 of Chapter III of the Charter cannot be applied to nations whose regimes have been established with the aid of the armed forces of countries that have fought against the United Nations, as long as those regimes continue in power.[1]

Spain as such was not mentioned, although the remarks of Delegate Quintanilla left not the slightest doubt that Spain was what he was talking about. The text itself is expressed in such language as to apply

---

[1] *United Nations Conference on International Organization — Documents,* Vol. VI, Commission I, General Provisions.

The argument developed by Luis Quintanilla and supported with enthusiasm by Paul Boncour of France, Evatt of Australia, M. Palladin of the Ukrainian Soviet Socialistic Republic, and James Dunn of the United States was objected to mildly by the Belgian who did not wish to exclude admissions on the basis of a principle such as the one laid down. The United States representative found nothing better to say than that "The U. S. delegation is in complete accord with the statement of interpretation made by the delegation of Mexico." It may not be without interest to observe the line of reasoning taken by Quintanilla. His fuller statement was as follows:

"Mr. President, it is a well established fact that military forces of Fascist Italy and Nazi Germany openly intervened to place Franco in power. And since this is a war to stamp out the last vestiges of the Axis, of which two members have already been defeated and the third, Japan, is about to be crushed, then it is not unreasonable to demand that no government imposed upon any nation by the military forces of the Axis be permitted to participate in a conference or in a society of United Nations.

"There was a time while the costly fight was going on, when some of the powers directly concerned with the military conduct of the war placed — or should I say, had to place — practical reasons of expediency above logical commitments, but fortunately, through the untold sacrifices of the great nations that comprise this Conference, the war in Europe is won. Mussolini is no more, and Hitler himself has disappeared. We can at long last speak uncompromisingly. We can now, without endangering the course of European military operations, speak the whole truth. And the historical truth, Sir, is that the military help given Franco by Mussolini's legions and by Hitler's air power is the main reason why the Republic of Spain is not represented here today.

"Moreover, it is ironical that the defeat of Hitler and Mussolini should lend itself to consolidate Franco's position in the post-war world. The military intervention of Italian and German armies in Spain constitutes a flagrant and criminal violation of the principle of non-intervention, which is so vitally important to Mexico and to all of the small nations of the world. In fact, we consider this principle so essential to the maintenance of a decent world order that, if we should make one single exception, the whole structure of collective security and international law would be seriously endangered. We would be the last to ask intervention in the internal affairs of Spain, but precisely because of this, we demand that those groups who benefited by the military intervention of the Axis powers be ignored in meetings of these United Nations."

to more than one nation, but the intention was perfectly clear and the approval of the resolution was the consequence of this understanding. In fact, the statement that Quintanilla advanced was fundamentally the text of the memorandum presented by a group of Spanish exiles regarding the internal and external affairs of Spain.

A Committee of *Friends of the Spanish Republic* was formed to diffuse the English text of the memorandum of the exiled Spaniards and this document, that formed the basis of the Mexican proposal and was circulated widely among the delegates, was couched in terms of the most violent hostility to the Madrid regime. "As the first government to declare war on Nazism and Fascism, republican Spain has a right to admission to the organization for universal security." The Spanish Republic was, continued the same document, "our first ally in the war" and as such was deserving of preferential treatment at the Conference. I can attest to the extraordinary activity of these emissaries of Spanish republicanism. Their press conferences, handouts and releases, consumed an endless amount of time and taxed one's already overflowing mailbox to capacity.

The actual proposals advanced at San Francisco against Spain were sometimes fantastic in their sweeping generalizations and in complete contradiction with the facts of the case. It was proposed seriously, although the Conference had the common sense not to debate it, that the following points be considered:

1. Repudiation of the present Spanish regime.
2. A seat in the conference for the representatives of the Spanish republican government in the Conference.
3. Sever diplomatic relations with Spain.
4. International recognition for a meeting of the Spanish Cortes in some country other than Spain.
5. Recognition of the republican government as the only legitimate Spanish regime.

The inclusion in the Charter of the Mexican proposal was responsible for the tiresome repetition of the Spanish case down through the succeeding years. Political passion, temporary expediency, passing contingency — all of these elements intervened to produce this remarkable declaration, the very contrary of what Chapultepec had decided upon and what President Roosevelt had asserted so solemnly in January of that same year. The United Nations was to be plagued and harassed by this item in its constitution, serving as a convenient handle for the endless efforts to intervene in Spanish domestic affairs.

Potsdam was the logical successor of San Francisco. The fact that Clement Attlee was there as the new Prime Minister of Great Britain constituted a matter of considerable hope to the Spanish exiles and their friends. After all, Attlee had paraded through the streets of Madrid, closed fist in air, in the company of Helen Wilkinson back in the days when besieged Madrid was the symbol of heroism and resistance to fascism of every left-wing group in the world. His every instinct might be expected to favor the petition of the anti-Franco Spaniards. Marshal Stalin, needless to say, was not expected to experience any serious qualms about denouncing the Franco government. The result of the pressure was not everything that the republicans desired, although it reiterated the original Quintanilla declaration in the following terms:

> The three governments feel bound however to make it clear that they, for their part, would not favour any application for membership put forward by the present Spanish Government, which having been founded with the support of the Axis powers, does not, in view of its origins, its nature, its record, and its close association with the aggressor states possess the qualifications necessary to justify such membership.

The statement that the Franco regime had come into power through Axis aid was insufficient, apparently. To this was added that the nature, history, and associations of this regime made it impossible to consider it as a future member of the United Nations. This expression formed the basis of the later accusations in the Security Council of the United Nations Organization. Under *nature* was listed the allegedly fascist character of the regime; under *history,* its alleged collaboration with Hitler and Mussolini in preparing for war; and, under *association,* aid that was presumed to have been given during the war to the Axis belligerents.

The Potsdam statement was an extraordinarily gratuitous attack on a government which formed no part either of the deliberations in occupied Germany or the United Nations. The Spanish government itself replied three days later in the following terms:

> In the face of the unheard-of allusion to Spain contained in the communication of the Big Three conference at Potsdam, the Spanish government rejects, as arbitrary and unjust, the expression regarding it, and considers them the result of the false atmosphere created abroad by the campaign of calumny carried out by the expatriate Reds and their collaborators.

Spain, in line with its policy of discretion and good will, regarding errors which do not directly affect it, chose to remain silent with reference to the agreements at San Francisco, taken when most of the European countries were not even present. But when in the present case the allusion is so palpably unjust, it feels obliged to declare that it does not beg for any place in the international assemblies nor would it accept any such participation not in accord with its past, its people, and its services to peace and culture.

Similar reasons led Spain in the days of the monarchy to abandon the League of Nations.

Spain once again proclaims its will to peace, its good will toward all peoples, and is confident that once the passions that war and propaganda intensified, the excesses of today will be submitted to a more calm judgment. Spain will collaborate once more in the work of peace, since one of her merits is to have remained neutral in the two most devastating wars in History.[2]

The Assembly of the United Nations, meeting in London in February, 1946, restated once more the text of the Potsdam agreement. In addition to the formal condemnation, a third paragraph was added which considerably modified if not the intent at least the execution of this agreement. It was stated that:

The Assembly, in endorsing this statement, recommends that the members of the United Nations act in accordance with the spirit and the letter of the statement in the conduct of their future relations with Spain.[3]

This item changed the meaning, for it was now the member nations who were "recommended" to conduct themselves regarding Spain in accordance with the declaration of Potsdam and the reaffirmation of this doctrine in London. This period of 1946 was one of active machinations against Spain. The full story of the organized propaganda, the synchronized calumnies, and the incredible distortions of the most obvious facts form a later part of this chapter. It was so ordered as to coincide with the deliberations in London and thus create the impression of an honest public opinion.

The innocuous character of the London statement was followed by pressure on the French government and the Quai d'Orsay proposed to Great Britain and the United States a common plan of action against Spain. The discrepancies between them were too great to overcome. On March 1, 1946, the French government closed the frontier between the two countries, cutting Spain off from land communication with the rest of Europe. This action was provoked by the various trade

[2] Full text in Manuel Jiménez Quílez, *Proceso irregular,* Madrid, 1947.

[3] *Resolutions adopted by the General Assembly during the first part of its first session from 10 January to 14 February, 1946,* Chap. XVI, Resolution 7, p. 39.

unions and imposed on a French government unable to resist their pressure.

On March 4, 1946, a Three Power statement was issued in Washington, London, and Paris:

> The Governments of France, the United Kingdom and the United States of America have exchanged views with regard to the present Spanish Government and their relations with that regime. It is agreed that so long as General Franco continues in control of Spain, the Spanish people cannot anticipate full and cordial association with those nations of the world which have, by common effort, brought defeat to German Nazism and Italian Fascism, which aided the present Spanish regime in its rise to power and after which the regime was patterned. There is no intention of interfering in the internal affairs of Spain, the Spanish people themselves must in the long run work out their own destiny. In spite of the present regime's repressive measure against orderly efforts of the Spanish people to organize and give expression to their political aspirations, the three Governments are hopeful that the Spanish people will not again be subjected to the horrors and bitterness of civil strife.
>
> On the contrary, it is hoped that leading patriots and liberal-minded Spaniards may soon find means to bring about a peaceful withdrawal of Franco, the abolition of the Falange, and the establishment of an interim or caretaker government under which the Spanish people may have an opportunity freely to determine the type of government they wish to have and to choose their leaders. Political amnesty, return of exiled Spaniards, freedom of assembly and political association and provision for free public elections are essential. An interim government which would be and would remain dedicated to these ends should receive the recognition and support of all freedom loving nations.
>
> Such recognition would include full diplomatic relations and the taking of such practical measures to assist in the solution of Spain's economic problems as may be practicable in the circumstances prevailing. Such measures are not now possible. The question of the maintenance or termination by the Governments of France, the United Kingdom and the United States of diplomatic relations with the present Spanish regime is a matter to be decided in the light of events and after taking into account the efforts of the Spanish people to achieve their freedom.[4]

This is one of the most extraordinary documents in the whole history of Spanish relations with the rest of the world, for it is a web of contradictory sentiments, overt threats, pious expressions, and intellectual dishonesty. Just how did the United States, France, and the United Kingdom propose to achieve the new temporary government under "liberal" direction, and at the same time invite the Spanish people to seek their own liberation and in so doing merit outside aid?

---

[4] Department of State Release, No. 151, Washington, D. C., March 4, 1946.

How can the bald statement that no intervention is intended possibly be reconciled with the first set of items presented? This is the clearest incitement in the world to domestic rebellion and the overthrow of the present regime. Unless the regime proved utterly unable to lift a finger in its own defense, the probability is that civil war would result. The three powers hope that the Spanish people may be spared this horror, to which they are contributing by this declaration. Moreover, no one could define what is meant by a "liberal" regime. Did it mean the exiled republicans? The great majority of them were anything but liberals. Were they to be imported as the advance agents of the powers exerting the pressure? This statement is merely one more glaring example of the hopelessly muddled, fatuous policy that governed almost every step taken by the major world powers regarding Spain.

The culmination of the campaign against Spain came with the meeting of the Security Council in April, 1946. Oscar Lange, head of the Polish delegation, addressed a request to this United Nations agency asking that the Spanish question be placed on the agenda, because he deemed it was necessary to take appropriate measures under Articles 34 and 35 of the Charter of the United Nations against the Franco regime in Spain.

On April 17, at the thirty-fourth meeting of the Council, Lange stated his case. In an obvious attempt to avoid the accusation of interference in the domestic affairs of a nation, he based his indictment on what he claimed were the "international frictions caused by the Franco regime and which threatened world peace and security." On the basis of Articles 39 and 41 of the Charter, the Polish member urged that all members of the United Nations maintaining diplomatic relations with the Spanish government should break them. Only the delegates of the Soviet Union, France, and Mexico supported this contention, and it was perfectly clear that common sense was certain to triumph in the eventuality of a vote. In the midst of infinite machinations, the problem was passed on to a subcommittee for study, to determine if Spain in reality was a "threat to the peace of the world." The task of the subcommittee was: (1) to investigate the charges and establish their validity or their absurdity as the case might be; (2) if the charges proved true, to recommend political measures which could be adopted by the United Nations. The most crushing proof of the purely political character of this effort, as contrasted with the juridical one which by the nature of things should have predominated, was that both Poland and France, which had been in the vanguard of the anti-Spanish campaign, were designated members of the subcommittee. In a word, two of the accusers were now called upon to judge the evidence.

The subcommittee met nineteen times and was the happy recipient of an avalanche of memoranda, statements, alleged statistics, information, and pure propaganda. This mass of material was brought together in a report presented to the General Assembly. It is important to note in this connection that during the entire period of the investigation, Spain itself was never invited to make known its position; no evidence was accepted from Spanish sources — unless they were the exiled republicans. The question now was either to adjourn all discussion of the matter or take definite action. The subcommittee replied to the question: Is Spain a menace to peace and security? in the following manner:

> Although the activity of the Franco regime does not constitute at this moment a threat to peace in the sense of Article 39 of the Charter, and therefore does not authorize the Security Council to take action under Articles 40 and 42, the regime does produce a situation which represents a potential danger to peace and security and therefore is a danger in the meaning of Article 34 of the Charter.[5]

This statement, despite the preconceived intention of doing everything possible to bring in an unfavorable verdict on Spain, reveals how farcical the whole process was. After weeks of effort, even the enemies of the Franco government could conclude that "The activity of the Franco regime does not constitute at the present time a threat to peace." The extraordinary part of this statement is that it is suggested that the Security Council take appropriate action on the basis of a "potential" threat to peace. In a word, not satisfied with the absence of evidence to show such a threat, the subcommittee was of the opinion that sometime in the future Spain might become such a threat, and action ought to be taken regarding it. If this doctrine prevailed in United Nations' circles, a new era in international conduct would unquestionably be ushered in; that of taking measures to solve situations that have not even occurred. The subcommittee suggested three steps to the Security Council:

1. That the potential threat to peace be taken into account.
2. That each member of the United Nations cease diplomatic relations with Spain.

---

[5] *Report of the subcommittee on the Spanish question appointed by the Security Council in April, 1946,* United Nations Document S/75, May 31, 1946.

3. That the General Secretary communicate these agreements to each of the member nations.

The matter was submitted to a vote, June 13, 1946. The Soviet Union vetoed the measures as far too moderate. The discrepancies in the Council made it impossible to arrive at a decision. Evatt of Australia proposed a compromise. This resolution stated baldly that the investigations of the subcommittee had "fully confirmed the facts that led to the condemnation of Franco at Potsdam and San Francisco, in the first General Assembly and in the Security Council," and that the subcommittee was of the opinion that the continuance of this state of affairs would endanger peace. Therefore Evatt suggested that the Security Council, without prejudice to the General Assembly and in conformity with the Charter, keep the Spanish question constantly before it and be prepared for the appropriate measures at any time.

The whole thing was a parody of justice from beginning to end. At no time was there the slightest evidence that the truth about Spain was sought, and the decision to adjourn action was a convenient avoidance of stating definitively whether Spain constituted or did not constitute a threat *then,* not at some future imaginary date, to the peace and tranquillity of the world. The truth was that even if the internal regime of Spain was the most outrageous in existence; even if the misery and corruption were what they were claimed to be, the Security Council was limited in its action to a definite, tangible, visible threat to peace. Even the stacked subcommittee, eager to bring together every morsel of evidence against Spain, was forced to acknowledge that it was not a threat to peace.

The problem was not allowed to rest. The General Assembly of the United Nations was expected to discuss the matter once more. The address of Secretary General Trygve Lie to the Assembly in which he openly charged Spain with bellicose intentions and demanded action against her, was startling in its implications. Although the Soviet-controlled bloc was obviously in the vanguard of the anti-Spanish motion, it was judged wise to entrust the actual conduct of the debate to a more neutral nation. Minister Spaak of Belgium was largely responsible for this effort. The resolutions that came out of these deliberations are one of the texts which does the least honor to the high motive and lofty purposes of the United Nations. The preamble of this declaration reiterates the fact that at San Francisco and Potsdam, the Franco regime had been condemned. It is the second part of this preamble that is of particular interest:

DRAFT RESOLUTION ON SPAIN

The peoples of the United Nations, at San Francisco, Potsdam and London condemned the Franco regime in Spain and decided that as long as that regime remains, Spain may not be admitted to the United Nations.

The General Assembly in its resolution of 9 February 1946 recommended that the Members of the United Nations should act in accordance with the letter and the spirit of the declarations of San Francisco and Potsdam.

The peoples of the United Nations assure the Spanish people of their enduring sympathy and of the cordial welcome awaiting them when circumstances enable them to be admitted to the United Nations.

The General Assembly recalls that in May and June 1946, the Security Council conducted an investigation of the possible further action to be taken by the United Nations.

The Sub-Committee charged with the investigation found unanimously:

"(*a*) In origin, nature, structure and general conduct, the Franco regime is a Fascist regime patterned on, and established largely as a result of aid received from Hitler's Nazi Germany and Mussolini's Fascist Italy.

"(*b*) During the long struggle of the United Nations against Hitler and Mussolini, Franco, despite continued Allied protests, gave very substantial aid to the enemy Powers. First, for example, from 1941 to 1945 the Blue Infantry Division, the Spanish Legion of Volunteers and the Salvador Air Squadron fought against Soviet Russia on the Eastern front. Second, in the summer of 1940 Spain seized Tangier in breach of international statute, and as a result of Spain maintaining an army in Spanish Morocco large numbers of Allied troops were immobilized in North Africa.

"(*c*) Incontrovertible documentary evidence establishes that Franco was a guilty party, with Hitler and Mussolini, in the conspiracy to wage war against those countries which eventually in the course of the world war became banded together as the United Nations. It was part of the conspiracy that Franco's full belligerency should be postponed until a time to be mutually agreed upon."

The General Assembly,

Convinced that the Franco Fascist Government of Spain which was imposed by force upon the Spanish people with the aid of the Axis powers and which gave material assistance to the Axis Powers in the war, does not represent the Spanish people, and by its continued control of Spain is making impossible the participation of the Spanish people with the peoples of the United Nations in international affairs;

Recommends that the Franco Government of Spain be debarred from membership in international agencies established by or brought into relationship with the United Nations, and from participation in conference or other activities which may be arranged by the United Nations or by these agencies, until a new and acceptable government is formed in Spain.

The General Assembly

Further, desiring to secure the participation of all peace-loving peoples, including the people of Spain, in the community of nations, and

Inasmuch as the United Nations, by the action they took in San Francisco, in Potsdam, in London, and more recently in Lake Success, have in fact collectively refused to maintain relations with the Franco regime,

Recommends that the Members of the United Nations take, individually, the same attitude they have taken collectively and refuse to maintain diplomatic relations with the present Spanish regime, and

Further recommends that the States Members of the United Nations report to the Secretary-General and to the next Assembly what action they have taken in accordance with this recommendation.

DRAFT RESOLUTION IN AID OF THE SPANISH PEOPLE

The General Assembly,

Recognizing that the majority of the Spanish people are in a situation of hardship because they are seriously deprived of food necessary to their existence,

Recognizing that the Franco regime exports considerable quantities of foodstuffs which are essential for the feeding of the impoverished Spanish people,

Recognizing that the Franco regime uses foreign exchange obtained from such exports to reinforce the political organization that has been repeatedly condemned by the United Nations.

Recommends that the Members of the United Nations should forthwith put an end to all imports from Spain of foodstuffs and their products until the United Nations is assured that these products are no longer an immediate necessity for the food requirements of the Spanish people.[6]

A great deal of the activity described above within the various agencies of the United Nations was promoted by the Soviet bloc, under the leadership of Satellite Poland and aided by the numerous Spanish refugees in America and associated with the republican government in exile. At the same time that the problem was up for debate within the United Nations, the most extraordinary campaign was being waged in the press and over the air outside official circles, to create the necessary moral climate for the condemnation of Spain. There are few cases in recent history in which the synchronized, sustained propaganda against a particular country has been more violent and unrestrained. There can be no doubt, on the basis of evidence, that the machinery of propaganda utilized against Spain was communist. The unhappy fact is not that communists were exclusively responsible for the anti-Spanish statements and publicity, but that many of those

---

[6] *United Nations. Official records of the second part of the first session of the General Assembly,* First committee, Summary record of the meetings, p. 359, Dec. 12, 1946.

who were not, innocently took their information from Marxist sources without the least effort to investigate the truth or falsity of the claims. Behind the whole thing was the hand of those who had been defeated in the civil war. The importance of this propaganda drive against the Franco regime is such that it may be useful to trace the complicated threads of the plot and demonstrate exactly how the operation was carried out.

During the spring of 1946 the Spanish government made repeated reference to the existence of such a propaganda plot. On March 2, Madrid denounced "once more the development of a new offensive of calumnies and lies against Spain under the guise of humanitarianism." In his address to the Cortes, May 14, 1946, General Franco stated that "Western sectarianism and Asiatic communism are responsible for the campaign abroad against our country." It might reasonably be suspected that this statement was a simple way of placing responsibility on that vague thing called the "Left Wing" forces in the world. Fortunately the evidence exists to prove that the campaign of calumny against Spain was in fact of communist inspiration and origin.

In early 1946 the first signs of this activity appeared, while within United Nations' circles, as we have observed, the question was being agitated. France was the center from which the campaign emanated for Toulouse, France, had long been the center of the various exiled Spanish communist groups; there the newspaper *Mundo Obrero* is published, the party has its headquarters, and preparations are made for infiltration into Spanish territory. On January 17, 1946, the Constituent Assembly of France passed a resolution demanding that relations be broken with Spain, and in the debate that accompanied this request, Jacques Duclos, French communist leader, took an active part, delivering violent diatribe against the Madrid regime. In support of the resolution, the extremists in France began the initial agitation which was aimed at forcing the French government, faced by public opinion, to act favorably.

The "case" selected as the central issue of the campaign was that of Cristino García. On January 22 the trial of Cristino García and sixteen other defendants took place in Alcalá de Henares. The indictment against them was for common law crimes, none of which could in any sense be considered as political. The French Communist Party seized on the sentences against Cristino García as the incident it needed to let loose a wild campaign of calumny against the Franco government. The details of this incident are highly revealing of the tactics and utter dishonesty of extreme Left methods, seeking to produce the atmosphere of violence and of tension in which to achieve their ends. But before describing how this came about, it may be well to explain just who Cristino García was before he was turned into a communist hero and the supposed victim of Franco tyranny.

On July 18, 1936, Cristino García was an obscure stoker on the merchant ship *Luis Adaro* which arrived a few days later at the port of Avilés. On leaving ship he joined the republican army in Asturias and became a sergeant in its ranks. When the northern front was smashed by the nationalists, García fled to France and from there went into Catalonia where he rejoined the army. When the Catalan front collapsed, he took definite refuge in France and sometime in 1943 joined the French underground and collaborated against the Nazi occupier. At the end of the war García had attained a position of some importance as a resistance leader in the south of France and had come in contact by this time with the Spanish Communist Party in exile and in all probability attended the school maintained in Toulouse by this group for the formation of terrorists. Designated head of a guerrilla band in Spain, García crossed the frontier clandestinely in April, 1945, and for some time headed a group that got as far as the Guadarrama Mountains. From then on his career became that of an ordinary highwayman. His first known crime was the murder of the owner of a bar in Canillejas; an act of cold-blooded assassination. On June 13, at Peguerinos, Ávila province, he shot a policeman who had demanded his papers and three days later attacked another civil guard post and shot two of its members. On September 6, García shot Gabriel León Trillo, a former communist who had renounced the party; on September 14, he attacked the railway station at Paseo Imperial and stole 21,000 pesetas; on October 9, with his gang he entered the branch of the Banco Central, on the Paseo de las Delicias, No. 121, and made off with 143,000 pesetas; and on October 15 liquidated one of his group, Alberto Pérez Ayala, who had refused to continue further the life of crime. He was caught shortly after, having on his person a number of papers showing the offices, factories, and banks he was preparing to loot; at the trial García did not attempt to deny his crimes.

The facts as revealed at the trial, the confession of García, and the solid evidence presented show him as a bandit and highwayman, and whatever political views he may have held were not on trial. This, however, was not the view of the universal left-wing press, despite the information released to the press and the international agencies in Madrid. From then on it became a race as to how grotesque the presentation of the Cristino García case could really become. The New York *Daily Worker* (Jan. 23, 1946) stated that the accused had been guilty of an attack on a Falange headquarters and underground activity. This same sheet on January 25, followed by *P. M.* on January 24, acknowledged that a couple of murders were involved, but they are explained away by the fact that the victims were "traitors to the party." The distortion of the news was universal in the French press. *L'Humanité* (Jan. 23, 1946) asserted that the death penalty was the result of García's attack on a Falange center and his leadership of the guerrilla fighters. *Combat,* of the same date, simplified the case even more by stating that the death sentence was the consequence of García's participation in the French underground during the war. The effort now was directed to glorifying García and presenting him as a hero of the democratic resistance against Franco, and every resource of the communist network was employed to advance this version. Antonio Mije, Spanish communist leader in Toulouse, cabled the various communist centers the world over that García was "the heroic leader of the underground" and that "Spanish Republican exiles appeal to the world to make every effort to save his life."[7] The Spanish communist organ in France, *Unidad y Lucha* (Jan. 26, 1946), proclaims Cristino García as "a hero of the French liberation movement." The paper *L'Espoir* of Bayonne (Jan. 26, 1946) entitled its chronicle of the García case, "The crimes continue," referring not to García and his numerous murders, but to the alleged crimes of the Spanish government against these heroes. The French papers *Front National* (Feb. 5, 1946), *France d'Abord* (Feb. 6, 1946), and *Voix Ouvrière* of Geneva (Feb. 5, 1946) echoed this claim faithfully and explained to readers that García had simply returned to Spain and upon arrival had been arrested and condemned to death. Not a word was said of his activities after crossing the frontier.

José Giral of the exiled Spanish republican government, not to be outdone by the communists, issued an appeal on January 26, demanding intervention to save Cristino García, "a commander of the French Interior Forces (FFI) who has been condemned to death." Moscow Radio on January 28 broadcast its own version with a stirring appeal to save the life of a liberator and solid democrat.

---

[7] *Daily Worker,* New York, Jan. 26, 1946.

The agitation was not limited to the press. Very soon popular demonstrations began to take place with the specific demand that the French government break relations with Franco Spain, and we are told that "The Federation of former Partisans of the Haute Garonne sent a telegram to Gouin stating their indignation at the new murder Franco is planning and demanding the immediate cessation of all relations with him."[8] The demand became very concrete in the words of one paper that "France must save Cristino García. France should intervene immediately."[9]

The communist press whipped its readers into a state of frenzy, and on the two meager pages available to the French newspapers, column after column was devoted to the tribulations of Cristino García and the monstrous miscarriage of justice that had been perpetrated in Madrid. The extremist organizations all over France poured forth protests and manifestos. *L'Humanité* (Feb. 3, 1946) records that the construction workers of the Paris area demanded that France intervene to liberate García. This paper explains its position and especially the "spontaneity" of the protests in this way: "Numerous resolutions should be voted and sent by the various organizations as well as all sincere democrats united in the defense of 'peace and liberty.' This is insufficient, however. The real fight for Cristino and the heroes of the Spanish people is to undertake without a moment's delay effective action to block the shipment of goods to Franco."

The United States, Sweden, Switzerland, and the United Kingdom were denounced for carrying on trade with Spain. The official sheet of the French Communist Party concludes in glaring headlines: "Not a single ship to Spanish ports! Not a single railway car to the Spanish frontier!" The emphasis on the rupture in relations with Spain was not limited to the diplomatic; they included rather the whole range of commercial and business operations between the two countries. On February 8, *L'Humanité* recorded the first concrete reaction to this wave of agitation and confusion. "The metallurgical workers of Dieppe have refused to load motors for Franco Spain. This is an example of how the workers appreciate the interests of France. It is necessary to break completely with him and his government of bandits." *Front National* (Feb. 5, 1946) proposed that the honor of France was involved in the García case and that the French government should offer him honorary French citizenship as testimony of admiration.

[8] *Le Patriote,* Jan. 26, 1946.
[9] *La Voix du Peuple,* Lyon, Jan. 31, 1946.

On February 9 the French government responded to this pressure and issued instructions to its representative in Madrid:

> In view of the important role played by Cristino García in the French resistance, the French government has given instructions to its representative in Madrid to intervene in his favor with the Spanish authorities. Cristino García has been condemned to death by a Spanish court for his political activity (*Le Populaire, Combat,* and others).

Ce Soir, a fellow traveler journal, reported elatedly on February 8 that the French government was prepared to take retaliatory measure against Spain even if the Anglo-Saxon power did nothing. On February 10 this semiofficial approval led to public demonstrations against Spain. It is not without interest that in this respect Maurice Thorez, as "an official representative of the French government" joined in these manifestations.[10] The French General Confederation of Labor was directly involved in the campaign. The socialists had been somewhat reluctant to follow the communist lead in this matter, but *Le Populaire* announced, on February 15, that the French socialists were profoundly moved by the news coming from Spain and urged that the government intervene with Franco. On February 17 a monster mass meeting gathered at the Salle Pleyel to support the rupture in relations between France and Spain. The French government was led to make an official statement in which its second *démarche* in Madrid was described: that the Ministry of Foreign Affairs take up with Franco the possibility of clemency for those who had so valiantly taken part in the liberation of France.[11] Both the socialist and communist journals heralded this new intervention in the most exultant terms; and both proclaimed the victims of the Spanish courts as "Spanish republicans." *L'Humanité* (Feb. 18), which has never been noted for its moderation, denounced "the crime that Franco is committing against our country . . . and the new Fascist aggressions being prepared on Spanish soil."

Jacques Duclos, French communist leader, participated in the Pleyel meeting at the side of Antonio Mije, General Modesto, and other Spanish exiles and did not conceal the basic reasons for the hostility to Franco: "Franco has set himself up as the enemy of communism. The liquidation of Franco is to us French the execution of an enemy."[12]

---

[10] *Daily Worker* (London), Feb. 11, 1946, and *Die Tat,* Zurich, Feb. 12, 1946.
[11] *Le Parisien Liberé, Le Populaire,* Feb. 17, 1946.
[12] *France Nouvelle,* Feb. 23, 1946.

At Strasbourg, on February 18, a meeting under C.G.T. auspices demanded the rupture of relations with Franco, and on February 21, various papers published the resolution of the C.G.T., couched in identical terms with the resolution approved at the Pleyel meeting, in which it was urged that "the lives of all former combatants of the French army be saved."[13]

The paroxysm of the press reached a new high point in the succeeding days as it was rumored that the seventeen condemned men would be reprieved. The French press exulted that pressure of the French government had led the Madrid authorities to moderate their condemnation.[14] On February 21 the Spanish government announced the execution of the more prominent among the condemned with a detailed list of the common law crimes of which they were guilty, while the less guilty were reprieved by act of General Franco. Almost none of the French papers published the entire Spanish statement with the aggravating circumstances, and in most cases the statement was reduced to the mere notice that the execution had been carried out. Even the more moderate press, *L'Aube, Le Figaro,* and others, expressed shock that French intervention had produced no effect.

Most of the Paris press simply eliminated any attenuating circumstances and published the bare announcement with the implication that the crimes for which the men had died were exclusively political.[15] Every newspaper without exception called them "republicans," some listed their contributions to French liberation, others that García was married to a French woman. *Paris Presse* stated simply that they had been executed for communist activity.[16] *Le Populaire* demonstrated its moderation and good will by playing up the story under the title, "Franco a murderer."

The session of February 22 of the Constituent Assembly found nothing better to do than approve a resolution deploring the executions in Madrid and expressing "indignation for the execution of Cristino García and his companions, shot because of the hatred of liberty on the part of the executioners."[17] The violent language of the extremist press increased in an *in crescendo* effect; parades, demonstrations, and a huge meeting in the Vélodrome d'Hiver, one of the

---

[13] *Front National, L'Humanité,* Feb. 21, 1946.
[14] *Le Populaire,* Feb. 22, 1946.
[15] *Le Monde, L'Ordre, Paris Matin, Le Populaire, Libération,* Feb. 23, 1946.
[16] *Combat, France Libre,* Feb. 23, 1946, and *Paris Presse* of the same date.
[17] *Le Populaire,* Feb. 23, 1946.

favorite meeting places of the communists, were announced. The response to the incitement was immediate, and among the first was the Postal Employees Federation which announced that "to indicate disapproval of the assassination of Cristino García, it has ordered its departmental branches to suspend as of today until tomorrow all telephone, telegraph, and postal communications with Spain, with the exception of strictly official communications."[18] The Spanish government protested against this act which contravened every international agreement signed by the two countries and which was a matter of the exclusive jurisdiction of the French government and not of a trade union. No reference to this protest based on international practice was even made except by *France-Soir* and *Le National* of February 28. Trade unions all over France continued to demand the breaking off of relations; the steelworkers, transport employees, railway workers, textile workers, all sent in their petitions, while *L'Humanité* faithfully reported this demonstration of solidarity with the victims of Franco tyranny. Thirty thousand persons demonstrated in Toulouse against Spain; five thousand in Perpignan, and in Morocco a demonstration at Rabat demanded action against the assassins of Cristino García.[19] *L'Humanité* reported during those days that a group of distinguished Frenchmen had signed a petition demanding the immediate cessation of relations with Spain. In the list are to be found the usual names of Albert Bayet, Louis Saillant, Irene Joliot-Curie, Louis Aragon, Marcel Cachin, and others. To this were added exuberantly the names of Pablo Picasso, Pierre Cot, and others of the same stripe.[20]

As might be expected, the republican government in exile was not idle while this indignation was being worked up. Manuel de Irujo, a member of the Giral government, addressed the British Foreign Office to the effect that if a single European country had recognized the exiled government, Franco would never have dared carry out the executions.[21] Giral himself, chief of the cabinet of the exiled government, compared the procedures in Spain to the worst that had come out of Dachau and Buchenwald. Dolores Ibarruri, the celebrated "Pasionaria," telegraphed Ministers Bidault, Bevin, and Secretary Byrnes imploring them to

---

[18] *Ce Soir, Franc Tireur, Le Populaire,* Feb. 24, 1946.
[19] *L'Humanité, L'Eco du Maroc,* Feb. 26, 1946.
[20] Feb. 24, 1946. *Ce Soir* and *Libération,* same date.
[21] *Ce Soir,* Feb. 24, 1946.

take steps to terminate the "assassination of militant democrats by the hangman Franco."[22]

The French press was busy demonstrating that elsewhere the same sort of protests were being organized. *Aurore* (Feb. 24, 1946) reported that in Rio de Janeiro there had been demonstrations; that President Grau San Martín of Cuba had been petitioned on behalf of the condemned men, that the friends of republican Spain in London had protested and had urged Bevin to take the proper steps to put an end to Anglo-Spanish relations.

The culmination of this prefabricated campaign was February 25, for on that date the representatives of the C.G.T. met with the railway, dock, and transport workers to examine specific measures to be taken against Spain.[23] The principal point under discussion was the most effective means for the immediate cessation of all traffic between the two countries. *Le Populaire* (Feb. 26, 1946), socialist Blum's organ, was quite frank about the result of the labor deliberations: "The rail, dock, and marine workers have decided to stop all traffic with Spain." On that same date the French government was informed of the action of the C.G.T., at that time under the direction of the communist, Benoît Franchon.[24] The French government was not violently enthusiastic about the prospect of a rupture. A right-wing paper, *L'Epoque,* commented that:

> It is no secret that the Ministry of Foreign Affairs considers a break inopportune, especially a unilateral rupture which will produce serious economic and financial complications for France (Feb. 26, 1946).

It must be recognized that Georges Bidault was not inclined to any such drastic measure, although the presence of the communists in the cabinet demonstrated that their pressure could not easily be withstood. This may be taken as further evidence, if such is necessary, of the total impossibility of a working arrangement with the communists in a mixed or Popular Front cabinet. The announcement was made that as of March 1 the frontier between France and Spain would be closed. The press was outspoken in its expression regarding the effects of this measure; *Ce Soir* (Feb. 27, 1946) opined that "it would have international repercussions. Not only will it deprive France of our exports and those coming through France,

---

22 *Ibid.,* Feb. 27, 1946.
23 *Combat,* Feb. 25, 1946.
24 *Franc Tireur.*

but it is virtually a denunciation of the commercial agreements between Paris and Madrid. Moreover this is the first step on the part of a great nation to protest against the Franco regime and its crimes. It is another move toward the breaking of diplomatic relations. The Council of Ministers had decided to warn the governments of Great Britain and the United States of the danger of Spain for international peace." *Libération Soir,* on the same date, was even more outspoken: "This decision merely confirms the resolution taken this morning by the trade unions on direct instructions from the General Confederation of Labor." Since the C.G.T. was communist dominated and since it was responsible by public confession of having given the orders for the resolution on the part of the trade unions, it is logical to conclude that the French government acted to close the frontier under direct and unequivocal pressure from the communists. It was a glaring example of the foreign policy of a major power determined by the irresponsible and partisan action of the extreme Left through methods which were dishonest and unscrupulous. *Cité Soir* (same date) claimed quite candidly that the "C.G.T. and the trade unions have mapped out the road for Félix Gouin to follow." *The New York Herald Tribune* (Feb. 27, 1946) reported that the "Government decision came after the General Confederation of Labor had ordered its members to cease all transport of products between France and Spain."

This by no means modest achievement was not sufficient to satisfy the Left. During the mass meeting at the Véledrome d'Hiver, Jacques Duclos demanded that further measures be taken; petitions to the United States and Great Britain, the organization of a blockade, and the isolation of Spain. "It is necessary to show the world that Franco is looked upon by the civilized world as a savage."[25] The Central Committee of the Communist Party issued a statement expressing the conviction "that all Frenchmen and Frenchwomen will see to it that nothing reaches Spain by land or sea or across Portugal. The order of the day is: Not a ship, not a train, not a car, no goods for Franco Spain. Down with Franco. Long live the Spanish Republic."[26]

The whole fictitious agitation in the case of Cristino García was the work of the French Communist Party. The repercussions abroad were not long delayed, due to the fact that Antonio Mije, of the

---

[25] *L'Humanité,* Feb. 27, 1946.
[26] *Ibid.,* March 1, 1946.

Spanish Communist Party, telegraphed the communist groups abroad, urging them to take action. We find in a periodical in Chile an unusually frank statement as to exactly how this world-wide protest was really provoked. In *Noticias Gráficas,* of February 25, the following message from the Pasionaria, as General Secretary of the Spanish Communist Party, to the Hispano-Chilean committee for the aid to the Spanish people reads:

> In spite of world demand and the protests of the Provisional Government of France, to save the lives of Cristino García and his companions, Franco has executed him together with nine other Republicans. Other lives are in danger. World democracy must save them and strike down the hand of the hangman. I urge, in the name of Spanish democracy, that the protests be intensified against these crimes and that every aid be given the militant Spanish democrats who are in danger of assassination by the Fascist dictatorship of Spain.

The official sheet of the Argentine Communist Party, *La Hora,* on February 26 promised solemnly that "in the name of Argentine anti-Fascism this demand of the Pasionaria will be heeded." The artificial character of the propaganda against Spain on the Cristino García issue is no more eloquently demonstrated than in the tirade of the Brazilian communist paper, *A Hora:*

> We demand that in every country the maximum effort be mobilized to save these valiant sons of the Spanish people. . . . We demand that messages and letters be sent the various United Nations embassies in Madrid, the foreign offices of London and Washington to obtain the intervention of these nations. . . . We demand an intense radio and press campaign to arouse public opinion against the Franquist terror (Feb. 19, 1946).

There is no hint in any of the quotations, or in the multitude of others that cannot be included, of an interest in discovering what was really happening in Madrid, nor did any of the extremist sheets express the slightest concern for anything but the maximum of confusion, agitation, and pressure. If the whole absurd business had been limited to the noisy, vulgar extreme left-wing press, it would have perhaps been of little consequence and would scarcely merit the space devoted to it here. But the fact is that this jarring, scandalous campaign made a deep impression on a public opinion that is normally far removed from the Marxist press. It created the atmosphere of distrust and prevented through sheer pandemonium a dispassionate and rational examination of the realities.

The usual front organizations moved into action immediately. The veterans of the Abraham Lincoln Brigade, the numerous cultural and relief groups in America, Britain, and elsewhere, all contributed their protest to this rapidly mounting chorus of invective. Boycotts were proclaimed here and there. Dock workers in Amsterdam refused to load a ship carrying potatoes to Spain.[27] Workers in Chile were reported as refusing to load or unload Spanish vessels.[28] Seventy Labor members of Parliament sent the Ministry of Justice in Madrid a telegram protesting against the execution of "patriots."[29]

Ironically enough the countries east of the Iron Curtain were not backward in protesting this alleged violation of basic human rights. "The Bulgarian Committee for the Defense of Spanish Democracy," whose president was Comrade Dimitrov, proclaimed that the "Bulgarian people are ready to do everything in their power to destroy this vile nest of Fascism, Franco Spain."[30]

The Spanish government was not inclined to take this verbal trouncing passively. On March 1 the government issued a formal statement, with special reference to the attitude of France. It reviews under fourteen points[31] the whole story of Franco-Spanish relations since the outbreak of war. After a number of points regarding the general attitude of Spain during the war, the communiqué listed certain specific incidents and situations that the French government tolerated without attempting to correct. These included:

1. Assaults on Spanish consulates in Algiers, and the south of France, the last at Sète on February 28, 1946.
2. Training and aid to Spanish Reds who have landed on the coast near Málaga with arms and explosives provided from French North Africa.
3. Constant aggression against our territory by Spanish exiles with the support of the local French authorities.
4. Kidnaping and murder of Spaniards living in France by Spanish communists with no intervention on the part of the French authorities.
5. Constant protection to Spanish guerrilla fighters crossing the frontier.
6. Existence in France of centers for the preparation of communist

---

27 *L'Humanité,* Feb. 24, 1946.

28 *Daily Worker,* New York, March 2, 1946.

29 Reported in *Libération Soir* of Paris, March 3, 1946.

30 *L'Humanité,* Feb. 14, 1946.

31 Full text of all points in *Apuntes para la Historia,* Oficina Informativa Española, Madrid, 1946, pp. 50–51.

terrorists with no attempt by the French government to suppress them.

7. Aggressions across the frontier at Chambéry and other points.

8. Unceasing campaign by the French in every international conference against Spain.

9. Constant defamation and calumny by radio and press against Spain with no corrective on the part of the French government.

The French press scarcely dignified the text of the Madrid statement with a reproduction. *Le Monde* reproduced it in its entirety (March 3, 1946). The rest of the press dubbed these accusations, "Franco agitation," "Franco lies," "Extravagant communiqué from Franco," "A ridiculous report."[32] Astonishingly enough, after this sampling of the French press the French representative in Madrid was instructed to protest to the Spanish foreign office against the tone of the Spanish press with reference to France.[33] The French government did not hesitate to receive José Giral, head of the Spanish government in exile and not recognized by France at all, officially and with all honors.[34] A few months later a Rue Cristino García was duly inaugurated in Paris, with the Pasionaria as the principal speaker.[35]

The uproar that accompanied this whole affair was amply summarized by such papers as the *Courrier de Genève* (Feb. 28, 1946), which suggested that the execution of Cristino García served as the flimsiest of pretexts for communist agitation within France. *The Irish News* of Belfast (Feb. 28, 1946) expressed the thought that if every execution of a criminal provoked the furor that accompanied the García case, Europe would find itself in a third world war in record time.

The most complete summary of the matter is that of *La Bourse Egyptienne* of Cairo, under date of April 9:

> We are witnessing a new offensive inspired by Moscow against General Franco. The recent initiative in France supported by the Soviet Union had not produced the desired result, namely the restoration of the Republican regime. The plain truth is that the Soviet Union hopes to create a communist Spain. Lenin always said that this was the first country in which to carry out his Marxist revolution. As long as General de Gaulle was in power he refused to take the steps demanded by the communists. When de Gaulle retired, President Gouin gave in to the pressure exerted by Maurice Thorez.

---

[32] *La Voix de Paris,* March 3, 1946. *Résistance, Ce Soir,* and others.

[33] *Ibid.,* March 18, 1946.

[34] *Le Populaire,* March 8, 1946.

[35] *Front National,* Aug. 6, 1946.

Obviously this propaganda was not aimed merely at arousing world sympathy for the victims of the so-called Franco "terror." The case described, however, served its purpose admirably. It focused attention in elementary terms on Spain and provoked an instantaneous reaction among large masses of people. It created what I would call the "climate" for action and for pressure. In this sense the work was not unfruitful. The immediate aims were the economic strangulation of Spain through agitation among workers and the isolation of the nation through the withdrawal of the normal diplomatic missions. In addition to these two objectives which have already been defined in connection with the pressure of the French labor groups for the closing of the frontier, there was the third and not less important motive of creating within each nation an atmosphere of revolution and of agitation, inspired by the Spanish question and admirably suited to the ends of the communist opposition.

Despite the relative failure of these incidents, the campaign against Spain continued unabated. The detailed story of the complex communist activity around the world would fill the pages of an entire book. The published sources, if carefully correlated, reveal beyond any doubt that this synchronization was the consequence of a well-conceived and cleverly operated propaganda machine. Moscow Radio called on February 28, 1946, for the unconditional rupture by all countries with Franco Spain. Both *Pravda* and *Izvestia* devoted much space during the succeeding months to information regarding anti-Franco demonstrations and protests all over the world. In Belgrade Minister Bakić stated that "Yugoslavia supports without reserve all action tending to put an end to the Franquist regime."[36]

The Czech cabinet expressed unconditional solidarity with "all democratic fighters against Franco."[37] Poland spoke out for the organization of all democratic peoples to overthrow the Spanish government.[38] Bucharest and Sofia responded to the call for action by mass demonstrations against Franco and protests at the terror alleged to reign in the peninsula.[39] The Belgian Communist Party launched a full-dress campaign for the isolation of Spain.[40] In the Netherlands, Denmark,

---

[36] Reported in *Le Messager,* Paris, March 1, 1946.

[37] *Daily Worker,* London, Feb. 28, 1946, and *Le Drapeau Rouge,* Brussels, March 1, 1946.

[38] *L'Humanité,* March 8, 1946.

[39] *Daily Worker,* London, March 1, 1946.

[40] *Mundo Obrero,* Toulouse, March 9, 1946.

and Great Britain the communist parties made the anti-Franco cause the leading issue in the spring of 1946. The Greek E.A.M. demanded that the government break with Franco in the name of democracy.[41] The press reports show that in Chile, Argentina, Brazil, Cuba, Colombia, Uruguay, and Mexico the same resolutions were being passed and the same pressure applied to the local governments.

In Italy the campaign reached almost grotesque proportions. The employees of the Rome slaughterhouse cabled their protest against the Franco regime. The "National Liberation Committee of the Public Markets of Rome" signified that, in protest against Franco, the markets would be closed down for fifteen minutes on a specified day.[42] Pietro Nenni, communist-sympathizing socialist, expressed himself in favor of the creation of a *cordon sanitaire* around Spain.[43]

In certain countries, such as Canada and Brazil, the anti-Spanish campaign was an excellent means for strengthening the position of the local communist parties. In the case of Canada the discovery of Soviet espionage had increased public sentiment against the extreme Left, and the agitation against Spain constituted an excellent antidote. *The Gazette* (March 1, 1946) of Montreal reported the usual demonstrations and petitions to the government for action. In the far-off Union of South Africa, the local labor organizations acknowledged the receipt of a communication from the World Federation of Trade Unions in Paris signed by the communist Louis Saillant, asking them to bring pressure to bear on the South African government for a break with Spain.[44]

The press agency, *France-Presse,* reported that on March 5 posters had been placed near the Spanish consulate in Shanghai, in English and Chinese, denouncing Franco.

Another immediate objective of this world-wide agitation was aggression against Spanish consulates and diplomatic missions. In Havana, Cuba, on January 14, 1946, a bomb was tossed at the Spanish embassy.[45] The consulate in Toulouse was attacked, and in Sète the consular quarters were occupied by republican exiles who hoisted the republican flag.[46] In Casablanca, Morocco, the consulate had to be protected

---

[41] *Le Drapeau Rouge,* March 2, 1946.
[42] *L'Unitá,* Rome, Feb. 28, 1946.
[43] Reported in *La Suisse,* Geneva, April 13, 1946.
[44] *Cape Times,* Cape Town, South Africa, March 7, 1946.
[45] *Washington Post,* Jan. 15, 1946.
[46] *Ce Soir,* Paris, March 1, 1946.

by police against demonstrators who filed past it menacingly.[47] In Copenhagen a hand grenade was thrown at the consulate.[48] In Buenos Aires, Oslo, and Liverpool similar incidents took place.

Great pressure was mustered to prevent ordinary commercial relations with Spain, for the idea of an economic blockade was very much in the air and did not subside for the next two years. A very frequent proposal, not only from communist sources, whose purpose was chaos in Spain, but from more conservative elements, is that Franco would be brought to his knees in short order if all foreign commerce was cut off. The communists utilized the unions in which their strength was great to produce the same effect that the transport workers in France had achieved in stopping trade with Spain. A picturesque case is that of the port of Rotterdam. The Dutch communist paper, *Da Waarheid,* demanded the complete boycott of Spain, and a strike was proclaimed in Rotterdam against all shipments to Spain. The mayor of the city, Oud, and the port captain met with the strikers; the former mayor with great common sense suggested that relations with Spain was a matter pertaining more properly to the Dutch government. Moreover, Holland was furnishing Spain seed potatoes, beet seed, and other similar products to be paid for by the Spanish with oranges, glass, cork, and wood. Was there any sense in allowing such perishable products as oranges to rot, simply because the dockers were not in sympathy with the government in Madrid?[49] The Dutch communists were of the opinion that "We can stand a few more months without oranges to be sure that Fascist bombs do not come with them."[50]

Moscow Radio contributed to the agitation by calling for a more vigorous effort everywhere, "for a boycott to asphixiate Spain through isolation." Every incident or situation was seized upon in the anti-Spanish campaign. Switzerland was denounced for selling armaments to Spain. *La Voix Ouvrière* (March 6 and 7) of Geneva raised its voice in indignation at the purchase by Spain of materials in the Hispano Suiza factory in Geneva. Moscow Radio joined in denouncing the purchase of war material, adding that it was for the purpose of arming 10,000 ex-Nazis who had fled across the Pyrenees after the war. Official sources in Switzerland revealed that Spain had actually

[47] *Le Courrier de Maroc,* Feb. 26, 1946.
[48] *Daily Worker,* London, March 1, 1946.
[49] *Trouw,* March 19, 1946.
[50] *Haagsche Dagblad,* The Hague, March 19, 1946.

purchased some 850,000 francs of materials, a trifling sum compared with the bloated figures diffused by the left-wing press. The alleged sale by the United States of planes and other materials to Spain was sufficient reason for a new wave of indignation to fill the communist press around the world. *L'Humanité* (Feb. 5) proclaimed that "the United States had sent fifty planes to Spain for the purpose of bombarding the guerrilla forces." Great Britain was similarly attacked from all sides for continuing trade with Spain.

Coinciding with the formal indictment of Spain at Lake Success, the communist propaganda machine began a violent attack against Franco as a threat to peace. In the preceding pages it has been pointed out that whatever may be the legitimate criticism of the Franco regime within Spain, only the wildest or the most dishonest imagination can present that government as a direct menace to the peace and security of the world. Outrageous as this may seem, the communists were quite prepared to reveal the so-called fact that Spain *was* such a threat. *L'Humanité* (Feb. 22) announced a few days before the closing of the frontier that "Spanish reinforcements are being concentrated on our frontier." The next day, the editorial writer in the communist sheet, M. Magnien, wrote that "Franco is sending Moorish, Hitlerite, and former Vichy militiamen to our frontier. This is clear evidence of hostile intentions against France. France has the right to demand that the Security Council take cognizance of this threat." The New York *Daily Worker* (March 2) found no difficulty in assigning a precise number to the Spanish troops thus concentrated, placing the figure at 250,000. The exiled Spanish communists upped the figure to 350,000.[51] On March 4 news was received from republican quarters in Hendaye to the effect that 400,000 troops were on the border.[52] The maximum estimate was finally 800,000, reported from a Spanish journal published in Bayonne.[53] The London *Daily Telegraph* (March 5) called attention to the nonsense that had been propagated by commenting that if the French were really menaced, they would increase the minute frontier guard now maintained along the Spanish border.

Despite the implausible character of all this information, the communists were not to be dissuaded. *L'Humanité* (March 3) went on insisting that Franco was preparing the invasion of France. It was now,

---

[51] *Franc Tireur,* Paris, March 1, 1946.
[52] *Le Populaire,* March 5, 1946.
[53] Reported in *Le Pays,* Paris, March 6, 1946, with comment regarding its evident absurdity.

not only hundreds of thousands of Spanish troops, but also 40,000 to 50,000 organized and armed Nazis who manned the frontier.

As late as the spring of 1947, the left-wing press was still publicizing the troop concentrations on the French frontier. The present writer can testify to the fact that a prolonged visit to a large number of frontier places, late in the spring of 1947, revealed that the maximum Spanish concentrations consisted of a handful of bored recruits doing their military service in the area north of Pamplona and near the Roncesvalles pass. There was not the slightest evidence of anything more than the normal contingent of soldiers likely to be found on any frontier in Europe. *L'Humanité* (March 15, 1946) published a map showing the positions of the Spanish troops to justify the accusations in the Security Council. Lange included this map in the documents presented against Spain. The leftish *P.M.* (April 18, 1946) did not hesitate to comment on the map with reference to its presentation before the Security Council. Moscow Radio seized on these points to assert that "Franco had an army of a million men, of whom 50,000 were Nazis."[54] Since the only question that could juridically be discussed by the Security Council was the alleged threat to world peace, it was indispensable to *prove* that Spain was a menace to peace and specifically to neighboring France. The extraordinary thing is that the *proof* can be directly traced to the official organ of the French Communist Party, in the form that it was later disseminated throughout the world.

The alleged presence of a vast number of Nazis in Spain is another phase of this whole incredible story. The Spanish Foreign Minister was obliged to state that there were perhaps 7000 to 8000 Germans in Spain, a large majority of whom had been there for over twenty-five years and that there was absolutely no truth to the contention that Nazis had flocked to Spain at the conclusion of hostilities. *L'Humanité* (Jan. 15, 1946) could not, of course, pass over this declaration in silence. After denouncing the Foreign Minister for minimizing the problem, the communist journal asserted that 100,000 Germans had found their way to Spain. "All are war criminals." From then on the figure 100,000 was taken as gospel truth by papers everywhere. *Ny Dag* in Stockholm, *France Nouvelle* in Paris, *Vorwärts* in Basel, and numerous others repeated, parrotlike, this alleged figure. Representative Savage in the United States congress asserted that 40,000 Ger-

[54] Reported in *Ce Soir*, Paris, April 13, 1946.

mans were enrolled in the Spanish army, and Representative Coffee went much further by stating that "Nazi-Falangist Spain is the laboratory of the atomic bomb for Fascism in the third world war."[55] The numbers began to climb astronomically. We now learn that there were 6000 scientific workers in Spain of German origin, 3000 espionage agents, and an army of 600,000 to 700,000 men on a war footing. Moreover, 30 German schools had been reopened.[56] The accusation regarding the atomic bomb became popular for a brief period. The New York *Daily Worker* (April 14, 1946) had no scruples in stating that Franco was concentrating on the bomb and these accusations were contained in the memorandum presented during the debate on the Spanish issue before the Security Council and signed by such friends of the defunct Spanish republic as Frieda Kirchway, William Shirer, and others, all of whom appeared to have swallowed the factually fragile reports that the former Republican Minister Alvarez del Vayo chose to supply.

The detractors of Spain have never been particularly concerned about the accuracy of their sources or even their existence. The story of the atomic research in Spain was supported by names and places, all of which gave an air of verisimilitude to the version that convinced or appeared to convince a considerable number of people. The fact that Spain did not have the money even to put the railway system of the country in proper shape; the fact that Spanish industry is insufficient to care for the basic needs of reconstruction; the fact that the ingredients of the atom bomb are not available to Spain even if the government proposed to set about making one — none of these obvious, known, and simple facts made the slightest difference to those who were bent solely on making a "case" — any case that would discredit the Franco regime and produce action in the Security Council. We are faced here, as in so many other ways, with an obdurate unwillingness to come to grips with reality when Spain is concerned. Bilbao, Ocaña, and other spots in Spain were stated to be the sites where atomic energy was being harnessed for military purposes. *Le Populaire* (April 12, 1946) tells us that "The United States is perfectly aware that near Bilbao there are installations for the manufacture of the atom bomb." The London *Daily Worker* descended to all the lurid details of this enterprise:

---

[55] *Times Herald,* Washington, D. C., Jan. 30, 1946.
[56] *Daily Worker,* New York, and *P.M.,* Feb. 28, 1946.

> Information received from the Spanish resistance movement states that an atomic energy research station under the direction of German experts exists at Portugalete, five miles south of Bilbao. The center is situated on a rocky mountain top almost inaccessible to everyone and is guarded day and night by members of the Security Police, a majority of whom are German speaking. No one can come near the works and the workers sleep and live within it. Trucks and buses circulate in that area but are under heavy guard. They never stop in the village and no one knows what they are carrying (April 14 and 15, 1946).

José Giral of the exiled republican government informed the subcommittee of the United Nations that Murcia and Granada were the centers of this atomic research, and a French review reported that studies had been made that show Spain is engaged in all seriousness in atomic research. *Heures Nouvelles* of Paris reported that the center is Oviedo and that others exist in Madrid, Barcelona, Bilbao, Valencia, and Málaga. The centers for experiments in the explosive qualities of the energy are in Vigo and Avilés and the manufacture of the mechanical part of the bomb is carried out in Cartagena, Alicante, and Burgos. V-2 bombs are also being made, says this source, and Spain already possesses some 100 of them. France, of course, will ultimately be the target of this effort.[57]

A scientific lecture by the brother of the Spanish foreign minister, José Ignacio Martín Artajo, professor of electrotechnics in the Naval Academy on atomic energy, led the Mexican newspaper *Ultimas Noticias* to cry out in alarm that the Spanish scientists were already talking of the atomic bomb and had knowledge of its construction. The journal's indignation was somewhat mitigated when it was revealed that Dr. Martín Artajo had shown slides and other material for his lecture made available to him as public property by the cultural relations section of the American embassy in Madrid. It is astonishing that this sector of public opinion apparently assumes that Spaniards are all illiterate and quite incapable of reading material made public by other governments or from foreign sources. After all, a considerable body of information can be pulled together on atomic energy from United States sources available to anyone who wishes to ask for it.

Another source of propaganda is the existence in Spain of guerrilla bands. There is no doubt that some exist and have existed ever since the end of the civil war. There is no doubt either that there is an

---

[57] Dated May 14, 1946. Sources cited are articles in the Swiss paper *Servir*, by one García Muñoz who is presumed to have been able to obtain this detailed documentation.

infiltration from France of some proportions. The Cristino García case showed that to be true. The communist propaganda has tried to depict Spain as torn by a sort of soundless civil war, with guerrilla bands all over the land and large areas virtually blocked off because of the unrest and disturbance within them. *Ny Dag* (Jan. 24, 1946) of Stockholm reported fighting in the streets of Madrid. *La Hora* in Buenos Aires and *El Siglo* in Santiago, Chile, echoed this information. It was stated in Geneva by the son of former republican Ambassador Azcarate in London, that the Spanish *maquis* were so active that the chief of police of Granada was assassinated every two or three months.[58] *Mundo Obrero* claimed that in certain areas such as Málaga, the unrest was so great that the government had been obliged to employ troops including Moors, Germans, and the Foreign Legion to maintain order. The Spanish communist leader, Antonio Mije, in the celebrated Pleyel meeting to which reference has been made, told his jubilant listeners that 25,000 regular troops were employed in the single province of Cáceres to put down the guerrilla fighters. *Mundo Obrero* (March 2, 1946) was never to be outdone in its dire prognostications of guerrilla success: "Nine thousand soldiers with dogs are hunting the guerrillas in the region of Talavera. . . . Three divisions of Moors were concentrated in the Santander-Asturias area. . . . Thousands of troops have been rushed to Galicia and León. . . . In Aragón seven divisions are operating."

Lister, who had participated so actively in the republican forces in the civil war days, announced loudly that Talavera, Navalmoral de la Mata, Arenas de San Pedro, and other areas had been declared war zones, while almost all Aragón was under martial law. Fighting took place in Madrid and bombs exploded in the Cibeles in the heart of the Spanish capital, while a battle occurred at the Central Post Office in Madrid between guerrillas and the regular forces.[59] One Jean Durkheim, writing in *Front National* (Feb. 7, 1946) of Paris, described the progress of the *maquis* against Franco. He quoted an interview with the guerrilla commander and delighted his French readers with the story of the advance of democracy in northern Spain.

The communists were far from modest; they published maps to show the precise location of the guerrilla bands and the areas "reconquered" from fascist authority. In the review, *Femmes Françaises* (March 1, 1946), two thirds of all Spanish territory was in the hands

58 *Le Peuple,* Geneva, Jan. 18, 1946.
59 *La Liberté,* Algiers, May 30, 1946.

of the so-called liberators: Barcelona, Tarragona, Alicante, Almería, Málaga, Cádiz, Coruña, Gijón, Valencia, Santander, Zaragoza, Seville, Córdoba, and Toledo. This map of the progress of the guerrillas was published everywhere by the communist and fellow traveler press. The wonder was that no one seemed to bother to reflect that, if this were true, the Spanish republican government in exile might easily have transferred its authority from Paris or Mexico to Spain, since so large a portion of the national territory was in its hands. The fact that the exiled government stuck closely to France might indicate that even in those quarters there was still some lingering doubt that this happy consummation were entirely true.

One could go on indefinitely with the false accounts in the left-wing press of revolts, insurrections, strikes, and disturbances everywhere in Spain. Photographs, too, were falsified, as in the case of *La Nación* (March 8, 1946) of Ciudad Trujillo, Dominican Republic, which published that of Franco and Hitler together at "the conference in Berlin between the Caudillo and the Führer which lasted for several days." The fact that General Franco was never in Berlin in his life made no difference at all. In Argentina, the newspaper *Córdoba* (May 5, 1946) found no more edifying picture to publish than that of General Franco with King Victor Emmanuel of Italy reviewing the Italian troops which had participated in the civil war. The minor detail that such a review never occurred and that General Franco had never laid eyes on the Italian monarch were not, of course, sufficient reasons for doubt as to the authenticity of the photograph.

The whole story is one of intrigue, false information, motivated and deliberately provoked scandal aimed at discrediting the Franco regime. The amazing thing is that serious and documented criticism of the government and its policy was rarely included. Pure fantasy and an imagination unrestricted by truth were given free play, to the detriment of Spain — but still more as testimony to the degree of degeneracy of serious and honest appraisal of public affairs in our day. This long account of exactly what happened when the extreme Left set out to create a world opinion should serve as something of an object lesson to those who are readily taken in by the spectacular and usually false accounts of what is happening in Spain.

There is no point in following through in full detail the weary debates in the Security Council and General Assembly regarding Spain between the years 1946–1949. The general development of the question may be indicated in broad lines. The position of the United States has been interesting, as one may judge by the official statements of the President during the years since the Polish proposal in 1946. In that year, in his annual report to the Congress on American participation in the United Nations, President Truman devoted considerable attention to Spain: "The United States representative expressed his Government's willingness to consider any action which in its opinion would further the elimination of the Franco regime and the restoration of a democratic regime without civil war." Moreover, the President acknowledged that the United States had furnished much of the material that went into the subcommittee report on Spain.[60] A year later in his report, the President recounted the steps taken to carry out the resolutions and commented that "The United States delegation opposed any proposal looking toward the application of sanctions since there was no factual basis for taking such action."[61] In 1948 the presidential report is beautifully laconic in its treatment of Spain: "The Security Council made brief reference to the Spanish question on June 25, 1948."[62]

The French publicist, André Siegfriend, in editing the annual volume *L'Année Politique,* comments that "the problem posed by the continuance in Spain of the Spanish regime occupied a very large place last year on the international scene. This year the question has been buried under a discreet silence."[63] But the Spanish question was hard to bury. In General Assembly of September 16 to November 19, 1947, Spain was dragged into the debate by the indefatigable Oscar Lange. The distinguished delegates flayed Franco for the Succession Law and Jan considered that Lord Templewood's book, *Complacent Dictator,* was a telling indictment of Franco. Bebler of Yugoslavia could find nothing better than to claim that "racial discrimination was being inculcated in the Spanish schools."[64] Fahy of the United States was not pleased with the Polish proposal and claimed it did not "aim at altering the situation in Spain by pacific means."[65] It is odd that after inciting a people to rebellion by international pressure, scruples suddenly develop that perhaps that method will not be entirely "pacific."

In 1948 at the Chaillot Palace in Paris, the Spanish issue was not

---

[60] *The United States and the United Nations,* Report Series 7, 1947, for the year 1946, Washington, 1947, p. 37.

[61] *Ibid.,* 1948, p. 39.

[62] *Ibid.,* 1949, p. 91.

[63] *L'Année Politique, 1947,* Paris, 1948, p. 212.

[64] *United Nations, Official Records of the Second Session of the General Assembly,* Nov. 11, 1947, p. 410.

[65] *Ibid.,* p. 412.

allowed to lie dormant and the Venezuelan delegate opined that "the Spanish question is hardly a problem of government. It remains a problem of the people."[66] His Colombian colleagues expressed the conviction that "since the question was referred by the General Assembly at its last regular session to the Security Council, and since the Security Council decided on June 25, 1948, not to include the question on its agenda, this means implicitly that there is no threat to the peace inherent in this question."[67] Delegate Costa du Rels of Bolivia expressed a very general sentiment among many in saying that: "As for Spain, we have been linked to her by bonds of blood, language, and faith. We, therefore, deplore once again the ostracism undeservedly forced on Spain."[68]

On November 15, 1948, the exiled Spanish republican government addressed a communication to the General Assembly for the fourth time, which was transmitted officially by the Secretary General to the delegates. This long document speaks of the "impossibility of believing in the insensitiveness of the United Nations" to the Spanish case and declares that "frivolity" cannot be the explanation for the inaction.[69] The document admits that the major obstacle to action is the "nonintervention policy," and decries the fact that "neither respect nor courtesy can hide the feelings that obliges it to decline all responsibility before the persistence in the error of keeping the Spanish problem outside the fundamental tasks of the United Nations." The sessions of the autumn of 1948 were distinguished by resolutions, joint draft resolution, votes affirmative, negative, and abstentious. The Spanish case became bogged down in a literal inundation of rhetoric.

When the General Assembly met at Flushing Meadow, in May, 1949, Malik of the Soviet Union expressed the conviction that "we must consider the question of Franco Spain, the importance of which is well known. It is a question which has not been acted upon by the General Assembly since 1947."[70] On May 4, Polish delegate Katz-Suchy called attention to the fact that the resolutions regarding Spain had produced no effect. They included:

---

[66] *Verbatim Report of the Hundred and Fortieth Meeting, General Assembly, Third Session,* Sept. 23, 1948.

[67] *Ibid.,* Sept. 28, 1948.

[68] *Ibid.,* Sept. 29, 1948.

[69] *United Nations, General Assembly,* Document A/781, Nov. 15, 1948.

[70] *General Assembly, Second Part of the Third Session,* May 2, 1949.

1. Condemnation at the San Francisco Conference;
2. Condemnation by General Assembly at first session;
3. Polish resolution to Security Council and subcommittee to recognize Franco Spain as a danger to international security;
4. On December 12, 1946, the resolution of the General Assembly was adopted, even if toned down by United States intervention;
5. Economic and Social Council withdrew the invitation to Spain to attend a penal law conference (Jan. 24, 1947);
6. On May 13, 1947, the International Civil Aviation Organization expelled Spain;
7. Resolution of December 12, 1947, invited nations to withdraw heads of diplomatic missions from Madrid and the Security Council to take measures if certain conditions had not been fulfilled within a reasonable time.

Two and a half years later, said the representative of peace-loving and presumedly "democratic" Poland, "Franco still defied the United Nations."[71] The extraordinary thesis was laid down that since General Franco did not step down instantly when the United Nations passed a resolution, he was a threat to the peace and engaged in defying the solemn will of that international institution. A number of Hispanic American delegates challenged this interpretation; Víctor Andrés Belaúnde, of Peru, and Urdaneta, of Colombia, proceeded to examine the problem from the point of view of intervention in the domestic affairs of a sovereign State and from the particular angle of the alleged threat to world peace of the Madrid government.[72] Much of the ensuing discussion became a verbal duel, of the customary sort, between the East and the West, with Byelorussians, Ukrainians, and the satellite representatives accusing the United Kingdom and various western states of supporting General Franco as part of their preparation for an anti-Soviet crusade.

In November, 1950, the General Assembly of the United Nations by an overwhelming vote abrogated the 1946 ruling regarding the maintenance of full diplomatic representation in Madrid. This was, in fact, merely the formal recognition that the whole absurd policy of cutting off one's nose to spite the face was a complete failure. The admission of Spain to the various specialized branches of the United Nations is another step in the obvious direction; the reintegration of Spain within normal international life.

---

[71] *Ibid.*, May 4, 1949.

[72] *Ibid.*, May 5, 1949.

Chapter 20. THE OUTLOOK

> The truth is that Spain is a little world apart and one must learn, in all cordiality to treat her in that light. The ignorance of this fact led Napoleon I to disaster. It is quite useless to exert pressure on the Spanish people either to get them to change their government or to adopt economic views that are not their own.[1]

THIS is the first and basic truth to bear in mind in examining the problem of Spain's future and its role in the modern world. Almost every step in policy that has been taken since 1939 by western European powers and the United States has been predicated on error — the tragic error that threats and denunciation are effective weapons to force the Spanish government and people to change. The torrent of diatribe directed against General Franco's government by the United Nations and almost every foreign office of any consequence in the world, stiffened resistance, brought out the inherent disdain of the Spanish for favors when national integrity is attacked, and made impossible the normal evolution of the present regime. Visible evidence of this was available before the concerted drive in 1945 to unseat the Generalissimo.[2]

The proposals for doing something about Spain run from the imposition of a new regime, preferably a Republic, to economic sanctions, slow strangulation, and ostracism. None of these policies of interference and needling will lead to anything but a hardening of Spanish antagonism, a more solid support of the present regime, and the passionate dislike of the Spanish people for those responsible for the prodding

---

[1] Jacques Chastenet, "Cosas de España," in *Gazette de Lausanne,* Lausanne, Switzerland, Aug. 19, 1949.

[2] Salvador de Madariaga has expressed this trait admirably: "We find ourselves faced with an element of Spanish character which can be observed in other cases — the tendency to renounce all interest and retire into silence and passivity when the circumstances make words and deeds useless" (*Spain* [London: Jonathan Cape, 1943; New York: Creative Age Press, Inc., 1943], p. 229).

process. This simple fact of psychology seems to have failed to penetrate the minds of statesmen and publicists everywhere. This attitude of a self-imposed mission to reform Spain is the basis of all the ineffectual efforts that have been made inside and outside the United Nations to ease the tension between Spain and the rest of the world. There seems to be some slight hope at present that in Washington, if not in London and Paris, it will be recognized that General Franco is not going to step down from power because Acheson does not like him, or because Georges Bidault holds certain mental reservations regarding him.[3] Moreover, Spaniards are singularly unimpressed by the stubborn hostility of the British Labor government, for they all remember — and the incident is enshrined in newspaper pictures — Clement Attlee marching through Madrid with his clenched fist in the air and saluting the British members of the International Brigades with rapture.

Unquestionably the effect of foreign ostracism on Spain has been very severe. Despite the fact that formal sanctions were never decreed and the present government has managed to work out a series of reasonably satisfactory trade agreements with a number of countries, the major characteristic at present (the winter of 1949–1950) is one of stagnation. Things in Spain go on, but there is a creeping paralysis, a scarcely perceptible slowing down of economic life, a profound feeling that the limit of domestic capacity has been reached. There is no danger of a crash in Spain; there is real danger of semi-strangulation as a result of the untenable position the country occupies in the world. Obviously, too, it is a great pity that Spain is cut off from the rest of the western world, for her own spiritual development is hampered and, what is even more important, her undeniable contribution to the solidarity of the West is lost. The latter is too frequently overlooked in the constant insistence on the strategic value of Spain. To depict the whole problem as a defense against communism is an oversimplification, and to talk of the Pyrenees as the natural defense line in west-

---

[3] Constantine Brown discovered at once that Spain had rallied behind Franco as the pressure was put on by the United Nations. "There seems to be no doubt in the minds of anyone who has carefully observed recent developments in Spain that the United Nations' decision to urge its members to withdraw their chiefs of mission from Madrid has strengthened General Franco's position. . . . The fact that foreign governments which are not concerned with how Spaniards live and are ruled, took it upon themselves to make such a demonstration caused a wave of genuine indignation. . . . I talked with many . . . especially those known to be hostile to the regime. They all said, Spain is not a liberated country and the members of the United Nations have no right to tell us how and when we shall change our government" (*Evening Star,* Washington, D. C., Feb. 24, 1947).

ern Europe is to put the whole question on a false basis. The Spanish themselves are not taken in by this sudden discovery. They do not relish the idea that normal relations with their government will be re-established simply because the Pentagon is convinced that an army on the Franco-Spanish frontier can hold the line until American military and naval aid comes to the rescue of the rest of Europe. Why, fundamentally, should the Spanish be so keen to rally to the defense of western Europe when for thirteen years that same western Europe, with the exception of Portugal, has denounced them as a menace to peace and tranquillity and the last refuge of defeated fascism? Is it small wonder that the Spaniard does not wax enthusiastic when his army and reserve power are measured in terms of what he can contribute to holding the Soviet forces off?

The intrinsic merit of the Spanish contribution to the twentieth century world reposes on the devotion to certain ideals which are potentially of inestimable value to the integrity of the West. In the first place, Spain is devoted to internal unity as never before. The official motto on the coat of arms, *Una, Grande Libre,* has become ingrained in the political temper of the people. This hard, solid unity makes of Spain a bastion against the type of internal disintegration that the country knew under the Republic and which gnaws at the "innards" of not a few of the other nations of western Europe. In the second place, the Spanish are convinced of the virtue of a larger *Hispanidad* than the peninsula, that is, a strong and effective union with Portugal and an extension of this solidarity to the Spanish- and Portuguese-speaking nations of the New World. This Iberian bloc or concert of nations may seem like a form of imperialism. It is, within the regional scheme of things, recognized as legitimate by the United Nations themselves, a logical and entirely justifiable aspiration.

We must be entirely frank on this second point. The tendency to speak of an "inter-American unity" between the United States and the other American republics is more of a fiction than a fact, as we all know deep in our hearts. We have tried valiantly to make of the accident of geography the basis of a spiritual and emotional kinship that does not exist and at the best can only be maintained by artificial stimulants. Between the United States and Hispanic America there are innumerable barriers of sentiment and a different set of values; between Spain and her former possessions in the New World there is the incredibly strong link of language, culture, religion, and the comradeship that derives from participation in the same particular tributary that feeds into the broader stream of western civilization. The superficial may decry the maintenance of strong Spanish relations with the Hispanic American as nothing but an effort to extend fascism to America; as a part of the campaign to bring Falangism to these shores. No one, unless he be motivated by that peculiarly blind prejudice against modern Spain and all it stands for, can conceive that Madrid has any political aspirations in America or the slightest pretension of regaining control over territories in this part of the world.

The difficulty is, of course, a relatively simple one, that ought to be brought out into the light of day. The Spanish approach to Hispanic America is on the basis of tradition, history, culture, and the Catholic faith. To the American who thinks that Hispanic America must be made over to the image and likeness of New Jersey, this basis of rapprochement is repugnant. Nevertheless, it is evident that every gesture made by Spain toward genuine cultural and spiritual contacts with America pays rich dividends. Every cultural gesture made from the United States is a decidedly uphill fight against tremendous natural odds. Moreover, there is no reason to believe that bad relations with Spain mean good relations with Hispanic America. Former Ambassador Hayes has expressed the idea admirably:

> I do not believe that we can successfully pursue one policy in Hispanic America and another in Spain. If we continue to convey the impression that we are a "bad neighbor" to Spain, we shall increase the difficulties and hazards of remaining a "good neighbor" to the other American Republics.[4]

The former American Ambassador calls attention to the very strong links that bind the peninsula to America; the hundreds of thousands of Spanish immigrants everywhere from Cuba to Chile, the wide acceptance of Spanish books and culture generally. Two facts perhaps ought to make him stop and reflect on the folly of our present hostility to Spain, insofar as it relates to our relations in the western hemisphere. One is that republic after republic in America has refused to obey the United Nations' ruling on diplomatic relations with Madrid and has either left its ambassador there or has sent one after the decision was made at Lake Success. The second is that the increase of travel to Spain from Hispanic America is astonishing; in 1949 there were over a thousand Hispanic American students in Madrid alone; in November a special residence hall was opened for Bolivians, whose number was already large enough to justify this step.

---

[4] Hayes, *Wartime Mission in Spain,* p. 312, copyright, 1945, by The Macmillan Co. and used with their permission.

The third passion of Spain after its own unity and its solidarity with the Hispanic world is its devotion to the idea of Christendom. Unfortunately this splendid word has fallen into disuse among English-speaking people and we prefer to prate about common democracy and common institutions, even when they do not exist, rather than place the emphasis on the common Christian heritage. To the Spanish, Christendom is a very live thing, pregnant with meaning for the modern world. An isolating factor unquestionably is that Spain is devoted to this idea, while the rest of Europe and the United States are willing to base their pacts for mutual aid and understanding on anything except the fact that all that we have that can be called civilization is the product of our Christian tradition.[5]

The Spanish have sometimes looked on the Pyrenees as a not unmixed blessing, shutting them off from the rest of Europe and particularly from France. The distinguished Catalan priest, Jaime Balmes, whose centenary was so widely celebrated in 1949, was wont to argue that the higher the Pyrenees the better for the mind and spirit of Spain. On the other hand, contemporary declarations are not lacking to indicate that Spain feels itself to be very much a part of the European continent and desirous of playing its part in the defense of that solidarity. "Spain is logically a part of the western world, for geographical, cultural, and economic reasons . . . and the efforts to exclude her can only weaken the forces facing the Soviet Union."[6] Whatever one may think of its form of government, there can be absolutely no doubt that Spain belongs to the western community of nations and that every interest of the country is closely tied up with the West. If Turkey can be arbitrarily incorporated into the western bloc, and if Iran can be looked upon as one of the links in the long defense chain that encircles the Soviet Union, it is impossible to conceive that Spain be left out.

The defense of what we call the West is not a single issue but a combination of them. We are not engaged in a struggle, popularly called the "cold war," against the forces of Marxism simply to retain the right to hold proper elections or to hold sessions of a parliament. We are engaged for that and a great many other things, including the right to believe that man possesses an immortal soul and that the

---

[5] This idea of the three passions of the contemporary Spaniard is brought out in Jacques Blondeau, "Visions d'Espagne," *L'Aube,* Paris, June 14, 1949.

[6] Statement of General Franco to Seymour Berkson, President of International News Service, reported in *La Prensa,* Barcelona, Nov. 7, 1949.

paternity of God means exactly what it says with the subsequent obligations on the part of mankind. There are innumerable Spaniards who are very little concerned with what happens to parliamentary democracy, and who are very much concerned with what happens to the Church; just as there are Americans and British whose concern over the fate of the Church is insignificant but whose distress is acute at the prospects for parliamentarianism. There ought to be a place in the line of defense of the West for those who want to defend the Church together with the values she has represented throughout western history. Spain has been excluded because of sheer bigotry and nothing else. The close examination of the reasoning on the Spanish case reveals beyond any doubt that a basis of principle is totally lacking. It is this precisely that the Spanish resent above everything else. If the major powers had proceeded along rational, logical, although mistaken lines, the situation would have been vastly different. We condemned Spain in 1945 for what we did not condemn her in 1940, although nothing had changed in between. Churchill praised Spain for her attitude during the war, and Bevin instructs British diplomats not even to exchange the ordinary amenities with their Spanish colleagues. The Spanish issue has been decided on the basis of slogans, propaganda, catch phrases, and the warmed-over emotionalism of 1936. It is, as Douglas Woodruff has very properly expressed it, "the clinging to the carcass of a dead policy."[7] The distinguished British writer puts the question very neatly when he asks, "The British attitude toward Spain opens up an even wider question: on what values are we going to stand in the defense of the West?"

If we talk of democracy as the basis for our international action and the link that binds the western nations into a solid phalanx against sovietism, then we are obviously in a perfectly untenable position. Anyone must realize that the inclusion of Turkey in the defense arrangements, meritorious as it may be on the strategic side, cannot be defended if we are going to demand simon-pure democracy as the acid test of all alliances. We seek the good will and understanding of the Arab countries, and engage in the closest kind of relations with Saudi Arabia, where, I daresay, the democratic processes are at the best somewhat stunted. We are not averse to entering into oil agreements or commercial treaties with almost any nation in the western hemisphere or elsewhere without regard to the purity of its political

[7] *The Tablet,* London, Nov. 27, 1948, Article, "Spain Revisited."

techniques. If we were consistently so scrupulous, we would have to break relations with at least half a dozen Hispanic American countries, not to mention a whole assortment of states elsewhere in the world.

But the height of folly and of illogic: the hilariously amusing case of unreason carried to the nth degree is the new United States policy toward Yugoslavia, coupled with the obstinate refusal to deal with Spain. I realize that in linking the two countries I am not flattering the Spanish. This is not meant to imply that the Marxist terror that passes for a regime in Belgrade belongs to the same category with Madrid. It is disconcerting, nevertheless, to observe the alacrity with which the press and public opinion of the United States have hastened to the defense of Tito, and at the same time refuse the smallest concession to Franco.[8] If the strategic argument is valid, it applies even more to Spain than to Yugoslavia. If we accept the idea that "the enemy of our enemy is our friend," then General Franco can claim an anticommunism that antedates by far that of anyone else on the continent. And certainly Spain represents a far more solid opposition to militant Marxism than Tito's heretical communist deviationism. If economic aid is to be given on the purely objective ground of aiding people who are willing to resist Soviet pressure, then there is no possible reason for denying to Spain what has been granted to Yugoslavia.

The total lack of logic, reason, and common sense in our Spanish policy to date is no better illustrated than through the popular press. The argument runs that Franco is not dependable because he holds power by desperate means, that there is an elaborate black market in Spain, and that workers, kept on starvation wages, directly benefit the members of the Falange. He has not popular mandate, is a self-proclaimed totalitarian and a burden on the conscience of western democracy. This is the indictment. If one examines it carefully, the utter shallowness of the argument becomes apparent at once. If we are to oust from the benefits of the Marshall Plan a country with a black market or administrative corruption, the sixteen nation group will shrink to rather lean proportions. There is a tendency to forget

[8] Constantine Brown sums this up as follows: "Neither General Franco, his advisers, nor his political opponents can understand why America, which is spending so many billions of dollars to create a wall against Soviet aggression purposely overlooks Spain, which is one of the best military bets in Europe. They cannot conceive that disapproval of a mildly dictatorial regime, much milder, for instance, than that of Marshal Tito, should blind us to the point of jeopardizing the defense of the West" (*Evening Star,* Washington, D. C., Nov. 14, 1949).

that the Marshall Plan was never conceived nor proclaimed as having anything to do with the internal regimes of the countries invited to participate, for the Soviet Union was so invited as were all the satellite countries. The purpose was to provide economic aid for the general recovery of Europe. The fact that the Soviet Union and satellites saw fit to reject the invitation does not modify in the least the intention. In a word, we were willing and eager to have Czechoslovakia, Poland, Hungary, and the Soviet Union itself in the E.C.A. program; we were absolutely unwilling because Spain is a dictatorship and does not pay the kind of wages we consider proper, to admit the latter country. This, I submit, is the height of absolute illogic.

What we have done is absurd and futile; a foreign policy dictated by left-wing mumbo-jumbo that still manages to convince too many of our people that democracy is hopelessly compromised if we have any truck with General Franco. The contradiction in all this was pointed out by General Franco himself in words that bear transcription because they apply so precisely to the present situation:

> Democracy in different countries takes on different forms. Some of the governments in the western hemisphere pass as democracies but are in fact omnipotent dictatorships very different from anything that in Europe is called democracy. The *coup d'état,* the falsification of electoral returns, the intervention of the President in every branch of the government, characterizes many of these governments, which are accepted, nevertheless, in international society as democracies.[9]

There is no chance whatever that the republicans will return to power in Spain. The best alternative for those who hope for the triumph of the extreme Left in Spain is the withholding of economic aid. The advocates of sanctions and strangulation believe, or suggest they believe, that Franco will fall and the "democratic forces" within the country will take over. In the first place, there are no internal democratic forces in the republican camp. Secondly, the republicans outside Spain have no chance whatever of achieving power. They are today unknown and forgotten by most Spaniards. If they were to return it would be on the coattails of an advancing army of occupation which in itself would be enough for the Spanish people to reject them. The refusal to grant economic aid does not weaken Franco; it merely weakens Spain and the Spanish people. Widespread hunger and an economic crisis is precisely what the communists want. Economic assistance to the

[9] Interview of General Franco with the Australian journalist Tom Jacob, published in *Solidaridad Nacional,* Barcelona, Nov. 24, 1949.

people of Spain will permit the nation to evolve as she pleases. With an injection of economic aid Spain will attain a more balanced structure and avert the possibility of a crisis. A collapse in the economic and social order, followed by a swift political change would benefit no one but the communists, for in the troubled waters of a chaotic Spain the probability of a left-wing dictatorship would be very great.

To many in Europe it is evident that the United States is torn between the convictions of the military and the reservations of the diplomats. The recent stream of members of the United States Congress through Spain demonstrated that the legislative branch of the government is aware that this anomaly cannot go on much longer. The argument for economic aid to Spain is so overwhelming, be it in the form of a government loan or the encouragement of private investment, that even Juan Negrín, who can certainly not be accused of pro-Franco sympathies, published his opinion that Spain today, without a change of regime, should be favored in the European Reconstruction Plan. In other words, the interests of the Spanish people come first and no end is to be served by humiliating them, coercing them, and arousing in them a profound distrust for the so-called democracies.[10]

Those who think that Spain will join the western bloc joyfully at the moment of danger may be sadly disappointed. It is not likely that after years of systematic humiliation by the foreign offices of most of the western States or after years of the denial of the ordinary financial assistance given to almost every country in real need — be it Turkey with its one-party system, Greece, Saudi Arabia, or Iceland — that Spain will rally to the support of the western bloc the moment the Soviet menace becomes more active. Spain has been busily cultivating closer relations with Argentina and certain of the Hispanic American countries. The visit of King Abdullah of Transjordan in September, 1949, sealed a long and carefully nurtured policy of friendship with the Arabs, with whom, incidentally, Spain maintains the most cordial contacts. "Spain at the present time has no intention of lining up militarily with any bloc. Her freedom of action is absolute."[11] In a word, years of disdain and hostility are not going to pay off in collaboration when war comes.

---

[10] The Negrín articles stating this point of view appeared in *The New York Herald Tribune* (Paris edition), April 1, 2, and 3, 1948.

[11] J. M. Creac'h, "Les nouvelles routes de l'Espagne," *Le Monde,* Paris, Sept. 3, 1948.

The most authoritative statement on Spain to come out of the Department of State recently was that of Secretary Dean Acheson in May, 1949. The major problem has been the designation of an ambassador in Madrid. Since the resignation of Norman Armour no American ambassador has resided in the Spanish capitol. No one has yet proposed a really convincing argument why we should leave an entire embassy functioning in Spain without a head, nor just how we expect to unseat General Franco by having merely a chargé d'affaires on the job. This is one of the major mysteries of our time and for which no satisfactory answer has yet been produced in official circles. We dislike a government, and want to see it changed; therefore we remove our chief of mission and deprive ourselves of a chance to have a first-class man on the spot to find out what is really going on.

The bankruptcy of our Spanish policy is nowhere more eloquently revealed than in the published remarks of the Secretary of State in reply to questions on Spain. The essence of Acheson's views may be boiled down to the following form:

1. The United Nations' resolution to withdraw full diplomatic representation from Spain was rooted in history, because Franco is the product of Hitler and Mussolini and is a fascist dictatorship.
2. The Spanish government is to be condemned because of certain specific violations of what we call basic human liberties: (*a*) no writ of habeas corpus; (*b*) no right of trial by jury; (*c*) no religious liberty; (*d*) no right of association.[12]

The Secretary of State said, quite rightly, that "the importance is not in throwing words around in talking about 'fascists' because other people call us fascist too. We do not get anywhere merely by using the word. The important thing is what goes on in Spain." On the basis of this indictment the Secretary concluded that "You cannot have an intimate working partnership with such a regime in the economic field and in the defense field." Now this extraordinary document defends the absence of an American ambassador in Madrid because there is no operation of the writ of habeas corpus as we know it in the United States. When the Secretary was asked if this was the proper basis for withdrawing an ambassador, how he explained the fact that we keep an ambassador in Moscow where no habeas corpus has been

[12] Full text in *The New York Times,* May 11, 1949.

heard of since the days of Kerenski, the Secretary of State dismissed the question derisively as "dialectics."[13]

In summary regarding a realistic and intelligent policy toward Spain, the following may be taken as points which would serve the cause of peace as well as the best interests of both Spain and the rest of the world:

1. Economic aid to Spain is necessary for the reconstruction of Europe and the defense of the West.
2. This aid should be granted at once by the United States, either within the framework of the Marshall Plan, or through direct loans, or through the encouragement of private investment on a large scale.
3. The present regime has possibilities of evolution and the maintenance of the present strained relations merely solidifies and freezes it.
4. The United States should resume normal diplomatic relations with the Spanish government, since only an illogical insistence on political and ideological affinities prevent it from doing so.
5. The fullest information regarding Spain will serve to inform public opinion of the realities and truth of Spain and eliminate the unfortunate holdovers of prejudice and *parti pris* that have heretofore prevailed.
6. The full support by Spain of the common defense can be assured only by readmission to the family of nations on a basis of absolute equality.
7. The maintenance of the present quarantine only serves the purposes of Soviet policy and divides the West at a time when it is desperately in need of consolidation.

Obviously the realization of this policy presupposes a new enlightenment regarding Spanish affairs. Certain simple ideas have become lodged in the minds of western peoples about Spain. Their dislodgment is no easy task, but a necessary one. They must be brought to realize that above General Franco and the temporary contingencies of the Spanish situation there are permanent values and devotion to larger ideals, to

[13] An excellent comment is contained in *Human Events,* Washington, D. C., July 15, 1949. This publication points out that "Today, Spain continues to furnish the inspiration for additional farcical attitudes among our officials." Another reason to deny a loan was that Spain devotes too much of its budget to the armed forces. This criticism appeared about the time that Defense Secretary Johnson demanded 15 billion dollars out of a total of 40 billion for defense.

which the people of Spain have demonstrated a century-long devotion. Without Spain, the West is incomplete and crippled. The permanent exclusion of the regime from all participation in normal international affairs merely contributes to the unrest of the Spanish and might, if pressed too far, lead to an explosion of political emotion that might conceivably end the present state of affairs only to lead to an abyss of confusion that would be the ideal muddied waters in which the Soviet Union fishes with such effectiveness.

Turning from Spain as an international question to the internal outlook, we find that we are faced fundamentally by the problem of what shape the potential opposition takes and what prospects there really are for a political change in the present regime. The first may be examined briefly in the light of the various tendencies that are eager for such a change. There are the monarchists of various persuasions on one side and the numerous leftist forces on the other. There are, in reality, no parties of any kind in opposition. There are segments of opinion, minor movements perhaps without much cohesion, and a certain number of nuclei and cells that are either maintained within the country or precariously fed by Spanish exiles from outside.

From time to time opposition forces are depicted as rising up to challenge the Franco regime. For a time, at the conclusion of World War II, it was guerrilla fighting by armed bands. Later it was bombing and terroristic activity within Spain. At others, attention was focused on the action of the so-called republican government in exile, either in Paris or at the United Nations. From time to time the monarchists come in for a spot of attention and rumors fly that Don Juan and the socialists have come to an agreement, or that Franco and Don Juan, having met on the waters of the Bay of Biscay, have ironed out their differences.

The fact is that an understanding of the forces opposed to the present regime must take the form of extreme subtlety, for it is vain to talk of formal opposition in some cases, because there is merely disagreement with particular aspects of the regime. In other cases the hostility is absolute and on every issue. There are strong monarchists who have ranged themselves unhesitatingly with the regime. There are other monarchists who have reservations and prefer an attitude of passive waiting. There are republicans who might be induced to come to terms with the monarchists, and there are others who refuse anything short of the restoration of the Constitution of 1931 and the re-establishment of a reasonable facsimile of the Popular Front.

The information regarding the leftist opposition usually mentions the *Alianza Nacional de Fuerzas Democráticas,* founded in the autumn of 1944. It was apparently a *potpourri* of republicans, socialists, and even anarchists. It is still incomprehensible, after the bitter experience of 1936–1939, that there are those who think the adherence of the anarchists is a source of strength. The communists up to 1946 had an organization of their own called the *Unión Nacional.* The *Alliance* issued its statement of principles and a program. Its activity has been largely that of maintaining some kind of organized group within Spain, but certainly neither in propaganda nor in influence has it reflected any deep-rooted movement of promise. The communists have the enormous advantage of their international connections. In general, the anarchists and the communists have constituted the most active underground movements in contemporary Spain, although this activity must be taken in a purely relative sense. There have been rumblings and minor commotion in the Spanish underground, but it cannot be said that for the first decade any group had managed to accomplish anything, and at the present writing there is no sign that it will.

The republicans outside Spain are divided and subdivided into infinite factions. Even the shadowy government they set up in Mexico suffered periodical crises and shifts, while its actual influence on public opinion abroad is nil. Within Spain it is still less, for no one takes it at all seriously. Whatever might happen in Spain, one thing is absolutely certain, that if Franco should fall tomorrow, José Giral will not take his place.[14]

The attitude of the monarchists is far more interesting because they are not clandestine, nor do they presume to destroy the present institutions in the vain effort to win their case. From time to time in this volume I have had occasion to mention the various divisions among the monarchists. The most serious group unquestionably is that which defends the position of Don Juan as King of Spain. It must be emphasized again that almost everyone in high position in Spain today is a monarchist. The real difference does not lie in their monarchism versus anti-monarchism, but in the procedure and method to bring

---

[14] A serious study of contemporary Spain was published in Brussels under the title, *Problème des relations internationales: L'Espagne,* 1948, by the *Institut des Relations Internationales.* In this co-operative study the conclusion is reached that "it must be remembered that the enemies of Franco abroad do not appear at all dangerous. Their campaign is limited to the purely verbal. The enemies of General Franco at home are no more dangerous than those abroad" (p. 27).

about the restoration. Spain has been proclaimed a monarchy. The issue now is how to bring about the transition in the best way, satisfactory to Don Juan and to Franco. Within the monarchist ranks there are many who feel strongly that Spain is standing still under the present regime and that as the years pass the psychological moment for the restoration is lost. There are others who have the keenest hopes of working from the inside of the regime and contributing from that vantage point to the normalization of Spanish institutions. The belief is strong among all that the return of a king is indispensable to give Spain an institutional structure that will resist the change when General Franco ceases to manage affairs.

I am personally convinced that the restoration is the obvious thing for Spain. The Republic did not work, and there is no sign that in Spain it ever will work. Monarchy provides the armor of stability, without which Spain is doomed to the convulsions which did it such great harm during both republican experiments. Just how the restoration can best be brought about is another question. I think the essential point of disagreement between Franco and Don Juan is this: the Generalissimo naturally is unwilling to have the King return as though the accomplishment of the past thirteen years did not exist, while the King, on the other hand, refuses to return to Spain as the Monarch of the Falange or as the creature of the regime, but rather as the King of all Spaniards. General Franco can hardly be expected to step down and sacrifice cheerfully the regime he has created out of civil war. This attitude is entirely understandable. On the other hand, Don Juan has felt strongly that to return as monarch, tied to the virtues and faults of the Franco regime, would weaken his position before he even began to exercise the royal powers.

The fact is, of course, that General Franco is in power, and that elementary reality cannot be overlooked. The meeting of General Franco and Don Juan in 1948 was primarily for the purpose of arranging for the schooling of the King's son in Madrid, and to establish cordial contacts between the two. Toward the end of World War II, when Don Juan proclaimed his belief in constitutional monarchy, perhaps to convince the western world that he was prepared to institute a regime similar to the British, General Franco was equally obdurate in asserting with absolute clarity his position. It may be summarized as follows:

1. The Monarchy abandoned authority to the Republic in 1931.

2. The National Movement was directed against the abuse of republicanism.
3. The Movement in 1936 was not primarily monarchical, but Spanish and Catholic.
4. General Mola, at the very beginning, made it clear that the Movement was not fundamentally monarchical.
5. Of the million enrolled in the nationalist ranks during the civil war, only a portion were pronounced monarchists.

General Franco defended his regime as the legitimate consequence of the civil war, with a sovereignty sanctioned by victory. The essential point in the *Caudillo's* position has been that Don Juan sought to separate the future of Spain from the national crusade that had brought it order and authority.

The monarchists, especially of the Don Juan persuasion, as well as the Carlist traditionalists have protested against the fact that despite the proclamation of the monarchy as the ultimate aim of the regime and the promulgation of the Succession Law, present-day Spain is a singularly uncongenial atmosphere for monarchist propaganda. The monarchists are not allowed to urge their case or to sustain a propaganda that they deem necessary to create the state of mind that will make the return of the King feasible and logical. The cases of restrictions are numerous. The Duchess of Valencia was fined heavily for monarchist activity; General Kindelán was confined to the barracks because of a speech. Father Santiago Hevia delivered a lecture at the *Ateneo* on the re-establishment of the Rota in which he maintained that the privileges granted by the Holy See to the present regime were less than those given the monarchs. In his general thesis he spoke openly in favor of the monarchical claims and was subject to molestation as a result. A Mass for the repose of the soul of Alfonso XIII, in February, 1948, was forbidden by the authorities, although at the same time a Mass was celebrated officially at the Escorial for the same purpose. I know of five or six cases of active monarchists who have suffered fines of 25,000 pesetas for their public pronouncements in favor of the restoration of this institution. These cases and their repetition have annoyed the supporters of Don Juan, who see in it a contradiction with the protestations of monarchism as contained in the Succession Law.

The visit of General Franco to Lisbon, in October, 1949, contributed to the strengthening of relations between the two countries. Despite the fact that the Generalissimo and Don Juan did not meet personally, the relations between the two have not changed since the original meeting. In a word, the dialogue is still open and the possibility of an arrangement is there.[15]

A fundamental difficulty in the restoration is, of course, the long years of exile of Don Juan and the problem of accommodating his return to the exigencies of practical politics. The present regime has built up an army of supporters and beneficiaries, while there are many who have devoted their lives to the cause of the restoration and could reasonably expect to enter public service if Don Juan were to ascend the throne. How can this situation be worked out realistically? One must add the fact that in the minds of some the restoration means primarily the re-establishment of the court and the rehabilitation of the aristocracy. If one thing is clear in contemporary Spain it is that the traditional aristocracy is looked upon with profound suspicion, both by the mass of people and by the regime. Could Don Juan accommodate himself to the demands of politics and at the same time bring about the reconciliation of all Spaniards, both Franquist and anti-Franquist? This must remain as one of the major incognita of the present day.

---

[15] "General Franco's visit to Lisbon," in *The Tablet*, London, Oct. 29, 1949.

Appendix 1. CHRONOLOGY OF SPANISH HISTORY AT ITS ZENITH

1474 — Death of Henry IV and Proclamation of Isabel, Queen of Castile.
1479 — Ferdinand, husband of Isabel became King of Aragón.
Peace signed with Portugal which had favored the succession of Juana.
1480 — The Inquisition set up at Seville.
1482 — Beginning of war against Granada.
1483 — Torquemada named Grand Inquisitor.
Revolt of Aragón against Inquisition as the instrument of the centralized monarchy.
1484 — The Christians took Málaga.
1491 — Beginning of siege of Granada.
1492 — The Jews expelled from Spain; discovery of America.
1498 — Fourth and last voyage of Columbus.
1504 — Death of Isabel and complete union of Castile and Aragón.
1509 — Oran forced to pay tribute to Spain.
1516 — Charles I ascended the throne of Spain.
1517 — Explorations of Yucatán.
1520 — Conquest of Mexico.
Insurrection of the Comuneros.
1521 — War with France in Flanders and in Italy.
1522 — Conquest of Milan.
1524 — Siege of Pavia.
1525 — Francis I of France taken captive to Madrid.
1529 — Conquest of Peru.
Treaty of Cambrai. Charles V renounced Bourgogne; Francis I, Naples.
1534 — Foundation of the Society of Jesus.
1535 — Foundation of Buenos Aires, Lima, discovery of Chile.
Conquest of Tunis.
War with France over Milan.
1542 — War with France allied with Lutheran Sweden.
1553 — Defeat of Charles V before Metz.
1556 — Abdication of Charles V. War with France.
1559 — Peace of Chateau-Bambrésis.
1562 — Teresa of Ávila founded reformed Carmelite convent at Ávila.
1563 — The construction of the Escorial begun.
1565 — Conquest of the Philippines.
1567 — Insurrection in the Low Countries.
1569–1571 — Moorish revolts. Lepanto.
1580 — Annexation of Portugal.
1588 — Loss of the Armada.
1598 — Death of Philip II.

Appendix 2. CHRONOLOGICAL TABLE OF VIA CRUCIS OF THE SPANISH CHURCH IN THE NINETEENTH AND TWENTIETH CENTURIES

1798 — Expropriation of Church properties under Charles IV. The confiscation and sale of properties belonging to the orders was authorized.

1805 — Sale of Church property against compensation by government bonds.

1809 — Reduction of number of religious houses under Napoleon.

1812 — Under the Constitution of Cádiz, it was ruled that certain restrictions should apply to the orders. It was forbidden to make appeals for funds to restore houses. The appropriation to the State of the property of all houses suppressed by the invasion was confirmed. Further suppression of smaller houses.

1814 — Under Ferdinand VII temporary restoration of properties and return of Jesuits.

1820 — Rebellion of Rafael Riego. Expulsion of Jesuits and decree against religious orders, October 25, 1820.

The impoverishment of the treasury was taken to make raids on the Church a patriotic necessity. Benedictines and Augustinians suppressed.

Parish priests reduced; numerous houses closed; suspension of benefices.

1822 — Suppression of all houses in villages of less than 450 inhabitants.

Between 1820 and 1822, bishops and priests forced to espouse Liberal constitution from pulpits in laudatory terms.

1834–1837 — Persecution, killings, and finally the Mendizábal *desamortización*. The expulsion of bishops and the suppression of eighteen bishoprics.

1843 — Restoration of a degree of normality.

1851 — The Concordat between Rome and Madrid.

1854 — A two-year period of progressive rule began, with a new anti-Church outburst. Expulsions and confiscations began again. The Vatican broke diplomatic relations with Spain.

1856 — Expropriation extended to all property possessed or enjoyed by individuals or corporations of an ecclesiastical character.

1868 — The revolution against Isabel II. All religious communities established since 1837 suppressed. Society of Jesus dissolved. Convents reduced to half their number.

The Constitution of 1869 and its strongly anti-Catholic inspiration.

1874 — Riots and antireligious demonstrations. The support of clergy allowed to fall into arrears.

1876 — New constitution and restoration of respect for Church.

1910 — "Padlock Law," restricting the entrance or formation of new religious communities in Spain.

1931 — The advent of the Second Republic and the outbreak of new disorders and persecution.

Appendix 3. DEVELOPMENT OF COMMUNISM IN LEFTIST-CONTROLLED SPAIN BEFORE THE CIVIL WAR

It has been made clear in the text of this book that communism as a movement and party never gained outstanding success in pre-civil-war Spain, nor did it compare in virulence to either socialism or anarcho-syndicalism. The importance that attaches to it springs from the fact that it was by far the best-knit, organized, and aggressive force among the extremist movements. The experience of the Asturian revolt in 1934 proved this. The factual study of growing communist control up to the time of the civil war is further evidence in the same direction.

Communism began to make headway in Spain as a positive influence on government and thought when the technique of the Popular Front became the accepted procedure, that is, after the Seventh Congress of the Communist Internationale in 1935. The decision to seek electoral alliances with other left-wing parties and particularly with bourgeois groups was the entering wedge which permitted communism to begin the slow climb intended to lead to full control. The fusion of the socialist and communist parties was unquestionably the goal in Spain. The youth organizations had achieved this perfect union in 1934, as will be described shortly. There remained the much more difficult task of welding together socialism and communism into a solid single party, representing supposedly all facets of the working class. *Pravda* (Feb. 19, 1936) had commented on the victory of the Popular Front in February, 1936, in the following terms:

"The triumph of the Popular Front is the beginning of the proletariat's offensive against the forces of fascism and reaction. . . . The primary need in annihilating fascism completely is amnesty for all imprisoned revolutionaries, the confiscation of the property of the aristocrats, the readmission of all workers dismissed for revolutionary activity in October, 1934, and the raising of the salaries of rural and urban workers. Spanish communists know that this program cannot be realized by the kind of left wing government that will probably be formed at first. Our task is to increase by every means the effectiveness of the working masses and the Popular Front. But we should not be content with the latter, but advance by every means the democratic revolution."

The French publication *La Vie Ouvrière* contains a great deal of material on Spanish affairs during the critical months after the Popular Front came into power. We find repeated allusion, for instance, to Francisco Largo Caballero, as the future leader of all Spanish working-class parties.

But first of all, it may be useful to describe the various divisions of the communist forces in Spain at the time. They may be classified as follows:

Partido comunista español. The most important nucleus of the communists and directly linked with the Comintern. It is the Spanish branch of the Communist Internationale. Its organ of expression was *Mundo Obrero.*

Partido comunista catalán. This was the official Catalan branch of the communist party, but of extremely limited influence.

Partido Obrero de Unificación Marxista. This is the P.O.U.M., the initials of which became so well known in the civil war days. It represented opposition communist forces, under the direction of Joaquin Maurín. Its influence was limited strictly to Catalonia. The official communist party considered this group as Trotskyite.

Bloque Obrero y campesino. Founded by Maurín after the break with the Central Committee of the communist party. Later fused with the P.O.U.M. The *Bloque* exerted considerable influence in Barcelona.

It was extremely difficult to determine with precision the communist strength in Spain up to 1936. Mauricio Karl in a little book entitled *El comunismo en España* gave the following figures: Communist party, Youth, etc., 280,000 members; Bloque Obrero, P.O.U.M., etc., 50,000 members.

It is highly probable that the first figure is reasonably accurate while the second is exaggerated. The more conservative estimates do not give the opposition communist forces much more than 10,000 members. *Mundo Obrero* (April 1, 1936) expressed its gratification at the "50,000 members of the party." The Central Committee of the Spanish Communist Party, meeting between March 28 and 30, 1936, spoke of "30,000 new members since the February elections." In this case the party prior to the triumph of the Popular Front had only some 20,000 members. José Díaz, General Secretary of the party, wrote in *La Correspondencia Internacional* (April 17, 1936) that the party was "60,000 strong." *Mundo Obrero* (April 28, 1936) informed all provincial groups of the need for the most accurate statistical information on new members, especially those who entered the party after February 16.

The figures for the other extremist groups are equally open to serious doubt as to their accuracy. These are often given as the following:

Socialist party, Socialist Youth, and U.G.T.	1,100,000
Federación sindicalista literaria and opposition unions to the C.N.T. (*Confederación Nacional del Trabajo*)	200,000
Regional Confederation of Asturias, León, and Palencia	90,000
C.N.T. and *Federación Anarquista Ibérica*	600,000
Semiorganized groups more or less affiliated with C.N.T.	200,000
Escamots separatistas (Catalan separatists)	30,000

The Spanish Communist Party operated clandestinely until the advent of the Republic. In June, 1931, it registered with the Home Secretary and became a legally recognized party, and in March, 1932, the fourth national congress was held at which time 11,000 was the number of members stated.

The Communist Party was favored in an extraordinary way by the Popular Front combination which permitted it to obtain 17 deputies in the Cortes. But infinitely more serious was the enormous infiltration of communist elements in the provincial governments, and very particularly in the municipal administration. Among the communists occupying seats in the Cortes in 1936, only a few have been recorded by history as playing a role of outstanding importance; José Díaz Ramos, deputy for Madrid and General Secretary of the party, a former baker and ex-anarchist, was looked upon as one of the figures of greatest prestige. Dolores Ibarruri, deputy for Oviedo, had a long and significant career as an agitator in Vizcaya, as the editor of *Mundo Obrero,* and as one of the most effective of the communist propagandists. Cayetano Bolivar Escribano was the only communist deputy in the Cortes up to the victory of 1936. Other leaders after that in parliament included Vicente Uribe, minority leader, and Jesús Hernandez Tomás, later to be Minister of Education of the Popular Front government. The communists made no effort to conceal their contempt for parliament and their primary interest in the mobilization of mass opinion for the Revolution:

"Our policy in the Cortes will differ from that of the other groups. We shall endeavor to link our parliamentary action with the struggle in the street. We do not consider parliament to be of fundamental importance since the vital thing is the mobilization of the masses, to which is reserved a far greater task than the work of their representatives in the chamber."[1]

As has been indicated, the most important single element for a proper understanding of the role of the extreme Left in the crisis of 1936 is the increasing collaboration between the communists and socialists. It was perfectly clear that the communists alone and unaided could not hope to capture a majority. The only solution was to operate in close co-operation with the socialists who had a far greater hold on the working masses. The extraordinary thing is that the socialists were willing to allow the communists to participate fully in the name of working-class unity, despite the familiar "boring from within" tactics of the latter. The communists devoted a great deal of attention to the creation of *Alianzas obreras,* that is, workers' alliances, which became in the rural areas *Alianzas obreras y campesinas.* This unity of action was frequently limited to a single factory or enterprise and circumscribed to specific demands. It nevertheless created little by little the atmosphere of co-operation toward which the communists were working. The ultimate goal was fusion with the socialists and above all perfect co-ordination among the various trade union groups.

The names and character of these organizations have already been indicated in the course of these pages. It will be remembered that the *Unión General de Trabajadores* (U.G.T.) was dominated by the socialists; the *Confederación General de Trabajo Unitaria* was communist created and was dominated entirely by them; and finally the *Confederación Nacional del Trabajo* (C.N.T.), whose doctrine and ideology was anarcho-syndicalist.

The approach to socialism in the republican period was complicated by the divisions within the socialist ranks themselves. There was the so-called right wing or reformist branch of socialism, led by Professor Besteiro and Indalecio Prieto, and the radical or revolutionary wing, of which Francisco Largo Caballero was the leader. It would seem that the latter tendency was steadily on the increase and the revolutionary doctrine was particularly strong among the socialist youth organizations.[2] The communist press was extremely laudatory of Largo

[1] *Mundo Obrero,* March 12, 1936. Statement of Dolores Ibarruri.

[2] The great fact in the communist offensive in 1936 was, of course, the Popular Front technique. In the case of Spain this was particularly necessary in view of the paucity of communist leadership. Therefore, it became evident that Francisco Largo Caballero was the leader, by the grace of the Communist International, that was to guide Spain toward communism. In a remarkable series of articles in the Madrid

Caballero, and everything seemed to indicate that if the union between socialists and communists really came about that he would be the accepted leader of the new Sovietized Spain. We discover on the communist side expressions such as the following:

"With the exception of the communist party and in large part, of the left wing of the socialist party, the leaders of the other parties forming the Popular Front consider it merely as an electoral combination and do not aspire to anything else. The right wing socialists have revealed themselves as the enemies of the united workers front."[3]

By the spring of 1936 the union of the communist trade unions and the U.G.T. had made notable progress. Largo Caballero indicated that this was a fact in an article in his paper *Claridad,* April 13, 1936. The problem of union with the anarcho-syndicalists of the C.N.T. was a much more complicated matter. The traditional hostility of the syndicalists for the "authoritarianism" of the communists and left-wing socialists came to the surface to obstruct the negotiations toward unity. The socialist and communist press devoted much space to praise the anarcho-syndicalists in the effort to bring their leaders around to the idea of union. In the Zaragoza congress of the C.N.T., May 10, 1936, the organization reiterated its acceptance of anarchism, its total disbelief in political solutions, and its uncompromising hostility to all active participation in the normal processes of the State. It appealed to the socialists to unite in a revolutionary pact, on the condition that they recognize the failure of parliamentarianism and refuse to collaborate further in the present government. The communists were not disheartened, as the editorial in one of their papers indicated: "The C.N.T. congress holds open a door of very great hope."[4]

But the really powerful achievement of communism and the one thing that assured it of an opportunity for the climb toward power was the union of the socialist and communist youth organizations. As early as July, 1934, the leaders of the two youth groups met to discuss the basis of unified action. In March, 1936, a delegation of the *Juventud comunista* and *Juventud socialista* traveled to Moscow to discuss the plans for a union. Early in April the respective federations decided to create a joint committee to be called the *Comision Nacional de Unificación.* On April 4 the agreement was made public with the expressed approval of the executive committee of the Communist Youth Internationale. This unity revealed its practical effects almost immediately. On April 4, the separate publications of the two youth movements were joined under the name of

---

paper *Ya,* Enrique Matorras, former secretary of the communist youth organization, describes in detail how Largo Caballero came to be chosen, how Julio Alvarez del Vayo became one of the leading spokesmen for the Left wing of socialism, and how the two socialist branches actually broke with the Largo Caballero wing and passed over to communism. "*Claridad,* the organ of revolutionary socialism, was forced out of the printing office *Gráfica socialista* and was then printed on the presses of *Mundo Obrero,* the property of the communist party. One of the positive results of the deliberations of the Communist International was to whitewash Manuel Azaña and present him henceforth as the hope of the extreme Left. The change in tone of the leftist press toward Azaña is extraordinary in 1935–36" (*Ya,* Jan. 28 and 30, 1936).

[3] José Díaz in *La Correspondencia Internacional,* April 17, 1936.

[4] *Juventud,* May 16, 1936.

Renovación y Juventud Roja. After May 1, the united front issued its magazine *Juventud.* There was much discussion about the appropriate uniform, and it was finally decided that the united youth groups should wear a blue shirt with a red tie. The revolutionary intention was crystal clear in the statement of *Renovación* (May 9, 1936):

"We believe that the political line of the Federation of Socialist Youth at the present time . . . ought to include the following: The creation of the Bolshevik Party with the fusion of the purged socialist party and the communist; the establishment of a single trade union organization with the fusion of the C.N.T. and U.G.T.; the increase of the workers and farmers alliances, all aimed at the proletarian revolution."

An aspect of the very greatest importance in the study of the communist campaign to win Spain was the number of organizations directly or indirectly controlled by the extreme Left. These may be listed as follows: the communist trade unions; Friends of the Soviet Union; International Red Relief; Workers Sporting Federation; National Committee for the Fight against War and Fascism; Association of Revolutionary Writers and Artists; Union of Students; Union of Proletarian Women; Pioneers Union; Federation of the Workers Theater and Cine Clubs; Artists International. This list, which is by no means all-inclusive, sounds strangely like something the congressional committee on anti-American activities turned up: the same front organizations, the same ambiguous title at times to catch the unwary, the same unscrupulous use of democratic terminology to cover the machinations of the communist party. The lesson that Spain learned thirteen years ago does not seem to have penetrated a great many other countries.

Spanish communism was behind any number of the incidents and constant agitation that characterized the Spain of the republican era. The general technique of the communists was to profit from social movements that were popular with the workers, and condemn those that were either a failure or likely to favor other left wing groups. Thus it was that the Central Bureau of the Spanish Communist Party condemned with severity the uprising in the Llobregat Valley, in 1932, denouncing the C.N.T. for provoking a movement that merely led to the repression of the working class. The records show that the communists were directly involved in the following number of strikes: 1930, 527; 1931, 3643; 1932, 2400; 1935, 775.

Direct communist provocation may be pointed out in a large number of cases where the proof can admit of no doubt. Some of the incidents which the communists engineered may be listed as follows:

April 13, 1931: Strike in Seville with complete tie-up and attack on the civil government.

May 10, 1931: Active participation of communists in events in Madrid and elsewhere in Spain and the general strike of May 11.

May 26, 1931: Strike in Pasajes and march on San Sebastián. Open conflict between communists and civil guard.

July 21, 1931: General strike in Seville. Communist assault on barracks of civil guard. Put down with machine guns.

1932: Communist participation in murder of civil guards at Castilblanco. Participated in incidents at Zalamea de la Serena, Jeresa, Epila y Arnedo.

Jan. 25, 1932: General strikes in Seville, Vizcaya, Málaga, Valencia, and Almería directed by communists.

May 1, 1932: Shooting in Madrid and general strike May 2.

May 25, 1932: General strike under communist direction in Seville, Cádiz, Ceuta, and Valencia.

July 8, 1932: Uprising in Villa de Don Fradique, Toledo province, where communism was proclaimed. The leader was Bolivar, later elected as communist deputy for Málaga.

Aug. 12, 1932: General strike in Seville declared by communists.

June 23, 1933: Communist bands were organized to seize and burn all emblems of the Sacred Heart that were displayed publicly by Catholics.

1934: Full communist participation in the Asturias uprising.

1935: During the Lerroux regime the communists were more quiet.

All these developments, it should be noted, had taken place well before the beginning of the civil war, July 18, 1936, under the republican administration.

It may not be without interest to note the explanation of the failure of the Asturias rebellion as given by the review *L'Internationale Communiste* (Nov. 20, 1934):

1. The Spanish proletariat is still too strongly influenced by socialist and anarchist leadership.
2. Sufficient work has not been done with the peasants.
3. The Catalan nationalist movement has been pre-eminently bourgeois.
4. Not enough has been done to assure army support for the people.
5. Absence of adequate organization. The strikes and rebellion all over Spain were not sufficiently unified and centrally directed. The communists gave the right kind of direction in Asturias and the Basque provinces where they are relatively strong.

By the time the Popular Front was in power, Spain was quite aware of the specialties of each extremist group. The anarchists were invariably involved in bomb tossing and armed holdups. The socialists and communists were much more addicted to attacks on political centers of the opposition parties and particularly church burning. The Logos News Agency drew up a list of the actual cases that were reported or about which authentic information could be obtained for the period between February 16 and April 20, 1936, under the republican administration. The constant censorship made it almost impossible for the daily press to keep up with the destruction and murders that occurred every day. The list of violent incidents in which communist participation is either completely established or reasonably presumed is as follows:

Churches totally destroyed	90
Churches partially destroyed or profaned	122
Newspapers totally destroyed	8
Newspapers partially destroyed	17
Political centers destroyed	15
Political centers assaulted and partially destroyed	97
Catholic Action centers destroyed	6
Catholic Action centers assaulted	20
Official offices destroyed	10
Official offices assaulted	9

Private residences assaulted and destroyed	23
Private residences assaulted	112
Violent deaths from attack	140
Wounded	620
Attacked without serious consequences	153
Holdups committed	81
Holdups that failed or were foiled	12
Bombs exploded	58
Bombs picked up before explosion	42

Between April 20 and May 15, still previous to the civil war which was soon to follow, communists and socialists were responsible for the attack on the street against eight nuns whose college in Cuatro Caminos was assaulted.

A word regarding some of the propaganda methods of Spanish communism in the months immediately preceding the civil war, before the Catholic liberation. One of the organizations to develop a curiously vigorous life was the "Friends of the Soviet Union." The Spanish section was established in April, 1933, and by 1936 already had a network of local and provincial centers all over Spain. There were, in the summer of 1936, about 50 major centers of this organization in the peninsula. Its magazine, *Rusia de Hoy,* was a powerful propaganda instrument. The headquarters of the Association was at Calle de la Flor Baja, 5, the main floor of which is devoted to the offices of the Communist Internationale.

The victory of the Popular Front produced a tremendous upsurge in the amount of communist propaganda and especially in the persistent deluging of the market with communist and Sovietophile literature. Communist-inspired literature began to appear in great profusion in 1931, and by 1932 and 1933 seemed almost to exert a monopoly in the field during this section of the republican regime. The number of book stalls on the Madrid streets selling this sort of thing was legion. The annual book fair was distinguished by the fantastic amount of Soviet or communist material. I recall personally the aspect of things in Madrid in the late summer of 1932. At every stand communist programs, historical works, treatises on economics, and volumes laudatory of the Soviet Union were available for as low as a peseta. The development of communist propaganda in Spain by means of books has followed a very definite course. After 1929 there was a considerable vogue of the German left-wing novel, pacifist and vaguely socialist, such as Remarque, Zweig, Johanssen, and the Frenchman Barbusse. The second period belonged to the novel with social content or a class-conscious message, American, German, and Soviet. The third period was a literal invasion of Soviet literature: Ehrenburg, Pilniack, Babel, Zochtchenko, and the first of the Spaniards writing in the same vein, such as Sender and others. The fourth stage was the period of communist propaganda unashamed — open, above board, and enormously voluminous. The major enterprise producing this type of literature was the *Editorial Europa-America,* which flooded the stands and especially the news and magazine carts that were so numerous in Madrid with cheap editions, many for as low as 10 and 50 centimos.

As an indication of the state of things in Spain in the spring and early summer of 1936, before the final outbreak of the civil war the following are some of the books most highly praised in the left-wing press and reviewed most frequently by the socialist and communist papers:

Juan Garcia Morales (an ex-priest), *El Cristo Rojo* (The Red Christ); J. Stalin, *La teoría de la revolución proletaria* (The Theory of Proletarian Revolution); F. Engels, *Orígin de la familia, de la propriedad privada y del Estado* (Origin of the Family, Private Property and the State); Fermin Galán, *Barbarie organizada* (Organized Barbarism); *Sexto congreso de la Internacional Juvenil comunista* (Sixth Congress of the International of Communist Youth).

An astonishing chapter in the story of the communist plot against Spain is the place won in the cinema world — in the film industry, cine clubs, and reviews devoted to the screen. One can readily imagine the very great effect on the younger generation of the popular cinema reviews more or less openly devoted to spreading the communist line. This is precisely what happened in Spain before 1936. Take the *Cine Teatro Club,* as an example. This organization whose first film séance took place on February 29, 1936, was devoted primarily to Soviet pictures and to low-priced showings of revolutionary films. The admission price of a peseta attracted vast numbers of workers who were dazzled by the propaganda of such productions as "The Cruiser Potemkin." Other film circles, such as the *Proa Filmófono,* showed Soviet pictures in great number: "Land," "October," and "Song of Life." There were some 25 centers of this character scattered about Spain, all assiduously engaged in promoting the showing of Soviet films or others slanted in the revolutionary direction. Even the Spanish film production was influenced by the Soviet model, and such producers as Tony Roman and Bunuel gave the public extremely tendentious interpretations of Spanish themes. The vogue of Soviet documentaries, such as "Wings," increased notably after the triumph of the Popular Front. There were various attempts to develop a typically revolutionary theater in Spain. For a time after the success of the proclamation of the Republic a few plays were shown in the workers quarters of Madrid, but their low artistic quality did not lead to anything permanent. The *Cine Teatro Club,* founded in February, 1936, by Jacinto Grau, Santiago de la Cruz, and César Falcon undertook to stimulate the revolutionary theater, especially in the Teatro Rosales. There were perhaps another half-dozen enterprises of this nature, although it was evident that the motion picture was a far more effective propaganda weapon than the legitimate stage. César Falcon wrote a play called "Asturias" of very pronounced revolutionary flavor and announced in the pages of *Mundo Obrero* (May 9, 1936) that only proletarian players, organized in co-operatives, would take part in the production.

The Friends of the Soviet Union made every effort to encourage Spanish listeners to tune in on Radio Moscow for the Spanish language broadcasts. The number of such broadcasts were stepped up during 1936 so that listeners in the Iberian peninsula were rarely deprived of the communist education to be secured by listening to the Soviet programs.

The communists did not overlook the possibilities of separate sporting groups, once they had brought about the alliance with the socialists. The importance of this phase of communist propaganda can scarcely be overemphasized. It will be recalled that on July 18, 1936, the first foreign volunteers — the precursor of the International Brigades — were a group of left-wing athletes, gathered in

Barcelona for a meeting with their Spanish comrades. Within a few months hundreds of local sporting clubs were formed all over Spain along strictly communist lines. There was even a special competition for what was called the "Thälmann Football Cup," in honor of the German communist leader. Much effort was made to organize the children and we discover in the sporting section of *Claridad,* the left-wing socialist paper, for May 14, 1936, a photograph and salutation to the "young children's team of Aranjuez, U.H.P."

The unified socialists and communists were quite aware of the importance of armed militia for the crucial moment when their forces would take to the streets, to use the genteel term of "The Pasionaria." It is conservatively estimated that these youth organizations represented some 100,000 members all over Spain. Santiago Carrillo, the socialist secretary, and Trifon Medrano, the communist, promised the communist party in March that by July they would reach this figure. On Sundays it was their practice to indulge in military exercises in the parks around Madrid and in the Sierra de Guadarrama. On May 17, 1936, for example, they engaged in shooting practice in the Pedriza de Manzanares. The government, needless to say, paid not the slightest attention to these demonstrations.

Communism in the schools is another problem entirely. In the gigantic effort to provoke social chaos and by this means launch the movement toward revolution, the combined communists and socialists had not overlooked the importance of infiltration in the school system. This was enormously enhanced by the legislation against the religious orders. The atmosphere of total secularism favored the new tendency, and the influx of improvised and ill-prepared teachers to take the place of religious gave the extreme Left a rare opportunity for its action. Part of the story has been told in a remarkable book, to which too little attention has been paid, Alfonso Iniesta, *Garra marxista en la escuela,* Burgos, 1939. In this work the author, himself a primary school inspector, traces the whole process of the Marxist assault on the school system. It is a shocking and disconcerting story indeed. The largest organization of communist teachers was the *Federación española de trabajadores de la enseñanza,* consisting of some 6000 members out of the total of 50,000 teachers in the entire country. How did this nucleus operate? The introduction of materialism and Marxism in the schools became more and more evident during the five years of the Republic. There are authentic cases, testified to by teachers, pupils, and parents, of schools where the clenched fist was the obligatory salute each morning. One teacher in Alcala de Henares demanded that his students salute him on arriving at school by saying, "There is no God," to which the teacher replied, "There never was." In March and April, 1936, there were numerous parades in the main streets of Madrid of small children with large banners stating that "We want teachers, not friars."

At one school in the Colonia de los Carteros in Madrid, the teacher insisted that the children call her "Comrade." It is obvious that the socialist and communist controlled city and provincial governments would make life intolerable for the Catholic schools. In some cases, too, the local lay teachers were forbidden to attend Mass, and in other cases were actually dismissed for having been seen at Mass. One Madrid teacher was denounced and suspended because he cited the case of St. Vincent de Paul as an example of charity. The Minister of Public Instruction declared Catholic teachers' associations illegal since the Constitution forbade anything "sectarian." The number of assaults and outrages against Catholic schools surpasses all listing. In the Madrid area alone these included Ciempozuelos, Torrelodones, Perales de Tajuna, Valdeguna, Villaconejos, Mejorada del Campo, Tetuán de las Victorias, Vallecas, Dehesa de la Villa, Bellas Vistas, Canillas, Cuatro Caminos, Carabanchel, and Chamartín — a total of seventeen schools.

Communist penetration in the public service was notorious. After the Republic was proclaimed, a union was formed of telegraph workers, nominally a professional group, but in fact dominated by the revolutionary idea. Within this organization a number of communists very soon became dominant, among whom were Julio Mangada and Martin Caire. The influence of these leaders in the Ministry was so far reaching as to include appointments and dismissals. There were efforts among the serious employees to get rid of this agitation, and in general it may be said that the telegraph and communications system remained reasonably free of contamination. A bizarre example of sovietism at work was the so-called *Hogar Telegráfico,* founded to care for the orphans of telegraph operators. This institution was totally communized to such an extent that the children dismissed ten directors in the course of a single year. By March, 1936, the institution was run by a board of students who selected and dismissed the teaching staff at will.

Communist activity extended to every effort to bring about the communization of dock workers, fishermen, and port employees. In most cases the propaganda was directed toward unification along the lines already realized in the youth groups. The communists did not overlook the possibility of separatism even in places as unpromising as Morocco. "Everyone recognizes the existence of strong currents of nationalism in Morocco which we, the proletariat, are in duty bound to support."[5]

Another phase of the "demoralization" of Spain was the incredible increase in the propaganda on behalf of atheism. It must not be thought that Spanish communism was merely a political or even economic force. It was dedicated to the complete Marxist ideal and included most prominently among its postulates the absolute eradication of religion. The situation in 1936 was most unhealthy. While religious institutions were burned, destroyed, and pillaged, no handicap was placed on the free dissemination of atheism in its most virulent form. The following is a list of the principal atheist newspapers and reviews published in Spain and sold on the newsstands, as of 1936: *Mirador,* inspired by Francisco Pujols; *La Rambla,* weekly with Granier Barrera as the principal collaborator; *El Ateo,* directed by Gines Bernades Franco; *El Lerrouxista,* directed by Antonio Sevilla; *El Be Negre,* satirical review against all religion; *Revista Blanca,* director, Federica Montseny; *Solidaridad Obrera,* organ of the anarchist F.A.I., with innumerable articles favorable to atheism; *El Diluvio,* daily under direction of noted atheist Luis Umbert Santos; *Renovación,* the well-known atheist, Alfonso Martiney Carrasco, director; *L'Hora,* Catalan atheist sheet; *Iniciales,* atheist paper of anarchist tendency; *Biofilia,* Laura Brunet, director; *Vida y Trabajo.*

---

[5] *Mundo Obrero,* April 4, 1936.

In Valencia there were a number of atheist papers and reviews as well as in the other provincial capitals of the peninsula. In Madrid, Calle de Roma 41, there was a "Godless Library" and an institution called the *Casa de los Sin Dios* (The House of the Godless) located at Ballasteros 8.

In December, 1932, the Godless League was founded in Spain with branches in all the provinces. The year before a kindred organization, the Liga Anticlerical Revolucionaria, had been set up. In 1935 there was founded the *Unión de Librepensadores proletarios* run by the communists, and a socialist counterpart called the *Liga de Librepensadores.*

The perversion of family life was another aspect of this same general trend. Immorality and corruption were commonplace. I have referred before to the appalling prevalence in every Spanish city of pornographic literature, sold to everyone without the least restriction and reaching a degree of shamelessness rarely matched anywhere. In a newsstand located in La Glorieta in the Madrid suburb of Cuatro Caminos, the most scandalous literature was offered for sale: *Communism and Morality, Communism and Marriage, Engels on the Family.*

The real danger of communism in 1936 was not that it would seize power suddenly. The anarchists were bitterly opposed to any communist monopoly of revolution. The pact with the socialists was still too fresh to give absolute assurance of harmony. The danger of communism was that it was the powerful contributing force to the demoralization of a people. Through every one of the methods described above, it was undermining morality, destroying the bases of the social order, and producing the kind of society that would have no defenses against the inroads of materialism and ultimately of the revolutionary overthrow of the established order. The evidence I have cited is a hundredth part of what is available to show how the extreme Left was out to destroy Spanish society and its way of life. This was the awful, appalling danger that appeared to men of good will in July, 1936. Against it there was no recourse but the recourse to arms.

The existence of a communist plot for the summer of 1936 has been amply demonstrated with documentary proof. The British writer, Arthur F. Loveday, in his *Spain 1923–1948* (p. 251 sq.), has done us the service to reproduce in English translation the full documentary evidence on this point. They are secret, confidential documents outlining the plans for the establishment of a Soviet regime in Spain. The details are illuminating in the precision with which they provide for every contingency. Largo Caballero, needless to say, was the president of the National Soviet so envisaged. An earlier book, published from English language sources, gives an excellent summary of the development of leftism in Spain up to the civil war.[6]

---

[6] G. M. Godden, *Conflict in Spain, 1920–1937,* London, 1937. This volume utilizes to advantage communist sources, reports of the Communist Internationale, and the communist press of England and the Continent.

BIBLIOGRAPHY

I

General Works

THE HISTORICAL BACKGROUND AND THE SPANISH SPIRIT

Aguado Bleye, P., *Manual de historia de España,* Madrid, 1947, Vol. I, 6 ed.

Alba, Santiago, *Problemas de España,* Madrid, 1916.

Altamira y Crevea, Rafael, *Historia de España y de la civilización española,* Barcelona, 1913–1914, 4 vols., 3 ed.

——— *A History of Spanish Civilization,* translated by P. Volkov, London, 1930.

——— *Psicología del pueblo español,* Barcelona, 1917, 2 ed.

Armstrong, E., *The Emperor Charles V,* London, 1910, 2 vols., 2 ed.

Asín Palacios, Miguel, *Huellas de Islam,* Madrid, 1941.

Atkinson, W. C., *Spain, A Brief History,* London, 1934.

Ballesteros, Antonio, *Historia de España y su influencia en la historia universal,* Barcelona, 1943–1948, 12 vols., 2 ed. The histories of Altamira y Crevea and Ballesteros are fundamental for the background of Spanish affairs. Both are monumental in their scope and treatment of the Hispanic past.

Balmes, Jaime, *Obras completas,* Madrid, 1948–1950, 7 vols. Father Balmes covered a multitude of subjects in his writings. This edition belongs to the famous Biblioteca de Autores Cristianos now in publication. To date seven volumes of Balmes have appeared. There are other complete editions of his works available.

Bayle, Constantino, S.J., *La expansión misional de España,* Barcelona, 1936.

Beltrán Rózpide, R., *La peninsula ibérica,* Madrid, 1918.

Bergua, J., *Psicología del pueblo español,* Madrid, 1934.

Bertrand, Louis, *Espagne,* Paris, 1934.

——— *Histoire d'Espagne,* Paris, 1932.

——— *Philippe II à l'Escorial,* Paris, 1929.

——— *Sur les vielles routes d'Espagne,* Paris, 1931. Louis Bertrand constitutes an excellent introduction to Spain. His *Philippe II à l'Escorial* is vivid; his *Sur les vielles routes d'Espagne* suggestive and penetrating.

Blázquez, A., *España y Portugal,* Barcelona, 1914.

Borrow, George, *The Bible in Spain or the journeys, adventures and imprisonments of an Englishman, in an attempt to circulate the scriptures in the peninsula,* London, 1891, 4 ed. Borrow is too well known to require comment. He is full of prejudice as well as shrewd observation. A *must* however for the student of Spain.

Bouissounouse, Janine, *Isabelle la Catholique. Comment se fît l'Espagne,* Paris, 1949. A new and readable life of the great Queen.

Calmette, Joseph, *Histoire de l'Espagne,* Paris, 1947.

——— *La formation de l'unité espagnole,* Paris, 1946.

Calvo Serer, Rafael, *España sin problema,* Madrid, 1949. A highly polemical essay that should be read together with Laín Entralgo for a view of what contemporary Spaniards think about the destiny of Spain.

Cambridge Modern History, Cambridge, 1907–1912, 14 vols.

Carbia, Rómulo, *Historia de la leyenda negra hispanoamericana,* Madrid, 1944.

Cardo, Carles, *Histoire spirituelle des Espagnes,* Paris, 1946. A study of "the Spains" by a Catalan canon. Useful as a reflection of the view of a Catalan nationalist.

Castro, Américo, *Aspectos del vivir hispánico. Espiritualismo, mesianismo actitud personal en los siglos XIV al XV,* Santiago, Chile, 1949.

——— *España en su historia. Cristianos, moros y judíos,* Buenos Aires, 1948. Suggestive essays from the pen of one of the most eminent of contemporary Spanish philologists and literary historians.

Chapman, C. E., *A History of Spain,* New York, 1925.

Churchill, Winston, *The Gathering Storm,* Vol. I, Boston, 1948.

Clarke, H. Butler, *Modern Spain, 1815–1898,* Cambridge, 1906.

Colección de Encíclicas y Cartas Pontificias, Madrid, 1942. A superb edition of the social, political, and other encyclicals of the recent Pontiffs with an excellent index issued by Spanish Catholic Action.

Coles, S. F. A., *Spain Everlasting,* London, 1946.

Cortada Reus, F., *Geografía económica de España,* Barcelona, 1946.

Corts Grau, José, *Motivos de la España eterna,* Madrid, 1946, 6th edition.

Cuadra, Pablo Antonio, *Entre la cruz y la espada,* Madrid, 1946. Essays on Hispanic topics by an outstanding Nicaraguan traditionalist.

Curiel, Luis, *Indice histórico de disposiciones sociales,* Madrid, 1946. A useful guide to the entire history of social legislation in Spain classified by years and covering the development from the Middle Ages to recent date.

Del Río, Angel, *Historia de la literatura española,* New York, 1948. One of the most recent general histories of Spanish letters. This one has the advantage of including sections on Catalan and Galician letters as well as a few pages on literary trends since 1939.

Diccionario de la literatura española, Madrid, 1949. Under the direction of Julián Marías and Germán Bleiberg. This is a publication of the *Revista de Occidente,* under the inspiration of José Ortega y Gasset.

Donoso Cortés, Juan, *Obras escogidas,* Buenos Aires, 1943. The complete works of Juan Donoso Cortés have been published in the Biblioteca de Autores Cristianos. I have used this selection of his works since the important essays such as his pronouncements on the situation of Spain, religion, etc., are to be found here.

Doussinague, José M., *Hispanidad y catolicismo,* Montevideo, 1939.

Ediciones Cultura Hispánica, *Fray Francisco de Vitoria, fundador del derecho internacional moderno,* Madrid, 1946. Of the many publications on Francisco de Vitoria on the fourth centenary, I have found this volume of lectures particularly useful.

Elías de Tejada, Francisco, *Las Españas: formación histórica, tradiciones regionales,* Madrid (n.d.).

Ellis, Havelock, *The Soul of Spain,* London, 1929, 11 impr.

Elorduy, Eleuterio, S.J., *La idea de imperio en el pensamiento espanol y de otros pueblos,* Madrid, 1944. A substantial examination of the "idea" behind the expansion of Spain beyond the seas.

España vista por los españoles, selections by C. Palencia, Mexico, 1947.

Ford, Richard, *Gatherings From Spain,* first published, London, 1846. Fundamental. Available in Everyman's Library, New York and London.

——— *Handbook for Travellers in Spain and Readers at Home,* London, 1845, 2 vols. By all odds one of the best books on Spain. A guide book in character it covers every aspect of Spanish life from roads and inns to history.

Ganivet, Angel, *Obras completas,* Madrid, 1943, 2 vols. Contains, of course, the famous *Idearium Español,* one of the outstanding essays of the 1898 period and a penetrating analysis of the Spanish character.

Gannon, E. D., *Portrait of a Spaniard,* published in the *British Survey,* London, Vol. VIII, No. 21, December, 1947. Although a pamphlet, this short analysis of the Spanish character is excellent.

García Morente, Manuel, *Idea de la Hispanidad,* Madrid, 1947, 3 ed. Indispensable for the contemporary traditionalist trend.

García Villada, Zacarías, *El destino de España en la historia universal,* Madrid, 1948, 3rd ed. A series of illuminating essays by the greatest modern ecclesiastical historian of Spain. His *Historia eclesiástica de España,* interrupted by his murder in Madrid in 1936 promised to be the most significant contribution to this subject.

Gescher, B. H., and F. M., *L'Espagne dans le monde,* Paris, 1937, translated from the Dutch.

Gómez de la Serna, *España y sus problemas,* Madrid, 1916.

Gómez Zamora, Matías, *Regio Patronato español e indiano,* Madrid, 1897.

Hume, M. A. S., *Modern Spain,* London, 1899.

——— *Philip II of Spain,* London, 1897.

——— *The Court of Philip IV. Spain in decadence,* London, 1927.

——— *Spain: its greatness and decay, 1479–1788,* Cambridge, 1925.

Jobit, Pierre, *Espagne et Hispanité,* Paris (n.d.). A suggestive little volume by a French priest, distinguished for his Hispanic activity at the Catholic Institute in Paris.

Juderías, Julián, *La leyenda negra. Estudios acerca del concepto de España en el extranjero,* Madrid, 1917.

Junco, Alfonso, *Sangre de Hispania,* Buenos Aires, 1944. Essays by one of the most distinguished of contemporary Mexican Catholic writers.

Laín Entralgo, Pedro, *España como problema,* Madrid, 1948.

——— *Sobre la cultura española. Confesiones de este tiempo,* Madrid, 1943.

Legendre, Maurice, *Nouvelle histoire d'Espagne,* Paris, 1938.

——— *Portrait de l'Espagne,* Paris, 1923.

——— *Semblanza de España,* Madrid, 1944.

Leiper, Henry Smith, *Christianity Today. A Survey of the State of the Churches,* New York, 1947.

Llorca, P. Bernardino, S.J., *Manual de historia eclesiástica,* Barcelona, 1946. An excellent survey of Church history with numerous references to Spain.

Madariaga, Salvador de, *Anarquía y jerarquía,* Madrid, 1935.

——— *Englishmen — Frenchmen — Spaniards,* Oxford. The brilliant essay of the distinguished Spanish liberal on the national mentalities of the three peoples.

——— *Spain,* London and New York, 1946, 2 impr.

——— *The Genius of Spain,* Oxford, 1923.

——— *The Rise of the Spanish American Empire,* London, 1947.

Madden, Marie R., *Political Theory and Law in Medieval Spain,* New York, 1930.

Maeztu, Ramiro de, *Defensa de la Hispanidad,* Madrid, 1946, 5 ed. Together with García Morente, fundamental for Spanish traditionalism.

Menéndez y Pelayo, Marcelino, *Historia de España,* Madrid, 1946, 5 ed. Selections by Jorge Vigon. A selected number of the essays of Menéndez y Pelayo on the history of Spain.

——— *La Ciencia española,* Madrid, 1948.

Menéndez Pidal, Ramón, *Historia de España,* Madrid, 1935–1950. Four volumes to date. This monumental history of Spain under the direction of Menéndez Pidal consists to date of the following:

Vol. I: *España prehistórica,* Madrid, 1947;

Vol. II: *España romana,* Madrid, 1935;
Vol. III: *España visigoda,* 1940;
Vol. IV: *España musulmana,* 1950.

Menéndez Pidal has contributed the brilliant introduction to Volume I which is one of the most effective examinations of the constants in Spanish history to be found anywhere.

——— *Idea imperial de Carlos V,* Madrid, 1940.

——— *The Spaniards in Their History,* translated by Walter Starkie, London, 1950.

Monsegú, Bernardo, C.P., *El Occidente y Hispanidad,* Madrid, 1949.

Moran, Catherine, *Spain, Its History Briefly Told,* London, 1931.

Mousset, Albert, *Histoire d'Espagne,* Paris, 1947.

Ortega y Gasset, José, *Obras completas,* Madrid, 1946–1947, 6 vols. Fundamental for many aspects of contemporary Spanish culture.

Orts González, J., *El destino de los pueblos ibéricos,* Madrid, 1932.

Palacio Atard, Vicente, *Derrota, agotamiento, decadencia en la España del siglo XVII,* Madrid, 1949.

Papini, Giovanni, *Lettere agli uomini del Papa Celestino Sesto,* Florence, 1946.

Peers, E. Allison, *Our Debt to Spain,* London, 1938.

——— *Spain, a Companion to Spanish Studies,* London, 1948, 4 ed. Professor Peers is the general editor of this useful handbook to Spanish studies.

——— *Spain, a Companion to Spanish Travel,* London, 1930. A delightful guide to Spain.

——— *Spanish Mysticism,* London, 1924.

Pérez Bustamante, *Compendio de historia de España,* Madrid, 1949, 4 ed.

Pérez Mier, Laureano, *Iglesia y Estado nuevo. Los concordatos ante el moderno derecho público,* Madrid, 1940. Fundamental for the history of the concordats and especially for the relations of Church and State in Spain. An enormous amount of material on these relations in numerous other countries.

——— *Sistemas de dotación de la Iglesia Católica,* Salamanca, 1949. Father Pérez Mier of the Pontifical University of Salamanca examines the fiscal policy and financial support of the Church in various countries, including Spain.

Petrie, Sir Charles, *Spain,* London, 1934 (Modern States Series).

Pfandl, Ludwig, *Historia de la literatura nacional española en la edad de oro,* Barcelona, 1933. A brilliant literary history by one of the greatest of German Hispanists.

Poesía española actual, Madrid, 1946.

Postius y Sala, Juan, *El código canónico aplicado a España,* Madrid, 1926, 5 ed. A veritable arsenal of information on every aspect of the Church problem in Spain. Disorganized and diffuse, this voluminous work contains a great deal that is not strictly Canon Law.

Rommen, Heinrich A., *The State in Catholic Thought,* St. Louis, 1947. Pages 594 sq., on tolerance and separation are particularly interesting with certain references to Spain.

Rubio, David, O.S.A., *The Mystic Soul of Spain,* New York, 1946.

Rubio, Julián M., *Los ideales y los hombres en la España imperial,* Madrid, 1942.

Ryan, John A., and Boland, Francis J., *Catholic Principles of Politics,* New York, 1943.

Sedgwick, H. D., *Spain, a Short History,* London, 1925.

Sitwell, Sacheverell, *Spain,* London, 1950. A travel book.

Soldevila, F., *Historia de Catalunya,* Barcelona, 1934–1935, 3 vols. Basic for the historical evolution of Catalonia.

T'Serstevens, A., *Itinéraire espagnol,* Paris, 1933.

Unamuno, Miguel de, *Ensayos,* Madrid, 1945, 2 vols. Indispensable, especially his *En torno al casticismo.*

Valbuena Prat, Angel, *Historia de la literatura española,* Barcelona, 1937, 2 vols.

Vilar, Pierre, *Histoire de l'Espagne,* Paris, 1947. A slender little volume in the collection, *Que sais-je?* An excellent summary of the general lines.

Vossler, Karl, *Estampas del mundo románico,* Buenos Aires, 1946. Published in the *Austral* collection of Espasa Calpe.

——— *Introducción a la literatura española del siglo de oro,* Buenos Aires, 1945.

——— *Formas literarias en los pueblos románicos,* Buenos Aires, 1944. These and other studies by the German Hispanist Karl Vossler are important for the understanding of Hispanic culture.

Zabala y Lera, P., *Historia de España y de la civilización española. Edad contemporánea,* Madrid, 1930, 2 vols. A continuation of the work of Altamira y Crevea.

II

RECENT HISTORICAL BACKGROUND

The following works have been consulted with reference to the period preceding the Second Republic. Obviously there is a good deal of overlapping and, although the majority of books touching on the Primo de Rivera dictatorship have been cited here, some find their place under the Republic itself because the content extends into that period. In general, I have included in this section works treating of the nineteenth century and of the events up to 1931. Clearly there is no intention of suggesting an exhaustive bibliography for the nineteenth century itself.

Alcalá Galiano, *La caída de un trono,* Madrid, 1933.

Antequera, J. M. de, *La desamortización eclesiástica considerada en sus diferentes aspectos y relaciones,* Madrid, 1885. Important for the problem of Church properties.

Araquistain, Luis, *El ocaso de un régimen,* Madrid, 1930.

——— *Entre la guerra y la revolución: España en 1917,* Madrid, 1917.

Aunós Pérez, Eduardo, *Itinerario histórico de la España contemporánea 1808–1936,* Barcelona, 1940.

——— *L'Espagne contemporaine,* Paris, 1939. Two basic works for Spanish history from Napoleon to the civil war.

Bec, Renée, *La dictature espagnole de Primo de Rivera,* Montpellier, 1933.

Benoist, Charles, *Cánovas del Castillo. La restauration rénovatrice,* Paris, 1930.

Bermejo, I. A., *Historia de la interinidad y guerra civil de España desde 1868,* Madrid, 1876–1877, 3 vols.

Blasco Ibáñez, Vicente, *Lo que será la república española,* Paris, 1925.

——— *Una nación secuestrada. El terror militarista en España,* Paris, 1925.

Bofarull y Romañá, Manuel de, *Las antiguas Cortes, el moderno parlamento, el régimen representativo orgánico,* Alcalá de Henares, 1945.

Calvo Sotelo, José, *Mis servicios al Estado. Seis años de gestión. Apuntes para la historia,* Madrid, 1931.

Canals, Salvador, *España, la constitución y la monarquía,* Madrid (n.d.).

Cantero, P., *La Rota española. Historia diplomática de las relaciones entre España y la Samta Sede en el campo jurisdiccional,* Madrid, 1946.

Capella, Jacinto, *La verdad de Primo de Rivera. Intimidades y anécdotas del Dictador,* Madrid, 1933.

Chapman, Huston, and Princess Pilar of Bavaria, *Don Alfonso XIII,* London, 1931.

Cigesx, Aparicio, M., *España bajo la dinastía de los Borbones, 1701–1931,* Madrid, 1932.

Costa, Joaquin, *Oligarquíax y caciquismo como la forma actual del gobierno en*

España, Madrid, 1902.
Deakin, F. B., *Spain Today,* London, 1924.
Desdevises du Dezert, G., *L'Espagne de l'ancien régime,* Paris, 1897–1904, 3 vols.
Erskine, Mrs. Steuart, *Twenty-Nine Years: the Reign of King Alfonso of Spain,* London, 1931.
Fernández Almagro, Melchor, *Historia del reinado de Alfonso XIII,* Barcelona, 1933.
Franco, Francisco, *Marruecos, diario de una bandera,* Madrid, 1922. The only published work of the present *Caudillo* of Spain.
Fugier, André, *Napoléon et l'Espagne,* Paris, 1930, 2 vols.
García y García de Castro, Rafael, *Vázquez de Mella; sus ideas. Su persona,* Granada, 1940. An important study of the thought and life of one of the outstanding representatives of Traditionalism.
Grandmaison, Geoffrey de, *L'Espagne et Napoléon,* Paris, 1908, 3 vols.
Güenechea, José, S.J., *Pobreza del culto y clero en España,* Bilbao, 1916.
Hernández Mir, F., *La dictadura ante la historia,* Madrid, 1930.
Hubbard, Gustave, *Histoire contemporaine d'Espagne,* Paris, 1869–1883, 6 vols. Strongly anticlerical in tone.
Jobit, Pierre, *Les éducateurs de l'Espagne contemporaine. I. Les Krausistes,* Paris, 1936. A most important phase of recent Spanish intellectual history. The educational reform and the influence of Krausism constitute a significant chapter in modern Spain's development.
Labra, R. M. de, *La orientación internacional de España,* Madrid, 1910.
La Orden, Ernesto, *Jaime Balmes, político,* Barcelona, 1942. A good study of this aspect of the personality of Jaime Balmes.
Lira, Osvaldo, *Nostalgia de Vázquez de Mella,* Santiago, Chile, 1942.
López Ochoa, E., *De la dictadura a la república,* Madrid, 1930.
López Peláez, *El derecho español en sus relaciones con la Iglesia,* Madrid, 1902.
Ludwig Ferdinand of Bavaria, Princess, *Through Four Revolutions, 1862–1933,* London, 1933.
Marco Miranda, V., *Las conspiracines contra la Dictadura,* Madrid, 1930.
Marvaud, A., *L'Espagne au XXième siècle,* Paris, 1913.
Maura Gamazo, G., *Bosquejo histórico de la Dictadura,* Madrid, 1930, 2 vols.
——— *Historia crítica del reinado de Alfonso XIII durante su menoridad,* Barcelona (n.d.), 2 vols.
Maura, Duque de, and Fernández Almagro, M., *Porqué cayó Alfonso XIII Evolución y disolución de los partidos históricos durante su reinado,* Madrid, 1948, 2 ed.
Maurín, J., *Los hombres de la Dictadura. De la monarquía absoluta a la revolución socialista,* Madrid, 1932.
Meléndez, L. M., *Cánovas y la política exterior española,* Madrid, 1944.
Mirkine-Guetzévitch, B., and Reale, E., *L'Espagne,* Paris, 1933 (Bibliothéque d'Histoire et de Politique).
Nicolau d'Olwer, Ll., *La lliçó de la dictadura,* Barcelona, 1931.
Peers, E. Allison, *Spain, the Church and the Orders,* London, 1945. This work may be classified either as historical or contemporary. It treats of the background of the modern Spanish Church and of the problems regarding it up to the Republic. It begins in 1700 and surveys the status of the orders down to the civil war. There is a chapter on the persecution during the war. The appendixes on Church wealth, numbers of religious, etc., are particularly helpful.
Pirala, Antonio, *Historia contemporánea (1843–1879),* Madrid, 1875–1880, 6 vols.
Primo de Rivera, *Epistolario del Dictador,* Madrid, 1930.
Ramos Oliveira, A., *Politics, Economics and Men of Modern Spain 1808–1946,* London, 1946.
Reig, Cardinal, *Principios y bases de reorganización de la Acción Católica española,*

Toledo, 1926. Important for the study of the evolution of Spanish Catholic Action.
Reparaz, Gonzalo de, *Alfonso XIII y sus cómplices,* Madrid, 1931.
——— *Política española en Africa,* Barcelona, 1907.
Rodríguez Solís, E., *Historia del partido republicano español,* Madrid, 1892–1893, 2 vols.
Romanones, Conde de, *El ejército y la política,* Madrid, 1920.
——— *Las responsabilidades políticas del antiguo régimen. De 1875 a 1923,* Madrid, 1924.
——— *Las últimas horas de una monarquía,* Madrid, 1931.
——— *Notas de una vida, 1868–1912,* Madrid, 1934, 2 vols., 2 ed.
——— *Los cuatro presidentes de la primera república española,* Madrid, 1939.
——— *Breviario de política experimental,* Madrid, 1944. The writings of the distinguished Monarchist leader are indispensable for the understanding of this epoch.
Ruiz Castillo, J., *Antonio Maura. 35 años de vida pública,* Madrid, 1917, 2 vols.
Salazar Alonso, R., *La justicia bajo la Dictadura,* Madrid, 1930.
Sencourt, Robert, *King Alfonso, a Biography,* London (n.d.). An excellent short biography of the last Spanish King.
——— *Spain's Uncertain Crown. The Story of Spanish Sovereigns 1808–1931,* London, 1932.
Shaw, Rafael, *Spain From Within,* London, 1910.
Tharaud, Jérome and Jean, *Rendezvous espagnols,* Paris, 1925.
Trend, J. B., *The Origins of Modern Spain,* Cambridge, 1934.
Varenne, Alberic, *Quand la France occupait l'Europe*, Paris, 1948.
Vázquez de Mella y Fanjul, *Juan Ideario,* Barcelona, 1930, 3 vols.
——— *Juan Política tradicionalista,* Barcelona, 1932, 2 vols. The writings of the traditionalist leader are indispensable for the background of Carlism and the revival of traditionalist sentiment since the end of the republic.

III

REGIONALISM

Almirall, Valentí, *La catalanisme,* Barcelona, 1886.
Alvarez y Blanco Gendín, S., *Regionalismo. Estudio general. El problema en Asturias,* Oviedo, 1932.
Aymamí i Baudina, L., *Macià. Trenta anys de política catalanista. Apunts per una biografia,* Barcelona, 1933.
Bofill i Mates, J., *Una política catalanista,* Barcelona, 1933.
Cambó, Francisco, *Actuació regionalista,* Barcelona, 1915.
——— *Catalunya i la solidaritat,* Barcelona, 1910.
——— *Per la concòrdia,* Barcelona, 1930. The writings of Cambó are fundamental for a knowledge of Catalanism.
Caro Baroja, Julio, *Los vascos,* San Sebastián, 1950. A fundamental work on the history and formation of the Basque people. Largely anthropological and historical.
Creus i Vidal, L., *Visió econòmica de Catalunya,* Barcelona, 1934, 2 vols.
Duran y Ventosa, Ll., *Regionalisme y federalisme,* Barcelona, 1905.
Dwelshauvers, G., *La Catalogue et le Problème Catalan,* Paris, 1926. Salvador de Madariaga comments on this book as written from the viewpoint of the "rash Catalan nationalist."
Estelrich, Joan, *Catalanismo y reforma hispánica,* Barcelona, 1932.
——— *Catalunya endins,* Barcelona, 1930.
——— *Felix o l'esperit de renaixença,* Barcelona, 1934.
——— *La Catalogue et le problème des nationalités,* Lausanne, 1929.

——— *La qüestió de les minories nacionals,* Barcelona, 1929.

Fernández Almagro, M., *Catalanismo y república española,* Madrid, 1932.

García Silvestre, *Història sumària de la literatura catalana,* Barcelona, 1932.

García, Venero, M., *Historia del nacionalismo catalán (1793–1936),* Madrid, 1944.

Gay de Montellà, R., *Catalunya, nació mediterrànea. Assaig sobre la formació historica de la nostra cultura,* Barcelona, 1933.

Graëll, Guillermo, *La cuestión catalana,* Barcelona, 1902.

Larcegui, F. de S., *Cataluña y la nacionalidad española,* Madrid, 1927.

Marvaud, Angel, *Le mouvement catalan,* Paris, 1913. With special attention to the cultural and spiritual revival.

Massó i Escofet, C., and Gay de Montellà, R., *L'Estatut de Catalunya. Text oficial comentat, amb referencies legals i notes de la discussió parlamentària,* Barcelona, 1933. The full text of the regional statute with commentary.

Nicolau d'Olwer, Ll., *L'Expansió de Catalunya a la Mediterrànea Oriental,* Barcelona, 1925.

Peers, E. Allison, *Catalonia Infelix,* London, 1937. This volume covers both the history of Catalonia and the experience of the region during the civil war. By all odds the best account in English.

Pi Sunyer, C., *L'Aptitud econòmica de Catalunya,* Barcelona, 1927–1929, 2 vols. Excellent account of the economic structure of Catalonia with good bibliography.

Pi y Margall, F., *Las nacionalidades,* Madrid, 1882.

——— *La federación,* Madrid, 1880.

Prat de la Riba, E., and Muntanyola, P., *Compendí de la doctrina catalanista,* Sadabell, 1894.

——— *La nacionalitat catalana,* Barcelona, 1910.

Rovira i Virgili, A., *Història dels moviments nacionalistes,* Barcelona, 1912–1914, 3 vols. Includes an account of the nationalist movements in various parts of Europe as well as in Spain.

——— *Catalunya i la república,* Barcelona, 1931.

——— *La constitució interior de Catalunya,* Barcelona, 1932.

——— *Resum d'història del catalanisme,* Barcelona, 1936. An indispensable one-volume work on the Catalanist movement.

Rubió Tudurí, M., and Mart, N., *Estat espanyol, societat anónima,* Barcelona, 1930.

Sieberer, Anton, *Katalonien gegen Kastilien. Zur innenpolitischen Problematik Spaniens,* Vienna, 1936. A first-class study on the problem of Catalonia and Castile.

Torras y Bages, J., *La tradició catalana,* Barcelona, 1892. The Bishop of Vich states the case for regionalism.

IV

SOCIAL AND ECONOMIC QUESTIONS

Aznar, Severino, *El catolicismo social en España,* Zaragoza, 1906.

——— *La cruzada sindical,* Barcelona, 1913.

——— *Estudios económico-sociales,* Madrid, 1946. The various publications of Severino Aznar are indispensable for an appraisal of the place in modern Spain of Catholic social doctrine.

Baratech Alfaro, F., *Los sindicatos libres de España. Su origen — su actuación — su ideario,* Barcelona, 1921.

Buenacasa, Manuel, *El movimiento obrero español, 1886–1926,* Barcelona, 1928.

Carrión, Pascual, *Los latifundios en España,* Madrid, 1932. The best handy volume for information regarding land distribution and holdings in Spain.

Colmeiro, Manuel de, *Historia de la economía política en España,* Madrid, 1863.
Coloma, Jesús, *El problema social de la tierra,* Madrid (n.d.).
Costa, Joaquîn, *Colectivismo agrario en España,* Madrid, 1898.
Eza, Visconde de, *El problema agrario en España,* Madrid, 1915. Indispensable.
——— *Agrarismo,* Madrid, 1936.
Garrido, Fernando, *Historia de las asociaciones obreras en Europa,* Madrid, 1870, 2 vols.
Gil Maestre, M., *El anarquismo en España y el especial de Barcelona,* Madrid, 1897.
González Posada, Adolfo, *El socialismo y la reforma social,* Madrid, 1904.
Halévy, Elie, *Histoire du socialisme européen,* Paris, 1948. An extremely useful one-volume account of the history and action of European socialism.
Hoyos Sainz, Luis de, *Riqueza agrícola de España,* Madrid, 1926.
Kaminski, H. E., *Michel Bakounine. La vie d'un révolutionnaire,* Paris, 1938. Of the many biographies of Bakunin, perhaps the most succinct and satisfactory.
La Iglesia y García, G., *Caracteres del anarquismo en la actualidad,* Madrid, 1909.
Lindholm, Federico, and Miñana, E., *El anarquismo,* Madrid, 1906.
López, Núñez, Alvaro, *Veinticinco años de legislación social,* Madrid (n.d.).
Lorenzo, Anselmo, *Criterio libertario,* Barcelona, 1903. Anarchism as seen by an anarchist.
——— *El proletariado militante,* Barcelona, 1901 and 1923, 2 vols.
Marvaud, A., *La question sociale en Espagne,* Paris, 1910.
Marx, Karl, and Engels, Friedrich, *Revolution in Spain,* London, 1939.
Mora, Francisco, *Historia del socialismo obrero español,* Madrid, 1902.
Morato, Juan José, *Historia de la sección española de la Internacional, 1868–1874,* Madrid, 1930.
——— *El partido socialista,* Madrid, 1931.
——— *Pablo Iglesias,* Madrid, 1931. Two very useful books for the socialist development and particularly for the character and personality of Pablo Iglesias.
Núñez de Prado, G., *Los dramas del anarquismo,* Barcelona-Buenos Aires, 1904.
Palomo, Emilio, *Uso y abuso de la tierra,* Valencia, 1930.
Reventós, Manuel, *Els moviments socials a Barcelona durant el segle XIX,* Barcelona, 1925.
Sergent, Alain, and Harmel, Claude, *Histoire de l'Anarchie,* Paris, 1949. Although devoting no specific attention to Spain, this general history of anarchism is very useful in following the development of the doctrine.
Stekloff, G. M., *History of the first international,* London, 1938.
Uña y Sarthou, J., *Las asociaciones obreras en España,* Madrid, 1900.
Valdour, Jacques, *L'Ouvrier espagnol,* Lille, 1919, 2 vols. An examination of the Spanish worker based on residence in the various parts of the peninsula. Interesting detail for the first quarter of the twentieth century.
Vicent, P. Antonio, *Cooperatismo católico. Cooperativas de consumo de crédito y de producción,* Valencia, 1905.
——— *Socialismo y anarquismo,* Valencia, 1893.
Zancada, Praxedes, *El obrero en España,* Barcelona, 1902.

V

THE SECOND REPUBLIC AND THE CIVIL WAR

Albornoz, Alvaro de, *Al servicio de la República,* Madrid, 1936.
Alonso, Bruno, *La flota republicana y la guerra civil de España,* Mexico, 1944.
Alvarez, Basilio, *Dos años de agitación política,* Alcalá de Henares, 1933, 2 vols.

Alvarez del Vayo, Julio, *Freedom's Battle,* London, 1940. Important as a presentation of the views of a prominent actor in the Spanish tragedy, to be supplemented with the same writer's *The Last Optimist,* New York, 1950.

Anon., *A qui la victoire? Un an de guerre en Espagne,* Paris, 1937.

Anon., *La justice du front populaire par trois députés aux Cortes,* Paris, 1937.

Anon., *La persécution religieuse en Espagne,* Paris, 1937. The author was the Catalan Dr. Joan Estelrich.

Anon., *La question basque et la guerre civile en Espagne,* Brussels, 1937.

Anon., *La religion dans l'Espagne de Franco,* Paris, 1937. A strictly propaganda publication issued by the *Editions des Archives Espagnoles* with the intention of demonstrating that the Catholic Church in nationalist Spain was fascist and subservient to the military leadership.

Anon., *Lo que han hecho en Galicia. Episodios del terror blanco en las provincias gallegas contadas por quienes los han vivido,* Paris (n.d.).

Araujo, García, and Grubb, Kenneth, *Religion in the Republic of Spain,* London, 1933. A useful survey from the Protestant point of view of the religious situation in Spain during the early period of the republic. Of particular importance in connection with the interest in the status of the Protestant denominations.

Arcaya, Francisco, *La reforma agraria del 15 de septiembre de 1932,* Madrid, 1933.

Arrabal, Juan, *José María Gil Robles: su vida, su actuación, sus ideas,* Madrid, 1933.

Arrarás, Joaquín, *Francisco Franco: The Times and the Man,* Milwaukee, 1938. Translated from the Spanish and one of the best biographies of the Spanish leader.

Arrese, José Luis de, *El estado totalitario en el pensamiento de José Antonio,* Madrid, 1945. An attempt to show that José Antonio Primo de Rivera did not conceive of the Falange as totalitarian in the Hitler or Mussolini sense of the term.

Atholl, Duchess of, *Searchlight on Spain,* London (n.d.). This book was written by a leading British Conservative and supported strongly the Spanish republicans. The antidote is supplied by Sarolea, Charles, *Daylight on Spain,* London (n.d.).

Azaña, Manuel, *Una política, 1930–1932,* Madrid, 1932. This and the following works of Manuel Azaña are indispensable as a reflection of the political thought and parliamentary action of the Prime Minister and President of the Second Republic. As several of the volumes are collections of speeches, they are handy in tracing the evolution of Azaña's public pronouncements.

——— *En el poder y en la oposición (1932–1933),* Madrid, 1934, 2 vols.

——— *Mi rebelión en Barcelona,* Madrid, 1935.

——— *Discursos en campo abierto,* Madrid, 1936.

——— *La velada de Benicarló,* Buenos Aires, 1939. Written in May, 1937, in Barcelona, the volume is an examination of the issues of the civil war in dialogue form. Illuminating as evidence of the views and state of mind of the republican leader.

Aznar, Manuel, *Historia militar de la guerra de España,* Madrid, 1940. Written by a leading nationalist newspaperman and present Spanish minister to the Dominican Republic.

Azpeitía, Mateo, *La reforma agraria en España,* Madrid, 1932.

Azpilikoeta, *Le problème basque,* Paris, 1938. A Basque nationalist statement of position during the civil war. A useful volume since it contains the address of José Antonio Aguirre on December 22, 1936 and the exchange of correspondence between the Basque leader and Cardinal Gomá.

Bahamonde y Sánchez de Castro, Antonio, *Un año con Queipo,* Barcelona, 1938.

Bardoux, Jacques, *Staline contre l'Europe,* Paris, 1937.

Barea, Arturo, *Struggle for the Spanish Soul,* London, 1941.

——— *The Clash,* London, 1945. This is the third part of an autobiographical trilogy which pretends to tell the story of "a Spanish generation, an age and a man." The first two parts are entitled *The Forge* and *The Track*. As a novel it contains considerable atmosphere of the civil war period.

Bayle, Constantino, S.J., *¿Qué pasa en España?*, Salamanca, 1937.

Belforte, Francesco, *La guerra civile in Spagna. Gli interventi stranieri nella Spagna rossa,* Rome, 1938. An extremely useful account of Italian participation in the civil war.

Berdión, Auxilio, *Madrid en tinieblas. Siluetas de la revolución,* Salamanca, 1937.

Berenguer, Dámaso, *De la dictadura a la república,* Madrid, 1946.

Bernanos, Georges, *Les grands cimitières sous la lune,* Paris, 1938. The celebrated novel of Bernanos in which he presents his reaction to the nationalist occupation of Mallorca.

Bernárdez Romero, B., *Calvo Sotelo, estudio crítico de su obra,* Vigo, 1937.

Berner, Rudolf, *Spansk rapsodi,* Stockholm (n.d.).

Bertrán Güell, Felipe, *Preparación y desarrollo del Alzamiento Nacional,* Valladolid, 1939.

Bloch, J. R., *Espagne, Espagne!,* Paris, 1937.

Bollati, Ambrogio, and Del Bono, Giulio, *La guerra di Spagna,* Turin, 1938.

Borkenau, Franz, *The Communist International,* London, 1939. There is a short chapter on the Spanish Communists in this survey.

——— *The Spanish Cockpit,* London, 1937. There is a long introduction on Spanish history while the major part of this book is devoted to the civil war itself. It is one of the best of the innumerable publications on the war itself. Salvador de Madariaga calls it one of the best of all the books and regrets that it falls short of outstanding excellence because of a number of serious deficiencies. Borkenau's book is weak when dealing with the Church and the religious problem.

Brandt, J. A., *Toward the New Spain,* Chicago, 1933. An optimistic account of Spain's evolution into republicanism.

Brasillach, Robert, and Bardèche, Maurice, *Histoire de la guerre d'Espagne,* Paris, 1939. A full-blown account of the civil war in detail with a good bibliography. The authors are decided partisans of the nationalists.

Brenan, Gerald, *The Spanish Labyrinth,* an account of the social and political background of the civil war, New York, 1943. One of the best accounts of the complex social and economic elements that made up the situation in Spain on the eve of the civil war. Good chapters on the anarchists and other extremist groups. A superb bibliography with critical notes.

Brereton, Goeffrey, *Inside Spain,* London, 1938.

Brongersma, *Voorproef in Spanje 1919–1939,* Utrecht-Brussels, 1946. One of the best accounts published in the Netherlands regarding modern Spain.

Brouwer, Dr. J., *Spaansche aspecten en perspectieven,* Rotterdam, 1939.

——— *De Spaansche burgeroorlog. Zijn oorzaken en mogelijke gevolgen,* Hilversum, 1936.

Brugmans, H., *Spanje en de democratie,* Assen, 1938.

Buckley, Henry, *The Life and Death of the Spanish Republic,* London. A pressman of long residence in Spain with considerable detail of events up to the outbreak of the civil war.

Caballero de Ronte, *Santander rojo,* Palencia, 1936.

Calvo Sotelo, José, *La voz de un perseguido,* Madrid, 1933. This and the other writings cited in this bibliography are important in the light of the significant position occupied by Calvo Sotelo up to the time of his assassination in 1936.

Campoamor, Clara, *La révolution espagnole vue par une républicaine,* Paris, 1937. A very interesting and often penetrating account of the deception of a Spanish republican and member of the Chamber of Deputies during the period before the outbreak of war. Good account of the atmosphere of Madrid during the weeks after the beginning of the hostilities.

Cánovas Cervantes, S., *Solidaridad obrera — apuntes históricos,* Barcelona, 1937.

Cantalupo, Roberto, *Fu la Spagna,* Milan, 1948. A fundamental book on the diplomacy of the Spanish war and on the internal conditions during the critical period of 1937. As Italian Ambassador to the nationalists, Cantalupo gathered together an impressive amount of information concerning Spanish affairs. His penetrating analysis of the Spanish temperament is invaluable in explaining the events of the time.

Cardell, Carlos, *Antología de José Calvo Sotelo,* Madrid, 1942.

Cardozo, Harold G., *The March of a Nation,* London and New York, 1937. One of the many journalistic accounts of Spain in wartime, strongly pro-nationalist.

Carreras, P. Luis, *Grandeza cristiana de España. Notas sobre la persecución religiosa,* Toulouse, 1938.

Carta Encíclica de S. S. Pío XI dirigida a España y declaración colectiva del episcopado español sobre la ley de congregaciones, Zaragoza, 1933.

Casado, S., *The Last Days of Madrid,* London, 1939. An account of the final days of Madrid when the Council of Defense was set up and preparations made for the surrender.

Casares, Francisco, *España y su revolución,* Buenos Aires, 1937.

Castillejo, J., *War of Ideas in Spain,* London, 1937. Particularly good for the movement of ideas in nineteenth-century Spain.

Castrillo y Santos, J., *La orientación de la República,* Madrid, 1933.

Castro Albarrán, A. de, *Guerra santa,* Burgos, 1938. This is one of the many more or less ephemeral publications of the time reflecting the sentiment and emotion of those engaged in the civil war. A certain number of books, both republican and nationalist, of this type are included as a source for the "climate" of the period.

Castro, Cristóbal de, *Al servicio de los campesinos: hombres sin tierra, tierra sin hombres,* Madrid, 1931, 2 ed.

Chaminade, Marcel, *Feux croisés sur l'Espagne,* Paris, 1939.

Chamsom, André, *Rien qu'un témoignage,* Paris, 1937.

Communist Atrocities. Second and Third Report. Preface by Arthur Bryant, London, 1937. A documented account of the atrocities committed by the republicans in southern Spain from July to October, 1936, and issued by the committee of investigation appointed by the national government at Burgos.

Conze, Edward, *Spain Today,* London, 1936.

Cordero Pérez, M., *Los socialistas y la revolución. Temas de actualidad,* Madrid, 1932.

Cortés Cavanillas, J., *La caída de Alfonso XIII,* Madrid, 1932.

Cossío, Francisco de, *Guerra de salvación,* Valladolid, 1937.

Cox, Geoffrey, *Defence of Madrid,* London, 1937.

Dautun, Yves, *Valence sous la botte rouge,* Paris, 1938.

De cardona, María, *La terreur à Madrid,* Paris, 1937.

De la Mora, Constancia, *Fière Espagne,* Paris, 1948. An interesting but highly colored account of the Spanish war and aftermath. Issued by a communist publishing house in Paris.

Deschamps, Bernard, *La vérité sur Guadalajara,* Paris, 1938.

Diez, Emilio, *General Franco,* Seville, 1940.

Domingo, Marcelino, *¿A donde va España?,* Madrid, 1930.

——— *La revolución de octubre,* Madrid (n.d.).

Duff, Katharine, *The Course of the War in Spain 1936–1937,* London, 1937.

Dundas, Lawrence, *Behind the Spanish Mask,* London, 1943. One of the more lurid accounts of the Spanish scene.

Duval, Général, *Les leçons de la guerre d'Espagne,* Paris, 1938. A study of the military operations of the civil war. The book carries a preface by General Weygand.

——— *Les espagnols et la guerre d'Espagne,* Paris, 1939.

Dzelepy, E. N., *The Spanish Plot,* London, 1937.

Echeandia, José, *La persecución roja en el país vasco,* Barcelona, 1945. A detailed account of the violence and persecution under republican rule in the Basque provinces. The book is particularly interesting because of the evidence of the astonishingly large number of Basques who suffered persecution at the hands of the republican government and who bore no apparent sympathy for the Basque separatist government installed in Bilbao.

Eliseda, Marqués de, *Fascismo, catolicismo y monarquía,* Madrid, 1935.

Enriquez, Nello, *La Spagna sorge,* Milan, 1937.

Epistolario Prieto y Negrín. Puntos de vista sobre el desarrollo y consecuencias de la guerra civil española, Paris, 1939. An important collection of exchanges revealing the hostility between the two republican leaders. The correspondence involves the problem of the treasure taken from Spain to Mexico and the determination of its ownership.

Esperabé de Arteaga, Enrique, *La guerra de reconquista española y el criminal comunismo,* Madrid, 1939.

Estelrich, Joan, *De la dictadura a la republica,* Barcelona, 1931.

Falcón, César, *Madrid,* Paris, 1939.

Faludi, Ivan, *I spanska folkets tjänst,* Stockholm, 1937.

——— *Med Madrid milisen,* Stockholm, 1937.

Farrère, Claude, *Visite aux espagnols (hiver 1937),* Paris, 1937.

Feliz, Victorino, *La conquista de la juventud obrera,* Madrid, 1935.

Fernández Almagro, Melchor, *Historia de la república española, 1931–1936,* Madrid, 1940. An excellent survey of the formation and decline of the Second Spanish Republic.

——— *Porgué cayó Alfonso XIII,* Madrid, 1948, 2 ed.

Fischer, Louis, *Men and Politics,* London, 1941. Contains numerous references to Spain and the civil war through the eyes of a well-known correspondent. Chapter XXIV, entitled "Ebro: River of Blood" is an interesting comment on the actual fighting.

——— *Why Spain Fights On,* London (n.d.).

Fonteriz, Luis de, *Red Terror in Madrid,* London, 1937.

Försvarsstabens Krigshistoriska Avdelning, *Det spanska inbördeskriget,* Stockholm, 1938. An absolutely first-rate analysis of the military operations of the civil war by a specialized Swedish organization, with numerous maps and explanation of the movements.

Foss, W., and Gerahty, C., *The Spanish Arena,* London, 1937. A five hundred page book published by the "Right" Book Club of London and strongly pro-nationalist. Well documented, with attention to foreign aid, the Guernica incident, etc.

Franceschi, Gustavo, *El movimiento español y el criterio católico,* Montevideo, 1937.

Franco, Comandante, *Madrid bajo las bombas,* Madrid, 1931. A description of the republican uprising at Cuatro Vientos under the leadership of the brother of General Franco.

Galíndez, Jesús de, *Los vascos en el Madrid sitiado,* Buenos Aires, 1945. Published by the Editorial Vasca Ekin of Buenos Aires which has issued a series of books under the title "Biblioteca de Cultura Vasca." This particular volume is an account of the activities of the Basque representatives in Madrid between September, 1936, and May, 1937.

Gannes, Harry, and Repard, Th., *Spain in Revolt. A history of the civil war in*

Spain in 1936 and a study of its social, political and economic causes, London, 1936. Typical of the prejudiced and uncritical accounts that appeared during the course of the civil war.

Garcerán, Rafael, *La Phalange de février 1936 jusqu'au gouvernement national,* San Sebastián, 1938.

García Alonso, F., *España roja,* Buenos Aires, 1937.

García Gallego, J., *¿Por donde se sale? El momento actual de España,* Madrid, 1931.

García Morato, Joaquín, *Guerra en el aire,* Madrid, 1940.

Garratt, G. T., *Gibraltar and the Mediterranean,* London, 1939.

Gay, Francisque, *Dans les flammes et dans le sang. Les crimes contre les églises et les prêtres en Espagne,* 12 ed., Paris, 1936. An excellent account of the religious persecution in republican Spain by the distinguished Frenchman of letters and political leader, recently French ambassador to Canada.

Germain, André, *La révolution espagnole,* Paris, 1931.

Gielen, A., *Das Rotbuch über Spanien. Bilder, dokumente, Zeugenaussagen, gesammelt und herausgegeben von der Anti-Komintern,* Berlin, 1937.

Giménez Caballero, E., *El genio de España,* Madrid, 1932.

——— *La nueva catolicidad,* Madrid, 1933. These two volumes have often been considered the intellectual case for Spanish fascism.

——— *Manuel Azaña, Profecías españolas,* Madrid, 1932.

Godden, G. M., *Conflict in Spain, 1920–1937,* London, 1937. This book is basically devoted to exposing the communist infiltration in Spain from the nineteenth century onward. It goes into considerable detail regarding the communist control in 1936 and 1937.

Gollonet, Angel, and Morales, José, *Sangre y fuego, Málaga,* Granada, 1937.

Gomá Tomás, Cardinal, *Antilaicismo,* Barcelona, 1935, 2 vols. These two volumes contain pronouncements and addresses by the Cardinal Primate of Spain. Although some of the materials deal with matters unrelated directly to Spain, the book is an arsenal of material on such matters as Church properties, relations with the republic, the school question, etc.

Gómez Málaga, Juan, *Estampas trágicas de Madrid,* Ávila, 1936.

González Ruíz, Francisco, *Yo he creído en Franco. Proceso de una gran desilusión,* Paris, 1937.

González Ruíz, N., *Azaña, sus ideas religiosas, sus ideas políticas, el hombre,* Madrid, 1932.

Graña, M., *¿Qué debe España a los religiosos?,* Madrid, 1932. A study of the work and influence of the religious orders in Spain and overseas, with abundant statistics on their activities.

Grondijs, Dr. L. H., *Spanje. Een voortzetting van de Russische revolutie?,* Leiden, 1937.

Guernica. *The official report of the commission appointed by the Spanish National Government to investigate the causes of the destruction of Guernika on April 26–28, 1937,* London, 1938. To be read together with the work on Guernica of Steer which contains the widely diffused version of destruction from the air. The official report details the reasons for believing that the major destruction was perpetrated on the ground by the retiring republicans.

Guest, Carmel Haden, *David Guest. A Scientist Fights for Freedom (1911–1938),* London, 1939. A communist publication eulogizing the sacrifice of a young British scientist for "freedom" in Spain.

Hamrin, Agne, *Spansk Horisont,* Uppsala, 1949. An attempt to interpret Spain without reference, as the author says, to "the Figaros and the Carmens." A series of observations on such matters as the anarchists, the Catalan question, and especially religion. A curious chapter is devoted to the devotion to the Blessed Virgin.

Hemingway, Ernest, *The Spanish War,* London, 1938.

Heredia, M. de, *Semblanzas. Figuras de la revolución española,* Madrid, 1933.

Héricourt, Pierre, *Arms for Red Spain,* London, 1937. The English version of the arguments contained in the other books of Pierre Héricourt in which he analyzes the substantial aid received by the republic from abroad.

——— *Pourquoi Franco vaincra,* Paris, 1936.

——— *Pourquoi mentir. L'aide franco-soviétique à l'Espagne rouge,* Paris, 1937.

——— *Les Soviets et la France, fournisseurs de la révolution espagnole,* Paris, 1938.

——— *Pourquoi Franco a vaincu,* Paris, 1939.

Hispanicus, *Foreign Intervention in Spain,* London, 1937. Published by the United Editorial, Ltd., of London, as part of a large number of works on Spain and especially in defense of the republic. Seven hundred and fifty pages are here devoted to showing German, Italian, and Portuguese intervention against the republic. Not a word is breathed about the Soviet Union or France on the republican side.

Ibarruri, Dolores, *Pour la victoire,* Paris, 1937. From the pen of the famous "Pasionaria."

Iniesta, Alfonso, *Garra marxista en la infancia,* Burgos, 1939. The appalling story of exactly how Marxist influence infiltrated in the schools of republican Spain. A considerable amount of specific factual information is contained in this book.

Iribarren, José María, *Mola. Datos para una biografía y para la historia del Alzamiento Nacional,* Zaragoza, 1938.

Jellinek, Frank, *The Civil War in Spain,* London, 1938. A very complete and detailed study of the civil war with a decidedly leftist bias.

Jiménez de Asúa, L., *Notas de un confinado,* Madrid (n.d.).

——— *Política, figuras, paisaje,* Madrid (n.d.).

——— *Proceso histórico de la constitución de la república española,* Madrid, 1932.

Joaniquet, Aurelio, *Calvo Sotelo. Una vida fecunda, un ideario político una doctrina económica,* Madrid, 1939.

Joubert, H., Vice-Admiral, *L'Espagne de Franco,* Paris, 1938.

——— *La guerre d'Espagne et le catholicisme,* Paris, 1937.

Jouve, Marguerite, *Vu en Espagne,* Paris, 1937.

Junco, Alfonso, *El gran teatro del mundo,* Madrid, 1937. Contains certain materials on the wealth of the Spanish republic that was transported to Mexico and whose use has been wrapped in considerable mystery.

Kaminski, H. E., *Ceux de Barcelone,* Paris, 1937. A good picture of the atmosphere of Barcelona in 1936 from a definitely leftist point of view. I have been unable to get the original French text and have used instead the Italian translation, *Quelli di Barcellona,* Milan, 1950.

Kizel, J., *Licht over Spanje,* Utrecht (n.d.). With an introduction by Cardinal Gomá.

Knoblaugh, H. Edward, *Correspondent in Spain,* New York, 1937. One of the soundest accounts of the early stages of the war. Remarkable for its conclusions and general impressions which stand the test of later developments.

Koestler, Arthur, *Spanish Testament,* London, 1937. Devoted primarily to demonstrating nationalist brutalities and violence. Mr. Koestler undertakes among other things to disprove the claim that a communist plot existed in 1936. French translation, under title, *Un testament espagnol,* Paris, 1939.

Kristensen, Tom, *En Kavaler i Spanien,* Copenhagen, 1945.

Lacruz, Francisco, *El Alzamiento, la revolución y el terror en Barcelona,* Barcelona, 1943.

La Iglesia y la guerra civil española (*documentos eclesiásticos*), Buenos Aires, 1947. A very useful collection of episcopal statements and the text of the response of

the national hierarchies all over the world to the appeal of the Spanish bishops.
Lakhovsky, Georges, *De Moscou à Madrid,* Paris, 1937.
Lamour, Philippe, *Sauvons, la France en Espagne,* Paris, 1937.
Landau, Katia, *Le stalinisme en Espagne,* Paris, 1938.
Langdon Davies, J., *Behind the Barricades,* London, 1936.
Largo Caballero, Francisco, *Un proceso histórico: Largo Caballero ante la justicia,* Madrid, 1936.
Last, J., *Brieven uit Spanje,* Amsterdam, 1936.
——— *The Spanish Tragedy,* London, 1939. Translated from the Dutch and reflecting an extreme left-wing sympathy.
Ledesma Ramos, Ramiro, *Discurso a la juventud de España,* Madrid, 1938.
Le Fur, Louis, *La guerre d'Espagne et le droit,* Paris, 1938.
Lerroux, Alejandro, *Al servicio de la república,* Madrid, 1930.
——— *La pequeña historia. Apuntes para la historia grande vividos y redactados por el autor,* Buenos Aires, 1945. A very useful account by one of the leading figures in the twentieth-century history of Spain.
——— *Trayectoria política de Alejandro Lerroux,* Madrid, 1934.
Lichtveld, L., *De sfinx van Spanje. Beschouwingen van een ooggetuige,* Rotterdam, 1937.
Lindskog, J., *Spanier Blöder,* Stockholm, 1937.
Loewenstein, Prince Hubertus Friedrich of, *A Catholic in Republican Spain,* London, 1937.
Lojendío, Luis María de, *Operaciones militares de la guerra de España, 1936–1939,* Barcelona, 1940. A detailed and voluminous account of the campaigns and military operations of the civil war.
López, Capitán Antonio, *Defensa de Madrid. Relato histórico,* Mexico, 1945.
Loveday, Arthur, *World War in Spain,* London, 1939.
——— *Spain, 1923–1948. Civil War and World War,* London, 1949. The second book is in a sense a revised and extended edition of the first. Arthur Loveday as a British businessman includes much interesting material on the economic life of Spain during the war and since 1945. One of the few English language summaries of recent events. Written in a somewhat chronological form, it provides a good review of what has taken place in Spain up to 1948.
Low, Mary, and Brea, Juan, *Red Spanish Notebook,* London, 1937.
Lunn, Arnold, *Spanish Rehearsal,* London, 1937. A most interesting combination of impressions of wartime Spain and pungent remarks on some of the issues of the day. Stimulating.
Maeztu, Ramiro de, *Em vísperas de la tragedia,* Madrid, 1941. A collection of articles by the famous author of *Defensa de la Hispanidad.* Useful as an indication of rightist thought on the eve of the civil war.
Manning, Leah, *What I Saw in Spain,* London, 1935.
Marañón, Gregorio, *Cuatro comentarios a la revolución española,* Madrid, 1931. Revealing commentaries by one of the intellectual fathers of the Second Republic.
Marquès-Rivière, Jean, *Comment la F. M. fait une révolution,* Paris, 1937. Freemasonry in the Spanish debacle.
Marsá Graco, *La sublevación de Jaca: relato de un rebelde,* Madrid, 1931.
Martín Blázquez, J., *Guerre civile totale,* Paris, 1937.
——— *I Helped Build an Army,* London, 1939.
Massis, H., and Brassilach, R., *Le siège de l'Alcazar,* Paris, 1939.
Mathieu, A. C., *Non! Ce n'est pas Franco qui a commencé,* Paris, 1939.
Mattioli, Guido, *L'Aviazione legionaria in Spagna,* Rome, 1938.
Maura Gamazo, G., *Dolor de España,* Madrid, 1932.
Maurín, Joaquîn, *Révolution et contre-révolution en Espagne,* Paris, 1937.

McCullagh, Francis, *In Franco's Spain,* London, 1937.

McNeill-Moss, Major Geoffrey, *The Epic of the Alcazar. A History of the Siege of the Toledo Alcazar, 1936,* London, 1937. A most detailed, day-by-day account of the siege of the Alcazar. Also analyses of the storming of Badajoz and comments on Guernica.

Medina y Togores, J. de, *Un año de Cortes constituyen tes. Impresiones parlamentarias,* Madrid, 1932.

Menage Challa, H., *Spanje. Verzamelde opstellen,* Amsterdam, 1937.

Mendizábal, Alfred, *The Martyrdom of Spain,* London and New York, 1938. Translated from the French of a former University of Oviedo professor. Expresses what may be called the "center" Catholic view on the war. Carries an introduction by Jacques Maritain.

Merin, Peter, *Spanien zwischen Tod und Geburt,* Zurich, 1937.

Miquelarena, Jacinto, *Traqué dans Madrid,* Paris, 1938.

Mira, José, *Un hombre: Durruti,* Barcelona, 1937.

Mitchell, Sir Peter Chalmers, *My House in Malaga,* London, 1938. A personal account of experiences during the early period of the civil war in Málaga. Decidedly leftist in sympathy.

Mola, Emilio, *Memorias de mi paso por la Dirección General de Seguridad,* Madrid, 1932, 2 vols.

Monserrat, Victor, *Le drame d'un peuple incompris. La guerre au pays basque,* Paris, 1937.

Montan, Luis, *Asalto y defensa heroica del Cuartel de la Montaña,* Valladolid, 1937.

——— *Martirio y reconquista de Vizcaya,* Valladolid, 1937.

Mora, Constancia de la, *In Place of Splendour. The autobiography of a Spanish woman,* London, 1940.

Moure Mariño, Luis, *Galicia en guerra,* Madrid, 1939.

Muro Zegri, D., *La epopeya del Alcázar,* Valladolid, 1937.

Nève, Edouard de, *Spanje, dapper Spanje!,* Bussum, 1937.

Newman, Bernard, *I Saw Spain,* London, 1937. A completely informal, personal account of Spain and Spanish Morocco on the eve of the civil war. No pretense to political acumen, but curiously revealing of the atmosphere.

Nicholson, Helen, *Death in the Morning,* London, 1937. The tribulations of a foreign resident of Granada during the early weeks of the civil war.

Norden, Henri, *L'Espagne trahie et la guerre qui vient. Bilan d'un mois de "Non-intervention,"* Brussels (n.d.).

Nunes, Leopoldo, *A guerra em Espanha,* Lisbon, 1936.

Núñez, Ignacio, *La revolución de octubre de 1934,* Barcelona, 1935, 2 vols.

Núñez Morgado, Aurelio, *Los sucesos de España vistos por un diplomático,* Buenos Aires, 1941.

O'Brien, Kate, *Farewell Spain,* London, 1937. Reflections by the distinguished Irish novelist on leaving Spain in civil war.

O'Donnell, Peadar, *Salud!,* London, 1937.

Oficina Informativa española, *El Orden en la República española,* Madrid, 1948. One of several publications of the Oficina Informativa and extremely good for the documentary presentation.

——— *Saqueo del tesoro religioso de España,* Madrid, 1948.

Oliveira, Mauricio de, *La tragedia española en el mar,* Cádiz, 1937–1938, 4 vols.

Oliveros, W. G., *Falange y Requetés,* Valladolid, 1937.

Ollivier, Marcel, *Les journées sanglantes de Barcelone,* Paris, 1937.

Orwell, George, *Homage to Catalonia,* London, 1938. Not having the English text at hand I have used the Italian translation, *Omaggio alla Catalogna,* Milan, 1948. The British novelist recounts experiences and observations in Catalonia in 1936.

Ossorio, A., *España de mi vida,* Buenos Aires, 1941.

Ostenberg, Axel, *Bakom Barcelonas Barrikader,* Stockholm, 1936.

Oudard, Georges, *Chemises noires, brunes, vertes en Espagne,* Paris, 1938.

Oyarzun, Román, *Historia del carlismo,* Bilbao, 1939. Of particular interest because of the participation of the Carlist traditionalists to such a large degree in the nationalist uprising.

Padelford, Norman, *International Law and Diplomacy in the Spanish Civil Strife,* New York, 1939.

Pascazio, Nicolo, *La rivoluzione in Spagna,* Rome, 1933. A good account of the advent of the Spanish republic.

Paul, Elliot, *The Life and Death of a Spanish Town,* New York, 1937. The famous account of Paul's impressions of the fate of a Mallorcan town when the civil war came.

Peers, E. Allison, *The Spanish Tragedy, 1930–1936. Dictatorship, Republic, Chaos,* London, 1936, 3 ed. Perhaps the best single account of the Republic and civil war as of its beginning. We are all indebted to Prof. Peers for this and his many other equally illuminating and scholarly studies of Spain.

Peiró, Joan, *Perill a la retaguardia,* Mataró, 1936. An important book by an outstanding Catalan anarchist and fundamental for an appreciation of the purposes and policy of the anarchists.

Peiró, P. Francisco, *El problema religioso-social de España,* Madrid, 1936. One of the best studies of the religious problem at the end of the republic. Unfortunately the bibliography on this subject is not extensive.

Pemán, José María, *Atención! Atención!,* Seville, 1937.

Pemartín, José, *Qué es "lo Nuevo." Consideraciones sobre el momento español presente,* Madrid, 1940, 3 ed. Fundamental for the doctrinal side of the nationalist movement. One of the most complete statements of what the New State was conceived to be.

Pérez Ferrero, Miguel, *Drapeau de France,* Paris, 1938.

Pérez de Olaguer, Antonio, *El terror rojo en Andalucia,* Burgos, 1938.

Pérez Serrano, N., *La constitución española,* Madrid, 1932.

Pérez Solís, Oscar, *Sitio y defensa de Oviedo,* Valladolid, 1938.

Pestaña, Angel, *El sindicalismo, qué quiere y adonde va,* Barcelona, 1933. An important statement of the Anarcho-Syndicalist position.

Piazzoni, Sandro, *Las tropas Flechas Negras en la guerra de España,* Barcelona, 1941.

Picard-Moch, G., and J., *L'Espagne républicaine,* Paris, 1933. A French socialist view of Republican Spain.

Pillement, Georges, *Romancero de la guerre civile,* Paris, 1937. Songs and verses of the civil war.

Pla, José, *Historia de la segunda república española,* Barcelona, 1940, 4 vols. An important work covering the entire history of the Second Republic. Contains long excerpts from public documents and statements.

Poncins, Léon de, *Histoire secrète de la révolution espagnole,* Paris, 1937.

Posada, Alfonso, *La reforma constitucional,* Madrid, 1931.

Prader, Jean, *Au secours de l'Espagne socialiste,* Paris, 1937.

Pradera, Víctor, *El Estado Nuevo,* Madrid, 1934. A basic work for the understanding of the Traditionalist position.

Priesto, Carlos, *The Spanish Front,* London, 1936.

Prudhommeaux, A. and D., *Catalogue 1936–37,* Paris, 1937.

Puig Mora, E., *La tragedia roja en Barcelona,* Zaragoza, 1938.

Rabasseire, Henri, *Espagne creuset politique,* Paris, 1938.

Ramos Oliveira, Antonio, *La revolución española de octubre,* Madrid, 1935.

Rasi, Giuseppe, *L'Inferno spagnuolo,* Milan, 1937.

Recaséns Siches, L., *El poder constituyente. Su teoría aplicada al momento español,* Madrid, 1931.

Report of the commission appointed to study the question of the illegitimacy of the government in power in Spain on the 18th of July, 1936. The English text of the investigation of the legitimacy of the Popular Front government in 1936.

Report of a group of Anglican and Free churchmen who visited Spain January 29 to February 9, 1937, London, 1937.

Rey Carrera, Juan, S.J., *El resurgir de España,* San Sebastián, 1938.

Reyes, Rodolfo, *De mi vida: La bi-revolución española,* Mexico, 1948. An important account of the situation in Spain before and during the first part of the civil war by a Mexican, long resident in Madrid.

Richard, Marthe, *Mes dernières missions secrètes, Espagne 1936–1938,* Paris, 1939.

Rivera y Pastor, F., *Nueva Práctica y estilo de la república,* Madrid, 1935.

Rogers, Theo., *Spain: A Tragic Journey,* New York, 1937. A very strongly pro-nationalist account by an American.

Rost, Nico, *Guernika, de heilige stad der Basken, bestaat niet meer,* Amsterdam (n.d.).

Rotvand, Georges, *Franco Means Business,* London (n.d.).

Rust, William, *Britons in Spain. The History of the British Battalion of the XVth International Brigade,* London, 1939. A communist account of the British participation in the International Brigades.

Saint Aulaire, Compte de, *La renaissance de l'Espagne,* Paris, 1938.

Sánchez Guerra, R., *Dictadura, indiferencia, república,* Madrid, 1931.

——— *Proceso de un cambio de régimen,* Madrid, 1932.

Santillán, D. A. de, *El organismo económico de la revolución,* Barcelona, 1936.

Sarolea, Charles, *Daylight on Spain. The Answer to the Duchess of Atholl,* London (n.d.).

Sencourt, Robert, *Spain's Ordeal, a Documented Survey of Recent Events,* London, 1938. One of the fundamental books on the civil war written from a conservative point of view.

Sender, Ramón, *Contre-attaque en Espagne,* Paris, 1937.

——— *The War in Spain,* London, 1937.

Sheean, Vincent, *The Eleventh Hour,* London, 1939. Deals in part with the situation in Spain.

Sieberer, Anton, *Espagne contre Espagne,* Geneva, 1937. A first-class study with emphasis on the factors of separatism and the struggle for regional expression in Spain. The author is an Austrian. This is a translation from the German.

Simon, O. K., *Hitler en Espagne,* Paris, 1938.

Smith, Rhea Marsh, *The Day of the Liberals in Spain,* Philadelphia, 1938.

Sommerfield, John, *Volunteer in Spain,* London, 1937.

Soner, Enrique, *Los intelectuales y la tragedia española,* Burgos, 1937.

Soria, George, *Trotskyism in the Service of Franco,* London, 1938.

Spanish Office of Information, *The International Brigades. Foreign Assistance to the Spanish Reds,* Madrid, 1948.

Steer, G. L., *The Tree of Guernika. A field study of modern war,* London, 1938. The most important study of the Guernica incident and the work responsible for the version that nationalist bombers destroyed the city.

Tangye, Nigel, *Red, White and Spain,* London, 1937.

Tennant, Eleonora, *Spanish Journey: Personal Experiences of the Civil War,* London, 1936. A British observer in nationalist territory.

Téry, Simone, *Front de la liberté,* Paris, 1938. A French communist newswoman gives her version.

Tharaud, Jérome and Jean, *Cruelle Espagne,* Paris, 1937.

Timmermans, R., *Heroes of the Alcazar,* London, 1937.

Toynbee, A. J., and Boulter, V. M., *Survey of International Affairs, 1937,* Vol. II, London, 1938. The subtitle is "The international repercussions of the war in Spain (1936–37)." An extremely important contribution for following the development of events in Spain.

——— *Survey of International Affairs, 1938,* Vol. I, London, 1942.

Tusquets, J., *Orígenes de la revolución española,* Barcelona, 1932.

The Unknown Diplomat, *Britain in Spain. A study of the national government's Spanish policy,* London, 1939.

Valdesoto, Fernando de, *Francisco Franco,* Madrid, 1943.

Vegas Latapié, Eugenio, *Escritos políticos,* Madrid, 1940. An important collection of political essays by a man who has been very close to Don Juan. They reflect the monarchist position.

Vigneau, Albert, and Orland, Vivienne, *F. M. et Front Populaire,* Paris (n.d.).

Volta, Sandro, *Spagna a ferro e fuoco,* Florence, 1937.

Volunteers for Liberty, publication of the International Brigades during the civil war, 1937–1938, New York, 1949.

Von Haartman, Carl, *En nordisk caballero i Francos armé,* Stockholm, 1939.

Wall, Bernard, *Spain of the Spaniards,* London, 1938.

Watson, Keith Scott, *Single to Spain,* London, 1937.

White, F., *War in Spain, a Short Account,* London, 1937.

Wintringham, Tom, *Deadlock War,* London, 1940.

Yáñez, T. R., *La soberanèia popular y su fuerza emancipadora. Ante la situación de España,* Madrid, 1931.

Young, Sir George, *The New Spain,* London, 1933.

Zugazagoitía, Julián, *Historia de la guerra en España,* Buenos Aires, 1940. A valuable source from the pen of a member of the republican government during the civil war. Highly useful for the account of internal affairs in Madrid during the conflict.

Zwingelstein, André, *Au pays de la terreur rouge,* 5 ed., Paris, 1937.

VI

SPAIN SINCE THE END OF THE CIVIL WAR

Albornoz, Alvaro de, *Páginas del destierro,* Mexico, 1941.

Alvarez del Vayo, *The Last Optimist,* New York, 1950. In this work the former republican minister of foreign affairs clings to his conviction that collaboration with the Soviet Union is possible.

Anon., *Cárceles españolas,* Madrid, 1948. A detailed study of the penal system issued by the *Oficina Informativa española.*

Anuario estadístico de España, Edición manuel, Madrid, 1948–1949. Published by the *Instituto Nacional de Estadística.*

Apuntes para la historia. La ofensiva comunista contra España, Madrid, 1947. Issued by the *Oficina Informativa española,* this is a detailed study of the campaigns against the Spanish regime abroad.

Aragón, Juan de, *Verdad s españolas: comunismo y democracia en la república y en el exilio,* Montevideo, 1948.

Arauz, Alvaro, *La Wilhelmstrasse y El Pardo (documentos secretos de la guerra de España),* Mexico, 1949.

Areilza, José María de, *Embajadores sobre España,* Madrid, 1947, 3 ed. An examination of the reflections of Sir Samuel Hoare, Carlton Hayes, etc., in their books on Spain.

Areilza, José María de, and Castiella, Fernando María, *Reinvindicaciones de España,* Madrid, 1941. A compendium of Spanish aspirations in Africa and elsewhere.

Arrese, José Luis, *La revolución social del nacional sindicalismo,* Madrid, 1943, 2 ed.

Ars skolkommissions, *Betänkande med förslag till riktlinjer för det svenska skolväsendets utveckling,* Stockholm, 1948. The report on the school question issued by the ecclesiastical department of the education ministry. Contains the detailed restrictions on Catholics.

Asociación de los hombres de Acción Católica. Consejo Superior. II reunión nacional de los secretariados patronales diocesanos. *Lecciones explicadas por el Excmo y Rvdmo. Sr. D. Angel Herrera Oría, Obispo de Málaga,* Madrid, 1947. An important series of lectures on social questions delivered by the present Bishop of Málaga.

Aznar, Severino, *Los seguros sociales,* Madrid, 1947. On social security.

Barents, Dr. J., *Het nieuwe Spanje,* Hilversum, 1941.

Bonnet, Georges, *Fin d'une Europe. De Munich à la guerre,* Paris, 1947.

Bouthelier, Antonio, *Legislación sindical española,* Madrid, 1945, 2 vols.

Bravo, Francisco, *Historia de la Falange española tradicionalista y de las J.O.N.S.,* Madrid, 1940.

Burns, Enile, *The Nazi Conspiracy in Spain,* London, 1937, translated from the German.

Cantero, Pedro, *Doce años de asistencia social en España. Labor del Estado Español 1936–1948,* Madrid, 1948. A good survey of the social legislation and activities of the Spanish regime.

Castro Delgado, Enrique, *J'ai perdu la foi à Moscou,* Paris, 1950, 11 ed. An excellent account of the official delegate of the Spanish communist party to the Comintern. It relates in detail the activity of the Spanish communists in the Soviet Union after the end of the civil war. The portrait of Dolores Ibarruri is particularly significant as a reflection of the intrigue and ruthless jockeying for favor that distinguished the many Spaniards who sought refuge in the U.S.S.R.

Catálogo de Revistas españolas, Madrid, 1948. Published by the Instituto de Cultura Hispánica and gives pertinent details regarding all contemporary Spanish literary and scientific reviews.

Causa General. La dominación roja en España, Madrid, 1943. A monumental volume with full details of left-wing terrorism in Spain. Accompanied by innumerable photostatic copies of documents and photographs.

Cavalli, S. J. F., "La condizione dei protestanti in Spagna," published in *Civiltá Cattolica,* Rome, April 3, 1948. A leading article on the status of Protestants in Spain.

Chase, Allan, *Falange. The Axis Secret Enemy in the Americas,* New York, 1943.

Chavaz, Edmond, *La situation du protestantisme en Espagne,* Geneva, 1949. Originally published in the *Vie Intellectuelle* of Paris.

Chávez Camacho, Armando, *Misión de prensa en España,* Mexico, 1948. A first-class report on Spain by a competent and observing Mexican journalist on post-civil-war Spain.

Chronicle of the National Trust of St. Paul, 1943–1947, Madrid, 1948. An excellent account of the program of the Trust on behalf of prisons and prisoners.

Ciano, Galeazzo, *L'Europa verso la catastrofe,* Milan, 1947. A fundamental work containing a large number of diplomatic pieces and other documents relating to Spain.

De la Cosa, Juan, *España ante el mundo. Proceso de un aislamiento,* Madrid, 1950. A general survey of the situation of Spain since 1945.

Del Rey, José María, *España y la democracia,* Montevideo, 1948.

Del Río Cisneros, Agustín, *Política internacional de España. El caso español en la O. N. U. y en el mundo,* Madrid, 1946.

Del Valle, Florentino, S.J., *Las reformas sociales en España,* Madrid, 1946 and 1948, 1 and 2 ed. A very handy compendium of Spanish social legislation.

Department of State Bulletin, Vols. XIV and XV, May and September, 1946.

Department of State of the United States, *The Spanish Government and the Axis. Official German documents,* Washington, 1946.

——— *Documents on German Foreign Policy, 1918–1945,* Vol. III, "Germany and the Spanish Civil War, 1936–1939," Washington, D. C., 1950. This collection of documents covering the civil war period appeared too late for inclusion in this book. Obviously an important source from the captured foreign office documents of information regarding German policy.

Diez Años de Cultura Española (1939–1948), Madrid, 1948.

Documentos, Conversaciones Católicas de San Sebastián, San Sebastián, 1949 and 1950, Vols. 2 and 4. This excellent publication of the famous Conversaciones Católicas includes numerous papers on the problem of tolerance and religious minorities.

Dos años de actuación al frente del Ministerio de Trabajo. Mayo 1941–43, Madrid, 1948.

Doussinague, José M., *España tenía razón (1939–45),* Madrid, 1950, 2 ed. An important book by a competent Spanish diplomat reviewing in detail the wartime diplomacy of the Spanish government.

Duff, Charles, *A Key to Victory: Spain,* London, 1940.

Eisenhower, General Dwight, *Crusade in Europe,* New York, 1948.

Escobar, Adrián C., *Diálogo íntimo con España,* Buenos Aires, 1950. The Spanish impressions of a former Argentine ambassador.

Feis, Herbert, *The Spanish Story. Franco and the Nations at War,* New York, 1948.

Foltz, Charles, *The Masquerade in Spain,* Boston, 1948. The author's thesis is that it is the "oligarchy" that rules Spain through General Franco.

Fraga Iribarne, Manuel, *Así se gobierna España,* Madrid, 1949.

Fuero de los Españoles, Edition published by the *Subsecretaría de Educación Popular,* Madrid, 1945.

Gay de Montellà, R., *El fuero del trabajo y sistema de Estado sindical-corporativo,* Valladolid, 1939.

Gomá, Cardinal, *Por Dios y por España,* Barcelona, 1940.

Guía de la vida social de España 1945–46, Madrid, 1946. Published by Fomento social and covering every aspect of the economic and political life of the country.

Hamilton, Thomas J., *Appeasement's Child. The Franco Regime in Spain,* New York, 1943.

Hermandad Obrera de Acción Católica, Primera semana nacional, Madrid, 1946.

Hermandad Obrera de Acción Católica, Segunda semana nacional, Madrid, 1947.

Hermanos, Juan, *La fin de l'espoir,* Paris, 1950. With a preface by Jean Paul Sartre. Claims to represent the torment of those who after 1946 have seen the prospect for the "deliverance" of Spain from Franco gradually recede.

Hernainz Márquez, Miguel, *Tratado elemental de derecho del trabajo,* Madrid, 1947.

Hoare, Sir Samuel, *Complacent Dictator,* New York, 1947.

Hughes, Emmet John, *Report From Spain,* New York, 1947. Important as the statement of a Catholic.

Instituto Nacional de Previsión. Disposiciones sobre previsión social, Madrid, 1945–1947, 2 vols.

Ippécourt, *Les chemins d'Espagne. Mémoires et documents sur la guerre secrète à travers les Pyrénées, 1940–45,* Paris, 1948.

Jiménez de Asúa, L., *La constitución de la democracia española y el problema regional,* Buenos Aires, 1946.
Jiménez Quílez, Manuel, *Proceso irregular,* Madrid, 1947.
Lange, Oscar, *The Problem of Franco Spain,* Washington, D. C. (n.d.). Issued by the Library of the Polish Embassy.
Langer, William L., *Our Vichy Gamble,* New York, 1947.
La Obra Penitenciaria española, Madrid, 1947. Issued by the Ministry of Justice, Department of Prisons.
Larraz, José, *La meta de dos revoluciones,* Madrid, 1946.
Leahy, William D., *I Was There,* New York, 1950.
Legaz y Lecambra, Luis, and Aragón Gómez, Bartolomé, *Cuatro estudios sobre sindicalismo vertical,* Zaragoza, 1939.
L'Eglise catholique en Suède, Malines, 1937. A brochure containing considerable information regarding the status of Catholics in Sweden.
Les lettres secrètes échangées par Hitler et Mussolini, Paris, 1946.
López-Aranda, Alfonso Esteban, *Alcance y finalidad de los seguros sociales obligatorios,* Madrid, 1945.
Los 26 puntos de la Revolución nacional, Barcelona, 1939. Pamphlet with statement of the Falangist program with commentary.
Ministry of Foreign Affairs, Madrid, *Réplica a la publicación hecha por el Departamento de Estados de los Estados Unidos de América de documentos relativos a Espana,* Madrid, 1946.
Mirandet, François, *L'Espagne de Franco,* Paris, 1948.
Mistral, Silvia, *Diario de una refugiada española,* Mexico, 1940.
The Nation Associates. The case for action against Franco and the recognition of the Spanish Republic by the United Nations, New York, 1946.
Nazi Conspiracy and Aggression, Washington, D. C., 8 vols.
New Leader, Vol. XXX, No. 4, January 25, 1947, New York, "The International Implications of the Spanish Problem." By Alfred Mendizábal.
Oficina Informativa española, *El Refrendo popular de la ley española de Sucesion,* Madrid, 1948.
Peers, E. Allison, *Spain in Eclipse 1937–43,* London, 1945, 2 ed.
——— *The Spanish Dilemma,* London, 1940.
Polnay, Peter de, *Death and Tomorrow,* London, 1942. An account of the prison camp of Miranda del Ebro.
Posada, Carlos G., *Los seguros sociales obligatorios en España,* Madrid, 1946, 2 ed.
Primo de Rivera, José Antonio, *Obras completas,* Madrid, 1942.
Reske-Nielsen, Erik, *Republik og Francostyre, 1931–1948,* Copenhagen, 1949.
Ruíz Morales, José Miguel, *La economía del bloque hispanoportugués,* Madrid, 1946.
Rumeu de Armas, Antonio, *Historia de la previsión social en España cofradías, gremios, hermandades montepíos,* Madrid, 1944.
Sánchez Barbudo, Antonio, *Una pregunta sobre España,* Mexico, 1945.
Sanness, John, *Den spanska fragan,* Stockholm, 1948.
Serrano y Serrano, Ignacio, *El fuero del trabajo. Doctrina y comentario,* Valladolid, 1939.
Serrano Suñer, Ramón, *Entre Hendaya y Gibraltar,* Madrid, 1947. A fundamental book by the former foreign minister.
Spanish Information Bureau, New York, *The Marshall Plan and Franco,* March, 1948. The Spanish republican information agency and its views on aid to Spain.
Suárez, Luis, *España comienza en los Pirineos,* Mexico, 1944.
Sutherland, Halliday, *Spanish Journey,* London, 1948. Travel comments of a British writer with special reference to Spanish prisons.

Torrente Ballester, Gonzalo, *José Antonio Primo de Rivera* (*antologia*), Madrid, 1942, 3 ed.

Torres, Manuel, *L'Oeuvre sociale du nouvel état espagnol,* Paris, 1938.

Unité Chrétienne et tolérance religieuse, Paris, 1950. A work in collaboration with an article on the Protestant question in Spain by Father Paul Couturier and the evangelical minister Delpech.

Verdades sociales, II Ciclo de conferencias de cultura religiosa, Barcelona, 1946. Lectures on social questions under the auspices of the diocesan organization of Catholic men.

Vizcarra, Zacarías de, *Curso de Acción Católica,* Madrid, 1947, 3 ed. Bishop Vizcarra as episcopal adviser to Catholic Action gives a detailed account of the activity and structure of Spanish Catholic Action in this book.

VII

PAMPHLETS

Obviously, a bibliography of pamphlets on Spain and its civil war would take more pages than those consumed in this entire book. I have consulted many of them in various languages. The following is a small selection concerning a variety of problems from many points of view:

Anon., *The Spanish War. Foreign Wings Over the Basque Country,* London, 1937.

Azaña, Manuel, *A Year of War in Spain,* London, 1937.

A Barrister, *I Accuse France,* London (n.d.). A short statement of the specific ways in which the French government was aiding the Spanish republicans.

Bartlett, Vernon, *I Accuse,* London, 1937.

Charlton, Air Commodore L. E. O., *The Military Situation in Spain After Teruel,* London (n.d.).

Cohen, Chapman, *Spain and the Church,* London, 1936. A freethinker pamphlet, the gist of which is contained in the remark, "In Spain the principal cause of decay was the preponderating influence of the Church."

De los Ríos, Fernando, *What Is Happening in Spain?,* London, 1937.

Dingle, Reginald, *"Democracy" in Spain,* London, 1937.

——— *Russia's Work in Spain,* London (n.d.).

——— *Second Thoughts on "Democracy" in Spain,* London (n.d.).

Fraser, Hamish, *The Truth About Spain,* London, 1950, reprint. A short statement by a former political commissar in the International Brigades. Interesting as evidence of a complete reversal of viewpoint since the experience of the civil war.

Godden, G. M., *Communist Operation in Spain,* London, 1936.

Greaves, H. R. G., and Thomson, David, *The Truth About Spain,* London, 1938. A "Left Book Club" pamphlet.

Gwynne, H. A., and Ramos Oliveira, A., *Controversy on Spain,* London (n.d.). A more than usually interesting polemic regarding the issues of the Spanish war.

Hart, Captain Liddell, *Britain and Spain,* London, 1938.

How Mussolini Provoked the Spanish Civil War. Documentary evidence, London, 1938.

In Spain With the International Brigade. A personal narrative, London (n.d.).

Intellectuals and the Spanish Military Uprising, London (n.d.). A pamphlet published by the Spanish embassy.

Langdon-Davies, John, *The Spanish Church and Politics,* London, 1937.

Leval, Gaston, *Social Reconstruction in Spain,* London, 1938.

Lloyd George, David, *Spain and Britain,* London, 1937.

MacKee, Seumas, *I Was a Franco Soldier,* London, 1938.
McGovern, John M. P., *Terror in Spain,* London (n.d.).
Moreno, Enrique, *Catholics and the Spanish State,* London, 1937.
Negrín, Juan, *The Will to Victory,* London, 1938.
Parker, A. A., *The Catholic Church in Spain From 1800 Till Today,* London, 1938. A collection of articles from *The Tablet.*
Spain Against the Invaders. Napoleon, 1808 — Hitler and Mussolini, 1936, London, 1936.
Spain: Catholic and Protestant Priests, Freemasons and Liberals Shot by the Rebels, London, 1937.
Stewart, Margaret, *Reform Under Fire. Social Progress in Spain 1931–1938.* London, 1938.
Stoye, Johannes, *Spanien im Umbruch,* Leipzig, 1936.
The Voice of the Church in Spain, London, 1936.
Zur Spanischen Revolution, Paris, 1937. Published by the *Marxistische Tribune,* of German communists in Paris.

VIII

NEWSPAPERS AND DOCUMENTARY SOURCES

Newspaper sources constitute a veritable mine of information for the recent history of Spain. Obviously the investigator must take into account the difficulties imposed by the often erratic censorship. The careful reading of the press of the Second Republic as well as of the civil war period itself constitutes an indispensable part of the task of culling out information regarding the issues at stake. The following are the newspapers consulted, sometimes frequently, sometimes only for occasional numbers. In some cases I have gone through entire collections of certain newspapers for given periods, such as the five years of the Republic or the three years of civil war:

Gaceta de la República, Madrid, 1931–1936. Indispensable for the official report of debates, decrees, and legislation.
El Socialista, Madrid.
El Debate, Madrid. The great Catholic daily, then under the direction of D. Angel Herrera Oría, now Bishop of Málaga.
A.B.C., Madrid, the monarchist organ.
El Liberal, Madrid.
El Sol, Madrid. Liberal in tendency.
Diario de Sesiones, Madrid, 1931–1936. The equivalent of the British *Hansard* or the American *Congressional Record.* The printed text often watered down.
Solidaridad Obrera, Barcelona. The anarchist sheet. Occasional numbers consulted.
Informaciones, Madrid. The number of daily papers in Madrid and Barcelona during the Second Republic was phenomenal. Most of them, as in France, reflected shades and nuances of political opinion as well as the position of the numerous political parties represented in the Cortes.
Vanguardia, Barcelona.
Claridad, Madrid.
Blanco y Negro, Madrid (magazine).
Gaceta de Madrid, Madrid.
El Liberal, Bilbao. The personal house organ of Indalecio Prieto.
Ahora, Madrid.
Heraldo de Madrid.

El Norte de Castilla, Valladolid.
Arriba, Madrid.
Mundo Obrero, Toulouse, France. The organ of the Spanish Communist Party in exile.
Revista de Estudios Politicos, Madrid. A fundamental review for following political thought since 1940.
El Correo Catalán, Barcelona.
Ecclesia, Madrid. Official organ of Spanish Catholic Action.
The Tablet, London.
The New York Times, New York.
The Times, London.
La France Catholique, Paris.
Témoignage Chrétien, Paris.
La Croix, Paris.
Evening Star, Washington, D. C.
Human Events, Washington, D. C.
Le Monde, Paris.
L'Aube, Paris.
Daily Worker, London.
Daily Worker, New York.
L'Humanité, Paris. In the analysis of the communist plot against Spain I have used clippings and occasional pieces from a large number of left-wing and Marxist papers from all over the world. In most cases only one or two items have been taken. No formal listing of all these newspapers, the names of which appear at the foot of the pages in the appropriate chapter, would seem necessary.
Boletín oficial eclesiástico del Arzobispado de Toledo.
Boletín oficial eclesiástico del Arzobispado de Sevilla.
Boletín oficial de las Cortes españolas.
United Nations Conference on International Organization — Documents.
Resolutions adopted by the General Assembly during the first part of its session from 10 January to 14 February, 1946.
Report of the Subcommittee on the Spanish question appointed by the Security Council in April, 1946, UN Document, No. S/75.
United Nations. Official records of the second part of the first session of the General Assembly, 1946.

INDEX